D0259241

KA 0011509 6

THE LION AND THE EAGLE

British and Anglo-American Strategy, 1900–1950

OTHER BOOKS BY BASIL COLLIER

THE DEFENCE OF THE UNITED KINGDOM

THE BATTLE OF BRITAIN

BARREN VICTORIES:
Versailles to Suez

THE BATTLE OF THE V-WEAPONS,
1944–1945

THE SECOND WORLD WAR:
A Military History

THE WAR IN THE FAR EAST,
1941–1945

THE LION AND THE EAGLE

British and Anglo-American Strategy, 1900–1950

by BASIL COLLIER

Macdonald · London

First published in Great Britain by
Macdonald & Co. (Publishers) Ltd,
49/50 Poland Street, London W 1

Published simultaneously in the United States of America by
G. P. Putnam's Sons, New York

SBN 356 03600 6

PRINTED IN THE UNITED STATES OF AMERICA

CONTENTS

Maps

Author's Note

The purpose of this book is to describe in greater detail than would be appropriate in a general history the strategic background of Anglo-American relations in an era which has seen the replacement of Great Britain by the United States as the leading Anglo-Saxon power. Its aim is not to challenge but to supplement accounts written by students of political, diplomatic, economic and social history.

The obvious point of departure for such a study is the abandonment by Britain of the two-power naval standard. At the beginning of the present century the British government of the day came to the conclusion that the country could no longer afford to maintain a battle fleet stronger than the combined battle fleets of its two most powerful naval rivals. From that decision, made necessary in the governments' estimation by the growing naval strength of Germany, Japan and the United States and the growing cost of naval armaments, flowed the Japanese alliance, the reduction of British naval strength in the Far East, the Mediterranean and the Western Atlantic and much else that helped determine the pattern of British diplomacy during the next fifty years and more.

No less momentous was the decision taken after the First World War to abandon the Japanese alliance, accept naval limitations imposed by the Treaty of Washington and rely on the United States to make common cause with Britain should British and American interest in the Far East and Western Pacific be seriously threatened by Japanese ambitions. This was a hazardous move, since the Americans had no first-class naval base west of Pearl Harbor and were unlikely to send any major part of their battle fleet to a British one. But the alternative, according to a British government soon to fall from office, was an arms race which would not only have been ruinously expensive but have carried the risk of a lasting disagreement with the United States.

Whether the right or the wrong decisions were made on these and other occasions the reader will decide for himself.

The text of the book was prepared for simultaneous publication on both sides of the Atlantic. By agreement between the American and British publishers the spellings—and in some cases methods of punctuation—more familiar in the United States than in Britain have been adopted. It is hoped that this gesture of Anglo-American solidarity will cause no inconvenience to British readers.

I am indebted to the British publisher for supervising the preparation of the maps and to friends and correspondents on both sides of the Atlantic for valuable comments and suggestions.

B. C.

These Yankees are most disagreeable Fellows to have to do with about any American Question. They are on the Spot, strong, deeply interested in the matter, totally unscrupulous and dishonest and determined somehow or other to carry their Point. We are far away, weak from Distance, controlled by the Indifference of the Nation . . . and by its Strong commercial interest in maintaining Peace with the United States. The result of this State of Things has been that we have given way Step by Step to the North Americans on almost every disputed matter.

—VISCOUNT PALMERSTON

No people respond more spontaneously to fair play. If you treat Americans well they always want to treat you better.

—WINSTON S. CHURCHILL

I

Before the Deluge

ON the eve of the First World War the British Empire covered a quarter of the habitable globe. Despite fierce competition from Germany and the United States, Great Britain still held the foremost place among the nations as an exporter of goods and services; London was still the world's most important financial and commercial center. Nevertheless, the situation of the British was in some respects extremely vulnerable. The British Isles were the homeland of some 40,000,000 people who depended on imports for more than half their food, on foreign trade and invisible exports to maintain their living standards. Agriculture was the largest single industry in Britain, but it gave employment to only a twelfth of the working population and furnished little more than a fifth of the wheat consumed in British homes. The 53,000,000 tons of imports which reached the United Kingdom in the last full year of peace included not only prodigious quantities of grain, meat, tea and sugar, but also raw materials needed by industries catering both to the domestic market and to export markets. Should supplies from overseas be cut off, the British would not merely be impoverished but would starve.

The structure of Britain's armed forces reflected, albeit imperfectly, the needs of a country which was, at one and the same time, the center of a far-flung empire, a focus of world trade, and an island kingdom compelled to look abroad for the means of keeping its people fed and its factories at work. A body of statesmen and strategists known as the Committee of Imperial Defence had been created and developed for the express purpose of harmonizing strategic doctrine with national and imperial aims and policies; from 1904 it was served by a permanent secretariat. But the deliberations of the committee were bound to be affected by the knowledge that, irrespective of theoretical needs, the peacetime strength of the British Army would almost certainly remain low by European standards. The British, like the Americans, were credited with an innate distrust of large standing armies. In recent years attempts had been made by the veteran Field Marshal Lord Roberts and others to persuade the country to accept the principle of compulsory military service. But most practical politicians remained of the opinion that no British government which sponsored conscription in time of peace could hope to stay in office.

By 1914 Britain's strategic problems were essentially defensive. Since the incorporation of the Transvaal in the Empire at the end of the South African War, the public had shown no taste for further annexations. Englishmen who called themselves imperialists no longer wished to extend the frontiers of the Empire. They had become people who advocated a system of tariffs designed to favor producers within the Empire at the expense of foreign rivals.

At a general election in 1906, even this form of imperialism was decisively rejected. The Liberal statesmen who were then confirmed in office were not imperialists in any sense. Tariffs were obnoxious to them. Far from wishing to extend the frontiers of the Empire, they looked forward to the assumption by overseas possessions of the Crown of a growing share of responsibility for their own welfare and a consequent lightening of the burden borne by the central government.

The fact remained that roughly a fifth of the world's inhabitants looked to armed forces controlled directly or indirectly from London as their ultimate safeguard against foreign aggression or internal strife. India, Australia, Canada, New Zealand, South Africa, and some of the Crown Colonies and dependencies could and did make valuable contributions to internal security and imperial defense, but all territories whose rulers owed allegiance to the British Crown relied on the Royal Navy to protect their external communications and ensure the safe passage of troops and supplies from one part of the Empire to another in case of need. Moreover, since roughly three-quarters of Britain's overseas trade at the beginning of the twentieth century was with countries outside the Empire,[1] the security of the trade routes linking the United Kingdom with foreign markets and sources of supply was no less important to the British than that of their imperial communications.

During the heyday of Britain's naval and mercantile supremacy in the Victorian era, her experts had reckoned that to ensure command of the sea, her battle fleet must be stronger than the combined battle fleets of her two most powerful naval rivals. For example, at a time when France and Russia mustered twenty-eight capital ships between them, the British had felt barely safe with twenty-nine. By 1901, however, the emergence of Germany and the United States as vigorous naval powers made it apparent to the British that they could not hope to maintain the two-power standard unless they were prepared to accept, within the next six years, a tenfold increase in the annual cost of the Navy since 1889.[2] At the same time, yet another naval power, Japan, was adding to her battle fleet in order to offset the growth of Russian power and influence in the Far East which followed Russia's occupation of Port Arthur in 1897.

Reluctance to adopt extreme courses where compromise seems possible is a recurrent tendency of British governments. To content themselves with a one-power standard and seek the friendship of one or more of the leading naval powers was the policy which, on the whole, seemed best to the Conservative or Unionist statesmen who held office from 1895 to 1905. The difficulty was to find a suitable ally. Public opinion in the United States was firmly opposed to any alliance with a foreign power; negotiations with Continental powers made slow progress at a time when relations were embittered by commercial rivalries, conflicting aims in Africa, and a remote but disquieting threat to the North-West Frontier of India from Russian advances in Central Asia. In 1902, after approaches to the United States and Germany had been rebuffed, Britain concluded with Japan an alliance which provided for mutual support should either country become involved in a Far Eastern war and be attacked by a power not originally a party to the conflict.

The signing of the Japanese treaty was followed by far-reaching naval conversations. Dispositions in the event of war were studied in detail; a system was devised whereby either a British or a Japanese admiral would be able to command a mixed force should the need arise; arrangements were made for the exchange of intelligence and the pooling of supplies. At the same time, the British were promised access to Japanese naval bases if they should require it. In the light of these assurances, they concluded that they could safely reduce their naval strength in Far Eastern waters. Thus it became easier for them to assemble in home waters the strong fleet needed to meet the challenge presented by the creation of a powerful German High Seas Fleet.

Largely on the advice of the Committee of Imperial Defence,[3] in 1905 the British affirmed and extended the Japanese alliance on terms which pledged Japan, in return for assurances of support against Russian aggression, to come to the aid of the British Empire in the event of an unprovoked threat to India. In 1911 the alliance was renewed for ten years, on the express understanding that nothing in its terms should compel the British or the Japanese to go to war with a country with which either party was linked by a treaty of general arbitration. This proviso, intended by the British to allay American misgivings, was inserted in contemplation of a far-reaching Anglo-American treaty of general arbitration then under negotiation. The new treaty was duly signed about a month after the renewal of the Japanese alliance, but in consequence of difficulties raised by the United States Senate it was never ratified. The less satisfactory Root-Bryce Treaty of 1908, which recognized the principle of general arbitration only with reservations, remained in force and was renewed in 1913, but its terms—again as a result of intervention by the Senate—were such as to make it improbable that the parties would, in fact, resort to arbitration in the event of a serious dispute about a major issue. The broad effect of the abandonment of the 1911 treaty of arbitration was that diplomatic assurances failed to convince a large section of opinion in the United States that there was nothing sinister about the alliance between Britain and Japan.

Meanwhile, the British continued their search for allies. In 1904 they reached agreement with the French about Moroccan, Egyptian, and other colonial questions which had long clouded relations between the two countries. In 1907, after the Russians had suffered a severe defeat at the hands of the Japanese in the Far East, they came to an understanding with the British about their interests in the countries bordering on India.

These developments greatly reduced the chances of a Russian attack on India, especially as the Russo-Japanese War was followed by serious internal disturbances in Russia. On the other hand, they exposed Britain to the risk of being drawn into a European war should France and her ally Russia fall out with Germany and Austro-Hungary. When Germany sought in 1905 to test the strength of the understanding between France and Britain by picking a quarrel with the French about Moroccan questions and threatening war, British statesmen asked themselves anxiously what would happen if German troops invaded France and especially if they sought to outflank the French fortified zones along the Franco-German frontier by marching through Belgium.

The British responded to the threat by giving diplomatic support to France at the conference held at Algeciras in 1906 to settle the dispute. On the initiative of the Foreign Secretary, Sir Edward Grey, they also entered into military conversations with the French. As the sequel to tentative approaches in 1905, staff talks began in 1906. In addition, conversations between the British and Belgian General Staffs were held in the late winter and early spring of that year. These exchanges led to the conclusion that if Germany did go to war with France, the French would need all the help they could get in repelling an advance by the right wing of the German armies. The outcome was that, after agreement had been reached with the Russians in 1907, tentative arrangements were made for the dispatch to the European mainland of a British Expeditionary Force of one cavalry division and six infantry divisions, originally intended for dispatch to India in the event of war with Russia. The Belgians proposed that any troops which the British might send to Europe should disembark at Antwerp and join the Belgian Army in falling on the right flank of the German Army.[4] The British, unwilling to risk troopships in the southern part of the North Sea at a time when Germany might be expected to have an undefeated fleet in being, thought it better that their troops should land in France and take up positions on the left of the French armies.

The Liberal statesmen who sanctioned the staff talks did not interpret this tentative plan as a firm undertaking to send the Expeditionary Force, or any part of it, across the Channel in the event of war. Their view was that if and when war did come, the decision to intervene or remain neutral would have to be made by the government in office at the time.

From 1909 formal exchanges between British and French officers were supplemented by off-the-record conversations between Brigadier General Henry Hughes Wilson, until 1910 commandant of the Staff College at Camberley, and General Ferdinand Foch of the École Supérieure de Guerre. Wilson spoke French fluently and was a warm advocate of friendship with France and support for the French Army. Between 1907 and 1913 he made repeated visits to the frontier area as far south as Belfort and as far north as Arnhem and beyond. Traveling in the guise of a tourist and covering long distances by bicycle or motorcar, he paid special attention to the eastern approaches to the Meuse.

Wilson's observations, supplemented by information from secret sources, convinced him that the Germans, if they did go to war with France, would wish to extend their right as far north as possible in order to make a wide sweep toward Paris but would be reluctant to add to the number of their enemies by marching through Holland. He was sure that, on the other hand, they would not hesitate to march through Belgium. The crucial question was whether they would try to cross the Meuse between Namur and the Dutch frontier (where the Meuse becomes the Maas) or confine themselves to the ninety-mile gap between Namur and the French fortified zone at Verdun. The French frontier defenses south of that point were not continuous but consisted of a chain of fortified positions designed to steer an invader along routes which would lead him into trouble.

The only points between Namur and the Dutch frontier at which substantial German forces might be able to cross the Meuse without recourse to elaborate bridging operations were at or in the neighborhood of Liège, Huy, and Namur itself. The crossings at Liège and Namur were commanded by powerful forts constructed in the 1880's; those at Huy by older fortifications which could doubtless be improved. On the whole, it seemed likely that the Germans would make their main effort between Namur and Verdun. The British, however, were never quite so confident that the Germans would not try to cross the Meuse in strength below Namur as the French High Command became in the last few years before the outbreak of war.

Wilson noted on the map, and inspected in person, seventeen

roads in the sector between Metz and Aachen by which German infantry could approach the Meuse without coming under fire from Verdun. Assuming that each would be used by three divisions and that German reserve divisions would march with the first line, he put the number of infantry divisions which the Germans could bring to bear in the crucial sector at fifty-one. This estimate, which the French thought excessive, proved very close to the mark.*

Wilson concluded that the Allies ought to aim at stopping the enemy well short of the river. The plan he envisaged in the summer of 1913, when he visited the frontier area with Colonel G. M. Harper, the future GSO 1 (Operations) of the Expeditionary Force, was that the British, after concentrating near Maubeuge, should move into the Ardennes and occupy a front of some twenty-five miles, with their right at Rochefort and their left on the Meuse at Andenne, about eighteen miles downstream from Namur. If the French Third, Fourth, and Fifth armies on their right came forward to prolong the line from Rochefort through St.-Hubert, Neufchâteau, and Longuyon to Verdun, this disposition would give the Allies some forty British and French divisions, exclusive of cavalry, with which to oppose the advance of rather more than fifty German divisions through wooded, rolling country which offered favorable positions for defense. Experience in South Africa and elsewhere suggested that the Germans would find so small a margin of superiority insufficient for a breakthrough.

Notwithstanding the shortcomings of this concept, its existence should be enough to dispose of the popular belief that the British blundered into war in 1914 with no clear idea of how their forces might be used to counter a German advance through Belgium. At the same time, it is obvious in the light of retrospect that Wilson's plan could have succeeded only if the French had hastened, as soon as they were free to enter Belgian territory, to prepare positions for themselves and their allies on the Verdun-Andenne line, and had helped and encouraged the Belgians to hold the line of the Meuse between Andenne and the Dutch frontier. Even then, the British could

* The number of infantry divisions actually used by the Germans in August, 1914, for their initial advance in the sector north of Metz was fifty-three. This figure was made up as follows: First Army (less two divisions held back during the initial advance), twelve; Second Army, twelve; Third Army, eight; total for the armies of the right, thirty-two; Fourth and Fifth armies (forming the armies of the center), twenty-one; grand total for the armies of the right and center, fifty-three.

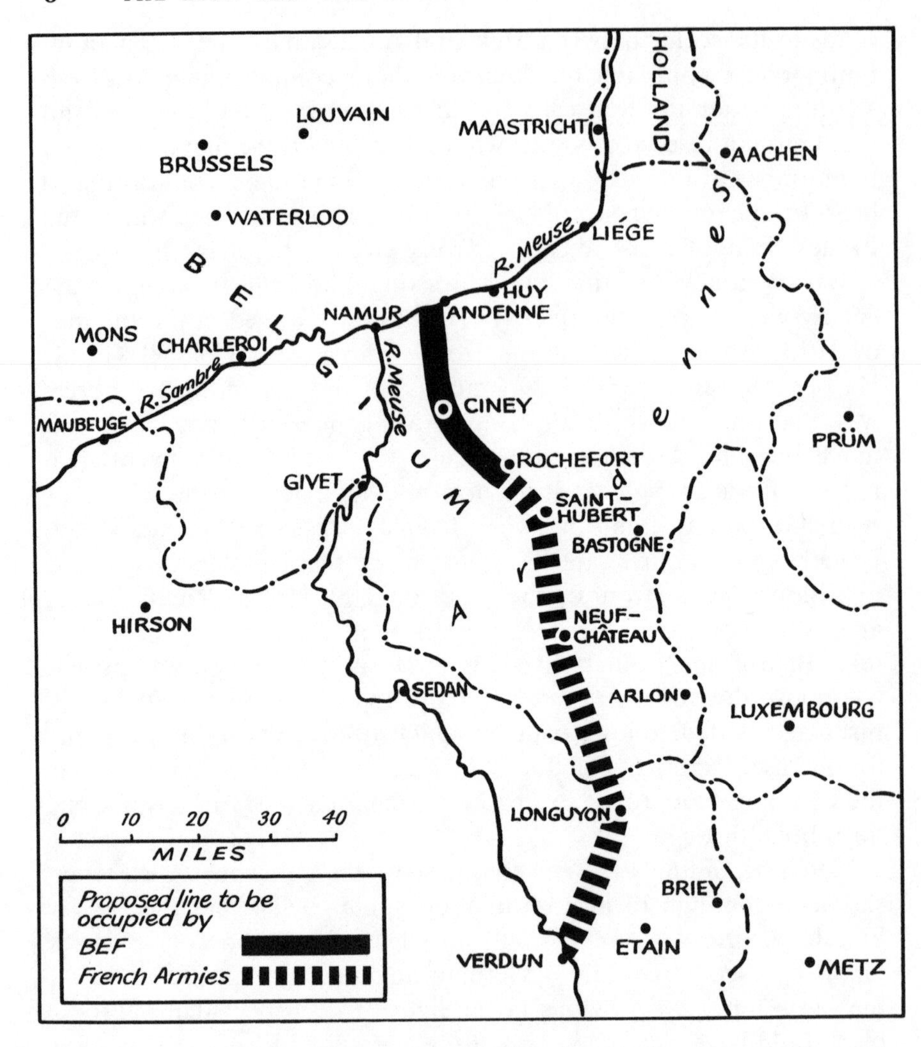

THE FRONTIER AREA

scarcely have reached the Ardennes with much time to spare. Moreover, the Verdun-Andenne line would have been tenable only if the Belgians, thus helped and encouraged, had succeeded in preventing the Germans from crossing the Meuse at Huy with substantial forces, and from bringing heavy siege guns within range of the Liège forts.

Wilson was only about halfway through his study of these problems when he was appointed Director of Military Operations at the War Office. Thus it fell to him to expound the views of the General Staff when, in the summer of 1911, an incident at Agadir, in Morocco, brought France and Germany to the verge of war for the second time since 1905. On a day of sweltering heat in August he had a long talk over the luncheon table with the Foreign Secretary, Sir Edward Grey, and the Secretary of State for War, Richard Burdon Haldane (afterward Lord Haldane). The sequel was a special meeting of the Committee of Imperial Defence on August 23. Besides Grey and Haldane, ministers present included the Prime Minister, Herbert Henry Asquith; the Chancellor of the Exchequer, David Lloyd George; the Home Secretary, Winston Spencer Churchill; and the First Lord of the Admiralty, Reginald McKenna.

Wilson, armed with a huge map and an impressive array of facts and figures, had no difficulty in showing that in a war between France and Russia on the one hand and Germany and Austro-Hungary on the other, nothing the Russians might do could prevent the Germans from aiming a heavy blow at France within the first few weeks. He went on to argue that since the French would almost certainly be outnumbered, the small British Expeditionary Force might be able to make a contribution out of proportion to its size.

In the afternoon the First Sea Lord, Admiral Sir Arthur Wilson, followed with a guarded exposition of the Admiralty's plans for war with Germany. Either in the interests of security or because he was uncertain about details, he did not give a full account of the Navy's program, which included the capture of islands in the neighborhood of the Helgoland Bight and the East Frisians, a major fleet action, and eventual landings on Germany's Baltic coast. Even so, he said enough to make it clear that the Admiralty contemplated a close blockade of German North Sea ports from captured bases. This concept did not square with the growing conviction of many naval strategists that the advent of the submarine had made the close blockade of an enemy's ports impractical. Moreover, the naval plan assumed that troops would be available for purposes utterly at variance with the plan just advanced by the General Staff.

Apart from these objections, the Admiralty's case was not well presented. Admiral Wilson was a distinguished seaman and a selfless patriot, but he lacked the persuasiveness of his military namesake.

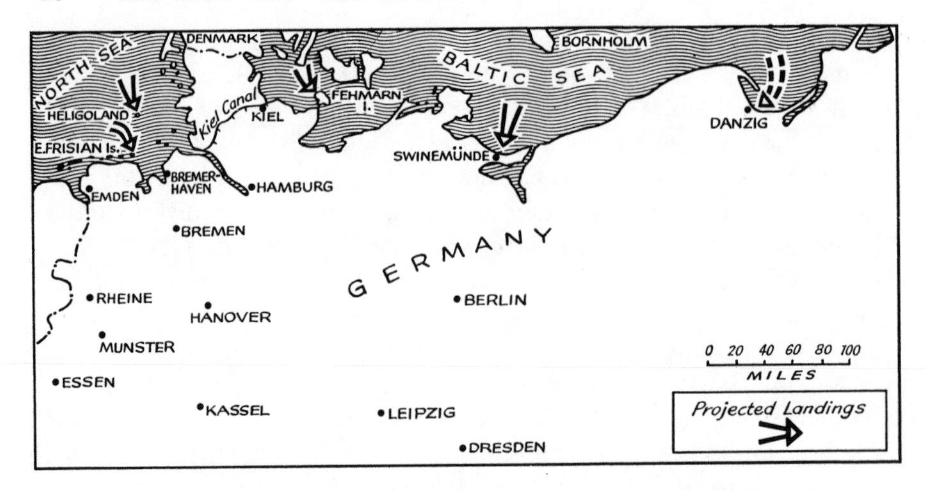

THE REJECTED BRITISH NAVAL PLAN (1911)

The result was that, in effect, the Committee of Imperial Defence rejected the Navy's plan and endorsed the Army's without giving much thought to the possibility that a third course—such as a landing in Belgium—might be preferable to either. Immediately after the meeting Haldane threatened to resign unless steps were taken to bring the Admiralty's strategy into line with his. The outcome was a Cabinet reshuffle which enabled the relatively youthful Winston Churchill to step into the congenial post of First Lord of the Admiralty. The sponsors of the rejected naval plan were not dismissed, but in due course the First, Second, and Fourth Sea Lords all were succeeded by officers thought likely to work in harmony with the General Staff.

In theory these decisions were not irrevocable. Theoretically there was nothing to prevent either the existing Cabinet or some future Cabinet from countermanding the Army's arrangements and adopting an entirely new plan for war with Germany. But for practical purposes the ultimate effect of the deliberations of the Committee of Imperial Defence in the summer of 1911 was to commit the country, in the event of its participation in a European war, to a land campaign in which the strategy of the British Army was bound to be subordinated, at any rate in the early stages, to that of the numerically stronger French Army.

At the same time, Henry Wilson's appearance before the committee considerably strengthened his influence with key members of the government. During the next few months he made it his business to impress upon Winston Churchill, Lloyd George, and others the "immense importance" attached by the General Staff to a friendly understanding with the Belgians and also to the prompt dispatch of the whole of the Expeditionary Force on the outbreak of war. In the spring of 1912 he was allowed to pay a flying visit to Ostend for the purpose of briefing the British military attaché in Brussels, Colonel G. T. M. Bridges, for a crucial approach to the Belgian General Staff. Bridges was to say that in the event of war with Germany, Britain could provide 150,000 troops at the decisive time and place, but to add that the Belgians would be expected to play their part by strengthening their defenses on the Meuse and by calling for help as soon as their country was invaded.

These overtures were unsuccessful. Six years earlier the Belgians had been more than ready to discuss the disembarkation of British troops at a Belgian port. By 1912 they had become so reluctant to jeopardize their neutrality that they refused even to enter into a fresh series of staff talks. The British had therefore to fall back on the hope that when the moment came, the Belgian Army would nonetheless be able and willing to fill the role assigned to it.

Meanwhile, a sense of urgency arising from the Agadir crisis had led the French to attempt a fresh approach to their strategic problems. General Michel, the Commander in Chief whom they had chosen to lead their armies in the event of war, expected the Germans to aim at a wide encircling movement through Belgium. He proposed to counter it by adopting a defensive deployment along the Belgian frontier. In the light of indications that the Germans meant to use reserve formations to swell their effort, he also proposed to use his own reserve formations in an active role. In the summer of 1911 the authorities allowed themselves to be persuaded by critics of Michel's strategy that these proposals were heretical. Thereupon they replaced Michel by a fifty-nine-year-old engineer officer, General Joseph Jacques Césaire Joffre.

Joffre, the son of a manufacturer of wine barrels in a small town in a remote province, was not a graduate of the École Supérieure de Guerre and had little experience of staff work. In the eyes of the group of officers who came to dominate French military thought between 1911 and 1914 he had, however, the great merit of subscribing to the theory that one of the hallmarks of a good commander is readiness to take the offensive even in outwardly unfavorable conditions. This age-old doctrine made a special appeal to Frenchmen of Joffre's generation, largely because its twentieth-century exponents in France were able to give it a new twist. Claiming that the French Army had been too much preoccupied with the defensive in 1870, they asserted that offensive tactics and an offensive strategy chimed better with the national temperament. Notwithstanding the lessons of the South African, Russo-Japanese, and Balkan wars—in all of which troops defending prepared positions proved extraordinarily hard to dislodge—they managed to convince themselves that French infantrymen, charging with the bayonet, would have a good chance of storming the enemy's lines before effective fire could be brought to bear against them.

Joffre's devotion to an offensive strategy was reflected in the notorious Plan XVII, completed by his staff and adopted by the French Supreme War Council in the spring of 1912.[6] This document was deemed so secret that it was neither communicated to the British nor shown in its entirety even to French army commanders. The preamble proclaimed the Commander in Chief's intention of "advancing to the attack with all forces united." Joffre planned to seize the initiative at the outset of a war with Germany by launching attacks both north and south of the German fortified zone between Metz and Thionville. In the south, the First and Second armies were to begin by advancing into Alsace and toward the Rhineland. In the north, the direction of Joffre's advance would depend on circumstances. If the Germans respected the neutrality of Belgium, as both France and Prussia had done in 1870, then the Third and Fifth armies, with the Fourth Army in reserve, would attack across the common frontier immediately south of the German fortified zone. If, on the other hand, German troops moved into Belgium and Luxembourg, then the whole of the Allied armies of the left would attack in a northeasterly direction through the Ardennes. The general intention was that in either case all the Allied armies should join eventually in an advance toward the heart of Germany, probably along an axis centered on Mainz.

The British General Staff learned about the time of Agadir that the French (as Henry Wilson put it) "were going to attack." Even so, they could scarcely foresee the extent to which the new doctrine

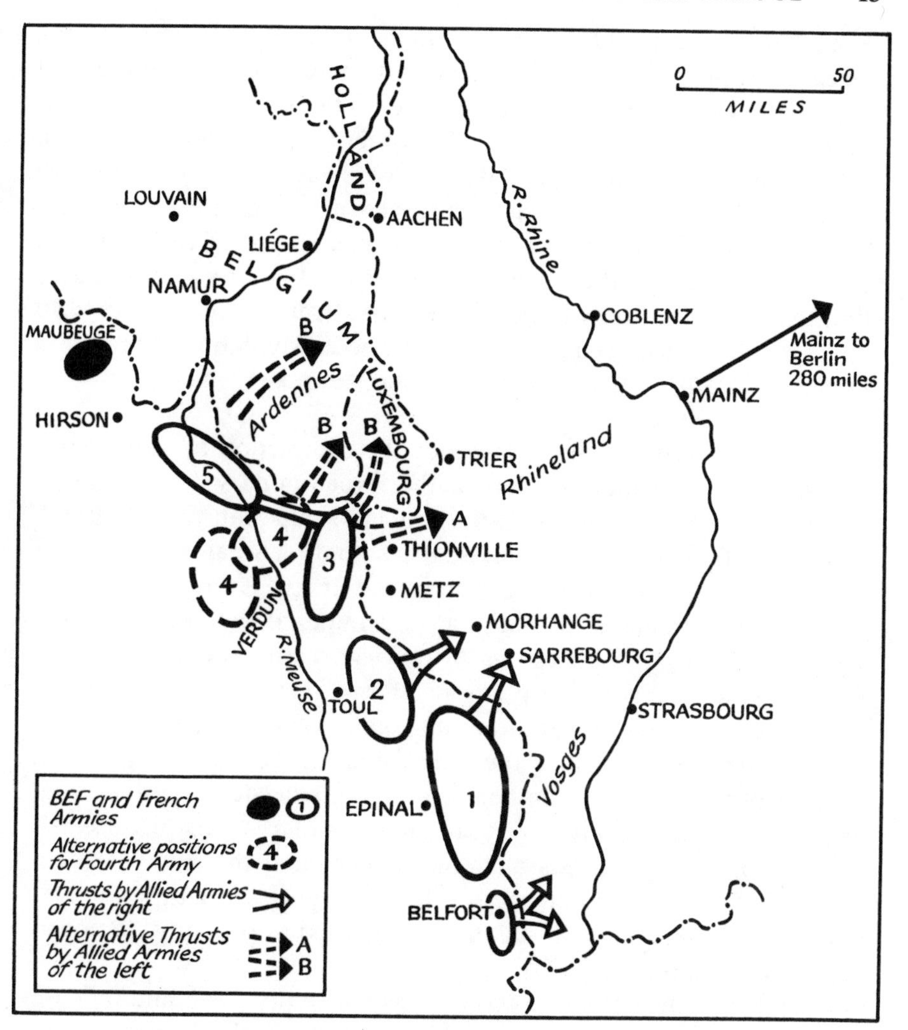

PLAN XVII

would affect not only the strategy, but also the major tactics of the French Army. Bitter experience in South Africa, reinforced by observation of events elsewhere, had convinced them that gallantry and resolution alone could not atone for a dearth of well-directed fire-power. They had learned in the same hard school the importance of improving the infantry's marksmanship and use of natural and artificial cover, and it did not escape their notice that progress in the design and manufacture of artillery and small arms during the past half century or so tended, on the whole, to favor the defender rather than the attacker. They assumed that other armies besides their own had learned these lessons, as indeed most armies had. The point they were inclined to overlook was that the French were not so much ignorant of such truths as determined to make light of them. British officers attached to the French armies in 1914 were astonished to find that it was not only at maneuvers that French troops omitted to dig trenches, exposed themselves needlessly, and sometimes launched infantry attacks without artillery support.

During the last few years of peace the completion of administrative plans for the mobilization of the Expeditionary Force and its dispatch to France was an important preoccupation of the British military authorities. Nevertheless, it was only a small part of their duties. The peacetime organization of the British Army was tailored to fit the requirements of national and imperial defense in a wide sense. Battalions of the Regular Army were scattered throughout the Empire for such diverse purposes as internal security, ceremonial parades, and punitive expeditions against hostile frontiersmen. For many years the strength of the land forces in the United Kingdom depended more on the number of battalions needed to provide reliefs or reinforcements for overseas garrisons than on any precise calculation of strategic needs at home. Except that the Army was responsible for the fixed defenses of defended ports both at home and abroad, defense against invasion was regarded as primarily the business of the Navy.

An attempt to define the Army's responsibility for home defense in more rational terms was made in 1908, when the Committee of Imperial Defence recommended that even though naval supremacy in home waters could be assumed, the strength and organization of the land forces in the United Kingdom should always be such as to compel an invader to mount an expedition too large to escape detection and interception before it reached the coast. The fact remained that mobilization of the Expeditionary Force would absorb practically all the Regular battalions likely to be at home at a given moment. Consequently, if the whole of the Expeditionary Force were sent abroad, the committee's proviso would not be met unless or until the Territorial Army became capable of filling the gap.

The Territorial Army consisted, apart from a nucleus of Regular officers and noncommissioned officers, of volunteer reservists who attended periodical drills and lectures and annual exercises. It was designed to provide on mobilization fourteen infantry divisions and fourteen mounted Yeomanry brigades; but these would be equipped in the first instance on a lower scale than corresponding Regular formations, and their fighting value was consistently underrated by professional soldiers who equated the new Territorial Army with the old Militia.

On the naval side, from the time when the policy of friendship with France was first adopted, the Admiralty's foremost aims were to build a modern battle fleet capable of mastering the German High Seas Fleet and to keep it concentrated for that purpose. With the exception of three or four battle cruisers to be assigned to the Mediterranean Fleet, practically the whole of the battle fleet would be stationed in or near home waters. Under the guidance of the eccentric Admiral Sir John Fisher, whose enthusiasms dominated naval opinion throughout his six years as First Sea Lord from 1904 to 1910, a massive investment was made in powerfully armed battleships of the Dreadnought and post-Dreadnought classes and in fast but vulnerable battle cruisers. Despite protests from Radical members of the government who argued that the diversion of funds from social welfare to naval armaments would merely stimulate the Germans to greater efforts, enough of the new ships were completed by 1914 to give the country a numerical superiority of roughly three to two both in battleships launched since 1906 and in capital ships of all classes.

Until 1916, when the only major fleet action fought by the Royal Navy since the age of sail revealed serious shortcomings in the design of ships laid down during the past decade and more, most British naval officers assumed that the British battle fleet would prove superior not only in numbers, but also in quality to the enemy's. Admiral Sir John Jellicoe, Commander in Chief of the Grand Fleet from August, 1914, to December, 1916, was one of the few who thought this a dangerous assumption. He issued a number of warnings both before and after he took up his appointment, but his attitude was generally ascribed to the natural tendency of a man in his position to exaggerate the difficulty of the task he has inherited or may inherit. A great many Englishmen took it for granted in 1914 that the Grand Fleet was the most powerful, the best manned, the best commanded, the most technically perfect array of fighting ships ever assembled under one flag. Brought up to believe that the Royal Navy was always in the forefront of progress and the British Army incurably conservative and reactionary, they would have been shocked if anyone had suggested that possibly the Expeditionary Force, with its unsurpassed standards of musketry and fire discipline and its severely functional uniforms and equipment, was in some ways the more advanced weapon.

The substitution of Germany for France as the potential enemy shifted the focus of strategic interest from the English Channel, the Bay of Biscay, and the Mediterranean to the North Sea, then still called the German Ocean. This change led after long debate to the conclusion that the main fleet should be stationed in time of war in Scottish waters. Ultimately Scapa Flow in Orkney was chosen in preference to Rosyth or Cromarty as the main war base of the Grand Fleet, largely because its remoteness and the strong currents in the channels leading to it were widely believed to make it secure against surprise attacks by light naval forces, including submarines. That view was not fully shared by Jellicoe or his subordinate commanders. Jellicoe insisted during the early months of the war that special measures should be taken to reduce the risk of underwater attack. Even thereafter he was seldom at ease unless the Grand Fleet was at sea.

From 1911, when Churchill succeeded McKenna as First Lord, the Admiralty accepted the principle that close blockade of German ports was not a practical operation of war. Apart from the risk that warships working for long periods off a hostile coast might be torpedoed, the Germans were known to be alive to the strategic importance of Helgoland and the East Frisians and to be taking steps which would make the capture of suitable bases there almost impossible, even if the necessary troops could be found without prejudice to the Expeditionary Force. In theory, close blockade by forces based on British ports, some 300 miles away, would still have been possible; in practice many more destroyers, working in relays, would have been needed to guard against attacks by the enemy's torpedo boats than the Navy could provide.

Accordingly, the plan adopted by the Admiralty in 1912 substituted for close blockade a distant blockade designed to strangle Germany's foreign trade and to make it difficult for her warships to break out of the narrow waters. Destroyers based on Dover, supported by battleships of the pre-Dreadnought era from Sheerness, would block the Dover Strait. A cordon of cruisers and destroyers covering the whole width of the North Sea between the east coast of the United Kingdom and the Norwegian coast was found by calculation and experiment to be impractical, but seaward patrols and occasional sweeps toward the far side of the North Sea would, it was thought, suffice to give warning of invasion or an attempted breakout by the enemy's main fleet, though not necessarily of raids by up to 20,000 men carried in fast ships which might attempt the crossing in darkness or thick weather. The Admiralty believed that these measures, reinforced by a close watch on merchant vessels trading with European ports, would impose so intolerable a strain on Germany's economy that sooner or later the High Seas Fleet would put to sea in an attempt to end the deadlock. It would then be brought to action by the Grand Fleet. Finally, British merchant shipping would be protected by "a policy of vigorous offence against the enemy's warships wherever stationed." Only in exceptional circumstances would recourse be made to the "cumbrous and inconvenient" method of convoy.[7]

The existence of these plans did not prevent British statesmen of all parties from earnestly wishing to reach agreement with Germany if agreement was possible. Nor did the statesmen feel that competition between British and German merchants in overseas markets need be a bar to such agreement. No factual basis can be found for the legend which depicts the British as engineering, with Machiavellian cunning, a European war so that Britain should have a chance of destroying a trade rival. There may have been Englishmen who believed in 1914 that war with Germany would be financially or economically advantageous, but they were not to be found in well-informed circles in Whitehall or the City. German competition in export markets was inconvenient, as indeed was American competition; but British exporters and financiers had so large a stake in the stability of foreign currencies that war with Britain's best European customer as a remedy for unsatisfactory trade returns would have struck most orthodox financiers as not merely a cure worse than the disease, but the height of insanity.* The decline in living standards which might result from a persistent loss of markets to German and American competitors was a danger recognized, and from time to time discussed, by British governments from the 1870's, but it was not one which seemed, as a rule, to call for more drastic action than an occasional shake-up in the consular and diplomatic services and at the Board of Trade.† What Englishmen who concerned themselves about such matters feared was not a gradual loss of markets but a swift catastrophe which might deprive the British people of the means of supplying themselves with food and raw materials. Should Germany use her powerful army to gain hegemony over Continental Europe and then turn with a formidable navy against a Britain not fully prepared for war, she might quickly put herself in a position to starve the British Isles into political and economic vassalage. Alternatively it was, some people thought, conceivable that she might launch a "bolt from the blue" against Britain without first settling with France and Russia and perhaps even without declaring war.

In 1912 the British made the last of a series of attempts to persuade the Germans to accept a "naval holiday." The gist of their proposals was that Britain and Germany should agree to make no further additions to their battle fleets during a given period. The Germans rejected these overtures on the ground that their High Seas Fleet was not, and never had been, intended to fight the British fleet and that they could not forgo the right to decide for themselves how many ships they ought to have. Thereupon Asquith and his colleagues reluctantly abandoned the hope of reaching an understanding with Germany about naval matters in the immediate future. They agreed with the French that in the event of war or an imminent

* Lloyd George pointed out in his *War Memoirs* that when war did come, he and his officials at the Treasury were deluged with pleas from financiers to "stop the war, or we shall all be ruined."

† An apparent exception was the founding of the Ottoman Bank (an institution underwritten by the British taxpayer) as a means of checking German economic penetration of the Ottoman Empire. The point here is that German economic penetration of the Ottoman Empire was regarded as not merely commercially but *strategically* undesirable. Similarly, the investment of public funds in the Anglo-Persian Oil Company was designed to serve a strategic purpose by ensuring a supply of fuel oil for the Royal Navy. Where purely commercial issues were at stake, British governments for a long time before 1914 were generally reluctant to intervene with guarantees or subsidies, on the principle that public funds should not be used to promote the interests of one particular group of investors rather than another. For a detailed study of this question see Platt, *Finance, Trade and Politics in British Foreign Policy, 1815–1914.*

threat of war with Germany, the Royal Navy should undertake to safeguard the north and west coasts of France. The French, who wished to devote their main fleet to the protection of communications between French North Africa and the mainland of France, would thus be free to do so without fear of a stab in the back from the German Navy. Grey claimed in a letter to the French ambassador, Paul Cambon, that neither this arrangement nor the plans for the Expeditionary Force pledged Britain to go to war in defense of French interests.[8] The naval and military understandings, as the inner circle of Asquith's Cabinet interpreted them, merely specified what was to be done if the two countries did decide to "assist each other by armed force."

By 1914 the United States had long ceased to be a mere federation of weak American states struggling to extend her frontiers to the west with the help of British capital and with varying degrees of acquiescence or approval from British governments. Toward the middle of the nineteenth century, war with Mexico and the settlement of a long-standing frontier dispute with Canada resulted in her adding to her continental possessions large tracts of territory in California, Nevada, Utah, New Mexico, Arizona, Wyoming, Colorado, and Oregon. Texas, which had broken away from Mexico but soon found itself obliged to choose between British and American support, was also annexed in due course by the United States.[9] By establishing a virtual protectorate over Cuba and acquiring further possessions and dependencies in Alaska, Puerto Rico, the Philippines, Hawaii, Samoa, Midway, Guam, and Wake, the United States went on to become an imperial power with both Western and Far Eastern interests. This she accomplished at the cost of going to war with Spain and thereby incurring the resentment of most foreigners except the British, who welcomed the extension of Anglo-Saxon law and order to hitherto ill-governed or undeveloped countries.

However, if the two Anglo-Saxon empires had more in common than language, their economic circumstances were very different. In 1914 free-trade Britain, even though her merchants had ceased to dominate some markets where German and American rivals could outsell them, was still statistically the most important trading nation and by far the greatest creditor nation in the world. British citizens, for the most part interested only in finding profitable outlets for their surplus capital and oblivious of the motives supposed by Marxist economists to determine the pattern of foreign investment in a capitalist-imperialist society, held overseas investments whose value has been estimated at £4,000 million or roughly $20,000 million.[10] The income from these investments, added to payments for services rendered to customers abroad by British shipowners, financiers, and insurers, played a crucial part in maintaining the supremacy of sterling in the world's money markets despite unfavorable trade balances. Conversely, protectionist America exported more goods than she imported but was still a debtor country.[11] Furthermore, by 1914 Britain had become so deeply dependent on imports for the necessities of life that she would have needed a strong navy to protect her sea communications even if not a scrap of territory outside the British Isles had been ruled from London. The United States, with ample supplies of most raw materials and not much more than twice Britain's population in an area twenty-five times as large, was under no such compulsion. Her foreign trade, although a valuable source of amenities and extremely important to those engaged in it, was not a vital factor in her economy.

To increase the volume of that trade was nonetheless among the aims of men whose power to influence national policy was at times substantial. According to the political economist Walter Bagehot, by the middle of the nineteenth century the old mercantile notion of fighting for markets or intriguing for exclusive access to them was completely dead in Britain. Even half a century later, it was not dead in the United States. At the time of the Spanish-American War and for some years after it, Americans who could claim to speak for their fellow citizens did not conceal their belief that the United States should lose no opportunity of increasing her power and influence outside her frontiers. "The trade of the world must and shall be ours," declared Senator Albert J. Beveridge of Indiana in a context which implied that the nation should not scruple, if the need arose, to use armed force to attain its ends.[12] "From the Rio Grande to the Arctic Ocean," added Senator Henry Cabot Lodge, "there should be but one flag and one country."[13]

Such uninhibited declarations of intent made no appeal to President Woodrow Wilson, the scholar turned politician who came to office in 1913. No less a patriot than Lodge or Beveridge, he hoped and believed that national aims would be better served by conciliation than by aggression. Yet even he could scarcely have denied that a nation which sought to increase its exports while heavily taxing imports and which in the course of a century or so had fought three foreign wars, acquired vast new territories at home, and founded an overseas empire, was not in a position to dispense with armaments, no matter how reluctant its leaders might be to use them.

To decide how large the armed forces of the United States ought to be and how they should be disposed and organized was always a difficult problem for her statesmen. Elected Presidents, aware that public opinion was often divided and that the Senate jealously guarded its ultimate responsibility for foreign policy, were seldom able to give free rein to their strategic conceptions, even when they held strong opinions about such matters.

However, on one point most voters were agreed. "Standing armies are dangerous to liberty" was an axiom so dear to Americans that it narrowly escaped being written into the Constitution of the United States. The American ideal was a small professional army designed to serve as a focus of military doctrine and a nucleus around which a powerful citizen army could be built when the need arose. This was in many ways an admirable concept, but it had the disadvantage of dating from a time when little more was needed to build a powerful army than a plentiful supply of recruits and a well-stocked store of ammunition and small arms. Even for the Americans, masters of the art of military improvisation as they were to show themselves to be in two world wars, it was out of date in an age of growing specialization and increased reliance on the firepower of artillery and automatic weapons.

Between the end of the Civil War and the outbreak of the First World War a number of attempts were made by patriotic citizens to inculcate a different attitude. Major General Emory Upton, a distinguished soldier, was sent around the world after the Civil War to study the organization and methods of foreign armies. The report which he completed on his return was not widely circulated, and an unfinished book in which he called for a stronger peacetime army was published only after he had been dead for more than twenty years. A Far Eastern specialist, Homer Lea, attracted some attention, but made no lasting impression, by pointing out in a book first published in 1909 that the Philippines could be adequately defended only by a combination of fixed defenses and naval and land forces.

Theodore Roosevelt, both as President and as private citizen, preached the doctrine that political aspirations must be matched by military preparedness, but by military preparedness he meant primarily a strong navy.

Since well-informed Americans saw no need of a large army for themselves, it was natural that they should regard the armies maintained by the leading European countries as dangerous luxuries and even as anachronisms. President Woodrow Wilson's confidential adviser, Colonel Edward Mandell House, was no soldier, despite the military rank conferred on him by the governor of his native Texas, but he was far better acquainted than most of his compatriots with European countries and their problems. Yet he agreed, or at any rate professed to agree, with other advocates of Anglo-Saxon solidarity that armies would become "mere sanitary police" if only the great powers—by which he meant primarily Britain, the United States, and if possible Germany—would combine to develop "the waste places of the earth" and to protect the poor and weak against the rich and strong.[14] House and his friends did not, however, specify the proportions in which the great powers were to contribute to the massive armed forces which they might well need before the rest of the world could be brought to accept so sweeping a solution of its problems.

In the meantime it was clear that even if the United States did not need a large army, she did need an adequate number of warships to protect her trade, her homeland, and her overseas possessions. It was also clear that where British and American interests did not clash, Britain's command of the sea could be expected to confer substantial benefits on the United States. American naval strategists, by no means uniformly pro-British in sentiment, recognized the importance of this factor. Admiral Alfred T. Mahan, the historian of sea power, stressed in his writings the advantages of "walking in agreement" with the British; the General Board of the Navy recorded in 1906 its opinion that the welfare of the United States was greatly enhanced by "strong ties of friendship and by unanimity of action with Great Britain." [15]

These views did not reflect a mere sentimental regard inspired by kinship. Apart from the benefits which all nations with overseas interests derived from the policing of the seas by British warships, American, as well as British, strategists recognized that an armed conflict between the two Anglo-Saxon powers would be highly inconvenient. It would be inconvenient for the United States because the British possessed naval bases within striking distance of her eastern seaboard and because they were good customers. It would be inconvenient for Britain because her citizens had a big stake in American prosperity and because a high proportion of her imports of grain, meat, and raw materials came from the Western Hemisphere. Furthermore, the facts of geography and the experience of the War of 1812 suggested that neither side could hope to press such a conflict to a successful conclusion. To fortify the long frontier between Canada and the United States was not a practical undertaking for either party. Even though Americans tended, on the whole, to be less pro-British than the British were pro-American, it was generally accepted in London and Washington between the end of the American Civil War and the outbreak of the First World War that Anglo-American relations must, as far as possible, be maintained on a basis of friendly disagreement where a common outlook was unattainable.

For the Americans, as well as the British, the rise of imperial Germany as an aggressive mercantile and naval power raised awkward problems. Germany, by acquiring the Marshall and Caroline islands and part of the Marianas, had put herself in a position to dominate American communications in the Pacific. Apart from possible effects on American trade, this might increase the difficulty of meeting the threat from Japan which was always in the background of American strategic thinking. German infiltration of Latin-American countries, German infiltration even of the United States itself were other dangers which American statesmen could not afford to leave out of their reckoning.

A more immediate danger was a European war, whose effects on the welfare of the United States could not be foreseen but would doubtless be disagreeable. During the early years of the Woodrow Wilson era Colonel House sought to avert such a calamity by working not merely to improve his country's relations with the leading European powers, but also to lessen the tension between them. The President, in his first years of office more interested in domestic issues than in foreign affairs but never an unqualified isolationist, encouraged these efforts in the belief that they not only would reduce the risk of American embroilment in a quarrel between powers with worldwide interests but might, if trouble did ensue, enable the

United States to play the honorable and perhaps even profitable role of arbiter. House succeeded in putting himself on terms of friendship and confidence with British statesmen but failed to convince the Kaiser and his ministers that Germany had anything to gain by modifying her naval programs in deference to British wishes.

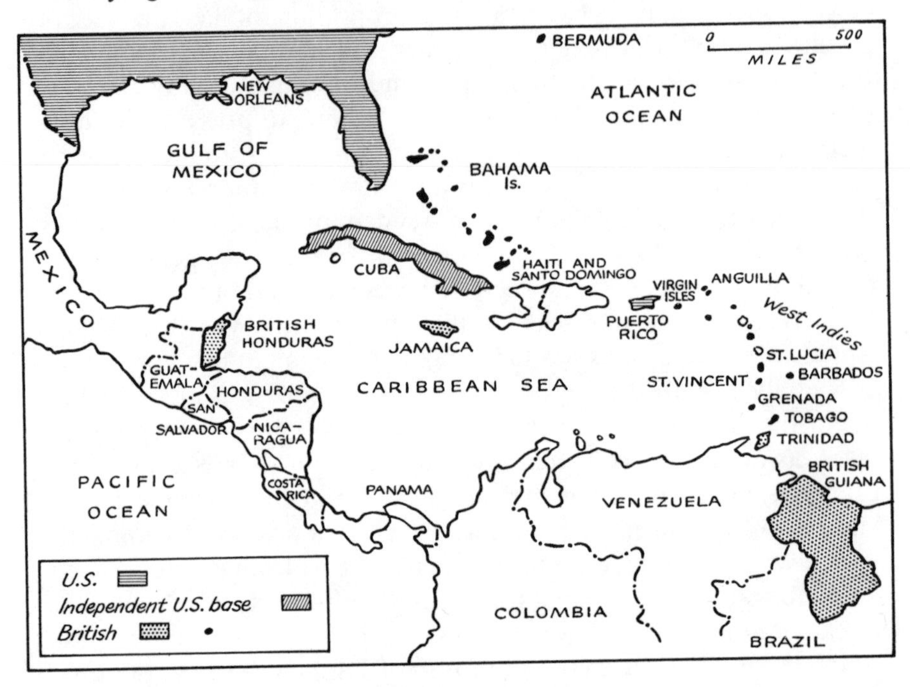

THE CARIBBEAN (1914)

With the President's approval, House also made strenuous attempts to strengthen the Western Hemisphere by shepherding the Latin-American countries into a "loose league of American states which should guarantee security from aggression and furnish a mechanism for the pacific settlement of disputes." [16] He began by tackling the Argentine, Brazil, and Chile. He made little progress, largely because the Chileans were doubtful starters and because disturbances in Mexico created conditions unfavorable for an outcome which could not, at best, have been achieved without great difficulty. Nevertheless, he and his chief continued to cherish the belief that the creation of a "mechanism" for the settlement of disputes could become a step toward the creation of a will to settle them.

In the field of strategy, the crucial question throughout the early part of the twentieth century was how the nation's naval strength should be disposed. Admiral Mahan recommended in 1903 that the main fleet should concentrate in the Pacific. Two years later the Joint Board of the Army and the Navy proposed that the battle fleet should be stationed in the Philippines and that a new naval base, which would replace or supplement the existing base at Cavite in Manila Bay, should be established for the purpose at Subic Bay.[17] This proposal was rejected partly on financial and partly on strategic grounds. The crux of the strategic problem was that the United States had two long coastlines and a number of outlying possessions to defend; at the same time, it was an axiom of naval doctrine that "the fleet should not be divided."

Clearly, a canal connecting the Atlantic and Pacific oceans would make the problem less baffling. Under the Clayton-Bulwer Treaty of 1850 with Britain, however, the United States had promised not to build such a canal except as one of the participants in an international undertaking. An important step toward the removal of that obstacle was taken in 1901 when the British, conscious of their isolation, made a bid for American goodwill by waiving the ban on an all-American canal. The Hay-Pauncefote Treaty, signed in November of that year and accepted by an overwhelming majority of the Senate in December, affirmed the right of the United States to build and operate a canal across the Isthmus of Panama and in effect to make herself responsible for its defense. In the outcome the physical difficulties proved so formidable that the canal was not ready until 1914.

Under the terms of the Hay-Pauncefote Treaty, the Panama Canal was to be accessible to ships of all nations on terms of "entire equality," without discrimination in respect of charges or otherwise. Nevertheless, Congress saw fit to pass, and President Taft to adopt in his last year of office, an act containing a clause which exempted American coastwise shipping from tolls. According to Walter Hines Page, from 1913 United States ambassador in London, this measure stamped Americans in the eyes of Englishmen as mean, stingy, peculiar, and given to queer freaks.[18] President Wilson was at first inclined to defend the exemption clause on grounds which would not have gained Page's approval. When he found that not only some of his political opponents but also many of his supporters disapproved of it, he boldly risked dissension by calling on Congress to repeal it. In return, the British deferred to American opinion by withdrawing the *de facto* recognition which they had extended to the Mexican dictator Victoriano Huerta in the belief that he might be able to restore the law and order which he had helped shatter by deposing his predecessor. This move was warmly welcomed by many Americans who disapproved of Huerta on moral grounds. It was also welcomed by some who suspected him of subserving British oil interests.

A more serious bar to complete accord between Britain and the United States was the possession by the British of colonies and naval bases in the West Indies, the Bahamas, and Bermuda and of sizable tracts of Central and South American territory in British Honduras and Guiana. As long as they held Bermuda, in particular, the British could always present a powerful threat to the United States by stationing a strong fleet there. The British did not renounce these possessions when they accepted the Hay-Pauncefote Treaty, but they did reduce their naval strength at the West Indies station in order to be stronger at home. Thus, in effect, they ceded local control of the Caribbean, at least for the time being, to the United States.

Hence the broad naval situation on the eve of the First World War was that Britannia still claimed to rule the waves but, in order to meet the threat posed by German naval expansion, had gone some way to delegate command of Far Eastern waters to the Japanese, of the western Mediterranean to the French, and of the Caribbean to the Americans. Simultaneously the Americans had moved perceptibly nearer to the ideal of a fleet capable of dominating both the eastern and the western approaches to their homeland. On the other hand, with no first-class naval base farther west than Hawaii, they were still not well placed to defend their interests in the western Pacific and the South Seas in the event of Japanese aggression. The Japanese had, however, pledged themselves by a "gentlemen's agreement" of 1908 not to flood California with immigrants, and in 1914 the British made it clear to the Japanese government that they regarded the Anglo-Japanese alliance as inoperative against the United States.

In one respect the British were determined to make no concession to American opinion. In 1907 the United States government, with the full assent of President Theodore Roosevelt but against the advice of the Navy Board and the Secretary of State,[19] joined a number of European governments in urging the British to agree that henceforth private property should be immune from seizure on the high seas in time of war. The British made it clear that they had no intention of renouncing the weapon of blockade which they had used against Napoleon. They readily agreed, however, that an international prize court should be set up to adjust claims by merchants or shipowners whose property was seized or detained, and they invited the powers to attend a conference in London for the purpose of codifying "the acknowledged principles of international law." At the London Conference in 1908 the powers drew up, and embodied in a document known as the Declaration of London, lists of goods which would always be treated as contraband of war, of goods which in some circumstances might be so treated, and of goods which would always be exempt from seizure. The Declaration of London was, however, rejected by the House of Lords. Thereupon President William Howard Taft refused to ratify it, although it had been accepted by the Senate. The consequences were that the international prize court did not come into existence and that the British were free, when war broke out in 1914, to make their own definition of contraband of war and to modify it as they pleased.

2

Disaster in Europe

AT the time of the Moroccan crisis of 1905–6 the Chief of the German General Staff, Count Alfred von Schlieffen, drew up an ambitious plan for war with France. Schlieffen had no faith in frontal assaults. These, he believed, could seldom do more than push an opponent's forces back without destroying them. The aim he set himself was to march his troops into central Belgium and make so wide a sweep through Flanders, Artois, and Picardy that "the last man on the right" would "brush the Channel with his sleeve." He would then encircle Paris and pin the main body of the French armies against the barrier formed by their own frontier defenses and by German columns advancing from southern Belgium and Luxembourg in the general direction of Rethel and Verdun.[1]

Schlieffen believed that this maneuver could succeed only if the German armies of the right were strong enough to carry all before them during their roundabout advance toward the heart of France. Since their strength would depend largely on the number of roads they could use for their approach march, it followed that their initial advance would have to be made on a wide front. At the same time Schlieffen believed that they would be unable to advance into central Belgium by crossing the Meuse exclusively in Belgian territory, for the Belgian forts at Namur and Liège were regarded in 1905 as impregnable. He decided, therefore, to cross the Meuse in Belgian territory only at Huy and to march the main body of the armies of the right across the narrow strip of Dutch territory which projects southward to Maastricht and beyond.

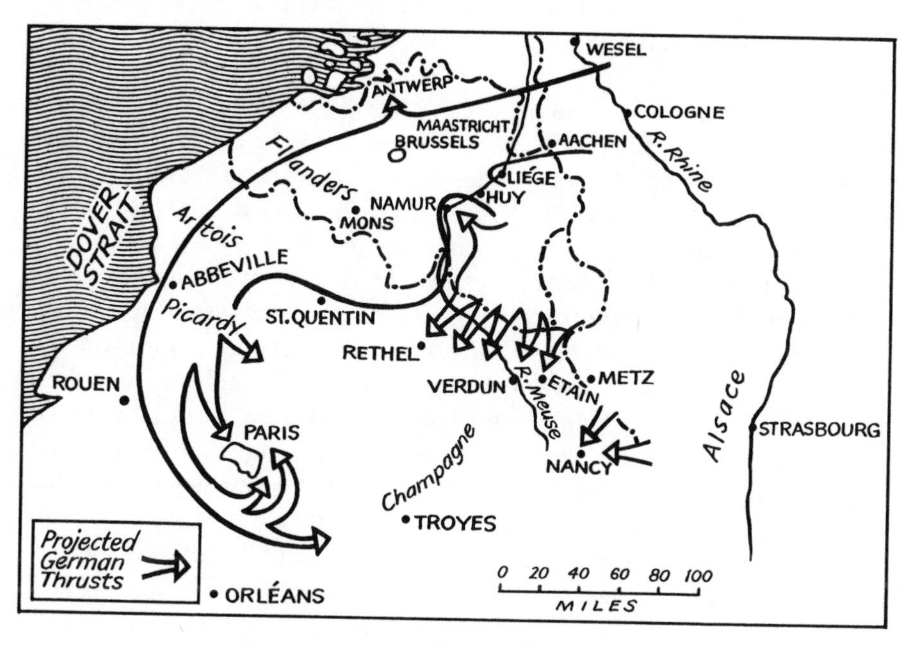

THE SCHLIEFFEN PLAN (1905)

This meant that if the Schlieffen plan were ever carried out, not only part of Belgium but also the part of Holland known as the Maastricht appendix would become a corridor for German troops. Schlieffen believed, however, that the Dutch could be induced by adroit diplomacy to offer no resistance. In his more sanguine moments he hoped that the Belgians, too, might succumb to diplomatic pressure backed by a show of force. On the other hand, he was keenly aware that the chances of success would be materially reduced if promises of British help should induce the Belgians to offer serious resistance. The advance of the German right through central Belgium, he wrote after his retirement, could "easily be blocked" by the British and the Belgians, "supported if necessary by a few French corps." [2]

Schlieffen was succeeded in 1906 by Helmuth von Moltke, a nephew of the Count von Moltke whose plans had laid the foundations of victory in the Franco-Prussian War. The younger Moltke, conscious that he was likely to be compared with his famous namesake, was far from confident that any such comparison would be to his advantage. On learning of his appointment he asked pointedly whether the emperor expected to draw the winning ticket twice in the same lottery.

Sustained until Schlieffen died in 1913 by a stream of advice and exhortation from his predecessor, Moltke nonetheless set to work to recast the plan in the knowledge that circumstances had changed since it was first conceived. The Dutch, he was warned, could no longer be relied upon to acquiesce in the invasion of their country. It followed that unless Moltke was prepared to fight them, as well as the French, the Russians, and possibly the Belgians and the British, the crossing of the Meuse by the First and Second armies, on the German right, would have to be made, after all, exclusively in Belgian territory. Since Namur and Huy, even if they could be reached and taken at an early stage, were too far from the First Army's assembly area north of Aachen to make convenient crossing places for that army, this meant that for practical purposes Moltke had no choice but to gamble on the prompt capture of Liège, with its six large and six smaller forts and its crucial road and rail bridges. Without the bridges, he could not hope to pass his troops across the river except after intolerable delays or to supply them during their advance through central Belgium and beyond.

Accordingly, a special detachment of the Second Army was given the task of seizing Liège as a corridor for the First Army. Mounted troops and infantry in motorcars were to race forward on the first day and do their best to take the place by a *coup de main.* They were also to exploit any opportunities that might arise of bypassing the forts by seizing bridges or establishing improvised crossings outside the town. Should the *coup de main* be unsuccessful, attempts would be made to take Liège by assault, if necessary with the aid of special siege guns. Guns of novel design were ordered from Krupp, and arrangements were made to borrow a number of exceptionally heavy guns from the Austrian Army. When the Liège forts and the bridges they commanded were safely in German hands the First and Second armies, ultimately twenty-six divisions strong exclusive of Landwehr brigades and cavalry, would cross the Meuse at Liège and Huy while the Third Army on their left, with eight divisions, made for Dinant. On the left of the Third Army the Fourth and Fifth armies, with twenty-one divisions, would advance through southern Belgium and Luxembourg and across the Franco-German frontier immediately north of the French fortified zone at Verdun. South of Metz the Sixth and Seventh armies, with twenty-one first-line or reserve divisions supplemented by six Ersatz divisions, four Landwehr regiments, and three cavalry divisions, were to stand on the defensive in the hope that the French would walk into a trap.[3]

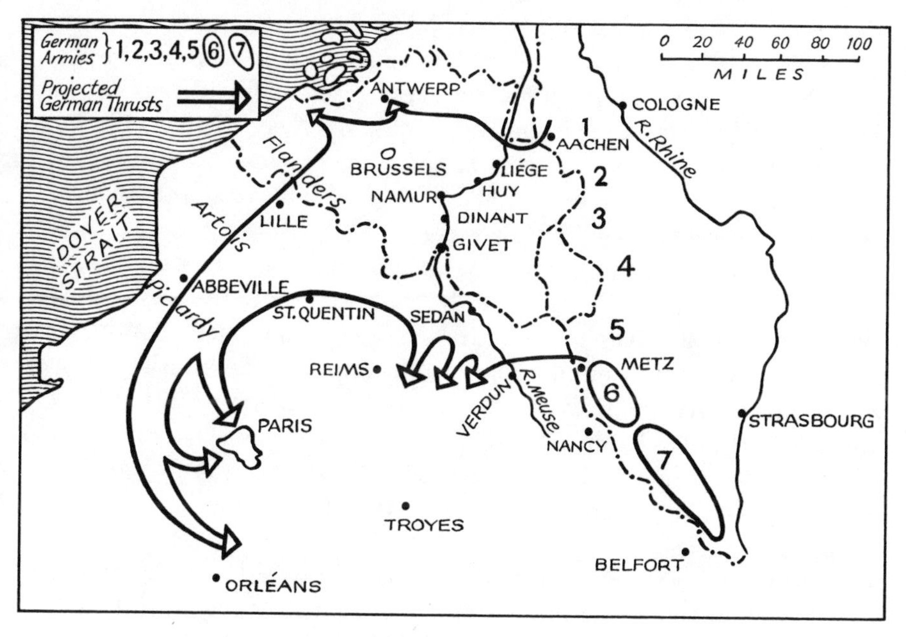

THE MOLTKE PLAN (1911–1914)

In the autumn of 1911 the French told the British of a document in their possession which purported to be a copy of the Schlieffen plan with annotations by Moltke.[4] Perhaps because a number of conflicting tales, possibly invented by the French to protect their sources, were circulated to account for their possession of this document, much doubt has been cast on its authenticity. However that may be, there is no reason to suppose that Joffre lacked the means of making an accurate assessment of Moltke's intentions.[5] The trouble was not that he was unaware of the danger to which his forces would be exposed if the Germans marched across the Meuse below Namur and threatened his flank, but that he made light of it. Partly because the Belgian forts were thought to be so strong, partly because Joffre refused to believe that German reserve formations would be able to keep up with first-line troops, he insisted that Moltke could not attempt such a maneuver without so weakening his center as to open the way for an Allied offensive.

In 1908 Austro-Hungary alarmed the chancelleries of Europe by annexing Bosnia and Herzegovina. These former provinces of the Ottoman Empire had, by international agreement, been administered since 1878 by Austrian officials with every appearance of success. Nevertheless, their annexation was resented in Russia and in Western Europe as a high-handed action which challenged the authority of the powers. Austria's action was, however, supported by the German emperor, who claimed afterward to have stood "in shining armor" beside his fellow sovereign.

Six years later Herzegovina was once more in the news. On June 28, 1914, the Archduke Franz Ferdinand, heir to the thrones of Austria and Hungary, was murdered at Sarajevo, the chief town of the province, by a youth named Gavrilo Princip. Princip and his fellow conspirators were believed to be agents of a Serbian secret society, the Black Hand, and the Serbian government was suspected of conniving at the crime in the interests of a Russian-inspired Pan-Slav movement which sought to challenge Austrian domination of lands inhabited by Slavs.

The Austrian Foreign Minister, Count Leopold von Berchtold, concluded that the time had come for a punitive expedition to Belgrade. This would teach the Serbs a lesson and would warn the leaders of the Pan-Slav movement that interference in the affairs of the Austro-Hungarian Empire would not be tolerated. His agents were unable to establish the complicity of responsible Serbian statesmen or officials, and the attitude of the Serbian government was conciliatory. Berchtold, sustained by past assurances of German support for Austria's foreign policy, nonetheless decided to force a crisis. He rejected offers of a friendly settlement, instructed the Austrian ambassador in St. Petersburg to warn the Russians that Austria would not "recoil from the possibility of European complications," and on July

28 persuaded the aged Emperor Franz Josef to declare war on Serbia.

The consequences were disastrous. On July 29 the Czar Nicholas II, alarmed by Berchtold's bellicosity, sanctioned a precautionary deployment of Russian troops along the Austro-Hungarian frontier; on the following day he ordered general mobilization. Thereupon the German government, determined not to be caught on the wrong foot should Berchtold's punitive expedition lead to a European war, issued an ultimatum calling on the Russians to restore their armies to a peace footing without delay. The czar, not unmoved by a personal appeal from the Kaiser, might conceivably have agreed to some such course had he not been warned that the Russian military machine would break down if put into reverse. As it was, he could do nothing. No reply had been received from the Russian government when the German ultimatum expired at noon on Saturday, August 1; some five hours later the Russian Foreign Minister, Sergei Sazonov, received from Count Friedrich von Pourtalès, the German ambassador, a note declaring war. Sazonov claimed afterward to have told Pourtalès that "the curses of the nations" would rest upon Germany for precipitating a war which she could easily have stopped by exerting pressure on Vienna.[6]

Almost simultaneously Moltke, 800 miles away in Berlin, received the mobilization order which gave him the signal for a two-front war against France and Russia.[7] About half an hour later the Kaiser was handed a telegram which the Foreign Ministry had received from Prince Lichnowsky, the German ambassador in London. This was to the effect that, according to Lichnowsky's understanding, the British would be willing to abstain from warlike measures and to urge the French to do likewise if Germany refrained from attacking France. The Kaiser, wrongly believing that he had been offered a free hand in Eastern Europe as long as he made no aggressive move in the West, thereupon recalled Moltke and asked whether troops assigned to the invasion of Belgium and Luxembourg could be switched to the Eastern Front. But he found, as the Czar of All the Russias had found a day or two earlier, that not even absolute power could arrest the march of armies. Although plans for war against Russia alone had in fact been considered by the German General Staff, Moltke replied that matters had gone too far. The Kaiser then tried, independently of Moltke, to halt a division whose forward troops were due to enter Luxembourg that evening but abandoned the attempt when he learned that the British offer was conditional on his abstaining from hostile action not only against France, but also against Russia. All he accomplished was to undermine the confidence of his Chief of the General Staff. Moltke, according to his own account, was so shaken by the Kaiser's interventions that he shed "tears of abject despair" and was "never the same thereafter." [8]

By nightfall on Sunday, August 2, strategic points throughout the Grand Duchy of Luxembourg were in German hands. Belgium had not yet been invaded, but at 7 P.M. the German minister in Brussels presented a note which threatened war unless the Belgians agreed within twelve hours to admit German troops and adopt an attitude of "benevolent neutrality." The Germans claimed in support of their case that they had been reliably informed of a French plan to invade Germany through Belgium but did not add that the French had no intention of giving effect to it unless the Germans entered Belgium first.

The Belgians had no difficulty in concluding that surrender to Germany's demands would compromise not only their honor, but also the country's ultimate future as an independent state. They were, however, not well placed to resist a German invasion without French or British help. Since the independence and neutrality of Belgium were guaranteed by a treaty signed in 1839 by England, France, Russia, Prussia, and Austria, they had felt it incumbent upon them until the outbreak of war to take no overt steps which might suggest that they expected to be attacked from one quarter rather than another. Consequently, the Belgian field army of six infantry divisions and one cavalry division was not concentrated to meet a threat from any particular direction, but was so disposed as to preserve an appearance of impartiality and to facilitate withdrawal to a central position should the country be invaded either by the Germans from the east, by the French from the south and west, or even by the British from the north. The forts commanding the principal crossings of the Meuse were manned by garrison troops not trained or equipped for a mobile role. In order that no provocation should seem to be offered to the Germans, little or nothing had been done to prepare infantry positions in the gaps between the Liège forts. Finally, the Belgians had practically no heavy artillery. They had ordered a number of heavy guns from Krupp, but these had not yet arrived when the Germans presented their ultimatum.

In accordance with the constitution, the thirty-nine-year-old King Albert of the Belgians became Commander in Chief on the outbreak of war. His appointment took effect on August 3. The king, a soldier by training, would have liked to concentrate the whole of the field army on the Meuse but came to the conclusion that too much time had been lost to make this feasible. It was agreed that the garrisons of Liège and Namur should each be supported by one infantry division and that the rest of the field army should concentrate near Louvain for the defense of Brussels. If driven from its positions, it would fall back on Antwerp.

Orders for the destruction of a number of bridges and tunnels were given on August 3. It was not, however, until after German troops had crossed the frontier on August 4 that the king appealed to the treaty powers and invited French troops to enter Belgium for the purpose of "ascertaining the direction of advance of the Germans and delaying their columns."

Joffre responded to the invitation by sending a substantial body of cavalry into southern Belgium. His troops moved rapidly along the right bank of the Meuse as far as a point almost within sight of Liège. They also reconnoitered a wide area on the left bank before turning for home. Since the Germans had not yet arrived in strength except in the immediate neighborhood of Liège, this reconnaissance served no useful purpose. On the contrary, its negative results tended to bolster Joffre's mistaken belief that the enemy would not try to cross the Meuse in force below Namur. Joffre took no steps to prepare infantry positions in the Longuyon-Rochefort sector, where his troops were soon to meet the Germans with disastrous consequences, and he made no serious attempt to help the Belgians at Liège or elsewhere.

In England, the Balkan crisis descended upon a government preoccupied with the aftereffects of an attempt to impose home rule on Ireland against the wishes of the Unionist inhabitants of Ulster. A number of Army officers had been asked in March to choose between the sacrifice of their careers and obedience to undisclosed orders which might involve them in hostilities against the Ulstermen.

The sequel was a controversy which threatened to split from top to bottom not merely Ireland but the whole of the United Kingdom. By the time of the murder at Sarajevo the Secretary of State for War, the Adjutant General, and the Chief of the Imperial General Staff all had resigned their posts, the last on the understanding that in all probability he would be recalled to command the Expeditionary Force in the event of war. As a temporary expedient the Prime Minister, who did not despair of convincing the Army that he had acted in good faith, had assumed immediate responsibility for War Office business.

At the end of a discussion of the Irish question on Friday, July 24, Grey told the Cabinet for the first time that he regarded the European situation as "very grave." He added that he hoped that negotiations between Russia and Austro-Hungary might yet lead to a peaceful settlement.[9] Four days later Austria declared war on Serbia.

The events of the next few days came as a great shock to most members of the government. Ministers outside the inner circle of Asquith's Cabinet, although aware of the general trend of the staff conversations with the French, had learned only in 1912 of the plans for the Expeditionary Force.[10] Dismayed by the prospect of British participation in a European war, many had taken refuge in the belief that the Foreign Office would know how to steer clear of so redoubtable a hazard. In these circumstances it was not to be expected that the Cabinet as a whole would agree in 1914 to declare war on Germany merely because conditional promises had been given to the French. On the other hand, concrete evidence that the sanctity of treaties and the independence of Belgium were at stake was likely, in the opinion of Grey and others, to unite all but a few extremists in favor of a resolute attempt to call the Germans to account, if necessary by force of arms. Hence it was not until news of Germany's demands on Belgium reached London late on August 2 that Grey was in a position to take a strong line without risking a disastrous split. Accompanied by Haldane, who had continued since he exchanged the War Office for the Woolsack in 1912 to take a keen interest in military affairs, he then called on Asquith and asked that the Expeditionary Force be mobilized without delay.

Monday, August 3, was a bank holiday in England. Large numbers of private citizens, impelled by some mysterious upsurge of patriotic feeling or merely out for a lark, appeared in the streets of London demanding war against Germany. The Belgians, it was learned, had rejected Germany's demands. Telegrams calling up reservists and Territorials were dispatched with Asquith's sanction. Germany declared war on France and concluded a secret alliance with Turkey. Grey, after convincing the House of Commons that Britain could not afford to disregard her obligations under the Belgian treaty, told Churchill that the next step was to send the Germans an ultimatum calling upon them to "stop the invasion of Belgium within twenty-four hours." [11] The ultimatum was not in fact sent until the following day, a good many hours after the invasion of Belgium had begun. It expired at midnight on August 4 by Central European time.

The government had next to find a full-time Secretary of State for War. Haldane seemed the obvious choice. Although his critics called him garrulous and glib, he was undeniably energetic and resourceful. As a former holder of the post, he had sponsored far-reaching reforms at the War Office and in the Army. Some of these were based on plans worked out in the lifetime of an earlier government, but still, it was he who had persuaded the Cabinet and the House of Commons to adopt them. He was widely, and on the whole not unfairly, regarded as father of the Territorial Army, the General Staff, and the Officers' Training Corps. No civilian had a better knowledge of the plans for the Expeditionary Force or a better understanding of the strategy they stood for. On the other hand, it was alleged against him that he had shown too keen an interest in German philosophy, and in recent years had taken too active a part in attempts to reach agreement with Germany, to be acceptable to the man in the street. Asquith did not claim to understand the views of the man in the street but was always willing to listen to a case. He decided to make a bid for national unity by offering the post to Field Marshal Lord Kitchener, famous for his conquest of the Sudan and his brush with the viceroy, Lord Curzon, during a spell as Commander in Chief in India.

Kitchener did his country an immense service by insisting from the outset that preparations should be made for a long war. Nonetheless, the appointment of a serving officer to a Cabinet post of crucial importance led to difficulties aggravated by Kitchener's autocratic outlook, dislike of argument, and reluctance to take civilian colleagues into his confidence. In comparison with these temperamental shortcomings it mattered little that Kitchener disliked the

French, was contemptuous of the General Staff, and distrusted on principle any proposal not initiated by himself. Such minor prejudices could have served, and to some extent did serve, as useful correctives to the tendency of such Francophiles as Henry Wilson to rely too much on the French and to regard the plans made for the Expeditionary Force as immutable. The real objection to the choice of Kitchener as Secretary of State for War was that it forced ministers to rely for their knowledge of military affairs on a warlord entirely out of sympathy with the principle of collective responsibility which Cabinet government stood for.

The future of the Expeditionary Force was discussed at an *ad hoc* "Council of War" on August 5 and a similar meeting on August 6. Each of these gatherings was attended by some sixteen or seventeen persons, some of whom knew little or nothing of the plans drawn up before the war.

The crucial question was whether the whole or only part of the Expeditionary Force should cross the Channel without delay. The Committee of Imperial Defence had recommended in 1908 that in the event of war, at least two divisions should stay at home until the Territorial Army was ready to assume responsibility for home defense. On the other hand, Asquith had given Henry Wilson to understand in May, 1914, that even in face of the Ulster crisis, he did not contemplate withholding more than one division in such circumstances as had now arisen.[12] The War Office representatives were therefore much put out when the government decided, without dissent from Kitchener, that after all only the Cavalry Division and four infantry divisions should move with the first wave. Furthermore, as the sequel to an incautious remark by Sir John French, who was to command the Expeditionary Force, Kitchener was only narrowly prevented from insisting that the force should concentrate not at Maubeuge, as had long been planned, but at Amiens, where a gap of 100 miles would have separated it from the left of the French armies.

In the course of the discussions the old notion of sending the force to Antwerp was revived, also by Sir John French, on the ground that the Germans were said to be marching across the Maastricht appendix and that a landing at Antwerp would enable the British to join forces with both the Belgians and the Dutch.[13] This proposal was dropped when the report was found to be without foundation. Accordingly the Expeditionary Force, reduced for the time being to roughly two-thirds of its planned strength and supported by some 300 field guns and four squadrons of aircraft for tactical and artillery reconnaissance, arrived in due course at Maubeuge. A directive from Kitchener instructed Sir John French that his primary task was to support the French Army but that he was not to take orders from any Allied general and must decide for himself whether to share in movements which might expose his force to undue risks. These instructions threw a heavy burden on Sir John, a notoriously impulsive and impressionable man who would not find it easy to decide just what constituted an undue risk.

One of the advantages claimed for sea power as Britain's principal weapon of home defense was that it provided security not only during a war, but also before was was declared. Unlike an army whose units had to be brought up to strength and organized in brigades and divisions before they could take the field, the fleet was supposed always to be ready.

This claim was broadly justified, inasmuch as the resources needed to put the Grand Fleet and the naval home commands on a war footing consisted largely of either First Fleet ships which were fully manned in time of peace or Second Fleet ships whose crews could be quickly brought to strength at the expense of shore establishments. Even so, the Admiralty's war plans could not be fully implemented without Third Fleet ships manned largely by reservists who would not normally be called out unless general mobilization or a state of national emergency was decreed. Hence it was important that the Admiralty should be ready with a scheme which would ensure that reservists from civilian life were swiftly and smoothly absorbed into the service when the moment came.

For reasons not connected with the crisis in the Balkans, the usual fleet exercises were replaced in the summer of 1914 by an exercise designed to test the mobilization scheme. In the middle of July more than 20,000 reservists reported to their depots. Ships of the Third Fleet then joined the First and Second fleets for a grand review at Spithead.

When Grey gave his historic warning to the Cabinet late on July 24, the test mobilization had just been completed. Reservists called to the Third Fleet had been released and were homeward bound.

The First and Second fleets were at Portland but were due to leave early on Monday, July 27. The First Fleet would then disperse by squadrons for tactical exercises at sea; ships of the Second Fleet would move to their home ports, where they would dismiss such officers and ratings as had joined from shore establishments. Thereafter some ships would go into dock for repairs or refitting, and some would be laid up.

The news from foreign capitals on Sunday, July 26, was far from reassuring. Churchill spent the day with his family more than 100 miles from the Admiralty but arranged that the First Sea Lord, Prince Louis of Battenberg, should "do whatever was necessary." [14] Prince Louis saw the importance of keeping as much as possible of the fleet together at a moment when a flare-up in the Balkans might put Russia and the Central Powers at each other's throats. He ordered the First Fleet to remain at Portland until further notice; ships of the Second Fleet, on reaching their home ports, were to stay there "in proximity to their balance crews." [15]

At Portland the First Fleet would be safe, either in peace or in war, as long as it stayed in harbor. Should it remain there until war was declared it would, however, run some risk of a surprise attack with torpedoes in the narrow waters of the Channel when it emerged. On July 28 Churchill and Prince Louis agreed that the best course was to move the most valuable ships to their war stations while the country was still at peace. With Asquith's sanction, the First Fleet left Portland on July 29. That night the fleet, forming a line of ships some eighteen miles long, steamed safely through the Dover Strait on its way to Scapa Flow.

As Scapa Flow is more than 500 sea miles from the Kentish Knock light vessel at the mouth of the Thames Estuary, the effect of this move was to put it out of the power of the main body of the Grand Fleet to intervene before the second day if the German High Seas Fleet should leave its base in the Jade Roads and head for the English Channel at a time when the Grand Fleet was in harbor. However, even without their best and strongest ships the British had powerful forces on the east coast and in the Thames Estuary and the Channel. The Lords of the Admiralty felt justified in assuming that if put to the test, their system of patrols and flotillas, backed by the ultimate sanction of the Grand Fleet, would prove effective against an enemy who would not willingly thrust his head into a noose. On August 2 the Cabinet sanctioned a fleet mobilization order issued by Churchill on his own authority on the previous evening. On the same day, after the Germans had declared war on Russia but some hours before they presented their demands to the Belgians, Grey handed Cambon a memorandum to the effect that the Royal Navy would resist any attempt by the German High Seas Fleet to enter the English Channel or the southern part of the North Sea for the purpose of bombarding the French coast or taking hostile action against French shipping.

This gesture went some way to relieve the French of the fear that Britain meant to leave them in the lurch, but it was not a complete answer to their naval problems.

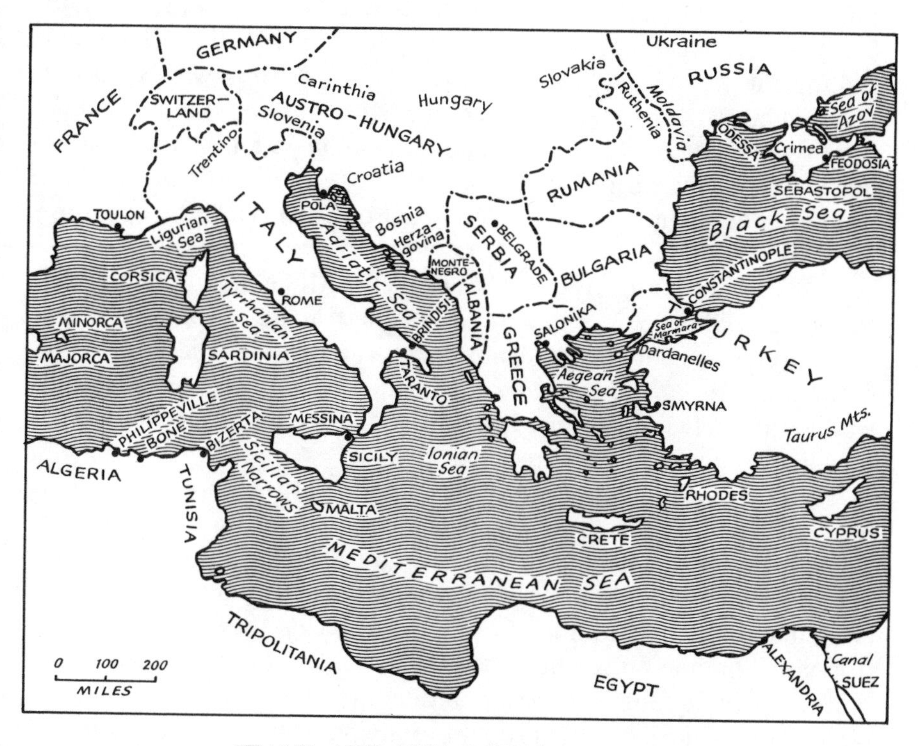

ITALY AND THE BALKANS (1914)

In the western and central Mediterranean France was the strongest naval power, with sixteen capital ships to three British, one German, and eight Austrian. At the same time, Italy's geographical position might, in certain circumstances, enable her or a power allied with her to dispute command of the Sicilian Narrows with the British and the French. Hence it was a matter of some importance that until the eleventh hour her attitude remained uncertain. Under the Triple Alliance of 1882 the Italians had pledged themselves to support Germany and Austro-Hungary should either be attacked by Russia, yet it was only at the expense of Austro-Hungary that they could gain advantages in the Adriatic which they were known to covet. Ultimately they declined to join the Central Powers on the ground that they were not bound to take part in an offensive war which Germany and Austro-Hungary had launched without consulting them.

The fact remained that the French, in spite of their superiority in numbers and tonnage over the combined German and Austrian fleets in Mediterranean waters, had no ship capable of catching and sinking the fast German battle cruiser *Goeben.* They wished to use their naval power to ensure safe passage for troops from French North Africa to the French mainland but feared that the *Goeben* might sink their transports and escape before their battle fleet, based in Toulon and commanded by Admiral Boué de Lapeyrère, could intervene.

On the other hand, Admiral Sir Berkeley Milne, commanding the British Mediterranean Fleet at Malta, had at his disposal no less than three ships capable of dealing with the *Goeben.* These were the battle cruisers *Inflexible, Indomitable,* and *Indefatigable,* each armed with eight twelve-inch guns. In addition, Milne had four heavy and four light cruisers and fourteen destroyers.

Accordingly, the Admiralty warned Milne at the end of July that his first task in the event of war would be to "aid the French in the transportation of their African army" by covering the *Goeben* and any other fast German ships which might appear. In order to make it clear that Milne would not be expected to tackle the Austrian battle fleet single-handed if it emerged from its base at Pola, near the head of the Adriatic, the Admiralty added that he must not, "at this stage," allow himself to be brought to action against superior forces, "except in combination with the French as part of a general battle." [16]

Admiral Wilhelm Souchon, commanding the German Mediterranean Squadron, had no base of his own, and his command consisted only of the *Goeben* and the fast light cruiser *Breslau.* Some weeks earlier he had put into Pola for repairs to the *Goeben*'s boilers. Not wishing to be bottled up in the Adriatic in the event of war, he decided at the end of July to move south. As a result of Italy's impending neutrality, he was coolly received in southern Italy and Sicily and was able to obtain coal only by drawing on the stocks of a German shipping firm at Messina and arranging for further supplies to be transferred to his ships outside Italian territorial waters.

Souchon learned on August 3 that Germany had declared war on France. By that time he had made up his mind that if war did come, he would begin by attacking ports of embarkation for French troops at Bône and Philippeville in Algeria. He was on his way there when a further signal from the German Admiralty informed him that Germany had concluded a secret alliance with Turkey and ordered him to take his squadron to Constantinople. He decided to complete the task in hand before complying with this order. Reaching the Algerian coast early on August 4 without interference from the French battle fleet, which was far to the north, the *Goeben* bombarded Philippeville while the *Breslau* tackled Bône. Both ships were sighted soon afterward from two of the three British battle cruisers, but Milne was powerless to intervene since the British ultimatum to Germany had not yet expired.

Milne, although prevented by fog from shadowing the German ships throughout the rest of the day as he was told to do, judged correctly that they would make for Messina. Neither he nor the Admiralty guessed, however, that a voyage to Constantinople was in prospect. Moreover, as Italy had now declared her neutrality, Milne was expressly forbidden by the Admiralty to venture within six miles of the coast. Expecting Souchon to break out to the west and either attack French shipping or make a dash for the Atlantic, he took station with two of his battle cruisers west of the Strait of Messina, sent the third battle cruiser to coal at Bizerte so that she would be ready to join him if he moved in that direction, and posted only a single ship, the light cruiser *Gloucester,* on the route which Souchon was likely to take if he went east. In addition, he ordered a squadron of heavy cruisers and destroyers under Rear Admiral Sir Ernest Troubridge to watch the mouth of the Adriatic lest the Austrians come out or the Germans try to enter.

At Messina, Souchon faced a cheerless prospect. If he stayed where he was, he risked the disarmament of his ships by the Italian authorities and the internment of their crews. If he put to sea, he would be lucky to escape interception by a superior British force. To make matters worse, soon after his return he learned that "for political reasons," his superiors no longer thought it desirable that he should go to Constantinople but expected him to make his own choice in the light of an express warning that he could expect no active cooperation from the Austrian fleet.

The background of this change was that the grand vizier and other Turkish ministers had refused to endorse a promise made by the pro-German Minister of War, Enver Pasha, that the *Goeben* and the *Breslau* would be allowed to pass the forts and minefields guarding the entrance to the Dardanelles and steam through the Sea of Marmara to Constantinople. The Turks, notwithstanding the agreement they had signed, were not prepared to part with the advantages of neutrality by siding openly with the Central Powers.

Souchon was unwilling to retreat ingloriously to Pola. In any case, he could not be sure of reaching Pola safely. Concluding that he might as well be hanged for a sheep as for a lamb, he decided to make a dash for Constantinople in the hope that if he succeeded in arriving at the entrance to the Dardanelles without disaster, the Turks might, after all, be persuaded to admit him. Leaving Messina in daylight on August 6, he headed northeast in order to give the impression that he was bound for the Adriatic. He was duly followed by the *Gloucester,* whose commander, Captain Howard Kelly, reported his course and speed to Milne and Troubridge.

Milne had no inkling of Souchon's destination. Expecting that the German squadron would either continue toward the Adriatic and be intercepted by Troubridge or double back in a desperate attempt to elude his battle cruisers, he made no change in his dispositions apart from sending an additional cruiser to join the *Gloucester.*

After nightfall Souchon was obliged to turn to starboard, since otherwise he would have gone so far out of his course as to be unable to make rendezvous with a collier which had been ordered to meet him off the coast of Greece. He had been unable to shake off the *Gloucester,* and in consequence, his change of course was signaled to the two British admirals. Milne, receiving the signal about midnight, thereupon decided to set off in pursuit. He was, however, too far behind to stand much chance of catching the German ships in a stern chase. On the other hand, Troubridge, by steaming south at high speed, might be able to head them off if they continued eastward and would still be well placed to intercept them should they turn to port and head toward him.

Troubridge was nonetheless in a difficult position. A great-grandson of one of Nelson's captains, he was noted for his interest in seamanship. He had received from Milne a copy of the Admiralty order forbidding action against superior forces. As the *Goeben* was capable, at any rate in theory, of sinking all or any of his ships at ranges which would preclude an effective reply, clearly she and the *Breslau* were a superior force. Troubridge came to the conclusion that, even so, he would be justified in engaging Souchon's ships if he could catch them in time to open fire at first light. Accordingly, he headed south at high speed until, in the early hours of August 7, a careful calculation convinced him that he could no longer hope to join action until the sun was well above the horizon. He then broke off the pursuit, reported by wireless that he had done so, and waited for one or more of Milne's battle cruisers to join him. No battle cruisers having appeared by 10 A.M., he put into a convenient port and prepared to resume the watch on the Adriatic which he was still under orders to maintain. Later in the day Captain Kelly of the *Gloucester* made a daring attempt to delay the German squadron by opening fire on the *Breslau* and thus inducing her consort to turn back in order to engage him, but Souchon, scenting danger, resumed his original course after firing a few ineffective rounds.

As things turned out, Milne might conceivably still have caught the *Goeben* if a clerk at the Admiralty had not chosen an inopportune moment to dispatch a routine signal authorizing the commencement of hostilities against Austria.[17] Souchon, on reaching the Aegean, paused while awaiting the reply to a message in which he asked the German naval attaché in Constantinople to put all possible pressure on the Turks to admit him to the Dardanelles. It came so late that he might have had difficulty in making his escape if Milne, interpreting the signal from the Admiralty as an order to prepare for action against the Austrian fleet, had not lost valuable time by steaming away from him until the mistake was discovered and put right. Even then, Milne still believed that Souchon was more likely to double back to the west than to seek asylum in neutral Turkey.

The answer to Souchon's message reached him on August 10. It was so cryptic that it brought him little enlightenment. Nevertheless, he presented himself that afternoon at the entrance to the Dardanelles and asked for a pilot. The outcome was a dramatic interview in Constantinople, 150 miles away, between Lieutenant Colonel von Kress of the German Military Mission and Enver Pasha. Kress asked that the Turkish commander on the spot should be ordered to admit the German ships. Enver began by insisting that the matter must be referred to the grand vizier but at length yielded to the argument that the local commander could not be kept waiting for an answer.[18] Finally he agreed that the ships should be allowed to enter. When asked whether British ships should be fired upon if they tried to follow, he hesitated a long time before giving an affirmative reply.

Since Turkey was still neutral despite her alliance with Germany, international law required that the ships should be disarmed unless their commander agreed to leave Turkish territorial waters within a day or two of his arrival at Constantinople. The Germans refused, however, to accept even the "temporary and superficial" disarmament proposed by the Turkish authorities. Someone then suggested that the ships should be deemed to have been sold to Turkey and should be given Turkish names. Perhaps partly because the British had caused resentment in Turkey by requisitioning two battleships built for the Turkish Navy in British shipyards, the Turks welcomed this proposal without reflecting until it was too late that they were throwing away their last chance of using their neutrality as a bargaining counter in negotiations with Germany on the one hand and the Entente Powers on the other.

The presence of the German warships, still under German command and manned by German crews, within gunshot of the Turkish capital proved a hideous embarrassment to those members of the government who did not concur wholeheartedly in Enver's pro-German policy. Souchon, as he afterward confessed, was determined to force Turkey, "even against her will," to enter the war on the side of the Central Powers.[19] In the last week of October he showed his hand. Accompanied by a Turkish cruiser and destroyers, he took his squadron into the Black Sea, sank a Russian gunboat, and bombarded Sevastopol, Odessa, and Feodosiya (afterward Novorossisk). The sultan's ministers, having told the world that Turkey had bought the *Goeben* and the *Breslau,* could not disclaim responsibility, although many of them would have liked to do so. The Russians were equally powerless to escape the consequences of Souchon's gesture.

At a moment when they would willingly have paid a large sum to keep Turkey neutral if they could have done so without forfeiting the support of their allies, they were forced by ineluctable circumstances to declare war on her.

If this was a calamity for the Turks, it was an unmitigated disaster for the Russians. War with Turkey, by closing the only route between the Black Sea and the Mediterranean to Russian shipping, deprived Russia at one stroke of all but a tiny fraction of her foreign trade. Since access to her Baltic ports was already barred by the German Navy, henceforth war material from overseas could reach her only through Vladivostok, Archangel, and Murmansk. Vladivostok was thousands of miles from the battlefront, Archangel was icebound for roughly half the year, and the railway which was to connect Murmansk with St. Petersburg was still under construction. In general, communications between these far-off ports of entry and the main centers of distribution were so inadequate and so badly organized that vast quantities of supplies were to accumulate during the next few years at all three places. Despite huge orders placed abroad by incompetent and often dishonest officials, only a trickle reached the armies whose leaders cried out for arms and ammunition to save them from defeat.

3

Mons to Ypres

THE German Chancellor, Theobald von Bethmann-Hollweg, confessed to the Reichstag on August 4, 1914, that his country's invasion of Belgium was contrary to international law. He added, not very convincingly, that the wrong done to Belgium would be righted as soon as Germany attained her "military goal." [1]

This admission did little or nothing to efface the bad impression created by Germany's repudiation of her obligations under the Belgian treaty. Moreover, the invaders of Belgium did not improve their image by adopting a policy of calculated harshness in the belief that this would shorten the war by making the Belgians more amenable. Tales of war atrocities are often exaggerated and sometimes baseless, but many outrages committed by the Germans in Belgium were well attested. On the pretext that civilians had opened fire on German troops and were cooperating with the Belgian Army, hostages were shot, villages were burned, and part of the city of Louvain, including a library containing irreplaceable books and manuscripts, was wantonly destroyed.[2] Apart from their obvious inhumanity, these measures contravened the principle, accepted by Germany under the Hague Convention, that only individual offenders whose guilt was proved could be held accountable for such acts and that collective punishments were illegal.

President Wilson was deeply shocked by reports of German atrocities in Belgium.[3] Although eventually he came to regard all the European belligerents as almost equally selfish and hence unworthy of his esteem, in the early part of the war he saw France and Britain as defenders of civilization against Teutonic barbarism. No decent man, "knowing the situation and Germany," he said privately, could be other than heart and soul with the Allies.[4]

This was Woodrow Wilson's view as a student of history and a private man. At the same time, as President of the United States he shared the aversion of his predecessors from "entangling alliances." He also shared with many of his fellow citizens a deep-rooted prejudice against British imperialism. The nation, he believed, stood to gain far more by remaining aloof from the struggle in Europe than by taking part in it. Advising Americans not only to act, but also to speak and even to think, as neutrals, he claimed that nonbelligerency would enable the United States to "serve humanity" by playing the part of "impartial mediator." [5] Some of his advisers pointed out that nonbelligerency need not prevent the government from strengthening the armed forces, if only as a precaution against the country's becoming ineluctably committed to war in response to some act of provocation which public opinion would not tolerate. Wilson shrank, however, from measures which he regarded as tantamount to "turning the United States into an armed camp." In the early winter of 1914 he was strongly urged by House and others to sanction plans for the expansion of the Army and, above all, to agree to measures designed to ensure that an expanded army would not be short of up-to-date artillery. He refused for the time being to do either, although in conversation with House he admitted that there was a good case for the creation of some kind of army reserve.[6]

On the whole, the President's attitude accurately reflected informed opinion in the United States. Not even the bellicose Theodore Roosevelt, not even the unregenerately pro-British Walter Hines Page seriously believed on the outbreak of the European war that the country should abandon its traditional aloofness from foreign quarrels.[7] Dr. Charles W. Eliot of Harvard proposed in August that the United States should join the British Empire, France, Japan,

Italy, and Russia in enforcing a blockade of Germany and Austro-Hungary. But ultimately he came to the conclusion that the Entente Powers would be able to win the war without outside help and that nations not already involved "had better keep out of the conflict." [8]

Apart from tradition and military unpreparedness, a powerful argument for neutrality was that as long as Britain and France were allied with Russia, American interests seemed unlikely to be served by an outright victory for either side. A triumph for Russian autocracy, many Americans felt, would be almost as bad—perhaps even quite as bad—as a triumph for German militarism. The American ideal was a "peace without victory" which would enable the United States, if not precisely to dictate terms to the exhausted belligerents, at any rate to earn the reward of an honest broker by helping them adjust their differences.

At a time when only a short war was expected, the President and his advisers could not foresee the transformation which the national economy would undergo in the course of the next few years. Nevertheless, even in 1914 some of the economic and financial advantages of neutrality were apparent. The war in Europe brought huge demands from all the belligerents for American raw materials and manufactured goods. Despite the awkward insistence of the British that American producers should not sell goods to their enemies as long as they had the power to prevent it, exports to the leading European countries increased almost threefold during the period of neutrality. Moreover, the vexatious interest shown by the British in the ultimate, not merely the immediate, destination of cargoes consigned to Europe did not prevent trade with neutral as well as Allied countries from rising sharply. The United States became, with almost bewildering suddenness, no longer a debtor but a creditor nation, with large gold reserves and an increased stake in the prosperity of foreign countries whose commerce, industry, and public utilities had hitherto been dominated by the British. At the same time, the growing prosperity of exporters and primary producers not only created surplus funds for investment and development, but also helped foster boom conditions in the home market by creating new demands for goods and services. The outcome was an upward spiral of incomes and prices which raised American living standards to a level hitherto unknown.

Neutrality did not prevent a large number of Americans from

viewing with unconcealed delight the resistance offered to the German armies by the Belgians. Moltke's troops, racing forward to Liège on the first day of the invasion, were met by rifle and machine-gun fire, and the *coup de main* was unsuccessful. As the Liège forts were almost impervious to shells from field guns, attempts to storm them with infantry supported by field artillery also failed. On August 6 a German brigade succeeded, however, in pushing through the gap between two of the forts on the east bank of the Meuse, and on the same day a zeppelin dropped bombs on Liège, killing nine civilians. Thereupon the Belgians, recognizing that they could not hope to hold the built-up area of Liège without help which the French War Minister, Adolphe Messimy, was willing to send but which Joffre was not,[9] withdrew their one field division from the neighborhood and ordered it to join the main body of their army at Louvain. On the following day they surrendered the obsolete citadel of Liège but not the forts, which continued to hold out. Moltke, already constrained to put back the start of his advance through central Belgium from August 10 to August 13, then played his last card by giving orders that the few outsize siege guns which could be made ready in time should be brought forward within the next few days.

The arrival of the first of the big guns on August 12 turned the scale. Projectiles lobbed high into the air and fuzed to explode after impact crashed through the roofs of the forts, filling casemates and control rooms with acrid fumes and showering the defenders with fragments of masonry and metal. By August 14 the Germans had captured all the forts on the east bank of the river and were able to start hauling the guns within range of those on the west bank. When the last of these fell on August 16 the Germans, with troops of the Second Army already across the Meuse at Huy, were free to begin the vast wheeling movement which would carry the First Army through Central Belgium and Flanders to Artois and Picardy.

These events did not shake Joffre's determination to commit practically the whole of his forces to an offensive strategy. On August 14, after a preliminary thrust near the Swiss frontier, the French First and Second armies launched their planned attacks in the Vosges and toward the Rhineland. In accordance with Moltke's avowed intention of luring the French into a trap, no serious attempt was made to halt these armies until they came up against prepared positions at Morhange and Sarrebourg. The First Army achieved some success at

Sarrebourg, but the Second Army was driven from Morhange with heavy losses. Both armies then retreated to the frontier area. Moltke, departing from his plan to the extent of sanctioning a vigorous pursuit, was faced thereafter with constant demands for the reinforcement of the German armies in the south at the expense of the crucial wheeling movement in the north.

Late on August 20, after learning of the setback at Morhange, Joffre ordered the Third and Fourth armies to advance on the following day in the general direction of Virton and Neufchâteau. Almost simultaneously he took three reserve divisions from the Third Army as the nucleus of a new Army of Lorraine, whose task was to prevent a breakthrough by forces pursuing the Second Army. He knew when he gave these orders that German troops were said to have reached the Ardennes in large numbers, but assumed that they were moving in a northwesterly direction toward Liège and that the southern part of the Ardennes would be only lightly held by the time his armies reached it. In fact, the German Fifth and Fourth armies were moving more or less due west toward Virton and Neufchâteau respectively, while the German Third Army was also moving westward with Dinant as its objective.

The outcome was one of the worst disasters ever suffered by French arms. The French Third and Fourth armies, blundering into the enemy in foggy weather on August 21, became caught up in a series of encounter battles extending over the greater part of three days. The French infantry, slow to take cover and conspicuous in the brightly colored uniforms which their leaders had insisted on retaining when other armies switched to field gray or khaki, suffered appalling losses. On August 23 the two armies fell back to the Meuse, leaving the rich iron fields of the Briey-Longwy region to be occupied by the Germans at their leisure.

The French Fifth Army, which ought according to plan to have advanced to Rochefort, was unable to take part in this adventure. In order not to be outflanked by German troops who were crossing the Meuse at Huy and Liège, it was forced to deploy on an L-shaped front of some fifty miles extending along the Meuse from the neighborhood of Fumay to Namur and thence along the south bank of the Sambre to a point southwest of Charleroi. A British advance to the Rochefort-Andenne line was thus ruled out. Indeed, the left of the Fifth Army was so close to the concentration area of the Expeditionary Force that the British would have had only a short distance to go had they merely been called upon to prolong the Allied line on the Sambre. That, however, was not the task assigned to them. Because Joffre insisted that since the Fifth Army could not advance into the Ardennes, it should attack northward, Sir John French was asked to conform with an advance in that direction by pushing forward along the axis of the Maubeuge-Mons-Soignies-Brussels road.

General Charles Lanrezac, commanding the Fifth Army, decided after some hesitation to begin his advance on August 21 and meanwhile to stand on the defensive. He had yet to go forward when troops of the German Second Army crossed the Sambre at two points between Namur and Charleroi. The French, who had no trenches or wire on the south bank and were out of their element in a defensive role, tried in vain to drive them back by charging with flags flying and bugles blowing.

As the main body of the British Expeditionary Force was approaching Mons on August 22, Sir John French learned that his cavalry was in contact with the enemy at Soignies and that a German infantry column was marching straight toward him along the road from Brussels. An air reconnaissance told him that there were also German troops on his left front. On his right, the Fifth Army's positions south of the Sambre were some nine miles in the rear of his leading troops; on his left, a gap of eighty miles between Mons and the coast was guarded only by a few French Territorial divisions of doubtful quality and an outmoded system of frontier defenses covering the chief towns. He had asked on August 16 that a French cavalry corps and two reserve divisions should be placed under his command to secure the exposed flank of the Allied armies, but his request had not been met.

That evening Lanrezac asked the British to launch an attack on August 23 in order to relieve the pressure on his front. French's reply was to the effect that he could not continue his advance without knowing more precisely what was in front of him but would hold his existing positions for twenty-four hours and would then decide on his future course of action in the light of reports from his "aeroplanes." [10]

The German troops on French's front were the spearheads of the First Army, commanded by General Alexander von Kluck. Kluck, constrained by orders from Moltke to conform with the movements of the Second Army on his left, had marched south-southwest from Brussels in spite of an uneasy feeling that by moving in that direction, instead of making a wide sweep to the west as he would have liked to do, he was exposing his army to the risk of being taken in the rear by the British, whom he believed until the last moment to have landed at Ostend, Dunkirk, and Calais. When the cavalry skirmish at Soignies told him that, after all, there were British troops to the south of him, his inclination was to edge westward and feel for their flank. Since this would have taken him farther from the Second Army than was permitted, he decided to aim at forcing the crossings of the Condé Canal, immediately ahead of him, in the hope of driving the British back to Maubeuge and there encircling them.

When a misty dawn broke on Sunday, August 23, the four British infantry divisions which the government had allowed to reach the battlefield were standing on a front of some twenty-seven miles close to the Franco-Belgian frontier. On the left the Second Corps (Lieutenant General Sir Horace Smith-Dorrien) held a fifteen-mile sector extending from the neighborhood of Condé along the south bank of the canal to a point northeast of Mons, where the canal makes a northward loop. On the right the line held by the First Corps (Lieutenant General Sir Douglas Haig) was bent back sharply to make contact with the left-hand corps of the Fifth Army. The Cavalry Division (Major General E. H. H. Allenby) was in reserve. Smith-Dorrien, a recent arrival, had been chosen by the War Office to succeed Lieutenant General Sir James Grierson, who had died of heart failure on his way to the front.

The German First Army, with fourteen infantry divisions under command, had some eight divisions, organized in four corps, in the forward area. Kluck ordered two corps to attack the sector held by Smith-Dorrien's two divisions. Later he ordered concerted attacks by the whole of his available forces, but his flanking corps were unable to arrive in time to make an effective contribution to the battle. His troops were met by rifle fire so rapid and so well coordinated that they believed it to come from machine guns. Notwithstanding a local superiority of more than two to one in men and guns, they could make no progress. Smith-Dorrien's troops in the salient formed by the loop of the canal were, however, under infantry and artillery fire from three directions. In the afternoon Smith-Dorrien ironed out the salient by withdrawing his troops from the loop and its immediate neighborhood to a new line of prepared positions two or three miles to the rear. The Germans made little attempt to follow up and at nightfall sounded the cease-fire.

This encounter between the largest German and the smallest Allied army imposed on the Germans the only significant check suffered by any of their armies on a day when all the French armies were retreating, or had retreated, before forces whose aggregate strength was not materially greater than theirs.* Moreover, as a result of the defensive tactics adopted by the British the losses of the Expeditionary Force were much lighter, in proportion to the numbers involved, than those inflicted on the French.[11]

The French Fifth Army had a particularly disastrous day. About midday General Lanrezac received the dire news that the only Belgian division still in the forward area was withdrawing from Namur. In the late afternoon he learned that the Germans were entering the city. His troops on the Sambre had suffered terrible losses and were falling back at many points; on the Meuse the spearheads of the German Third Army had crossed the river and were enlarging a bridgehead from which he could not know that they were about to be dislodged. Although unaware that the Fourth Army on his right was withdrawing in a direction which would uncover his flank, he saw the risk of a double enveloping movement which might force him to reenact the tragedy of 1870 by surrendering his army in the field. Without consulting French, he ordered a general retreat which would open a huge gap on the British right.

That evening the British, believing that there were at most four German infantry divisions on their front, planned a counterattack for the following day. On learning about 8 P.M. that Joffre's intelligence officers put the enemy's strength much higher, French countermanded the plan and announced his intention of standing the enemy's attacks on August 24 on the ground already occupied by his troops. Three hours later the British liaison officer with the Fifth Army, Lieutenant E. L. Spears, arrived with the news that Lanrezac was retreating and the Expeditionary Force in deadly peril.

Before the battle, French had considered taking refuge behind the

* The aggregate strength of the five French armies was approximately 1,060,000 of all ranks; that of the German Second, Third, Fourth, Fifth, Sixth, and Seventh armies was approximately 1,100,000 of all ranks. The French were not engaged during the frontier battles by the German First Army, whose attacks fell entirely on the British.

old-fashioned fortifications of Maubeuge if he was driven from his positions, but his staff had warned him that by doing so, he would put his head into a noose.[12] On learning of Lanrezac's retirement he decided to fall back in a southwesterly direction and stand on August 26 on a line through Cambrai and Le Cateau. Hundreds of French civilians and all available headquarters troops were put to work digging trenches on that line. However, on August 25 the British made slow progress, largely because roads allotted to them were blocked by French troops moving to their flanks. Furthermore, the lay of the land forced Haig to take a route which diverged from Smith-Dorrien's. After "tremendous discussion," French ruled that the retreat should be continued on the following day to Busigny.

Haig's troops were approaching Landrecies on August 25 when some of them were engaged by elements of the German First Army. Only a skirmish followed, but Haig, believing in the confusion of the moment that he was seriously threatened, obtained permission to continue his retreat during the next few days by a route which would take him still farther from the Second Corps and the Cavalry Division.

On the same day Smith-Dorrien's troops reached Le Cateau, with the Germans close behind them. General Allenby, whose cavalry was covering their retreat, warned Smith-Dorrien that by the following morning their line of march might be commanded by the enemy and urged him to get away before daybreak. Since units were still coming in long after nightfall, Smith-Dorrien knew that he could not hope to do so. After consulting his divisional commanders he decided, in the teeth of advice from GHQ, to turn and face the enemy with troops whom he described as "too tired to march but not too tired to fight." Taking the Cavalry Division and the newly arrived but incomplete Fourth Division temporarily under command and helped by French troops who had reached his outer flank, he succeeded for the second time in halting Kluck's army for the best part of a day. Many of the trenches dug by French civilians were, however, very shallow. Smith-Dorrien was so hard pressed at some points that he had to start disengaging without waiting for darkness to fall on August 26, and his losses were much heavier than those he had suffered at Mons.

Lanrezac, too, interrupted his retreat to turn and fight. Orders from Joffre compelled him to make a complex redistribution of his forces and commit himself, on August 29, to the confused series of engagements known as the Battle of Guise. Haig was willing to help but was not allowed by French to do so. During the battle Joffre spoke of ordering Lanrezac to "go on to the end" but was strongly urged by Henry Wilson, on behalf of the British, to attempt no prolonged stand until he was ready to reinforce his left on a major scale at the expense of his armies in the south. Eventually Joffre sent Lanrezac a message ordering him to disengage, but it was delayed in transit and did not arrive until the following morning.

Thereafter Joffre, no longer able to hope that a joint effort by the Expeditionary Force and the Fifth Army might hold the German First and Second armies either on the Somme or on the Aisne, resigned himself to a long retreat, if necessary beyond the Seine. He was persuaded with some difficulty to provide a substantial force for the defense of Paris by placing the Sixth Army, formed from the Army of Lorraine, under the orders of the military governor, the veteran General Joseph Simon Gallieni. On September 2 the French government left Paris for Bordeaux. The United States ambassador, Myron T. Herrick, was advised by the Germans to leave also but declined to do so. He planned to use his position as neutral custodian of the German Embassy to bargain with the invaders for the safety of museums and buildings of architectural or historic interest. Herrick was even willing, should the need arise, to venture forth and parley with the Kaiser or his representative on the outskirts of the city.[13]

Sir John French was so shaken by Lanrezac's unheralded withdrawal from the Sambre and the perils of the retreat from Mons that toward the end of August he moved his main base from Le Havre to St.-Nazaire and spoke of taking his whole force out of the line to refit. Kitchener, wearing the uniform of a field marshal, made it clear to him at a prickly interview in Paris on September 1 that notwithstanding the discretion given to him in his directive, he must regard himself as under orders not to desert the French. Meanwhile, a flash of strategic insight had led the government to consider sending the one division of the Expeditionary Force still in the United Kingdom to Ostend, where it would be well placed to threaten Kluck's flank and might also help Belgian and French garrisons to secure the Channel ports. Kitchener, at first favorably inclined to the project, eventually decided that the division could not be spared until it was replaced by troops from India and should then go to France. As a last resort, three battalions of marines were sent in the last week of August to join 6,000 Belgians carried to Ostend in British ships. The Belgians proved unsuitable for the role assigned to them, and the marines were soon withdrawn.

At that stage French could see little but disaster ahead of him. His army and the Fifth Army on his flank were in full retreat; he had no faith in Lanrezac; his Chief of Staff, Sir Archibald Murray, had fainted on learning of Haig's encounter at Landrecies. When Murray's deputy, Henry Wilson, assured a French officer that the Germans were pressing the pursuit too fast and were bound to make a mistake which would give Joffre his chance, he seemed to be uttering mere words of empty comfort.

Wilson's guess was nonetheless well founded. The plan on which Moltke was relying to give him a decision in the West by the fortieth day of mobilization was still a long way from completion after three-quarters of that period had elapsed. Despite the disastrous failure of Joffre's offensives in Alsace and the Ardennes, the French armies of the right and center were fighting tenaciously in the frontier area after a bad start; the swift withdrawal of the Fifth Army and the Expeditionary Force, although contrary to Joffre's wishes at the time, proved the sound strategic move which Lanrezac always said it was. Opposing the Germans stoutly not only at Mons and Le Cateau, but also in subsequent rearguard actions, the British escaped crippling losses, and on September 3 they withdrew with their strength substantially unimpaired behind the Marne. The Fifth Army, which crossed the Marne on the same day, was not prevented by its setbacks on the Sambre and Meuse from giving a good account of itself at Guise. "My army can fight . . . but is not in brilliant condition," was the verdict of General Louis Franchet d'Esperey, who succeeded to the command when Joffre decided, also on September 3, that the too argumentative, too highly strung Lanrezac must go.

Mons, Le Cateau, and Guise were not decisive battles by any definition. They were not comparable in scope or duration with the battles fought in August and early September by the French armies in the frontier area. Even so, their influence on German strategy was far from negligible. The time available for Kluck's wheeling movement, already curtailed by setbacks at Liège, was further reduced by delays at Mons and Le Cateau. At the same time, the German armies of the right were weakened by four divisions transferred to the

Eastern Front, where the Russians had launched a short-lived but crucial offensive in East Prussia, and by the equivalent of six divisions retained in Belgium or close to the Franco-Belgian frontier. The remaining troops were tired by forced marches, often in blazing heat and on cobbled roads, through hostile country where food and fodder were hard to find. ("There is hardly a horse in our army," Moltke complained on September 4, "which will go out of a walk.")[14] Despite poor lateral communications across war-torn Belgium, Moltke could doubtless have reinforced his right at the expense of his left. By doing so, he would, however, have tacitly relinquished the faint, beguiling hope of a vast double enveloping movement in which the armies of the left could join.

Kluck's wide sweep west of Paris was the essence of the project bequeathed by Schlieffen to his successor. Hitherto it had always figured in Moltke's plans. In an order of August 28 he affirmed, once more, his intention of carrying out this movement but went on to hint at its abandonment by adding that, in certain circumstances, "a wheel of the armies from a south-westerly to a southerly direction" might be necessary.[15]

When Lanrezac's army streamed from the battlefield of Guise on August 30, the temptation to force a climax by renouncing the time-consuming Schlieffen maneuver became irresistible. Kluck and his neighbor, General von Bülow of the Second Army, believed that Lanrezac was beaten and that any threat from the Expeditionary Force and the French forces on the outer flank could be discounted. To allow Kluck and Bülow to close by the shortest route with an enemy ripe for envelopment seemed to Moltke sound strategy. Besides offering him virtually his only remaining chance of gaining a decision within the allotted time, a wheel to the south would tend to reduce the gaps that had opened between the First and Second and the Second and Third armies. Furthermore, by making the possibility of a double enveloping movement slightly less remote, it might help stifle doubts about the wisdom of his refusal to weaken his left in order to "make the right wing strong."

With Moltke's sanction, the First and Second armies began on August 31 a turn which changed the direction of Kluck's advance not merely from the southwest to the south but ultimately to the southeast.

Late on September 2 Kluck's right-hand corps, exhausted by yet another forced march, staggered to a halt in the neighborhood of Chantilly, barely twenty miles northeast of the outskirts of Paris. Moltke's orders for the next stage of the advance were that the First and Second armies should drive the enemy to the southeast, away from Paris, but that the First Army should protect the outer flank of the armies of the right against a possible counterattack from the west by remaining in echelon behind the Second. Kluck obeyed one of these commands but not the other. On September 3 he swung to the left in order to continue his pursuit of Bülow's old opponent Lanrezac. On the following day he crossed the Marne, leaving only one reserve corps as rear guard east of Paris.

On September 4 Moltke became alarmed by reports that the French were passing troops from east to west across their rear. At the same time it struck him that his armies of the right had little to show in the way of prisoners or booty for their supposedly victorious sweep toward the heart of France. Concluding that the Allies were still far from beaten, he decided to form a defensive front east of Paris by halting the First and Second armies. The pursuit toward the Seine would be continued by the Third Army.

By the time the appropriate orders were transmitted to the armies on September 5 Kluck had already resumed his advance with some eight divisions on a thirty-mile front. He did nothing about the order until, in the evening, an emissary from the headquarters of the High Command at Luxembourg, Colonel Hentsch, arrived to explain why a change of plan was considered necessary. Kluck and Hentsch then agreed that on September 6 the First Army should begin a leisurely withdrawal to the north bank of the Marne.

Meanwhile the French had learned that Paris was not Kluck's immediate objective. As early as Seplember 1 they took from the dead body of a German officer a map which indicated that the First Army would swing to the southeast after completing its crossing of the Oise.[16] On September 3 they saw that Kluck, by carrying out this maneuver within a day's march of the outer suburbs, was offering his flank to Gallieni. As the outcome of earnest discussions that evening and on the following day, arrangements were made for a concerted effort by the Sixth Army (General Michel Joseph Maunoury); the British Expeditionary Force; the Fifth Army under Franchet d'Esperey; and a new Ninth Army, commanded by Foch, on the Fifth

Army's right. Orders to the Fourth and Third armies to join in the offensive were issued later.

The crucial question was when the offensive should begin. Gallieni and Franchet d'Esperey came independently to the conclusion that the Sixth Army's attack on Kluck's flank ought to be launched on September 6, and should be made north of the Marne. Joffre would have liked Maunoury to start on September 7, after crossing the Marne from north to south, but eventually he succumbed to Gallieni's arguments. A plan was then drawn up by Joffre's staff on lines proposed by Franchet d'Esperey after consultation with two British officers.* It was not, however, until late on September 4 that the plan received Joffre's sanction. By that time Sir Archibald Murray, apparently influenced by the belief that room would have to be found for the Sixth Army on the south bank of the Marne, had issued orders to the Expeditionary Force for a further retreat of ten to fifteen miles on the following day. During the morning of September 5 Henry Wilson nonetheless succeeded in persuading Sir John French to take part in the offensive. At a dramatic interview with Joffre in the early afternoon, French promised that his troops would "do all that it was possible for men to do." [17]

After a preliminary skirmish on September 5, Maunoury duly attacked Kluck's rear guard on September 6. He was soon in action on a wide front south and southeast of Chantilly. Kluck's retirement across the Marne was transformed in consequence from the leisurely affair discussed with Hentsch to a desperate attempt to raise the strength of his forces on the right bank to a point which might enable him to defeat the Sixth Army before the Fifth Army and the British could break through his front or envelop him. Maunoury, reinforced by newly arrived troops of whom about 6,000 were rushed to the front in the famous "taxis of the Marne," tried hard to push Kluck's rear guard to the east and cut him off, but Kluck succeeded in keeping his communications open at the cost of widening the gap between the First and Second armies. On Kluck's left, the Second and Third armies became locked in hard-fought encounters with the French Ninth Army and part of the Fifth. Still farther east, "devastating" artillery fire from the French Third and Fourth armies

* These were Major General Henry H. Wilson and Colonel Macdonogh, respectively Sub-Chief of the General Staff and GSO 1 (Intelligence) of the Expeditionary Force.

pinned the German Fifth and Fourth armies to the ground between the upper reaches of the Marne and the frontier area.

About 10 A.M. on September 8 Colonel Hentsch, vested by Moltke with plenary powers, set out on a further round of visits to the German armies of the right and center. After reporting hopefully on the state of the Fifth, Fourth, and Third armies, he reached Bülow's headquarters in the evening. A long talk with Bülow and his staff convinced him that Bülow's situation, although serious, was not hopeless and that the Second Army need not make a further retreat unless the enemy crossed the Marne in strength and appeared in the rear of the First Army.

On the following day the French made little progress and in some sectors were even driven back. The British, however, succeeded in getting the greater part of their infantry, as well as cavalry, across the river. Thereupon Bülow countermanded an attack planned on the previous evening, ordered the withdrawal which he had agreed to make if the enemy crossed the Marne in strength, and warned Kluck that "four long infantry columns" had arrived on the north bank. He claimed afterward that his prompt action averted a disaster for the whole of the armies of the right.

At six o'clock that morning Hentsch left Bülow's headquarters southwest of Épernay for Kluck's, northeast of Meaux. He found the roads in Bülow's rear so jammed with baggage columns "retiring in wild haste" that the journey of less than fifty miles by motorcar took five hours. On arrival he learned that Kluck had decided, even before he received Bülow's message, to pull back his left under cover of a delaying action and a renewed attack on the Sixth Army. Hentsch, concluding about an hour later that this was not enough, used his authority as Moltke's envoy to order Kluck to retreat on Soissons.

The German armies of the right then fell back to the Aisne. A slow pursuit enabled them, on reaching the right bank and the heights beyond it, to establish themselves in entrenched positions from which the Allies failed to dislodge them.

The retreat from the Marne left Moltke so visibly shaken that the Kaiser was persuaded with difficulty not to dismiss him on the spot. He was succeeded soon afterward by General Erich von Falkenhayn, the former Minister of War, who complained that he had "a lost war" on his hands but nonetheless refused to admit defeat.

At that stage British concern with the Channel ports, never long dormant, reasserted itself. With Joffre's consent the Expeditionary Force moved from the Aisne, where its place was taken by French troops, to the neighborhood of St.-Omer. As the sequel to visits by Winston Churchill to Dunkirk and Calais a brigade of marines, accompanied by a mounted Yeomanry regiment and equipped with motor buses and some armored cars, arrived at Dunkirk in the second half of September to take part in the local defense of French towns and to "confuse the enemy with the idea of British as well as French troops being in this area." [18]

In the meantime, much thought was given in London to the possibility of helping the Belgians hold Antwerp as a bastion on which the left of the Allied armies might rest. The chief obstacle, apart from the difficulty of persuading Kitchener and Joffre to release British and French troops for the purpose, was that the communications of a force large enough to hold the place would be precarious unless supplies could be carried by sea through Dutch territorial waters at the mouth of the Scheldt. Churchill proposed in September that troops of the Territorial Army should be used and that the Dutch should be pressed to open the Scheldt to Allied military traffic; but Kitchener considered the Territorials unsuitable, and Grey was unwilling to put diplomatic pressure on the Dutch. Eventually it was agreed that the whole of the Royal Naval Division of marines and the newly formed Third Cavalry and Seventh (Infantry) divisions should move to Antwerp by way of Dunkirk, Ostend, and Zeebrugge and that a French offer of one or two Territorial divisions and a brigade of marines should be accepted.[19]

The British marines, preceded by Churchill as emissary of the British government, began to arrive on October 4. By that time the outer defenses of Antwerp had crumbled under sustained artillery fire. The Belgians feared that their escape route to the west through Ghent might not long remain open. Late on October 6 they decided to withdraw all but one of their field divisions to the west bank of the Scheldt. The remaining division followed on October 8. The Belgians formally surrendered the city on October 10, about five days later than they would have done but for Churchill's encouragement and the hope of powerful British and French support.[20]

The fall of Antwerp freed Kluck's forces for an attempt to turn the Allied left in Flanders but did not enable him to make up the time already lost. The retreating Belgians, joined by French troops diverted from Antwerp and supported by British warships off the coast, succeeded in halting the Germans on the Yser. Farther south the Third Cavalry and Seventh divisions, also diverted from Antwerp and moving to the left of the main body of the Expeditionary Force, played a crucial part in blocking the route from Ghent through Ypres to Dunkirk and Calais. A month-long series of desperate battles, afterward called First Ypres, cost the Germans their last chance of reaching the Channel ports before the spring of 1918, but left the British standing in an awkward salient dominated by low hills to the south.

So ended the first phase of the war on land in the Western theater. Events since August had falsified many opinions held before the war. Among these was the belief, too readily accepted by British planners, that the Belgians would be able to hold the line of the Meuse below Namur and that no weapons likely to be available to the Germans in 1914 would suffice to reduce the Liège forts except after a prolonged siege. The British, when drawing up their plans for war with Germany, also erred in placing too much reliance on the offensive capacity of the French Army and the strategic insight of its leaders. On the other hand, their planners made no mistake when they asserted that a small force sent promptly across the Channel might make a contribution out of proportion to its size. The French put many more troops in the field than the British, their share of the fighting was much heavier, their losses were much greater. The fact remains that but for delays imposed on Kluck's army by fear of what the British Expeditionary Force might do and by what it did, Moltke's hope of a lightning victory in the West might well have been fulfilled. In that case the British would have faced in 1914—as they were ultimately to do in 1940—the problem of preventing Germany from establishing a lasting hegemony over a great part of Europe.

As it was, by the end of the year the German and Allied armies were confronting each other along a continuous line of entrenched and wired positions from the North Sea to the Swiss frontier. The British, with well over 300,000 men in the field by December, still held little more than twenty miles of that line and were under pressure to do more, either by extending their front or by making a push in support of offensives by French troops. Sir John French favored an attempt to advance along the Belgian coast to Ostend and Zeebrugge, but for this he needed reinforcements and also the cooperation of the Belgians and the French.

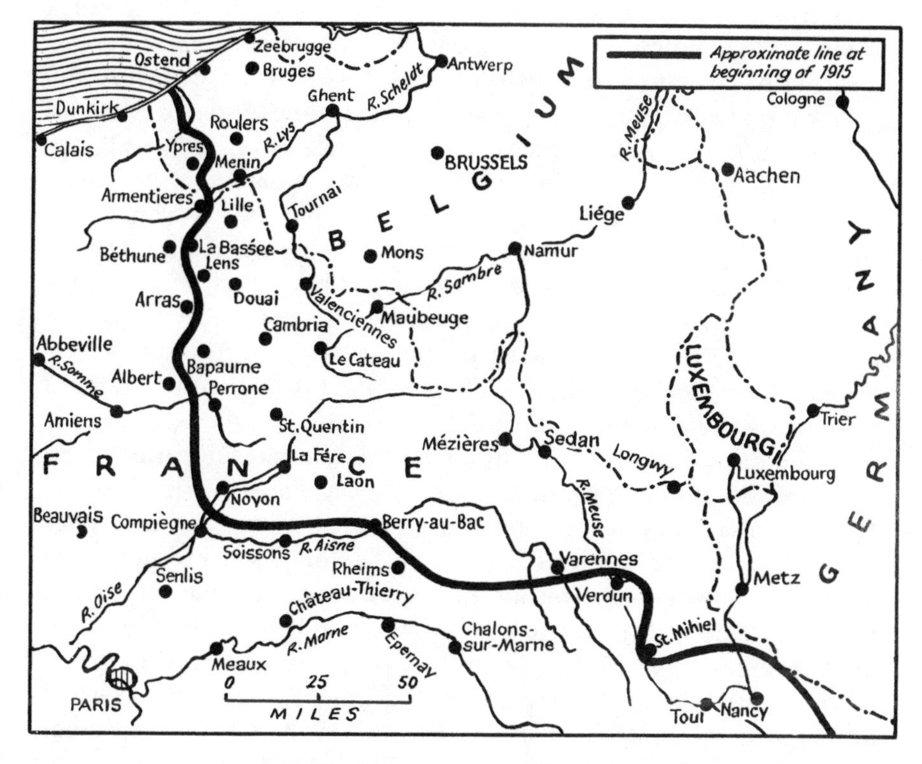

THE WESTERN FRONT (JANUARY, 1915)

In the meantime, Kitchener had disrupted prewar plans for expansion of the Army by sending Territorial battalions abroad piecemeal,[21] but was taking advantage of a huge flow of volunteers to the recruiting offices to form new armies which would give him a total of seventy divisions by the spring of 1916. The first of these were expected to be ready twelve months earlier, but this proved too hopeful an estimate. To train, equip, and clothe a million raw recruits was a formidable undertaking, especially since volunteers from all walks of life were being accepted without regard to the effects on industry.

In any case, there was no certainty that mere numbers would enable the Allies to drive the enemy from France and Belgium. On the contrary, the failure of the Germans to reach the Channel ports in the early winter suggested that in the conditions prevailing on the Western Front, both sides might find it impossible to achieve a breakthrough unless they could devise new methods of capturing trenches protected by thick belts of barbed wire. A few British strategists were already thinking in terms of such innovations or revivals as body armor, smoke screens, flamethrowers, and, above all, the tracked and armored fighting vehicles which came to be called tanks.[22] War Office experts reported in 1915 that the problem of designing and producing a vehicle capable of battering a way through wire and crossing trenches was insoluble,[23] but naval constructors, encouraged by Churchill and afterward by Arthur Balfour, his successor at the Admiralty, took up the project with enthusiasm. Nevertheless, it was not until early in 1916 that the first experimental tanks were ready to show their paces.

In the meantime, men as various in outlook and temperament as Asquith, Lloyd George, Churchill, Kitchener, and Colonel Maurice Hankey of the Committee of Imperial Defence saw that the Allies had only a remote chance of achieving anything worthwhile on the Western Front with the resources likely to be available during the next twelve months or so. In the last week of 1914 Hankey devoted his Christmas leave to the preparation of a memorandum in which he called attention to "the remarkable deadlock which has occurred in the western theatre of war" and reviewed the situation in other theatres.[24] A few days later, on January 2, 1915, Kitchener wrote to Sir John French that there was a growing feeling in London that while the Allies must continue to defend their existing line in France and Belgium, troops not needed for that purpose would be better employed elsewhere.[25] Almost simultaneously, Asquith recorded his profound dissatisfaction with the waste of life and money in fruitless enterprises on the western front, and Lloyd George and Churchill independently proposed offensives in other theaters.[26] At the same time German successes in Eastern Europe, reinforced by Russian pleas, made it clear that the Russians, already short of ammunition and raw materials, were not likely to hold out indefinitely against the Central Powers unless the British and the French could give them effective support.

Asquith and his colleagues were afterward accused of failing to act resolutely on the conviction that the Western Front had become, for the time being, an unprofitable theater. It must, however, be admitted that their difficulties were considerable.

In the first place, Britain was not conducting an independent war but fighting as the ally of France and Russia. Joffre, whose eyes were firmly fixed on the Western Front, became so popular a figure in France after the Battle of the Marne that the French government dared not risk his disapproval. This meant that no strategy which threatened to relegate his forces, even temporarily, to a secondary role could be proposed by the British unless they were prepared to risk a time-consuming wrangle with French statesmen. At the same time, the difficulty of dealing with potential allies in the Balkans was increased by the need to defer to Russian susceptibilities. This problem was further complicated by the difficulty of establishing physical contact with the Russians, who could be reached from November, 1914, only through Archangel. Grey pointed out in August, 1914, when the Greeks offered to join the Entente powers, that their intervention might precipitate hostilities by Bulgaria and Turkey.[27] When Turkey entered the war and the British decided that the time had come to unite the Balkan countries against her, their failure to do so was brought about not only by their own mistakes, but also by the insistence of Russian statesmen that Greek troops should not be used in the neighborhood of Constantinople.*

The Asquith government was also handicapped by the lack of any effective means of dealing promptly and authoritatively with strategic problems as they arose. Constitutionally, responsibility for all such matters rested on the Cabinet. A Cabinet between two and three times as large as Pitt's was not, however, a very suitable instrument for the purpose. Most of its members were immersed in departmental duties, and few were qualified to pronounce upon military questions without expert guidance. The Cabinet had no means of recording its decisions apart from handwritten reports rendered by the Prime Minister to the Crown.[28] There was no check on the accuracy of these reports, since they were not shown to the men whose opinions they purported to reflect. Sometimes ministers did not know at the end of a meeting what had been decided, even in relation to matters affecting their own departments.[29]

The difficulties to which this system would give rise in time of war

* See p. 84.

had been foreseen. One remedy tentatively proposed before the war was that responsibility for the conduct of military affairs should be delegated on or after the outbreak of hostilities to the Committee of Imperial Defence. This high-level committee had played so important a part in prewar planning that leading statesmen on both sides of the House confessed that they did not know how their predecessors had done without it. It had the advantage of being a flexible body, whose composition the Prime Minister was free to vary at his discretion, and of being served by a permanent staff well qualified to provide objective data for the study of strategic problems.

That course did not appeal to Asquith. He seems to have feared that, apart from obvious objections to the transfer of power to a body supposed to be purely advisory, so many ministers would insist on attending meetings of the committee if its responsibilities were enlarged that it would soon become as unwieldy as the Cabinet. The solution he adopted in November was to set up a War Council consisting in the first place of himself, the Chancellor of the Exchequer, the Foreign Secretary, the First Lord of the Admiralty, the First Sea Lord, the Secretary of State for War, the Chief of the Imperial General Staff, and the former Unionist Prime Minister, Arthur Balfour. Later additions brought the number of persons who regularly attended meetings of the council to ten and finally to thirteen.[30]

This was a step in the right direction, but no more. Asquith saw that a handier instrument than the Cabinet was needed to deal with big strategic issues. He neither created nor wished to create an organization capable of keeping the operations of the armed forces under constant review from a standpoint distinct from that of either of the service ministries. The War Council met at irregular intervals and sometimes at short notice. No agenda papers and very few written reports or appreciations were circulated before meetings. On one occasion the council did not meet for eight weeks.[31] In these circumstances no continuous review of operations would have been possible, or was attempted. Day-to-day decisions continued to be made by the service ministries with or without reference to higher authority and not necessarily in the context of any grand strategic plan.

Coordination was not made easier by the departure to France on the outbreak of war of a number of officers who had hitherto held key positions at the War Office. Inevitably, in view of Kitchener's conception of his role as Secretary of State for War, the outcome was a decline in the power and influence of the General Staff. At the Admiralty, attempts to found a body analogous to the General Staff had been opposed by officers who feared that the prerogatives of commanders in chief would be invaded, and a small War Staff created by Churchill had yet to find its feet. To make matters worse, ill-judged comments by people outside the Admiralty led Prince Louis of Battenberg to resign his post at the end of October for fear that his German antecedents might embarrass the government and harm the Navy. Thereupon Churchill, not content with losing an excellent First Sea Lord, made a rod for his own back by insisting that the elderly but still explosive Fisher should be recalled from retirement to fill the vacancy.

4

The Way Around

AT least one British spokesman ventured to suggest before the First World War that while Britain was compelled by her dependence on foreign trade, her imperial commitments, and the smallness of her army to maintain a powerful navy, the High Seas Fleet was something of a luxury for Germany. The German homeland was guarded by so strong an army that no combination of European powers was likely to launch an unprovoked attack on Germany. Unless she meant to look for trouble by herself attacking Britain, France, or Russia, she had nothing to fear at home or abroad as long as Britannia ruled the waves.

The Germans retorted, with some heat, that Germany, like Britain, was a great imperial and mercantile power with worldwide commitments. Like Britain, she needed a powerful navy to maintain her place in the sun.

The fact remains that Germany made no attempt in 1914 to use her battle fleet to protect her foreign trade or overseas possessions. Her merchantmen, confined to the Baltic or immobilized in neutral ports, disappeared in a few weeks from the world's trade routes. Her colonies beyond the seas were left almost entirely to their own devices.

Japan, still smarting from humiliations inflicted on her by German diplomacy in the nineteenth century, declared war on Germany within a fortnight of the invasion of Belgium. She quickly seized the naval base established by the Germans at Tsingtao in the Chinese province of Shantung and the whole of Germany's colonial possessions in the Pacific north of the equator. German colonies and trading posts in the Pacific south of the equator were occupied by Commonwealth forces from Australia and New Zealand. In addition, British, Allied, or Commonwealth expeditions were mounted against the German colonies in East and West Africa. So far as the British were concerned, the primary object of these enterprises was to deprive the Germans of bases and signal stations for commerce raiders. A secondary motive was to gain possession of territories which might, if the need arose, be exchanged at the peace conference for any part of Belgium still occupied by German troops.[1]

Nor did the German Navy do much in 1914 to interfere with the assembly of British, Allied, and Commonwealth troops. Admiral Souchon's bombardment of Bône and Philippeville before his flight to Constantinople did not prevent the French from ferrying their African Army across the Mediterranean without further molestation. The British Expeditionary Force crossed the Channel without the loss of a ship or a man. Large numbers of British and Commonwealth troops were carried without interference from India and Canada to the United Kingdom and from the Antipodes to Egypt, where the Anzac Corps of Australians and New Zealanders was to complete its training.

Meanwhile, orders from the High Command restricted the High Seas Fleet to brief sorties of little or no strategic value. The nearest approach to a major engagement came on December 16, when battle cruisers supported by battleships bombarded towns on the east coast of England. The British, warned by intercepted wireless traffic that something was in the wind but uncertain of its scope, just missed bringing the raiders to action as they withdrew. The bombardment killed or injured more than 500 civilians at Hartlepool, Scarborough, and Whitby but did no significant military damage. The chief effects in Britain were to put the Admiralty on its mettle, strengthen an impression that the Germans were queer folk, and stimulate recruiting.[2]

Other operations by home-based German naval units in the early stages of the war included the illegal laying of undeclared minefields off the British coast, and sporadic attacks by submarines both on merchant shipping and on warships. On October 27 the battleship *Audacious* struck a mine off Northern Ireland and sank in full view of a liner crowded with passengers. Some of the German minefields proved, however, more useful than harmful to the British, who soon located them, improved them, and used them for defensive purposes.

German submarines were another matter. In September, nearly a month before the first British merchant vessel succumbed to this form of attack, a single U-boat torpedoed three cruisers in swift succession near the eastern approaches to the Channel. Still worse, from the British point of view, than any material loss was the knowledge that U-boats might be met where German surface ships would not dare to go. In 1914 the fear of underwater attack affected British naval officers much as the fear of air attack affected their successors a quarter of a century later. In October Admiral Jellicoe, believing that U-boats were coming after the Grand Fleet in harbor, withdrew from Scapa Flow and announced his intention of staying either in Irish waters or on the west coast of Scotland until he was satisfied that Scapa Flow was safe.

In 1914 the problems with which unrestricted submarine warfare would ultimately confront the British were, however, still in the future. The biggest threat to Allied interests in the early stages of the war came not from U-boats or from the High Seas Fleet, but from surface raiders on distant trade routes. On the outbreak of war eight German cruisers suitable for a *guerre de course* were based on foreign stations from the Atlantic to the Yellow Sea. Among them were two ships, the *Scharnhorst* and the *Gneisenau,* whose armament put them almost in the battle cruiser class. In October all were still at large in various parts of the world. More than seventy British, French, and Russian cruisers were available to deal with them, but the problem was to find and catch them before they did incalculable damage. The cruiser *Emden*, detached from the China Squadron to the Indian Ocean, alone sank more than 70,000 tons of Allied shipping before she was cornered and destroyed at the Cocos Islands by the Australian cruiser *Sydney* in November.

Admiral Maximilian von Spee, commanding the China Squadron, had left Tsingtao well before the outbreak of war for a destination unknown to the British. The force left to him after he parted with the *Emden* included the *Scharnhorst* and the *Gneisenau.* These ships were seen on August 5 near the Solomon Islands; on August 9 they were reported coaling at Ponape in the Caroline Islands, then still in German hands though soon to be captured by the Japanese. Subsequent reports suggested that Spee was moving in the general direction of Cape Horn, possibly for the purpose of attacking trade in the south Atlantic or the southeast Pacific.

Steps taken to deal with Spee's squadron included a watch in the neighborhood of the Strait of Magellan by a force based on the Falkland Islands and commanded by Admiral Sir Christopher Cradock. The Admiralty intended that Cradock should avoid splitting his force and that any ships with which he engaged the *Scharnhorst* and the *Gneisenau* should include his only battleship, the *Canopus.*

These intentions cannot have seemed as clear to Cradock as they did to Churchill and the First Sea Lord. When Spee approached the coast of Chile at the end of October with five ships, Cradock was close at hand with a weak cruiser force, but the *Canopus* was 300 miles away. Cradock, without waiting for the *Canopus* or for reinforcements to reach him from a squadron off Montevideo, engaged Spee on November 1 off Coronel. He suffered a crushing defeat and went down with his flagship.

The Admiralty responded to the news of this disaster by sending two battle cruisers from the Grand Fleet to the south Atlantic and appointing Admiral Sir Doveton Sturdee, hitherto Chief of the Naval War Staff, to take charge of operations on the spot. Sturdee, flying his flag in the battle cruiser *Invincible* and accompanied by her sister ship the *Inflexible,* arrived on December 7. On the following day Spee approached the Falkland Islands, presumably in the belief that he would have to deal only with the remnant of Cradock's force. Sturdee, emerging from harbor, sank four-fifths of Spee's squadron. The cruiser *Dresden* escaped but was later blown up by her crew after being cornered in the southeast Pacific.

The Battle of the Falkland Islands ended the threat from German surface raiders. Thus it came about that when stagnation was seen to threaten the Allied armies on the Western Front, the British were able to make their naval dispositions in the knowledge that, for all practical purposes, they need take account of no German surface ships outside the North Sea, and the Helgoland Bight, the Baltic, the Sea of Marmara.

Apart from expeditions to German colonies and purely naval enterprises, the only military operation of any consequence undertaken by the British in 1914 outside France and Belgium was a landing at the head of the Persian Gulf, followed by the capture of the Turkish administrative district (vilayet) of Basra. The initiative came from the Admiralty,[3] which depended on the Anglo-Persian Oil Company's installations in western Persia for supplies of fuel for its oil-burning ships. Largely at the prompting of the First Lord, the British government had recently acquired a controlling interest in the company.

The strengthening of British influence in the neighboring Arab states seemed to the British authorities in India even more important than the guarding of the oil installations. When the project was discussed in London on September 26, the Military Secretary of the India Office suggested that the landing should be made "ostensibly" to protect the company's assets, "but in reality to notify to the Turks that we meant business and to the Arabs that we were ready to support them." [4]

The Cabinet sanctioned the enterprise on October 2. A brigade group of the Indian Army arrived off Bahrain on October 23 but waited for Britain to declare war on Turkey in the first week of November before taking further action. The troops then landed on the Persian island of Abadan to secure the company's refinery. Reinforced by further arrivals from India, they advanced thence to the mainland, secured the port of Basra, and by early December reached the confluence of the Tigris and the Euphrates. The local inhabitants were assured by a proclamation that they would never be returned to Turkish rule.[5]

As things turned out, the landing at Abadan was not the first notification given by the British to the Turks that they "meant business."

At the beginning of November none of the Entente Powers was at war with Turkey. The Russian ambassador had, however, demanded his passports, and the British had delivered an ultimatum which made war extremely probable. Accordingly Vice Admiral Sackville H. Carden, who had succeeded Admiral Milne as British naval Commander in Chief in the Mediterranean, was ordered on November 1 to bombard the outer forts of the Dardanelles on the first suitable occasion.[6]

For reasons which have never been satisfactorily established, the execution of this order was not postponed, like the Abadan landing, until Britain and Turkey were formally at war. Russia declared war on November 2; France and Britain followed on November 5. The bombardment was delivered on November 3, apparently in the belief that prompt action was needed not only to test the strength of the forts, but also to demonstrate to the Turks the unwisdom of their flirtation with the Germans. Who decided that the attainment of these aims—if they were attained—would justify opening fire before a declaration of war had been delivered is not known.[7]

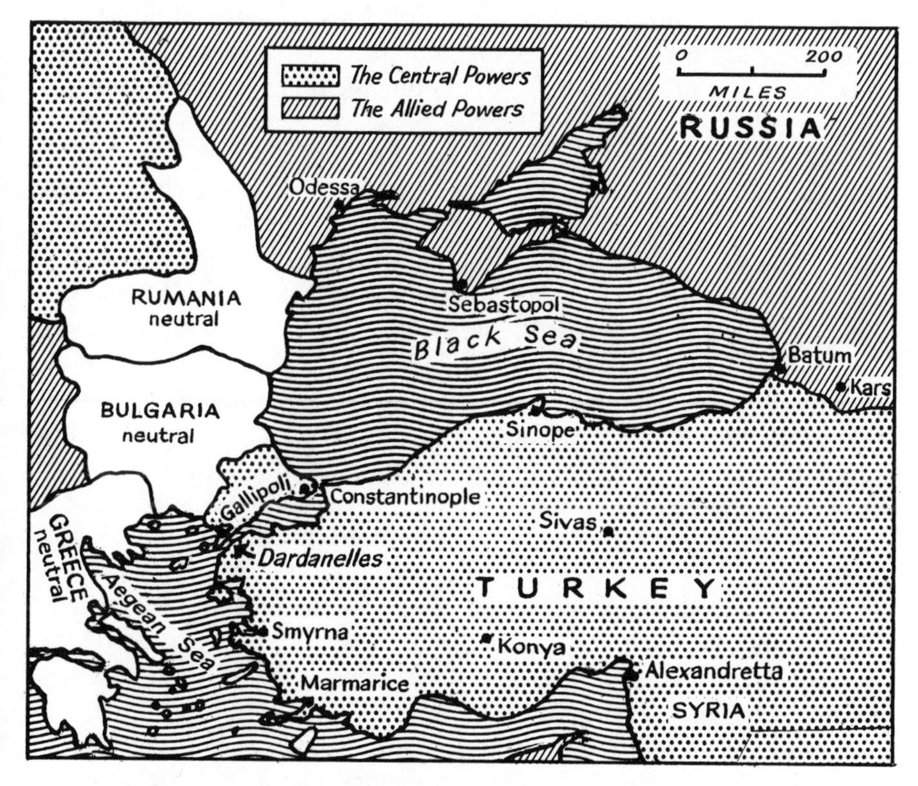

THE DARDANELLES AND THE NEAR EAST (1915)

In fact, they were not attained. The forts sustained a fair amount of damage, but the conclusions drawn by the British were misleading since they gave rise to unsound estimates of the chances of forcing the Dardanelles by naval action. As for the effect on Turco-German relations, it was roughly the opposite of that intended. Instead of convincing the Turks that their alliance with the Germans was a blunder, the bombardment helped reconcile them to the necessity of improving their defenses with German help.[8] The task eventually undertaken by the Allies at Gallipoli was made not easier but harder by the Navy's premature move.

Early in 1915 the British government and the War Council in particular faced the problem posed by Hankey's December memorandum and by proposals from Churchill, Lloyd George, and others. The Expeditionary Force, augmented since the outbreak of war by two divisions of the Indian Army, nineteen Territorial battalions, and three Regular divisions formed from troops recalled from overseas garrisons, was already twice as large as the largest army which Britain had previously undertaken to put into the field. The Canadian Division was in England, the Anzac Corps of two divisions completing its training in Egypt. Other formations at the disposal of the War Office included a further Regular division formed from battalions withdrawn from distant garrisons and the equivalent of seven or eight Territorial divisions.* According to forecasts current in January, the first of Kitchener's New Armies would be ready in March or April, the rest later. The crucial question was whether these troops, less the essential minimum needed for home defense, should go to swell the Allied armies across the Channel, stay at home as a strategic reserve, or (in Kitchener's phrase) be "employed elsewhere."

One point on which there was general agreement was that in any case there should be no complete or permanent severance of the British Army from the Western Front. The essence of the strategy outlined by Hankey was that the existing line in France and Flanders should be held, but that troops not needed for that purpose or for home defense should be used, in the first instance, to defeat Austro-Hungary and Turkey in partnership with Russia, Serbia, and perhaps some or all of the other Balkan states and Italy.[9] When that had been done, they could, if the government saw fit, be moved to the West to join the French in administering a final knockout blow to Germany.[10]

* Nominally there were still ten Territorial divisions in the United Kingdom after four had been sent to various parts of the overseas Empire for garrison duties. These had, however, been mulcted of some thirty battalions for a variety of purposes.

Lloyd George's proposals were broadly similar to Hankey's. Like Hankey, Lloyd George believed that mutual distrust would prevent the Balkan states from cooperating against the Central Powers unless direct participation by a British force assured them of a fair division of the spoils. Even if the Bulgarians held aloof, the landing of a substantial British or Franco-British force at Salonika or on the Dalmatian coast would, he thought, suffice to rally nearly 1,000,000 Greek and Rumanian troops in support of more than a quarter of a million Serbs who had fought extremely well in the early stages of the war.[11] In contrast with the Germans on the Western Front, the Austrians would be forced to defend an immensely wide front which they could not hope to make impregnable by digging multiple lines of trenches in every sector. Furthermore, a great many of their soldiers were Poles, Czechs, Slovaks, Ruthenians, Slovenes, or Croats who might not feel much enthusiasm for a campaign waged against fellow Slavs at the behest of German and Magyar overlords.

Lloyd George also proposed that British troops should land in Syria to cut off a Turkish force advancing toward the Suez Canal and incidentally to gain control of an area from which many people would like to see the Turks expelled on grounds of religion or sentiment.[12] Kitchener agreed that Turkish communications should, if possible, be cut, but postponed discussion of Lloyd George's project by suggesting that consideration should be given to a proposal of his own which called for the landing of a smaller force farther north. This effectively killed both projects. A plan was prepared, but no action had been taken when, early in February, the Turks reached the canal and were put to flight by the forces already in Egypt.[13]

A project sponsored by Churchill but inspired by Fisher amounted to the revival, in a modified form, of the old idea of a close blockade of Germany, to be preceded by the capture of one or more islands off her North Sea coast and followed, if all went well, by landings in Schleswig-Holstein or farther east.[14] A Russian army might, it was suggested, be put ashore in Pomerania once control of the Baltic had been gained.[15] With such aims in view, the Admiralty had begun as long ago as November to build a fleet of more than 200 self-propelled barges and some 400 other ships designed for use inside the Baltic.[16] Attempts to produce a workable plan showed that nonetheless, the consensus inside and outside the Admiralty did not support the view that entry into the Baltic through the narrow waters of the

Great Belt or the Sound was a practical operation of war while the Scandinavian countries remained neutral and Germany undefeated.[17]

A more promising proposal, since it appealed to Kitchener, as well as to Churchill, was that an attempt should be made to gain control of the Dardanelles with a view to the capture of Constantinople and the reopening of communications with Russia through the Sea of Marmara. This would ease the problem of supplying the Russian armies, bring down the price of wheat, and free a mass of shipping locked up in the Black Sea.[18] It would also help Russia's finances by reviving her foreign trade.

The Dardanelles venture and Lloyd George's Balkan enterprise were regarded at first as complementary rather than rival projects. They came to be viewed as competitors only when it was seen that troops could not be found simultaneously for both undertakings, if indeed they could be spared for either.

Lloyd George's Balkan proposals were discussed by the War Council on January 8 in the context of Hankey's memorandum. At that meeting the council agreed that, although the British Army must continue to make its main effort beside the French armies as long as France was seriously threatened, a projected advance by the Expeditionary Force along the Belgian coast to Zeebrugge, for which Sir John French was demanding a reinforcement of two Regular divisions and fifty Territorial or "New Army" battalions, should not be made.[19] In the light of an appeal from French, the ban was lifted five days later, but only on condition that the final decision was deferred until the beginning of February and that in any case the War Office should not be required to send more than the two Regular divisions and two Territorial divisions without artillery.[20] At the earlier meeting the Balkan project was criticized on the ground that a landing on the Dalmatian coast or elsewhere in Austria would be too hazardous in view of the danger from submarines and mines.[21] A landing at Salonika was not open to the same objections but would be feasible only if the Greeks were prepared to throw in their lot with the Entente Powers and the Entente Powers to face the consequences of bringing them in.

A further objection, which threatened to be decisive, was that a substantial force would be needed to rally the Balkan states to the Allied cause and that Kitchener professed his inability to find more than a brigade.[22] He did not regard the Territorials as suitable for employment in the Balkans; the time was not yet ripe for the Australians and the New Zealanders to leave Egypt. The Canadian Division would have to be sent across the Channel in the near future; the only remaining Regular division, the 29th, Kitchener wished to retain as a strategic reserve in the United Kingdom if he could escape sending it to French.

At first the same lack of troops seemed likely to rule out any prospect of gaining control of the Dardanelles. The Committee of Imperial Defence had reported in 1907 that if an attempt were made to force the Dardanelles in the event of trouble with Turkey, "the operation of landing an Expeditionary Force on or near the Gallipoli Peninsula would involve great risk, and should not be undertaken if other means of bringing pressure to bear on Turkey were available." [23] This was not known to the War Council in January;[24] but the subject had been raised by Churchill with Kitchener in August, 1914, studied by the General Staff at the War Office in September, and discussed by the War Council at its very first meeting in November.[25] On that occasion Churchill remarked that a landing at Gallipoli would be a difficult operation requiring a large force.[26] When the War Council discussed the matter again on January 13, Kitchener estimated that roughly 150,000 men would be required.[27]

Clearly, nothing like that number of British troops would be available. However, after a long discussion Churchill revived flagging hopes by suggesting that the Dardanelles might be forced by naval action. Something of the sort had been attempted during the Napoleonic Wars, when Admiral Sir John Duckworth entered the Sea of Marmara to make a demonstration intended to hearten the Russians and intimidate the Turks. As things turned out, the consequences were almost the opposite of those intended, largely because Duckworth, although he succeeded in forcing the Narrows, did not secure them, with the result that his squadron was badly knocked about on the return voyage. The plan sketched by Churchill in the light of an exchange of signals with Admiral Carden was quite different. His proposal was not that Carden should try to rush the Narrows, as Duckworth had done, but that he should destroy the Turkish forts by systematic bombardment, using about twelve old battleships in addition to two battle cruisers and the brand-new battleship *Queen Elizabeth.* Once the forts had been silenced and the Turkish minefields cleared, the fleet would steam to Constantinople and sink the *Goeben*.[28]

The War Council liked this plan. The appearance of a British fleet before Constantinople would, it was thought, so shake the Turks that even if they did not sue for peace, the government might well fall and be replaced by one unfavorable to the German alliance.[29] Kitchener remarked at the time that the naval attack was "worth trying," later that it was "vitally important."[30] Balfour confessed at the next meeting of the War Council that he found it hard to imagine a more helpful operation.[31] The moral effect on the wavering Balkan states of a successful attack on the Dardanelles could scarcely fail to be decisive. As for the military aspect, Grey thought that the Turks would be "paralyzed with fear" when they heard that their forts were falling, while Asquith seems to have assumed that the passage of the fleet, by isolating Gallipoli, would compel the garrison to surrender.[32]

At the close of the meeting on January 13 the War Council agreed that (in Asquith's words) the Admiralty should "prepare for a naval expedition in February to bombard and take the Gallipoli peninsula, with Constantinople as its objective."[33] On January 28 the council was given to understand that the bombardment would begin about February 11, but on February 9 ministers learned that as a result of bad weather and other mishaps, the opening day had been put back to February 15. Eventually the start was postponed, with unfortunate consequences, until February 19.

The War Council did not know, when it sanctioned this expedition, that the government's principal naval adviser was vehemently opposed to it. Fisher believed that, in general, warships ought not to be used to fight forts unless the intention was to force a decision at sea and, in particular, that the Navy ought not to be expected to "take" Gallipoli.[34] At the same time he held the curious belief that he was under an obligation not to express such views at meetings attended by his chief unless he intended to resign. This did not prevent him from communicating his differences with Churchill to men in close touch with the Prime Minister and other members of the government. Some days after the meeting at which the decision to prepare for a naval expedition was taken, he complained to Hankey that Churchill "out-argued" him.[35] On January 25 he completed, with help from Hankey and others, a memorandum setting forth his objections and asked that it should be printed and circulated to members of the War Council before the next meeting.[36]

This was not permitted. When the subject of the Dardanelles was raised at the War Council's meeting on January 28, Fisher rose from his seat with the intention of writing out his resignation on the spot but was persuaded by Kitchener not to do so.[37] The result was that although the existence of differences between the First Lord and the First Sea Lord was known, ministers received the impression that they had been patched up. This was true up to a point. Fisher did agree, at an interview with Churchill after the meeting on January 28, not to press his objections to the Dardanelles venture.[38] But his assent was given against his better judgment. He was willing that old battleships should be used to bombard the Turkish forts but still thought that only troops could take and hold Gallipoli. He agreed to the operation in the form implied by the War Council's resolution not because he liked it, but because, once again, Churchill succeeded in "out-arguing" him by appealing to his loyalty and reminding him of the good work he could continue to do if he remained at his post.[39]

By January 28 it was known in London that Sir John French had failed to gain Joffre's support for his Zeebrugge offensive. The project then lapsed until Haig revived it in 1917. Ministers would have liked to withhold at least three of the four divisions promised as reinforcements for the operation but knew that the French were counting on them to send all four "for the purpose of strengthening the line and providing a mobile reserve." [40] Kitchener proposed that he should either send the four divisions but reserve the right to withdraw them in a month or retain them on the understanding that they would be rushed across the Channel in an emergency.[41] French, when consulted by Churchill on the government's behalf, insisted that the four divisions should be sent but offered to hold two of them in reserve so that Kitchener could withdraw them after the middle of March if he still wished to do so. Under pressure, he afterward accepted a third Territorial division in place of the 29th Division.

As the sequel to conversations with the French Foreign Minister, Théophile Delcassé, the War Council agreed on February 9 that the 29th Division should go to Salonika as the British contribution to an Allied force.[42] The French promised a division; the Russians, who were known to be short of ammunition and had suffered serious setbacks since German troops joined the Austrians in Galicia, declared their inability to send more than 1,000 Cossacks. Grey then undertook to draft, in consultation with Kitchener, a telegram to Athens to the effect that the British government thought it imperative that Greece should go to the aid of Serbia and that Britain, France, and Russia proposed to send an Allied force to Salonika for the purpose of helping her to do so and protecting her communications with the Serbian front. Delcassé, who was still in London, promised a similar telegram on behalf of the French government.

The War Council intended that the presentation of messages on these lines by the British and French ministers in Athens should coincide with the news that Admiral Carden (with French, as well as British, warships under command) had begun to bombard the Turkish forts at the entrance to the Dardanelles.[43] As things turned out, the impact of the messages was much weakened by Carden's inability to begin the bombardment until four days after they were presented. The result was that a diplomatic gesture which might, with better timing, have rallied Rumania, as well as Greece, to the Allied cause failed to stir either country to action. The Greeks, aware that the Russians were in difficulties and alarmed by the news that Bulgaria had raised a large loan in Germany, flatly refused to enter the war or receive an Allied force without a firm assurance of Rumanian support; the Rumanians remained unresponsive.[44] A proposal from Lloyd George that a special diplomatic mission should visit the Near East to negotiate a military convention with Greece and Rumania was coolly received by Grey and Asquith.[45]

For the British the only consolation to be gleaned from the failure of their *démarche* was that it left the 29th Division uncommitted. On February 16 Asquith decided in consultation with Kitchener, Churchill, Fisher, Lloyd George, and Grey that the division should be sent to the neighborhood of the Dardanelles so that it would be available, "in case of necessity," to support the naval attack. Two battalions of marines were already being sent for the purpose of capturing torpedo tubes which formed part of the Turkish defenses. In addition, a force would be sent from Egypt if it were needed. Finally, the Admiralty was asked to provide transports and barges for a landing by up to 50,000 men.

These decisions, reached only twenty-four hours after the Greeks had refused to help the Serbs, were deemed to be decisions of the

War Council, although not all members of the council were summoned to the meeting at which they were made.[46] Among the absentees were the Chief of the Imperial General Staff and the experienced Haldane and Balfour.

However, Kitchener soon changed his mind. Fearing that a Russian collapse might enable the Germans to reinforce their armies in the West, he refused at the next meeting of the War Council on February 19 to abide by the decision to send the 29th Division to the Aegean but renewed his offer to send the Australians and New Zealanders from Egypt.[47] These troops, with the Royal Naval Division and some independent marine battalions, should, he thought, suffice for a purpose which (although he did not say so) had yet to be made clear. Rejecting Lloyd George's argument that the Germans were more likely to attack Serbia than move divisions to the Western Front if Russia did collapse, he persisted until the second week in March in his refusal to release the 29th Division.[48]

The naval bombardment, when at last it was launched, made a good beginning. On the first day a number of forts were damaged and no hits were scored on Allied ships; by February 25 all the outer forts on both sides of the entrance to the Dardanelles were silenced. Furthermore, the moral effects in Allied and neutral countries exceeded expectations in all respects except that the bombardment came too late to bolster the Salonika proposal. On February 22 the French offered to send a division to the Dardanelles.[49] The Russians, delighted to find that the Turks were withdrawing troops from the Caucasus to reinforce Gallipoli, promised that their Black Sea Fleet and an army corps should contribute to the capture of Constantinople, with the proviso that Carden's fleet should first reach the Sea of Marmara.[50] The Balkan countries responded so favorably to the bombardment that British hopes of uniting them against the Central Powers revived. For the time being the threat of a hostile Bulgaria receded; early in March Italy took the first step toward joining the Entente Powers.[51] Above all, on March 1 the Greek Prime Minister, Eleutherios Venizelos, proposed that three Greek divisions should be put ashore on the Gallipoli Peninsula.[52]

This proposal was defeated by the very power which stood to profit most from it. The Russians had everything to gain from an Allied success at the Dardanelles and the bringing together of the Balkan states against the Central Powers. Yet so strong was their desire to see the Russian flag planted on the shores of the Bosporus without help from Greece that on March 2 Sazonov, their Foreign Minister, informed the Russian minister in Athens and the Russian ambassadors in London and Paris that Russia would "in no circumstances . . . allow Greek forces to participate in the Allied attack on Constantinople." [53] On the following day the Greek General Staff announced that "the moment had passed." [54] A few days later Venizelos fell from office and was succeeded by the pro-German Gounaris.

The Russians went on to lay claim to Constantinople, a small part of Turkey in Asia, the Turkish islands in the Sea of Marmara, two islands off the entrance to the Dardanelles, and substantially more of Turkey in Europe than was needed to secure control of the Straits. Sazonov did not ask that France and Britain should publicly announce their readiness to accede to these proposals but only that they should agree not to oppose them.[55]

Russia was felt to have behaved badly in regard to the Greek offer. On the other hand, France and Britain were indebted to her for drawing two German corps from the Western Front by invading East Prussia early in the war. What was more, they were counting on her for further efforts. Lloyd George, who saw more clearly than many of his colleagues the importance of the Russian contribution, proposed that Grey should seize the opportunity of thrashing out the whole problem of relations with Russia and the Balkan states by conferring with Sazonov and Delcassé on Greek soil or aboard a British warship in the Aegean, but he argued in vain. Asquith felt that a prompt decision was needed to avert ill will which threatened to hamper the Allied war effort.[56] At a meeting of the War Council on March 10, no objection was raised to Sazonov's proposals by the Admiralty, the War Office, or opposition statesmen who attended the meeting at Asquith's request.[57] Accordingly, a favorable reply was given through diplomatic channels.

This did not mean that Russia could be sure of obtaining the territories she coveted. It meant merely that the British joined the French in pledging themselves not to oppose her claims at the peace conference should Turkey be defeated. The Russians promised in return to respect any wishes which their Allies might express in regard to other parts of the Ottoman Empire and to look favorably on proposals for other territorial adjustments.

Meanwhile, the opening of the naval bombardment had transformed the attitude of British statesmen to the Dardanelles venture. Kitchener had said on January 28 that one of the merits of the scheme was that the naval attack could be broken off if it were unsuccessful.[58] On February 24 he argued that, on the contrary, the publicity given to the bombardment after the first day meant that there could be no going back and that the Army would have to take a hand if the fleet could not get through the Straits unaided.[59] Similar views were expressed by Grey and Churchill.[60] Lloyd George thought that the Allies were committed by the bombardment to some operation in the Near East, though not necessarily to a siege of the Dardanelles.[61]

One consequence was increased pressure on Kitchener to release the 29th Division. He held out until March 10, when he agreed that the division should go to the Aegean. He then produced figures to show that nearly 130,000 troops were "available against Constantinople." [62] But this total included nearly 50,000 Russians who would not, in fact, be available unless and until the fleet reached the Sea of Marmara. Even if no troops were put ashore on the Asian side of the Dardanelles, the number of troops available for landings on the Gallipoli Peninsula after the arrival of the 29th Division would not be more than about 75,000. This was one-half the force which Kitchener had thought might be needed when the matter was discussed in January. The Greeks, too, when drawing up a plan for a landing at the Narrows, had come to the conclusion that 150,000 troops would be needed to capture the peninsula.[63]

General Sir Ian Hamilton, an experienced staff officer and commander in the field whom Kitchener had long had in mind as a possible successor to French, was chosen to command what was at first called the Constantinople and later (at Hamilton's request) the Mediterranean Expeditionary Force. He was given a two- to three-year-old manual on the Turkish Army, a prewar Admiralty report on the defenses of the Dardanelles, and an inaccurate map of the Gallipoli Peninsula, but no detailed, up-to-date appreciation of the problem of advancing to Constantinople by way of Gallipoli.[64] The number of Turkish troops defending the peninsula was estimated at 60,000.[65]

Hamilton, with fewer than 80,000 troops including the French contingent, was not well placed to open a way to his objective by hammering methodically at the Turkish lines. Churchill suggested that without waiting for the 29th Division, he should try a *coup de main* with some 40,000 troops already on the spot.[66] That course was, however, ruled out by the written instructions which Hamilton received from Kitchener. These instructions, dated March 13, were not shown to the War Council, although their tenor was known to Asquith.[67] In effect, they ordered Hamilton to await the arrival of the 29th Division before attempting any serious undertaking on the peninsula, and not to use his forces "on any large scale" unless the fleet failed to get through the Straits after every effort had been exhausted. Once the Straits had been forced, he would be free to use some of his troops to hold the neck of the peninsula at Bulair in order to prevent the Turks from bringing reinforcements beyond that point.[68] At the same time, Kitchener made it clear that he had no intention of abandoning the project, even if the naval attack proved unsuccessful.

An obvious weakness of this plan was that Hamilton's resources were clearly insufficient—or at any rate were not clearly sufficient—for the task which would fall to the Army if the Navy failed. The number of troops allotted to him was not based on any scientific assessment of his needs, but was merely the number that happened to be available.

In the meantime Carden, troubled by fire from guns which he could not locate until he had more aircraft and by the difficulty of sweeping mines with small craft manned by civilians, had broken off the naval attack after a cautious attempt to subdue forts immediately outside the Narrows. Under pressure from the Admiralty, he agreed about the middle of March to make a further attempt but reported that in his opinion (which was also Fisher's) the time had come to use troops as well as ships.[69] An unsatisfactory exchange of signals with the Admiralty culminated in his replacement by Vice Admiral J. M. de Robeck, hitherto his second-in-command.

A fresh attack on the forts was launched on March 18 with sixteen ships. Two old battleships and a French battleship were sunk and three ships damaged, mostly by contact with a single row of mines. Although few lives were lost, Robeck broke off the action and reported that his fleet had suffered a disaster. The War Council ruled on the following day that he should be invited to renew the attack if he thought fit but that the decision should be left to him.[70] He responded by announcing on March 23 that he proposed to suspend operations until the Army was ashore and had gained control of the peninsula. Churchill then drafted a signal directing Robeck to resume the attack, but the Admiralty War Staff (with two dissentients) held that the man on the spot could not be ordered from London to adopt a course of action which he deemed impractical on technical grounds. Asquith, to whom Churchill appealed, agreed that the naval attack ought, if possible, to be renewed, but upheld the War Staff's view that the signal should not be sent.[71]

No further meeting of the War Council was held until May 14. The crucial decision to attempt the capture of the Gallipoli Peninsula with land forces was made by Hamilton and Robeck at a conference aboard the *Queen Elizabeth* on March 22. The two commanders in chief agreed that the time had come to "turn to the land scheme." [72] This departure from the principle that Hamilton's troops should help the Navy "take" the peninsula but should not be used on a large scale until the fleet had "exhausted every effort" was approved by Kitchener, who consulted Asquith and others; but it was never sanctioned or even discussed by the War Council. Attempts to persuade Asquith to summon the War Council before the troops went ashore on April 25 were made by Fisher and independently by Hankey, who proposed that a committee of naval and military experts should be appointed to draw up a plan of campaign and work out the number of troops required to give effect to it.[73] Both men found the Prime Minister unresponsive.

This, perhaps, was only to be expected. The government was engaged in delicate negotiations with the Balkan states and Italy at a time when Grey was troubled by failing sight. A military success or at least a demonstration in the Near East was needed to help these negotiations. The naval attack had failed, and Robeck was unwilling to renew it. Kitchener, an acknowledged master of the military art, was prepared not only to send troops to the Dardanelles, but to sanction their use in an offensive role. Not unnaturally, a government grateful for his complaisance saw little reason to question his strategy.

Even so, had a committee of experts been appointed it might well have recommended that Hamilton's assault should be postponed until more troops were available. Whether additional troops could have been assembled and shipped to the Dardanelles in time to meet the government's wishes is another question. Certainly the troops themselves could have been found had Kitchener been able and willing to restrict the forces in France to a defensive role.

That, however, was not done. On March 10 Sir John French, stung by Joffre's comments on his failure to support a French offensive in December and his refusal since the beginning of the year to extend his line, delivered an attack at Neuve-Chapelle although an advance by French troops who were to have cooperated with him had been called off. The initial assault achieved surprise and was brilliantly successful. A brief but heavy bombardment destroyed the enemy's wire, and the leading troops of Haig's First Army broke through on a narrow front to a depth of about a mile and a quarter. Reserves under corps and divisional headquarters were waiting to push through the gap made by the infantry, but they could not be summoned in good time because the German counterbombardment had destroyed Haig's telephone lines from front to rear. An attempt to retrieve the situation by throwing in Smith-Dorrien's Second Army at short notice led to substantial losses, only partly offset by an inconsiderable advance.

The War Council had not been consulted about the Neuve-Chapelle attack.[74] Even though success was admitted to have been very near, its failure strengthened the belief of many ministers that offensives on the Western Front were useless. Nevertheless, Kitchener agreed, at a conference at Joffre's headquarters on March 29, to give French two more Territorial divisions so that he could contribute to a major attempt to break through the German lines in the Artois sector which Joffre was planning. This brought the strength of the Expeditionary Force to well over half a million men.

The Artois offensive, launched on May 9, failed at a cost of roughly 160,000 French and some 30,000 British casualties. Heavy fighting continued until well into June, but little progress was made after the first day or two. Kitchener reported on May 14 that a breakthrough in existing circumstances had been shown to be impossible.[75]

Meanwhile, Hamilton had put his force ashore at the Dardanelles, despite misgivings on the part of his divisional commanders. The troops succeeded in establishing and consolidating their lodgment areas after a shaky start but were soon brought to a halt by a garrison believed to outnumber them by roughly two to one. On May 9, less than a week after Kitchener had told Asquith that success was certain, Hamilton announced that he could not hope to occupy the Gallipoli Peninsula without reinforcements.[76]

By the middle of May the government's failure to adapt its grand strategy to changing needs was thus made manifest. On the Western Front, as Kitchener admitted, no worthwhile objective was attainable by the strongest push of which the British and the French between them were capable. At the Dardanelles the Allies had the prospect of a brilliant success which promised to open the way to Constantinople, revive Russia's declining fortunes, and range the Balkan states behind the Entente Powers. The Turks had shown that by entrenching themselves on favorable slopes, they could prevent a numerically inferior force from storming the heights which commanded the Narrows, but they could not be expected to hold the slender Gallipoli Peninsula indefinitely against a determined enemy with command of the sea and enough troops and supporting fire to launch simultaneous attacks at a number of widely separated points. Yet the British had 546,000 men on the Western Front, which they persisted in calling the "main front." At the Dardanelles, which had become for the time being the "decisive point" they sometimes talked about, there were fewer than 80,000 Allied troops.

At this crucial moment, when a change of emphasis became imperative, the government's vision was clouded by preoccupations which obscured, for at least a fortnight, the paramount need to rush reinforcements to a front where they could be usefully employed.

The unexpected scope and duration of the war forced all the leading belligerents to increase their output of arms and ammunition. A big increase was harder to achieve in Britain than in France or Germany, because the British armaments industry was not geared in peacetime to the needs of a large standing army and because the response to Kitchener's recruiting drive far exceeded expectations.[77] Furthermore, some manufacturers handicapped themselves by accepting large orders from Russia at a time when they were working flat-out to meet demands at home and had lost some of their best men to the armed forces. Industrial disputes and absenteeism arising from the abnormal demand on labor in certain industries and other departures from routine also threatened, in some cases, to disrupt production schedules.

At the same time, trench warfare created new demands for heavy guns and also for large quantities of high-explosive ammunition to support what were, in effect, siege operations. These needs had not been foreseen in any country at a time when a short war of movement was expected. Nonetheless the Germans were better provided than the British or the French with big guns and high-explosive shells, because they had always known that they might have to tackle the Belgian forts on the Meuse and perhaps such fortified towns as Antwerp and Lille.

Almost from the beginning of the war, Sir John French asked for more ammunition for his field guns and also for a higher proportion of high explosive to shrapnel. Such requests were made on at least ten occasions between September and November, 1914.[78] Finally, on December 31 French warned the War Office that supplies were so inadequate as to rule out offensive operations, "even on a small scale." [79]

He gave rather a different impression at his interview with the War Council a fortnight later. When asked whether he would have enough artillery support for his proposed advance to Zeebrugge, he said that although he was counting partly on the Navy and the Belgians and would like more heavy guns, he was saving six rounds a day for each of his field guns and hoped to do still better in February.[80] Again, when discussing the coming offensive in Artois with Kitchener on May 2, he said that "the ammunition would be all right." [81] Admittedly he attributed the breaking off of his advance at Neuve-Chapelle partly to want of ammunition, but the explanation was thought to be that no reserves had been accumulated in the Second Army's area because originally only the First Army was to have taken part in the offensive.

The result was that although ministers knew that output was far from satisfactory in view of the need to arm and equip the new armies that were coming forward, some of them received the impression that shortages were potential rather than actual. On the strength of a letter written by Kitchener after consultation with French, Asquith denied in a speech at Newcastle on April 20 that operations were being hampered by any failure on the part of the government to provide the necessary ammunition.[82]

This proved a most unlucky statement. When the British went forward at Festubert in the May offensive, the infantry found that they were asked to take positions which a preliminary bombardment with shrapnel had left almost unscathed. The Germans, in deep trenches with concrete emplacements for their machine guns, had come to little harm. In some places the German wire was still intact.

After the battle, French and his staff pointed out that the infantry's task would have been less difficult, and their losses lighter, if the gunners had had plenty of high explosive. They also complained of poorly made shells, defective fuzes, and, once again, a dearth of heavy guns. French, who had begun to speak of Kitchener, half-seriously, as "the Arch-Fiend," was not content with protests sent through the usual channels. He made disclosures to the press which led to serious charges against the government. Kitchener was accused of starving the Expeditionary Force of shells, Asquith of hiding the truth in his Newcastle speech. These charges could have been met only if Asquith had been willing to say that Kitchener had unwittingly misled him and to confess—as Kitchener afterward did in the House of Lords—that the cause of the trouble was not that supplies were being withheld but that output was unsatisfactory.

The immediate cause of the Liberal government's downfall was not, however, the munitions scandal, but a crisis at the Admiralty. In the second week of May Robeck sent a signal asking whether he should make a fresh attempt to force the Dardanelles by naval action because the army had failed to capture the forts. Fisher threatened to resign if an affirmative answer were given but was assured that no action would be taken without his concurrence. He emerged well satisfied from an interview with the Prime Minister on May 13.[83]

Late on Friday, May 14, Fisher was asked to agree to the dispatch to the Aegean not only of two monitors intended to replace the *Queen Elizabeth*, on whose recall he had insisted, but also of a number of submarines and minesweepers. His response was to leave the Admiralty on the following day and take refuge at his club. He also told Lloyd George that he had resigned and was leaving for Scotland, wrote letters to Churchill and Asquith tendering his resignation, and took care that the leader of the opposition, Bonar Law, was informed of his supposed resignation and departure.[84]

This was irregular. Fisher would have been within his rights in asking to be relieved of his post. He was not entitled to absent himself from duty on the strength of a proffered resignation which might not be accepted.

The effect was to bring down the government after more than nine years of Liberal rule. Bonar Law, after consulting Lloyd George, offered Asquith the choice between "some change in the constitution of the government" and a damaging debate in the House of Commons. Asquith agreed to form a new government in which ministerial posts would be found for leading members of the Unionist opposition and for one representative of the Labor Party.

From the military point of view, the change could scarcely have come at a worse moment. When Hamilton replied, on May 17, to a signal asking him what reinforcements he needed to complete his task, the Liberal Cabinet was in dissolution and the War Council had ceased to exist. More than three weeks elapsed before the new Cabinet agreed to send him the three divisions he asked for, roughly seven weeks before a revised figure of five divisions was adopted.[85] Meanwhile, his original force, already depleted by battle casualties and sickness, suffered further wastage in a climate which became progressively less favorable for offensive operations as the season advanced toward high summer.

With the five divisions promised, Hamilton would have for his second attempt to capture the peninsula about 150,000 men, including two French divisions and two divisions in reserve. His troops already ashore were well entrenched and in vigorous contact with the enemy, but all their supplies had to be landed at points within artillery range of the Turkish lines. Intense heat, swarms of flies, and the lack of any recreation except bathing from beaches intermittently under fire made their lot unenviable.

The starting point of Hamilton's plan was a deception scheme designed to give the impression that troops were being withdrawn from Anzac Cove and that a new landing was to be made in Turkish territory far from the Dardanelles. When the stage was set, the troops at Anzac Cove, secretly reinforced by night, were to thrust across the waist of the peninsula in order to cut off the Turkish forces near its tip, seize the Kilid Bahr plateau with its forts commanding the Narrows, and bring the enemy's communications on the far side of the Straits under artillery fire. Because the beachhead at Anzac Cove could not accommodate more than three to four divisions and also because a sheltered anchorage would be needed if the Allies stayed until the winter, one corps of two divisions (less one brigade) would land farther up the coast at Suvla Bay. Its task was to seize a line of hills about four miles from the shore, help the troops from Anzac

Cove capture the crucial Sari Bair Ridge should help be needed at that point, and then push on toward the Straits. British and French troops already ashore in the Cape Helles area were to make diversionary attacks for the purpose of confusing the enemy and pinning him to his trenches near the southwestern extremity of the peninsula.

Hamilton asked that two energetic corps commanders who had served on the Western Front should accompany his reinforcements, but Kitchener insisted that appointments should be based on seniority. Command of the corps which was to land at Suvla went to a senior lieutenant general with no recent experience in the field.

D day was August 6. The main advance from Anzac Cove was stoutly resisted by experienced troops in strong positions. The landings at Suvla, on the other hand, came as a surprise to the Turkish High Command and were opposed only by weak local garrisons. But the opportunity thus offered to the British was not taken. The corps commander at Suvla did not go ashore with his troops but remained with his staff aboard the flagship of the officer responsible for the naval side of the expedition. His subordinate commanders, drawing an unsound inference from reports of the fighting in France and Belgium, carried to absurd lengths the principle of a step-by-step advance. The troops, instead of seizing the hills in front of them at the earliest possible moment, stayed so long on the beaches that the Turks were able to bring up reinforcements by forced marches. The result was that Hamilton's chance of overcoming a check to his right by thrusting with his left had already disappeared by the time he arrived at Suvla on August 8 to see for himself how things were going. A few units from Anzac Cove pushed far enough to gain tantalizing glimpses of the Straits before they were withdrawn for lack of support.

The failure of the Suvla-Anzac operation did not prove that the Allies were incapable of getting to Constantinople. It did suggest that they were unlikely to do so without more troops, more ammunition, and better generals. All these could have been provided had the authorities at home been willing to act resolutely on the assumption that, while progress at the Dardanelles was difficult, progress on the Western Front was next to impossible. This they were not prepared to do. For a time the British government, advised by a Cabinet subcommittee called sometimes the Dardanelles Committee and sometimes the War Committee, did contemplate giving Hamilton further reinforcements on the understanding that the French would raise their contribution from two to six divisions. But the project lapsed when the British and French governments, on learning that the Bulgarian Army was mobilizing, agreed that on political grounds an Allied force must, after all, be sent to Salonika to help the Serbs. Eventually such a force was sent, but it arrived too late to save the Serbian Army from being overwhelmed by an offensive concerted between the Bulgarians, the Austrians, and the Germans. Almost simultaneously, a British Indian force which had advanced from Basra toward Baghdad was besieged by Turkish troops at Kut-el-Amara, where it was afterward forced to surrender in humiliating circumstances.

On October 27 General Sir Charles Monro, an officer described by Hankey in his diary as "a cheery old fellow . . . but not very quick," arrived at Hamilton's headquarters with orders to relieve Hamilton of his command and "report on the Near Eastern situation."[86] On October 31, after a hurried visit to the Suvla, Anzac, and Cape Helles beachheads, he advised the government that the force now under his command could not withstand a determined attack and should be withdrawn. Kitchener let it be known on November 3 that he "absolutely refused" to sign an order for withdrawal but changed his mind after traveling to the Dardanelles later in the month to see Monro and inspect the beachheads.[87] Despite a warning from Hankey that withdrawal would free the whole of the Turkish Army for attacks on Mesopotamia, the Caucasus, or Egypt and that the Russians might even sign a separate peace, Monro's troops withdrew from Suvla and Anzac on December 20 and from Cape Helles just over a fortnight later. Both withdrawals were accomplished almost without loss.

In the meantime, the Cabinet had decided, on July 3, that for the time being offensive operations on the Western Front should be discouraged. If nonetheless the French insisted on taking the offensive, the Expeditionary Force was to give, with its existing forces, such support as it could render without risking undue losses.[88] Despite the reference to "existing forces," Kitchener agreed at a conference with the French at Calais a few days later to send large numbers of "New Army" divisions across the Channel in the near future. According to President Raymond Poincaré, he promised six divisions by the end of the month and a further six each month thereafter.[89]

In August reports of spectacular advances by the German armies in Poland led Kitchener to depart still further from the decision of July 3. After telling French and his army commanders that, because the Russians might collapse, they must do their utmost to help France even at the cost of "very heavy losses indeed," he persuaded the Cabinet to accept the argument that even though the offensive which Joffre was planning for September promised no military success, the British must take part in it for fear that otherwise not only Russia but even France might drop out of the war.[90]

Joffre's plan was to hammer at both ends of the huge German salient between Artois and the Argonne by attacking in the south with thirty-four divisions, in the north with twenty-seven divisions supported by nine British divisions. The launching of these attacks on September 22 and 25 was followed by weeks of futile endeavor which cost the Allies a quarter of a million casualties and 10,000,000 shells in return for an inconsiderable adjustment of the German line. Haig, whose army delivered the British attack at Loos, claimed after the battle that he could have done much better had French not insisted on retaining control of the reserve formations needed to exploit an initial success. On December 4 French relinquished his command at the government's bidding. Just over a fortnight later Haig succeeded him.

Kitchener, on his return from the Dardanelles at the beginning of December, also offered to resign but found that Asquith had other plans. On December 23 General Sir William Robertson, a dour professional soldier who had risen from the ranks to the top of the military hierarchy without ever commanding troops, assumed the post of Chief of the Imperial General Staff with enlarged powers carved from Kitchener's. On his first day in office he recommended that the Cape Helles beachhead at the Dardanelles should be given up on the ground that its retention violated the principle of concentration.[91] Thereafter he made it his business to frustrate almost any proposal which threatened to divert troops from the Western Front.[92] Starting from the premise that the best way of winning a war was to defeat the enemy's armies in the field, he argued that the Western Front was the decisive theater for France and Britain.

Once the Allies had decided to leave the Dardanelles this argument was hard to counter, because there was no longer an alternative strategy which promised a reward comparable with the capture of Constantinople. No decisive success was likely to come of attacks on the Turkish forces in Mesopotamia, Syria, or Palestine; communications northward from Salonika would not suffice for more than a limited offensive which could no longer materially affect the situation in the Balkans. Italy, in return for the promise of substantial gains at the expense of Austria and Turkey, was about to declare war on Austro-Hungary, and later on Germany, but the Italians had all the troops they could deploy on their restricted front. To adopt a defensive strategy on all fronts, devote a bigger share of the national output to the Navy, and rely on the economic blockade to bring the Central Powers to their knees was, for the British, an attractive but not a practical solution. Steps had already been taken to build a substantial army which would be needed when the time came to drive the Germans out of France and Belgium. In the meantime, some employment had to be found for it which would satisfy not only the British, but also the Russians and the French, that Britain was making an adequate contribution to the war.

In the light of these considerations the government agreed in the last week of December that the British Army must make its main effort in 1916 on the Western Front.[93] In Egypt and Mesopotamia a defensive strategy would be adopted. No offensive in the West was to be launched without further reference to the government, but Robertson was authorized to prepare for one. Ministerial misgivings were only partly set at rest by the hope that more and better guns and more ammunition for the artillery might make the infantry's task less difficult than in 1915.

In effect, these decisions condemned the Expeditionary Force to participation in a perilous attempt to wear down the enemy's forces by sacrificing British, French, Italian, and Russian lives in the hope that the losses of the Central Powers would be even heavier. Although this implication was not yet fully apparent to the government, there was a grim logic in the Cabinet's decision, on the same day, to consider some form of compulsory military service.[94] After prolonged debate, the principle of compulsion was accepted by the Cabinet on April 29.[95] The National Military Service bill was introduced in the House of Commons on May 2, passed its second reading without a division on the same day, and became law on May 25. By that time more than 2,500,000 men had enlisted voluntarily in the armed forces since August, 1914. Compulsion brought roughly another 2,000,000 during the remaining three and a half years of war.[96]

5

Blockade and Attrition

SINCE neither Britain nor the United States had ratified the Declaration of London when the First World War began, there existed in 1914 no up-to-date and comprehensive definition of contraband of war by which all the belligerents were bound. In other respects the conduct to be expected of civilized nations engaged in a war at sea was fairly well established by rules derived from earlier declarations or conventions and from long-standing custom. Thus it was generally accepted that a belligerent was not entitled to sow mines in the open sea, lay minefields dangerous to noncombatant shipping without declaring their existence, or sink merchant vessels of any nation without providing for the safety of passengers and crews. As long as these conditions were observed, a belligerent had the right to board any merchant vessel for the purpose of establishing its nationality, confiscating it for the duration of the war if it was found to belong to a citizen of a hostile nation, and seizing goods intended to assist an enemy's war effort. This right not only was recognized by all the leading maritime powers but had been freely exercised by the British in the Napoleonic Wars, by the United States in the Civil War and the Spanish-American War, and by the French and the Dutch in earlier wars.

The right of seizure was, however, qualified by the Declaration of Paris, accepted by the leading European powers in 1856. This provided that an enemy's goods, carried in a neutral vessel, should be exempt from seizure unless they were contraband of war; but the Declaration of Paris contained no satisfactory definition of contraband of war, and in any case its terms had been expressly rejected by the United States.

According to the definitions attempted in the Declaration of London, copper and cotton were not contraband of war, while food and fodder could be seized only if they were intended for the use of a belligerent's armed forces. Even then they were exempt if consigned to a neutral port. Had the declaration been ratified by all parties, the Germans would thus have been free to import as much copper and cotton for the manufacture of shells and explosives as could be shipped to them in neutral vessels. They would also have been free to receive cargoes of grain, meat, sugar, cocoa, edible fats, and other comestibles consigned to them through neutral ports or even through German ports unless the Allies could show that the ultimate consignee was an agency concerned with the prosecution of the war. It was therefore much to the interest of the Central Powers to secure the practical adoption of the terms of the declaration by exerting pressure on the Allies through neutral governments whose nationals were ready and willing to sell goods to both sides. At the same time, the United States government was concerned to know whether the British intended to use their command of the sea to interfere with the shipment to Germany, or to neutral countries trading with Germany, of cargoes which would have been exempt from seizure if the declaration had been ratified.

On August 6, 1914, the United States government asked all the leading belligerents whether they were willing to abide by the terms of the declaration during the war that had just begun. The Central Powers, not surprisingly, expressed their readiness to do so if other belligerents did the same. The British, observing that the Germans were already breaking the rules by their indiscriminate use of mines, replied after consulting their Allies that they proposed to adopt the terms of the declaration with "certain modifications and additions." [1] Since this was tantamount to a refusal, the State Department instructed the United States ambassador in London to press for unconditional acceptance. After four times presenting a demand which he knew would be rejected and himself regarded as unreasonable, Page proposed a compromise. At his suggestion, the United States government published on October 22 an announcement to the effect that it proposed to rest its rights not on the declaration but on the existing provisions of international law and on treaties duly ratified. The British then accepted the terms of the declaration with modifications whose essential feature was a new and greatly extended list of goods to be regarded as contraband of war.[2]

About the same time, the British placed in the United States large orders for raw materials and manufactured goods. American copper producers, in particular, were thus assured of a profitable market for practically the whole of their exportable surplus.[3]

The Allied blockade continued, nonetheless, to be a source of irritation and annoyance to the Americans. The State Department complained on many occasions that the interests of United States citizens were adversely affected by the detention of ships, cargoes, or mails or by delays in settling claims arising from such acts. The British, although vexed by these complaints, could not afford to disregard them. They were determined that the blockade should cause the Central Powers as much "inconvenience, loss, dislocation of trade and finance, expenditure of effort, depression, and despair" as possible.[4] At the same time they recognized that if American industrialists and shipowners suffered more inconvenience than they were prepared to tolerate, the United States government might be forced to restrict exports to Allied countries or perhaps to send American merchantmen across the Atlantic under naval escort. The first would greatly hamper the Allied war effort; the second might make the blockade unworkable. They decided to aim, therefore, at what Grey called "the maximum of blockade that could be enforced without a rupture with the United States." [5]

The Germans replied to the Allied blockade by instituting a blockade of their own, to be enforced by submarines. On February 4, 1915, they announced that they proposed to regard the whole of the waters around the British Isles as a "war zone" which neutral vessels would enter at their peril unless they followed a prescribed route and in which all Allied vessels would be sunk. On February 18 they followed up this declaration by formally proclaiming a "submarine blockade."

From that date an avowed aim of both the Entente and the Central Powers was to win the war partly by depriving their enemies not merely of war materials, but of supplies of every kind, including food for men and cattle. As Grey pointed out to the United States government, the difference between their policies was that the British and the French, unlike the Germans, proposed to attain their ends without sacrificing neutral ships or noncombatant lives, and without "inflicting upon neutrals the damage that must be entailed when a vessel and its cargo are sunk without notice, examination or trial." [6]

Count von Bernstorff, the German ambassador in Washington, could not fail to know that unrestricted submarine warfare was bound, in the long run, to do great harm to his country's relations with the United States. He therefore proposed a compromise. On Bernstorff's initiative,[7] President Wilson suggested on February 20 that in return for an undertaking by the British not to interfere with cargoes of food or animal feeding stuffs consigned to approved agencies for distribution to the civil population through licensed retailers, the Germans should agree not to make submarine attacks on merchant vessels of any nationality "except to enforce the right of visit and search." Bernstorff's superiors effectively killed this proposal by insisting that raw materials which would have been exempt from seizure under the Declaration of London should be included in the scheme and by refusing to forgo the use of minefields for offensive purposes, as they were asked by the Americans to do.[8]

In the meantime, Wilson and House had come to the conclusion that no chance of ending the war by mediation ought to be passed over. An outright victory for the Entente Powers would, House thought, be a disaster if it led to the crippling of Germany and the consequent domination of Europe by czarist Russia.[9] On January 30 he left for Europe in the hope of extracting from the British tentative proposals which he would then present in Berlin as a possible basis for a negotiated peace.

House reached London a few days after the Germans had announced their intention of treating the waters around the British Isles as a war zone. He met many prominent men, including Asquith, Balfour, and Curzon, and had long talks with Grey and his private secretary, Sir William Tyrrell. In the course of these conversations Grey and Tyrrell told him that they thought that if the termination of the war and the signing of the peace treaty were followed by an international convention governing the conduct of future wars, Britain would agree that merchantmen of all nations should be free to ply their trade without molestation.[10] Grey did not consult the Cabinet, the War Council, or the Admiralty before expressing this opinion,[11] and he failed to make it clear that no British government was in the least likely to renounce the weapon of blockade except in the context of a general agreement to disarm. Such an agreement, he might have added, was not likely to be reached unless Germany was first thoroughly defeated and made harmless.

In March House traveled to Berlin by way of France and Switzerland. On March 27 he told the German Chancellor that Germany and the United States had a common interest in persuading the British to give free passage to all goods which were not strictly implements of war.[12] He proposed that the United States government should bring pressure to bear upon them to make this concession "at the final settlement." [13] The Chancellor could then tell the German people that Belgium could be safely restored to its rightful owners, "since England was being brought to terms." [14]

The Germans responded to these hints by launching a campaign of propaganda in favor of what House (adapting a term familiar to European jurists) called the freedom of the seas. If England granted the freedom of the seas, then Belgium, they said, would be given up; if she refused to do so, then Germany would "establish a permanent fortified base on the English Channel." [15] These pronouncements, which seemed to stamp the freedom of the seas with the label "Made in Germany," did not help House convince the British that they would gain by making concessions to the Central Powers. By the last week in April not even Grey believed that the freedom of the seas was "a fair proposition" if it meant freedom for Germany to wage war in the knowledge that henceforth her trade would be exempt from seizure. Only if she joined after the war "some League of Nations where she would give and accept the same security that other nations gave and accepted" might it be possible, he wrote on April 24, to come to some such arrangement as House had in mind.[16]

Less than a fortnight later a German submarine sank the British liner *Lusitania* off the coast of Ireland. More than 1,000 noncombatant passengers, including women and children, were drowned. Among them were more than 100 citizens of the United States. Since the nation was neither equipped for war nor ready to forfeit its neutrality, the President contented himself with a protest which inaugurated a lengthy correspondence with the German government. Only after another British liner, the *Arabic,* had been sunk in circumstances which made it self-evident that she was not carrying contraband of war did the Germans announce that orders had been given to U-boat commanders not to sink further passenger vessels without warning and without provision for the safety of noncombatants.[17] This announcement was warmly welcomed in Washington, though the effect was somewhat marred by the sinking of yet another liner, the *Hesperian,* only three days after it was made. Moreover, the Germans refused to admit that their attack on the *Lusitania* was illegal, and they did not promise not to resume unrestricted submarine warfare when it suited them to do so.

House was not easily discouraged. Eleven days after the sinking of the *Lusitania* he proposed that the Germans should abstain from submarine attacks on merchant shipping in return for an undertaking by the British to allow foodstuffs to go without question to neutral ports. They were also to renounce poisonous or asphyxiating gases such as they had already used against the British in April. The German Foreign Minister's reply, given orally to the United States ambassador in Berlin, was to the effect that a similar proposal had been made and declined in February, and that Germany was not short of food.[18] House considered, as did Grey, that this answer effectively disposed of the argument that Germany's submarine offensive was justified by hardships inflicted on the civilian population by the Allied blockade.[19]

The failure of House's attempt at mediation put President Wilson in a difficult and even dangerous position. The lack of enthusiasm shown by the belligerents for a negotiated peace implied that both sides believed that an outright victory was within their powers. By the summer of 1915 enough had been seen of German methods to convince unprejudiced observers that an outright victory for the Central Powers would be a disaster for the United States and for the world. Even so, the President was still not reconciled to the prospect of an outright victory for their opponents. Had he headed a strong, united country, his best course might have been to join the Entente Powers without delay and thus earn the right to insist that Germany should not be crippled when the war was won. But he did not. The United States Army was small and weak, its leaders had little or no experience of modern war, and opinion in the States was divided. While some Americans, especially on the eastern seaboard, favored intervention on behalf of the Allies and others insisted that the Allied blockade should be challenged even at the risk of a rupture with Britain, the majority of the President's supporters in the South and West were either resolutely neutral or indifferent. To prepare the nation for war, both morally and physically, would take at least two years, and a Presidential election was due in little more than one.

The outlook did not improve when documents intercepted by the British revealed a plot by agents of the Central Powers in the United States to damage factories producing war material for the Allies. The President insisted on the recall of envoys implicated in the affair but refused to sever diplomatic relations with Germany and Austro-Hungary as long as there was anything to be gained from two-way communication with Berlin and Vienna. The incident strengthened the distrust of Germany already felt by the well-informed, but it did not lessen pressure on the President and the State Department to take a firm line with the Allies in regard to their blockade. One result of the *Lusitania* crisis was, however, that William Jennings Bryan, the great apostle of neutrality, resigned his post as a protest against the bias in favor of the Allies which he thought was shown by some members of Wilson's Cabinet. He was succeeded as Secretary of State by Robert Lansing, hitherto counselor in the State Department. Lansing, a faithful, though sometimes reluctant, servant of the President, was careful not to allow his correspondence with the British government to be colored by the strong sympathy with the Allies which he claimed afterward to have felt throughout the war.

In the late summer of 1915 the President made up his mind that the time had come to give serious consideration to the strengthening of the armed forces, especially in view of demands from naval experts for the creation of a navy as strong as any in the world. On the other hand he was not prepared to enter the war, unless forced to do so, without making a further attempt at mediation. House proposed, and the President agreed with reservations, that he should try to bring the belligerents to the conference table by threatening hostilities should one side or the other either refuse to negotiate or stand out for unreasonable terms.[20]

With this aim in view, House completed early in 1916 another round of visits to London, Paris, and Berlin. He found that while the

Germans were in no mood to offer terms which anyone outside Germany or Austro-Hungary would think reasonable, he was able to reach a substantial measure of agreement with the British on the kind of settlement that seemed likely to promote a stable peace.[21] The terms of such a settlement would have to include, in his view and Grey's, the restoration of Belgium and Serbia, the return to France of her lost territories in Alsace and Lorraine, and the creation of a League of Nations for the purpose of settling future disputes without recourse to war. Constantinople, it was agreed, would have to go to Russia.

With the President's express sanction, given by cable on March 7, House agreed with the British before leaving London that the United States government should propose, when the Allies judged that the moment was opportune, a conference to "put an end to the war." Should the Allies accept but the Central Powers reject the proposal, or should the conference be held but the Central Powers prove unreasonable, then the United States would "probably" enter the war against Germany.[22]

Unfortunately for the President's hopes, the opportune moment never came. The Allies, it seemed, thought so little of his offer of mediation that they were willing to forgo a chance of getting the United States into the war on their side rather than allow him to make the attempt.[23] Already irritated almost past bearing by the Allied blockade[24] and always inclined to impute sinister motives to European statesmen, Wilson suspected that the reason was that the Allies believed that if left to themselves, they could press the war to a successful conclusion and inflict harsher terms on their enemies than he would countenance. The result was that from 1916 on, he became increasingly distrustful not only of the Russians and the French, but also of the British.

Here he was less than fair to the Allies. If they believed that attempts at mediation would be a waste of time, the reason was not that they doubted the value of American support or cherished unreasonable hopes. It was that they were sure that they had no chance of extracting from the Central Powers an offer of peace terms which either they or the President would think acceptable. There they were undoubtedly right. It is certain, for example, that Germany would not have agreed in 1916 to withdraw her troops from Belgium except on terms which would have reduced the Belgians to economic servitude.[25]

Soon after his return from Berlin in February, House predicted that the Germans would open an offensive on the Western Front in the near future and that possibly Verdun might be their objective.[26] French intelligence officers had indeed already reported signs of an impending attack in that sector. Joffre, intent on preparations for his own offensive, was nonetheless reluctant to move large reinforcements to a part of his line which was generally regarded as exceptionally strong.

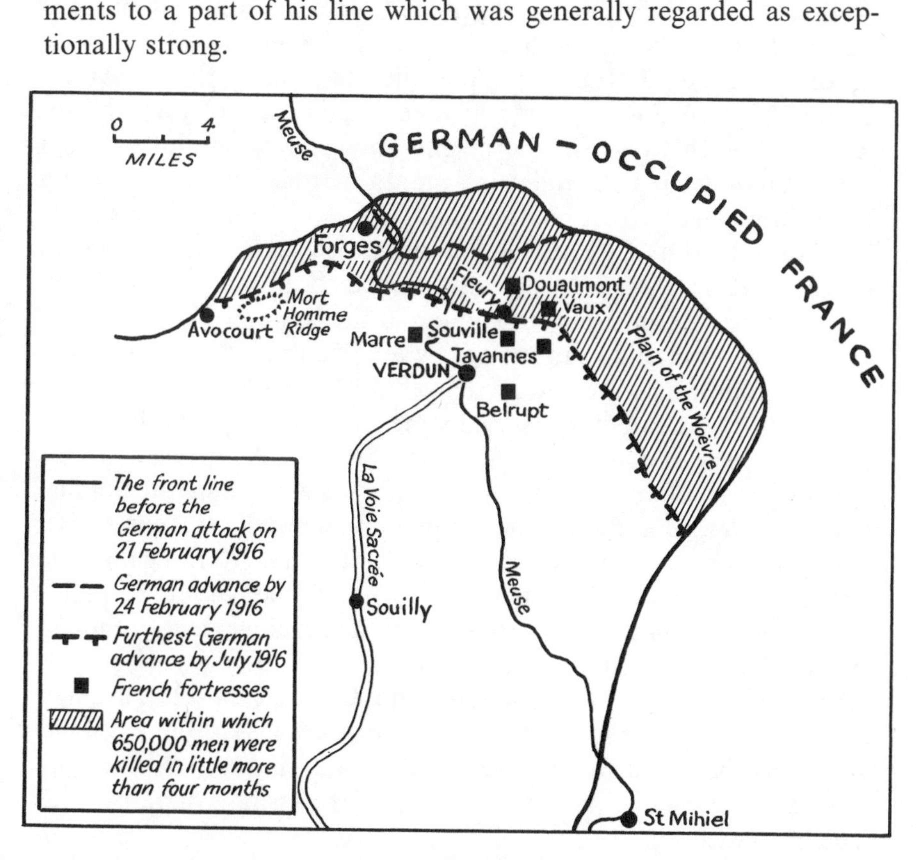

VERDUN

On February 21 the German Fifth Army launched a violent offensive at Verdun for the twofold purpose of shattering the Allied line and inflicting such losses on the defenders that France would be "bled white." About 1,400 guns, massed on an eight-mile front, supported the initial assault. Heavy fighting, in which the French suffered even more crippling losses than the Germans, continued for many months, but no breakthrough was achieved.

As a result of the German offensive, the British were compelled not only to extend their line so as to free French troops for a defensive role, but also to renounce the strategy of limited attacks and economy of manpower which ministers had hoped to impose on Robertson and Haig. Early in April the French asked that in order to relieve the pressure at Verdun, Haig should be instructed to concert an offensive with Joffre. Thereupon the government gave Haig authority to proceed with plans which envisaged a joint effort by British and French troops in the neighborhood of the Somme. When Joffre announced in the following month that he no longer feared a breakthrough at Verdun, matters had gone too far for the decision to be reversed. Thus the British found themselves committed to an offensive undertaken for a purpose which had ceased to be valid by the time their troops went into action at the beginning of July.

The general intention in the spring and summer of 1916 was that simultaneous attacks should be delivered by the Russians in Galicia and north of the Pripet Marshes, by the Italians in the Trentino, and by the British and the French on the Somme. As a result of the preoccupation of the French with the fighting at Verdun, the Somme offensive became in the outcome a predominantly British enterprise.

Preparations for the offensive were conducted in April against the background of a rebellion in Dublin. This did not improve Anglo-American relations, since the Irish nationalist movement, although exploited since the outbreak of war by the Germans, was known to have drawn much of its revenue from the United States. Englishmen convinced that all or most of the genuine grievances of the Irish had long since been redressed were not favorably impressed when the United States Senate passed a resolution expressing sympathy with rebel prisoners.[28]

Meanwhile, the long-standing dispute between the State Department and the German government about the sinking of the *Lusitania* was still unsettled. The Germans were willing to pay compensation, but they did not agree that unrestricted submarine warfare was illegal. Their case was that the existing rules of maritime warfare assumed that the right of search would be exercised by warships capable of overpowering a merchant vessel which disregarded a warning and that this did not apply to submarines. A submarine, if it did not get its blow in first, could easily be sunk by an armed merchantman or might even be rammed by an unarmed one.

Robert Lansing, the new Secretary of State, was slow to admit that the German case amounted to a confession that submarines were unfit for use as commerce raiders. Feeling that the submarine had come to stay, he suggested that merchant ships might be forbidden to carry arms, so that U-boat commanders should not be tempted to sink them without warning.

The Germans responded to this artless proposal by announcing on February 10 that with effect from March 1 they intended to treat all armed merchant vessels as warships.[29] The President, taking a firmer line than some of his supporters thought desirable, thereupon insisted that Lansing's proposal, which he described as merely tentative, should be dropped. He also stoutly opposed a measure which would have prohibited citizens of the United States from traveling in ships which the Germans might attack. Masters of American merchantmen were, however, required thereafter to testify that any armament they carried was purely defensive.[30]

On March 24 the Germans brought matters to a head by torpedoing the unarmed Channel steamer *Sussex* at a moment when American citizens were among those aboard her. Most of the passengers were rescued, but some eighty were killed or injured. Lansing, repenting of his former leniency, thought that a break with Germany was now inevitable.[31] The situation remained critical until, in May, the Germans at last promised to sink no more merchant vessels without warning or provision for the safety of passengers and crews unless they offered resistance or tried to escape.[32] This guarded pledge did not prevent Germany from resuming unrestricted submarine warfare early in 1917, but it did enable the President to postpone the severance of diplomatic relations for eight months.

In the meantime, little had been heard of the German High Seas Fleet since early in 1915, when an encounter between British and German battle cruisers near the Dogger Bank went in favor of the British. The first sign of a new departure came on April 25, 1916, when the Germans resumed their naval raids on English seaside places by sending a cruiser force to bombard Yarmouth and Lowestoft. Just over a month later the German Commander in Chief, Admiral Reinhard Scheer, took his fleet to sea with the intention of seeking battle.

Since the British were numerically superior both in battleships and in battle cruisers, Scheer did not expect to win a straight fight with the whole of the Grand Fleet. Inasmuch as he failed to stay out of the way of Jellicoe's battleships, the Battle of Jutland went no more according to plan from the German than from the British point of view. Scheer's intention when he put to sea on May 30 was to lure the British battle cruisers into an encounter with his own and then to fall on them with his battle fleet. He could not hope to win a decisive victory by avoiding contact with the enemy's main fleet. By concentrating his strength against the battle cruisers, he might nonetheless do something to reduce the all-round superiority which enabled the British to dominate the North Sea and exert a stranglehold on German trade.

As things turned out, intercepted signals told Jellicoe at an early stage that German battleships, as well as battle cruisers, were at sea. Ordering a strong battle cruiser force, under Vice Admiral Sir David Beatty, across the North Sea from the east coast of Scotland, he followed late on May 30 with the main body of the Grand Fleet from Scapa Flow. His intention was to join the battle cruisers in a general action after Beatty had made contact with the enemy and located his main fleet.

The battle began during the afternoon of May 31 with a hard-fought engagement between Beatty's battle cruiser force (which included a small proportion of battleships) and the German battle cruisers under Vice Admiral Franz von Hipper. This lasted about two hours. It was followed after a brief lull by a general engagement, lasting about three hours and generally called the battle fleet action, although battle cruisers, as well as battleships, took part in it. A gathering mist helped Scheer to disengage as dusk approached, but part of his fleet became embroiled after nightfall with elements of the Grand Fleet which had moved between him and his base. This final encounter led to a confused action in which at least two ships were sunk by collision and others by gunfire.

During the first phase the British found to their dismay that the magazines of their battle cruisers were not proof against the effects of hits on the turrets immediately above them. Furthermore, Jellicoe was unable to extract from Beatty as prompt and accurate an account of the whereabouts of the enemy's main fleet as he seems to have expected. Nonetheless he attempted, in the second phase, an elaborate maneuver designed to put his battle fleet in a position of overwhelming tactical advantage. Good shooting by the Germans, the toughness of the German capital ships, and an early dusk all helped Scheer score a tactical success by knocking out three battle cruisers, three heavy cruisers, and eight destroyers for the loss of one battleship, one battle cruiser, four light cruisers, and five destroyers.

The strategic consequences of the battle, on the other hand, were such as might have been expected to follow a resounding victory for the British. The loss of eleven ships was a far more serious matter for the Germans than the loss of fourteen ships for their opponents. Moreover, the German High Command could not fail to know that another two hours of good visibility might have brought disaster to Scheer's battle fleet. The High Seas Fleet never again sought battle with the Grand Fleet as long as the war lasted, and there were no more cruiser raids on east coast towns.

However, at the time these benefits were not apparent to the British. An official communiqué, published by the Admiralty before the fate of all of Scheer's ships was known, stressed Beatty's losses and gave the impression that the enemy had been allowed to escape after only a brief exchange of shots with the main fleet. The public was bitterly disappointed by Jellicoe's failure to sink a large number of German battleships; the confidence of British naval officers in their ships was shaken by the knowledge that the battle cruisers had proved vulnerable. In foreign countries, too—perhaps not least in the United States—the mantle of invincibility hitherto supposed to clothe the Royal Navy was felt to have slipped a little.

In the spring of 1916 the Russians were contemplating a major offensive within the next few months, although they were known to be short of ammunition and even rifles. Having exhausted credits granted in the previous September, they were also short of money. They nonetheless continued to order vast quantities of goods and raw materials for which they would be unable to pay unless the Allies gave them further help.

The British government concluded that the time had come for a frank talk with the czar and his ministers. A mission to be headed by Lloyd George was planned, but Lloyd George was asked by Asquith after the Easter Rising in Dublin to turn his attention to the Irish problem. Kitchener left without him for Archangel and was drowned when the cruiser *Hampshire* struck a mine near the Orkney Islands on June 5.

Asquith thereupon resumed the direct responsibility for War Office business which he had relinquished on the outbreak of war. Later he saw an opportunity of placating Lloyd George, who had become so seriously dissatisfied with the government's conduct of the war that he was contemplating resignation, by offering to make him Secretary of State for War. On July 5 Lloyd George accepted the post, with obvious eagerness according to some contemporary observers, with grave misgivings according to his own account.[34]

The change had no immediate effect on British strategy. Haig's proposals for an offensive on the Somme had been accepted in April. By the time the new Secretary of State for War was installed in office the battle had begun.

Haig's plan for the offensive was to pave the way for his assault troops with a massive artillery bombardment, extending over six days. He believed that after such thorough preparation, the assault troops would need only a few hours to break through the enemy's forward positions on a relatively narrow front and reach the farthest line of German trenches northeast of Albert. Beyond that line was open country with no obstacles. As soon as it was occupied, one cavalry division would ride straight through to Bapaume and seize the German headquarters there, while four more cavalry divisions formed defensive flanks to right and left of the captured sector. Infantry reserves, advancing immediately behind the cavalry, would then pour through the gap and roll up the German line from south to north.

The preliminary bombardment began on June 25 and continued until the morning of July 1. It churned up the battlefield so thoroughly that the enemy's forward positions became almost unrecognizable, but it did not knock out his artillery or prevent the bulk of his frontline troops from finding a secure refuge in deep dugouts. When the shelling stopped and the British were seen through trench periscopes to be massing for the assault, large numbers of German infantrymen and machine gunners came out of hiding and took up improvised positions in shell craters or manned concrete machine-

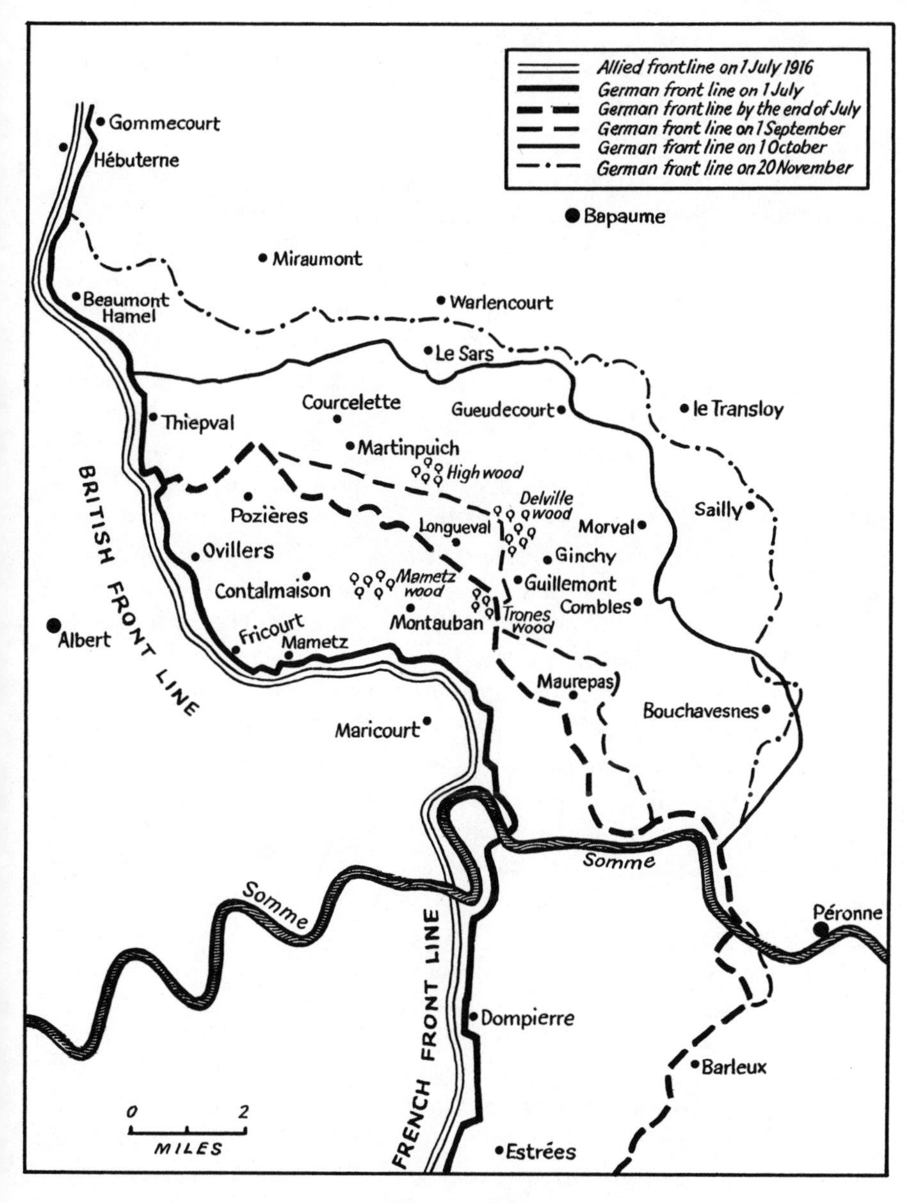

THE SOMME

gun posts which had survived the bombardment. Aided by a brisk counterbombardment, they put up such a strong defense that the assault troops suffered heavy losses and made slow progress. The line which ought, according to the timetable, to have been occupied well before noon on the first day was not reached until many weeks had passed. The cavalry were unable to go forward, and the plan collapsed.

French troops on Haig's right fared better, largely because the Germans expected the French High Command to be fully occupied with the fighting at Verdun and were taken by surprise.

A second attempt to force a breakthrough in the British sector about a fortnight later was no more successful. The assault troops, starting before dawn, made a good beginning, but the two divisional commanders who were to decide in consultation when the cavalry should be summoned were unable to agree. An appeal to higher authority delayed the decision by about twelve hours. Toward the end of the day a number of cavalry units advanced beyond the line reached by the assault troops, but the positions they captured were afterward abandoned, for lack of orders, by the infantry who relieved the cavalry at nightfall.

In the course of a further attempt in September Haig used tanks for the first time in battle, although some of his advisers had urged him not to do so until much larger numbers were available. About fifty tanks were expected to be ready, but only thirty-two reached the starting point. Fourteen of these succumbed to mechanical shortcomings or were ditched, and only half the remainder kept up with the infantry. They terrified the enemy, but were too few to turn the scale. Specialists who complained that the secret of the new weapon had been given away in circumstances which promised no return were made still more indignant by Haig's insistence on using tanks in small numbers throughout the rest of the campaigning season.

Despite such setbacks, Haig continued to hammer at the German lines until the middle of November. In the first three weeks alone he lost more men than the Mediterranean Expeditionary Force had lost in the whole of its eight months at Gallipoli.[35] When rain and mud at last compelled him to call a halt, about 125 square miles of war-scarred territory had changed hands at the cost of well over 1,000,000 British, French, and German casualties.

Whether the battle was a bigger disaster for Britain or for Germany was afterward hotly debated in the light of statistical comparisons. The fact remained that huge losses did not convince any of the leading belligerents that the time had come to give up the struggle.

General Paul von Beneckendorff und Hindenburg, who succeeded Falkenhayn as Chief of the German General Staff in August, saw that a breakthrough on the Western Front would be extremely difficult, but did not despair of ultimate success. When a French deputy suggested in September that France had suffered enough and might do well to seek a negotiated peace, the French Prime Minister, Aristide Briand, replied that such an outcome would be an outrage to the memory of the dead.[36] Lloyd George, once notorious for his pacifism, told an American press correspondent in the same month that Britain was determined to fight to a finish and would "tolerate no outside interference." [37]

Allied offensives on other fronts were no more decisive than the offensive on the Somme. The Italians, grappling with the Austrians in the Trentino and on the Isonzo, made little progress. The Russians drove the Turks back in Transcaucasia and made a spectacular advance in Galicia; but their main offensive north of the Pripet Marshes was unsuccessful, and their casualties were extremely heavy. Rumania, encouraged by the success of the Russians against the Austrians, declared war on Austro-Hungary, but her intervention brought no profit to herself or to the Entente Powers. Hindenburg's preoccupations on the Somme did not prevent him from finding enough troops to deal effectively with the situation in the Balkans. In face of a joint effort by German, Austro-Hungarian, and Bulgarian forces, neither a halfhearted Anglo-French advance from Salonika nor anything the Russians were prepared to do could prevent Rumania from going the way of Serbia. The Central Powers thus gained access to new sources of much-needed oil and grain.

On the other side of the account, the Portuguese agreed in August to send an expeditionary force to the Western Front, while the Greeks, although still torn between allegiance to the pro-German King Constantine and faith in the pro-British Venizelos, became on the whole more responsive to British and French influence as a result of the changed situation in the Balkans. In the Near East, Sherif Husein of Mecca undertook to lead a revolt against the Turks in return for British subsidies and the promised creation of an independent Arab state or group of states. To support his guerrilla operations near the Red Sea coast, the British forces defending Egypt would advance their front from the Suez Canal to the head of the Gulf of Aqaba and prepare for a further advance at some future time.

However, any satisfaction which the Allies could derive from these developments was more than offset by the fear of a disastrous setback in Russia. The Russians, even after calling up 13,000,000 men by the end of 1916, still had large reserves of manpower, but their war effort was very badly organized. Their armies not only were short of weapons and of such necessities as wire cutters and entrenching tools, but were so poorly provided with transport and services that units could seldom count on the prompt arrival of rations, ammunition, and medical supplies, even when these were available at base. These evils arose from a variety of causes. A minor one was the failure of some British firms to meet delivery dates early in the war. More potent sources of trouble were the closing of Black Sea ports to Russian shipping and the administrative incompetence which hampered attempts to overcome this handicap. Millions of rubles had been spent before and since the outbreak of war on up-to-date arms factories, but most of these were hopelessly mismanaged by functionaries who were often not only inefficient, but corrupt. The state of the railways was chaotic. A big backlog of manufactured goods and raw materials shipped by British, French, and American suppliers was building up at Vladivostok and Archangel; completion of the long-planned Kola railway, which served Murmansk, had been delayed by an unedifying conflict between vested interests. A further consequence of the disorganization of the railways was that although there was no lack of food in Russia, its distribution became increasingly difficult as the third winter of the war approached. Shortages and rising prices affected chiefly the poorer inhabitants of large towns, but others, too, were discontented. The well-informed resented the czar's refusal to consider even the most necessary reforms and to rid himself of irresponsible advisers. Before long, aristocrats and members of the intelligentsia were at one in hoping that somehow or other he might be persuaded to abdicate before worse befell.

Lloyd George had long been an advocate of close cooperation with Russia and vigorous action in the Balkans. He believed that if Grey and Kitchener had shared his views, no insuperable difficulty would have been found in shipping large quantities of arms and ammunition to Russia early in the war. He thought, too, that prompt steps could and ought to have been taken to establish an Allied force at Salonika and improve communications between Salonika and the Balkan hinterland. Adroit diplomacy and resolute action could, in his opinion, have swept aside the difficulties which Grey found so baffling. Had Grey and Kitchener grasped the nettle, Greek hesitations could have been overcome, Serbia would not have been overrun, and Bulgaria, as well as Rumania, would have joined the Entente Powers or taken refuge in benevolent neutrality.

On becoming Secretary of State for War, Lloyd George found that Robertson did not share these views. Furthermore, his attitude was not merely uncooperative but obstructive. When Lloyd George proposed that an Allied military conference should be held in Russia and that Robertson should be the British representative, Robertson not only refused to go but told Hankey that he would fight Lloyd George "without kid gloves on." [38]

This quarrel threatened to come into the open at a time of intense anxiety for the government. Haig's losses on the Somme were becoming a nightmare; Britain's dollar resources were threatened with exhaustion; poor harvests in North America forced the British to lock up a higher proportion of their shipping in the long haul from Australia at a moment when dwindling tonnage was causing a great deal of worry. In 1916 merchant shipping losses exceeded new production by nearly 1,000,000 tons.[39] Moreover, the Germans were known to be introducing improved oceangoing submarines with an extended range. Admiral Sir Henry Jackson, the First Sea Lord, could suggest no remedy, and the Navy's image was not improved by Jellicoe's insistence after Jutland that in view of the danger from submarines and mines, the Grand Fleet should not venture south of the Dogger Bank unless directly challenged.

Asquith, unwilling to break with Balfour but convinced that changes must be made, did his best to meet the difficulty by dismissing Jackson, bringing Jellicoe to London as First Sea Lord, and replacing Jellicoe as Commander in Chief of the Grand Fleet by the less cautious Beatty. He did not, however, venture on a similar cure for the friction between Lloyd George and Robertson. No suitable replacement for Robertson was in view, and in any case his dismissal would almost certainly have precipitated a clash with critics whom Asquith did not wish to challenge. In circles hostile to the government, there was already strong support for the dangerous argument that in wartime statesmen should leave strategy to the service chiefs and confine themselves to questions of manpower, organization, and supply.

The government's difficulties were increased by the fact that Lloyd George, although totally opposed to this view of the statesman's role in war, was himself keenly critical of the way in which the war was being handled. He told Hankey in November that he could not remain in office if his colleagues continued to support Robertson's policy of concentration on the Western Front but, in order not to embarrass them, would accept some post which carried no direct responsibility for strategy.[40]

In preparation for a summit conference to be held in Paris in the middle of the month, Lloyd George wrote a long memorandum which amounted to a scathing denunciation of British and French strategy since the Battle of the Marne.[41] Asquith agreed to place an expurgated version before the conference, but instead of introducing it at a plenary session, he read it to Briand at an informal meeting before the conference began.[42] The conference achieved little, since the service chiefs were allowed to meet independently of the heads of government and record their own decisions. They paid lip service to the principle of a vigorous effort in the Balkans but failed to convince Lloyd George of their sincerity.[43]

On his return to London, Lloyd George sounded first the Unionist members of the Cabinet and afterward Asquith about a possible reconstruction of the government. With the exception of the Ulster leader Sir Edward Carson, none of the Unionist ministers wished to put Asquith out of office, but all agreed that the existing War Committee ought to be replaced by a smaller and better organized body, capable of dealing with the war from day to day and of ensuring that its decisions were not sidetracked by departments. Lloyd George proposed that the new committee should consist of the First Lord of the Admiralty, the Secretary of State for War, and a minister without portfolio and that one of the three should act as chairman. Asquith thought that the Prime Minister should be chairman, and he also differed from Lloyd George in wishing to retain Balfour as First Lord. However, on Sunday, December 3, he accepted Lloyd George's proposals with modifications designed to safeguard his own position.[44] It was agreed that the agenda and resolutions of the committee should be submitted to the Prime Minister for approval or veto and that he would be entitled to attend meetings if he chose to do so. The chairman would report to him daily, and he would have power to direct the committee to consider particular topics or proposals. The personnel of the committee was to be discussed at a further meeting between Asquith and Lloyd George on the following day.

On Monday, December 4, there appeared in the London *Times* a leading article purporting to reveal the substance of Lloyd George's plan and commenting on it in unfavorable terms. The article is now known to have been written by the editor, Geoffrey Dawson, on his own initiative but in the light of information communicated by Carson.[45] Asquith believed at the time that it was inspired by Lloyd George and that it pointed to a conspiracy between Lloyd George and Lord Northcliffe, proprietor of *The Times,* to bring down the government. He refused to see Lloyd George, summoned all other Liberal members of the Cabinet to a meeting, and informed Lloyd George by letter that he had the king's authority to call for the resignation of all his colleagues and to form a new government. He added that he had come to the conclusion that after all, the new War Committee could not be made "workable and effective" unless the Prime Minister were chairman.[46]

On the following day Asquith learned from Bonar Law, in circumstances which afterward aroused much controversy, that the Unionists were not prepared to support his attempt to form a new government on terms which contravened his agreement with Lloyd George.[47] The king then sent for Bonar Law. Law proposed an all-party government under Balfour, but Asquith refused to serve under Balfour on the ground that he ought not to be asked to take "a secondary position" after holding the first place for eight years.[48] He also refused to serve under Bonar Law. Thereupon the king, on Law's advice, invited Lloyd George to form a government. Lloyd George, nothing if not courageous, agreed to do his best in the knowledge that roughly half his own party were against him and that, notwithstanding his uneasy truce with the Unionist leaders, he was widely regarded among the rank and file of the Unionist Party as a dangerous demagogue.

Thus the year of Verdun, Jutland, and the Somme was beset with perils and frustrations for the British. It was also a troubled year for

President Wilson. The failure of his attempts at mediation emphasized the weakness of his position as ruler of a nation which he had hoped to make neutral in thought, word, and deed but had succeeded only in making nonbelligerent. British sea power did not directly threaten any American interest. On the contrary, it provided the sanction for an eastward flow of commodities and manufactured goods which brought large profits to American producers and raised the standards of living of almost every section of the community. The fact remained that command of the sea enabled the British to shape the pattern of American trade with Europe by insisting that goods which they chose to regard as contraband of war should be shipped only to recipients of whom they approved. At the same time, vexations arising not only from the depredations of German submarines but also from the Allied blockade made relations with both the Entente and the Central Powers far from satisfactory. In the meantime, Japan, long suspect in the United States by reason of her expansionist aims, had not improved her image by making sweeping demands on the weak Chinese Republic soon after the outbreak of the European war. The service chiefs and the State Department, observing the ease with which she had gained possession of the German dependencies in the Pacific north of the equator, could not contemplate without dismay the prospect of an eventual confrontation in the Far East.

The obvious conclusion was that for a nation rich in raw materials and industrial potential, averse to foreign alliances, yet reluctant to curtail her foreign trade and deeply conscious of her imperial commitments, true neutrality would always be next to impossible until she possessed the physical means of ensuring safe passage for her cargoes to markets of her own choosing.

The President applied the lesson. In September he received from Congress authority to restrict exports and loans should he find it necessary to take reprisals for the seizure of American mails. In the same month, Congress accepted a long-term program of naval expansion which promised, if it were ever completed, to put the United States in the forefront of the world's naval powers. House, reminding his chief that Germany had challenged British naval supremacy with dire consequences for all peace-loving nations, predicted that Britain would never allow the United States to draw level with her if she could prevent it. The President was unabashed. "Let us build a navy bigger than hers," he said, "and do what we please." [49]

Wilson was afterward accused of insincerity because at the very moment when he was advocating a policy of firmness and had sanctioned large additions to the Navy, he stood for reelection as the man who kept the United States out of the war. The reproach was unjust. When he went to the polls, Woodrow Wilson still hoped for peace.[50] He even believed that he might still be able to force the belligerents to come to terms by threatening them with his displeasure if they failed to do so.[51] There was logic in the argument that adoption of the naval program and an unbending attitude toward the belligerents on both sides would tend to make these aims not harder but easier to attain.

Immediately after his reelection, the President favored an immediate appeal to the belligerents to stop the war "in deference to the necessities and welfare of mankind." [52] House, on the other hand, was against any further attempt at mediation unless the Allies asked for one in accordance with the arrangement made earlier in the year. The United States still had only a small army without heavy artillery or air support, and no part of the new naval program was due for completion within the current year or for many months after it. A premature plea for peace would be bound, House thought, to give the impression that the President was eager to buy the Germans off with the tacit promise of a favorable settlement before they forced his hand by stepping up their submarine campaign.[53]

The President, although not convinced by this argument, was considerably shaken by it.[54] He made substantial alterations to the "peace note" he had drafted and was still awaiting a favorable moment for its dispatch when the Germans forestalled him by handing a "peace note" of their own to the United States chargé d'affaires in Berlin. In this they boasted of their conquests, proclaimed their "indestructible strength," and offered to make peace on terms not stated.[55]

Nearly a week of diplomatic activity behind the scenes divided the arrival of the German note on December 12 from its formal submission to the British government on December 18. During this period the British not only consulted the French, the Russians, the Italians, the Belgians, and the Japanese, but also took soundings in Holland,

Sweden, Switzerland, and the United States and at the Vatican. They found that while most Allied statesmen thought that an offer without terms could not be taken seriously, neutral advisers were unanimously of the opinion that the German note ought not to be rejected without inquiry.[56] No authoritative explanation of Germany's intentions was, however, forthcoming from any neutral source. House, to whom the British applied for a confidential account of what the German government had in mind, could only suggest that if the British would wait another five or six days, he might seek enlightenment from the German ambassador in Washington, who would doubtless need to consult his superiors in Berlin before replying.[57]

The British could not wait so long before making an interim statement about the government's attitude to peace negotiations. House appears to have believed that this was because the Foreign Office was in a great hurry to reject the German offer for fear that its details, once disclosed, might prove so superficially attractive as to make subsequent rejection difficult.[58] The true explanation would seem to have been merely that Lloyd George, as a Prime Minister newly installed in office, could not risk antagonizing the House of Commons by withholding information to which members might feel they were entitled. Not for the first or the last time, a serious misunderstanding between Britain and the United States arose largely from the difficulty which Americans and Englishmen always had in understanding that the limitations imposed on the governments of their respective countries by the relationship between executive and legislature were not the same.

On December 19, Lloyd George duly told the House that the government would not enter into negotiations with the Central Powers without knowing what terms and guarantees they had to offer. This decision was warmly endorsed by the large section of the Liberal Party which continued to follow Asquith's lead and was not challenged by the pacifist section of the Labour Party under Ramsay MacDonald and Philip Snowden.

On the following day President Wilson issued his own "peace note." He disclaimed any intention of dictating terms or even of acting as mediator but suggested that the belligerents should say what they were fighting for. He added, very unwisely in the opinion of some of his friends, that the objects which the statesmen on both sides claimed to have in view seemed very much the same.[59]

At a moment when they were preoccupied with plans for the coming year and when the French had followed the example of the British by reorganizing their government, the Allies had therefore to concoct replies to both the German and the American notes.

Their reply to the German note was drafted at an Anglo-French conference in London immediately after Christmas. It informed the Central Powers that the Allied governments could not regard as a serious offer of peace "a mere suggestion, without statement of terms, that negotiations should be opened." [60] This formula, ultimately accepted by all nine of the countries at war with Germany as an adequate expression of their views, was largely the work of Paul Cambon, the French ambassador in London, and Philippe Berthelot of the French Foreign Ministry.[61]

The Allied reply to the American note was considered at the same conference. The British, who had already rejected as "too vague and too evasive" a draft submitted by the French, were of the opinion that the reply should include a candid and explicit statement of war aims.[62] Arrangements were made at the conference for a fresh draft to be considered by all the Allied governments and for their diplomatic representatives in Paris to take part in the preparation of the final text. In the carefully considered note which emerged on January 10, the Allies defined their aims substantially as follows:

1. Restoration, with compensation, of Belgium, Serbia, and Montenegro.
2. Withdrawal of the armies of the Central Powers from the invaded territories of France, Russia, and Rumania, with "fitting reparation."
3. Restitution of provinces or territories (*e.g.*, Alsace) torn from the Allies before the war by force or against the wishes of the inhabitants.
4. Creation of an autonomous Poland in accordance with a promise already given by the czar.
5. Liberation of Italians, Slavs, Rumanians, Czechs, and Slovaks from "foreign domination." (This referred primarily to territorial claims to be made on Austro-Hungary, but the clause was so worded as to leave room for negotiation in regard to the status of minorities which might remain within the frontiers of a reformed Austro-Hungarian Empire or federation.)
6. Expulsion of the Ottoman Empire from Europe and liberation

of its non-Turkish subjects. (In other words, Russia to have Constantinople and the Straits, and an Arab state or group of states under Allied tutelage to be established in the Middle East.)

7. Abolition of the German military machine.

8. Reorganization of Europe, under international guarantee, on lines which would reflect not only the principle of nationality, but also economic and strategic needs.

To this declaration of intent, the Allies added a commentary to the effect that they had no thought of exterminating or subjugating the German people but were determined to rescue Europe from the menace of Prussian militarism and were ready to go on fighting until their objects were attained.

On the whole, the Allied note made a favorable impression in those parts of the United States where the Allies, or at any rate the British and the French, were already in good repute. The President gave the Allies a good mark for their candor, but was nonetheless dismayed by the extinction of his last remaining flicker of hope that somehow or other they might be induced to sign a blank check in favor of the Central Powers and allow the United States to insert the words and figures. His characteristic response was to cable to London, Paris, Berlin, and St. Petersburg the text of an address which he proposed to deliver to the Senate. In this he expressed the hope that the war would be followed by an era of universal democracy, in which each nation would be free to fulfill its destiny without outside interference. He added that these benefits were unlikely, in his opinion, to be forthcoming unless hostilities ended without a decisive victory for either side.[63] The Allies gave the President credit for his good intentions, but they had some difficulty in understanding how Germany's neighbors were to be free to fulfill their destinies without interference if she were not decisively defeated.

The President delivered his address on January 22, after discussing it with the Secretary of State and the chairman of the Senate Foreign Relations Committee.[64] Nine days later the German ambassador in Washington informed the United States government that with effect from the following day, Germany proposed to sink all ships trading with Allied countries and that consequently neutral vessels would enter at their peril designated zones surrounding the British Isles and bordering on France and Italy. On certain conditions the United

States would, however, be allowed to send one ship a week to Falmouth. In a letter to House, the ambassador added that Germany was not prepared to publish any peace terms. He went on to make it clear that she had no intention of withdrawing her armies from France and Belgium unless the Allies withdrew from the small part of Alsace occupied by French troops and granted her far-reaching financial, economic, and strategic benefits.[65] In other words, her price for ending the war was that her enemies should reward her for violating their frontiers, expropriating their territories, and exposing millions of their citizens to the hardships of a ruthless military occupation.

These disclosures upset the President so much that he felt "as if the world had suddenly reversed itself . . . and that he could not get his balance." [66] He agreed with his advisers that the time had come to sever diplomatic relations with Germany but was not convinced that war must follow. "I refuse," he said, "to believe that it is the intention of the German authorities to do in fact what they have warned us they will feel at liberty to do." [67]

American shipowners were not so sanguine. Although assured that their rights were unaffected by the German declaration and that they were welcome to take such defensive measures as might seem good to them, some refused to send their ships to sea unless the government provided some form of protection. A bill empowering the President to furnish weapons for the arming of merchant ships was passed by the House of Representatives, but opposition from a small group of Senators prevented a vote from being taken in the Senate.

This experience brought out a combative streak in Wilson. The government, relying on the President's executive authority, announced after Congress had adjourned that it would provide an armed guard for every American merchantman traversing the waters from which Germany sought to banish vessels trading with the Allies.

Meanwhile, the State Department learned from the British that in January the German Foreign Ministry had cabled the German minister in Mexico City, instructing him that in the event of war between Germany and the United States, he was to arrange an alliance with Mexico on the understanding that she would be helped to reconquer New Mexico, Texas, and Arizona. A transcript of the cablegram, published in the American press and afterward admitted by the German Foreign Ministry to be authentic, did a great deal to reconcile the public to the necessity of war.

Proof that the Germans did mean to sink as many Allied and neutral ships as possible was soon forthcoming. Between February 27 and March 19 not only the liner *Laconia* but also four American cargo vessels were sunk without notice. The crew of one ship saved their lives by taking to the boats and rowing to the Scilly Islands.

The President—still so reluctant to lead his country into war that he asked despairingly, "What else can I do? Is there anything else I can do?" [68]—accepted the inevitable. On April 2 he advised Congress to declare that a state of war existed between the United States and Germany.

6

Soldiers and Statesmen: I

ON becoming Prime Minister of the United Kingdom in December, 1916, Lloyd George established what was sometimes called "a dictatorship in commission" by setting up a small War Cabinet charged with the conduct of the war. Its members consisted in the first instance of himself as chairman; the Unionist leaders Andrew Bonar Law, Lord Milner, and Lord Curzon; and the Labor leader Arthur Henderson. Law, besides taking office as Chancellor of the Exchequer, relieved his chief of day-to-day responsibility for parliamentary business by acting as leader of the House of Commons; Curzon, as Lord President of the Council, and Milner and Henderson as ministers without portfolio, had no departmental duties.

An important consequence of this reform was that the Prime Minister, although still bound by the principle of collective responsibility and still subject to the will of Parliament, was no longer debarred from initiating action on major issues until they had been discussed with a score of colleagues, many of whom were not qualified to make any useful contribution. Moreover, the services of a permanent secretariat ensured that, for the first time in history, the decisions of a British Cabinet were independently recorded and that ministers were punctually informed of any action that was expected of them.

Effective control over strategy continued, nonetheless, to elude the Cabinet even under the new dispensation. The crux of the problem was that constitutional safeguards, intended to prevent misuse of the armed forces by either Crown or Parliament, put a good deal of power into the hands of the First Sea Lord and the Chief of the Imperial General Staff. As long as these posts were held by men who regarded governmental intervention in the field of strategy as an invasion of their prerogatives, the instrument designed by Lloyd George for the supreme direction of the war was bound to fall short of its creator's aims.

In this respect British and American practice differed widely. The President of the United States, as head of government and also head of state, was ex officio Commander in Chief of the Army and the Navy. A British Prime Minister, as head of government only, enjoyed no such status. The Army and the Navy, although nominally the armed forces of the Crown, were not for practical purposes unreservedly at the disposal of the ministers on whose advice a constitutional monarch was bound to act. In the remote past the reigning sovereign had been accustomed to appoint a Lord High Admiral directly responsible to him or his successors; but that post had long been in abeyance, and its duties had devolved upon a Board of Admiralty composed partly of civilians and partly of serving officers. The post of Commander in Chief of the British Army, on the other hand, had continued until modern times to be filled by a serving officer who was often a member of the royal family; but after the South African War the post had been abolished, and an Army Council, also composed partly of civilians and partly of serving officers, had then assumed the powers hitherto shared between the Commander in Chief and the War Office. The broad effect of these arrangements was that while the First Lord of the Admiralty and the Secretary of State for War were responsible to Crown and Parliament for all the business of the Admiralty and the War Office respectively, operational orders to commanding officers at sea or in the field could not, according to the consensus in naval and military circles, be transmitted without the concurrence of the First Sea Lord or the Chief of the Imperial General Staff. Even the broad directive given by Kitchener to Sir John French soon after the outbreak of war would doubtless have been regarded by sticklers for constitutional propriety as issued not on his authority as Secretary of State for War, but on that of the Army Council, of which he was the head.

Lloyd George chose as Secretary of State for War Lord Derby, a popular landowner who had served as a junior minister in the preceding government. Derby, born to great wealth, respected Robertson as a man who had raised himself from the ranks to the top of his profession. He believed that the War Cabinet had the right to choose the men best fitted to carry out its military policy. At the same time he made it clear that he would almost certainly resign if Robertson were superseded merely because he gave honest advice unpalatable to the government.[1]

As successor to Arthur Balfour at the Admiralty Lloyd George appointed the Ulster leader Sir Edward Carson, a stormy petrel whom he could not afford to offend by excluding him from office. Balfour, whose experience made him invaluable in council although he had not done well as First Lord, agreed to serve as Foreign Secretary on the understanding that since foreign affairs were closely linked with strategy, he would be free to attend meetings of the War Cabinet at his discretion, not merely by invitation. Carson accepted the post but soon declared war on the government he had joined by publicly announcing that he was determined to protect Jellicoe and the Naval War Staff from assaults by "amateur strategists." [2]

Since the Admiralty had failed conspicuously in recent months to steer clear of dangers which threatened the ship of state with irremediable disaster, this challenge was ill timed. British merchant ship losses from enemy action in the last four months of 1916 exceeded the total for the whole of the preceding eight months; in the first four months of 1917 they were higher still.[3] In conversation with Admiral William S. Sims of the United States Navy, Jellicoe confessed in April that continued losses at the current rate would "make it impossible for us to go on with the war." [4] Nevertheless, he could see no solution to the problem. When asked why the time-honored method of convoy, invariably used when troop transports or valuable warships had to be protected, could not be applied to groups of merchant vessels, he and the director of Anti-Submarine Warfare, Admiral Sir Charles Duff, replied that cargo ships sailing together would present a huge target to the enemy and would be unable to keep station or take evasive action.[5] They added that in any case it would be impossible to find enough warships for escort duties without denuding the Grand Fleet of its cruisers and destroyers.[6]

This conclusion was based on returns which showed that each week about 2,500 vessels entered United Kingdom ports.[7] As the returns included every vessel, no matter how small, which made passage from one port to another, in point of fact they gave no indication of the number of escorts that would be needed to safeguard ocean trade. It was only when a relatively junior officer was ordered, at the request of the French authorities, to look into the possibility of escorting ships which carried coal to France that the true situation came to light. Inquiries which ought to have been made in the first instance then revealed that the number of oceangoing vessels which arrived each week was only about 140 at the most.[8] Moreover, experiments with groups of ships escorted to Brest, Cherbourg, and Le Havre by armed trawlers yielded results which contradicted the Admiralty's assumptions at almost every point. In March, April, and May more than 4,000 voyages through waters where submarines were known to be active were completed for the loss of only nine ships.[9] Experimental convoys between Norway and the Humber were less successful, but even so the number of ships lost between April and December was not much more than 1 percent of the number of voyages completed.[10]

In the middle of April stocks of wheat in the United Kingdom fell to the equivalent of about nine weeks' consumption, and it was reckoned that one out of every four ships which left home waters would never be seen again.[11] On April 22 Jellicoe submitted to the War Cabinet a long memorandum on "The Submarine Menace and Food Supply." Admitting that the situation called for immediate action, he asked that the United States Navy should be urged to send as many destroyers as possible to strengthen his patrols. He did not mention convoy, although not only amateur strategists but also such authorities as Beatty and the American Admiral Sims were known to favor its introduction.[12]

The War Cabinet considered Jellicoe's memorandum at three meetings on April 23 and 25.[13] It seemed to them so unsatisfactory that after the third meeting, Lloyd George caused the Board of Admiralty to be informed that he proposed to visit the Admiralty in the near future for the purpose of going into the whole question of antisubmarine warfare and would claim the right to question any officer, irrespective of his rank.

On the following day, Admiral Duff recommended to Jellicoe that convoy should be adopted.[14] Jellicoe agreed on April 27 that at any rate the system should be tried.[15]

A chastened Board of Admiralty greeted the Prime Minister when, accompanied by Hankey, he arrived on April 30 to exercise, for a single day, the functions of Lord High Admiral. A family luncheon party with Jellicoe and his wife and their four small daughters revealed an attractive side of Lloyd George's complex character.[16] After a talk with Jellicoe and Duff he recorded, somewhat hopefully, that "complete accord" had been established between the Admiralty and the War Cabinet.[17] He then turned to an attempt to lighten Jellicoe's task by giving him a staff with clearly defined duties. Hitherto practically the entire burden of framing naval policy, giving orders to ships and squadrons, and drafting telegrams to naval stations throughout the world had fallen on the First Sea Lord and the Chief of the Naval War Staff. In consequence, both were overworked, neither was free to devote himself for more than a few hours at a time to questions which called for prolonged study, and visits to the fleet by senior officers serving at the Admiralty were rare. Lloyd George insisted that the two offices should be amalgamated and that many duties should be delegated to officers over whom the First Sea Lord would exercise only general supervision. A Deputy Chief of Staff, Vice Admiral Sir Rosslyn Wemyss, was appointed to take care of movements of ships and squadrons; immediate responsibility for long-term planning and for providing intelligence for current and future operations was parceled out on lines suggested by experience at the War Office. A final recommendation was that more room should be found at the Admiralty for officers with "war experience." [18]

The U-boat problem was by far the most urgent and important that had faced the Admiralty since the outbreak of war or perhaps ever. Other preoccupations included the problem of maintaining efficiency and keenness in a body of highly trained professional seamen who could not hope to distinguish themselves in action as long as the British and German battle fleets continued to keep out of each other's way. Officers serving with the Grand Fleet had tended since Jutland to range themselves in two schools of thought which looked to Jellicoe and Beatty respectively for inspiration. Beatty, who wore his cap at a jaunty angle, had married an American heiress, and was reputed a hard rider to hounds, personified in the eyes of his admirers the virtues of boldness, enterprise, and resolution. Conversely,

Beatty's critics saw in the less flamboyant Jellicoe a classic example of the prudent commander whose refusal to take unwarrantable risks is apt to be mistaken for excessive caution.

Lloyd George thought that the existence of two currents of opinion in the Navy was no bad thing but that only a First Lord willing to listen to both sides could hope to take advantage of it. A man in Carson's position ought, in his estimation, to be a master of the art of keeping himself informed without giving senior officials the impression that he was bypassing them. Himself a great believer in sounding opinion at all levels, he complained that Carson seldom consulted serving officers outside a small circle of privileged advisers and that even when he could be brought to admit that suggestions from junior officers deserved serious attention, he was incapable of overcoming the "stolid resistance" of Jellicoe and other diehards.[19]

In the summer of 1917 Lloyd George was determined that the U-boat menace should be resolutely tackled. He was also determined that sympathetic consideration should be given to a proposal that the Navy should bombard the Belgian coast for the purpose of making Ostend and Zeebrugge untenable as bases for U-boats and destroyers. A night attack on the Dover Patrol in the previous October by destroyers from Zeebrugge had caused intense alarm in naval circles and had led to the temporary suspension of cross-Channel traffic.[20]

Jellicoe, arguing that the right way of dealing with Ostend and Zeebrugge was to use the Expeditionary Force to capture them, showed no enthusiasm for a naval offensive. He denied that (except in battleships) the Royal Navy and the United States Navy had the "overwhelming preponderance" over the German Navy which Lloyd George claimed. He added that in any case no port could be made untenable for more than a few days. Lloyd George, unwilling to provoke a crisis by dismissing Jellicoe, decided to circumvent him by appointing a First Lord who would "force his will on his subordinates."[21] After a struggle, Carson submitted in July to relegation to the War Cabinet. His place as First Lord was taken by Sir Eric Geddes, a railway magnate who had joined the Admiralty as controller within the past few weeks, but was better known for his work as director of Military Railways at the War Office and director general of Transportation to the Expeditionary Force.* Jellicoe, often at

* As controller, Geddes was responsible for shipbuilding not only for the Royal Navy, but also for the Mercantile Marine.

odds with Lloyd George and Geddes, lingered on as First Sea Lord until December, when he stepped aside in favor of the more genial and broad-minded Wemyss. By that time the attempt to take Ostend and Zeebrugge by an overland advance had been made and had failed disastrously.

Lloyd George came to office convinced that Robertson's preoccupation with the Western Front was strategically unsound. The German armies were firmly established in France and Flanders and would never, he thought, be dislodged by frontal assaults as long as they were backed by secure communications and a broad-based economy. In his estimation, the right way of bringing the German colossus to the ground was to start by "knocking away the props." The time for a frontal assault would come when Germany was weakened and isolated by the elimination of Austro-Hungary and Turkey. In the meantime, the Central Powers would be weakened, too, by the effects of the blockade.

Lloyd George also believed that cooperation between the Entente Powers ought to be much closer and that the Allies should think seriously of pooling their resources. A mere synchronization of offensives on the Western, Russian, and Italian fronts would never bring victory as long as the German lines in the West were too strong to be pierced and the Russian and Italian armies too poorly equipped to follow up any success they might achieve. "Stitching," said Lloyd George, "is not strategy." [22] The Russians and the Italians had plenty of men but were short of guns. The British—and to a lesser extent the French—commanded large industrial resources but suffered, for that very reason, from manpower problems, since the same men could not be fighting in the trenches and also working in the factories. It seemed to Lloyd George only common sense that if the British and the French could save guns and ammunition by abstaining from costly offensives on the Western Front, the surplus should be given or lent to the Russians and the Italians. For that reason and also because he thought that the Allied governments would set a dangerous precedent if they allowed their military advisers to dictate to them, he maintained that crucial strategic issues ought to be thrashed out at high-level conferences between statesmen.

As the price of Unionist support Lloyd George was compelled, however, to promise that there would be no immediate change in the High Command of the land forces.[23] This pledge was extracted from him not because Milner or Curzon or Bonar Law believed wholeheartedly in Robertson's policy of concentration on the Western Front, but because they and other Unionists feared that Lloyd George, by hastily dismissing Robertson and Haig, might provoke a nationwide crisis in which a powerful section of the press would be ranged against the government. In the early summer of 1917 Lloyd George went some way to settle this issue by persuading his colleagues to agree that Lord Northcliffe, the most redoubtable of the press lords, should be sent to the far side of the Atlantic to coordinate the work of the numerous missions which British government departments had set up in Washington.

Lloyd George did not always find it easy to agree with the rest of the War Cabinet about strategic questions.[24] Inasmuch as "knocking away the props" implied a bigger effort against Turkey and insofar as the collapse of the Ottoman Empire might create opportunities for the extension of British power and influence in the Levant and east of Suez, at least one aspect of his military doctrine had obvious attractions for men whose political philosophy inclined them to believe that the war would not have been fought in vain if it left the British Empire united by stronger political and economic ties than ever. On the other hand, one of the traditional tenets of the Conservative or Unionist Party was that imperial interests were best served in peacetime by a policy of friendship with Turkey and tolerance of her shortcomings. In any case it would be wrong to picture the Lloyd George-Unionist coalition as *initiating* an "Eastern" strategy in deference to the imperialist aspirations of its Unionist members. Even though the Allies had decided, after their setbacks at the Dardanelles and in Mesopotamia in 1915, to go on the defensive in the Near Eastern theater, the renewal of attempts to eliminate Turkey from the war was implicit in decisions taken long before the new government came into existence. The Arab revolt was launched six months before Asquith fell from power. It had its origin in negotiations begun in the summer of 1915 and foreshadowed by a conditional promise made to Sherif Hussein as soon as Turkey entered the war.[25] Similarly, the much-criticized inter-Allied agreements for the dismemberment of the Ottoman Empire were negotiated not by the

Lloyd George-Unionist coalition but while Grey was Foreign Secretary and were signed on various dates in the spring and summer of 1916.[26]

When the new government took office in December of that year, the situation in Mesopotamia was that Lieutenant General Sir Frederick Stanley Maude, a new commander appointed after the fall of Kut in April, had received authority to depart from a purely defensive posture as soon as he judged that he could safely do so with his existing resources.[27] Maude began a cautious advance within three days of the first meeting of the War Cabinet. On learning early in February that the Grand Duke Nicholas, commanding the Russian Army of the Caucasus, proposed to send some of his troops into Persia and thence toward Baghdad and Mosul, Robertson suggested that Maude should push on faster, even at the cost of heavier losses. On March 11 Maude's force occupied Baghdad well in advance of the Russians. British and Russian troops made contact in Turkish territory west of the Persian frontier about three weeks later.

The only other front on which British troops were in contact with the Turks was the Egyptian frontier area. The situation there in the first week of December was that Sir Archibald Murray, the former Chief of Staff in France, was authorized by the instructions given to him in the previous summer to push his left as far as El Arish, southwest of Gaza but in Egyptian territory. During the next few days he duly occupied El Arish, established control of practically the whole of the Sinai Peninsula by defeating the Turks in battles at Magdhaba and Rafah, and took up positions along the line of the frontier.

Meanwhile Lloyd George and his colleagues considered the case for a further advance. They found that while Murray was willing to move against the Turks in Palestine with two additional divisions, the General Staff in London considered that he would need three additional divisions and that his operations might cut across arrangements for the summer offensive in France.[28] Accordingly, Robertson recommended that no major offensive should be attempted before the autumn of 1917. In the light of a rather flattering estimate of Turkish strength, the War Cabinet accepted this recommendation "in principle." [29]

Murray had, however, been told earlier that the government expected him to do as much as he could with his existing resources while the weather was still unsuitable for operations on the Western

Front. In the hope of making his railhead at El Arish more secure, he attacked the Turkish positions at Gaza on March 26. His forward troops made excellent progress and would almost certainly have been successful if the local commander had been informed in good time that GHQ in Cairo had intercepted a signal indicating that the Turks were on the point of surrender.[30]

In the light of this experience, the War Cabinet passed a resolution to the effect that Murray should be ordered to submit plans for the capture of Jerusalem. Nonetheless, he remained under the impression that he would be expected to manage without reinforcements.[31] In April he made a second attack on Gaza but was unsuccessful. The Turks had strengthened their garrison since March, and Murray was forced to withdraw after a four-day battle.

The government then decided to relieve Murray. They offered the appointment to the South African General Jan Smuts, who was not a professional soldier but had fought against the British in the South African War and against the Germans in South-West Africa and East Africa. Smuts declined after learning from Robertson that although Lloyd George attached a good deal of importance to the campaign in Palestine, the War Office regarded it as a mere sideshow.[32] Eventually the post went to General Allenby, a forceful commander with an independent cast of mind. In accordance with Lloyd George's policy of associating the overseas Empire more closely with the war effort, room was found for Smuts as an additional member of the War Cabinet.

When Allenby took up his command toward the end of June, the Turks were holding a line from Gaza to Beersheba with some five divisions. Allenby had four divisions, exclusive of cavalry. Not knowing that the Turkish divisions were much under strength, he asked for reinforcements and eventually received two divisions removed from Salonika with grudging consent from the French. A division newly formed in Egypt gave him a total of seven divisions and six cavalry divisions. Additions to his air arm helped him to build up an accurate picture of the Turkish defenses, but estimates of the rifle strength of the Turkish divisions continued to be unreliable. Contact with Arab supporters on the desert flank was maintained through intelligence officers attached to Allenby's staff and in particular through Captain T. E. Lawrence, who was on good terms with members of Sherif Hussein's family. Lawrence, who had done some archaeological work in Turkish territory before the war, held a temporary commission in the British Army and had taken part in abortive negotiations with the Turks before the surrender of Kut.

Allenby's observations convinced him that he could not hope to break through the strong Turkish defenses at Gaza without heavy losses. The eastern extremity of the Turkish front at Beersheba, on the other hand, had little depth. Allenby began, therefore, by simulating preparations for an assault on Gaza. At the same time he carried out a series of armed reconnaissances designed to foster the impression that he was concerned to divert attention from that sector. Command of the air helped make these ruses so effective that he was able to shift troops to his right without disclosing his intention to the enemy. At the end of October a surprise attack on the weakest part of the Turkish line put him in possession of Beersheba. A turning movement which threatened to roll up the Turkish front from east to west then forced the Turkish commander to withdraw from the whole of his remaining positions for fear of encirclement. In little more than a week the Turks were in full retreat, and Gaza was in British hands.

In the meantime, Robertson had asked Allenby what reinforcements he would need to make sure of reaching Jerusalem and Jaffa. Allenby, apparently under the impression that the Turks could muster as many as twenty divisions for the defense of Jerusalem and Jaffa by drawing on reinforcements intended for a counteroffensive in Mesopotamia, replied that he would need another thirteen divisions.[33] This estimate was soon shown by Allenby himself to be a gross overinsurance. Helped by Arab irregulars moving on his flank to harass communications behind the Turkish lines, he drove the retreating enemy beyond the Jerusalem-Jaffa line. The garrison of Jerusalem withdrew to escape encirclement, and on December 9 a British divisional commander accepted the surrender of the city. Besides capturing the prize which Saladin had wrested more than seven centuries earlier from the heirs of the Crusaders, Allenby thus disrupted Turkish plans for the reconquest of Mesopotamia and southern Palestine.

Meanwhile, the British government had made a bid for the support of influential Zionists on both sides of the Atlantic by declaring in November that it favored the establishment in Palestine of a "national home for the Jewish people." This announcement—the famous Balfour Declaration—was not regarded at the time as inconsistent with promises made to the Arabs or with inter-Allied agreements for partition of the Ottoman Empire. The Sykes-Picot Agreement between Britain and France provided for an international zone in central Palestine, and Sherif Hussein had been warned —albeit in vague terms—that areas which were the subject of negotiations with the French would be excluded from the proposed Arab state or group of states.[34] Lloyd George and his colleagues were so far from foreseeing the protests which Jewish immigration would evoke that Allenby's troops were furnished with copies of the Balfour Declaration for distribution among the predominantly Arab inhabitants of Jerusalem. The immediate aim of the British was to gain the support of anyone who could help the Allied cause on the battlefield or in the international money market; their long-term aim was to safeguard the approaches to India by ensuring that the Near East fell into friendly hands when its Turkish overlords withdrew.

British progress in the Near East in 1917 was accompanied by a striking improvement in the outlook at sea. Regular convoys on the North America, Gibraltar, and Dakar routes were introduced in July and August. In September the tonnage of British merchant shipping sunk by enemy action was the lightest for many months. Thereafter losses were serious, but no longer crippling.[35]

The introduction of convoy was a triumph for Lloyd George; success in Mesopotamia and Palestine at least a partial vindication of his theories. Much to his disappointment, he failed nonetheless to convert the Allies or even his own military advisers to his policy of avoiding frontal assaults on strongly held positions. The lessons he had to teach they were willing to learn only from the enemy.

At the conference in Paris in November, 1916, which Lloyd George found so frustrating an experience, the Allies had agreed that preparations for a new offensive on the Western Front should be completed by the middle of February.[36] At the subsequent conference held in London in December, Lloyd George was not in a position to challenge this decision in principle without bringing a storm about his ears, and the time was not yet ripe to criticize in detail a plan of which the War Cabinet knew little.[37] He proposed, therefore, that the Allied statesmen, with their military advisers, should meet again in Rome in the near future, ostensibly to discuss the situation in the Balkans. Armed with the better knowledge of the French proposals which he hoped to acquire during the journey south in company with Briand and his experts, he would then do his best to release the Allies from the "fatal net" in which they had enmeshed themselves.[38]

When the Rome Conference opened on January 5, the situation in the Balkans had gone from bad to worse. Rumania had collapsed. In Greece, Venizelos had set up a provisional government in opposition to King Constantine, but although the British (but not the French) had recognized the provisional government on December 19, the Allies were still negotiating with Constantine. Furthermore, Greek and Allied forces had come into open conflict on December 1. Since that date the Greeks had agreed to withdraw their troops from the danger area, but the French complained that they had not done so. General Maurice Sarrail, the Allied force commander, was pressing the British and French governments for permission to turn on the Greeks and rout them.

Lloyd George handled this complex situation with considerable address. He pointed out that failure to take vigorous action while there was still a chance of helping the Rumanians had led to a state of affairs which called not for offensive measures but for a sound plan of defense. Lack of shipping made it impossible to carry British troops to Salonika except at a cost which might include suspension of deliveries of coal to France and Italy. He proposed, therefore, that the Italians should send two divisions by the short sea route from Brindisi to Santi Quaranta and thence by road to the Allied front at Monastir. The Italians were not enthusiastic, but agreed to cooperate with the French in developing routes by which Allied troops could reach the Balkan front through ports in southern Italy. Partly as the result of a satisfactory interview between Lloyd George and Sarrail, it was also agreed that the Greeks should be given an ultimatum requiring them to withdraw their troops to the Peloponnesus within a fortnight but that meanwhile Sarrail should hold his hand. In general, the Allies would abstain from measures likely to increase tension between the Royalist and Venizelist factions or involve the Greeks in hostilities against their will.

Lloyd George made it clear that his object in summoning the conference was not merely to settle the Balkan question, but to raise the whole question of Allied strategy. The Allies commanded greater material and moral resources than their opponents, but Germany had the advantage of central control. Allied strategy as hitherto practiced stood condemned by the fact that the efforts of the British and the French on the Western Front, the Italians on the Southern Front, and the Russians on the Eastern Front had not prevented an inferior enemy from overrunning first Serbia and then Rumania. Turning to the future, he asked what the Central Powers would do in 1917. Would they push deep into the heart of Russia, perhaps with Petrograd or Odessa as their objective? Would they use part of their forces to drive the Allies from Monastir? Or would they, before or after dealing with the Russians, strike at the Italians? No doubt, he added, each of the Allied commanders on the various fronts had a plan for the defense of his own sector, but what was the plan of the Allies as a whole? What preparations had been made, what preparations ought to be made, to move troops to a threatened front? What had been done, what could be done, to ensure that the Central Powers did not once again strike at the Allies where they were weak while France and Britain wasted the greater part of their resources on the Western Front?

Lloyd George went on to answer some of these questions by confessing that so far as he knew, the Allies had "absolutely no plan, except for each General to continue 'punching' on his own front." [39] Helping the Russians would be difficult, because the amount of material assistance that could reach them was limited by bottlenecks at Archangel and Vladivostok; even so, the Western Allies ought, in his opinion, to be prepared to make sacrifices in order to strengthen the Eastern Front if they found that nonetheless Russia could increase her intake. The Italians, on the other hand, could easily be helped not merely to defend themselves, but to move on Vienna by way of Ljubljana or perhaps to take Trieste. Lloyd George, pointing out that reinforcement of the Southern at the expense of the Western Front would make no demands on shipping and that the British had twice as many heavy guns in France as in the summer of 1916, offered to lend 250 to 300 heavy guns if the Italians would undertake to make good use of them.[40] Troops, as well as guns, could be sent if they were needed.

The Italian Commander in Chief, General Luigi Cadorna, showed a strange reluctance to close with this offer. He said that the guns would not be worth having if they had to be returned in three months' time and offered a number of other excuses. Not only Lloyd George but also the judicious Hankey, knowing that Robertson was bitterly opposed to the project and had visited Cadorna on the first day of the conference, concluded that Cadorna had been "got at." [41]

Their suspicions were well founded. Robertson is known to have boasted during the journey to Rome that he would "knock out L. G.'s wonderful proposal" by insisting that the French should send as many guns to Italy as the British and that all should be sent back in the spring.[42] Since Cadorna admitted that his impression that he would have to return the guns "in three months' time," or "by May," was derived from conversations with Robertson and the French,[43] the source of his inspiration is obvious. He may also have been influenced by the fear that British and French help might draw the Germans to his front.

French opposition, lack of support from his own military advisers, and Cadorna's halfheartedness defeated Lloyd George's attempt to persuade the Allies to reconsider their plans for the coming year. Nevertheless, the Rome Conference was not barren of results. Besides relieving the British of the fear that Sarrail might attempt a disastrous *coup de main* against the Greeks, agreement between the British and French governments in regard to the Balkan problem improved the lot of the Allied force in Macedonia by giving it, for the first time, a clearly defined task which was within its powers. More important still, Lloyd George's insistence that Italian and French experts should study the problem of carrying troops to the Balkans by way of southern Italy resulted in arrangements which made it possible to rush reinforcements to the Southern Front when the Italians were overwhelmed at Caporetto later in the year.

On his return from Rome, Lloyd George decided to make the best of a bad job. Since the French were not to be dissuaded from attacking the Central Powers on their strongest front, all possible steps must be taken to give their offensive the best chance of success.

In the meantime, the French had rid themselves of Joffre. Their new Commander in Chief, General Robert Nivelle, was described by his former chief and eventual successor, General Philippe Pétain, as "my best pupil." [44] In two local offensives at Verdun he had employed, with startling success, a method of attack which depended on meticulous artillery preparation and in particular on a creeping barrage which moved directly in front of the assault troops. He was a Protestant, his mother was British, and he spoke English fluently.

Nivelle expounded his plan to Haig, both orally and in writing, on December 20 and 21. In his letter of December 21 he asked Haig to extend his front in order to release French troops for an offensive role. Haig refused to do so unless he was strongly reinforced. At the Anglo-French conference in London a few days later the French asked the British to overrule him, but this they declined to do pending consultation with him and Robertson and further negotiations between Haig and Nivelle.[45] Lloyd George also declined to allow Nivelle to put the case to him when he passed through Paris on his way back from Italy, on the ground that he could not discuss the matter in Haig's absence.[46] Accordingly, Nivelle traveled to London in the middle of January for talks with Haig, Robertson, and the War Cabinet. After a series of meetings on January 15 and 16 the War Cabinet endorsed his proposals, and he and Haig then signed an agreement which was also signed by Robertson.[47]

The essence of Nivelle's plan was tactical surprise. He proposed to deliver, under cover of holding attacks by British and French troops between Arras and the Oise, a sudden blow at the German front in the limestone country between Rheims and Soissons. He chose this sector partly because he thought the Germans would not expect him to attack a ridge honeycombed with fieldworks, partly because an elaborate trench system on the French side of the lines offered him a chance of assembling his forces without detection. In the light of his experiences at Verdun he believed that his assault troops, supported by a short but devastating bombardment, would be able to punch a gap in the German lines by the second day. A strategic reserve of twenty-seven divisions, organized in nine corps and three armies, would then pour through the gap and engage "all available hostile forces" in a decisive battle.[48] Finally, British as well as French troops would advance on a wide front in pursuit of a beaten enemy.

To enable him to form such a reserve, Nivelle asked Haig to complete the extension of his line "at the latest" by January 15. Since that date had already passed when the plan was accepted by the British, Nivelle was in difficulties from the start. Subsequent delays in carrying out the extension were attributed by Haig to the shortcomings of the French railway system, by the French to the vastness of

Haig's demands for rolling stock. Nivelle and his experts, apparently unaware that Haig's figures included the transport needed to prepare for the offensive he hoped to carry out when Nivelle had shot his bolt, did not understand why the British asked for twice as many locomotives and wagons as they themselves needed to move nearly twice as many troops.[50]

On February 26—nearly a fortnight after the date fixed in November for the completion of all preparations for the spring offensive—Lloyd George traveled with Robertson and Hankey to Calais to thrash the matter out with Haig, Nivelle, and the French ministers. At the end of a discussion of technical problems he asked Nivelle whether he was satisfied and to say frankly what he wanted. Nivelle "got red in the face" and took refuge in generalities but later in the day submitted a scheme which would give him virtual command of the Expeditionary Force and reduce Haig to a cipher.[51] Hankey, who agreed with Robertson and Haig that the scheme was "outrageous" but saw that Lloyd George seemed to like it, then drafted a memorandum which provided that Haig should conform with Nivelle's "general strategical plans" and that this should apply not only to active operations, but also to preparations. Hankey's formula was accepted on February 27 by the soldiers and statesmen on both sides, and all of them then signed the memorandum.[52] Robertson claimed afterward that his signature did not imply acceptance of the principle of unified command, but merely of Hankey's method of giving effect to it if the statesmen insisted on adopting it.

Relations between GHQ and Nivelle's headquarters continued to be so unsatisfactory that in March yet another high-level meeting, at which Lloyd George strongly deprecated the peremptory tone of letters addressed to Haig by members of Nivelle's staff, was needed to soothe ruffled feelings. A liaison mission, headed by Henry Wilson, was then appointed to keep the peace between the two headquarters.

Meanwhile, such prospects of success as ever existed were receding into the limbo of the might-have-been. By the last week in February the Germans knew that a French offensive in Champagne was highly probable.[53] In the course of the next five to six weeks they withdrew on a front of more than seventy miles between Arras and a point north of Soissons to a new line of prepared positions which the British called the Hindenburg Line. Since they left behind them a belt of devastated country some fifteen to twenty miles wide, the

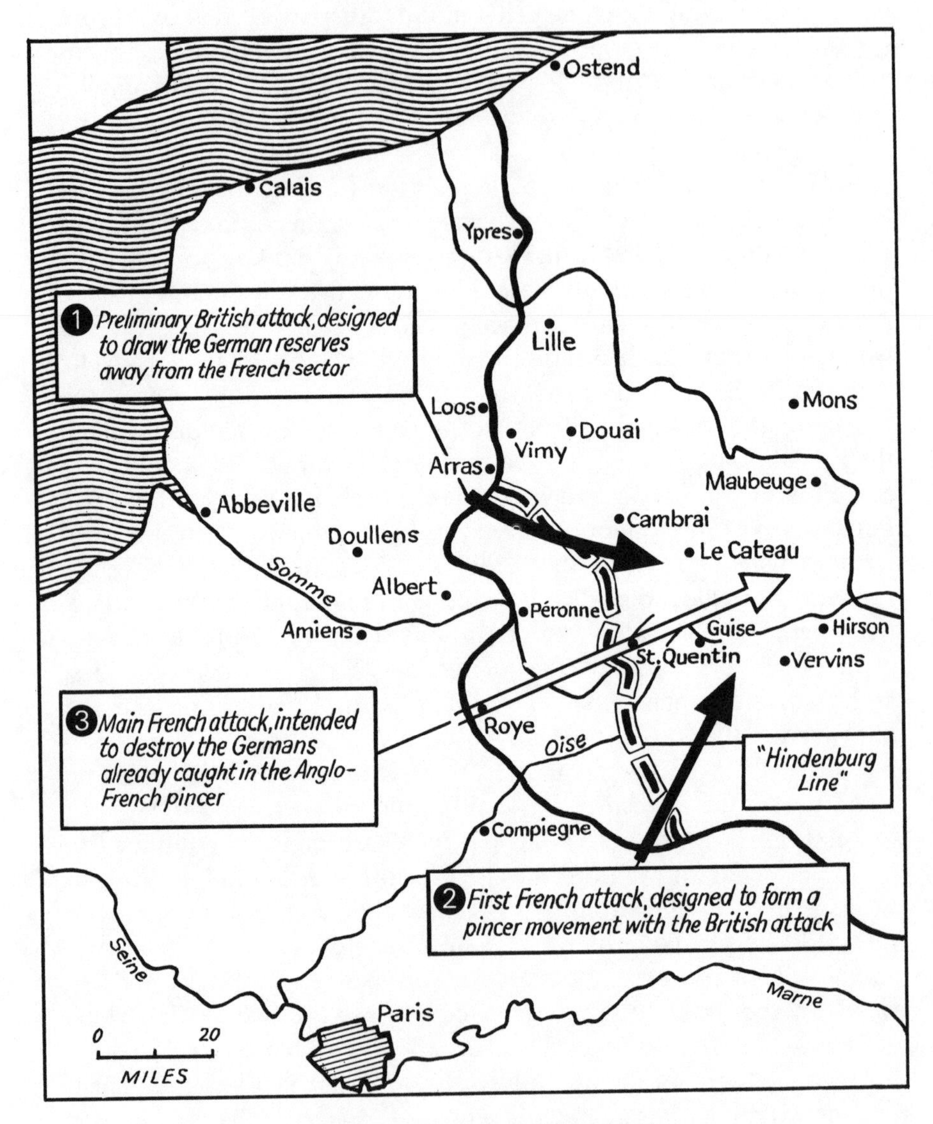

THE NIVELLE OFFENSIVE

holding attacks which were to be delivered in that sector had perforce to be postponed while contact was reestablished and guns were laboriously hauled to new positions by horses, mules, or steam-driven traction engines. Besides conferring this benefit on the Germans, withdrawal to a shorter and stronger line made it easier for them to shift troops to the threatened sector in Champagne. Between February and April the number of German divisions on or immediately behind the front chosen by Nivelle for his main attack rose from eight to forty.[54]

In March and April Nivelle's position was further complicated by momentous happenings at home and abroad. The Russian Revolution began on March 12 with upheavals whose ultimate consequences could not be foreseen, but which ruled out any immediate prospect of synchronized offensives on the Eastern and Western fronts. A change of government in France a few days later compelled Nivelle to justify his proposals in the eyes of a new War Minister, Paul Painlevé, who disapproved of great offensives and thought that Nivelle ought not to have been chosen to succeed Joffre.[55] Finally, President Wilson's address to Congress on April 2 led some Frenchmen to argue that since the Americans were about to take an active part in the war, no attempt to force a decision on the Western Front ought to be made until they arrived in strength or at any rate until their plans and intentions were known.

Within the next few days the French military authorities learned that on the night of April 4 the Germans had captured a noncommissioned officer who had in his possession a document which revealed the corps objectives of one of the army groups assigned to the offensive.[56] At a time when some of Nivelle's subordinate commanders were already dubious about his plan, this calamity greatly strengthened the argument for recasting it. Nivelle continued, nonetheless, to assert that he could force a breakthrough and in forty-eight hours would be ten miles behind the German lines.

At a conference with Nivelle and his army group commanders on April 6, leading members of the French government considered the case for abandoning the offensive in Champagne and adopting some such alternative as Lloyd George's proposed offensive on the Italian front. According to Painlevé, he and his ministerial colleagues were not told that a crucial document must be presumed to have fallen into German hands.[57] Even so, they knew of the withdrawal to the Hindenburg Line, and they also knew that some of Nivelle's ablest and most experienced generals were openly critical of his leadership.

Nevertheless they came to the conclusion that they could not countermand the offensive at a time when the preliminary bombardment in the British sector had already begun.

Haig's holding attack at Arras on April 9 found the Germans unprepared for a push so far north. His troops captured the important Vimy Ridge and advanced up to six miles on a ten-mile front. Had Nivelle's plan been flexible enough to allow him to switch his reserves to the British sector, a big success might have come within his grasp. As it was, Haig's follow-up was too slow to prevent the Germans from rebuilding their shattered front.

Nivelle launched his offensive in Champagne on April 16. By the end of the day it was obvious that he had failed to subdue the enemy's machine-gun posts and that the "broadening out into the decisive battle" which he had predicted was not likely to come to pass.[58] Philippe Pétain, an outspoken critic of Nivelle's refusal to change his plan when surprise was known to have been lost, became Chief of Staff in Paris at the end of April. A fortnight later he succeeded Nivelle as Commander in Chief.

Meanwhile, it became widely known in the French Army that Nivelle's troops had been committed to the assault against the better judgment of men in responsible positions. In more than fifty divisions the rank and file of regiment after regiment showed their disapproval by absenting themselves from duty, threatening to set up soldiers' councils on the Russian model, or taking part in more or less orderly demonstrations. About 20,000 men were posted as deserters. Most of the troops were willing to defend the soil of France by manning the trenches, but they insisted that no more attempts should be made to storm impregnable positions.

Pétain dealt with this situation by punishing a few ringleaders, promising regular leave, and letting it be known that he had no intention of risking heavy losses for doubtful gains. His policy as Chief of the General Staff and later as Commander in Chief, was to content himself with local advances until the arrival of the Americans and the weakening of the Central Powers by the partial or complete collapse of Austro-Hungary, Turkey, and Bulgaria made it worth his while to attempt a knockout blow.

At a conference in Paris on May 4, the British accepted this policy in the context of an agreement to continue offensive operations on the Western Front without attempting a decisive breakthrough. Pressure on the enemy was to be maintained for the purpose of "wearing down and exhausting" his resistance.[59]

When the British learned that the French Army was in poor shape, they concluded that most of the wearing down would have to be done by British troops. The question was whether they should make their contribution by undertaking the advance toward Ostend and Zeebrugge for which Haig had long been preparing or by some other means.

On June 7 Haig launched a preliminary attack designed to capture the high ground near Messines which dominated the Ypres salient. Thanks to careful preparation by General Sir Herbert Plumer of the Second Army and his Chief of Staff, Major General Sir Charles Harington, the operation was brilliantly successful; but its success did not make the statesmen's task any easier. They still had to decide whether to sanction two or three limited advances on the lines of Plumer's or one big push as proposed by Haig or whether to adopt some other course.

At a time when shipping losses were causing intense anxiety, a strong argument in favor of Haig's proposals was that, according to the Admiralty, the capture of Ostend and Zeebrugge would greatly ease the naval situation.[60] These places, it was claimed, could be reached by a series of step-by-step advances.[61] The fact remained that, even to bring Ostend within reach of his long-range guns, Haig would have to push nearly twice as far as he had managed to do on any previous occasion. Taking into account the poor state of the French Army, the statesmen doubted whether the Allies had enough superiority in firepower to make this possible.* Lloyd George would

* Current estimates of comparative strength on the Western Front were as follows:

	Combatant strength	*Field guns*	*Heavy guns*
British	1,127,000		
French	1,310,000		
Belgian	131,000		
Portuguese	25,000		
Russian	18,000		
	2,611,300	9,126	6,614
German	2,149,000	4,556	7,520

have preferred an offensive on the Italian front to a push in Flanders, but could not be sure that the French would agree with him.

Early in June Henry Wilson was summoned to London to report on the state of affairs in France. He told the War Cabinet on June 8 that "the French would not stick it much longer" unless some striking military or diplomatic success put fresh heart into them.[62] He suggested that an attempt might be made to detach Turkey or Bulgaria from the Central Powers.

In the second half of the month Haig expounded his plan to a War Policy Committee consisting of Lloyd George, Curzon, Milner, and Smuts. He proposed to begin by capturing the Passchendaele-Staden ridge, ten miles northeast of Ypres. This would be the task of the Fifth Army (General Sir Hubert Gough), supported on its right by the Second Army (Plumer), on its left by the French First Army (General François Anthoine). When his troops were established on a line through Passchendaele and Staden to Dixmude, Haig would aim at capturing Ostend by converging movements from that direction and along the coast. Thereafter he hoped to push his center to Bruges or farther, his right toward Courtrai, and his left in the general direction of Zeebrugge. He believed that, once the Passchendaele-Staden ridge was in his hands, opportunities might arise for the employment of "cavalry in masses." [63]

A serious objection to this program was that notwithstanding Haig's disclaimers, it seemed likely to commit him to yet another attempt to force a breakthrough at a heavy cost. A further objection was that, according to statistics in the possession of his staff but not disclosed to the War Policy Committee, the weather in Flanders "broke early each August with the regularity of the Indian monsoon." [64] Much of the country between Ypres and the Belgian coast was reclaimed marshland, kept cultivable in peacetime by an elaborate drainage system. The dikes and sluices, already in poor shape after three years of war, were bound to be further damaged by the preliminary bombardment. Since the troops would not be ready to start before the last week in July, the outlook could scarcely be called promising.

While Haig was in London, his principal liaison officer with the French, Henry Wilson, toured the French front from Verdun to Belfort and beyond. He found that in Alsace the war seemed curiously remote. Apart from intermittent artillery fire, there had been little fighting for some months; on both sides of the line, the fields were cultivated right up to the front. The civil population seemed heartily tired of the war and longed for peace. At a village conveniently close to the Swiss frontier, a man introduced to Wilson as "the principal secret agent of the French" told him that the Germans were visibly encouraged by recent events. They were not seriously alarmed by the prospect of American intervention, which they thought was unlikely to become effective within the next twelve to eighteen months.

On the return journey, Wilson called on Pétain, Foch, Nivelle, and Joffre. He found Joffre anxious about the state of the Army and the country. Nivelle admitted that there had been "considerable trouble" in the army but seriously underestimated its extent. Pétain made a similar confession but said that the worst was over and that now "only the politicians were dangerous." Foch, who had succeeded Pétain in Paris, was more explicit. According to him, the politicians were indeed so dangerous that even a hint of trouble with the British might lead them to seek a separate peace with Germany.

Wilson, fresh from these encounters, reached Haig's headquarters late on June 27. He had a long talk that evening with Lieutenant General Sir Launcelot Kiggell, the Chief of Staff. Kiggell, an experienced staff officer who had served at the War Office under Robertson, outlined the plan for the Flanders offensive. He claimed that Haig could take Ostend, Zeebrugge, Bruges, and Ghent, stressed the importance of obtaining an early decision from the government, and countered the objection that the French would prefer an extension of the British line by pointing out that Pétain was now so well disposed toward the offensive as to be willing to lend troops for it.

Hitherto Wilson's private opinion had been that Haig could do far more for the French by extending his line than by taking the offensive. He still did not believe that Haig would reach any of the places mentioned. In the light of Kiggell's other arguments, he nonetheless promised to support Haig's proposals on the understanding that the offensive would be called off if it proved too expensive and in any case would be discontinued when the weather became prohibitive, which Wilson thought would happen in October. He repeated his promise to Haig before leaving for London in the morning.

Accordingly, Wilson told Milner on June 30, and the War Policy Committee on July 3, that he thought Haig ought to attack "up to the mud time" and then take over more line from the French. Possibly because Kiggell had told him that Pétain now approved of the Flanders offensive, he did not add that both Pétain and Foch had spoken slightingly of Haig's proposals some four to six weeks earlier. He was somewhat shaken by the news that British casualties since April were twice as heavy as he had supposed but said that he saw no reason why Haig should have heavy losses if he went carefully, stayed within the shelter of his guns, and made good use of his aircraft. He told the War Policy Committee that the plight of the French was "not desperate" but added in a written report to the War Office that, although unrest in the French Army was "not yet serious," France was "beginning to die away" and needed careful handling.[65]

Wilson carried away from his interview with the War Policy Committee the impression that Lloyd George, Curzon, Milner, and Smuts all thought, as he did, that Haig had no chance of pushing the Germans out of Belgium. That impression was substantially correct. None of the statesmen believed that Haig's strategic objectives would be attained.[66] At the same time, they were not prepared to overrule their military advisers in the absence of any alternative to the Flanders offensive on which all could agree. Lloyd George hoped until the eleventh hour that support from the French might enable him to push through his proposal for an offensive on the Italian front, but he found that no Anglo-French conference could be held before the last week in July. Since Haig expected to complete his preparations about that time, the War Policy Committee agreed on July 16 that he should be told that he could begin his offensive when he was ready, but that it must not be allowed to degenerate into a long-drawn slogging match like the Battle of the Somme.[67] Should that danger arise, the offensive would be stopped and Lloyd George's Italian alternative would be tried.

In the outcome, Haig completed his preparations only just in time to launch his assault on the last day of the month. On July 29 and 30 his preliminary bombardment was hampered at a crucial stage by low clouds which made artillery observation from aircraft almost impossible. On July 31 a light drizzle began soon after midday and turned in the late afternoon to drenching rain. In the sector southeast of Ypres, where a strong thrust toward the Gheluvelt plateau by Gough's right-hand corps was needed to cover his advance to the Passchendaele-Staden ridge, the assault troops were halted by a cluster of strongpoints which the bombardment had left almost untouched. The result was that progress elsewhere left Gough with an uneven line which would have to be straightened before any further advance could be attempted.

Heavy rain continued to fall throughout the night of July 31 and the first few days of August. Haig noted in his diary as early as August 1 that the ground was "like a bog." [68] As a result of his bombardment and the German counterbombardment, it was also thickly honeycombed with craters, which soon became full to the brim with slime and water. Men and animals risked death by drowning if they diverged from a network of recognized tracks on which wooden duckboards or transverse lines of planks were laid. Where these were shattered by the enemy's artillery fire or succumbed to wear and tear, vehicles sank up to their axles and men up to their knees. The pace of the infantryman with his sixty-pound pack was reduced to a crawl, guns could be emplaced only with the utmost difficulty, and even to bring up supplies and move the wounded became a prodigious task.

By the middle of August conditions were so appalling that Gough recommended that the offensive be called off on the ground that tactical success had become impossible or would be inordinately expensive.[69] Haig insisted that further attempts to inch toward the elusive ridge should be made in the second half of August. On September 2, after these had been launched in drenching rain and had failed with heavy losses, he agreed to suspend offensive operations for the best part of three weeks. This decision was followed by a spell of fine weather which dried the surface of the ground but left the subsoil still waterlogged.

Meanwhile, Cadorna had repented of his lukewarm attitude to the offer of 300 British heavy guns but found that he had lost his chance of receiving more than some forty which the British had agreed in the spring to send him. On August 17 he began the last of a series of attempts to push the Austrians back in the Isonzo River sector with an army deficient in siege weapons and poorly supplied with ammunition for its field artillery. He made such a good beginning that early in September the French decided to send him 100 guns which they at first proposed to take wholly from Anthoine's army, on Gough's left. Lloyd George was thus presented with an opportunity of reminding his colleagues that the War Policy Committee had

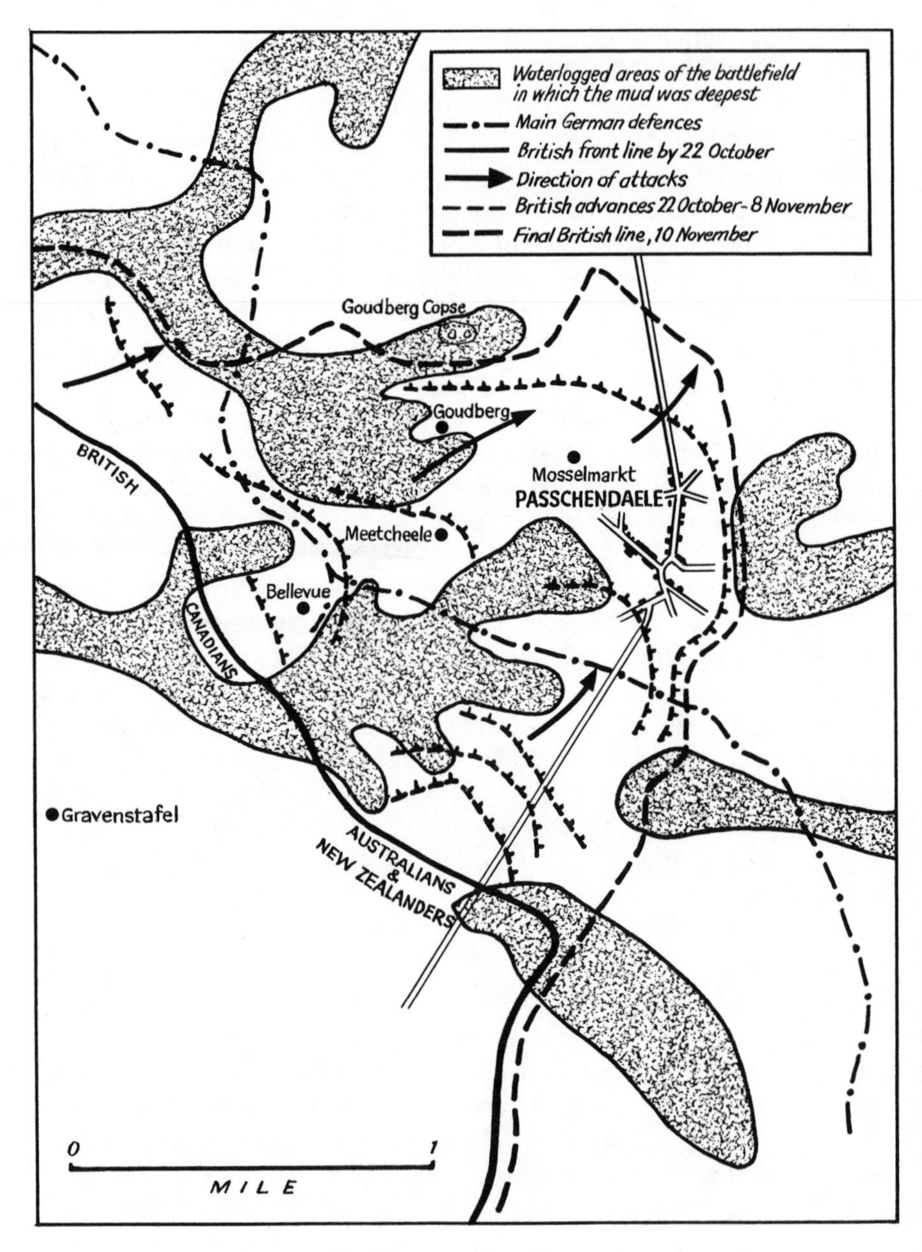

PASSCHENDAELE

agreed to call off the Flanders offensive and see what could be done on the Italian front if Haig were unsuccessful, but he postponed a decision pending discussion of a renewed offensive against Turkey. A few days later, lack of ammunition forced Cadorna to discontinue his attacks and go on the defensive.

Almost simultaneously the German Foreign Ministry made peace overtures to France and Britain through an intermediary in Brussels. These followed abortive negotiations between Britain, France, and Austro-Hungary, whose new ruler, the Emperor Karl, was more than willing to come to terms but was fatally handicapped by his obligation not to conclude a separate peace. Since the Germans were believed by the French to have acceptable terms in view, representatives of France, Great Britain, Italy, Japan, Russia, and the United States agreed on October 8 to notify Germany that the British government was prepared to receive any communication which the German government cared to make.[70] No reply was received, and the project lapsed when the German Foreign Minister announced publicly on the day after the Allies had sent their message that Germany would in no circumstances renounce her claim to the territories ceded by France at the end of the Franco-Prussian War. It is now known that the German High Command intended to stipulate that German troops should remain in Belgium for "several years" after the signing of the peace treaty and that Germany would almost certainly have insisted not only on reducing Belgium to economic vassalage but also on retaining the Briey iron fields.[71]

In the meantime, Plumer, with Gough's former right-hand corps and sector added to his command, had drawn up plans for a series of limited advances. Each advance was to be preceded by a massive bombardment and supported by a creeping barrage. By concentrating on a narrow front and attempting no deep penetration, Plumer succeeded on September 20, and again on September 26 and October 4, in reaching his objectives without suffering losses greatly in excess of those inflicted on the enemy. On the second of these occasions Lloyd George spent part of the morning following the progress of the battle on a map at Haig's headquarters. As evidence of the state to which Haig claimed to have reduced the German Army, Lloyd George and Hankey were shown later in the day a batch of newly taken prisoners which did not include a single man of robust physique.[72]

Lloyd George and his colleagues had recoiled from the odium of overruling their military advisers by stopping the Flanders offensive in August, when it was going badly. They were still less inclined to intervene when the outlook seemed more promising. Furthermore, they soon became preoccupied with other problems. The result was that, despite a break in the weather which ruined Plumer's next attempt to go forward on October 9, Haig was not restrained from keeping the offensive going until well into November. By that time, and indeed much earlier, the state of the ground was so bad that a wave of resentment against commanders and staff officers who sent men to fight in such conditions swept through the middle and lower ranks of the Expeditionary Force. The village of Passchendaele was captured on November 6, but the northern part of the Passchendaele-Staden ridge remained in German hands.

Haig was then persuaded to try his luck elsewhere and to use his tanks for the first time in large numbers. An attack with massed tanks at Cambrai on November 20 shattered the German lines on a front of three or four miles, but no infantry reserves were available to exploit the breakthrough. The Germans, counterattacking a week later, regained most of the ground they had lost and in some places pushed the British behind the line they had held before the battle.

When offensive operations were at last suspended in December, Haig had nothing tangible to show for his efforts except a substantial bag of prisoners and two small salients which were bound to crumble if attacked in force.[73] He believed that his losses were lighter than the enemy's, but official statistics published a few years after the war put British and German casualties between July and December at 448,614 and 270,710 respectively.[74] Many years later, experts with access to the original sources asserted that these figures were misleading, that British casualties attributable to the Flanders offensive and to "normal wastage" did not exceed 250,000 and that German casualties were probably of the order of 400,000.[75] The existence of such widely different sets of figures throws a strange light on the circumstances in which Haig decided to continue his offensive despite early setbacks. If the ratio between British and German losses was still in dispute many years after the war was over, what solid basis can Haig have had in 1917 for his belief that he was hitting the enemy harder than the enemy was hitting him?

Haig's defenders claimed after the war that in any case he was bound to continue the offensive after his initial attempt to capture the Passchendaele-Staden ridge had failed, because in his estimation the French were incapable of repelling the attacks which would otherwise have been made upon them.[76] His critics denied that the state of the French Army after midsummer was as bad as he supposed. The French were able to launch an offensive at Verdun as early as August 20, they fought doggedly there and elsewhere in September and October, and the contribution made by Anthoine's First Army to the Flanders campaign was far from negligible. Moreover, the success of Haig's attack at Cambrai in November suggested that, if he had to help the French by continuing to fight on the offensive after the middle of August, he might have found better ways of doing so than by plunging deeper into the mud of Passchendaele.

The fact remains that according to German accounts, the Flanders offensive did put a heavy strain on the defenders. Whether the moral effects of months of desperate fighting in appalling conditions were worse, in the long run, for the Germans or the British can only be, in the final analysis, a matter of opinion. One lesson which does seem to emerge clearly is that Haig was treading on very uncertain ground when he invoked the doctrine of attrition to justify the continuance of his offensive long after it became apparent that the objectives he had hoped to reach were unattainable.

7

Soldiers and Statesmen: II

HAIG'S failure to capture the Passchendaele-Staden ridge at an early stage of his offensive brought home to Lloyd George the disadvantages of a system which made the Prime Minister ultimately responsible in the eyes of his fellow citizens for committing the British Army to an unsuccessful enterprise, yet prevented him from choosing a new Commander in Chief of the Expeditionary Force and a new Chief of the Imperial General Staff without risking a political crisis which might put him out of office. Toward the end of August he asked Field Marshal French and Henry Wilson to visit him at the house in Sussex at which he was staying as the guest of his old friend Sir George Riddell. He told Wilson that he was "profoundly dissatisfied" with Robertson and was thinking of forming a committee of three soldiers to overhaul his work. Wilson assured him that such an arrangement would be grossly unfair to Robertson and was out of the question. In his view the statesmen, instead of sheltering behind their military advisers, ought to accept without question their responsibility for grand strategy. He suggested that they might begin by setting up an Inter-Allied Council, headed by the prime ministers of Britain, France, and Italy, to "draw up plans for the whole theatre from Nieuport to Baghdad." [1]

Lloyd George's reply was to the effect that such a council might perhaps be formed when France had a stronger government. The project then lapsed until the petering out of Cadorna's offensive for lack of British and French support, the prospect of imminent collapse in Russia, and Haig's lack of progress made action imperative. In October Lloyd George gave Hankey something new to think about by pointing out that in view of events in Russia, Germany was not likely to be decisively beaten before 1919, when the Americans could be expected to arrive in strength. Since Britain would not be able to speak with authority at the peace conference unless she had a strong army in the field when the time came for the decisive blow, the national interest required that her manpower should not be frittered away by fruitless offensives in the meantime.[2]

In the light of these considerations, Lloyd George decided to adopt the remedy discussed with Wilson. Since he could not rid himself of Haig and Robertson without risking a controversy which might undermine the nation's confidence in his administration, he would outwit them by transferring major decisions of strategy to the international level.

Invoking the precedent set by Asquith when he summoned a Council of War in 1914, Lloyd George arranged that French and Wilson should attend a meeting of the War Cabinet on October 11. There they were asked to put their views on paper. While awaiting the outcome Lloyd George ascertained, at an informal meeting with Foch and the French Foreign Minister, that the French would look with favor on the establishment of an Inter-Allied War Council advised by a permanent military staff.[3] A few days later French and Wilson submitted memoranda in which they strongly recommended the setting up of such a body.[4]

At that stage, events provided a striking vindication of Lloyd George's plea in January for both offensive and defensive preparations on the Italian front. On October 24 the Austrians, reinforced by six German divisions from the Eastern and Western fronts, routed the Italian Second Army at Caporetto in the Julian Alps. A thick fog hampered the artillery on which the Italians were accustomed to rely, commanders and staff officers soon lost touch with the situation, and all ranks were demoralized by rumors to the effect that the Germans, having defeated the Russians and taken the measure of the British and the French, were about to shift their main effort to the Southern Front. In sixteen days the Italians retreated seventy miles from the Isonzo and lost well over half a million killed, wounded, prisoners, and deserters.[5] They left behind them about 3,500 guns, in addition to many rifles and large quantities of food and ammunition.

Confronted with this disaster, Lloyd George's British and French colleagues agreed that, subject to Italian assent, the proposed Inter-Allied War Council should be formed with the least possible delay. It would be known as the Supreme War Council and would consist of the Prime Ministers of Britain, France, and Italy and one other member of each government. The statesmen would meet at least once a month, and would be advised by a full-time staff headed by a permanent military representative of each country. The existing general staffs and commanders in chief would continue to be responsible to their respective governments, but would be required to submit their "general war plans" to the Supreme War Council for comment and approval.[6]

In the first week of November Lloyd George traveled by way of Paris to Rapallo, where he conferred on November 6 and 7 with the Italians and the French. In addition to Smuts and Hankey, he took with him Henry Wilson as prospective British Permanent Military Representative. Robertson was already in Italy.

The Supreme War Council came formally into existence on November 7, when it met at Rapallo to consider the situation arising from the Caporetto disaster.[7] Robertson, who had proposed to send two British divisions to Italy, was told to order Haig to part with five. A new front for the defense of Venice and the Adriatic coast was then established with British and French help on the Piave. The French promised six divisions. Cadorna became Italian Permanent Military Representative and was replaced as Commander in Chief by a little-known corps commander, General Armando Díaz.

The strong French government postulated by Lloyd George as a prerequisite of this reform did not yet exist, but its advent was not long delayed. The British were told when they passed through Paris on their way to Rapallo that the Radical Georges Clemenceau "was likely to come into office for a time." On November 16 he duly became Prime Minister.

Almost simultaneously two former Russian exiles, V. I. Ulyanov and L. Bronstein (better known as Lenin and Trotsky), seized power in Petrograd. They succeeded after a brief struggle in gaining control of Moscow and other industrial centers in European Russia. One of their first acts was to negotiate an armistice agreement with the Germans, who had helped Lenin and other Communist exiles to return to Russia some months earlier. By the Treaty of Brest-Litovsk, which followed in March, 1918, Russia renounced large tracts of territory in Finland, the Baltic provinces, and Russian Poland. About 60,000,000 former subjects of the Czar ceased to be Russian nationals, and the territories renounced fell largely under German control.

At this fateful moment, an American mission headed by Colonel House arrived in London to exchange views with the British before traveling to Paris to attend a conference designed to inaugurate a new era of intimate cooperation between the Allied and Associated Powers. Its members included the Chief of Staff of the United States Army, the Chief of Naval Operations, and representatives of the Treasury, the War Trade Board, the Shipping Board, the War Industries Board, and the Food Administration.*

Lloyd George, receiving the American delegates on November 20 in the room in which Lord North had directed the policy that led to the loss of the American colonies, told them that in his opinion and that of his colleagues and advisers, manpower and shipping problems came first among the many difficult questions the Allied and Associated Powers had to face.[8] Reviewing the military situation in the light of recent events, he estimated that the collapse of Russia would enable the Germans to move thirty or forty of their best divisions to the West at a time when the British and the French had been compelled to send eleven divisions to Italy. In these circumstances it

* The mission was composed as follows:

Head of Mission and Personal Representative of the President:

Edward M. House

United States Army:	General Tasker H. Bliss
United States Navy:	Rear Admiral William S. Benson
United States Treasury:	Oscar T. Crosby
	Paul Cravath
War Trade Board:	Vance C. McCormick
Shipping Board:	Bainbridge Colby
War Industries Board:	Thomas Nelson Perkins
Food Administration:	Alonzo R. Taylor

Secretary: Gordon Auchincloss

could no longer be assumed that the Allies were strong enough to hold the Western Front unaided until a powerful American army joined them in dealing a knockout blow to the enemy in 1919.[9] He begged the Americans not to content themselves in the meantime with the valuable contributions they were making to the blockade of Germany and the financing of the Allied war effort, but to send across the Atlantic without delay the troops, guns, and aircraft needed to make the Western Front secure.

The Americans recognized the need to strengthen the Western Front in view of events in Russia. For that very reason they had raised from twelve to twenty-four the number of divisions they hoped to deploy in France by the summer of 1918. At the same time, they did not want their army to be used piecemeal to plug gaps in the Allied line. Their intention was to assemble in Europe, and supply from the United States, a large, self-contained expeditionary force capable of making an independent contribution to the war with Germany. They also recognized that shipping was likely to be the crucial factor. They believed, however, that by suspending their capital-ship program and concentrating on the production of cargo ships, destroyers, and submarines, they might be able to put themselves in a position to carry half the twenty-four divisions across the Atlantic if the British would carry the other half.

This belief was unrealistic. In November, more than seven months after the declaration of war, the number of American troops in France was only about 126,000, and only one American division had reached the front. Furthermore, the tonnage allotted by the Shipping Board to the armed forces would not suffice to maintain more than six to eight divisions at most.[10] Even if the large number of troops needed to complete the twenty-four-division program could somehow be shipped across the Atlantic by the following midsummer, the American authorities would still be unable to supply so large a force with the means at their disposal.

In the course of the meeting Lloyd George was obliged to warn the Americans not to assume that Britain could fill the gap.[11] He pointed out that three-fifths of the British merchant fleet was already wholly engaged in war service on behalf of Britain and her allies.[12] Food production in France had fallen to 40 percent of the peacetime standard, Russian granaries were closed to the Western Allies, and Italy's economy was disrupted by the suspension of trade with Central Europe. Britain, herself dependent on imports for four-fifths of her wheat and for much else besides, was obliged to export food and raw materials to France and Italy in order to keep their people fed and their armies in the field.

In the light of these disclosures the Americans reverted to their original target of twelve divisions by the summer of 1918. At the conference in Paris, which opened on November 30, they proposed that these divisions should cross the Atlantic at the rate of two a month and that half of them should travel in British or Allied ships. Meanwhile, the British, too, had given further consideration to the problem. In view of the great importance attached not only by their own experts but also by the French to the strengthening of the Western Front during the next six months, they came to the conclusion that they must do everything they could to hasten the arrival of American troops, even at the cost of allowing stocks of food and raw materials to run down. They therefore offered to carry, in addition to their share of the twelve divisions, a further 150 infantry battalions, on the understanding that these would be brigaded with British troops and fed and trained by the British until American divisions were ready to absorb them. By this means the infantry component of more than a dozen divisions, over and above the original twelve, could be transported across the Atlantic in the same number of ships as would be needed for three whole divisions complete with transport, services, and staff.[13] Moreover, since battalions could be trained much faster than divisions, the troops would be ready to fight in three to four months, as compared with six or more. Finally, the attachment of American battalions to British divisions, even for a few months, might help the War Office by doing something to reconcile divisional commanders and their staffs to a recent decision to reduce the establishment of a British infantry division from twelve to nine battalions.[14]

The military authorities in Washington were inclined to accept this offer, but agreed with the President that General John Pershing, Commander in Chief of the United States Expeditionary Force in Europe, must be allowed to make such arrangements with the British as seemed best to him.[15] Pershing, fearing that his force might lose its national identity if American troops served in British divisions, utterly refused to allow his men to be shipped to Europe by battalions. After lengthy discussion the British, unable to shake him, agreed that such shipping as they could spare after the needs of the two-divisions-a-month program had been met should be used to carry complete divisions. On arrival the infantry, auxiliary troops, commanders, and staffs of these divisions would be attached to British formations for training and to gain experience.[16] Artillery units would train in France under American direction, using French equipment. This was not a satisfactory solution from the Allied point of view but was accepted by the British with the philosophical reflection that at any rate it would do something to speed the arrival of American forces which would doubtless not be withheld from the battlefront in a dire emergency.

Before this question was settled, the Supreme War Council met for the first time at its permanent headquarters at Versailles. The proceedings opened on December 1 with a speech delivered by Clemenceau but drafted by the British.[17] The Permanent Military Representatives were then invited to hammer out proposals for the coming year.

Meanwhile, the Allied governments had to consider not only the military consequences of the Russian defection, but also the effects of events in Russia on public opinion in Allied countries. Long before the Leninist *coup d'état*, Russian leaders who saw no hope of continuing the struggle against the Central Powers had begun to pave the way for a separate peace by casting doubt on the motives of statesmen in all countries who wished to go on fighting. As early as May, 1917, the Russian Provisional Government implicitly condemned the revisionist aims of the Western powers by calling for a "general peace," without annexations or indemnities. At the same time international Socialism, dormant since 1914, raised its head again. In Britain not only extremists of the Independent Labour Party but also moderate Socialists urged British workmen and soldiers in June to follow the Russian example by setting up local councils; in August the British Labour Party voted by a large majority in favor of attendance at a conference of Socialist parties of all countries, to be held in Stockholm for the purpose of discussing ways and means of making peace.

Lloyd George saw a difficult time ahead. The experts believed, and he agreed, that Germany was unlikely to be decisively beaten before the spring or summer of 1919. To keep the country at war for another eighteen months or more, with only minor successes in Mesopotamia and Palestine to brighten the outlook in the meantime, would be impossible unless organized labor was solidly behind him.

At the same time, Lloyd George's attitude toward the Russians differed from that of many of his colleagues. To the French, the armistice negotiations between Germany and Russia seemed a hideous betrayal. Lloyd George could not altogether share that view. Almost from the beginning of the war he had felt that the Allies, in not pooling their resources with the Russians, were making a mistake which would cost them dear. Now that he had been proved right, he was not inclined to judge the Russians harshly.

The fact remained that, as long as Lenin and his collaborators were still struggling to assert their authority over local councils and regional governments, there was no single body of men in Russia whom the Allies could recognize as the *de facto* government of the country. Consequently the Russians were not represented at the conference in Paris. Lloyd George felt that, even so, no opportunity of making contact with men who might be able to form such a government ought to be neglected. At his request, the Russian ambassador in Paris was summoned to a meeting of heads of government and was asked whether he thought the Allies could help by formally releasing Russia from her obligation not to make a separate peace.[18] The ambassador did not believe that such a gesture would do anything to strengthen the moderate elements in his country, but suggested that the Allied and Associated Powers might make a bid for Russian goodwill by publicly declaring that they were not engaged in a war of conquest. None of the spokesmen of the assembled nations was, however, able to hit upon a formula to which everyone, the ambassador included, could agree. This was not surprising. The Italians could not honestly have claimed that they were not fighting for territorial gains at the expense of Austria, or the French that they did not hope to regain their lost provinces.

Colonel House felt when the conference was over that its usefulness had been greatly diminished by the failure of the Allied and Associated Powers to define their aims in broad terms which everyone opposed to German domination of Europe could accept.[19] In the absence of concerted action, he advised his chief to set a good example by making such a statement on behalf of the United States. At the same time, he and his colleagues warned the President that the Allies might be beaten within the next six months or so if they did not improve their teamwork or if the United States failed to give them the help they were expecting. All the leading members of the mission agreed that while much good work had been done in Paris by the setting up of various inter-Allied councils and committees, the United States government must do its utmost to make up for time lost through inexperience, imperfect coordination between departments, and ignorance of the true needs of the European Allies.[20]

In face of these warnings, the President thought of sending House back to Europe to sit with the British, French, and Italian Prime Ministers at meetings of the Supreme War Council. Ultimately he decided to content himself with an observer from the United States Embassy in Paris. He did, however, send Bliss to sit with the Permanent Military Representatives.

Lloyd George, too, felt that the time had come when the Allied and Associated Powers, separately if not together, should review their war aims in the light of the new situation created by the Russian Revolution. He decided to prepare a statement designed not so much to impress world opinion as to ensure continued support for his government from the trade unions and to scotch rumors to the effect that the war was being prolonged in order to provide British capitalists with new sources of raw materials in the Ottoman Empire and the German colonies. By consulting both his Cabinet colleagues and the leaders of the Opposition, he made sure that his statement was not likely to be repudiated by any British government which might be in office at the end of the war.

Lloyd George delivered his speech at a conference of trade union delegates in London on January 5, 1918.[21] So far as the terms of an eventual settlement with Germany were concerned, his proposals did not differ greatly from those foreshadowed a year earlier in the Allied reply to President Wilson's "peace note." He did, however, make it clear that Britain would not willingly become a party to any attempt to foist on Germany a system of government not chosen by the Germans themselves. He also expressed the opinion that the German colonies ought to be administered after the war in accordance with the wishes of the native inhabitants, as expressed through tribal chiefs and councils, and that their exploitation for the benefit of European governments or capitalists ought to be prevented. He dealt tactfully with French demands on Germany by avoiding any discussion of the historical background of the French claim to Alsace and

Lorraine and advancing the argument that France had every reason to ask for the return of territories whose incorporation in the German Empire after the Franco-Prussian War had poisoned her relations with Germany for nearly half a century. Similarly, he did not dwell on the ethnic basis of Italian demands on Austro-Hungary but promised British support for claims to territories racially or linguistically Italian, insofar as such claims were "legitimate." While disclaiming any intention of disrupting Austro-Hungary, he insisted that "genuine" self-government should be granted to those national groups within the Austro-Hungarian Empire that desired it. Finally, Russia's renunciation of her claim to Constantinople and the Straits enabled him to drop his former demand for the expulsion of the Turks from Europe and affirm the right of the sultan or his successors to retain control of "the homelands of the Turkish race." He offered to discuss the future of Arabia, Armenia, Mesopotamia, Palestine, and Syria in the light of circumstances to which existing agreements between the Allies no longer applied.

When this speech was delivered, President Wilson had begun to put his own declaration of war aims into its final shape. His proposals—the famous Fourteen Points—were drafted independently of Lloyd George's, but Lloyd George and House had discussed the subject of war aims when House was in Europe some weeks earlier.[22] On reading a report of Lloyd George's speech on the day of its delivery, the President thought the views expressed in it so like his own that he wondered for a time whether there was anything left for him to say. House convinced him that, on the contrary, he had everything to gain by making his speech at a moment when Lloyd George had paved the way for it. Accordingly, he delivered it as an address to Congress on January 8.

Unlike Lloyd George's, the President's speech was not a definitive statement of national policy. Wilson himself referred to his proposals, in a later speech, as a "provisional sketch." When gathering his material, he drew heavily on the services of a panel of American experts on political geography, economics, and international law. He also consulted foreign envoys and submitted the text of his speech to the Secretary of State. But the relationship between President and Congress was so different from that between Prime Minister and Parliament that Wilson—in any case reluctant to admit outsiders to his confidence—did not have the same opportunities as Lloyd

George of satisfying himself that his principles would be endorsed by the legislature when the time came to apply them. About all that could be confidently predicted of his proposals was that since they involved a radical departure from the American tradition of aloofness from the affairs of the Old World, they would not be accepted without a struggle.

Despite striking resemblances between the Fourteen Points and the aims outlined by Lloyd George in his speech to the trade unions, there were marked divergences between British and American attitudes toward some of the issues involved. Both the British and the Americans thought, for example, that there could be no lasting peace in Europe until Germany ceased to believe that she could dominate Europe by force of arms; the difference between them was that while the British were at least outwardly content to hope that somehow or other the Germans could be "turned aside from schemes of military conquest," the President's views were colored by the opinion of his experts that Germany could be forced, by the threat of economic penalties after the war and of exclusion from the League of Nations, to "renounce imperialist policies" and perhaps even to become a peace-loving democratic state.[23] The problem of the German colonies, too, was approached by the British and the Americans from different angles. The British thought, or at least professed to think, that after the war the German colonies ought to be administered, as India had been administered since the middle of the nineteenth century, primarily in the interests of the native inhabitants and that the first duty of their rulers should be to prevent their exploitation by foreigners. The President and his advisers believed that, on the contrary, the colonies ought to be exploited for the benefit of "the society of nations" but that the rights of the inhabitants should be safeguarded by strict regulations in regard to conditions of labor, profits, and taxes.[24]

Again, the President spoke of the removal of economic barriers and the freedom of the seas, but he did not mean that if his proposals were adopted, the United States would stop taxing imports or that the seas would in fact be free. According to a commentary prepared under the direction of House, all that was meant was that no member of the proposed League of Nations would be allowed to treat any other member better or worse than the rest in the matter of tariffs or port restrictions and that the right of search would be exercised in the interests of the League of Nations rather than individual states.[25] Yet many Americans, including eventually the President himself, interpreted the freedom of the seas quite differently.

The President's speech was widely acclaimed in the United States. The New York *Tribune*, hitherto critical of his policies, praised him highly for pledging his country to fight for the liberation of Belgians, Poles, Rumanians, and Serbs. Comparing him with Lincoln, the *Tribune* depicted him as struggling to free "the long suffering populations of Alsace-Lorraine and Italy Irridenta" from "a slavery worse a thousand times than that of the negro." [26] With reservations, the speech was also well received in Britain and France, though not in Italy.* It did not, however, make a favorable impression on the Russians, nor did it persuade the Germans to seek a negotiated peace without delay. The President had therefore to reconcile himself to the knowledge that he could not hope to exercise much influence on the conduct of the war until he had a substantial army in the field.

At the end of the third week in January the Permanent Military Representatives submitted the proposals they had been asked to make.[27] They reported that the safety of France and Italy in 1918 could be assumed on certain conditions, of which the most important were that the Allies should be steadily reinforced from the United States, that the whole of the Western Front should be treated as "a single strategic field of action," and that Allied reserves should be disposed accordingly. They did not think that any offensive action which the Allied and Associated Powers could take on the Western Front before the end of the year would be decisive unless some unforeseeable contingency arose, but they strongly recommended a "decisive offensive" against Turkey. For this no reinforcement from the Western Front of the troops already in Palestine and Mesopotamia would be needed.

The Supreme War Council considered these recommendations at the end of January and the beginning of February. The proposal to renew the offensive against the Turks was adopted in spite of objections from Robertson, who displeased Lloyd George by making his protest at a formal meeting after the project had been discussed at

* In Point IX of the Fourteen Points, the President proposed that the frontiers of Italy should be redrawn "along clearly recognizable lines of nationality." This adjustment would have given the Italians only part of their claim under the Treaty of London, at the cost of saddling them with an indefensible frontier in the Alps.

length in London. Robertson explained afterward that he had felt that if he remained silent, he might expose himself to reproaches similar to those incurred by Fisher in consequence of the Dardanelles fiasco.[28]

The council then turned to the proposed creation of a General Reserve for the Western, Balkan, and Italian fronts. Even Robertson agreed that such a reserve was desirable in principle; the difficulty was to decide who should control it. A committee of Chiefs of Staff or their equivalent seemed the obvious answer, but this would not have been a practical arrangement since it was essential that the reserve should be controlled by men who could be summoned at short notice. The Permanent Military Representatives satisfied that condition, but the French did not consider that their Permanent Military Representative, General Maxime Weygand, had the necessary standing. Eventually it was agreed that the General Reserve should be controlled by an Executive War Board consisting of Foch, Wilson, Cadorna, and Bliss, with Foch as chairman.[29] Wilson, Cadorna, and Bliss were already working under one roof at Versailles, and Foch could be brought from Paris in half an hour.

Finally, the council discussed a proposed extension of the British front in France and Flanders. In 1917 the French were holding a front three times as long as the British with troops not more than a third stronger. They agreed that the disparity was justified, to some extent, by the strength of the German forces opposite the British front, the lack of room for maneuver behind it, and the importance of the industrial objectives which the British were defending.[30] Even so, they thought the burden ought to be more evenly divided. In deference to their wishes, Haig had agreed in October to extend his front, when the Flanders offensive was over, to Barisis, just south of the Oise, and this adjustment was completed by the end of January. The French now wished him to make a further extension of some thirty miles to Berry-au-Bac, a village on the Aisne where there had been fierce fighting in 1914 and 1917. Finding that this did not suit Haig, the Permanent Military Representatives proposed a compromise by which he would make an extension of roughly a dozen miles to a point where the Ailette, a tributary of the Oise, crosses the Laon-Soissons road. Lloyd George began by defending Haig's refusal to go beyond Barisis but afterward supported the Permanent Military Representatives' solution in the belief that Haig had agreed to it.[31]

The council then adopted the Ailette plan, with the proviso that their resolution to that effect was not to be regarded as "an order requiring immediate action." [32] Clearly Haig did not so regard it, for in fact he never extended his front beyond the point reached at the end of January.

During the next few weeks the British government was fiercely assailed by its critics in the press and Parliament and in clubs and drawing rooms. The War Cabinet was accused, among other crimes, of forcing Haig to extend his front against his will, starving him of troops, and acquiescing in measures which threatened to put British troops under the control of foreigners. At the same time Robertson, asserting that the British Military Representative at Versailles ought to be no more than the "subordinate and representative" of the Chief of the Imperial General Staff, raised strong objections to the arrangements made for control of the General Reserve, although he had acquiesced in them at the Supreme War Council's meeting.

Lloyd George and his colleagues knew that they had not forced Haig to extend his front against his will. The decision to push his right as far as Barisis was his own, and the War Cabinet had studiously refrained from ordering him to go to Berry-au-Bac or the Ailette. In view of the efforts they had made to replace his losses despite acute manpower problems, they believed, too, that they could not justly be accused of starving him of troops.

On the other hand, the complaints made by Robertson and others about the General Reserve and the relationship between the Chief of the Imperial General Staff and the British Permanent Military Representative raised an issue of some importance. The government could not deny that the British Military Representative ought to be subject to guidance from the Chief of the Imperial General Staff as military spokesman of the Army Council, for that was obvious. But it seemed to the government equally obvious that such guidance must conform with the needs of a new situation. The point which Robertson and his fellow critics seemed to miss was that Britain had joined a coalition of Allied and Associated Powers and that this imposed new duties and new responsibilities on the government's military adviser. The Chief of the Imperial General Staff was now responsible for advising ministers not only in their capacity as members of the War Cabinet, but also in their capacity as members of the Supreme War Council. He was also responsible for ensuring that the British Permanent Military Representative was correctly briefed. At the same time, he must be prepared to submit his plans to the Supreme War Council for approval and comment. If Robertson were unable or unwilling to discharge these additional duties and responsibilities, then he ought, in Lloyd George's opinion, to make way for a successor more diligent or more amenable.

The fact remained that even if these points were conceded by the government's critics, the existence of the Executive War Board would still deprive the Chief of the Imperial General Staff of immediate and effective control of the British component of the General Reserve. But this did not seem to the government a valid objection, for the same could be said of any reserve which might be put at the disposal of a commander in the field. If indeed an arrangement which put British troops under the strategic control of a committee headed by a Frenchman was unconstitutional, then the constitution ought, in the government's view, to be changed in the interests of common sense. The French, as Lloyd George pointed out, had not found it impossible to put their First Army at Haig's disposal during the Flanders offensive in 1917.

However, Lloyd George's conviction that his critics were wrong did not make their attentions less troublesome. Some of the most telling attacks made on the government in connection with the General Reserve and the Executive War Board were the work of Lieutenant Colonel Charles à Court Repington, military correspondent of the right-wing *Morning Post*. Repington was a man of great promise who had been forced to leave the Army long before the war in consequence of an affair of honor which culminated in a bitter dispute with his brother officers and an abrupt severance of his relations with Henry Wilson, formerly one of his closest friends. He had acted as Haldane's confidential emissary when the first tentative approaches were made to the French in 1905. He was on good terms with Haig and Robertson, who were suspected of inspiring some of his pronouncements.

On February 8 a telegram sent by Repington from Paris, which referred in disobliging terms to "decisions of the recent inter-Allied War Council regarding the control of British troops in the field," was published in the *Morning Post* and reprinted in an evening newspaper, the *Globe*.[33] The *Globe* expressed the hope that the House of Commons, and Asquith in particular, would challenge a move which threatened the supremacy of Haig and Robertson. Two days later the editor of the *Morning Post* submitted to the official Press Bureau a long article in which Repington criticized in detail resolutions adopted by the Supreme War Council at a meeting of which only an intentionally uninformative account had been released to the press.[34] The editor was warned that the article contravened the Defense of the Realm Act and was contrary to the spirit of a recent request to the press to refrain from public discussion of the General Reserve.[35] Nevertheless, it appeared in the newspaper on the following morning with only slight amendments.

Repington's disclosures revealed knowledge which he could only have gained from a privileged informant. They therefore made a powerful impression on men who might otherwise have been reluctant to take Lloyd George's part in a quarrel with the General Staff. After reading the telegram and comment in the *Globe*, Milner advised Lloyd George to rid himself without delay of Robertson, if necessary even at the cost of losing Haig as well.[36] In the light of the article in the *Morning Post* a few days later, he went further. On February 12 he hinted that he might resign if the government did not change its military adviser.[37]

Lloyd George could not afford to disregard these warnings from one of his most influential supporters. At the same time, he was reluctant to break entirely with Robertson, whom he regarded as a poor strategist but an able administrator and a good organizer. Moreover, he feared that Derby, as well as Haig, might resign if Robertson were dismissed and that possibly as many as three or four Unionist members of the government might follow Derby's lead.[38] On February 9 he summoned Henry Wilson from Versailles, sounded Derby and also Haig about possible changes at the War Office, and made up his mind to offer Robertson the post of British Military Representative, on the understanding that he would sit with Foch, Cadorna, and Bliss on the Executive War Board and that Wilson would take his place as the government's military adviser in London.[39]

Robertson, scenting a trap, refused to purchase a share in the control of the General Reserve at the cost of becoming Wilson's spokesman. Lloyd George then made a further attempt to escape the odium of dismissing him: he gave him the choice of going to Versailles while retaining his seat on the Army Council and remaining as Chief of the Imperial General Staff without the special powers conferred on him in 1915 to foil Kitchener. Again Robertson declined. Thereupon Lloyd George, still reluctant to have it said that he had rid himself of Robertson in order to put Wilson in his place, offered the post of Chief of the Imperial General Staff to Plumer. Plumer excused himself, adding that his sympathies were with Robertson. This left Lloyd George with no choice but to tell the king's private secretary, Lord Stamfordham, that either Robertson or the government must go.[40] On Saturday, February 16, the government announced after Lloyd George had spent an hour with the king that Sir William Robertson had been replaced as Chief of the Imperial General Staff by Sir Henry Wilson.

Thus the agile-minded Wilson succeeded the dour but not unattractive Robertson as senior military member of the Army Council and the government's principal military adviser. As a youth, Wilson had failed twice for Woolwich and three times for Sandhurst before entering the Army by the back door of the militia. On making up his mind to marry on a subaltern's pay and a small allowance from his father, he had qualified for the Staff College and gone on to become the youngest staff officer in the British Army. He had served with distinction in the South African War and had made outstanding contributions to the organization of the General Staff and the preparation of the Expeditionary Force for a European war but had not done particularly well during a brief spell as a corps commander on the Western Front. In the spring of 1914, when the Ulster crisis threatened to undo his work by embroiling the Expeditionary Force in a civil war, he had done his best to avert a clash by warning the Secretary of State for War that the Ulstermen were determined to resist coercion and at the same time impressing on them and their supporters the importance of staying within the law and avoiding provocation. As Permanent Military Representative at Versailles he had proclaimed himself a convinced Westerner but had nonetheless backed Lloyd George's policy of defeating the Turks before attempting a knockout blow against the Germans.

On the day of Robertson's dismissal, Haig presided over a conference in France before leaving for England. He was warned by his chief intelligence officer that the greater part of the German reserves in the West were opposite his front but told his army commanders that he thought the main effort would be against the French.[41] On the following day he reported to Lloyd George that he expected the British front to be attacked and was anxious lest any of his reserves should be moved away from it. Lloyd George assured him that he could trust Foch, as chairman of the Executive War Board, to make the right decision.[42]

During the next few weeks Haig refused to contribute to the General Reserve, on the ground that he was short of troops and had agreed with Pétain on a scheme of mutual reinforcement. Wilson told the government that he thought Haig was wrong in principle and was acting against his own best interests but that it would be better to do without the General Reserve than quarrel with him on the eve of a crucial attack.[43] Since Pétain also withheld his quota and was backed by Clemenceau, the Supreme War Council had to save its face by pretending that all the British and French divisions in Italy formed part of the General Reserve.[44]

By the end of February the Germans were making visible preparations for a big attack between the Scarpe and the Oise, in the sectors held by the British Third and Fifth armies. Their plan was to reverse the verdict of the Marne, before the Americans arrived in strength, by smashing first the British Expeditionary Force and then the whole of the French armies. They believed that a decision must be gained in 1918 because their allies would not be able to hold out for another year or more, even if their own armies could.[45]

Despite accurate forecasts by his intelligence officers of the direction and timing of the German offensive, Haig made very inadequate preparations to meet it. He gave Gough's Fifth Army only fourteen divisions to defend a front of forty-two miles on either side of the Somme and as far south as Barisis. The Third and First armies, on Gough's left, were each allotted sixteen divisions on fronts of twenty-eight and thirty-three miles respectively; the Second Army received as many divisions as the Fifth to defend a twenty-three-mile front in Flanders which was not immediately threatened and was unlikely to be attacked until fine weather dried the ground. In comparison with the other armies and in relation to the length of the front for which he was responsible, Gough was also poorly provided with engineer companies and labor battalions. The result was that his rear positions were still far from complete when the long-expected crisis came.[46]

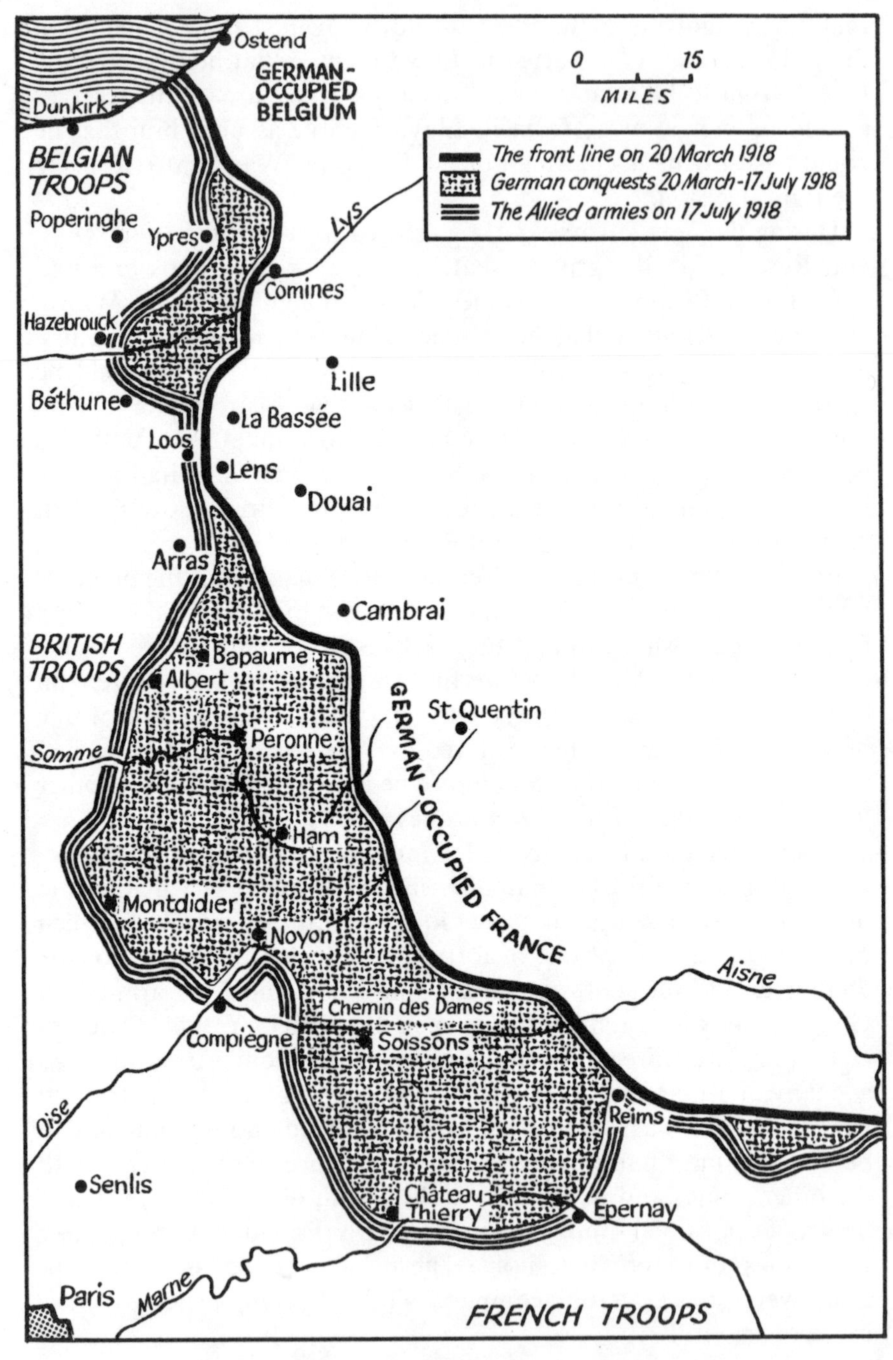

THE GERMAN SPRING AND SUMMER OFFENSIVES (1918)

The Germans launched their offensive on March 21 at the place and almost at the hour predicted by Haig's staff. By the evening of March 24 they had advanced up to twenty miles on a front of fifty miles. In some places fog helped them push through gaps which would otherwise have been commanded by crossfire, but the British were so thin on the ground, especially in Gough's sector, that even without the fog the situation could have been saved only by the prompt arrival of fresh troops.

In this respect Haig was handicapped by the absence of the British and French divisions which Foch would have placed in reserve at Amiens had Haig and Pétain carried out the orders of the Executive War Board.[47] As it was, Pétain responded generously to Haig's call for help, but the first of his reinforcing divisions did not reach Gough's front until the third day of the battle. Two more French divisions arrived on the following day, but without their artillery and transport. In the meantime, Gough had to depend on his own reserves and on the one British division which reached him from GHQ Reserve before he was relieved of his command. Gough was afterward exonerated by a War Office inquiry of blame for the setback to his army and was pronounced eligible for a fresh command.

On Saturday, March 23, the British government learned that the Germans had broken through the Fifth Army's forward and battle zones and that Gough was still falling back. Lloyd George urged the War Office to scrape up all the reinforcements it could find, including 50,000 youths under nineteen years of age whom the government had promised not to send abroad except in a national emergency. The War Cabinet decided that Milner should go to France, see Clemenceau, and do his best to restore the authority of the Supreme War Council in order to ensure the creation of a strategic reserve effectively controlled by Foch. Lloyd George would stay in London to direct the flow of reinforcements.

When Milner reached Versailles on March 24, the Germans were less than thirty miles from Amiens. Haig wrote on the following day that "it could only be a question of time" before the British and French armies were driven apart;[48] Pétain told Clemenceau on March 26 that the enemy would first defeat the British in the field and then defeat the French.[49]

On Monday, March 25, Wilson crossed the Channel in time to reach Haig's headquarters before noon. He found Haig so much shaken by his setback that he was willing to accept almost any arrangement which would bring French troops promptly to his front.[50]

Wilson arrived at Versailles soon after 8 P.M., saw Milner about 9 P.M., and later that evening visited Foch in Paris. Wilson and Foch agreed that at an Anglo-French conference to be held on the following day at Doullens, Wilson should propose that Foch be asked by the British and French governments to "co-ordinate the military action" of Haig's and Pétain's forces.[51]

Wilson urged this policy on Milner during the journey to Doullens. Milner pointed out that his instructions from the War Cabinet did not cover the appointment of a coordinator, although undoubtedly the British government would like to see Foch in effective control of a revived General Reserve.

On arrival at Doullens, Milner found that Haig, sobered by his experiences and primed by his talk with Wilson, was willing to work with Foch.[52] Since Pétain had begun to seem to Clemenceau a defeatist, while Foch was full of fight, the circumstances favored Wilson's proposal. After some discussion, the statesmen agreed that Foch should "co-ordinate the action of the Allied armies on the Western Front." He was to "work to this end with the Commanders-in-Chief," who were asked to "furnish him with all necessary information." [53]

This formula did not confer on Foch the powers of a supreme commander. Even so, his appointment substantially reduced the enemy's chances of driving a wedge between the British and French armies by exploiting the conflict between Haig's concern with the Channel ports and Pétain's with Paris. Foch, hitherto not an outstandingly successful commander in the field, rose to the level of his new responsibilities by insisting that everything must be done to ensure that the Germans did not separate the two armies by taking Amiens.

Almost simultaneously, the British addressed an urgent appeal to President Wilson. On March 21 there were about 300,000 American troops in France. One fully trained American division was in the line, two divisions were training in quiet sectors of the French front, and a fourth was in reserve. The British asked that all four divisions be used in an active role and that for three months from April 1 120,000 infantrymen and machine gunners a month should be sent from the United States. The President, in consultation with the Department of the Army, agreed in principle to send infantry and machine gunners at that rate, and indeed offered to extend the period from three months to four, but stipulated that Pershing should have a free hand to allot the troops as they arrived to British, French, or American divisions.[54]

Pershing was told by the British of this offer during a visit to London on April 22. At first he refused to believe that the President could have made such a concession without consulting him.[55] After studying the proposals in detail, he pointed out that if all the ships available to rush American troops across the Atlantic were used for months on end to carry only infantry and machine gunners, the date when he could form a balanced force would be indefinitely postponed. After a good deal of discussion it was agreed that in May, and again in June, priority should go to the infantry and machine gunners of six divisions. Any further shipping would be devoted first to the balance of the six divisions and only when those divisions were complete to the transport of more infantry and machine gunners. Lloyd George, when reporting this decision to Washington for the information of the United States government, added that such problems could be solved with much less difficulty if the United States were represented at meetings of the Supreme War Council by a plenipotentiary such as House.[56]

In the event the President's and Lloyd George's figures were far exceeded. As the result of prodigious efforts by the American, British, and inter-Allied authorities in the United States, 949,601 combatant troops and divisional or nondivisional details crossed the Atlantic between April and July. Later additions brought the ration strength of the United States forces in France on November 1 to 1,868,000. More than half these troops were carried in British-owned or British-controlled ships. This remarkable spurt, coming after an almost inconceivably slow start, enabled Pershing to form some forty large divisions and to contribute more than twenty divisions to the final push against the Germans between September and November. On the other hand, his hope of commanding a force capable in all respects of playing an independent role was not fulfilled. Even at the end of the war he had, with trifling exceptions, no American-made tanks or field guns, and all his aircraft were of foreign design, although some of them had been built in the United States.

Within a few days of the Doullens Conference, Foch complained that his powers were insufficient. He pointed out that his authority to coordinate the actions of Haig's and Pétain's armies did not enable him to initiate preparations for future action. Accordingly, at a conference at Beauvais on April 3, to which Bliss and Pershing, as well as the British and the French, were summoned, Foch was charged with the "strategic direction" of military operations on the Western front.[57] The British government did not agree until some ten days later that he should be called Allied Commander in Chief, but from that moment he became, in effect, Supreme Allied Commander in the West.

A day or two after the Beauvais Conference, the first phase of the German offensive came to a standstill. Both the Fifth and the Third armies had retreated with heavy losses, but the enemy's losses were still heavier. Amiens was under long-range artillery fire but had not fallen, and communications between London and Paris by way of Calais and Boulogne were intact. Above all, no gap had opened between the British and French armies.

On April 9 the Germans launched an attack north of La Bassée with eight divisions. It fell on a sector held by a Portuguese corps which was being relieved by British troops and had only one division in the line. The Germans, exploiting an unexpected success, advanced about six miles on the first day and extended their front of attack to left and right. On the southern flank the British held firm at Givenchy. Farther north, the Germans pushed through Merville, Armentières, and Bailleul to threaten the railway linking Ypres with the British and French sectors south of the Lys. Haig at first regarded the attack as only a demonstration but by the third day of the battle was exhorting his troops, in his famous "backs to the wall" order, to "fight on to the end." In the light of ominous reports from his headquarters, the statesmen felt bound to consider whether, in the event of a serious reverse, the Expeditionary Force should join the French in a general retreat to the south, as in 1914, or fall back on the Channel ports. At an Anglo-French conference at Abbeville on May 2, Foch confessed when cornered that he would rather lose the Channel ports than uncover "the battlefield of the Allies" but insisted that the need for so desperate a choice would never arise.[58]

By that date the danger had in fact receded. About the end of April the Germans, hampered as Haig had been in 1917 by the softness of the ground and the consequent difficulty of bringing up equipment and supplies, decided to break off their offensive in Flanders, turn their attention to the French front on the Aisne, and strike a further blow at the British when they judged that the Allies had used up their reserves. The Flanders offensive had, however, already involved them in such difficulties that nearly a month elapsed before they were ready to pass to the next stage. Moreover, the Allied blockade had begun to tell not only on civilians but also on the troops. German commanders complained that some of their men, instead of following up successes, stopped to look for British rations. They might have added that these were so much better than German rations that the failure of the U-boat offensive could no longer be disguised.

A few days after the Abbeville Conference, the British government was attacked on familiar ground but from an unexpected quarter. In a letter published in a number of newspapers on May 7 Major General Sir Frederick Maurice, until the end of April Director of Military Operations at the War Office, accused ministers of misleading the House of Commons.[59] In particular, he charged Lloyd George with making a statement on April 9 which wrongly implied that Haig's fighting strength on the eve of the German offensive in March was greater than in 1917 and Bonar Law with incorrectly stating on April 23 that the Supreme War Council had not dealt with the "particular matter" of the extension of Haig's line to Barisis. He claimed, too, that Lloyd George had misinformed the House about the number of white divisions in Mesopotamia and Egypt.

Lloyd George and Bonar Law were amazed that Maurice, long Robertson's right-hand man, should have put himself in the wrong by writing a letter which, even if his allegations were true, was a flagrant breach of discipline. They offered to appoint a panel of judges to investigate the charges. Asquith brushed the proposal aside and pressed for an inquiry by a select committee.

Maurice's first charge against Lloyd George is said to have been based on the knowledge that 86,000 British troops in Italy had been inadvertently included in figures prepared by a department of the War Office to enable a junior minister to answer a question bearing on the subject of Lloyd George's statement and that the mistake had never been disclosed to the House although the government must be presumed to know that it had been made.[60] If that is so, the indictment was very badly framed. Lloyd George had said on April 9 that the army in France was considerably stronger on January 1, 1918, than on January 1, 1917. That statement was literally true, and its truth could not be affected by a statement made by another minister on another occasion.* Whether it bore the implication Maurice put upon it could only be a matter of opinion. Even if it did, Maurice could not hope to convict Lloyd George of wilfull misrepresentation in view of the notorious difficulty of defining fighting strength in terms applicable to a war in which the old criterion of rifle strength had ceased to be valid.†

Maurice's attack on Bonar Law was still wider of the mark. Maurice implied, by claiming that he was "at Versailles" when the Supreme War Council decided the matter of the extension of Haig's line, that he had attended the meeting in question. Had he in fact been present, he would have known that the matter discussed was not the extension to Barisis, which Haig had settled with Pétain earlier, but the proposed further extension to Berry-au-Bac or the Ailette. That was not the "particular matter" referred to by Bonar Law in the statement which Maurice challenged.

The motion for the appointment of a select committee was debated in the House of Commons on May 9. Neither the government nor the Opposition raised the question of the inclusion or omission of the troops in Italy. The gist of Lloyd George's argument was that the officer on whom the War Cabinet had been accustomed until the end of April to rely for information about the strength of the forces in France was Maurice himself, that for three weeks after April 9 Maurice had attended meetings of the War Cabinet and had seen or spoken to its members almost daily, and that throughout the whole of that time he had never suggested that the statement made by the Prime Minister on April 9 was wrong and ought to be corrected. He had challenged that statement only after his removal from his post, when he no longer had access to the figures and could know nothing

* According to figures quoted by Lloyd George in his *War Memoirs* and to official statistics published after the war, the ration strength of the British Expeditionary Force was 376,000 higher on January 1, 1918, than on January 1, 1917; the ration strength exclusive of certain nonmilitary labor units was about 237,000 higher. These figures included a proportion of noncombatants which tended to grow as the Army came to depend more and more on tanks, aircraft, and other mechanical devices which needed men to maintain and service them.

† On the basis of figures quoted by Lloyd George himself in his defense, the combatant strength of the BEF, as defined by the War Office but after deduction of the troops in Italy, would seem to have been 41,000 lower on January 1, 1918, than on January 1, 1917 (not 45,000 higher as Lloyd George believed or claimed to believe). On the other hand, Haig had more tanks and aircraft in 1918 than in 1917.

about them not already within his knowledge when he was Director of Military Operations. Turning to the number of white divisions in Mesopotamia and Egypt, Lloyd George said that he had relied on a communication made to him by the Chief of the Imperial General Staff in Maurice's presence and afterward reduced to writing and shown to Maurice; that if the information was incorrect, Maurice had failed in his duty by not saying so while he was still at the War Office; and that if it was incorrect because a promised substitution of Indian for British troops had not been punctually carried out, then the military authorities must bear the blame. As for the allegation against Bonar Law, Lloyd George had no difficulty in showing that Maurice was guilty not merely of getting his facts wrong, but of bolstering an unjust charge with a constructive falsehood.

Since Lloyd George was, on his own confession, apt to be led astray by figures,[61] doubtless a good deal could have been said on the other side. But the shortcomings of Maurice's case were so glaring that Asquith must bitterly have regretted his decision to challenge the government on the strength of it. The motion was not supported by a single Unionist and was defeated by 293 votes to 106. Asquith emerged from the debate as leader of a party which had ceased to be capable of either effective government or effective opposition.

Eighteen days later the Germans launched an attack in morning mist on a thirty-mile front between Rheims and Soissons. The French, although not greatly outnumbered, had most of their troops in forward positions and were overwhelmed by a short bombardment which took them by surprise. The Germans advanced up to twelve miles on the first day. By the end of the month they had taken nearly 40,000 prisoners and were less than forty miles from the outskirts of Paris. The British, their confidence in the French Army shaken by a setback even more spectacular than that which had overtaken their own Fifth Army, discussed ways and means of withdrawing the whole Expeditionary Force from France should the need arise.[62] Lloyd George was for fighting on, even if the French collapsed; Wilson proposed that in any case Haig should shorten his lines, at the cost of abandoning Dunkirk and Ypres, by retreating behind inundations to the neighborhood of St.-Omer.

Milner, who had taken over the War Office when Derby went to Paris as ambassador in April, joined Wilson early in June in pressing this proposal on the French.[63] Foch remained unalterably opposed to voluntary withdrawals. At a moment when the Germans had reached Château-Thierry for the second time in the war and the sound of their guns could be heard from the terrace at Versailles, he astonished the British by insisting on preparations for a counter-offensive.[64]

Lloyd George, too, refused to believe that defeat was possible. In the second week of June he predicted that the situation would remain critical for another two months and would then improve.[65]

On June 9 the Germans launched a fresh attack on a twenty-mile front between Noyon and Montdidier but were checked by a counterattack after advancing about three and a half miles. In the middle of July they made a further attempt to overcome the French, as the preliminary to a renewed assault on the British front in Flanders, by attacking east and west of Rheims. Foch, forewarned by his intelligence officers, assembled eighteen French and two American divisions in wooded country near Villers-Cotterêts, adding two British divisions in reserve. On July 18 this force, supported by massed tanks, moved forward without a preliminary bombardment and fell on the western flank of the salient created by the German push to Château-Thierry and across the Marne. The Germans, convinced until too late that the French had committed all their reserves to the defensive battle, were surprised and caught off-balance. After some days of desperate fighting, to which the Americans and the British made important contributions, they succeeded in withdrawing with heavy losses, but with the bulk of their forces still intact. But the drain on their reserves was so great that they were obliged to countermand the offensive in Flanders on which they had been counting to give them a decision.

Meanwhile, relations between Soviet Russia and the outside world had reached a difficult stage.

The broad situation in Russia after the ratification of the Treaty of Brest-Litovsk was that Russian Poland, Estonia, Finland, and Latvia all had achieved nominal independence but in fact were controlled largely by the Germans. The Bolshevik government had promised the Germans access to Russian territory for the purpose of buying food and raw materials urgently needed by the Central Powers; but it had little or no authority east of the Urals, and some of the most productive parts of European Russia were outside its jurisdiction. The Ukraine had proclaimed itself an independent republic and had

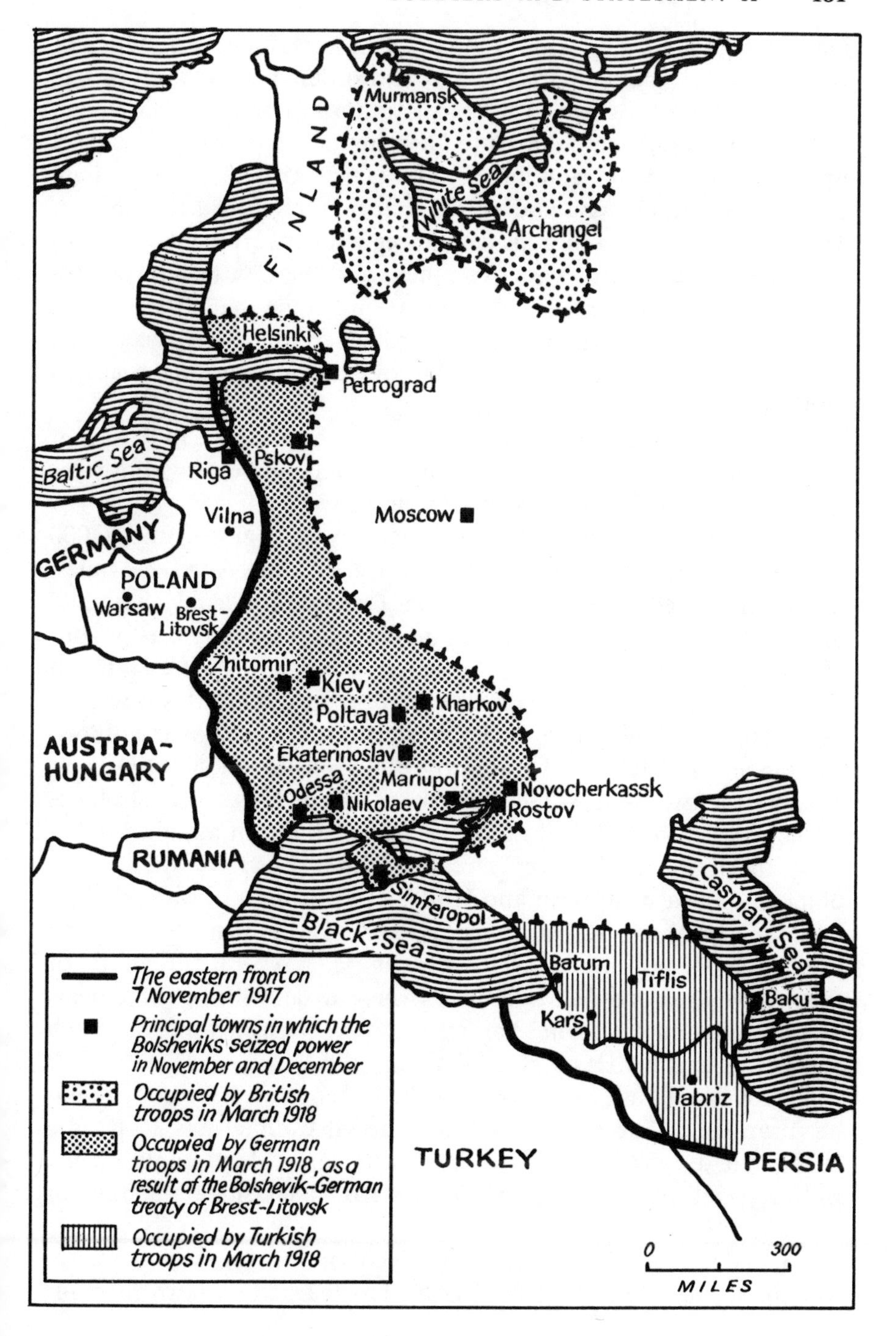

THE EASTERN FRONT (1917–1918)

made a separate treaty with the Central Powers. Its government discouraged economic penetration and had ordered the inhabitants to surrender stocks of grain to the local authorities or to destroy them, rather than allow them to fall into German hands. Bessarabia had set up the independent republic of Moldavia. Armenia, Azerbaijan, Daghestan, and Georgia had united to form the Federal Republic of Transcaucasia, but each had its own regional government, and attitudes toward the Bolshevik government and the Central Powers differed from government to government and sometimes from day to day. Even in regions nominally controlled by the Bolsheviks there was much opposition to the central government from the peasants and sometimes from local Soviets.

The situation was further complicated by the presence in Russia of large numbers of Austro-Hungarian nationals, some of whom were loyal subjects of the emperor, while others were not.

While Russia was still at war, a Czechoslovak Legion, some 40,000 to 60,000 strong and intended for service with the Russian armies, had been formed on Russian soil from Czechs and Slovaks who had lived in Russia before the war or had entered the country as prisoners of war or deserters. Later the self-styled Czechoslovak National Council, which was responsible for the organization of this force, arranged that it should move to the Western Front. The Soviet authorities agreed that it should travel by the Trans-Siberian Railway to Vladivostok, where it would embark in Allied ships. Long stretches of the Trans-Siberian Railway were, however, out of action.

By the terms of the Treaty of Brest-Litovsk, the Russians were obliged to release Austrian and Hungarian prisoners of war who had remained loyal to the Hapsburg dynasty. These men regarded the Czechoslovak legionaries as traitors. In May several trainloads of them passed through Chelyabinsk, where a detachment of Czechs was awaiting entrainment. The result was a clash in which a Czech was struck and his Hungarian assailant killed.

Thereupon Trotsky decreed that the Czechoslovak Legion should be disarmed.[66] The Czechoslovak National Council passed on the order, but the men refused to obey it, occupied key points on the railway, and eventually gained control of a considerable tract of western Siberia.

To understand the sequel, it is necessary to go back to early March. At that time the Bolshevik leaders feared that notwithstanding their negotiations with the Germans, German troops might march on Petrograd from Finland. An advance from that direction might also threaten Murmansk, where there were large dumps of war matériel shipped by the Allies. Accordingly, Trotsky ordered the local authorities to cooperate with the Allies against the Germans.[67] In response to an appeal from the Murmansk Soviet, the British sent a cruiser to Murmansk and invited the French and the Americans to do the same. The local authorities then put their naval force of three destroyers at the disposal of the Allied and Associated Powers for use against German submarines off the Murman Coast, while British marines joined Russian soldiers in opposing German and Finnish forces on land.

Thus the Allied and Associated Powers intervened in northwest Russia not as enemies of the Bolshevik government, but in accordance with its wishes. However, as time went on, it became apparent to the Bolshevik leaders that they had underestimated the resistance their doctrines would meet not only outside but also inside Russia. In June a bitter quarrel between the Bolshevik Party and its former supporters on the left wing of the Social Revolutionary Party inaugurated a reign of terror.[68] In these circumstances the central government became so distrustful of non-Communist intervention that it ordered the local authorities to expel the British, French, and American forces which had reached Murmansk since March. Instead of complying with the order, the Murmansk Soviet summoned a mass meeting which voted for a break with Petrograd and Moscow. The result was that the Allied forces on the spot found themselves in opposition to a government with which their respective countries were not at war and which the Allied and Associated Powers did not recognize.

There were also about 1,000,000 tons of undistributed stores at Archangel. In March the head of the British Military Mission there proposed that the Allies should send a substantial force for the purpose of removing or safeguarding the stores and securing the port as a place of egress for refugees. Early in May the British and the French decided that, if such a force were sent, elements of the Czechoslovak Legion still west of Omsk should be asked to make contact with it instead of trying to reach Vladivostok. In this way they could help form a more effective barrier against German penetration of northern Russia than the small force at Murmansk could provide, and eventually they would be withdrawn through Archangel or Murmansk.

This plan was never carried out so far as the Czechs were concerned, but British and French troops reached the neighborhood in June and July, occupied Archangel on August 2, and were joined on the following day by an American contingent. More American troops followed in September. The expedition was successful insofar as the stores at Archangel did not fall into German hands but in other respects achieved little.

In the extreme south the collapse of the Russian armies started a race between Turkish and German troops for the oil fields of the Caucasus. It also gave a new twist to the perennial problem of the defense of India. The British sent a small force (Dunsterforce) from Mesopotamia to northwest Persia to keep open the route from Baghdad to the Caspian, and a similar force (the Malleson Mission) from India to southern Turkmenistan to watch the railway from Krasnovodsk to Merv. Turkish troops, advancing through Armenia into Georgia, occupied Batum in April; the Germans, with farther to go, arrived in June. Georgia signed peace agreements with Germany and Turkey in that month, but the government was overthrown in July by an anti-German and anti-Turkish faction which appealed to the British for support. Dunsterforce responded by repelling a Turkish attack on Baku in August but withdrew in the following month to its base at Enzeli, in Persian territory.

There remained the problem of rescuing the Czechoslovak Legion and removing or safeguarding the stocks of war matériel, largely American in origin, which had accumulated at Vladivostok. This problem was linked, in the minds of Allied statesmen, with that of preventing Germany from adding to her strength by "gradually swallowing Russia like a boa constrictor." [69] Furthermore, in the early summer of 1918 it seemed possible to the British that France and Italy might drop out of the war. Lloyd George was determined that if they did, Britain should not follow their example but should carry on the struggle against the Central Powers with Japan and the United States as partners. To do so would be difficult if there were no front in Europe or Asia on which German and Allied forces were still in contact.[70] Intervention in Siberia offered the prospect of keeping such a front in being even if British forces had to withdraw from Western Europe. It would also provide opportunities for the employment of Japanese troops, hitherto debarred by distance and lack of shipping from making a major contribution to the war on land. Finally, the British hoped that if the Americans could be induced to share in such an enterprise, cooperation with the Japanese in a common task might help break down prejudices which threatened to stand in the way of a working alliance between Japan and the two Anglo-Saxon powers.

An expedition to Siberia was first mooted toward the end of 1917. In a joint note written in December, the Permanent Military Representatives stressed the importance of supporting "all national groups" in Russia who were willing to oppose the Germans but added that resistance could not be prolonged indefinitely unless the Allied and Associated Powers succeeded in opening a route to the Eastern Front either through the Caucasus or the Dardanelles or, alternatively, by way of Vladivostok and the Trans-Siberian Railway.[71] In the same month the British sounded the Americans and the Japanese about opening a route through Siberia, but they did not immediately press the matter when they found that the former were as dubious as the latter were enthusiastic.

In response to a proposal from their ambassador in Tokyo the British did, however, order the cruiser *Suffolk* from Hong Kong to Vladivostok. Her commanding officer confirmed reports to the effect that Russian armed forces in the neighborhood were in a state of anarchy and that anti-Bolshevik and anti-German elements in eastern Siberia were hoping for Allied support. In February the British government decided to grant a subsidy to a local leader named Grigori Semenov, who afterward became a puppet of the Japanese.

After the signing of the Treaty of Brest-Litovsk the French recommended very strongly that a Japanese expedition should be sent to Siberia without delay to extricate the Czechoslovak Legion so that it could move to the Western Front. The British were determined that no such expedition should be undertaken without American approval. They agreed to put the case to Washington but found, not unexpectedly, that President Wilson was not disposed to put Japanese troops into Siberia without knowing when—or even whether—they would come out again.[72] Well-informed observers on both sides of the Atlantic believed, too, that Japanese intervention might throw Russia into the arms of Germany.[73] The British, arguing that these objections would have less weight if the expedition were a joint one, then proposed that Japan, the United States, and Britain all should contribute to it. They thought it just possible that if this condition were fulfilled, the Bolshevik leaders might be persuaded to give tacit approval to the enterprise.

The Allies could not claim, however, that their sole purpose was to succor the Czechoslovak Legion. To the British, at any rate, it was clear that they must aim at advancing far enough into Russia to form a new front against the Germans.[74] Moreover, by midsummer it seemed unlikely that the legion would, in any case, be allowed to depart without a struggle. Almost from the beginning the legionaries had suspected that the Bolsheviks were arming released Austrian and Hungarian prisoners to fight them.[75] Their suspicions seemed to be confirmed when, at the end of June, a detachment of the legion fought its way into Vladivostok and claimed the capture of 600 Hungarians.[76]

Meanwhile, the Czech leader, Thomas Masaryk, had arrived in Washington to plead his cause at the highest level. On June 12 he lunched with House "to discuss Russia." [77] In the same month the United States government departed from its former policy of cautious support for Czechoslovak and Yugoslav aspirations by announcing that it favored not mere autonomy, but "complete independence of German or Austrian rule" for "all branches of the Slav race."

In July the President at last succumbed to the importunity of the Allies. At the end of the month he agreed with the Japanese that Britain, Japan, and the United States all should send troops to Siberia to help the Czechs and Slovaks "against the armed Austrian and German prisoners who are attacking them" and to "steady" any attempts at self-government or self-defense which the Russians might be willing to make with outside assistance.[78] This formula came dangerously near support for the policy of armed intervention against the Bolsheviks which the Allied and Associated Powers had hitherto been careful to disavow.

The Americans understood their agreement with the Japanese to mean that each country would contribute 7,000 troops.[79] This was not what the British had in mind. Their intention when they first made their proposal was that Britain and the United States should each contribute enough men to give the expedition an international character and that Japan should provide the rest of the troops needed to ensure success. One of the chief reasons for accepting Japanese cooperation in the first place was that Japan, alone among the Allied and Associated Powers, was able and willing to ship substantial forces to Vladivostok.

As things turned out, the Americans sent about 9,000 troops, noncombatants included.[80] The Japanese seized the excuse to increase the strength of their own contribution, ultimately to nearer 70,000 than 7,000.[81]

Preceded by a battalion from Hong Kong which the British had decided to send while the President was still hesitating, the international force began to go ashore in August. The American commander, Major General William S. Graves, was virtually restricted by his orders to a watching role, while the Japanese seemed more intent on making contact with anti-Communist Russians than on helping the Czechs. The Hong Kong battalion, on the other hand, made rapid progress. Soon after the middle of October it reached Omsk, 4,000 miles by rail from Vladivostok. When the Allied and Associated Powers granted Germany an armistice some three weeks later, a picket line of anti-Communist Russians, Czechs and Slovaks, British, Japanese, and United States troops and British and Japanese marines stretched right across Siberia from Vladivostok to the Urals.

Lloyd George claimed many years later that although the Siberian expedition disappointed Allied hopes of reviving the Eastern Front, it was justified as an insurance against the eastward expansion envisaged by the Germans.[82] After the armistice the Allied and Associated Powers did, in fact, form a new front on Russian soil, but for a different purpose.

The Allied Permanent Military Representatives had predicted in January that the Allied and Associated Powers would be able to strike a decisive blow on the Western Front in 1918 only if some unforeseeable contingency arose. When the unforeseeable contingency did arise some six months later, the Allies did not recognize it. The success of their counteroffensive in July ended German hopes of defeating the British and the French in turn before the Americans arrived in strength, but neither this fact nor the vast difference it made to the strategic outlook was apparent to their experts at the time. The Chief of the Imperial General Staff, in a memorandum written toward the end of July, stressed the importance of attempting a decisive stroke in the summer of 1919 and of accumulating machine guns, tanks, and aircraft for the purpose.[83] The French, too, believed that the decisive battle would be fought in 1919 and that it would be essentially a battle of tanks and aircraft.[84]

Foch was nonetheless determined that all possible pressure should be maintained on the enemy throughout the rest of the summer. He planned a series of offensives in which British, French, and American troops would take part. Haig proposed that the British contribution should begin with an offensive east of Amiens. Foch agreed but stipulated that the attack should be delivered on a wide front and that the French First Army should be added to Haig's command.[85] The plan as finally approved included an assault by more than 400 tanks.

Haig, attacking on August 8 after a brief bombardment, advanced between six and eight miles on the first day. In a week's fighting he took about 30,000 prisoners. The effects on the German Army were so calamitous that on August 14 the Kaiser spoke of finding a suitable moment to come to an understanding with the enemy, preferably through the King of Spain or the Queen of the Netherlands.[86]

At the end of August the Austrian Foreign Minister, Count Burián, was persuaded with some difficulty to postpone an independent approach to the Allied and Associated Powers. In the middle of September, unable to wait longer, he proposed that the belligerents should enter into a confidential, nonbinding discussion of terms at a conference to be summoned for the purpose. His offer is now known to have been a heartfelt cry for peace. At the time its effect was marred by a bellicose speech in which the German Vice-Chancellor declared that the treaties imposed by Germany on Russia and Rumania must stand, that Alsace-Lorraine would not be given up, and that all German, Austro-Hungarian, Bulgarian, or Turkish territories in Allied hands must be returned to their former rulers. The British declined to embark on a peace conference under such unfavorable auspices, while the Americans pointed out that the peace aims of the United States had already been stated in President Wilson's Fourteen Points.[87] On the other hand the German Foreign Minister, Admiral Paul von Hintze, thought the opportunity might well be taken to organize a peace conference in Holland.

In the meantime the French proposed that General Franchet d'Esperey, who had succeeded to the command once held by General

Sarrail, should try to knock Bulgaria out of the war by taking the offensive in the Balkans. Henry Wilson was not enthusiastic. Lloyd George insisted that since the Bulgars were known to be dissatisfied with their treatment by the Germans, the attempt was well worth making.[88]

Franchet d'Esperey opened his attack on September 15 with massive air support provided by the British along his whole front. The British and Greek divisions on his right met stiff opposition during the first few days and made slow progress; on his left the French and the Serbs swept irresistibly into Serbia. After little more than a week's fighting the plight of the Bulgarian armies was so desperate that on September 26 the Bulgars asked the British for an armistice and were referred to Franchet d'Esperey. On the same day Foch launched a new series of offensives by American, Belgian, British, and French forces on a wide front from Flanders to the Argonne. Especially in the British sector, these soon forced the Germans to abandon positions long regarded as impregnable.

Almost simultaneously Allenby, also with overwhelming air superiority, defeated the Turks at Megiddo, in northern Palestine, and went on to rout the whole of the Turkish armies in Palestine and Syria.

The collapse of Bulgaria, foreshadowing the loss of Rumanian corn and oil, convinced the German military authorities that the war must be brought to an end without delay. At a conference at Spa on September 29 they proposed that in order to gain a respite for the German Army, the Allied and Associated Powers should be asked to grant an immediate armistice and that this request should be linked with an offer to make peace on terms. When the Foreign Ministry insisted that a more democratic constitution was needed to carry through peace negotiations, the Kaiser was persuaded to sign a decree associating the majority parties in the Reichstag with the government. At the same time he accepted the resignation of the unbending Chancellor, Count Georg von Hertling. Hertling was succeeded after some delay by a less reactionary statesman, Prince Max of Baden.

On the day of the conference at Spa, Bulgarian envoys dispatched to Franchet d'Esperey's headquarters agreed to an armistice on terms amounting to surrender. Franchet d'Esperey then proposed to move most of the British contingent to his left and send it in the general direction of Vienna, leaving one British division to advance on Constantinople in company with one French and three Greek divisions, the whole under a French commander. This plan seemed to the British so unsatisfactory that they contemplated removing their troops from Franchet d'Esperey's command and putting them under Allenby.[89] Foch, when asked for his advice, expressed the opinion that Franchet d'Esperey should think first of isolating the Turks by cutting communications between Constantinople and Berlin. Only when that had been done, and when the disarmament of Bulgaria was assured, should he prepare for further action against Turkey.[90]

On October 4 Lloyd George, accompanied by Hankey, left London for Versailles, where he was to meet the Chief of the Imperial General Staff and discuss these matters with the French and the Italians. About 5 P.M. on the following day, Clemenceau brought the news that the Germans had asked the Swiss government to convey to Washington a request for an armistice and an offer to treat for peace on the basis of the Fourteen Points and President Wilson's subsequent speeches about war aims.[91] A similar request had been made by Austro-Hungary.

8

War and Peace

IN the famous "peace note" which reached the White House on Sunday, October 6, 1918, Prince Max of Baden asked President Wilson to summon the belligerents to a peace conference for the purpose of opening negotiations on the basis of the Fourteen Points and the President's subsequent pronouncements about war aims.[1] He also asked for an immediate armistice "on land and sea and in the air."

Colonel House urged the President to make no direct reply to this communication but to announce that he would consult the Allied governments and to send House to Paris for that purpose.[2] Wilson disregarded this advice. Without consulting the Allies, he dispatched on October 8 a note in which he declined to ask the Entente Powers to stop fighting while German troops were on their soil or to summon a peace conference without knowing whether Prince Max meant that he unequivocally accepted the points made in the President's speeches and was ready to discuss their practical application.[3] He hinted strongly at reluctance to negotiate with any but a democratic German government by adding that he felt justified in asking whether Prince Max was speaking merely for the "constituted authorities" who had hitherto conducted the war on Germany's behalf.

Copies of the President's reply reached the Allied statesmen through diplomatic channels on October 9, after they had read about it in their newspapers. Clemenceau, delighted that the President had made a point of the withdrawal of German troops from Allied territory, saw no need for any immediate action on the part of the Allied governments. Lloyd George did not agree. He thought that, if the Allies made no comment on the President's note, they might give the impression that they regarded the Fourteen Points as a suitable basis for a settlement. In fact, they had never been asked whether they viewed the President's proposals in that light.[4]

The statesmen then agreed to send two messages to Washington.[5] In the first, they pointed out that the terms of any armistice must be settled in consultation with their military advisers.[6] Moreover, they must be such as to ensure that the Germans did not withdraw without molestation to a shorter line and there renew the struggle on more favorable terms. In the second message, the statesmen asked the President to send a fully accredited envoy to Europe.

Wilson agreed that the drafting of armistice terms called for expert guidance. He also agreed to send House to Paris with a twofold mission as special representative in Europe of the United States government and personal representative of the President.[7] House was, however, unable to reach Paris much before the end of the month. Since no decision to suspend hostilities could be taken in his absence, the belligerents had no choice but to go on fighting in the meantime.

President Wilson had been urged as early as the previous January to appoint a plenipotentiary to sit with the Allied heads of government at meetings of the Supreme War Council. Nevertheless, it would be wrong to assume that had he acceded to this reasonable request, there would have been no delay in the granting of an armistice to Germany when she asked for one in October. The Germans, even after telling the President on October 12 that they accepted the propositions laid down in his speeches and were willing to withdraw from the occupied territories, continued to allow their U-boat commanders to sink passenger ships without warning and their retreating troops to do needless damage to Allied property.[8] The Allies suspected, not without reason, that Germany's real object when she first proposed an armistice was not so much to end the war as to gain a respite which would enable her armies to retreat safely to the frontier area, leaving a broad tract of devastated territory behind them. Her forces would then be well placed to fight a series of defensive battles whose outcome might compel the Allied and Associated Powers to grant her favorable terms.[9]

This was not true, however, of Germany's allies. Austro-Hungary, in particular, was clearly more than willing to lay down her arms if she could find a means of doing so without dishonoring her pledges. The Emperor Karl, who had succeeded to the thrones of Austria and Hungary on Franz Josef's death in 1916, was married to a Frenchwoman, professed liberal principles, and had expressed his readiness to transform the empire into a federation of autonomous states which might become a useful barrier against German domination of Central Europe.[10] But the failure of a number of attempts to come to terms with him had led the Allied and Associated Powers, the United States in particular, to doubt whether they would ever succeed by such means in detaching him from the German orbit. At an interview with the First Lord of the Admiralty, Sir Eric Geddes, about the middle of October, President Wilson confessed that in any case his commitments to the Czechs and the Yugoslavs were such that the breakup of the Austro-Hungarian Empire had become "an absolute necessity."[11] In a tardy reply to the Austro-Hungarian "peace note," which Wilson dispatched on October 18 without formal consultation with the Allies, he dealt a blow to the emperor's hopes by observing that circumstances had changed since he enunciated the Fourteen Points.[12] Less than a week later the Italians, encouraged by the diversion of Austrian divisions from their front to Bosnia and Herzegovina to meet the oncoming Serbs, launched in the neighborhood of Vittorio Veneto an offensive which soon drove the Austrians to seek an armistice in the field.

Meanwhile, the Allies and the Americans were eagerly studying Germany's reply to the President's note of October 8. After a long talk with their naval and military advisers, the Allied statesmen agreed on October 13 that the President must be asked to disabuse the Germans of the notion that withdrawal from occupied territories was the sole prerequisite of an armistice.[13] The President did so on the following day. He added, on his own initiative, a further strong hint to the effect that Germany would be well advised to turn her back on autocracy and entrust the management of her affairs to a popularly elected government.[14]

This addition caused some disquiet in London.[15] The radical

Lloyd George did not much like Germany's autocratic regime, but the question was whether one ostensibly more democratic would be truly representative. The British did not want to be forced to treat with a makeshift government thrust into office for the purpose of striking a bargain which the real rulers of Germany might repudiate when they felt strong enough to do so.

The Germans replied on October 20 to the President's note of October 14. They assured him that arbitrary power had been abolished in Germany. They added that orders would be given to their armed forces to spare passenger vessels and respect private property. Finally, they agreed that the terms of their withdrawal from Allied territory and of the armistice must be settled by the military advisers of the Allied and Associated governments. Alsace and Lorraine were not mentioned.[16]

The British, studying this answer on October 21, came to the conclusion that they must ask the President not to send any more telegrams to Germany without consulting the Allies.[17] Two days later Wilson formally transmitted to the Allied governments the whole of his correspondence with the German Chancellor. In a final message to the Germans, he made some disobliging remarks about "military masters and monarchical autocrats." [18]

On October 26 House arrived in Paris to do battle for the Fourteen Points as modified by the President's subsequent pronouncements. Himself not unfavorably disposed toward the Allies, he came as the envoy of a government and a country riddled with dislike of European ways and resentment of Britain's naval and mercantile supremacy. American distrust of British intentions, never long dormant, had been aroused in recent months by the inclusion in Lloyd George's government of Unionists who favored a system of tariffs designed to promote the interests of producers within the Empire and by signs of an active concern with foreign markets. Washington had not failed to take note of a recent visit to South American countries by a British mission whose purpose was to affirm Britain's continued interest in that part of the world.[19]

House found that almost everyone he met in Paris believed that the chance of bringing hostilities to an end ought not to be missed. Among the soldiers, only Pershing thought the war should be fought to a finish.[20] House found, too, that the drafting of armistice terms had reached an advanced stage. The military terms, as eventually approved by the Allied and Associated governments, included the surrender by the Germans of 5,000 guns, 25,000 machine guns, and 1,700 aircraft and the occupation by Allied or Associated troops of bridgeheads on the right bank of the Rhine. The naval terms included the surrender of all U-boats and the internment in neutral or other designated ports of sixteen capital ships, eight cruisers, and fifty destroyers.[21]

These were not peace terms. They were merely the terms on which, if the Germans still wished for an armistice, the Allied and Associated Powers would be willing to order a cease-fire. Even so, the Germans would be in no position to resume hostilities if such terms were accepted and could be enforced. Furthermore, once an armistice was signed, the Allied and Associated Powers would be extremely reluctant to call on their troops to make war on an apparently defeated enemy. It therefore remained for House to convince the Supreme War Council that the Allied and Associated Powers could safely and legitimately invite the Germans to disarm themselves on the strength of a promise that the terms of the subsequent peace treaty would conform with the principles laid down by President Wilson in his speeches.

This was not likely to be an easy task. When House reached Paris, the President's proposals had not yet been formally submitted to the Allied governments as a basis on which peace might be made.[22] Admittedly no more than a "provisional sketch," they did not purport to represent the views of the Congress and people of the United States, but merely those of the President and of such advisers as he had chosen to consult. A commentary which House had caused to be prepared showed, too, that some of them were not meant to be interpreted as people who had not seen the commentary would be likely to interpret them.[23] If the Germans accepted an armistice in the sole context of the correspondence between the Chancellor and the United States government, the proposals would nonetheless become the basis of a legal contract between Germany and the Allied and Associated Powers.[24]

Furthermore, it was far from certain that the Congress and people of the United States would endorse the President's proposals if they were ever asked to do so. While House was on his way to Europe, Wilson had publicly exhorted his fellow citizens to vote only for Democratic candidates at the forthcoming Congressional elections.[25]

This gratuitous appeal to the partisan spirit had aroused widespread resentment. Moderate Republicans who had hitherto been inclined to support the President's policies in the interests of national unity were no longer prepared to do so; the less moderate did not hesitate to describe his pronouncements about war aims as pretentious rubbish. The former President Theodore Roosevelt, a man much respected in Europe, openly advised the Allies to disregard Wilson's unctuous platitudes and make peace with the Central Powers on their own terms.[26]

The President and House believed that, even so, they could put strong pressure on the Allies to accept the Wilsonian program. Apart from the tacit threat of economic discrimination after the war, House was in a position to point out that refusal to negotiate on the President's terms might lead to a separate peace between the United States and one or more of the Central Powers. This might be preceded by a public announcement of the causes of the dispute between the President and the Allied heads of government. If the worse came to the worst, House could also make it clear that in the event of a serious challenge to the President's proposals, the United States government might be driven to complete the 1916 capital-ship program and perhaps make even larger additions to the Navy than were contemplated in that program.[27]

The chief conflict between House and the Allied statesmen arose in connection with Point II of the Fourteen Points, relating to the freedom of the seas. At his first meeting with the heads of government, House asked whether they accepted the Fourteen Points. Lloyd George replied that he could in no circumstances agree to any proposal which threatened to abolish the right of blockade. House pointed out that, according to his interpretation of Point II, the intention was not that the right of blockade should be abolished but that it should be exercised by a League of Nations. Lloyd George said that he could not relinquish belligerent rights in favor of an organization which had yet to be created and might never come into existence. If he did accept Point II, the nation would repudiate his leadership and he would find himself replaced by a less amenable successor.[28]

Lloyd George knew that not all Americans accepted the definition of the freedom of the seas proposed by House. He was also aware that President Wilson attached great importance to British adherence to the proposed League of Nations. Fortified by this knowledge, he made it clear at subsequent meetings that Britain would much rather forgo membership in such a league than forfeit the belligerent rights which had enabled her to survive two great wars with Continental powers. His French and Italian colleagues gave him valuable support by blandly proposing, when House showed signs of stress, that the Supreme War Council should address itself to the question of an armistice and leave peace terms to be discussed later.[29] When House fired his big gun by threatening the Allies with a separate peace between Germany and the United States, Lloyd George said that such an outcome would be regrettable, but that even so he could not accept Point II.[30]

Faced with united opposition, House gave way rather than jeopardize the whole of the President's proposals. Although empowered to warn the British that if they did not accept the principle of the freedom of the seas, they could count on the United States to build "the strongest navy that our resources permit," he agreed to drop the question for the time being in return for a promise by the British to discuss it on some future occasion.[31] A clause reserving for the Allies complete liberty of action at the peace conference with respect to Point II of the Fourteen Points was then added to the correspondence which afterward became a vital part of the contract between Germany and the Allied and Associated Powers.[32]

The Italians wished to add a reservation with respect to Point IX, relating to the frontier between Italy and Austro-Hungary. They pointed out that President Wilson's proposal that the frontier should be redrawn along clearly recognizable lines of nationality would neither satisfy their claims under the Treaty of London nor give them a secure frontier. House was determined that objections to the Fourteen Points should be kept strictly within bounds, while Lloyd George and Clemenceau insisted that the point was one which concerned not the armistice with Germany but the armistice with Austria.[33] Since the Austrians negotiated an armistice in the field while the terms of the armistice with Germany were still under discussion, the outcome was that the Italian reservation, although discussed in draft by House and the Allied statesmen, was never formally submitted to the Supreme War Council or communicated to the Austro-Hungarian government.[34] Furthermore, as the Austrians had asked for peace on the basis of the Fourteen Points but had received no satisfactory reply when they laid down their arms, their right to such protection as the President's proposals could give them remained uncertain.

Further problems arose in connection with the President's demand that invaded territories should be not only freed but "restored." Lloyd George thought that Germany should be made to accept responsibility for all direct damage done to Allied property by her armed forces and that this should include compensation for injuries suffered by British seamen in consequence of her illegal submarine warfare.[35] He also thought that these questions should not be raised in connection with the armistice but should be reserved for the peace conference. President Wilson and his advisers were of the opinion that since the invasion of Belgium was clearly illegal, the Belgians might well ask to be reimbursed not only for the devastation of their towns and provinces, but also for the whole cost of their war effort.[36] After some discussion, the Supreme War Council agreed on a reservation defining restoration as compensation for "all damage done to the civilian population of the Allies and their property" by Germany's armed forces.[37] In addition, a passage was added to the financial clauses of the armistice agreement to the effect that nothing in them should preclude the Allied and Associated Powers from making subsequent claims or concessions.[38]

By the time all these points were settled a month had elapsed since Germany first asked for an armistice. During that time both sides had suffered heavy losses. The German armies had been pushed back considerable distances, but they were still on French and Belgian soil. They continued to fight bravely, but there was a good deal of confusion in their rear. As a result of the Allied blockade, meat and edible fats were scarce. German civilians were poorly fed, and in consequence of transportation problems, the relatively generous but unappetizing rations allotted to the troops did not always reach them.

On November 4 the Supreme War Council communicated to President Wilson the armistice terms and the two reservations regarding the Fourteen Points on which House and the Allied statesmen had agreed. On the following day the President passed the reservations to the Germans and invited them, if they still wanted an armistice, to send accredited representatives to Foch.

A German delegation headed by Matthias Erzberger, leader of the

Center Party in the Reichstag, left Berlin on November 6. On November 7 the delegates entered the Allied lines under the protection of a white flag by following a prescribed route from the German headquarters at Spa. Foch, accompanied by the First Sea Lord, Admiral Sir Rosslyn Wemyss, received them on the following day in a railway carriage at Compiègne.

After studying the armistice terms, the disconsolate delegates asked to be allowed to send a copy to Spa. Fire from the German lines was so heavy that their courier had to take refuge at a French divisional headquarters and was unable to complete his journey until the following day. By that time disorders fomented by left-wing agitators, allegedly with covert support from the German High Command, had broken out in various parts of Germany. The Kaiser, advised by the High Command to abdicate in the national interest, fled with the crown prince to Holland, and an infant republic sired by President Wilson upon the reluctant body of the German Reich was born in dolor. On November 10 a newly installed Socialist government, "sitting bewildered in the high places" authorized Erzberger by wireless to accept the terms.[39]

At the grisly hour of 5 A.M. on November 11, Erzberger and his colleagues affixed their signatures to the armistice agreement. Thereby they undertook on behalf of Germany that she would withdraw her troops from Belgium, Luxembourg, and France, the whole of the former French provinces of Alsace and Lorraine included; surrender large quantities of war matériel; allow Allied or United States troops to occupy German territory west of the Rhine and bridgeheads at Mainz, Coblenz, and Cologne; and make such reparation for damage done to Allied property as might thereafter be thought suitable. In return the Allied and Associated Powers pledged themselves, by the hands of Foch and Wemyss, to enter into discussions with the Germans for the purpose of making peace on the basis of the Fourteen Points and the rest of President Wilson's pronouncements about war aims, as qualified by his correspondence with the German government and the reservations appended to it.

9

Versailles and After

ABOUT a fortnight after the cease-fire on the Western Front, Colonel House fell ill and was forced to spend a week or so in bed. At a meeting on December 2 which he was unable to attend, the British, the French, and the Italians agreed that they could best honor their engagements under the armistice agreement with Germany by meeting to draft terms which they would then discuss with the Germans at a conference of all the belligerent powers.[1] President Wilson had suggested before House left for Europe that such a conference should be held at Lausanne. House and Lloyd George subsequently agreed that Geneva would be a more suitable place.[2] Clemenceau proposed Versailles but did not press the matter when he found that House and Lloyd George had already decided on Geneva.[3]

Almost simultaneously, the Allied statesmen learned to their dismay that President Wilson proposed not merely to put in a formal appearance at the peace conference but to take an active part in the proceedings there and at the preliminary meetings between representatives of the Allied and Associated Powers. Although warned that, as a head of state, he would be out of place at meetings of heads of government and foreign ministers, he refused to take the hint.

Since he was not familiar with the give-and-take of diplomatic conferences and had become accustomed to regard himself as the chief figure at any gathering he attended, one consequence was that the preliminary meetings assumed a rather different character from that envisaged when they were first mooted.

Another was that the venue had to be changed. On November 8, only a few weeks after Wilson had suggested that the peace conference should be held at Lausanne, he declared that Switzerland was "saturated with every poisonous element and open to every hostile influence."[4] The pliant House, after privately recording his belief that it would be almost impossible to make a just peace "while sitting in the atmosphere of a belligerent capital," then arranged that the preliminary meetings should be held in Paris and the peace conference proper at Versailles.[5] This was not hard to do, since the French were more than willing and the rest of the Allies either indifferent or reluctant to make difficulties.

After these arrangements had been set in train, Wilson learned to his "complete confusion" that it would be impossible for him to preside over a conference held on French soil. When the news was broken to him, he offered to propose at the first meeting that Clemenceau should take the chair. He had to be told that his intervention would not be needed. Clemenceau, as chief plenipotentiary of the host country, would preside as of right and by long-standing custom.

The decision to hold the peace conference at Versailles was thus unfortunate on more counts than one. In the first place, since France and Germany were still at war and would remain so until the peace treaty was signed, it meant that the German delegates would attend the conference as men under surveillance. Second, to summon them to the very town, indeed to the very building and the very room, where the German Empire had been proclaimed at the end of the Franco-Prussian War might be an act of poetic justice but was not good diplomacy. Third, the decision meant that President Wilson would come to the conference knowing that his ignorance of protocol and fear of "hostile influences" had combined to rob him of the position he felt to be his due. Had the plenipotentiaries met in Switzerland, the President of the Swiss Federal Republic would have welcomed them with a brief speech and then withdrawn, leaving Wilson to take the chair as *doyen* of the statesmen entitled to attend all meetings.

At that stage the situation was further complicated by electoral hazards. The elections held in the United States in November gave the Republican Party not only a majority in the House of Representatives, but also control of the Senate and its Foreign Relations Committee. This need not have been disastrous for Wilson if he had listened to advisers who urged him to allot to prominent Republicans at least two of the five places at the peace conference to which the United States was entitled. As it was, he chose as sole representative of the Republican Party Henry White, a respected public servant who was not an enthusiastic party man. The remaining places went to Lansing, House, and Bliss. Lansing and House could scarcely have been excluded, but Bliss and White might well have been replaced by elder statesmen of the caliber of Elihu Root and William Taft. Both Root and Taft were keenly interested in the proposed League of Nations, and both were staunch Republicans whose support would have ensured a sympathetic hearing in the Senate for any proposals which the President might bring back from Europe. The inclusion of either might have changed the course of history.

The general election held almost simultaneously in Britain went overwhelmingly in favor of Lloyd George. But a victory so sweeping as to leave the government with no excuse for any failure to redeem promises made by overzealous canvassers was not an unmixed blessing. During his election campaign Lloyd George was led in the heat of the moment to endorse demands that Germany should be made to meet practically the whole cost of the war. Thus he was placed in an equivocal position. As a practical statesman, he knew that Germany could not and ought not to be made to pay huge indemnities. On the contrary, from the moment when the last shot was fired on the Western Front, British interests required that the French should be prevented from permanently upsetting the balance of power in Europe by completing her disruption. This he failed, however, to make clear to the general public. The result was that his attempts to secure reasonable treatment for Germany during and after the peace negotiations, although strictly orthodox according to the traditional British way of thinking, were bound to seem to some of his supporters perverse and even paradoxical.

After seeing his party defeated at the polls, President Wilson wished to address Congress before leaving for Europe. The British general election was held in the middle of December, but the need to collect and count the votes of men serving abroad compelled the authorities to postpone announcement of the results until nearly the end of the month. In France, Clemenceau needed time to sound parliamentary opinion before determining his policy. For all these reasons, the preliminary meetings between plenipotentiaries of the Allied and Associated Powers—officially styled the Preliminary Peace Conference of Paris but often misleadingly called the Peace Conference—could not begin until the middle of January. By that time men of almost every nation were clamoring for an end to be put without delay to a state of affairs which was neither peace nor war and which threatened every day to make the resumption of normal trade more difficult.

In the meantime, President Wilson paid a series of ceremonial visits to England, France, and Italy. On his way to Europe he told members of the United States delegation who traveled with him that they would be the only disinterested persons at the peace conference and that the men they were going to meet did not represent their own people.[6]

During a great part of the Paris Conference the President was preoccupied with future relations between the great powers, and particularly with the proposed League of Nations, to an extent which made other issues seem of secondary importance.[7] As a patriotic American he came to Europe determined to transform the situation which had long enabled Britain to play a dominant role in the world's affairs by asserting her command of the sea in face of repeated attempts to challenge it. Entering the First World War at a moment when the advent of the submarine and the aircraft seemed to have cast doubt on the supremacy of the battleship, he had agreed to suspend the 1916 capital-ship program in order to build more of the ships needed to carry American troops to Europe.[8] Even so, he had found himself still dependent on the British for much of the shipping needed for that purpose. More recently, his failure to shake the British in regard to the freedom of the seas had convinced him that a new world order would not be created without a struggle. To ensure the adherence of the Allies to the League of Nations, he was willing to threaten them and the British in particular not only with completion of the 1916 program, but also with a further program of naval expansion presented to Congress shortly after the signature of the armistice agreement with Germany.[9]

The broad naval situation at the time of the Paris Conference was such that even if only the 1916 program were completed, the United States could expect to attain between 1923 and 1925 a substantial degree of superiority over the British in capital ships of the most modern design, although not in warships of all categories.* On the other hand, should France and Britain continue their wartime partnership and the Anglo-Japanese Alliance remain in force, Britain and her allies would still be in a position to dominate the world's trade routes. Thus the Americans, if they wished to end Britain's command of the sea, would have to aim not only at discouraging her from building in competition with themselves, but also at detaching her from Japan.

When declaring his war aims, President Wilson had, however, committed himself to the view that armaments should be reduced to the lowest level consistent with domestic safety. American naval experts were therefore obliged to devote much ingenuity to attempts to show that massive additions to the United States Navy would not be incompatible with that principle.[10] The British found their arguments unconvincing. Lord Robert Cecil, the leading advocate among the British of a strong League of Nations, pointed out in a letter to House that while the United Kingdom depended on imports for four-fifths of its cereals, two-thirds of its meat and most of its wool and cotton and hence could be starved out in a month should the Royal Navy lose command of the sea, the United States was amply provided with all the necessities of life and could never be effectively blockaded.[11]

Two minor skirmishes in the cold war between the United States and the British Empire were fought in connection with the feeding of Germany and the disposal of warships to be surrendered by the Germans.

The Allied and Associated Powers insisted on reserving in the armistice terms the right to maintain their blockade of Germany until the peace treaty was signed, as the only practical means of enforcing the terms after the cease-fire. Recognizing that nonetheless the Ger-

* At the end of the First World War Britain had some sixty to seventy effective capital ships in commission, the exact number depending on the sense given to the term "effective." Germany had forty-five, the United States thirty-nine, France twenty, Japan twenty, Italy fourteen. Four capital ships which would reflect the experience of Jutland had been laid down in Britain, but work on all of them except the battle cruiser *Hood* had been suspended in 1917. The 1916 program would add sixteen modern capital ships to the United States Navy; the 1918 program, in its definitive form, the same number.

mans must be fed and that shipping was the crucial factor, they suggested that German merchant ships lying idle in various ports should be put at their disposal for the purpose of carrying food to Germany. The Germans proposed, as an alternative more acceptable to themselves, that the blockade should be relaxed so that the ships could be used to carry supplies bought in the open market. This the Allied and Associated Powers refused to allow at a time when the Germans were still technically at war with them and hence debarred from trading with their nationals. The Germans then agreed to release their ships as a condition of the renewal of the armistice.

However, they did not hasten to carry out their bargain. Meanwhile, British soldiers in the Rhineland reported that many German families were desperately short of food and that Germany was in danger of drifting into anarchy. On March 3 the Chief of the Imperial General Staff warned the king and afterward repeated to the Prime Minister that failure to act without further delay might lead to "the most awful chaos the world has ever seen." [12] Five days later Lloyd George read to the Supreme War Council a telegram in which General Plumer, commanding the British Army of Occupation, disclaimed responsibility for discipline as long as his troops continued to be distressed by the sight of starving children.[13] At a conference with German delegates in Brussels in the second week of the month the First Sea Lord promised substantial deliveries of grain and meat if the Germans renewed their promise in regard to their merchant fleet, and a few days later the first food ships reached Hamburg.[14]

Allegations to the effect that the Allied and Associated Powers prolonged the blockade in order to hamper Germany's economic recovery were not upheld in later years by responsible historians in Germany or elsewhere. In retrospect it seems obvious that the chief cause of the delay was the inability of the German government to impose its will on shipping magnates understandably reluctant to part with control of their property to foreigners. Even so, the failure of the Allied and Associated Powers to overcome such difficulties until four months after the signing of the armistice was harmful to their relations not only with Germany but also with each other. Americans who had always regarded the blockade as a weapon aimed obscurely at the foreign trade of the United States believed that they saw in its continuance evidence of European greed and guile; Frenchmen anxious that Britain and the United States should not combine to veto French proposals for the dismemberment of Germany primed the British with reports to the effect that the Americans were seeking to trade with the enemy under the guise of relief, had sent hundreds of commercial travelers disguised as officers to Berlin, and were "exploiting Europe under the flag of victory." [15] Englishmen were doubtless the readier to believe such allegations in the light of evidence that a forthcoming campaign of murder and intimidation in Ireland was being financed largely from the United States.

Trouble about the disposal of warships to be surrendered by the Germans began with a proposal that such ships should be shared in proportion to losses incurred during the war. The American Admiral William S. Benson, whose patriotism was so wholehearted that he would have liked the Germans to retain a strong fleet as a challenge to British command of the North Sea, objected that this arrangement would give Britain by far the largest share; consequently the United States would have to build still more ships to attain equality. The British then proposed that all surrendered warships should be sunk in deep water within three months of the signing of the peace treaty.[16] This was acceptable in principle to the Americans, but not to the French or the Italians, who were anxious not to miss an opportunity of augmenting their navies at little cost. Eventually it was agreed that, with certain exceptions, all surrendered ships should be sunk or broken up under international supervision. The exceptions would allow France and Italy each to take and keep five cruisers and ten destroyers. In addition, ten submarines would be allotted to the French, and a number of destroyers and torpedo boats to the smaller Allied powers. The British and the Americans would receive an agreed number of major warships and a few submarines but would keep them only for a limited period and then sink them.[17]

In the meantime, the sixteen capital ships, eight cruisers, and fifty destroyers interned under the terms of the armistice agreement were escorted to the Firth of Forth for lack of a suitable neutral port. Later they were moved to Scapa Flow. Throughout the spring and early summer of 1919 they remained at Scapa Flow on terms which did not give the British rights of visit and search. On June 21 the German commander, Admiral Ludwig von Reuter, gave orders for the scuttling of the ships at a moment when the Senior Naval Officer Afloat at Scapa, Admiral S. R. Fremantle, was at sea with his battle squadron. One battleship and some cruisers and destroyers were successfully beached by the British, but the rest were lost. Admiral von Reuter, when reproached with a flagrant breach of the armistice conditions, replied that the ships were still German property until the signing of the peace treaty and that no principle of international law debarred a commander from sinking his fleet to escape capture.

The sinking of these ships on the eve of the signing of the Treaty of Versailles aroused much indignation in Paris. Nevertheless, it was the Germans, not the Allied and Associated Powers, who lost by it. Since even Lloyd George, while anxious that Germany should not be made to pay huge indemnities or make vast territorial concessions, had long been of the opinion that she should be deprived of most of her armed forces, the inevitable consequence of Reuter's gesture was that the Supreme War Council refused to count the scuttled ships as surrendered. The Allied and Associated Powers insisted that most of Germany's remaining warships should be given up and that a number of floating docks and a substantial volume of merchant shipping should be thrown in as a makeweight.[18] Under the terms of the treaty the Germans were allowed to keep a few old battleships, but not to build new heavy ships, cruisers, and destroyers of more than 10,000, 6,000, and 800 tons respectively or to build or otherwise acquire submarines. The British advocated a universal ban on submarines, but their proposal was rejected by the French after the Americans had been persuaded with some difficulty to support it.[19] The French argued that nations which could not afford large battle fleets ought not to be prevented from defending themselves with submarines as long as they used them in accordance with the laws and customs of war.

Other clauses in the treaty stripped the German Army of its heavy artillery and limited its strength to seven infantry and three cavalry divisions recruited by voluntary enlistment. At the same time, Germany's right to use and manufacture aircraft was restricted to an extent which Sir Henry Wilson considered "fantastically severe and illogical." But the British were not well placed to insist on better terms for Germany in that respect, since France could be reached by German bombers while Britain could not.

The principle of voluntary recruitment for the German Army, on which the British did insist, was open to the objection that it would create a body of picked men which might become the nucleus of an exceptionally efficient conscript army. The British met this criticism by pointing out that no such transformation could occur as long as conscription was barred. Even so, they recognized that nothing could *permanently* prevent Germany from once more becoming a great military power if she had the will to do so.[20] Lloyd George made it clear to his intimates that when he advocated the reduction of the German Army to a relatively small force of professional soldiers, he was aiming at much more than merely gratifying the French by weakening Germany. His intention was that the change should pave the way for a general scaling down of land forces and an eventual rejection of the principle of compulsory military service by all the leading European powers.

Agreement on such points was reached only after prolonged negotiations. In these negotiations Clemenceau, Lloyd George, and President Wilson played the leading parts. Unanimity of outlook on the part of three popularly elected statesmen representing widely divergent interests was not to be expected. Moreover, none of the three possessed the intimate knowledge of foreign affairs which had enabled Castlereagh to present the British case at the Congress of Vienna with only a staff of fourteen to assist him.* The result was that although the Germans were not called in until the Allied and Associated Powers had agreed upon the terms to be proposed to them, the Treaty of Versailles was just as much a patchwork of compromise solutions as doubtless it would have become had representatives of the Central Powers been present from the outset. Indeed, it has been argued that in some respects their presence might have been both morally and practically an advantage. For example, at an early stage of the preliminary discussions the French proposed to advance their strategic frontier to the Rhine by detaching the Rhineland and the Palatinate from Germany, if necessary on terms which would allow the inhabitants to choose between independence and reunion with Germany at the end of a stated period. Had the Germans been present, the French might still have advanced this obviously unacceptable proposal, if only in the hope of earning the right to sympathetic treatment where other issues were concerned by gracefully withdrawing it when opposition to it became manifest. As it

* The British delegation in Paris in 1919 numbered about 200, exclusive of clerks and typists. The American delegation was not much smaller. The French, sitting in their own capital, could call on all the resources of the Foreign Ministry and other branches of the administration. Hence they did not need such a large delegation.

was, they clung to it tenaciously, refusing to withdraw it unless Britain and the United States agreed to guarantee a politically acceptable frontier against German aggression. The result was that President Wilson effectively, though unintentionally, wrecked the treaty even before it was signed by giving a guarantee which a more perspicacious statesman would have known was very unlikely to be ratified by the Senate.

When the statesmen came to consider how much Germany should pay by way of reparations, they faced problems which seemed almost insuperable. Clemenceau and Lloyd George knew that they could not hope to extract from the Germans an indemnity on the scale envisaged by many of their fellow citizens. At the same time, they were reluctant to disappoint their supporters by naming a lower sum. Some of Lloyd George's well-wishers hoped that he would take the House of Commons and the public into his confidence, remind them that he had never promised to claim more from Germany than she could pay without doing irreparable harm to international trade, and tell them that it would be inexpedient, as well as wrong, to saddle the Germans with a debt which could not be extinguished within a generation. However, if Lloyd George had taken that course, he would still have to reckon with Clemenceau. Eventually the Allied and Associated Powers adopted, in substance, a proposal made by a junior member of the American team, John Foster Dulles. This was that no sum should be stated in the treaty and that a commission should be appointed to determine "at its leisure" first how much the Germans owed and second how much they could pay.[21] The statesmen doubtless hoped, when they chose this course, that the consequences of deferring a decision until passions had cooled would be beneficial. But they overlooked the disadvantages of burdening the Germans with an unknown liability. An imponderable item in the national balance sheet was bound to impair Germany's credit in the international money market. At the same time, her citizens were not encouraged to work and save, or the guardians of her finances to put their house in order, by the knowledge that any success they might achieve was likely to increase the sum they would ultimately be called upon to remit to their former enemies.

Fairly rapid progress toward the creation of a League of Nations was made in the early stages of the Paris Conference, largely because a good deal of thought had already been given to the project on both sides of the Atlantic. President Wilson's ideal was an international court which would settle all disputes between sovereign states and would call, if the need arose, on an international force to impose its will on recalcitrant nations. Since this was too remote a goal to be reached in the course of a single conference, he recommended that a start should be made by the drafting of an agreement on general principles to which all civilized nations could adhere.[22] This agreement would be called not a treaty or a convention but a "covenant." No curtailment of national sovereignty or territorial integrity would be involved, except insofar as territories administered by or on behalf of the proposed League of Nations might perhaps be regarded as belonging to it. ("Nothing," said Wilson, "stabilizes an institution so well as the possession of property.")[23] Pending the creation of an international force, nations which contravened the spirit or the letter of the Covenant might be punished by economic sanctions and the denial of postal and cable facilities. For the time being no provision would, however, be made for compulsory arbitration. The President hoped that small nations would undertake the management of territories which fell to be administered by the community of nations in accordance with a system of "mandates" proposed by Smuts and others, but he contemplated close supervision of their stewardship by a permanent council on which the great powers would be strongly represented.[24]

In the light of these and other proposals, the Supreme War Council formally agreed on January 25, 1919, that a League of Nations should be established to promote international cooperation, ensure the fulfillment of international obligations, and provide safeguards against war.[25] Membership of the League would be open to "every civilized nation which can be relied on to promote its objects." The members would meet from time to time "in international conference," and a permanent organization served by a full-time secretariat would carry on business between meetings.

Largely on the initiative of the President (not against his wishes, as was afterward alleged by his biographer), the drafting of the Covenant was entrusted to a committee consisting in the first instance of two members each from Britain, France, Italy, Japan, and the United States and one each from Belgium, Brazil, China, Portugal, and Serbia.[26] Representatives of Czechoslovakia, Greece, Poland, and Rumania joined the drafting committee later. Disagreements about procedure threatened at one time to make progress very slow, but these were resolved in time for the committee to hold its first meeting on February 3 and present an agreed draft some ten days later.

Difficulties also flowed from the President's insistence that the system of mandates should be applied not only to parts of the Ottoman Empire to be ceded by Turkey, but also to the former German colonies in Africa and the Pacific. William Hughes and William Massey, Prime Ministers of Australia and New Zealand respectively, claimed that their countries ought to be allowed to annex the German colonial possessions in the Pacific south of the equator which their troops had occupied. Eventually they were persuaded, with some difficulty, to accept the mandatory principle. Australia then received the mandate for eastern New Guinea, the Bismarck archipelago, and the Solomon Islands as far south and east as Bougainville, New Zealand the mandate for the part of Samoa formerly under German rule. The mandate for Nauru went jointly to Australia, New Zealand, and the United Kingdom. Somewhat unexpectedly, Wilson seemed content that the mandate for Germany's former possessions in the Pacific north of the equator should go to Japan, although the effect was to place the Japanese across communications between the continental United States and the Philippines. The United States government claimed later that the President had entered a reservation with respect to the island of Yap in the Carolines, but no such reservation was recorded in the minutes circulated immediately after the meeting in question.[27]

The question of Germany's membership in the League caused some difficulty. Lloyd George thought she should be invited to join immediately after the signing of the peace treaty. The French pointed out that only nations which could be relied upon to promote the objects of the League were eligible, and on that ground the invitation was deferred. One consequence was that for some years proposals for an international force could not be entertained, for fear that the League might come to be regarded as merely an instrument for enforcing compliance with the peace treaties. A plan for a League navy, to be formed wholly or partly from ships surrendered by the Germans, was considered by American naval experts but was not endorsed by the United States government or formally proposed.[28]

While the first draft of the Covenant was in preparation, the Japanese proposed that it should give formal recognition to the principle of the equality of races. After several attempts, they produced a formula which seemed to their British and American colleagues unobjectionable. The proposal was, however, so vehemently opposed by William Hughes, who saw in it a challenge to Australia's policy of selective immigration, that eventually the Japanese decided, on American advice, to leave the matter in abeyance.[29]

On February 14 President Wilson, as chairman of the drafting committee, read the draft of the Covenant to delegates of the Allied and Associated Powers at a plenary session of the Preliminary Peace Conference. He then went home to consult Congress. During his absence House raised with the British and the French the question of the method by which the peace terms were to be presented to the Germans. He proposed that to save time, the German delegates should be summoned to Versailles only for the purpose of receiving the draft treaty and of signing the treaty when their government authorized them to do so.[30] The multilateral peace conference envisaged in the pre-armistice correspondence with the German Chancellor would thus be reduced to a formal ceremony at which a treaty already agreed upon would be signed. The Allied and Associated Powers, notwithstanding their implicit promise to enter into discussions with the Germans for the purpose of deciding on the detailed application of Wilson's principles, accepted the substance of this proposal, and in due course the Germans were warned that they would be expected to make only written comments on the draft presented to them.

As a means of enlisting Republican support for the Covenant, the President's visit to the United States in February and March was not a great success. At a dinner party at the White House to which all members of the Foreign Relations committees of the Senate and the House were bidden, some of the guests maintained an ominous silence when their host invited them to interrogate him on points of detail.[31] In New York, he made an unfavorable impression by asserting that the Covenant was so intertwined with the peace treaty that the two could not be separated.[32]

These and other incidents suggested that Congress was unlikely to accept the Covenant as it stood. Support might, however, be forthcoming if the League were expressly debarred from concerning itself with the internal affairs of member states or contravening the Monroe Doctrine and if provision were made for any member to leave the League on giving two years' notice. On his return to Paris in the middle of March, the President faced the problem of reconciling the Allies to amendments on these lines.[33] To secure the support of the French, he was obliged to make concessions with respect to such matters as the occupation of the Rhineland and the future of the Saar. He was also obliged to agree to the insertion in the peace treaty of the notorious "war guilt" clause, by which Germany accepted responsibility for all the loss and damage suffered by the Allied and Associated Powers in consequence of the war. Since the Germans had already undertaken to pay for damage done by their armed forces, this clause served no useful purpose and was gratuitously insulting and provocative.

The British, too, demanded their price. They noted with satisfaction that President Wilson had allowed the question of the freedom of the seas to drop, ostensibly on the ground that the existence of a League of Nations would put a stop to "private" wars in which the rights of neutrals would have to be protected.[34] Even so, they wished to know whether the United States government had abandoned its intention of building a strong fleet in direct competition with the Royal Navy. On March 28 they made it clear that they would not accept the revised Covenant unless they received a satisfactory assurance in that sense.[35]

The receipt of this ultimatum coincided with a crisis in the President's negotiations with the French about reparations, the Rhineland, and the Saar. On the very day of its delivery, Clemenceau walked out of a conference with him after calling him pro-German.[36] A few days later, Wilson succumbed to an attack of influenza which confined him to his room from the evening of April 3 until the afternoon of April 8. On April 5 House recommended that if no agreement with the French were in sight by the end of the following week, the American delegation should withdraw from the Preliminary Peace Conference, leaving the Allies to make a separate peace with Germany.[37] By April 6 Wilson was well enough to see House, Bliss, White, and Lansing in his bedroom. The five American plenipotentiaries then agreed that unless their differences with the French were resolved within the next few days, the President should tell the Allied heads of government that he must either go home or insist that all future meetings of the Preliminary Peace Conference should be plenary sessions, attended by representatives of all the powers and fully reported in the press.[38] On the following day Admiral Benson asked the Navy Department by cable how soon the *George Washington*, which had carried the American delegation to Europe in December, could arrive at Brest.[39]

In the outcome the President found it better to make concessions than to fall back on threats. On April 8 he accepted a tentative settlement of the reparations question on lines proposed while he was ill; by the middle of the month his other differences with Clemenceau also yielded to compromise solutions. In each case it was he, not Clemenceau, who proved the readier to give ground.[40] Similarly, the British were induced to accept the revised Covenant by oral and written exchanges in which the Americans undertook to suspend their 1918 program and consider the possibility of postponing the construction of ships of the 1916 program not yet laid down.[41] The Americans did not promise that the 1916 program would not be completed, but their naval experts made it clear to British colleagues that they had received strict instructions not to raise the question of the command of the sea until after the signing of the peace treaty with Germany. House believed that the two governments might then be able to reach agreement about naval strengths and that meanwhile the British could rely on the intention of the President not to build in competition with them.[42]

President Wilson's need of support in the matter of the revised Covenant also provided an opportunity for the Japanese to revive their proposal about the equality of races. At a meeting of the drafting committee on April 11, eleven of the nineteen members voted in favor of an amendment affirming "the principle of the equality of nations and the just treatment of their nationals." Six members voted against the amendment; the two American members withheld their votes. President Wilson, as chairman, thereupon declared that, for want of unanimity, the motion had not been carried.[43] The Japanese, with admirable restraint, accepted this ruling and refrained from raising the matter at a plenary session. Largely because they were willing to relinquish their amendment while continuing to support amendments sponsored by the Americans, the revised Covenant was formally adopted by the Preliminary Peace Conference without the outburst from Hughes which many delegates expected.

The exclusion of the Japanese amendment aroused a good deal of indignation in Japan. Consequently the part played in these transactions by the Japanese plenipotentiaries, Baron Nubuaki Makino and Viscount Sutemi Chinda, gave them a strong claim on the goodwill of their American colleagues. Thus the Americans found themselves awkwardly placed when Makino and Chinda urged them to agree that Japan, besides receiving the mandate for the German colonies in the Pacific north of the equator, should succeed to the German concession in Shantung. The Japanese offered, if their proposal was accepted, to restore the Shantung peninsula in full sovereignty to China, retaining only the right to operate mines and railways formerly operated by the Germans, provide capital for two more railways, and establish a settlement at Tsingtao on terms which would not prevent the Chinese government from granting similar privileges to other nations. They undertook that the land on which the railways were built would remain Chinese, and they promised to surrender all military control over the peninsula, including an area around Tsingtao in which the former holders of the concession had insisted that only German troops should be stationed.[44]

Had the Allied and Associated Powers been free to dispose of the Shantung concession as they pleased, no serious objection could have been made to this proposal. The British, whose interests in China far exceeded those of any other foreign power, thought well of it; from the American point of view, there was much to be said for a policy of diverting the attention of the Japanese from the South Pacific and the Philippines by encouraging them to seek outlets for their trade and surplus population in East Asia. Indeed, as recently as November the United States Naval Planning Staff had gone so far as to suggest that Japan should be allowed to acquire territory in Siberia.[45] But the Chinese did not agree that the Shantung concession could be regarded as an asset which the defeat of Germany had placed at the disposal of her enemies. They argued that, if Germany's rights had lapsed, then they must be deemed to have reverted to China. In that case it was for the Chinese government to decide whether, and on what terms, a new concession should be granted. As it happened, the Chinese authorities were not unwilling that Japanese capital should be invested in Shantung, and from that point of view the proposal was not unwelcome. The crux of the matter was that China felt that she would lose face if the sovereignty she claimed were restored to her not as of right, but merely by favor of Japan.

In the light of this argument and in view of the interest taken by the government and people of the United States in the welfare of the Chinese Republic, President Wilson was very unwilling that the Shantung concession should go to Japan. However, on April 22 Viscount Chinda made it clear that Japan would not sign the treaty with Germany if the point were not settled in her favor.[46] Two days later a dispute with Italy about Adriatic questions reached such serious proportions that Vittorio Orlando left Paris without saying whether or when he would return. The Japanese, seeing their opportunity, thereupon renewed their request for an early decision about Shantung.[47] Wilson feared that the future of the League of Nations might be seriously prejudiced if the Japanese, and perhaps also the Italians, refused to sign the treaty. Moreover, the German delegates had already been summoned to Versailles in the belief that the treaty would be ready for signature about the middle of the month, and they could not be kept waiting indefinitely while the Allied and Associated Powers wrangled about a matter which must seem to most of the world of small importance. Wilson, bowing once more to expediency, agreed in the last week of April that the concession should go to Japan.[48]

There remained the question of Italy's claims on Austro-Hungary and her successor states. The matter had been shelved for some weeks while the terms of the treaty with Germany were discussed, but it came to the fore when, early in April, Lloyd George proposed that representatives of the Croats and the Slovenes should be asked to attend a conference about matters in dispute between Italy and Yugoslavia. Since the Italians regarded the Croats and the Slovenes as enemies, this proposal did not please them.

The crux of the problem was that the Treaty of London, on the strength of which Italy had entered the war on the side of the Entente Powers, dated from a time when the utter collapse of the Austro-Hungarian Empire was neither expected nor desired. It recognized Italy's interests in the Trentino, Trieste, Istria, and part of northern Dalmatia but did not mention the Croatian port of Fiume. When Austro-Hungary fell to pieces, the Italians, alarmed by the emergence of an independent Yugoslavia which might challenge their prospective dominance of the Adriatic, advanced a claim to Fiume on the ground that some 25,000 Italians lived there.

This claim seemed to Wilson utterly without merit. On the other hand, much as he disliked some features of the Treaty of London, he recognized that Italy's claim to the Trentino had some force. Admittedly it would put a number of German-speaking Tyroleans under Italian rule and to that extent was incompatible with Point 9 of the Fourteen Points, but Wilson admitted that since the Austrians had accepted an armistice without receiving a favorable response to their offer to negotiate on the basis of the Fourteen Points, the Italians were not bound to make peace with them on that basis.[49] When announcing to Orlando that he could not agree that Italy should have Fiume, he sought to sugar the pill by offering to back her claim to the whole of the Trentino as far north as the Brenner Pass. He failed, however, to make it clear that this offer was conditional on no more being said about Fiume.[50] The result was that Orlando held him to his promise so far as the Brenner frontier was concerned but claimed Fiume too.

Lloyd George and Clemenceau agreed with Wilson that Italy's claim to Fiume was not well founded. Nevertheless, they were reluctant to join him in giving a flat denial to the Italians. They foresaw that if they did so, Orlando would retaliate by insisting on his full rights under the Treaty of London. In that case they and the President might well find at the final reckoning that they had saved Fiume for the Yugoslavs only at the cost of giving Italy other tracts of Yugoslav territory to which she had no better right.

In the third week of April Lloyd George tried to break the deadlock by proposing, on the initiative of House, that Italy should receive everything to which she was entitled under the Treaty of London as far south as Istria and that Fiume and all disputed territories beyond Fiume should be held jointly by the great powers as trustees for the League of Nations, pending a settlement to be made by the League in the light of mature reflection.[51] Orlando rejected this solution, arguing that the Italian people would not understand why the Allied and Associated Powers should deny them Fiume after making major concessions to the French. Wilson's response was to publish a manifesto in which he appealed to the Italians not to abandon the principles for which he conceived the war to have been fought. Orlando then left Paris, and for nearly a fortnight he and Baron Sidney Sonnino, the Italian Foreign Minister, absented themselves from meetings of the Preliminary Peace Conference.

In the outcome Italy received the Trentino, Trieste, Istria, and the

Dalmatian port of Zara. Fiume was seized and held for a time by Italian extremists led by the poet Gabriele d'Annunzio but was afterward restored to Yugoslavia.

Relations with the Italians were further complicated by promises made to them and the French of spheres of influence in southern Anatolia. When Russia collapsed, the plans made in 1915 and 1916 for partition of the Ottoman Empire became impracticable, but that did not prevent the powers from continuing to take a keen interest in the subject. The fate of Constantinople and the Straits was a matter of concern to all the naval powers. The British were pledged to uphold the rights of Arab chieftains from Aden to Aleppo, had undertaken, in addition, to forward Zionist aspirations in Palestine, and, above all, were determined to safeguard the approaches to India and the Persian Gulf. The French claimed Syria and a sphere of interest in Cilicia. The Italians expected either a sphere of interest in the region of Adalia or its equivalent elsewhere. The Americans had never declared war on Turkey and were not parties to the Turkish armistice, but they nonetheless appointed a Senior Naval Officer, Turkey, whose duties were largely concerned with the furtherance of American commercial interests.[52]

Britain's policy in face of this potentially explosive situation was to keep a firm hold on as much as possible of the Ottoman Empire pending a settlement sanctioned by international agreement. When the French proposed early in 1919 to send troops to Lebanon, they were told in unmistakable terms that no reinforcements not called for by the British commander of the occupation forces would be allowed to disembark there or in Syria.[53] They were also warned that any attempt on their part to gain control of Syria without the consent of the inhabitants might have disastrous consequences.[54]

Even so, the British could not undertake to guard for an indefinite period an empire nearly half the size of the continental United States. They hoped for a time that the Americans might be willing to share the burden with them, but to retain large forces in Europe or the Near East after the conclusion of hostilities with Germany was no part of American policy.[55]

In these circumstances Lloyd George allowed himself to be persuaded that Greece had at least as good a right to protect the interests of Greek settlers in Anatolia as France or Italy had to develop its economic resources. Expert advisers warned him in vain that not

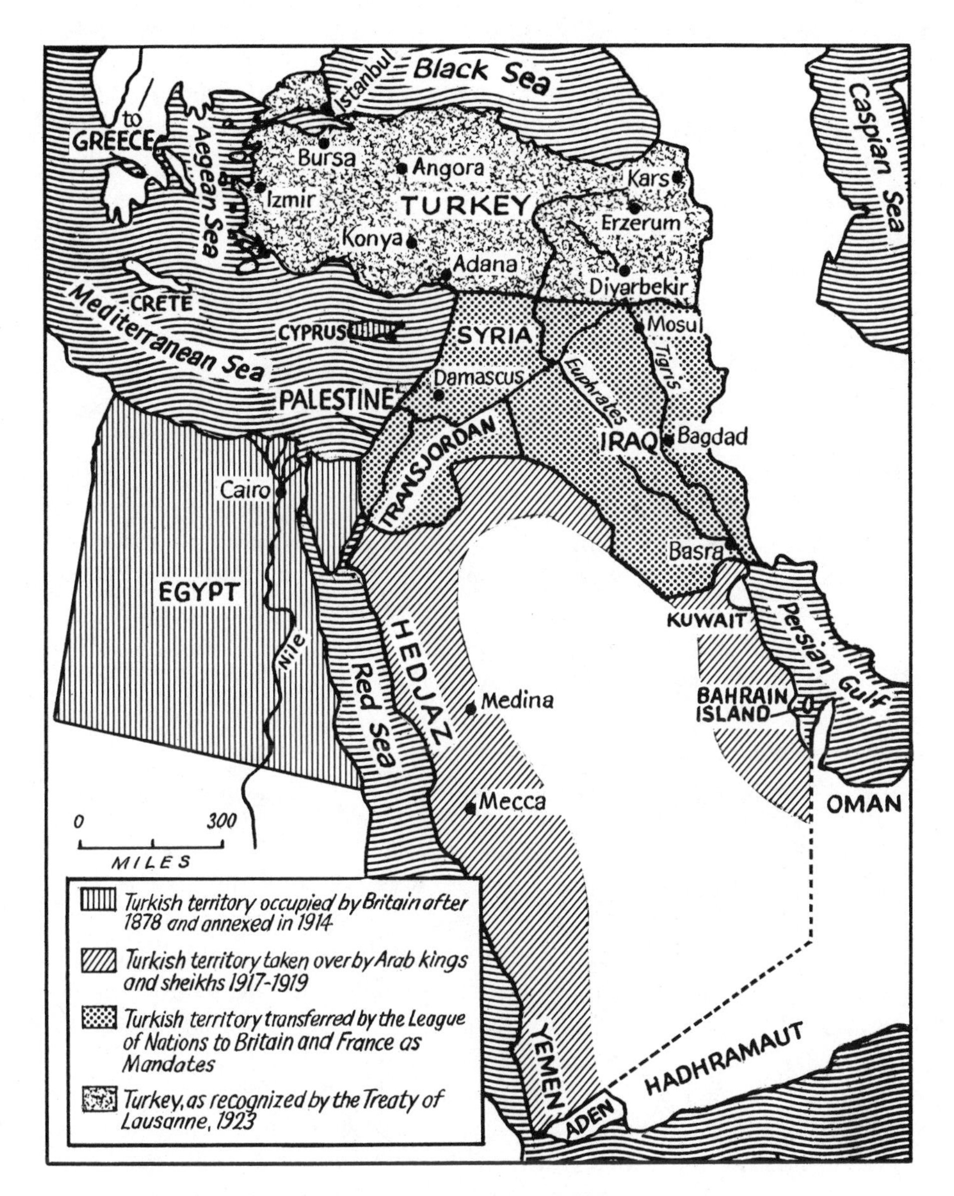

THE OTTOMAN EMPIRE

even a defeated Turkey would tolerate Greek interference in Asia Minor.

On Friday, May 2, Lloyd George asked the naval authorities to send a British and a Greek warship to Smyrna for the purpose of protecting the lives and property of its many Greek inhabitants.[56] On the following Monday he proposed to Clemenceau and Wilson that the division of the Ottoman Empire contemplated in the wartime agreements should be replaced by a system of mandates under the aegis of the League of Nations. The gist of his proposals was that the United States should take care of Constantinople and Armenia, France of Syria, Britain of Mesopotamia and Palestine, and Greece of Smyrna and its hinterland. The Italians, who had already been approached and had proved more tractable than might have been expected, were to drop their claim to a share of southern Anatolia and be compensated by a sphere of influence in Transcaucasia.

At a further meeting on May 6 Lloyd George, Clemenceau, and Wilson decided in the name of the Supreme War Council that one or two Greek divisions should be sent to Smyrna without delay. Sir Henry Wilson, according to his diary, protested that "this meant starting another war" but was overruled and ordered to prepare plans in consultation with American and French officers and the Greek Prime Minister Venizelos. Admiral Sir Somerset Gough-Calthorpe, the British Naval Commander in Chief in the Mediterranean, was told of the plan on the following day.[57] Four days later he was ordered to proceed to Smyrna. On that day an American battleship, accompanied by four destroyers, reached Smyrna on the orders of the President.[58]

The Supreme War Council intended, when these orders were given, that the Italians should be told of the expedition to Smyrna about twelve hours before the troops which were to land there left the Greek port of Kavalla. British and American officers called in at the planning stage felt that longer notice should be given. As things turned out, Orlando returned to Paris before the expedition was launched. It then transpired that news of the affair had already reached the Italian government. In the light of this discovery, the statesmen agreed that Italian troops should be allowed to land at Adalia at the same time that Greek troops went ashore at Smyrna.

On May 15 the Greeks duly disembarked at Smyrna under the guns of American and Allied warships. The landing was unopposed, but a number of Turks were killed when the Greeks opened fire on their hereditary enemies as the sequel to disorders which followed their occupation of the city. Soon afterward indignation in Turkey reached such a pitch that Mustapha Kemal, an officer sent by the sultan's government to supervise the execution of the armistice terms, was moved to raise the standard of revolt, defy the sultan, and establish a rival government at Ankara. The Allied and Associated Powers appointed an international commission under an American admiral to inquire into the alleged massacre of Turkish civilians at Smyrna, but no action was taken on its report.[59]

Meanwhile, the Allied and Associated Powers agreed, after many delays, on the terms to be offered to Germany. The draft treaty was presented to the German delegates at Versailles on May 7. Clemenceau opened the proceedings with a brief address; Count Ulrich von Brockdorff-Rantzau, the leading German delegate, read a long memorandum in which he protested vigorously against the "war guilt" clause. Clemenceau rose to deliver his formal speech, but Brockdorff-Rantzau observed the usual procedure at diplomatic conferences by making his contribution from a seated position. The Germans were thereby exposed to some ill-conceived reproaches. Brockdorff-Rantzau was an experienced diplomat. Although he is said to have been slightly lame, he would doubtless have risen to his feet had he foreseen that his failure to do so would be interpreted by President Wilson and other newcomers to diplomacy as a studied insult.

The Germans followed with written comments on the draft presented to them. The substance of their criticisms was that the terms proposed were not those which President Wilson's speeches had led them to expect. The Allied and Associated Powers did not admit that the terms were inconsistent with the President's principles but made a number of concessions. The most important was an undertaking to hold a plebiscite before deciding whether the coal fields of Upper Silesia should remain German or become Polish.

While the negotiations were in progress, the Allied and Associated Powers made arrangements to send troops across the Rhine, with the line of the Weser as their first objective, should their proposals be rejected. On June 23, amid political upheavals in Germany, the Germans agreed to sign the treaty. Some difficulty was experienced in finding delegates willing to affix their signatures to the document, but on Saturday, June 28, the ceremony was performed before a mixed audience. On the same day President Wilson left Paris for the United States, where he faced the task of persuading the Senate to ratify both the treaty and his undertaking to guarantee the new Franco-German frontier. When taking leave of the President, House urged him to "meet the Senate in a conciliatory spirit" but received a far from reassuring answer.[60]

Many features of the Treaty of Versailles were unsatisfactory from more points of view than one. Much the same was true of the treaty concluded with Austria in the following September. Austria, bereft of Hungary, Bohemia, Moravia, Slovakia, Ruthenia, Slovenia, Croatia, Bosnia, Herzegovina, the Trentino, Trieste, and Istria, was forbidden to safeguard her economic future by allying herself with Germany, even to the extent of concluding a customs union. Czechoslovakia, a country created ostensibly in the interests of self-determination, embraced within her frontiers 3,250,000 Austrian Germans, 3,500,000 Slovaks, Magyars, Ruthenians, and Poles, and 7,500,000 Czechs. To give Poland access to the sea, a corridor was driven through Germany, dividing Pomerania from East Prussia. Perhaps worse still, the disarmament terms imposed on the Germans were so harsh as almost to invite evasion. Yet they did not satisfy the French craving for security, since Germany's manpower and industrial potential were still far greater than those of France.

Despite such shortcomings, Lloyd George had some reason to feel when he returned to London that he had emerged from the Paris Conference with a balance of credit in his favor. The awkward problem of reparations had been shelved, albeit at a price not yet apparent. The French had been prevented from disrupting Germany by seizing the Rhineland and the Palatinate and from gaining permanent possession of the Saar unless the inhabitants voted at the end of a fixed period for union with France. Provision had been made in the Covenant of the League of Nations to alter territorial settlements which proved unjust or unworkable, and the promised adherence of the United States made it likely that edicts of the League would not be flouted. Admittedly the disarmament clauses of the Treaty of Versailles bore more hardly on German pride than seemed desirable; but the naval disarmament of Germany seemed a clear gain for Britain, and the military and air clauses would lose much of their sting if the French, reassured by American and British guarantees, could be persuaded to play their part in a general scaling down of armaments. Above all, Lloyd George could claim to have handled with every appearance of success the difficult question of Anglo-American naval rivalry. He had avoided an open clash with the United States, paved the way for a naval agreement without committing the country to any particular course of action, and obtained from an authoritative source an assurance that meanwhile he could count on President Wilson not to build a fleet in competition with the Royal Navy.[61]

Lloyd George recognized that, even so, agreement with the United States would be difficult unless the Irish problem were first disposed of. Subversive activities in Ireland, although financed partly by subscriptions wrung from Irish landowners and shopkeepers by appeals to patriotism or threats of violence, were known to be heavily subsidized by American sympathizers. Complaints had been made, too, of anti-British propaganda by citizens of the United States sent to Ireland on a fact-finding mission.

In letters written from London and Paris after the President's departure, House warned his chief that the British were beginning to think of the United States very much as they had thought of Germany before the war. In those days Germany was forging ahead as a great industrial power with worldwide economic and commercial interests, but she had thrown everything away by her arrogance and lack of statesmanship.[62] The United States, House thought, was now in a comparable position and must guard against the same mistakes. He added that Britain and France faced serious financial problems. Since any reduction in their spending power would have adverse effects on international trade, the United States had everything to gain by helping to put them on their feet.[63] He urged the President to reach agreement with the British about belligerent rights in a future war, summon a meeting of the League of Nations to discuss disarmament, and warn the people of the United States not to expect loans made to Entente countries during the war to be repaid in full.[64] After the Napoleonic Wars, Britain had waived repayment of most of the money advanced to her Continental allies and had gained immeasurably in the long run by doing so. House, without citing this precedent, proposed that the United States should follow it by writing off as war expenditure an unspecified proportion of her advances to the Allies. The balance should be repaid on terms which ought, in his opinion, to take account of Germany's capacity to meet her liability for reparations.[65]

However, to initiate such a policy, President Wilson would have had to begin by gaining the confidence of the Senate. He made no visible attempt to do so. When he appeared before the Senate Foreign Relations Committee in August, he seemed unable or unwilling to provide the reasoned account of his transactions which Senators expected.[66] Moreover, he strained credulity beyond its limits by asserting that he had known nothing before his arrival in Paris of the so-called secret treaties between the Entente Powers.* In point of fact, the British had offered, when the United States entered the war, a full disclosure of these wartime agreements; later the Russians had published long extracts in an attempt to discredit statesmen who wished to continue the war. In any case, the "secret treaties" were notoriously not secret. Since they had been the subject of comment and speculation in diplomatic and governmental circles on both sides of the Atlantic almost from the moment when they were signed, it was inconceivable that a statesman with President Wilson's sources of information should have known nothing about them until the eve of the Preliminary Peace Conference.

The President, although visibly shaken in health and spirits by his brush with the Senate, was nonetheless determined that his fellow citizens should demonstrate their faith in the Covenant of the League of Nations by wholeheartedly endorsing his acceptance of the Treaty of Versailles. Early in September he set forth, against medical advice, on a strenuous speechmaking tour of the Western states. After delivering thirty-seven speeches in little more than three weeks, he collapsed at Pueblo, Colorado. He was hurried back to Washington, where he suffered a seizure which left him half-paralyzed.

Almost simultaneously House succumbed, as he was leaving Paris, to an illness which kept him from the scene of action for many weeks. Thus the Democratic Party was without effective leadership at a time when Senators were called upon to choose between outright rejection of the treaty and ratification of a version qualified by more than a dozen reservations sponsored by the Republican Senator Henry Cabot Lodge. The President, an invalid shielded from contact with his political advisers, sent from his sickbed a message to the effect that he would regard acceptance of the treaty with the Lodge reservations as tantamount to its nullification.[67] The result was that when a motion for ratification with the Lodge reservations was put

* This lapse has never been satisfactorily explained. It has been conjectured that the President may have thought that a question put to him referred merely to a British promise to support the Japanese claim to the Shantung concession. There is ample evidence that he was aware, when he enunciated the Fourteen Points, of the provisions of the Treaty of London, the Sykes-Picot Agreement, and the Treaty of St. Jean-de-Maurienne.

to the Senate in November, loyalty to their ailing chief impelled the Democrats to vote against it, at the risk of losing their only chance of securing ratification on any terms. A motion for unconditional ratification was still more decisively rejected.

House then wrote two letters in which he proposed that the President, without expressly withdrawing his opposition to the Lodge reservations, should let his supporters know that he would not object to ratification of the treaty in any form acceptable to the European signatories. A confidential message in that sense would release Democratic Senators from any obligation to resist proposals for the amendment of the treaty merely because they were sponsored by Republicans. At the same time, it would place on the Senate the onus of reducing its proposals to a formula which the European signatories could accept. The President would then be in a position to counter any reproaches from Allied statesmen by pointing out that he had done his best to secure ratification of the treaty in its original form and was not accountable for any decision on their part to adopt a different version in order to meet the wishes of his political opponents.[68]

President Wilson did not reply to either of these letters. House had not seen him since the previous June, and the two were never again to meet. A motion for ratification of the treaty with substantially the same reservations as those proposed in November was put to the Senate in the spring of 1920, but without success. Twenty-three Democrats voted against the motion, and it failed by seven votes to gain the necessary two-thirds majority. In the light of these figures the Senate was not asked to ratify the document by which the President had undertaken to guarantee the frontier between France and Germany, and in consequence both the American guarantee and the parallel guarantee given by the British became invalid.

This outcome was fatal to Lloyd George's hopes of a Franco-German reconciliation and a general scaling down of armaments. The French, deprived of the American and British guarantees for which they had renounced their claim to a strategic frontier on the Rhine, insisted on maintaining a large army. A new guarantee by Britain alone was mooted, but the British, although willing to consider a short-term agreement couched in general terms, would not commit themselves to the long-term military alliance which the French thought necessary.

From the British point of view, a further disadvantage of the breach between President and Senate was that it ruled out any immediate prospect of concluding the proposed naval agreement. Some weeks before the President was stricken, Walter Long, who had succeeded Sir Eric Geddes as First Lord of the Admiralty in the previous January, asked his colleagues what assumptions regarding future relations with foreign powers he should make when preparing revised financial estimates to meet the transition from war to peace. The Cabinet, not yet in a position to know that the United States would repudiate the Treaty of Versailles and refuse to join the League of Nations, thereupon decided that the service departments should base revised estimates for the financial year 1920–21 on the assumption that the British Empire would not be involved in any great war during the next ten years.[69] The Admiralty, in particular, was directed to reduce its expenditure from an estimated £171,000,000 in the current year to a maximum of £60,000,000.[70] Only a few months later, the government learned to its dismay that the United States Navy Department was seeking approval for the construction of three capital ships and twenty-five smaller warships not included in the current version of the 1916 program.[71]

Since Congress provided no funds for new construction in 1919 and 1920, the ultimate effect of this proposal on American naval strength was negligible. Even so, the 1919 program, although far less ambitious than the abandoned 1918 program, seemed to the British a clear contravention of the spirit of the House-Cecil correspondence. Furthermore, their faith in American goodwill was severely shaken in the following months by events in Ireland and immoderate expressions of anti-British sentiment in the United States.

In the context of these anxieties—augmented by signs of unrest throughout the Moslem world and persistent reports of Communist-inspired attempts to foment industrial disturbances at home—the British government gave earnest consideration in and after the summer of 1920 to the situation that would arise when the American 1916 program was completed. Figures produced by the Admiralty pointed inescapably to the conclusion that unless British shipyards began building new capital ships without delay or the Americans could be persuaded to modify their aims, the United States Navy would attain within the next three to five years an overwhelming preponderance in post-Jutland battleships and battle cruisers.[72]

10

Between the Wars: I

AT the end of the First World War Britain, if no longer the richest, was certainly the most powerfully armed nation in the world. When the cease-fire sounded on the Western Front, more than 4,000 British or British-controlled warships, auxiliaries, and light naval craft were in commission; the British Army numbered about 3,000,000 of all ranks; the Royal Air Force, formed in 1918 by fusion of the Royal Flying Corps with the Royal Naval Air Service, mustered a first-line strength of some 3,000 aircraft, backed by more than 20,000 aircraft in training and holding units.[1]

As soon as the war was over, this vast accretion of armed strength became a burden which the national economy could not support. So huge an army, in particular, was quite beyond the nation's means. Except that roughly 1,000,000 conscripts had to be retained for a limited period so that Britain could contribute her quota to the armies of occupation, the United Kingdom soon reverted to its former dependence on a small professional army supplemented by a Territorial Army not permanently embodied.

The British, as pioneers of armored warfare, recognized that tanks supported by aircraft employed in a tactical role were likely to play a crucial part in any future war on a European or a global scale. Reforms designed to put the British Army in the forefront of technical progress were proposed soon after the armistice and again in 1926, when General Sir George Milne announced on becoming Chief of the Imperial General Staff that he intended to mechanize the army, form a number of armored divisions, and restore the tactical mobility of infantry formations by providing them with armored fighting vehicles. These proposals met some opposition from reactionary elements within the Army, but it was not this which played the chief part in delaying their adoption until almost the eve of the Second World War. From 1919 to 1932 the War Office was under orders to frame its annual estimates on the assumption that there would be no great war involving the British Empire for at least ten years; thereafter until the spring of 1939 the overriding assumptions were that Britain's chief contribution to any future European war would be made at sea and in the air and that no more than a token force of perhaps two infantry divisions and a tank brigade would be sent across the Channel.[2] During the greater part of the period between the wars the War Office was therefore not called upon, indeed was expressly forbidden, to form the large, highly mechanized expeditionary force which would be needed if Britain were to make a major contribution on land to a European war. Its primary task was to provide, on a limited budget, such forces as were needed to maintain order in a scattered Empire and provide a small reserve against the unforeseen.

During the first few years of peace the Royal Air Force, too, was drastically pruned in the interests of economy. In 1918 its resources included bomber, fighter, and reconnaissance squadrons for army support and maritime cooperation; an "independent" or "strategic" force of eleven bomber squadrons intended for attacks on German rail centers and centers of production; and a home-based fighter force of sixteen squadrons placed at the disposal of the Commander in Chief, Home Forces, for the purpose of repelling air attacks on the United Kingdom. Two years later so little of all this remained that the Air Force could scarcely meet the needs of the Army and the Navy for direct support. The "independent" bomber force had been swept away, and not one fighter squadron was specifically assigned to air defense.

Air Chief Marshal Sir Hugh Trenchard, Chief of the Air Staff from 1919 to 1929 and also for a brief period in 1918, foresaw that demands from the War Office and the Admiralty for direct control of squadrons cooperating with the Army and the Navy might lead to the extinction of the Air Force as a separate service unless he could show that it was capable of playing an independent role. A rebellion in Mesopotamia (afterward called Iraq) gave him an opportunity of proposing in 1920 that air attacks should be substituted for punitive expeditions by land forces as a means of keeping order in unsettled territories. The method he advocated would involve the bombing of villages, forts, or strongholds after due warning had been given. The system was introduced experimentally in 1922 in Mesopotamia and Transjordania, was afterward extended to Aden, and was also tried for a time on the North-West Frontier of India. It proved, on the whole, an effective, economical, and relatively humane method of punishing wrongdoers in places which columns of troops could have reached only at the risk of provoking conflicts with trigger-happy tribesmen on the outward and return journeys.[3] Its chief disadvantages were that it exposed the government to charges of punishing the innocent with the guilty and that repeated bombing of undefended targets in favorable conditions gave the Air Force a highly misleading impression of the tasks it would face in war.

Trenchard also proposed that the Air Ministry should become responsible for coordinating countermeasures to seaborne assaults on the United Kingdom and for repelling air attacks. The government did not agree that naval and land forces used to repel seaborne raiders or invaders would be best controlled by an air officer; but a standing subcommittee of the Committee of Imperial Defence, under Arthur Balfour, gave a sympathetic hearing to the rest of Trenchard's case. Trenchard pointed out that since 1918 the War Office had disbanded or diverted to other uses all the antiaircraft artillery and searchlight units formerly employed for the air defense of London and had ceased to call on the Air Force to provide fighters for the purpose. In consequence, London was exposed to the risk of attack by the French Metropolitan Air Force, believed to be about 300 bombers and roughly the same number of fighters strong.

When reporting these observations to his colleagues, Balfour added that in the event of trouble with France, "a continuous torrent of high explosives at the rate of seventy-five tons a day for an indefinite period" might paralyze the War Office and the Admiralty.[4] This was not a very convincing picture. The French were pursuing aims in Syria of which the British did not approve and were putting more pressure on Germany to meet her liability for reparations than the British thought advisable; but there was no reason to suppose that they would ever use their Metropolitan Air Force to bomb London, or that it was intended for such a purpose. If they did take so improbable a course, a naval bombardment of French ports would, in the Admiralty's opinion, provide a fairly effective countermeasure.[5] Even so, there was something in the argument that Britain's lack of air defenses must tend, in the long run, to weaken her diplomacy. Furthermore, the government was aware that aircraft manufacturers hit by postwar economies were in low water and that the future of British civil, as well as military, aviation would be prejudiced if they went out of business. Partly in deference to Trenchard's wishes, partly as a means of indirectly subsidizing the aircraft industry, Lloyd George and his colleagues agreed in 1922 to form a small Metropolitan Air Force of nine fighter and fourteen bomber squadrons.[6] This would be supplemented by antiaircraft and searchlight units to be provided by the War Office but controlled by the Air Force. Bomber squadrons were included because Trenchard insisted that the best way of securing immunity from air attack was to possess the means of carrying the war into the enemy's country.

These decisions were made against a background of unemployment and industrial strife at home and to the accompaniment of dire events in the Near East.

After the Greek landing at Smyrna in 1919, Mustapha Kemal gained such an ascendancy in Asia Minor that the chances of enforcing the peace treaty concluded between the Allies and the Sultan of Turkey at Sèvres in 1920 began to seem remote even before the treaty was signed. France and Italy, abandoning their claims to spheres of influence in Anatolia, soon came to terms with Kemal. Lloyd George, believing that Kemal could still be brought to his knees by the Greek Army, continued to back the Greeks despite warnings from colleagues and service advisers that persistence in his pro-Greek policy would unite all patriotic Turks more firmly than ever behind Kemal.

In the summer of 1920, after British seamen had occupied Constantinople with the consent of the Supreme War Council, Kemalist forces approached the Asian shore of the Bosporus and the Sea of Marmara, but they soon withdrew in face of a vigorous bombardment by British warships and attacks by shipborne aircraft.[7] Lloyd George then persuaded the Supreme War Council to agree that the Greek Army should be allowed to advance in the general direction of Ankara. After reaching Bandirma on the Sea of Marmara, the Greeks were halted at the request of the French and the Italians. In August Venizelos reported that Kemalist forces were massing for a counterattack and that he would soon need financial support. Two months later he offered to drive Kemal from Ankara and Trebizond in return for subsidies in cash and kind.

Soon afterward the young King Alexander of Greece, who had come to the throne in 1917 when Venizelos deposed the pro-German Constantine, died from blood poisoning brought on by the bite of a pet monkey. The Venizelist party was heavily defeated at the elections which followed, and Constantine's return from exile forced Venizelos to seek political asylum in France.

On Constantine's orders, the Greek forces in Anatolia resumed the offensive early in 1921. Weakened by the dismissal of officers suspected of undue partiality for Venizelos, they made little progress. In September, after suffering heavy losses in a long-drawn battle west of Ankara, they broke off their attacks. The Allies declared their neutrality and offered mediation, but the French and the Italians were known to be supplying Kemal with arms and ammunition.[8] Contrary to expectations, the Soviet government gave him little help.

In the following summer the Greeks strengthened their forces in Thrace with the obvious intention of overrunning what was left of Turkey in Europe. The Greek government asked at the end of July to be allowed to send troops into Constantinople, but the British made it clear that they intended to hold Constantinople for the sultan and that no such encroachment would be allowed.[9] The Kemalists, profiting by the transfer of Greek troops from Asia Minor to Thrace, then fell upon Constantine's remaining forces in Anatolia and drove them in wild disorder back to Smyrna. Thousands of Greeks and Armenians who fled before Kemal's troops were rescued by British and American warships, but many perished in a disastrous fire which broke out in the Armenian quarter of Smyrna and swept to the waterfront. Political upheavals in Athens then forced Constantine to abdicate for the second time, and a military government favorable to Venizelos came to office.

Lloyd George, often accused in the past of sheltering behind the

Greek Army, responded to the news of its collapse with a reckless courage which did nothing to placate his critics. On September 8 the Admiralty informed Admiral Sir Osmond Brock, who had succeeded Robeck in command of the Mediterranean Fleet, that the Cabinet regarded control of the Straits as a cardinal British interest and that any attempt by Kemalist forces to cross them must be resisted.[10] General Sir Charles Harington, the British commander of the Allied land forces on both sides of the Straits, received similar instructions. Although empowered to withdraw to the European side at his discretion, Harington was left in no doubt that the government would regard the abandonment of his positions at Chanak, on the Asian shore of the Dardanelles, as a grave setback.[11] The government arranged to reinforce Harington by one division, Brock by three battleships and a battalion of marines, in addition to a number of cruisers, destroyers, and other warships. Appeals to the self-governing Dominions for material and moral support were coolly received, perhaps not surprisingly since the Dominions had not been consulted when Lloyd George, Clemenceau, and Woodrow Wilson decided to put the Greeks ashore at Smyrna in 1919.

Appeals to European powers were not much more successful. The French agreed that a joint note, hinting at a settlement on terms more favorable to the Turks than the abortive Treaty of Sèvres, should be dispatched to Ankara, but they were clearly unwilling to fight Kemal should he refuse the bait. Britain, as the Admiralty had already warned Brock, might have to act alone.

Brock and the Admiralty agreed that the only sure method of preventing the Kemalists from crossing the Straits was to deprive them of ships or sink such ships as they managed to secure.[12] Sir Horace Rumbold, the British high commissioner on the spot, pointed out that Constantinople depended largely on shipborne supplies. Drastic interference with shipping might be so much resented that the British garrison would be imperiled. Accordingly he asked that he and the two service chiefs should be allowed to act as they thought best. The government replied that it had "complete confidence" in Rumbold, Harington, and Brock.[13]

This message was dispatched on September 25, 1922. By the following day substantial numbers of Kemalist troops had entered an area at Chanak which the Allies had designated as a neutral zone and were so close to Harington's lines that only tact and patience on both sides averted a clash. A conference which might lead to a peaceful settlement was in prospect when, on September 29, the Cabinet instructed Harington to deliver an ultimatum threatening war if the Kemalists did not withdraw. Harington, stoutly backed by Rumbold, decided to withhold the ultimatum and continue his attempt to arrange a conference. As a result of his and Rumbold's efforts, representatives of Britain, France, Greece, Italy, and Kemalist Turkey met early in October at Mudanya, on the Sea of Marmara, to negotiate a convention by which Kemal agreed to withdraw his troops from the neutral zones at Chanak and elsewhere. In November the sultan, recognizing that Kemal had become the effective ruler of Turkey, sought British protection and left Constantinople in a British warship. The Treaty of Lausanne, signed in the summer of 1923 after prolonged negotiations in which Curzon's peculiar talents proved of great value to the British, ended a long squabble for control of Constantinople and the Straits by leaving the Turks in possession on terms generally regarded as fair.

Thus a new war in the Near East was averted largely through the good sense of Harington and Rumbold. But Lloyd George's attempt to force the pace was too much for supporters already exasperated by his high-handedness, his lavish bestowal of honors on subscribers to party funds, his wayward handling of Irish and foreign affairs, and his failure to grapple to their satisfaction with economic and financial problems. As the sequel to a meeting at which a speech by the relatively obscure Stanley Baldwin made a powerful impression, the Conservative or Unionist Party withdrew its support from the coalition government soon after the Chanak crisis. A general election in November brought Bonar Law to power as the first Conservative statesman to form a government since Balfour's resignation in 1905. When Bonar Law fell mortally ill in the following year, Curzon was summoned in haste to London but found on arrival that not he but Baldwin was to be the next Prime Minister.

Among many misdemeanors of which the Conservatives accused Lloyd George was his failure to summon frequent meetings of the Committee of Imperial Defence. Either because the Prime Minister was preoccupied with other matters or because, as was sometimes alleged, he was reluctant to hear his Near Eastern policy called in question by the Chiefs of Staff, most of the functions of the committee were discharged between 1919 and 1922 by Balfour's standing subcommittee. One of the new government's first acts was to demonstrate its keen interest in national and imperial defense by appointing a committee under Lord Salisbury, Lord President of the Council, to look into the whole question of cooperation between the fighting services. The Salisbury Committee was also asked to say how strong it thought the Metropolitan Air Force ought to be.[14]

Almost simultaneously the French decided, in the teeth of British dissent, to invade the Ruhr in the hope of establishing a lien on mines and factories as security for the payment of reparations. The Salisbury Committee, after hearing evidence from Trenchard, came to the conclusion that prompt action was needed to remedy the "menacing position" created by the disparity between British and French air power.[15] In the light of this rather alarmist verdict, the government decided in the summer of 1923 to raise the strength of the Metropolitan Air Force to thirty-five bomber and seventeen fighter squadrons with a first-line establishment of 598 aircraft.

In the following year a committee of experts recommended that a new command, to be called Air Defence of Great Britain, should be established to administer the Metropolitan Air Force and control not only home-based bomber and fighter squadrons, but also some 200 to 300 guns and 600 to 700 searchlights to be provided by the War Office. An Observer Corps, staffed by civilian volunteers with the status of special constables, would be created to report movements of aircraft in parts of the country open to air attack. Air Defence of Great Britain would retain direct control of bomber squadrons but would delegate control of fighter squadrons, guns, and searchlights to a subordinate command called Fighting Area.

The government believed in 1923 that the system would be ready for use about the end of 1928.[16] In 1925 Stanley Baldwin's second Conservative government, in office after a brief period of Labor rule, learned that nearly half the bomber and fighter squadrons would be ready within the next few months but that even so, the scheme could not be completed before 1930. In the same year a committee headed by Lord Birkenhead, then Secretary of State for India but afterward Lord Chancellor, expressed the opinion that in view of the improved relations between Britain, France, and Germany which a series of talks at Locarno had created, completion could safely be deferred for some years but that the scheme ought not to be abandoned.[17] The government then decided to aim at completion in 1936. In 1929

Ramsay MacDonald's second Labor government sanctioned a further postponement, this time until 1938.[18]

These changes made the formulation of equipment and training programs rather difficult. In any case the progress of the fifty-two-squadron scheme did not accurately reflect progress over the whole field of air defense. For many years recruiting for units of the Territorial Army which would man the antiaircraft guns and searchlights was hampered by financial restrictions, a general distaste for war and warlike measures, and a marked disinclination on the part of many members of the public to believe that the air defenses could in any case be made effective. Territorial units assigned to air defense were also handicapped by infrequent opportunities of rehearsing their wartime roles. Even though their annual periods in camp could generally be made to coincide with air defense exercises by bomber and fighter squadrons, much of their time had to be devoted to general military training. Guns left over from the First World War were fairly plentiful, but practice with weapons and equipment known to be obsolete or obsolescent did little to stimulate interest in antiaircraft gunnery at a time when scoffers were only too ready to assert that destroying aircraft by fire from the ground was next door to impossible.

In these circumstances, progress was very uneven. When the ten-year rule was suspended in 1932, the Metropolitan Air Force had reached about four-fifths of its planned strength. Much thought had been given since 1924 to measures of passive air defense, such as public air-raid warnings, dispersal, the maintenance of essential services under air attack, the treatment of casualties, and protection against poisonous or asphyxiating gases.[19] The network of posts to be manned by the Observer Corps was incomplete, but not so seriously imperfect that the system could not have been put into effect in an emergency.[20] Air defense formations administered by the War Office, on the other hand, were so much behind schedule that they could not have manned more than about a third of the equipment needed to complete the scheme designed to go into effect on the outbreak of war.[21] The standard weapon was still the 3-inch antiaircraft gun of the 1914–18 era, and the whole of the air defenses depended for early warning of the approach of hostile aircraft on sound locators whose shortcomings would soon become glaringly apparent.

Since Britain was not seriously threatened between 1922 and 1932 by any air force within striking distance, these deficiencies were significant only insofar as they had some effect on subsequent developments. The question of Anglo-American naval rivalry was far more urgent and important.

When the British government enunciated the ten-year rule in 1919 and ordered the Admiralty to keep expenditure in the coming year within close limits, Lloyd George and his colleagues still hoped that notwithstanding President Wilson's illness and the Senate's repudiation of his policies, a naval agreement with the United States could be negotiated in the not too distant future. As a first step they asked Sir Edward Grey, who had become Viscount Grey of Fallodon, to undertake a special mission to Washington. Grey failed to see the President but reported that the United States Navy was "very short of personnel." [22] Early in 1920 he advised the government to set the Americans a good example by adopting moderate naval estimates for 1920–21.

This the government had already made up its mind to do. In the outcome the Admiralty was unable to come down to the modest figure of £60,000,000 proposed for 1920–21 but agreed to lop part of the difference from its provisional estimate for the current year. When presenting revised figures to the Cabinet in the autumn of 1919, the Board of Admiralty pointed out, however, that Britain would soon drop to the position of second naval power if no new construction were undertaken in the near future and if the Americans completed their 1916 program. In other words, either the government must accept relegation to second place or it must choose between coming to terms with the United States and adopting a program of new construction whose effects on American policy could not be foreseen.[23]

Within the next few months the First Lord of the Admiralty, Walter Long, persuaded Parliament without much difficulty to accept both his final estimate for the current year and a revised figure for 1920–21. As no provision was made for new construction, there was nothing in his proposals to excite hostility in the United States. He did, however, excite the suspicions of the influential American oil lobby by making some unguarded references to the strategic importance of oil in a speech delivered at the Institution of Petroleum Technologists in London.[24] The oil resources of Mesopotamia and the Persian Gulf, which presumably he had in mind when he spoke of securing "the supplies of oil now available in the world," were very small compared with those under American control, but his remarks, which were far more widely reported than might have been expected, were bound to seem provocative at a time when rumors were circulating in the United States to the effect that the oil deposits of the New World were approaching exhaustion.

In the meantime Beatty had succeeded Wemyss as First Sea Lord. He pointed out in the summer of 1920 that the Admiralty had no mandate to depart from the one-power standard repeatedly affirmed since the beginning of the century. If the principle that the Royal Navy should not be inferior in strength and firepower to any of its rivals were not to become a dead letter, new construction *must* be undertaken. Should no battleships or battle cruisers be laid down in the near future, Britain would possess in 1925 only one post-Jutland capital ship, the *Hood.* By that time the Americans, if they went on with their 1916 program, would have at least six battleships and six battle cruisers superior in firepower to any British ship. By the same date the Japanese, unless they modified their current programs, would have completed four battleships and four battle cruisers comparable with those which the Americans were building.[25]

Accordingly, Beatty proposed that four capital ships should be laid down in 1921 and the same number in 1922. Ships of other classes already on the stocks, including the aircraft carriers *Eagle* and *Hermes,* should be completed, and the battle cruiser *Furious* should be transformed into a carrier. The cost of the capital ship and carrier program, to be spread over five years, was estimated at £82,000,000.[26]

This was not a very large sum for the taxpayer to be asked to find in order to bring the Navy up to date. In the course of the controversy aroused by Beatty's proposals the minds of Lloyd George and his colleagues were, however, powerfully affected by the fear of starting an armaments race whose ultimate consequences could not be foreseen. When the Committee of Imperial Defence met in December to consider whether Britain should start building in direct competition with the United States, Lloyd George described the question before the committee as the most important and most difficult it had ever had to face.[27]

The substance of the case against Beatty's proposals was that Britain could not afford to make an enemy of the United States. Charles

Evans Hughes, the new American Secretary of State, had already threatened to stage a "Congressional demonstration" in favor of the Irish nationalist movement if Britain refused to drop the Japanese alliance.[28] For that reason, among others, far more was at stake than the cost of a few capital ships and aircraft carriers. The Americans, undisguisedly bent on creating "a navy second to none," would doubtless respond to any challenge by redoubling not only their naval effort, but also their attempts to undermine British power and influence by other means. With roughly twice Britain's population, they could raise twice as much money by imposing the same rate of taxation and thus could build more ships than the British.[29] Moreover, if Britain adopted a policy which involved even a remote risk of war with the United States, well-defended bases capable of accommodating a modern fleet would have to be developed in Bermuda and probably on the west coast of Canada. Such measures would be expensive, unpopular, and provocative.

On the other side of the case it was argued that while war with the United States might be "unthinkable," subservience to a foreign power whose government might become the tool of a ruthless commercial oligarchy was equally repugnant. Advocates of a strong navy pointed out that any advantages which the Americans derived from their ability to raise large sums by taxation might be offset by alliances. Also, there were means short of war by which the American eagle's claws might be blunted if the need arose. The United States, with her mixed population and large black minority, her extreme laissez-faire economy and her uneasy relations with Mexico and Spain, might prove extremely vulnerable to the weapon of subsidized propaganda which was being used against the British in Ireland, Egypt, and elsewhere.

This reasoning did not convince the government that direct competition with the United States in capital-ship construction would be wise. There remained the possibility that the Americans might be outmaneuvered. If Britain could find a way of retaining command of the sea without exciting American suspicions by saddling herself with a large, expensive, and possibly useless post-Jutland battle fleet, her statesmen would not need to defer to the American oil lobby, the Navy League, the Senate, or the State Department. The question of renewing or dropping the Japanese alliance could then be decided on its merits.

Accordingly, toward the end of 1920 the government invited a subcommittee of the Committee of Imperial Defence, under Bonar Law, to consider whether a combination of aircraft, submarines, and cruisers could provide adequate protection for British trade in the absence of a powerful modern battle fleet. The subcommittee found, after interrogating scores of witnesses, that it could not reach agreement on all points; but none of its members was prepared to say that the capital ship had ceased to be the arbiter of naval power. The subcommittee did not expressly endorse Beatty's proposals, but provision was made in the estimates for 1921–22 for £2,500,000 to be spent on "replacement of obsolete ships." [30]

The future of the Japanese alliance was discussed in ministerial and official circles on many occasions between the early winter of 1919 and the summer of 1921. Until the eleventh hour these discussions were based on the assumption that since the treaty with Japan had been renewed for ten years in the summer of 1911, it would expire in the summer of 1921 unless renewed. Almost at the last moment, expert scrutiny of the text revealed that the treaty was intended to remain in force after the end of the ten-year period unless denounced.[31] This discovery had little practical effect. The Japanese, well aware of American hostility to their alliance with Britain, knew that for all practical purpose the treaty would lapse unless positive action were taken to renew it.

The issue appeared to some of Lloyd George's critics much simpler than it did to him. In their view, the question was whether Britain should continue to support Japan in accordance with her traditional policy of preserving the balance of power by upholding the weak against the strong or should turn her back on tradition and throw her ally overboard at the behest of the United States because the Americans were rich and the Japanese comparatively poor. If she sacrificed honor to expediency by taking the latter course, her reputation for fair dealing would be lost, and she would cease within a generation to be a world power.

This was not the light in which the government viewed the matter. To Lloyd George and to many of his colleagues, it did not seem beyond the bounds of possibility that the Japanese alliance might be renewed on terms which would reconcile the Americans to its existence or inappropriate that pressure should, if necessary, be put upon the Japanese to accept such terms. Some ministers professed to see no reason why Britain should not afterward maintain good relations with both countries.

Strategists tended, on the whole, to regard this as too artless a view. The government, they thought, must choose between appeasing a power-hungry United States and retaining the goodwill of Japan; it could not do both. Even so, it would be wrong to suppose that there was a clear-cut division of opinion between statesmen on the one hand and soldiers and sailors on the other. Nor were misgivings about the effect on Britain's future of renewed ties with Japan confined to civilians. It was not a civilian minister but a naval officer, Admiral Jellicoe, who advanced the proposition, during a tour of the overseas Empire in 1919, that Britain could rely on the friendship of the Americans and that Japan was "the nation with which trouble might conceivably arise in the future." [32] The trouble he had in mind was an attempt by the Japanese to invade Australia. This, he thought, would be preceded by attacks on Hong Kong and Singapore and attempts to establish advanced bases in New Guinea and the Indonesian archipelago or farther east. Adding that it would be unwise to count on American help, he proposed that an imperial fleet of sixteen capital ships, with other warships, should be based in Singapore.[33]

Many years later Jellicoe was given credit for predicting the events of 1941 and the early part of 1942. But he did not foresee the circumstances in which Japan would go to war with the British Empire and the United States or that she would do so not primarily for the purpose of invading Australia but of establishing her claim to a dominant position in East Asia. His report was thus not so much an exercise in foresight as a reflection of somewhat ill-considered opinions put before him in Australia at a time when Japan's future relations with the Anglo-Saxon world were still in the melting pot.

Jellicoe's conclusions were promptly repudiated by his superiors.[34] Nevertheless, the Admiralty agreed that, *if it were decided that the British Empire should prepare for war with Japan,* Singapore and Sydney would be suitable bases for an Eastern Fleet.[35] The fact that no such decision had been made did not prevent the Admiralty from thereafter assuming, for purposes of administrative planning, that a powerful fleet would one day be needed at Singapore. In the early summer of 1921 the Naval Staff completed "a full study of the supply problems involved in the despatch of a large fleet to the Far East, working on the assumption of war with Japan in 1930." [36] This document was accepted by the Board of Admiralty on May 26 as a basis for future planning.[37] In the same month the Admiralty submitted to the Overseas Defence Subcommittee of the Committee of Imperial Defence "detailed and specific" proposals for the development of a naval base at Singapore.[38] The substance of these proposals came in due course before Balfour's standing subcommittee. The outcome was that on June 16, four days *before* the opening of an imperial conference summoned to discuss, among other matters, the future of the Japanese alliance, Balfour obtained the Cabinet's assent to the development of the Singapore base "as funds became available." [39]

These facts may be thought to lend some color to complaints that the Cabinet made only perfunctory and insincere attempts to sound informed opinion before embracing a policy which implied hostility to Japan. On the other hand, it must be admitted that those of the government's advisers who were best qualified to weigh the strategic disadvantages of terminating the Japanese alliance failed conspicuously to present a united front. The Admiralty, when consulted by the Foreign Office early in 1920, replied after the Naval Staff had "deliberated the issues involved" that renewal of the alliance seemed "neither necessary nor desirable." [40] The reason given was that the Navy could not provide the "powerful squadron" which the Foreign Office thought should be sent to Singapore "to strengthen the hands of our negotiators." This advice was directly contrary to that tendered by the Chief of the Imperial General Staff, who argued that Britain could secure Japanese support on terms of equality or even superiority but could make friends with the United States only at the cost of accepting an inferior position. It was also contrary to the advice given by Sir Auckland Geddes, the British ambassador in Washington. The ambassador (a brother of Sir Eric Geddes) thought that renewal of the alliance could not make the Americans much more hostile than they had already shown themselves to be. He proposed that the alliance should be renewed for a limited period on terms which would bring it into harmony with the Covenant of the League of Nations.[41]

Conflicting opinions were expressed, too, by spokesmen of the self-governing Dominions. Jellicoe's proposal that Japan should be regarded as a potential enemy was understood to be inspired largely by statements made to him during his visit to Australia. Yet the Australians, when they came to London for the Imperial Conference in 1921, spoke strongly in *favor* of renewing the Japanese alliance.[42] Since they still wished to be assured that preparations would be made to accommodate a large fleet in the Far East in case of need, in effect the policy they advocated was that the British should extend the hand of friendship to the Japanese while proclaiming their fear and distrust of Japan by making visible preparations for a Far Eastern war. William Massey of New Zealand went so far as to predict that "the next naval war" would be fought in the Pacific.[43] The Canadians differed from the Australians in vehemently opposing renewal of the Japanese alliance, but that was only to be expected since they were under strong pressure from the United States.[44]

Thus the Imperial Conference led to no agreement on whether the Japanese alliance should or should not be renewed. On the other hand, the government was left in no doubt that although the Dominions still looked to British sea power to protect their external communications, as well as those of the home country, they were not prepared to contribute to the cost of the Royal Navy on terms which would give the Admiralty undivided control of an imperial fleet.[45] In these circumstances Lloyd George and his colleagues decided to withhold judgment pending an international conference on Far Eastern and Pacific affairs which they proposed to hold in London. Simultaneously the Americans, in particular the Secretary of State, were thinking in terms of a conference on naval armaments, to be held not in London but in Washington. In order not to be forestalled, they announced their intentions while the Imperial Conference was still sitting. They also widened the scope of their proposed conference to include the problems which the British had in mind.[46] Indeed, they would willingly have discussed all aspects of the disarmament problem, as well as Far Eastern and Pacific affairs, had so comprehensive a program been generally acceptable. The French made it clear, however, that they were not prepared to consider any reduction of their land forces as long as the guarantees for which they had bargained at the Preliminary Peace Conference continued to be withheld.

The representatives of Britain, France, Italy, Japan, and the United States who met later in the year in Washington to discuss the limitation of armaments had therefore to confine themselves, for practical purposes, to the naval aspect of disarmament. Representatives of Belgium, China, the Netherlands, and Portugal joined them when Far Eastern and Pacific questions were discussed. Since the United States had not yet recognized the Soviet government, the Russians were not asked to attend any of the meetings, despite their legitimate interest in Far Eastern affairs. The Germans, having parted with most of their Navy and all their colonial possessions and concessions in the Far East and the Pacific, were not considered eligible.

Charles Evans Hughes, who led the American delegation and was supported by Senators Elihu Root, Henry Cabot Lodge, and Oscar W. Underwood, insisted that the conference should be essentially a gathering of statesmen. Officers of the armed forces who attended meetings did so as technical advisers.[47] The seventy-three-year-old Arthur Balfour led the British delegation; he was supported by Walter Long's successor at the Admiralty, Lord Lee of Fareham, in addition to Sir Auckland Geddes and representatives of Canada, Australia, and New Zealand. Beatty headed a team of British naval experts, but the task of drafting proposals for submission to the naval conference was delegated to the Assistant Chief of Naval Staff, Rear Admiral Alfred Ernle Chatfield.[48]

When preparing for the conference, the British were conscious of the difficulty of knowing what to expect of a Republican government recently installed in office after a long period of Democratic rule. During the lifetime of the previous government, anti-British feeling in the United States had reached such a pitch that members of the British ambassador's family in Washington had feared to go outside the embassy without police protection. Little was known of the new President, Warren G. Harding, or of Edwin Denby, who had succeeded Josephus Daniels as Secretary of the Navy; Hughes, the new Secretary of State, was notable for his threat to stage a Congressional demonstration in favor of Irish nationalism if the Japanese alliance was renewed.* An announcement by Lloyd George in the summer of 1921 that he was willing to observe a truce in Ireland pending a settlement of the Irish problem did something to placate Irish-Americans; but acts of lawlessness continued for some weeks after the truce was supposed to have begun, and it was not until the Washing-

* See page 238.

ton Conference was well under way that the government was able to come to a precarious agreement with a nationalist delegation for the partition of Ireland.

The British guessed that the Americans, following the example set by Asquith's government in its dealings with Germany before the war, might propose a ten-year "naval holiday." Any such proposal ought, in the Admiralty's opinion, to be resisted.[49] Almost exactly five years had elapsed since the *Hood* was laid down in 1916. If Britain abstained from capital-ship construction for another ten years, practically the whole of her battle fleet would be obsolete by the end of that period. Thereafter its deficiencies would have to be made good by a massive program of new construction which the government of the day would be obliged to force through Parliament at the risk of provoking dissent at home and alarm and resentment abroad. Furthermore, to prevent shipbuilders from going out of business in the meantime, money which ought to go toward new production would have to be spent on subsidies or on modifications to ships with only a few more years of useful life.

For these reasons, and because the situation in 1921 was very different from that existing in 1912, when both Britain and Germany had already provided themselves with modern battle fleets, British naval experts felt very strongly that any agreement to restrict numbers or tonnage should provide for the steady replacement of obsolete ships. At the same time, the consensus in the Admiralty and the Committee of Imperial Defence was that limitation of capital fleets was the only restriction likely to prove both practical and generally acceptable.[50] No limitation of the total permitted tonnage of warships of all classes would suit British requirements, since any such restriction would force Britain either to reduce the size and hence the power of her capital ships or to make do with an inadequate number of the smaller warships needed to protect her trade.

Since authority had already been given for the expenditure of £2,500,000 on the replacement of obsolete ships in the current year, the Admiralty took the precaution of ordering, almost on the eve of the conference, the first four of the eight capital ships contemplated in Beatty's program. This would ensure that Britain at least had something to bargain with when the conference began.[51]

American preparations for the conference were prolonged and secret. The General Board of the Navy, when first approached on the subject, paid lip service to the principle of naval limitation but proposed that in any case the current program should be completed.[52] This would give the Navy nearly 1,000,000 tons of capital ships after obsolete ships had been scrapped. Later the board proposed that expansion should cease when a net figure of approximately 820,000 tons was reached. Since the Secretary of State's intention was to *reduce* naval armaments, not increase them, neither of these proposals seemed to him appropriate.[53] The proposals eventually put before the conference were essentially his rather than the Navy's.

The board included in its report to the State Department a somewhat overemphatic account of the supposed aims and policies of the leading naval powers. Britain was described as determined to maintain her dominant commercial position and likely to resent any challenge to it. Although this was substantially true, the framers of the report might with advantage have added that Britain was still a free trade country and that the function of the Royal Navy, according to the British way of thinking, was not to fight for markets but to preserve the territorial integrity of the British Empire and to maintain uninterrupted access to ports throughout the world for her shipping and for that of every other nation not at war with her or engaged in traffic with a nation at war with her. As for Japan, the board believed that her aim was territorial expansion, "by conquest if necessary," and that she would "take sides against America" in the event of war between Britain and the United States.[54]

With more sober realism, the board added that should the Japanese fortify their mandated islands in the Pacific, the United States would have to "fight every inch of the way" to the Philippines and the South Seas in the event of war.[55] Neither the board nor the State Department, however, drew the obvious inference that in that case the United States would do well to abstain from any action which might increase the risk of war with Japan and especially from wounding Japanese susceptibilities by insisting that her alliance with Britain should not be renewed. On the contrary, the board continued to view the alliance with unconcealed dislike, while the State Department was willing to go to extraordinary lengths to induce the British to drop it.

At the first plenary session of the Washington Conference on November 12, 1921, Hughes astonished the British and Japanese delegates by offering to scrap all capital ships under construction in the United States. The gist of his proposals was as follows:

1. The United States to scrap fifteen battleships of the pre-Dreadnought era and all capital ships of the 1916 program except the recently completed *Maryland* (32,600 tons). Eighteen capital ships totaling 501,000 tons to be retained.

2. Britain not to proceed with the four capital ships ordered in the previous month and to scrap nineteen of her older capital ships. Twenty-two capital ships, totaling 604,000 tons but generally older and technically less advanced than their American counterparts, to be retained.

3. Japan not to proceed with eight capital ships contemplated but not laid down and to scrap seven capital ships under construction and ten pre-Dreadnought battleships. Ten capital ships totaling 300,000 tons to be retained.

4. No capital ships to be built during the next ten years. Thereafter, replacement of capital ships more than twenty years old by new ships of not more than 35,000 tons to be permitted.

5. Replacement programs to be so framed that the strengths of the capital fleets of the powers would not exceed:

Britain	500,000 tons
United States	500,000 tons
Japan	300,000 tons
France	175,000 tons
Italy	175,000 tons

6. The same principles to apply, *mutatis mutandis,* to other warships.

At the second plenary session, on November 15, Balfour responded so cordially to the spirit of the American proposals that the French suspected Britain and the United States of having agreed to share command of the sea and present a united front to the other naval powers. Even so, he made it clear that he and his advisers did not favor a ten-year ban on capital-ship construction and that Britain needed more ships to protect her trade than would fall to her lot if she accepted parity with the United States in cruisers and destroyers.[56]

To his colleagues in London, Balfour put the case against the ten-year holiday still more strongly. The more the technical objections to the holiday were examined, he told the Foreign Secretary in a cabled message, the more formidable they appeared.[57] Much to the indignation of Lloyd George, who thought it "disgraceful that admirals should combine against their governments," American naval officers were found to share the Admiralty's misgivings. Nevertheless, the Cabinet insisted that the State Department's offer should not be turned down.[58] The result was that the ten-year ban on capital-ship construction was accepted not only against Balfour's better judgment, but also in the teeth of advice from naval experts on both sides of the Atlantic.

A minor concession was, however, made in response to a plea from the Japanese that they should be allowed to keep the 33,800-ton *Mutsu.* This battleship had been paid for partly by public subscription and was so near completion that the Japanese could not bring themselves to scrap her. After some discussion it was agreed that Japan should retain the *Mutsu* but scrap an additional older battleship. To preserve the agreed ratio, the British would be allowed to build two battleships within the 35,000-ton limit, while the Americans would scrap their two oldest Dreadnoughts but complete two of the fifteen capital ships of the 1916 program still under construction and retain these ships—the *Colorado* and the *Washington*—in addition to the *Maryland.* This arrangement was not altogether satisfactory to the British, who would have preferred to build two of the substantially larger ships envisaged in Beatty's program.[59] Two 33,900-ton battleships, the *Nelson* and the *Rodney*, were nonetheless laid down in 1922 and completed in 1927. They were armed with 16-inch guns but were slower than some battleships built during the First World War.

The Japanese proposed to make it a condition of their acceptance of the 5:5:3 ratio that the Americans should agree not to fortify Manila, Guam, or Hawaii. They offered in return to renounce plans to fortify Formosa, the Pescadores, and Oshima. The upshot of these proposals was that a loosely worded ban on fortifications in "the region of the Pacific" was inserted in a treaty intended to replace the Anglo-Japanese alliance and known as the Four-Power Treaty. By the terms of this treaty, signed while the naval treaty was still under discussion, Britain, France, Japan, and the United States agreed to preserve the status quo in the Pacific, refer any dispute between them to a joint conference, and make common cause should any of them be threatened by a power not a party to the treaty. These terms appear to have been drafted, at any rate so far as the Americans and the British were concerned, by civilians imperfectly aware of the strategic implications of so far-reaching an agreement. The treaty created no machinery for the discussion of disputes or problems of mutual defense, it made no provision for compulsory arbitration or staff talks, and the reference to fortifications was so vague that a supplementary agreement was needed to make it comprehensible.[60] Eventually the powers principally concerned agreed that it should be interpreted as follows:

1. The United States should not establish new fortifications or naval bases or extend existing facilities in her insular possessions in the Pacific other than the Hawaiian Islands. These restrictions would not apply to islands (other than the Aleutians) in the immediate neighborhood of the continental United States, Alaska, or the Panama Canal.

2. Japan should not establish new fortifications or naval bases or extend existing facilities in the Kurile Islands, the Ryukyu Islands, Formosa, or the Pescadores. These restrictions would not apply to the Japanese homeland or islands immediately adjacent to it.

3. Britain and the British Empire should be free to develop and fortify Singapore, but not to establish new fortifications or naval bases or extend existing facilities at Hong Kong or in insular possessions in the Pacific east of a line through Hainan and the western extremity of Borneo. These restrictions would not apply to islands in the immediate neighborhood of Australia, New Zealand, or Canada.

4. The ban on fortification of mandated islands, created by the terms of the mandates, should be observed. Thus the Australians would not be free, for example, to fortify New Guinea, or the Japanese to fortify the Carolines, as long as the agreement remained in force.

5. The signatory powers should not be precluded from maintaining existing facilities in a reasonable state of repair by replacing worn-out equipment.

Turning to warships other than battleships and battle cruisers, Hughes proposed that the total displacements of carrier fleets should be limited to 80,000 tons each for Britain and the United States and

48,000 tons for Japan. After the experts had been heard, it was agreed that more suitable figures would be 135,000 tons each for Britain and the United States, 81,000 tons for Japan, and 60,000 tons each for France and Italy. In principle, no carrier should exceed 27,000 tons. Since the Americans wished to save two battle cruisers of the 1916 program from the scrapyard by completing them as 33,000-ton carriers, provision was made for each power to build up to two carriers of not more than that size as long as the total displacement allotted to that power was not exceeded. This concession enabled the Americans to complete as carriers the *Lexington* and the *Saratoga*, which ultimately proved invaluable although many American naval officers considered them too large, and the Japanese to transform two projected capital ships, the *Akagi* and the *Kaga*, into carriers comparable in size and lift with their American counterparts.* The British, on the other hand, remained faithful to the widely held belief that the optimum displacement for a carrier was well below the permitted maximum. Of the six British carriers commissioned between 1918 and 1930, none exceeded 22,600 tons. The *Hermes*, which alone of the six was designed from the outset as a carrier, displaced only 10,850 tons.

Where cruisers and destroyers were concerned, no agreement to restrict total tonnages was reached. Restrictions were proposed by Hughes, but his figures were not accepted by the British or the French. An upper limit to the displacement of individual cruisers, on the other hand, was clearly desirable, if only to ensure that none of the powers evaded restrictions on capital-ship construction by building outsize cruisers which would, in effect, be battle cruisers. The figure of 10,000 tons, which the British seem to have been the first to propose, was readily accepted by the Americans, who foresaw a need for cruisers of that size in a war fought over vast distances in the Pacific.[61] An unlooked-for consequence was that 10,000 tons came to be regarded as not merely the maximum but the optimum displacement. For some years the powers vied with each other in equipping themselves with 10,000-ton cruisers which proved less useful to the British than an equivalent tonnage of smaller vessels might have been.[62]

* When completed as carriers, the *Lexington* and the *Saratoga* displaced nearly 36,000 tons. Whether they were outside the legal limit depended on the interpretation of a clause which would have made the excess tonnage permissible had they been completed as capital ships.

Finally, the British proposed the abolition of submarines, not with much hope of success but because they had agreed among themselves before the conference began that the attempt was worth making. Their offer to scrap "the largest, most modern and most efficient submarine fleet in the world" if other nations would follow their example met with no response from the Americans or the French.[63] Moreover, the French made it clear that if restrictions on total tonnage were proposed, they would stand out for a figure calculated to wreck the chances of agreement. Clauses affirming the duty of submarine commanders to visit and search merchant vessels before sinking them were accepted, but the French afterward refused to ratify them.[64]

The conclusions reached at Washington were embodied in an elaborate series of treaties and supplementary agreements or resolutions. The most important of these were the Naval Treaty, the Four-Power Treaty, the supplementary agreement on fortifications and naval bases, and a Nine-Power Treaty by which Belgium, the British Empire, France, Italy, Japan, the Netherlands, Portugal, and the United States agreed to respect the sovereignty, rights, interests, and integrity of China. Japan was compelled by the terms of the Nine-Power Treaty to relinquish her special position in Shantung and withdraw from Siberia, but rights and privileges conferred by treaties or conventions to which the Chinese had assented were not affected.

Inasmuch as it was pressure from the United States which induced the British, the French, the Italians, and the Japanese to subject their naval programs to international scrutiny at Washington in 1921 and 1922, the holding of the Washington Conference must be reckoned a triumph for American diplomacy. Nevertheless, the United States derived no strategic benefit from the Washington agreements. The Naval Treaty debarred Japan from building as large a capital fleet as the United States while it remained in force, but as long as the United States had no first-class naval base west of Hawaii, the Japanese with up to 315,000 tons of capital ships would always be better placed to attack American possessions in the western Pacific and the South Seas than the Americans with up to 525,000 tons were to defend them. The strategic disadvantages to which the agreement on fortifications and naval bases exposed the United States could have been offset only by the conclusion of an Anglo-American alliance and the dispatch of a strong British, American, or Anglo-American fleet to Singapore.

The Naval Treaty—regarded in American naval circles as so disastrous that Edwin Denby spoke a month after it was signed of rescuing the Navy from "the worst smash it ever got" [65]—failed, too, to put an end to Anglo-American naval rivalry. American naval experts, accepting after Washington the axiom that the western Pacific had become the focus of strategic interest, agreed that success in a war against Japan would depend on the ability of the armed forces to hold Manila Bay as an anchorage for the main fleet. Yet the Japanese Navy did not replace the Royal Navy as the yardstick by which they measured the strength and weakness of their own service. In 1922 the General Board of the Navy called for substantial additions to the cruiser force, not because the Japanese were building cruisers, but on the ground that the British were well provided with them.[66] Distrust of Britain and the British Empire continued to exercise such a hold on the minds of responsible Americans that an attempt by the successors of Lord North to recapture the American colonies, although admitted to be wildly improbable, remained long after the Washington Conference was over a contingency for which the inter-service Joint Planning Committee felt bound to provide.[67]

Other contingencies considered by the Joint Planners during the early part of the period between the wars included war with both Britain and Japan and war with Japan alone. The planners recognized that in either case the United States would be seriously handicapped by her renunciation of the right to add to her naval bases and fortifications in the western Pacific. Until war broke out or the Washington agreements lapsed, she would be precluded, for example, from either developing Cavite as a permanent base for modern oil-burning capital ships or building the alternative base at Subic Bay which had been proposed before the First World War. To make planning possible at all, the planners had to assume that if and when war did come, the Army would be able not only to defend the western seaboard of the United States, the Panama Canal Zone, and Alaska, but also to hold the shores of Manila Bay for *four months* pending the arrival of reinforcements which the Navy could not undertake to put ashore and supply without first gaining command of the sea. Thereafter, if all went well, Japan would be isolated and defeated by the destruction of her battle fleet and the severance of her external communications by naval and air forces.[68]

No knowledge of this plan was needed to tell the British that the Americans would have great difficulty in fighting Japan from bases as far away as Hawaii and California. They concluded that if the Japanese did threaten American interests in the western Pacific, the United States might be glad of an opportunity of making common cause with Britain to avert the danger. In 1925, when the Committee of Imperial Defence discussed Japan's supposed designs on China in the context of plans for Singapore, the Foreign Secretary, Austen Chamberlain, expressed the opinion that any threat to British interests in the Far East would also jeopardize American interests and that joint representations by Britain and the United States should suffice to keep Japan on the rails.[69] British strategists thought that should such representations nonetheless be unsuccessful, Britain ought not to count on effective intervention by American naval forces in view of the distances involved.[70] In that case, everything might turn on the prompt arrival of a British fleet at Singapore.

However, despite the attention lavished on Singapore by British planners throughout the period between the wars, the naval base was still a long way from completion when, in 1931, a financial crisis brought to office a national government pledged to a program of strict economy. In the meantime, power was exercised in turn by Conservatives, who aimed at restricting public expenditure in order to maintain the value of sterling, and by Socialists, to whom all expenditure on armaments was repugnant. These circumstances did not favor the swift transformation of a mangrove swamp many thousands of miles from Westminster into a first-class naval base. From the time when the project was first mooted, about nine years elapsed before agreement was reached on the choice of site and the installations to be provided. Even when such points were settled, another ten years were expected to go by before the base was ready.[71]

The realization of plans for an effective system of imperial defense was hampered, too, by doubts about whether aircraft or long-range guns provided the best means of protecting ports and harbors against attack from the sea and by rivalries and disputes which bore not only on this point but also on the whole question of cooperation between the services. When the Royal Air Force was formed in 1918, the Admiralty relinquished control of the world's largest and most efficient naval air service. At the same time the post of Fifth Sea Lord, created for the study of air matters and the supervision of the naval air service, was abolished. Within a few years of the armistice, unification was seen to have gone too far. The Air Ministry conceded, in guarded terms, the principle that air squadrons serving with the fleet ought to be naval squadrons, but many years elapsed before the Admiralty gained effective and undisputed control of such squadrons and of operations by shore-based squadrons assigned to maritime cooperation.[72] A long delay in reaching agreement about such matters not only embittered relations between the Admiralty and the Air Ministry for many years, but almost certainly impeded the growth of a powerful air arm. Ten years after Washington, the British had twice as many carriers as the Americans, but far fewer airmen trained and equipped for service with the fleet.[73] Furthermore, while in Britain the emphasis was still largely on spotting for ships' guns, the Americans were developing efficient torpedo bombers and dive bombers. Airmen claimed, not unjustly, that the poor performance of aircraft assigned to the Fleet Air Arm was attributable to the Admiralty's old-fashioned insistence on multipurpose designs. They might have added that the failure of the Sea Lords to keep abreast of technical developments was itself an argument against the system adopted in the interests of unified service.

The Salisbury Committee failed in 1923 to close the breach between the Admiralty and the Air Ministry but took an important step forward by recommending that the professional chiefs of the fighting services should sit together from time to time as "a Super-Chief of a War Staff in Commission." [74] The Chiefs of Staff Committee was formed in the light of this proposal, and in 1926 each member was given a formal warrant charging him with individual and collective responsibility for advice tendered by the committee. Subcommittees comparable with the American Joint Planning Committee were created to deal with interservice planning, intelligence, and other matters of joint concern.

The creation of a Ministry of Defence was proposed soon after the armistice. Contrary to popular belief, the proposal received some support from the service chiefs but was rejected by Lloyd George's government as politically inexpedient. Later, when the project was revived, it aroused so much dissent in service circles that many years elapsed before it became feasible.

Meanwhile, successive British governments clung to the hope of reconciling a victorious but war-weary France with a defeated but resilient Germany. At Locarno in 1925 the Germans agreed to regard their frontier in the West as permanent and to seek a readjustment of their frontier in the East only by means short of war. Britain and Italy, but not the British Dominions, pledged themselves to go the aid of Germany or France should either country become the victim of an unprovoked attack by the other. In the following year Germany was admitted to the League of Nations. Nevertheless, the French continued to put more faith in their Army and in alliances with Belgium and the small states of Eastern Europe than in German promises and British and Italian guarantees. In 1927 they began building along their frontier with Germany the system of defended positions known as the Maginot Line.

In 1930, with the end of the ten-year holiday in sight, the Washington powers met in London to negotiate a new naval treaty. Since an earlier exchange of views had revealed marked divergences of outlook between the Admiralty and the United States Navy, agreement might have been impossible if the British Prime Minister, Ramsay MacDonald, had not satisfied himself by a visit to the United States that American goodwill was worth more than cruisers. The French and the Italians, convinced that once again the Anglo-Saxon powers were conspiring against them, took a largely negative part in the proceedings. The British, the Japanese, and the Americans agreed to prolong the naval holiday until 1936, Britain and Japan accepted parity with the United States in destroyers and submarines, and the British assented, at Ramsay MacDonald's behest, to a limit of fifty cruisers in place of the seventy regarded by the Admiralty as the essential minimum. The Americans were well pleased with these arrangements, the British accepted them with customary phlegm, and France and Italy proclaimed their dissent by refusing to ratify the treaty. In Japan, ratification of the treaty exposed the government to bitter reproaches and led to allegations that advice tendered by the emperor's constitutional advisers had been unlawfully set aside.[75]

11

Between the Wars: II

AMONG the extraterritorial rights in China retained by Japan after her renunciation of the Shantung concession was the privilege of stationing in the neighborhood of Tientsin a force capable of providing a legation guard at Peking and protecting communications between Peking and the coast. In common with other treaty powers she was entitled, too, to station a small force at Shanghai for the protection of the persons and property of her nationals in the International Settlement. She also claimed and exercised the right to maintain a force known as the Kwantung Army for the protection of her economic interests in Manchuria.

On September 18, 1931, a mysterious explosion damaged a short stretch of the South Manchurian Railway. Troops of the Kwantung Army exchanged shots with Chinese soldiers, whose officers afterward accused the Japanese of engineering the explosion for the sole purpose of provoking a clash. The Kwantung Army then occupied strategic points at Mukden and elsewhere in Manchuria.

On September 21 China referred her dispute with Japan to the League of Nations. Since Japan appeared, on the face of the matter, to have violated her treaty obligations by her action in Manchuria, the Council of the League called upon her on September 30 to withdraw her troops pending an investigation.

The consequences were far-reaching. Japan was already suffering from the effects of the decline in international trade which followed the disastrous Wall Street crash of 1929. Criticism of the acceptance by civilian ministers of the terms of the London Naval Treaty of 1930 had shaken confidence in the government and had left a legacy of resentment against the Western powers. The League's insistence that Japan should withdraw her troops before an investigation had shown whether she was in the wrong seemed unfair and insulting. The result was that the leaders of the Kwantung Army, instead of being censured by public opinion for exceeding their authority, were acclaimed as heroes. Thus encouraged, they went on to occupy the whole of Manchuria and set up the puppet state of Manchukuo.

At the same time, the League's widely publicized intervention reduced the chances of successful mediation by the Western signatories to the Nine-Power Treaty. The action taken by the League and the popular presumption of Japanese guilt which it created did not encourage the Western powers to risk charges of undue partiality toward Japan by offering to help the Japanese government to come to an amicable agreement with the Chinese if it would reassert its authority over the Kwantung Army and undertake to respect Western interests. With the eyes of the world upon them, the Western powers had to choose between waiting for the League to pronounce upon the dispute and taking some action in the meantime to prevent the conflagration from spreading.

As things turned out, it was not until the spring of 1933 that the Assembly of the League of Nations passed, in the light of a prolonged investigation by a commission appointed for the purpose, a resolution condemning Japan as the aggressor. By that time Hitler had come to power in Germany, the British were making a vain attempt to persuade the French and the Germans to accept drastic limitations of their land forces, and so much had happened in the Far East since the autumn of 1931 that Japan was irremediably cast in the eyes of the Western world as the villain of the piece.

Nevertheless, war against Japan was not seriously contemplated between 1931 and 1933 by any of the great powers. Of the signatories to the Nine-Power Treaty, Britain and the United States alone had navies capable of dealing with the Japanese fleet. Singapore was not yet ready to accommodate a large fleet in safety, and no other base available to the British or the Americans was suitable for operations against Japan. In any case, neither of the Anglo-Saxon powers was prepared to embark on a course which would almost certainly entail long-drawn hostilities. The American Secretary of State, Henry L. Stimson, did propose to the British Foreign Secretary, Sir John Simon, that economic sanctions might be imposed on Japan, but in terms so vague that a successor highly critical of Simon confessed that Simon could not be blamed for his lack of response.[1] Stimson and Simon could not fail to know that little support could be expected on either side of the Atlantic for an embargo on trade with Japan at a time when millions of men were out of work, factories were closing for lack of orders, and vast quantities of raw materials remained unsold. Moreover, such measures might themselves lead to war.

As a reprisal for the Kwantung Army's occupation of Manchuria, the Chinese instituted toward the end of 1931 a boycott of Japanese goods. After a riot at Shanghai on January 18, 1932, the Japanese demanded withdrawal of the boycott and the suppression of anti-Japanese associations. The Chinese did not reply. The Japanese then presented an ultimatum and arranged to strengthen their force in the International Settlement. The Chinese accepted the ultimatum, but their troops exchanged shots with Japanese marines moving to positions immediately outside the settlement. Thereupon the Japanese disembarked an expeditionary force whose leading troops advanced about twelve miles before American, British, French, and Italian mediators were able to arrange an armistice.

The Japanese withdrew their expeditionary force about the end of May. Almost simultaneously, demonstrations against a government accused of putting the interests of commerce, industry, and the urban proletariat before those of farmers, landowners, and peasants culminated in the assassination of the Prime Minister. The emperor, advised by the sole surviving member of a college of elders but indirectly influenced by a group of army officers who distrusted the party political system, then appointed a nonparty government with an admiral and a general as its leading members.[2] Four months later the new government formally recognized Manchukuo.

Early in the following year Japan gave notice of her withdrawal from the League of Nations at the end of the stipulated two years. In the same year she began to modernize her Army, hitherto deficient in tanks, aircraft, and up-to-date automatic weapons.[3] The Kwantung Army, after tightening its grip on Manchuria, proceeded to occupy the adjacent province of Jehol and encroach on the Chinese homeland south of the Great Wall.

Thus by 1933 the Chinese Nationalist leader, Chiang Kai-shek, faced a double threat from the Japanese and from Communist warlords with whom he was intermittently in conflict. In the summer of that year he seized an opportunity of making a truce with the Kwantung Army. Part of North China was then declared a demilitarized area. At the same time a political council for the provinces of Hopei and Chahar, created ostensibly as a concession to the Japanese, enabled Chiang to enter into relations with Manchukuo without formally recognizing its existence. Thereafter he was torn between the hope of using the Kwantung Army as a barrier against Communism and the fear of offending those of his supporters who disliked the Japanese more than they disliked Communists.

Japan's aim under the new government was not to embroil herself in a prolonged war with China, for which her existing Army of seventeen divisions and four independent brigades was insufficient. It was to bring about a situation which would compel Chiang and the treaty powers to concede her claim to a special position as the dominant power in the Far East.[4] From 1935 spokesmen of the Foreign Ministry urged the Chinese Nationalist government at Nanking to recognize Manchukuo, suppress anti-Japanese propaganda, and make common cause with Japan against Communism. At the same time Britain and other Western powers courted Chiang with credits and offers of advice, while the Communists subjected him to a rough wooing by arranging for him to be kidnapped, indoctrinated in the principles of international Socialism, and then released.[5] Relations between the Nationalist government and its Communist rivals improved so markedly after this elopement that Japanese statesmen had to reckon with the possibility of an anti-Japanese alliance between Nanking and Moscow.

In Britain, the Chiefs of Staff responded to the Sino-Japanese dispute by warning the government in 1932 that the Shanghai incident was "the Writing on the Wall." [6] They urged their political chiefs to cancel the ten-year rule and start providing for "purely defensive" commitments without delay. The government agreed to cancel the ten-year rule, sanctioned completion of the Singapore base by 1936, and invited a high-level committee to report on the state of the coast defenses throughout the Empire. Whether other measures must be taken would depend on the outcome of the Disarmament Conference which assembled at Geneva on February 2. Only toward the end of 1933, when failure at Geneva was seen to be imminent, did the government appoint a Defence Requirements Committee to advise it how to meet the worst of the deficiencies to which the ten-year rule had given rise.

The Defence Requirements Committee reported in the following February that although for the moment the chief danger lay in the Far East, the "ultimate potential enemy" was Germany.[7] The General Staff believed that Germany might be ready for war by 1938 or 1939. By concentrating on air power, Hitler might be able to provide himself with a formidable offensive weapon by that time. Clearly, if he attacked France or her allies in the hope of reversing the verdict of 1918, Britain might be implicated by her obligations under the Locarno treaties. Accordingly the committee recommended that the fifty-two-squadron scheme for the Metropolitan Air Force should be completed as a matter of "first importance." Consideration should be given to the provision of additional squadrons for the defense of ports and for maritime cooperation; moderate sums should be spent on the Navy and the coast defenses; and the public should be told about the measures of passive air defense which had been studied in secret for the past eight years and more. Finally, an expeditionary force of four infantry divisions, one cavalry division and one tank brigade, supported by two antiaircraft artillery brigades and an air component drawn from the Metropolitan Air Force, should be prepared for dispatch to the Continent in case of need. With such a force at her disposal, Britain would be able to cooperate with Continental powers in securing the Low Countries as an advanced base for the air defense of the United Kingdom.[8]

The capital cost of the program, to be spread over five years, was estimated at £71,000,000. This was equivalent to an annual expenditure for five years of approximately five shillings and eightpence for each inhabitant of the British Isles.

When the scheme was examined by a ministerial committee, the Chancellor of the Exchequer, Neville Chamberlain, declared that it was beyond the nation's means. The government decided to reduce the cost by cutting out the expeditionary force and spending part of the money saved on expansion of the Air Force. The effectiveness of air bombardment in a future war could not be foretold with any approach to scientific accuracy, but it was assumed that the knowledge that Britain was building a substantial air force would suffice to give pause to potential aggressors and to Hitler in particular.

Air Expansion Scheme A, adopted in the summer of 1934, was intended to provide a total of 43 bomber and 28 fighter squadrons based at home by the end of 1938 or early in 1939. With the addition of 13 general reconnaissance, maritime cooperation, and Army cooperation squadrons also based at home, these would give the Metropolitan Air Force a first-line strength of 960 aircraft. Twenty-seven squadrons serving overseas would bring the grand total for the Royal Air Force to 111 squadrons with a first-line strength of 1,252 aircraft.[9] These figures did not include 213 aircraft of the Fleet Air Arm.

The chief merit of Scheme A was its cheapness. This was also its chief defect. The scheme would provide a small immediate reserve of aircraft, but not the stored reserves which the Air Force would need if it went to war for more than a brief period. Since this could be inferred from published estimates of its cost, an intelligent foreigner might conclude that the British government wished to make a show of strength but did not intend to engage in prolonged hostilities.

About the end of 1934 the Germans had 565 military aircraft of first-line type in various stages of completion, but only 146 were held by operational units of the Luftwaffe already in existence. The British Air Staff believed, correctly, that the Luftwaffe was aiming at an operational strength of 576 aircraft by October, 1935, and of 1,368 aircraft by October, 1936. The second figure included an immediate reserve of 342 aircraft. Without these, the first-line strength of the Luftwaffe on October 1, 1936, would be 1,026 aircraft.[10]

When the government's proposals were debated in the House of Commons in November, 1934, Winston Churchill attacked them on the ground that Germany was already approaching air parity with Britain and that hence they were inadequate. He predicted that the Luftwaffe would be fully as strong as the Royal Air Force by November, 1935, nearly half as strong again by the end of 1936, and by 1937 almost twice as strong. Stanley Baldwin, replying for the government, said rightly that Churchill's fears were groundless so far as the existing situation and the probable situation toward the end of 1935 were concerned. Turning to the more distant future, however, he confused his audience, and ultimately himself, by saying that he "could not look more than two years ahead." This could be taken to mean either that he could not look as far ahead as the end of 1936 (which was almost certainly what he meant) or that he *could* look as far ahead as November or December of that year, but no farther. Since he failed to make it clear in the course of the debate that he did not accept the latter interpretation, he was obliged later to retract the assurance of a comfortable margin of superiority at the end of 1936 which he was thought to have given.

Further confusion arose from a visit to Berlin by Sir John Simon and Anthony Eden in the early spring of 1935. Hitler told Simon and Eden that he was aiming at parity with the French air forces in France and North Africa. In response to a question from Simon, he added "after a moment's hesitation" that Germany had already reached air parity with Britain.[11] This assertion flatly contradicted British estimates, now known to have been reliable. Nevertheless it filled Eden with "grim foreboding." [12]

Subsequent explanations by German officials, supplemented by information from other sources, satisfied the Air Ministry that the Luftwaffe was expanding at precisely the rate predicted in 1934. This meant that Scheme A had failed to deflect the Germans from their path. Accordingly, the government adopted in 1935 an accelerated program designed to give the Metropolitan Air Force the same first-line strength in the spring of 1937 as the Luftwaffe was expected to attain. Scheme C, as the new scheme was called, would provide a home-based air force of seventy bomber, thirty-five fighter, and eighteen other squadrons with a first-line strength of 1,512 aircraft. Again no provision was made for stored reserves, and completion of the scheme by 1937 would be possible only if some of the bomber squadrons were equipped with aircraft incapable of reaching worthwhile targets in Germany unless they flew from Continental bases.[13]

Furthermore, air defense exercises showed that the existing method of gaining early warning of the approach of hostile aircraft, which relied on sound locators and acoustic mirrors, was already out of date. When faster bombers were introduced, it would be quite useless. The search for a better system led R. A. Watson Watt of the National Physical Laboratory to propose the method afterward called radar. At the request of Air Marshal Sir Hugh Dowding, Air Member for Research and Development at the Air Ministry, Watson Watt demonstrated his method at Weedon, in Northamptonshire, on February 26, 1935.[14] In the light of experiments in Suffolk, the installation of radar stations at points around the coast began in 1936.

In the same year the government adopted a much-improved scheme of air expansion, Scheme F. This would provide by the spring of 1939 seventy bomber, thirty fighter, and twenty-four other home-based squadrons, with a first-line strength of 1,736 aircraft. Provision was made for £50,000,000 to be spent on immediate and stored reserves and for substantial additions to the Fleet Air Arm and to forces overseas.[15]

During the London Naval Conference of 1930, the Washington powers agreed to meet again in 1935 for the purpose of negotiating a further treaty. When preliminary discussions began in 1934, the Japanese demanded parity with Britain and the United States as the price of their active participation in the negotiations. Their claim was rejected, although some members of the British government argued that in order to avert the danger of simultaneous war in Europe and the Far East, an attempt ought to be made to improve relations with Japan even at the cost of offending the Americans.[16] Japan went on to announce that she would consider herself no longer bound by the existing naval agreements on the expiration of the two years' notice which she was required to give.

In the following year, relations between Britain and Italy became uneasy in consequence of the failure of repeated attempts by the British, and later by the League of Nations, to persuade Benito Mussolini to abandon a scheme for the conquest of Abyssinia which he had long been turning over in his mind. Besides reinforcing the Mediterranean Fleet, the British strengthened the antiaircraft and local seaward defenses of Malta and Alexandria at the cost of denuding themselves of material earmarked for home defense.[17] Highly colored accounts of the decline of Britain's armed strength circulated in Italy. The French Prime Minister and sometime Foreign Minister, Pierre Laval, was suspected by the British of having given Mussolini to understand that France and the powers associated with her would not oppose his Abyssinian venture, although he strenuously denied the charge.[18] Laval claimed that he had given Mussolini a free hand only "in the economic sphere."

These events cast a shadow over the naval conversations. The Italians, like the Japanese, refused to take an active part. The treaty negotiated by Britain, France, and the United States had little practical effect, since it contained escape clauses of which both the British and the Americans soon availed themselves.

While the conversations were still in progress, Hitler followed up Simon's and Eden's visit to Berlin by offering the British a naval agreement in place of the air pact for which they had been angling. Largely on the advice of the Admiralty the British government, without consulting the French or the Italians, conceded to Germany in the early summer of 1935 the right to build up to 35 percent of Britain's strength in surface ships and in certain circumstances up to 100 percent of her strength in submarines.[19] When the French protested, the British replied that they had not intended, when the negotiations began, to sign an agreement without reference to Paris and Rome but that the Germans had insisted on an immediate decision.[20] They claimed, not very convincingly, that Germany's offer to limit her naval expansion was one which no British government could have refused. The French pointed out that the agreement contravened the Treaty of Versailles and was contrary to the spirit of a public announcement by which the British and French governments had pledged themselves in the previous February to discuss the whole question of armaments, pacts of mutual assistance in Eastern Europe, Germany's return to the League of Nations, and joint action in the event of unprovoked air attacks.[21]

Britain and France were still immeasurably stronger than Germany on land, at sea, and in the air. Their partnership was, however, weakened by French resentment of the Anglo-German Naval Agreement and by British distrust of Laval and lack of confidence in Pierre Étienne Flandin, Foreign Minister in the government which succeeded Laval's. Italy was not yet Germany's ally. But she had embarked on a course which brought her into conflict with the League of Nations, and her Abyssinian commitment was bound to diminish her capacity to fulfill her obligations under the Locarno agreements. Mussolini had made common cause with Britain and France when Hitler seemed on the point of annexing Austria in the summer of

1934. Whether he would be able or willing to do so should a comparable crisis arise in 1936 was another matter.

Toward the end of 1935 the Germans were known to be dissatisfied with a state of affairs which prevented them from establishing air bases in the Rhineland. At Locarno Germany had accepted without demur the obligation not to build fortifications or bases in the demilitarized zone created by the Treaty of Versailles, but once she was openly rearming, these restrictions became irksome. German spokesmen claimed that a pact with Russia, signed by Laval in May, violated the spirit of the Locarno agreements. They hinted that Germany would be justified in remilitarizing the Rhineland if the pact were ratified.

EUROPE UNDER THE TREATY OF VERSAILLES

In December Simon's successor at the Foreign Office, Sir Samuel Hoare, was forced to resign as a result of his sponsorship of unacceptable French proposals for the partition of Abyssinia, and Anthony Eden became Foreign Secretary at the early age of thirty-seven. Eden's policy was to restore good relations with France and to maintain the authority of the League of Nations by taking a firm line with Italy. One of his first acts was to assure Turkey, Yugoslavia, and Greece that they could count on the cooperation of the British Mediterranean Fleet should economic sanctions, imposed on Italy at the League's request, lead Mussolini to attack them.[22] He believed that Britain should do everything she could to aid Germany's economic recovery and should seek a *modus vivendi* with Germany, but that she should not make concessions "merely to keep Germany quiet." [23] In view of Hitler's obvious intention of making Germany once more the dominant power in Europe, the speedy completion of Britain's rearmament programs seemed to Eden a "vital need." [24]

Early in 1936 Flandin and the German Foreign Minister, Baron Konstantin von Neurath, visited London for the funeral of King George V. Neurath assured Eden on January 27 that Germany had no quarrel with France and would honor her Locarno pledges as long as other powers did the same. He added that Germany would be vulnerable to concerted air attacks from France, Czechoslovakia, and Russia if the Franco-Soviet pact were ratified. He professed to agree with Eden that this made an agreement to limit air armaments all the more desirable but said that ratification of the pact would make the negotiation of such an agreement more difficult.[25]

Later on the same day, Flandin told Eden that he expected the Chamber of Deputies and the Senate to ratify the Franco-Soviet pact within the next three months. Adding that "it certainly looked as though the German government were preparing to take some action" in the demilitarized zone, he asked in effect what he ought to do.[26] Eden replied that Flandin and his colleagues ought first to decide whether they wanted to preserve the status quo at all costs or would prefer to come to a new arrangement "while the existence of the zone still had value in German eyes." In the light of Neurath's remarks earlier in the day, neither Eden nor Flandin thought it probable that Hitler would take any "precipitate action" in the near future.[27]

During the next four weeks the French neither approached the Locarno powers with proposals for a new deal in the Rhineland nor took steps to oppose any attempt that might be made to alter the state of affairs by unilateral action. They asked their military adviser, General Maurice Gamelin, what compensation he would expect if the right to exclude Germany's armed forces from the Rhineland were surrendered, but they did not order him to draw up plans or earmark forces to resist a German coup.[28]

On February 27 the Chamber of Deputies gave its approval to the Franco-Soviet pact after hearing a speech in which Flandin offered to submit the question of its compatibility with the Locarno agreements to the Permanent Court of International Justice at The Hague. A few days later, Flandin told Eden at Geneva that he feared that German troops might move into the demilitarized zone.[29] If they did, he would at once inform the League of Nations and consult Belgium, France, and Italy, but France had to reserve the right to take preparatory measures, "including military ones," pending receipt of their views.[30] Eden thereupon returned to London, consulted his Cabinet colleagues, and raised the subject of an air pact with the German embassy in the hope that an amicable discussion of the future of the demilitarized zone might follow.[31]

On Saturday, March 7, the German ambassador, Leopold von Hoesch, called on Eden by appointment to deliver "a communication of very great importance." This turned out to be a denunciation of the Locarno agreements insofar as they related to the existing demilitarized zone, and an offer to contribute to a new demilitarized zone on Belgian, French, and German territory. Germany also offered to return to the League of Nations, join a "western air pact," and enter into pacts of nonaggression with France, Belgium, and a number of other countries, including Lithuania and possibly the Netherlands. The ambassador added "casually" that a few small German detachments were moving into the Rhineland on that day.[32]

In fact, about 30,000 German troops were used. Columns ordered to move on Aachen, Trier, and Saarbrücken were to fall back if attacked, and the whole force was to be withdrawn should French troops cross the frontier.

But the French had made no plans to send troops swiftly into Germany. Consequently, the Germans were able to complete the occupation of the principal towns and strategic points throughout the Rhineland without interference. Once that was done, the French could see no hope of restoring the situation by force of arms without incurring risks which could be accepted only if general mobilization were ordered. Not many Frenchmen were willing to see the army mobilized merely to drive a few tens of thousands of German troops from territory indisputably German.

Similarly, the British came to the conclusion that they would have to ensure against a general war by mobilizing all three services if they were to make even a token contribution to military action against Germany.[33] Flandin suggested that financial and economic sanctions might be used to compel the Germans to withdraw their troops. The British thought that such methods would work too slowly to be effective.

The French had therefore to content themselves, as best they might, with a formal condemnation of Germany's action by the League of Nations and a reaffirmation by Belgium, Britain, and France of their obligations under the Locarno agreements. As a warning to Germany that action would be taken if French or Belgian territory were invaded, Belgian, British, and French staff officers met in London on April 15 and 16 to exchange information about forces available, port and transport facilities, airfields, codes, and signals.

The fact remained that Germany had not been prevented from remilitarizing the Rhineland without paying the least regard to French or Belgian interests. Nations which had hitherto looked to France for protection drew their own conclusions.

Soon afterward a general election gave France a Popular Front government led by Léon Blum, a left-wing intellectual with ample private means. Blum and his Foreign Minister, Yvon Delbos, had no difficulty in establishing good relations with British Conservative statesmen but were much disliked by many Frenchmen of the prosperous middle class.

Meanwhile, a liberal use of poison gas and the bombing of open towns enabled the Italians to make good progress in Abyssinia. Organized resistance ceased about the beginning of May. The British government agreed in June that the rather ineffective economic sanctions imposed on Italy in the previous October should be discontinued as soon as the League of Nations gave the word, but Eden insisted that *de jure* recognition of the King of Italy as Emperor of Ethiopia should not be granted except in return for some solid benefit.[34]

Hopes of a period of relative calm in the Mediterranean were soon dashed by events in Spain. In the middle of July dissension between church and Army on the one hand and a left-wing Republican government on the other erupted in a rebellion organized by a group of army officers led by General Francisco Franco. Monarchists, landowners, dignitaries of the church, and many members of the professional and commercial classes supported the insurgents; Basque separatists, whose ranks included a number of industrialists and shipowners, threw in their lot with the Communists, Socialists, and Liberals who stood behind the government. In Catalonia, traditionally separatist, the rebellion was quickly and ruthlessly suppressed. Thus the Republicans were able to draw on the commercial and industrial resources of Bilbao and Barcelona even when much of the rest of Spain was overrun by Franco's troops.

Germany and Italy actively supported the insurgents from the outset. Without help from the German Air Force, Franco could scarcely have hoped to win. Russia supported the Republicans, but the rather grudging scale of her effort gave rise to suspicions that Stalin was aiming not so much at a Republican victory as at prolonging the struggle in order to exploit to the utmost its disruptive effect on European capitalist society. The Republicans also received much help from Englishmen, Frenchmen, Americans, and others who offered their services in the belief that a victory for Franco would be a disaster for the cause of freedom.

Blum, aware that he had little or no hold on the affections of Frenchmen of the right and center, recognized within the first fortnight that France might be split from top to bottom if he succumbed to demands from his left-wing supporters that the French government should intervene on behalf of the Republicans. On July 26 he announced that France could not take sides in what was still essentially a Spanish civil war. A week later he proposed that Britain, France, and Italy should give formal pledges to abstain from intervention in Spain and to ban the export of arms to either side. The British suggested that Germany and Portugal, too, should be brought into the scheme. On August 15 the British and French governments exchanged notes in which they agreed to prohibit the export of war matériel to Spain as soon as Germany, Italy, Portugal, and Russia came into line. Four days later, the British decided to set the rest of Europe an example by imposing such an embargo without further ado. By that time rumors were circulating in left-wing circles in London and elsewhere to the effect that the policy of nonintervention had been foisted upon Blum by the British government.[35] Despite official denials, this belief persisted in some quarters for at least a quarter of a century.[36]

Within the next few weeks twenty-seven nations, including Britain, Germany, Italy, Portugal, and Russia, accepted the substance of Blum's proposals with or without unspoken reservations. Again on the initiative of the French government, a Non-Intervention Committee was established in London to supervise the working of the scheme. Attempts were made by various means to control the flow of arms through Spanish ports and frontier stations, but both sides continued to be well supplied with weapons and ammunition. At the same time, German, Italian, and Russian soldiers, airmen, and technicians continued to pour into Spain in the guise of volunteers. British ministers considered but rejected a proposal that Britain, as the strongest naval power in the Mediterranean, should offer to keep guard over the seaward approaches to Spanish ports and harbors.[37] The Non-Intervention Committee then adopted a system by which Britain, France, Germany, and Italy each agreed to maintain a naval watch in a given area. Allegations that nonintervention was a device intended to ensure a victory for Franco led to so much industrial unrest in France that reequipment of the French Air Force was seriously delayed. Supporters of Franco complained with equal vehemence that nonintervention was designed to make it impossible for him to win.

Meanwhile, an influential group of British ministers pressed the Foreign Office to seek better relations with Italy, on the ground that Britain could not afford to be simultaneously at odds with the Germans, the Italians, and perhaps the Japanese. Eden, not convinced that Mussolini could be transformed into an effective ally against Hitler, stood out against *de jure* recognition but agreed that something would be gained if the Italians could be persuaded to call off the campaign of anti-British propaganda conducted in recent months by government-sponsored newspapers, periodicals, and radio stations. Mussolini expressed his readiness to negotiate what he called a "gentleman's agreement." The sequel was a joint declaration by which Britain and Italy disclaimed any intention of modifying the status quo in the Mediterranean, undertook to respect each other's rights and interests, and promised to discourage activities likely to "impair the good relations which it is the object of the present declaration to consolidate." [38]

The declaration was signed on January 2, 1937. Two days later Eden learned that a fresh batch of Italian troops had just arrived in Spain.[39] In March a press agency reported that, according to German sources, nearly 40,000 Italians had taken part in a recent battle northeast of Madrid. Thereafter the Italians stepped up their anti-British propaganda in Arab countries, poured troops into Libya, and proclaimed their intention of reviving the glories of the Roman Empire, presumably by seizing Tunisia and Egypt. The British had therefore to think seriously of strengthening the garrison which they were entitled, under the terms of an Anglo-Egyptian treaty signed in the previous August, to maintain in the Suez Canal Zone and to reinforce in case of need. No decision had been made to prepare an expeditionary force for dispatch to Europe, but a campaign fought in the Western Desert of Egypt or elsewhere in the Middle East began to seem to well-informed British Army officers not unlikely.[40] This possibility, which afterward became a reality, had important effects on British planning and tactical doctrine during the remaining months of peace.

In the early summer of 1937 Stanley Baldwin handed the reins of office to his successor, Neville Chamberlain, after remarking that Hitler and Mussolini were "two madmen loose in Europe" and that "anything might befall." [41] Chamberlain, convinced that only improved relations with Germany and Italy could avert a disastrous war, thereupon embarked on a collision course with a Foreign Secretary who did not believe that any good could come of attempts to appease the dictators by concessions which they would interpret as a license to formulate fresh demands.

Soon afterward the German cruiser *Leipzig* was attacked by a submarine in Mediterranean waters. The Germans, assuming that the submarine was Spanish, urged the powers to address a sharp remonstrance to the Republican government. When this request was refused on the ground that the nationality of the aggressor had not been established, they withdrew their warships from the nonintervention patrols. The Italians followed their example. More attacks by submarines, this time on merchant vessels, followed in August.

Early in September a British destroyer was attacked by a submarine now known to have been one of some fifteen Italian submarines which were rightly suspected at the time of responsibility for most of the attacks.[42] At a conference at the Swiss town of Nyon, which the Germans and the Italians did not attend, nine powers agreed on September 11 that British and French warships should patrol the Mediterranean trade routes with orders to sink any submarine which attacked a non-Spanish ship and that no submarine of any of the nine powers should put to sea unless accompanied by a surface vessel. Britain and France would provide more than sixty destroyers for the purpose and, if necessary, would call on Greece, Yugoslavia, Russia, and Turkey for reinforcements. These arrangements not only put an end to attacks by submarines but went some way to restore faith in British and French leadership among the smaller nations. The fact remained that by 1937 the British had good reason to believe that Germany—by definition the "ultimate potential enemy"—was spending annually about as much on armaments as they themselves expected to spend in the whole of the next three years.[43]

In the following November Hitler unfolded to a select gathering of diplomatic and military advisers an ambitious program of eastward expansion involving the absorption of Austria and Czechoslovakia. Field Marshal Werner von Blomberg, the Minister of Defense, and General Werner von Fritsch, Commander in Chief of the German Army, joined Neurath in stipulating that nothing should be done to provoke a conflict with the Western democracies. All three were relieved of their posts on various pretexts within the next few months.

Meanwhile, Japan, alarmed by Chiang's flirtation with Communism, had accepted from Germany the offer of a pact which bound both countries to give no help to the aggressor should either be attacked or threatened by Russia. After the pact was signed, the Japanese perceived that it had brought them little benefit, since nothing in its terms pledged Germany to give them positive assistance should they find themselves at war with either the Chinese or the Russians or with both. At the same time, they recognized that their adherence to the pact had not improved their relations with Russia. They concluded that they must take care to avoid any move which might increase the risk of an alliance between Nanking and Moscow. In the light of these reflections, the General Staff in Tokyo sent an emissary to North China in the summer of 1937 for the express purpose of warning the Garrison Army against embroiling itself with the Chinese as the Kwantung Army had done in 1931.[44]

At that time the broad situation in North China was that the Garrison Army was some 7,000 strong and comprised one infantry brigade with supporting arms. With the consent of the Chinese Twenty-ninth Army, one battalion had taken up a position astride the Peking-Tientsin railway a few miles south of Peking. Minor disputes had arisen between the Garrison Army and local residents, who complained of too-frequent maneuvers and persistent attempts to persuade them to sell or lease their land for military purposes. Furthermore, Chinese officials were not altogether satisfied that the Garrison Army ought to be allowed to establish itself in permanent quarters from which it could dominate the approaches to Peking. On the other hand the Japanese commander, General Tashiro, was on such good terms with his opposite number, General Sung Cheh-yuan, that a clash between the Garrison Army and the Twenty-ninth Army seemed improbable.

Neither of these officers was, however, on duty early in July. General Tashiro had been stricken by an illness from which he was never to recover; General Sung, perhaps aware that trouble was brewing—although of this there is no evidence—had gone on leave for the time-honored purpose of "sweeping the tombs of his ancestors." * The commander of the Japanese infantry brigade, whom the emissary from Tokyo had been particularly careful to warn against putting himself in a position which might lead to a conflict with the Twenty-ninth Army, was also away from his headquarters, having departed on a tour of inspection.

During the night of July 7 a Japanese officer complained to the staff of the Twenty-ninth Army that a company on night maneuvers near the Marco Polo Bridge had been fired upon. The Chinese refused to allow Japanese troops to enter the neighboring town of Wanping in search of a man alleged to be missing but promised a joint investigation. Permission to enter Wanping was again sought and again refused. Shots were exchanged on July 8, and on the following day the Japanese launched an attack at approximately battal-

* The Chinese equivalent of "urgent family affairs" and often the pretext for a diplomatic absence.

ion strength, allegedly in response to persistent fire from the Chinese lines.[45]

Unfortunately for the reputation of the Japanese, this attack attracted far more publicity than the earlier incidents. Blame for the clash on July 8 is hard to apportion, but two points which seem clear are that the Twenty-ninth Army was determined to keep the Garrison Army out of Wanping and that the competent Chinese authorities, including General Sung when he returned from leave, accepted responsibility for the incident on the night of July 7.[46] The Japanese were rather unlucky in being stamped in the eyes of British and American statesmen as aggressors on the strength of an attack delivered some thirty-six hours after the trouble had begun.

Attempts were then made to settle the dispute by negotiation between the Garrison Army and the Chinese authorities at Peking. On July 11 the Chinese agreed to apologize for the incident on July 7, punish those responsible, and replace their troops in the neighborhood of the Marco Polo Bridge by lightly armed militia.[47] By that time, however, four Chinese divisions were said to be moving toward the scene of the dispute, and in consequence the Japanese Cabinet had agreed to reinforce the Garrison Army by three divisions from Japan, two brigades from Manchuria, and a division from Korea. The Prime Minister, Prince Fumimaro Konoye, was against so provocative a move but gave way rather than face a political crisis which might make matters worse.

On learning that agreement had been reached at Peking, the Japanese authorities countermanded the move of the three divisions from Japan but allowed their orders to the forces in Manchuria and Korea to stand. The result was that Japanese reinforcements began to reach North China at a time when the Chinese Nationalist government at Nanking was not yet formally committed to the Peking agreement.

The consequences were far-reaching. On July 16, five days after announcing that the negotiations at Peking had proved fruitful, the national government demanded the withdrawal of the Japanese reinforcements and invited the signatories to the Nine-Power Treaty to take note of an alleged violation of the treaty by Japan. Three days later Chiang Kai-shek publicly accused the Japanese of "engineering" the Marco Polo Bridge incident in the hope of creating another Manchukuo in Hopei and Chahar.[48]

In these circumstances, expressions of mutual esteem by local dignitaries were not enough to avert further clashes between units terrified of falling short of their responsibilities. These caused so much alarm in Tokyo that the authorities again ordered to North China the three home-based divisions set aside for the purpose. They also authorized Tashiro's successor, Lieutenant General Kiyoshi Katsuki, to demand a limited withdrawal of the Twenty-ninth Army's forces in accordance with the spirit of the Peking agreement. Katsuki duly delivered an ultimatum in that sense but exceeded his instructions by occupying the whole of the Peking-Tientsin region when the Twenty-ninth Army failed to withdraw by the stipulated time.

Thus the government faced a situation not unlike that which had arisen when the Kwantung Army took the bit between its teeth in 1931. Konoye and his colleagues concluded that they must at all costs reassert their authority over the too-zealous Katsuki before another three divisions were added to his strength. Taking only a few members of the General Staff into their confidence, they impressed upon their ambassador at Nanking the supreme importance of reaching agreement with Chiang before August 20, when the three divisions were due to complete their concentration. The ambassador was empowered to offer, in return for the withdrawal of all Chinese troops except militia from a delimited area, full restoration of the sovereignty of the Nationalist government throughout North China, and reduction of the Garrison Army to its normal permitted strength. He was also to propose, at his discretion, that Chiang should recognize Manchukuo, join an anti-Soviet pact, and suppress anti-Japanese activities in return for the withdrawal of Japanese support from secessionist movements in Inner Mongolia.

Chiang decided, largely on military advice, to reject these terms and fight Japan.[49] In the second week of August he moved substantial forces, including at least two complete divisions trained by German officers, to an area adjoining the International Settlement at Shanghai, where the Japanese had disembarked their expeditionary force in 1932.

On the Japanese side, the General Staff decided in the last week of July to earmark two divisions for the protection of Japanese lives and property at Shanghai and Tsingtao. Soon afterward the Inner Cabinet recorded the obvious conclusion that the Hopei-Chahar area and the neighborhood of Shanghai would be suitable places for the employment of land forces in the event of war with China.[50] Nevertheless, no orders incompatible with a genuine wish to come to terms with the Chinese government seem to have been issued during the next few weeks. On learning that substantial Chinese forces were moving to the Shanghai area, the Japanese authorities contented themselves with adding about 1,300 marines to the 2,000 or so who provided Japan's contribution to a scheme for the defense of the International Settlement. Even when reinforced, the marines were greatly outnumbered by Chinese forces assembling in close proximity to the settlement.

By August 8 rumors were current in diplomatic circles at Nanking to the effect that trouble was impending at Shanghai.[51] Hints dropped by highly placed informants suggested that the Chinese authorities either had foreknowledge of an impending Japanese attack or were setting the stage for some drama of their own devising.

On the following day two Japanese marines, one of them an officer, were killed by Chinese soldiers in the outskirts of Shanghai. The Japanese stated that the marines were performing routine duties under the International Defense Scheme, that the officer was unarmed, and that his companion carried only a revolver. The Chinese asserted that the men had tried to enter a military airfield without permission and had killed a sentry, whose body they produced as evidence. According to a Japanese source, an autopsy showed, however, that the sentry had been killed by a rifle bullet.[52] The Japanese concluded that the marines had been murdered and that false evidence had been adduced to shield the guilty and perhaps as part of a plan to discredit Japan in the eyes of the treaty powers.

The Chinese 87th and 88th Divisions completed their assembly at Shanghai on August 12. On the following day Chinese forces clashed with Japanese marines in the immediate neighborhood of the International Settlement; by August 14 a full-scale battle was in progress. A week later Chiang concluded with the Soviet Union a nonaggression pact which brought him immediate help in arms and ammunition and credits to the value of $250 million over the next two years.[53]

At the outset the Chinese had a big advantage in numbers, but this was partly offset by lack of room to deploy large forces. The Japanese, with command of the sea and the lower reaches of the Yangtze River, were in a position to supply and add to their forces at will. They decided to send an expeditionary force of two divisions, followed by piecemeal reinforcements which brought its strength to five divisions by the beginning of October. At the same time they offered, through British and German intermediaries, to make peace with Chiang on terms which would not compel him to renounce his pact with Moscow as long as he agreed to the creation of a buffer state between Soviet-controlled Outer Mongolia and China proper.

Chiang declined these proposals in the belief that not only the Russians but also the Americans and the British would be willing to reward him for fighting Japan by helping bolster his shaky economy. On the whole, his confidence was well founded. In Western eyes, Japan seemed almost as much at fault in 1937 as in 1931 and 1932. On October 6 the Assembly of the League of Nations adopted a report which described her action since July as "out of all proportion to the incident that occasioned the conflict." The Japanese, disgusted by what seemed to them the willful refusal of the Western democracies to give them credit for their attempts to come to terms with Chiang, declined to attend a meeting of signatories to the Nine-Power Treaty and other powers with Far Eastern interests at Brussels in November. They went on to drive Chiang's forces in disorder from Shanghai, and in December their troops entered Nanking to the accompaniment of an orgy of massacre, rape and arson.[54] In the autumn of the following year they took Canton by an overland advance from Bias Bay, northeast of Hong Kong. Almost simultaneously they occupied Hankow, seat of the Chinese government since its expulsion from Nanking. Chiang, deprived of the port through which he had hitherto drawn most of his foreign supplies, withdrew to Chungking, deep in the Yangtze gorges. The Japanese then announced that since the Chinese Nationalist government had sunk to the status of a local regime, they proposed to institute a new order in East Asia.

The Western powers were deeply disturbed by these developments, but none of them was well placed to take separate action against Japan. The United States, despite her powerful Navy, was still handicapped by the lack of a first-class naval base west of Hawaii. President Franklin D. Roosevelt, elected for a second term after putting through a massive program of economic and social reform, was conscious of the need to develop bases for a possible Far Eastern war. He was also alive to the danger of a gradual penetration and subversion of the Western Hemisphere by totalitarian ideas and ideologies. But Roosevelt viewed the contemporary scene in the light of information not available to the great mass of his compatriots. To millions of American voters, the Abyssinian War and the Spanish Civil War seemed to offer clear proof of the soundness of their conviction that American governments ought to concern themselves as little as possible with the world outside the continental United States. When the President made a speech in 1936 denouncing Fascist aggression, he was careful to add a reference to American neutrality. He was unable to prevent the legislature from adopting measures designed to make it difficult for belligerents to obtain supplies from the United States, and he failed to persuade Congress in 1937 that Guam should be developed as a base for the main fleet. Congressmen were willing that the fleet should be strengthened and that moderate sums should be spent on seaplane bases in Alaska and the Aleutians and as far west as Wake. They were even willing that minor additions should be made to defense works at existing naval bases such as Pearl Harbor and Cavite. They were not willing to fortify Guam at the risk of provoking Japan.

The British were in a stronger position, inasmuch as their naval base at Singapore was near enough to completion by 1937 to be capable of accommodating a substantial fleet. On the other hand, they could not afford to send more than a small proportion of their naval strength to the Far East while there was a risk of war in Europe.[55] They were also hampered, like the Americans, by the knowledge that their gunboats in the Yangtze River were completely at the mercy of the Japanese.

The fact remains that Britain and the United States could, by pooling their resources, have confronted the disputants with an almost overwhelming preponderance of naval strength. They could also, by joint action, have deprived Japan of more than half her foreign trade and denied her essential raw materials. Opinion on the wisdom of imposing economic sanctions on Japan was, however, deeply divided on both sides of the Atlantic. On the British side Eden, as Foreign Secretary, proposed in a message to the United States government measures amounting to "some form of economic boycott"; Chamberlain, as Prime Minister, toned down the message before dispatching it.[56] On the American side, Roosevelt recommended in a speech which afterward caused him some embarrassment "a quarantine of the patients" as a curb on "world lawlessness"; Cordell Hull, the Secretary of State, could not unsay these words, but he did his best to explain them away by repudiating any intention on the President's part of advocating measures which might lead to war.[57] The Brussels Conference revealed all too clearly the inability of the Western powers to agree on any course of action which promised to cut short the conflict between Japan and China. Indeed, the conference actually prolonged the fighting by exciting so much resentment in Japan that members of the government who wished to reduce the Army's commitment in China after the fall of Nanking were powerless to insist that Chiang should be offered acceptable terms.

Eden, recognizing that the conference had failed, pointed out to the United States government when it was over that infringements of the rights of the treaty powers were likely to continue, and perhaps grow worse, if nothing was done to mend matters. He proposed naval conversations and an Anglo-American naval demonstration to which Britain would contribute eight or nine ships, including the two capital ships which were all she could spare. In the light of these proposals the President received the British ambassador, Sir Ronald Lindsay, on December 16, three days after Japanese aircraft had sunk the American gunboat *Panay* in the Yangtze River. Roosevelt welcomed the prospect of naval conversations and proposed, in the event of further outrages by the Japanese, a naval blockade designed to deprive Japan of raw materials and thus bring her to her knees after a lapse of perhaps eighteen months.[58] A mere demonstration would, he thought, have no effect on the Japanese military authorities, although it might make some impression on civilian members of the government. For the time being the British would, in his opinion, be well advised to keep their capital ships in European waters, but cruisers, destroyers, long-range submarines, and possibly one or two battleships would be needed if the blockade he had in mind were put into effect.

In consultation with the Chief of Naval Operations, Admiral William D. Leahy, the President followed up his interview with Lindsay by briefing Captain R. E. Ingersoll of the United States Navy for conversations with the Admiralty. He also announced his intention of advancing the date of forthcoming maneuvers off Hawaii and of sending three cruisers on a visit to Singapore.[59]

On reaching London, Ingersoll explained, at a preliminary interview with the Foreign Secretary, that the primary purpose of his visit was to exchange information about British and American naval dispositions in "certain eventualities." [60] When asked whether his government thought that joint action should be taken immediately, or only in response to further developments, he said diplomatically that in any case nothing could be done unless full preparations were made to meet any eventuality, including war. Any political decisions which might have to be taken would be more easily made if the ground were first prepared by a technical examination.

Roosevelt's next step was to send through the embassy in Washington a confidential message to the British government. This was to the effect that he was deeply disturbed by a manifest decline in the influence of the European democracies. Small states which had hitherto looked to France and Britain for leadership and would still prefer to do so were gravitating into the orbit of the dictators. At the same time, standards of international conduct had declined. The President recognized that in the existing state of public opinion in the United States, he could intervene in the affairs of Europe only to the extent of exerting moral pressure. He therefore proposed, if the British government assured him by January 17 of its wholehearted approval, to summon all members of the diplomatic corps in Washington to the White House on January 22. He would ask them to urge their governments to agree that, in the common interest, armaments should be reduced, the laws of warfare should be respected, and all nations should have equal access to raw materials. He would add that some features of the post-1918 settlements might have to be changed in the interests of dissatisfied nations, but the implication would be that such concessions must be made only in return for guarantees of good behavior.[61]

Roosevelt's message reached London on January 12. It was followed by telegrams in which the British ambassador expressed the opinion that the President's proposal offered a chance of aligning American opinion behind the European democracies. Lindsay, a distinguished public servant with a wide experience of foreign affairs, recommended prompt and cordial acceptance.[62]

Eden was in the south of France, taking a spell of leave which he had postponed in order to meet Ingersoll. Called home by the permanent officials of the Foreign Office on January 14, he arrived on the following day to find that Chamberlain, without awaiting his return or consulting any member of the Cabinet, had sent Roosevelt a discouraging reply.[63] Chamberlain hoped to win Mussolini to his side by offering *de jure* recognition of his Abyssinian conquest and later to improve relations with Germany by inviting Hitler to recite his grievances. Knowing that opinion in the United States did not favor *de jure* recognition, he feared that Roosevelt's gesture might make negotiations with the dictators more difficult.

Chamberlain and other members of the Cabinet were unfavorably impressed, too, by what seemed to them the artlessness of Roosevelt's proposal. They pointed out that an appeal to the common interest was unlikely to make much impact on Hitler or Mussolini. Eden recognized the force of that argument, but such objections did not strike him as a valid reason for refusing an offer of American cooperation. Since the end of the First World War the United States had refused to join the League of Nations, passed stringent immigration laws, clung to punitive tariffs, pursued aims that were essentially, even narrowly American. By pouring cold water on Roosevelt's project, Chamberlain risked driving her back into an isolation from which she seemed to be just emerging.

At an interview with Eden on January 30, Chamberlain admitted that attempts to come to terms with the dictators might not succeed and that Britain's only safe course in that event might be to "encircle" Germany by concluding an alliance with Russia.[64] Nevertheless, he insisted on opening conversations with Italy without delay. Moreover, when Hitler gained control of the Austrian police by procuring the appointment of an Austrian National Socialist, Arthur von Seyss-Inquart, as Minister of the Interior, Chamberlain refused to be shaken by indications that Mussolini had already given his fellow dictator to understand that Italy would not oppose his designs on Austria.[65] Eden, on the other hand, insisted that formal exchanges should not begin until the Italians did something to honor the promises they had made more than a year earlier under the "gentleman's agreement." In particular, he was not prepared to consider *de jure* recognition unless Mussolini demonstrated his good faith by making a start with the withdrawal of "volunteers" from Spain.[66]

On February 20 Eden, finding that his differences with Chamberlain were irreconcilable, told his colleagues that he had no choice but to resign. His successor, Lord Halifax, was a man of the highest integrity, but shared Chamberlain's belief that Britain stood a reasonable chance of reaching agreement with the dictators on terms by which they would abide.

Less than three weeks later, German troops marched into Austria with Mussolini's tacit consent. Thereupon the British government, abandoning the principle that rearmament must not be allowed to interfere with normal trade, adopted a new scheme of air expansion designed to provide, by the spring of 1940, a Metropolitan Air Force with a first-line strength of 1,352 bombers, 608 fighters, and 413 other aircraft.[67] As the outcome of nonbinding staff conversations with the French, a tentative plan was made for the dispatch to France, in the event of war, of an expeditionary force of two infantry divisions and an Advanced Air Striking Force of either ten or twenty bomber squadrons. The two divisions, hitherto intended as an imperial reserve, had yet to be equipped on a scale suitable for war in Europe.[68]

Meanwhile, Roosevelt, dismayed by Chamberlain's lack of enthusiasm, allowed his project to lapse. After Hitler's invasion of Austria the President set up a committee to coordinate strategy with foreign policy, but most of its attention was given to quasidomestic issues such as the security of the Panama Canal and the safeguarding of Latin-American countries against Fascist penetration.[69]

During the next few months Hitler belligerently championed the claims to autonomy or union with Germany of the German-speaking inhabitants of the part of Czechoslovakia commonly called the Sudetenland. A group of senior officers of the German Army sent an emissary, Ewald von Kleist-Schmenzin, to London in August with a warning that the Führer was interested in wider issues than the fate of a few million Sudeten Germans and an offer to depose him as soon as he gave orders for the invasion of Czechoslovakia if the British government would promise to declare war on Germany in that event.[70] Kleist did not succeed in obtaining an undertaking to that effect from any authoritative source but was reminded that Chamberlain had already said that Britain might not stand aside if Czechoslovakia were attacked.

Even so, British and French statesmen were justly thought to be very reluctant to fight for the Czechs. To some extent their reluctance was attributable to the knowledge that the framers of the peace treaties, in order to give Czechoslovakia a defensible frontier, had flagrantly disregarded the principle of self-determination by which they professed to be bound and that therefore the Sudeten Germans had something of a case. But it also reflected a lively fear of the powerful bomber force which Hitler was rightly believed to have at his disposal. The Czechs were well armed so far as their land forces were concerned, but they had only a small air force and no radar. The French were deficient in modern fighters and antiaircraft guns and their early-warning system was archaic. Britain's air defenses were potentially very strong, but they were still some way from completion. Prague, Paris, London all could be reached by German bombers.

Accordingly, the British and French governments put strong pressure on the Czechs to accept a compromise solution. When negotiations came to a standstill in September, Chamberlain flew to Germany to ascertain, from the Führer himself, the price of peace. After returning to London to consult his colleagues, he found, on a second visit to Germany, that Hitler had raised his terms. Thereupon the British government mobilized the fleet; ordered a precautionary deployment of the air defenses; distributed 35,000,000 gas masks to civilians; and sent its most experienced fighting soldier, General Sir Edmund Ironside, to Cairo to report on the chances of holding the Suez Canal and the Middle East in general.

Mussolini, fearing that he might be dragged into a European war for which he was unprepared, then proposed the conference at Munich at which Czechoslovakia's rights in the Sudetenland were signed away.

Chamberlain declared on his return from Munich that he had secured a lasting peace. Nevertheless, the recent crisis had revealed such glaring deficiencies in the armed forces that completion of the rearmament programs seemed more important than ever. The strengthening of the air defenses, in particular, became a major preoccupation of the British government.

The lessons of Munich and its aftermath were not lost on President Roosevelt and his military advisers. In the course of the next twelve months the Joint Board of the Army and the Navy and its Joint Planning Committee revised their plans for war with Japan. They also drew up, in broad outline, plans to meet the various contingencies that might arise should the United States, either alone or in partnership with France and Britain, find herself at war with Japan, Germany, or Italy or with any combination of the three.[71]

In the following March, Hitler destroyed the last shred of Chamberlain's faith in his integrity by occupying Bohemia and Moravia. Clearly, he had begun the eastward drive foreshadowed in his book *Mein Kampf*. How Russia would respond to the threat became a burning question for the European democracies.

Britain's relations with Soviet Russia had never been easy, partly because the Soviet authorities greatly resented the support given by Lloyd George's government after the Revolution to anti-Communist movements in Siberia, the Ukraine, and elsewhere. In recent years a Westernized Russian Foreign Minister, Maxim Litvinov, had professed himself a keen supporter of the League of Nations, eager to cooperate with France and Britain against the dictatorships. At the same time, the British government received many reports of attempts by Communist agents to undermine British influence throughout the world.[72] It was also aware of the distrust with which Russia was regarded by her neighbors. A view widely held in Britain was that, while the Soviet Union might be genuinely anxious to oppose the march of Fascism, the recent execution or dismissal of large numbers of Russian officers suspected of anti-Communist leanings must greatly have reduced her ability to do so.

Even so, the British wished to be informed of Russia's attitude to German encroachments in Eastern Europe. Three days after Hitler entered Prague, they sounded the Soviet government about the matter. The Russians proposed a conference at Bucharest of representatives of Britain, France, the Soviet Union, Poland, Rumania, and Turkey; the British favored a joint declaration by the first four countries that any fresh act of aggression against a European state would be resisted. The Poles, however, were reluctant to enter into any arrangement which might have the effect of admitting Russian troops to Polish territory. Their plea for an explicit guarantee by France and Britain, coinciding with the news that Hitler had already committed a fresh act of aggression by seizing Memel from Lithuania, induced Chamberlain to announce on March 31, without further reference to Moscow, that the democracies would support Poland against any action which clearly threatened her independence. Almost immediately after he had decided to make such an announcement if the French were willing, he learned from a reliable source that Hitler had discussed a projected invasion of Poland with his military advisers.[73]

Chamberlain and his colleagues went on to double the establishment of the Territorial Army and introduce a limited form of compulsory military service. After some delay, they also set up a Ministry of Supply for the purpose of furnishing the army with such weapons, equipment, and supplies as a civilian minister who was not a member of the Army Council might think fit to provide. Meanwhile they extended their guarantee to Rumania and—in the light of an Italian invasion of Albania—to Greece.

The rape of Czechoslovakia cost France and her allies some forty Czech divisions. It also added the well-equipped Skoda arms factory to Hitler's war potential. In these circumstances the French, although still willing to provide the bulk of the land forces for the defense of Western Europe, insisted that the British should make a gesture tantamount to a formal renunciation of their oft-declared policy of contributing only naval and air forces. The British still had only two divisions more or less ready for service overseas but expected to have four by September. Further divisions, including two or three armored divisions, would be formed as equipment became available. Eventually it was agreed that four infantry divisions and an Advanced Air Striking Force of ten medium bomber squadrons should cross the Channel as soon as possible after the outbreak of war. Two armored divisions would follow when they were ready. Ten medium bomber squadrons based at home would cooperate with those in France. The British also agreed that collaboration with the French Army and the French Air Force should become the primary task of their entire bomber force during "any critical phase" of an invasion of the Low Countries by the Germans. Very few British fighters would, however, be available to cooperate with the bombers or provide escort or cover for them. The Air Component of the Expeditionary Force would consist mainly of reconnaissance aircraft, with only a handful of fighter squadrons drawn from the Metropolitan Air Force.

Throughout the spring, Members of Parliament on both sides of the House urged Chamberlain and his colleagues to cast aside ideological prejudices and seek a firm alliance with Russia. They pointed out that Britain had promised to support Poland and Rumania and that little or no help could be given to either country without the cooperation of the Russians. Nevertheless, it was not until the summer that the government made any serious attempt to follow up its earlier approaches to Moscow. By that time not even the most enthusiastic advocate of Anglo-Soviet concord could rate Chamberlain's chances of striking an honest bargain with Stalin very highly. In the first week of May Litvinov was replaced as Russian Foreign Minister by Vyacheslav Molotov, a former President of the Council of Commissars. A few days later the French ambassador in Berlin, Robert Coulondre, predicted an alliance between Russia and Germany.[74] Although this warning does not seem to have been taken very seriously, the British could not fail to know that they had little to offer to a Soviet government whose rejection of Litvinov's pro-Westernism was all too apparent. Chamberlain and Halifax, chastened by the failure of their attempt to appease Hitler at the expense of the Czechs, were in no mood to woo Stalin by sacrificing the interests of small nations even more terrified of Russia than of Germany. Hitler had no such scruples. In return for Russian assent in the dismemberment of Poland he offered a share of the spoils, far-reaching economic benefits, and acquiescence in Soviet penetration of the Baltic states and the "rectification" of Russia's frontiers with Finland and Rumania.

This offer proved decisive. On August 23, as the sequel to a trade agreement signed a few days earlier, Germany and the Soviet Union sealed their bargain with a political pact. Thereupon Hitler ordered his armed forces to attack Poland on August 26. The British, forewarned of the pact and of Hitler's designs on Poland, began on August 22 to move warships and reconnaissance aircraft to war stations and to requisition trawlers.

On learning some forty-eight hours later that Britain meant to fight and that Italy, although bound to Germany by a "Pact of Steel" signed in May, refused to do so except on prohibitive terms, Hitler countermanded the order and told his intimates that he needed time to sort out the political situation. On August 31 he directed that the assault on Poland should begin at dawn on the following day.

12

The Second World War: Phase One

BRITAIN went to war in 1939 in pursuance of her traditional policy of preserving the balance of power in Europe and preventing the Low Countries and the Channel ports from falling into the hands of a hostile state. Her immediate aim, however, was to help the Poles. In the absence of an agreement with the Soviet Union to form an Eastern Front against Hitler, she could have fulfilled that aim only by launching a vigorous offensive in the West. She was not equipped to do so. Her Expeditionary Force was highly efficient and, unlike the bulk of the French and German Armies, was fully mechanized. But it was very small and was committed to a defensive strategy under the direction of a French generalissimo, General Gamelin. Her Navy could put pressure on Germany only by the slow method of blockade. Her statesmen had delayed the creation of a strong Expeditionary Force in order to build a powerful bomber force, but the bomber force she possessed in 1939 was soon found to be incapable of performing, except at a prohibitive cost, any of the tasks envisaged for it by the government's air advisers.

Britain could not, therefore, prevent Hitler and Stalin from seizing and dividing Poland. On the other hand, her strong Navy, her big industrial potential, her standing in the international money market, and her reputation for always winning the last battle made it not unreasonable to suppose that, in the long run, her ultimate aim of defeating Germany and restoring the balance of power would be attained. President Roosevelt and his military advisers recognized the force of that argument when they agreed, some six weeks after the outbreak of war, that in certain circumstances the national interest might require that United States forces should be sent to Africa or Europe to cooperate with British and French forces in effecting the decisive defeat of Germany or Italy or of both countries.[1]

No immediate partnership with the European democracies was, however, contemplated by the United States government. Legislation intended to safeguard American neutrality precluded belligerent states or their nationals from raising loans in the United States or acquiring warlike stores or supplies from American sources unless they paid for them in cash and carried them in their own ships. The British had therefore to meet the cost of American supplies by depleting their gold and dollar reserves, requisitioning and liquidating foreign investments which could be sold for dollars, and maintaining dollar-earning exports at the highest level compatible with their war effort. This factor had important effects on Britain's war economy and even on her strategy. Malayan tin and rubber, for example, were such valuable dollar earners that the output of these commodities had to be kept up and if possible increased, even though this meant that, in some cases, the labor needed for defense works became unobtainable. While deploring at home the "business as usual" attitude which had hampered rearmament programs until the spring of 1938, in Malaya the British had positively to encourage it.

For the Poles the Russo-German pact was a disaster in more ways than one. Although unwilling to admit Russian troops to Polish territory, they had always counted on receiving supplies from Russia in the event of war with Germany. Since there were few good defensive positions in western Poland, their intention was to withdraw under cover of delaying actions to the line of the Vistula and accept the loss of important centers of production west of the river. The pact struck at the roots of this plan, for without supplies from Russia the Polish armies would be unable to hold even the strongest line for more than a few months if the centers of production in western Poland were sacrificed.

On reflection the Polish Commander in Chief, Marshal Edward

Smigly-Rydz, came to the conclusion that an eventual retreat to the Vistula could not be avoided but that he must try to postpone the loss of the whole of western Poland by holding for a time an intermediate position along a line of lakes and waterways between Bydgoszcz in the north and Katowice in the south. When driven from the Bydgoszcz-Katowice line, he would hope to hold out on the Vistula or at any rate somewhere in Poland until the Germans succumbed to pressure from the British and the French. Since the French Army was still regarded, even by German officers, as the best in Europe, that hope did not seem altogether unreasonable.

In the outcome, Smigly-Rydz was unable to hold either the Bydgoszcz-Katowice or the Vistula positions. A hot summer, following a succession of abnormally snow-free winters, had so dried the ground that tracked and even wheeled vehicles could go almost anywhere in western Poland, easily circumventing such natural or artificial obstacles as existed. The speed of the German advance, the effectiveness of German air power belied all expectations. Experience in Spain had taught the Germans to use their Air Force largely as an Army support weapon. In forty-eight hours the Luftwaffe drove the Polish Air Force from the skies by destroying or crippling many of its aircraft on the ground and forcing surviving units to disperse so widely that they ceased to be capable of coordinated action. The two air fleets assigned to the campaign then turned their full weight to the task of accelerating the Army's progress by attacking troop concentrations, strongpoints, gunsites, and ammunition dumps in or near the battle area; pockets of resistance which German troops had bypassed; and road junctions, rail centers, bridges, barracks, and other vital points behind the Polish lines.

Smigly-Rydz's task was made still harder by factors which he could not have been expected to foresee. During the afternoon of August 29, the Polish government told the British and French ambassadors in Warsaw that it had decided on general mobilization. The ambassadors asked that the mobilization order should be postponed for a few hours to give more time for mediation.[2] Since the day was already well advanced, the government could meet this request only by deferring the posting of notices calling out reservists until the morning of August 30 and postponing the first day of mobilization from August 30 to August 31. The delay had very unfortunate consequences for the Poles. Some reservists in frontier areas failed to reach their depots before they were overrun; reserve formations on which Smigly-Rydz was relying for a substantial proportion of his strength were unable to complete their assembly while their communications were still open. Furthermore, large bodies of Polish troops, finding themselves already in contact with the enemy, refused or were unable to carry out orders to fall back to the east. In consequence there were wide gaps in the fronts on which the Commander in Chief had intended to fight.

On September 14 Smigly-Rydz, recognizing that he had lost his chance of holding the line of the Vistula, proposed to the Allied governments that he should try to retain a bridgehead on Polish soil by withdrawing to a shorter line in the southeast.[3] Three days later Russian troops crossed the eastern frontier of Poland. The government and the Commander in Chief then took refuge in Rumania, leaving field and garrison commanders to fight on or surrender to the Germans or the Russians at their discretion.

Warsaw held out until September 27, when the garrison commander asked for terms after the Germans had switched a heavy air and artillery bombardment from outlying defense works to built-up areas of the city. About 120,000 troops in the neighborhood of the capital made their formal submission on the following day; organized resistance in other parts of the country ceased a few days later. The Polish Army, which Gamelin had expected to hold out at least until the spring of 1940, had been defeated in a month.

The Russo-German pact and its aftermath enabled the Russians, with German assent, to advance their frontier between 100 and 200 miles to the west and to improve their strategic position by forcing Estonia, Latvia, and Lithuania to accept "mutual assistance" pacts which gave Russia the right to establish naval, military, and air bases in all three countries. When the Finns refused to grant similar facilities, the Russians picked a quarrel with them, and on November 30 they declared war on Finland. Their attempt to overwhelm the small but well-trained Finnish Army in December failed at a cost in killed, wounded, and missing which far exceeded the cost to the Germans of their victory over the Polish Army in September.

Meanwhile, the Allied forces on the Western Front maintained an essentially defensive posture. The British contributed four divisions on the outbreak of war and ten by the following spring, while the French provided eighty and ninety-four respectively.* Thus they were in no position to challenge the theory of the French High Command and General Staff that success could be ensured by a continuous defensive line and a firm refusal to take the offensive until the enemy had exhausted himself by attacking it. Gamelin's sole contribution to the relief of the Poles in September was a limited advance on a front of sixteen miles in the Saar. This was followed by the withdrawal of all but covering troops to their original positions on the French side of the frontier. The Allies then prepared to wait for as long or as short a time as might ensue before the enemy felt strong enough to attack them. The Germans took advantage of the respite to increase their strength on the Western Front from fewer than 50 divisions at the end of the third week in September to more than 130 by the spring of 1940. By waiting until the spring, they were able to mass in the West some 2,600 tanks; about 3,500 first-line aircraft, of which roughly half were bombers or dive bombers; and nearly 500 transport aircraft.[4]

During the autumn, winter, and early spring of 1939–40 the Allied armies were deployed along a line which followed the Maginot Line as far as its terminus at Longuyon and extended thence along the Belgian frontier to the sea. Nevertheless, it was understood and accepted that should Belgium be invaded and the Belgians call for help, the British would advance into Belgian territory to join hands with the Belgian Army. In the second week of November Gamelin proposed a more ambitious plan by which, if the summons from the Belgians came in time, not only the British Expeditionary Force but also the French First and Ninth armies would swing forward to a line running more or less from north to south along the Dyle River between Antwerp and Wavre, thence across the Gembloux gap between the Dyle and the Meuse, and up the Meuse to a point in French territory between Givet and Sedan. The sector between that point and Longuyon would be defended by the Second Army, standing in its existing positions on and forward of the Meuse. In appropriate circumstances the French Seventh Army, hitherto in reserve, would race forward on the left of the British to make contact with Dutch forces in the neighborhood of Breda.

* These figures do not include divisions on the Italian front and overseas.

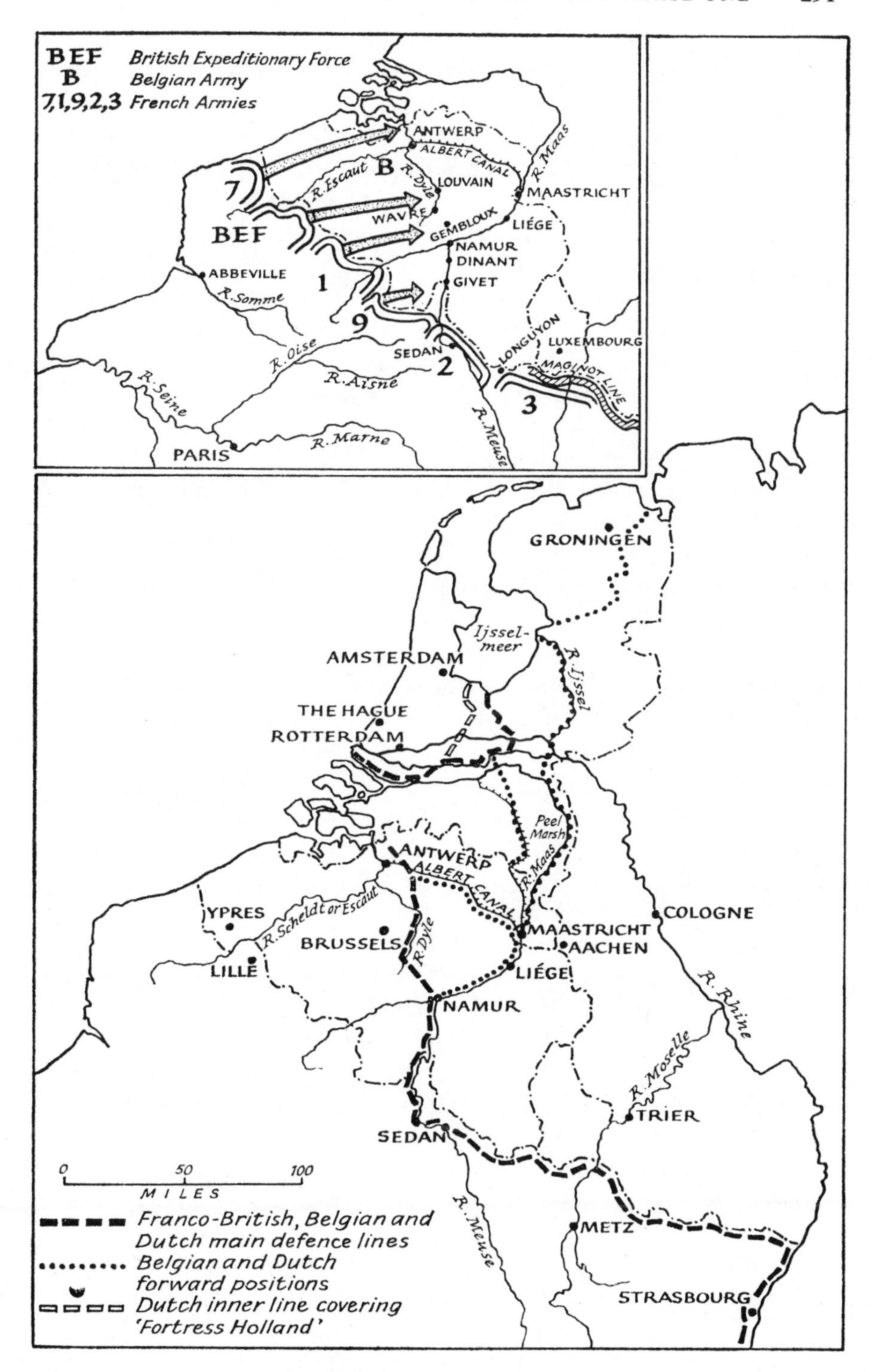

BELGIAN, BRITISH, FRENCH AND DUTCH DEFENSE PLANS (1939–1940)

One of Gamelin's main objects in making this proposal was to ensure that the defense of the Gembloux gap was not left to the Belgians but was undertaken by the French First Army. He believed that the Germans would make their main thrust in that sector. He did not exclude the risk of powerful attacks in the Ardennes but thought that the nature of the country would prevent the Germans from bringing up their artillery and armor fast enough to take the Second and Ninth armies by surprise. Furthermore, the Meuse, some sixty yards wide at Sedan and too deep to be forded, seemed likely to prove an effective barrier.

Thus the First Army played a crucial role in Gamelin's plan. To reach the Gembloux gap, it would have to advance about fifty miles at short notice. The Seventh Army, if sent to Breda, would have to go still farther. Gamelin allotted to these two armies, and to reserves earmarked for the First Army, the lion's share of his mobile formations, mechanized artillery, and motor transport. He also made generous provision for the manning of the Maginot Line. The result was that after setting aside five divisions to meet a possible attack through Switzerland, he was left with only ten divisions in general reserve, and with only twelve divisions to cover the ninety-five-mile front assigned to the Second and Ninth armies. The Second and Ninth armies also had four light cavalry divisions, but these were only partly mechanized and were suitable only for reconnaissance and skirmishing.

Gamelin also handicapped himself by persuading the government to agree early in 1940 that General Alphonse Georges, hitherto Deputy Commander for the Northeast Front, should become Commander in Chief of the forces on that front. Gamelin himself retained overriding responsibility for the land forces as a whole, including those on the Italian front and overseas. This reform had two evil consequences. In the first place, responsibility for staff work was divided, on lines which were not always clear, between two major headquarters, both distinct from Gamelin's own headquarters in the outskirts of Paris. Second, Gamelin became reluctant to give orders to Georges, for fear of offending him or undermining his authority. In effect, he abdicated his responsibility for the crucial front between the Swiss frontier and the North Sea.

As the months went by, the shortcomings of a strategy which surrendered all initiative to the enemy became apparent to the Allied governments. The bulk of their land forces were concentrated on the Northeast Front, where they had nothing to do but train and improve their positions while waiting for the Germans to make the first move. The French had nine divisions on the Italian front and substantial forces in North Africa and Syria; the British, who had planned in the event of war with Germany and Italy to tackle the Italians first, had in Egypt and elsewhere in the Middle East one incomplete armored division, the headquarters of two infantry divisions, and about twenty battalions of combat troops, with supporting arms. But no action could be taken against Italy or her African possessions, since she had not declared war and the Allies were unwilling to provoke her at the risk of surrendering control of the central Mediterranean to the Italian Navy. There remained the chance that the Allies might be able to use their naval power to outflank the Germans in the north.

During the first few months of war the Allies had to make a wide dispersal of part of their naval strength in order to deal with the German pocket battleships *Admiral Graf Spee* and *Deutschland*, which had gained the high seas before war was declared and were acting as commerce raiders. At the same time, the fear of air and underwater attacks led the British to remove the better part of the Home Fleet from Scapa Flow to temporary anchorages on the west coast of Scotland until Scapa Flow could be made safer. The outlook improved considerably from the Allied point of view in November and December, when the *Deutschland* returned to Germany and the *Graf Spee* was cornered by British cruisers off the Plate River, where her captain afterward scuttled her. On the other hand, the success of the *Deutschland* in eluding British reconnaissance aircraft on both her outward and homeward voyages doubtless played some part in fostering German hopes of a successful invasion of Norway. In October and December Grand Admiral Erich Raeder, the German Naval Commander in Chief, pointed out to Hitler that by occupying Norway, he could put himself in a position to use Norwegian bases for his U-boats, cut off Allied supplies from Scandinavia, and forestall any attempt by the Allies to dominate the approaches to the Baltic by themselves sending troops to Norway. On December 14 Hitler sanctioned preliminary work on the problem of seizing both Norway and Denmark.[5]

Thus the thoughts of the Germans and the Allies turned almost simultaneously toward the Scandinavian countries. The Allies were particularly interested in denying the Germans supplies of iron ore from Swedish iron fields at Kiruna and Gällivare. In summer, ore was shipped from Sweden to Germany through the port of Luleå, on the Gulf of Bothnia. In winter, when Luleå was icebound, it was taken by rail to the Norwegian port of Narvik. During the winter of 1939–40, ships carrying ore from Narvik to German ports dodged the Allied blockade by hugging the coast. The Allies hoped to stop this traffic by telling the Norwegians that they must either forbid such an abuse of their territorial waters or allow them to mine the passage called the Leads.

When Russia declared war on Finland, a more drastic method of plugging the hole in their blockade suggested itself to the Allies. They planned to disembark at Narvik, with the assent of the Norwegian and Swedish governments, a force which would advance along the railway for the twofold purpose of helping the Finns and gaining control of Kiruna and Gällivare. In addition, small forces would go ashore at Trondheim, Bergen, and Stavanger. These would deny port and airfield facilities to an aggressor and would establish at Trondheim a base for up to 150,000 British and French troops which could be used, if the need arose, for the defense of southern and central Scandinavia against German or Russian forces.

On February 5, 1940, the Allied Supreme War Council accepted this plan on the understanding that it was to be put into effect only if the Finns asked for help and if the Norwegians and the Swedes were willing. The enterprise would be managed by the British.

Nine days later the German auxiliary warship *Altmark*, carrying nearly 300 British seamen captured by the *Graf Spee* and illegally detained when others were released, took refuge in Norwegian territorial waters. Norwegian officers, asserting that the *Altmark* was unarmed and that no British seamen had been found aboard her when Norwegian officials searched her, rejected a British request that she should be taken to a Norwegian port under joint escort pending an inquiry. The British destroyer *Cossack* then entered the fjord where the *Altmark* was lying, and after a struggle a boarding party released the prisoners. The *Altmark*, which had run aground in the course of an attempt to ram the *Cossack*, was found to be armed with pom-poms and machine guns which must have been visible to the Norwegians who searched her, even if the 299 British seamen locked in cabins and storerooms escaped their notice.

In the light of this incident Hitler, fearing that he might be forestalled if he did not hurry, gave orders that preparations for the invasion of Denmark and Norway should be completed by March 20. At the same time, the Allies, although still unwilling to incur the odium of intervening in Finland unless they were expressly asked to do so, began to wonder whether they would be justified in disembarking troops at Narvik without an invitation from the Norwegians. They were still wondering when, early in March, the Finns succumbed to a series of massive attacks by the Russians on their defensive positions in Karelia. On March 12 Finland signed a peace treaty by which she ceded to the Soviet Union a small part of Karelia and some territory north of Lake Ladoga.

The Allies then reverted to their earlier plan which envisaged the mining of the Leads. Six battalions of British troops were held ready to go ashore at Narvik, Trondheim, Bergen, and Stavanger, but they were not to land unless the Norwegians invited them to do so or the Germans responded to the mining of the Leads by invading Norway. The troops were not organized or equipped to land in face of serious opposition. The Narvik force, if it did go ashore, was not to advance beyond the Swedish frontier. After some debate, which revolved around French objections to a British proposal to float mines down the Rhine, April 8 was fixed as the day for the mining of the Leads. By the morning of April 7 all the troops which were to land in Norway if called upon had embarked or were about to do so, cruisers were standing by to give such help as might be needed, and British, French, and Polish submarines were patrolling the southern part of the North Sea with orders to keep watch for German warships. The main part of the Home Fleet had returned to Scapa Flow and was ready to intercept the enemy's heavy ships if they put to sea.

The German plan was far more ambitious. Hitler proposed to disembark in Norway not six battalions but six divisions. To carry the first wave of roughly 9,000 men to destinations as far apart as Narvik, Trondheim, Bergen, Stavanger, Kristiansand, and Oslo, he was willing to risk practically his entire surface fleet. Equipment was to be carried partly in warships and transports, partly in outwardly harmless merchant vessels which were to lie in Norwegian ports until the invasion began. Transport aircraft would be used to carry a lim-

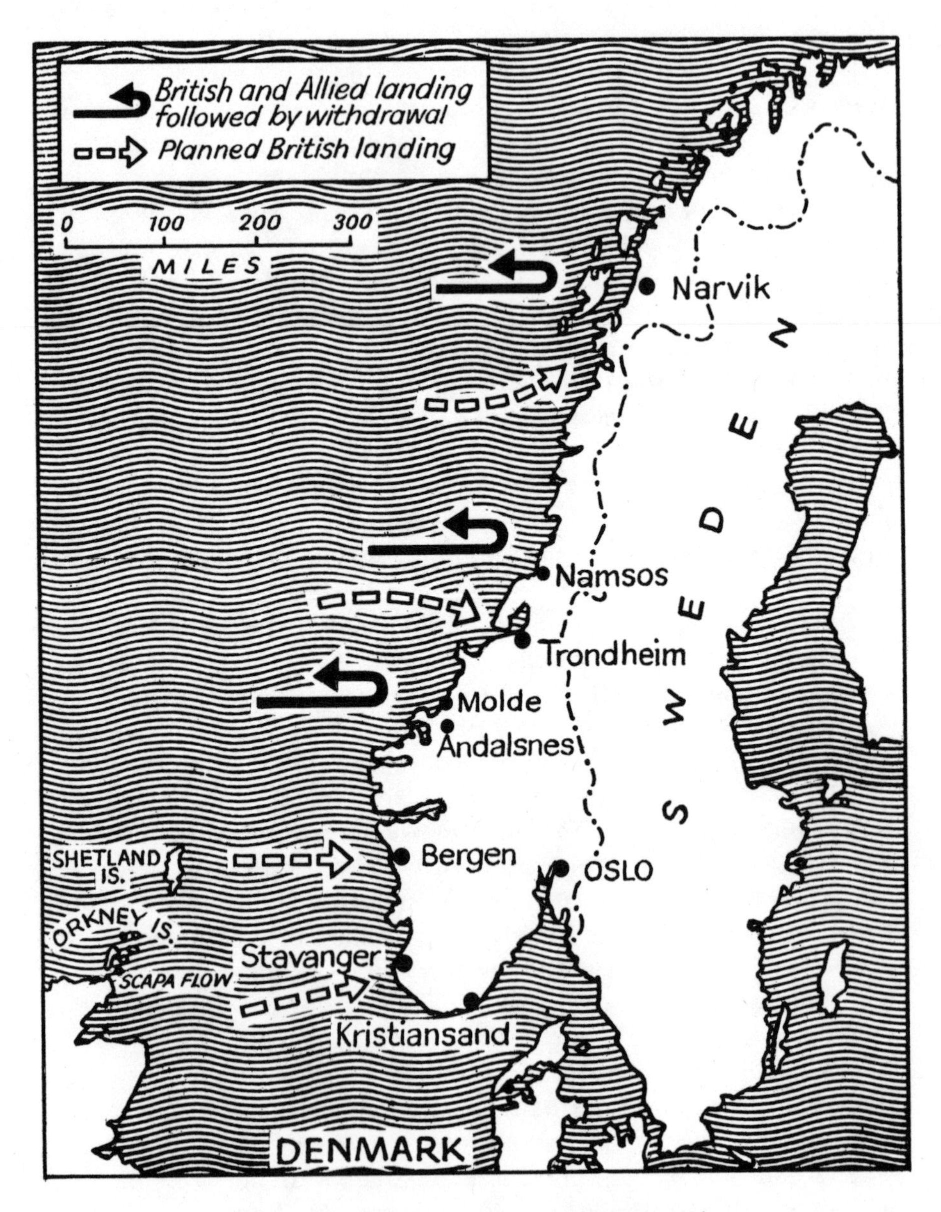

THE NORWEGIAN CAMPAIGN (1940)

ited number of airborne troops and some supplies. The main body of the six divisions would follow when the assault phase was over and would be routed through Oslo. Denmark was to be occupied by troops which would cross the frontier from Schleswig-Holstein and by seaborne and airborne forces.

By the morning of Sunday, April 7, the British were in possession of a good deal of information which pointed to an impending invasion of Norway by the Germans. This included a circumstantial report, received from a neutral source about midday on April 6, to the effect that troops carried in warships were expected to reach Narvik on April 8 and that Denmark, as well as Norway, was to be invaded. But the Admiralty regarded an attempt by German naval forces to break into the Atlantic as both a more probable and a more formidable threat to Allied interests.[6] Reports which suggested that Norway was the enemy's objective were viewed with skepticism. When German warships were seen off the west coast of Denmark, on April 7, heading north in the direction of Norway, aircraft were sent to attack them, but Admiral Sir Charles Forbes, Commander in Chief of the Home Fleet, decided to await news of the attack before taking his fleet to sea. When he did put to sea that evening after learning that the attack had failed, he set a course designed to enable him to intercept the German ships if they made for the Atlantic. The central part of the North Sea was left uncovered.[7]

By the following morning Admiral Forbes was convinced, according to his subsequent account of the matter, that a German invasion of Norway had begun. Even the Admiralty admitted that the report which mentioned the dispatch of German troops to Narvik might be well founded.[8] Nevertheless, orders were passed to the 1st Cruiser Squadron, which had embarked British troops due to land at Bergen and Stavanger if the enemy invaded Norway, to disembark the troops at Rosyth, even without their equipment, and join the fleet at sea.[9] A cruiser and six destroyers which were to have escorted troop transports to Narvik and Trondheim were also ordered to join the fleet. Thus the plan to carry at least a token force of British troops to Norway as soon as it appeared that the Norwegians needed help was shelved at the very moment when Allied intervention became appropriate.

In the course of the next forty-eight hours Narvik, Trondheim, Bergen, Stavanger, Egersund, Kristiansand, Arendal, and Oslo all were occupied by German seaborne forces, supplemented at Oslo and Stavanger by airborne forces. A number of German warships, including three cruisers and all ten of the destroyers used to carry troops to Narvik, were sunk or otherwise accounted for by the Norwegian coast defenses or British naval forces; but Allied naval superiority did not prevent the Germans from putting the greater part of their troops ashore in accordance with their plan. Except at Narvik, where 2,000 troops which arrived on April 8 were seriously hampered by the loss of nearly all their supplies and some of their equipment, subsequent attempts to turn the invaders out could have succeeded only if the Allies had been willing to use much larger forces than they thought fit to employ, and to take much bigger risks than seemed to them acceptable. About 6,000 British and French troops who went ashore at Namsos, in central Norway, with orders to move on Trondheim were withdrawn after they had suffered only 157 casualties, because the risk of air attack was considered unacceptable. British troops which landed farther south at Aandalsnes and Molde, also with Trondheim as their ultimate objective, were diverted to an attempt to bar the routes from Oslo to Trondheim to the Germans. Ultimately this force, too, was withdrawn on orders from London. Allied troops took Narvik in the last week of May, but only for the purpose of demolishing port facilities before withdrawing. A frontal assault on Trondheim by seaborne forces was contemplated but was not made because the British feared that valuable warships might be sunk by German aircraft or by Norwegian shore batteries manned by German crews.

Hitler's Scandinavian venture cost Germany the temporary eclipse of her small surface fleet. Immediately after the Allied withdrawal from Narvik the only German warships fit for use outside the Baltic were three cruisers and four destroyers; three months later the figures were four and eight respectively. Since the British never had fewer than eleven cruisers, eighty destroyers, and four or five capital ships in or near home waters, it is not surprising that Hitler, when he decided in July to prepare for an invasion of Britain, was unable to contemplate putting troops ashore without first gaining command of the air.

At the time, however, the results of the campaign seemed to the Allies far from satisfactory. The British, in particular, were powerfully impressed by the speed with which the Germans had gained control of the principal Norwegian ports and had established bomber, fighter, and reconnaissance squadrons on captured airfields. This pointed to a degree of cooperation between the services which was conspicuously lacking on the British side. On the outbreak of war Chamberlain had brought Churchill into the government as First Lord of the Admiralty and had set up a War Cabinet whose members included the three service ministers. The Chiefs of Staff had continued to sit in committee and had also regularly attended meetings of the War Cabinet. Until the first week of April the government had been able to call in addition on the services of a Minister for the Coordination of Defence, Admiral Chatfield, who was himself a member of the War Cabinet and from November chairman of its Military Coordination Committee. Chatfield had then resigned, Churchill had succeeded him as chairman of the Military Coordination Committee while remaining First Lord of the Admiralty, and the post of Minister for the Coordination of Defence had been left vacant. Since his resignation cooperation between the services had been noticeably poor, and some egregious blunders had been made. At the outset of the Scandinavian campaign the Admiralty had conspicuously failed to make the best use of the information at its disposal,[10] orders given to the 1st Cruiser Squadron at Rosyth had made havoc of the government's plan to send troops to Bergen and Stavanger,[11] and an admiral dispatched to the neighborhood of Narvik had received oral instructions which conflicted with the written directive handed to the general with whom he was to concert his plans. Finally, Churchill had used his authority as chairman of the Military Coordination Committee to insist that a brigade on its way to the Narvik area should be diverted to Namsos, although he was warned by the Chief of the Imperial General Staff that confusion might ensue.[12]

All this was horribly reminiscent of the Dardanelles fiasco, even to the part played by Churchill in both campaigns. After the withdrawal of the last Allied troops from central Norway early in May, criticism of the government's handling of the Norwegian campaign became so intense that Chamberlain handed the reins of office to his irrepressible lieutenant. Churchill had, however, not yet been installed in office when the Germans launched, on May 10, their long-awaited offensive on the Western Front.

As First Lord of the Admiralty since the outbreak of war and chairman of the Military Coordination Committee since early April, Churchill bore at least as much responsibility for the late government's wartime mistakes as any member of it. On the other hand, he had the great advantage of not being implicated in Chamberlain's peacetime negotiations with the dictators. Respected on both sides of the House for his rugged patriotism, he succeeded in forming the three-party coalition government which Chamberlain had never commanded wide enough support to bring about.

As Prime Minister, Churchill saw the need to concentrate executive authority—as distinct from the overriding responsibility for policy which belonged to the War Cabinet—in the hands of a small body of experienced men. The method he adopted was to allow the post of Minister for the Coordination of Defence to fall into abeyance, assume the office of Minister of Defence, and goad the Chiefs of Staff into acting together as an instrument for the implementation of agreed decisions. The Chiefs of Staff continued, when they sat together under one of their own number as chairman, to be joint advisers to the government. When they sat with Minister of Defence as chairman, they became members of a Defence Committee whose conclusions, reinforced as necessary by the authority of the War Cabinet, provided sanction for the action they were called upon to take.

This reform was crucial. Under Churchill's direction the Chiefs of Staff Committee, hitherto inclined to degenerate into a forum for inconclusive debate, became a war-winning weapon.

The German offensive against France and the Low Countries, although long expected and much talked about, swept the Allies off their feet. The Belgian forward positions on the line of the Albert Canal were turned on the first day by the loss of undemolished bridges to airborne infantry and paratroops. The Dutch, relying largely on fixed lines of defense and with few antitank or antiaircraft weapons, were quickly overwhelmed. The French were handicapped by an outmoded tactical doctrine and an unsound disposition of their forces, and the British could not escape the consequences of French mistakes.

Originally the Germans intended to make their main thrust through central Belgium, as predicted by Gamelin. Some 40 divisions were allotted to Army Group B (General Fedor von Bock) for that purpose, little more than half as many to Army Group A (General Karl von Rundstedt) for a covering attack on Bock's left. Rundstedt and his Chief of Staff, Lieutenant General Erich von Manstein, criticized this plan on the ground that Bock's thrust would drive the enemy's forces back without destroying them. After some tinkering with the original plan, Hitler adopted in February a new plan which gave Rundstedt the task of thrusting with 44 divisions from the Ardennes to Abbeville and annihilating Allied forces in northern France and Flanders. Bock, with 28 divisions, was to provide the anvil for Rundstedt's hammer by advancing into Belgium and Holland while Army Group C, with 17 divisions, stood on the defensive opposite the Maginot Line. With 45 divisions in general reserve, the Germans would have 134 divisions, of which 10 were armored.

The Allies had 94 French and 10 British divisions on the Northeast Front. About 8 Dutch and some 22 Belgian divisions gave them approximately the same strength, in terms of major formations, as the Germans. Belgian and Dutch plans had not, however, been formally communicated to the British or the French when the Germans opened their offensive. The French had about 2,400 modern tanks, in addition to 600 old tanks used for the defense of airfields, but roughly half their tank battalions were distributed among infantry formations. The rest were divided among a number of light mechanized divisions and 4 armored divisions, one of which was still forming and was much under strength when it first went into action (under Colonel Charles de Gaulle) on May 17. A British tank brigade and some mechanized cavalry were serving in France when the German offensive was launched, and the incomplete 1st Armored Division began to disembark at Le Havre on May 19.

Thus the Germans had no marked superiority over the Allies in numbers of divisions or of armored fighting vehicles, although their armor was much more effectively disposed. In the air, on the other hand, their 1,700 bombers and 1,200 fighters on the Western Front gave them a substantial advantage. The French had about 150 bombers.[13] The British had, on paper, about 500 on both sides of the Channel; but the serviceability of their bomber forces was low, and their heavy bomber squadrons were not trained or equipped for an army support role. Most of the Advanced Air Striking Force was equipped with the Battle, an obsolescent medium bomber which might have been more accurately described as a light bomber. The other British medium bomber, the Blenheim, had been chosen largely for its speed, but it was not fast enough to outpace the single-seater monoplane fighters of 1940. The French fighter force was roughly 700 aircraft strong, but its effectiveness was reduced by defective arrangements for the allocation of squadrons to sectors.[14] The British had 53 effective fighter squadrons, but only six of these were in France on May 10. Reinforcements equivalent to a further ten or eleven squadrons followed in the course of the next few days. Even if the British had been willing to reduce their strength at home below the danger level, they could not have sent substantially larger reinforcements without dangerously overcrowding the airfields allotted to them.[15]

The launching of the German offensive gave Gamelin and Georges the signal to swing their left into the Low Countries. On reaching the Gembloux gap, the French forward troops found that little work had been done on the defensive positions they expected to find. The result was that Georges became more intent than ever on making the First Army amply strong. This he did partly by allowing the two fully mechanized cavalry divisions which had covered its advance to be broken up and their tanks to be distributed along its front.[16] On the First Army's left the British Expeditionary Force, less one division in the Maginot Line, reached the Dyle without mishap. Farther north, the Seventh Army hastened to Breda but found no Dutch forces there and had to be withdrawn. The effect of this move was to deprive Georges of seven of his best divisions at a critical stage of the campaign.[17]

Meanwhile the tank units, motorcyclists, lorried infantry, and other components of Rundstedt's force raced westward through the Belgian Ardennes, using the full width of the roads and quickly clearing or circumventing unmanned obstacles erected by the Belgians. Leading elements of the 19th Panzer Corps (General Heinz Guderian) reached the right bank of the Meuse at Sedan on May 12. The left bank was held by the French 55th Division (Second Army), with the artillery of two divisions, supplemented by corps and army artillery—a total of about 140 guns.[18] On the following day a preliminary bombardment by bombers and dive bombers left the defenders so shaken that Guderian's assault troops were able to cross the river in collapsible boats and occupy a bridgehead about four miles deep by four miles wide. Possibly because the assault troops belonged to an armored formation, wild rumors spread among the French to the effect that German tanks had already reached the left bank. The greater part of the 55th Division melted away, leaving its commander "almost alone with his reserve troops." [19] Early on May 14 Guderian started passing his armor across the river by a bridge rebuilt during the night.

In the sector held by the Ninth Army, forward troops of the 41st Panzer Corps (General Reinhardt) reached the right bank of the Meuse at Monthermé on May 13. Assault troops, attacking without bomber support, managed to reach the left bank later in the day, but they were soon pinned to a small bridgehead by French colonial troops. Farther north, in the neighborhood of Dinant, the 15th Panzer Corps (General Hoth) was more successful. Motorcyclists of the 7th Panzer Division (Major General Erwin Rommel) found on reaching the right bank of the river near Dinant on May 12 that a footbridge across a weir was still intact. Since it was left undefended after nightfall, they crossed the river without difficulty. Crossings in boats were made on May 13 and 14, and by dawn on May 14 pioneers completed a bridge suitable for tanks.

Thus by the morning of May 14 there was German armor on the left bank of the Meuse at two points some fifty miles apart. No one could doubt that a critical situation, calling for intervention by the whole of the British Bomber Command, had come about. Since the outbreak of war, however, the British had discovered, and had warned the French, that their heavy bombers were not suitable for the daylight offensive for which they had been designed. The assumption that bombers would be able to escape punitive losses by flying in tight tactical formations had been proved wrong.[20] The heavy bomber force had therefore been relegated to night bombing, a task for which both aircraft and crews were ill equipped.[21]

On May 14 the Battles and Blenheims of the Advanced Air Striking Force, which had already suffered heavy losses in attacks on German columns in Luxembourg and Belgium and on bridges over the Albert Canal, joined French bombers in attacking the bridge repaired by the Germans at Sedan. British and French aircraft provided some degree of fighter cover, but nearly half the British bombers dispatched were shot down, mostly by antiaircraft fire.[22] A similar effort on the following day brought the number of sorties flown by the Advanced Air Striking Force since May 10 to roughly 200 and the number of aircraft lost to seventy-three. The heavy bombers were withheld until May 15, when the War Cabinet authorized Bomber Command to attack objectives "east of the Rhine." [23] * Ninety-nine bombers were dispatched that night to attack oil installations and railway targets in the Ruhr, with negligible results.[24]

Counterattacks intended by the French to break up the enemy's armor while it was still assembling west of the Meuse came to nothing. All three fully equipped armored divisions were to have been employed, but none of them was able to make any useful contribution. The 1st Armored Division, previously allotted to the First Army and ordered to make its way to the Ninth Army's sector, lost most of its tanks in chance encounters with elements of the 15th Panzer Corps before it was ready to go into action. The 2d Armored Division, also intended as a reinforcement for the First Army, ceased to be an effective fighting formation when its tracked vehicles became separated from its wheeled vehicles during the journey south. The 3d Armored Division was to have attacked the Sedan bridgehead but found itself relegated to a defensive role. Thus the Panzer formations were able to complete their assembly with little interference and from May 16 to drive a corridor through the Allied armies by making at high speed for the Channel coast. After a few days, however, their situation became precarious, since they were separated by huge gaps from the main body of Rundstedt's infantry and had to draw on their own resources to protect their flanks.[25]

Gamelin, at first thrown off-balance by the swiftness of the breakthrough, was reported as saying on May 16 that "all was lost." [26] Later he recovered his poise. In 1914 he had been Joffre's operations officer at the Battle of the Marne. In 1940 he saw that the Panzer formations were bound to be much stretched by the time they reached the Somme. On May 19, after air reconnaissance had confirmed that the German infantry was a long way behind them, he gave Georges a "secret and confidential instruction" calling upon him to strike southward at their rear and northward to cut their communications

* The War Cabinet, hitherto reluctant to initiate "strategic" bombing, was strongly influenced by a German air attack on Rotterdam on May 14. It is now known that roughly ninety long-range bombers were sent to Rotterdam, possibly on Hermann Göring's initiative, after an attack by the same number of dive bombers had been countermanded by the commander of the land forces assigned to the capture of the city. About half the bomber crews failed to see or disregarded flares which warned them not to drop their bombs. About 30,000 civilians were believed at the time to have been killed or injured, but this figure was almost certainly a gross exaggeration.

at the crossings of the Meuse.[27] The lack of a general reserve was not an insuperable obstacle, since there were plenty of good troops north of the corridor and in the Maginot Line who had yet to fire a shot.

Gamelin's instruction was so tactfully worded that Georges did not regard it as an order. Furthermore, about ten hours after signing it, he was relieved of his post. Paul Reynaud, the Prime Minister, had made up his mind some time earlier to get rid of Gamelin and replace him by the veteran General Maxime Weygand, but had been unable to persuade the Minister of War, the former Prime Minister Édouard Daladier, to make the change. Having himself assumed the office of Minister of War, Reynaud told Gamelin late on May 19 that he must go. Georges continued, therefore, to busy himself with minor matters while awaiting the orders of a new generalissimo. Eventually many more divisions than would have sufficed for Gamelin's maneuver were moved from the Maginot Line to the Aisne-Somme front, but only to be used in a defensive role after all hope of success had gone.

On May 20 Ironside visited General Lord Gort, Commander in Chief of the Expeditionary Force. Gort's communications with his base were severed on that day by the arrival of the Germans at Amiens and Abbeville. Ironside proposed that Gort should free himself by striking toward Amiens with his whole force. Gort said that he must maintain contact with the Belgian Army and could spare only two of his nine divisions for a counterattack. He added that, although his force was supposed to be part of the First Army Group (General Billotte), he had received no orders from Billotte for a week or more.[28] Ironside, a man of commanding presence who spoke excellent French, then interviewed Billotte, "shook him by the button of his tunic," and told him that he must attack at once with all his forces.[29] Thereupon Billotte ordered the First Army to support Gort's counteroffensive by attacking in a southerly direction with two divisions.[30] The French Cavalry Corps of three light mechanized divisions, which was trying to recover the tanks taken from two of its divisions after the advance to the Gembloux gap, was to bridge the space between the French right and the British left.

Neither of the French infantry divisions and only one of the three light mechanized divisions completed its preparations in time to support Gort's thrust on the following day. Gort, falling on the flank of the 7th Panzer Division in the neighborhood of Arras with two infantry battalions and supporting arms which included seventy-four tanks of his tank brigade, made such an impression on the Germans that they believed at the end of the day that they had been attacked by large forces with hundreds of tanks.[31] Such an effort could not, however, be decisive. The French, when they attacked belatedly on May 22, also made good progress but withdrew their small force of one infantry regiment and some reconnaissance units when they learned that the enemy had been reinforced.[32]

On the day of Gort's attack, Weygand flew north for the purpose of convincing Gort, the King of the Belgians, and Billotte that a vigorous attempt must be made to cut through the German armor and that the Belgians must be prepared to extend their line in order to release the British. A southward thrust was to be made in the first instance by six French and at least two British divisions; simultaneous thrusts in a northerly direction would be made by forces south of the corridor. The corridor was only about twenty-five miles wide at the crucial point, and only two good roads ran through it from east to west. The chances of success would therefore be good if a resolute offensive could be launched before the German infantry arrived in strength. So far as the French were concerned, no resolute offensive would, however, be possible unless commanders at all levels could bring themselves to meet the Germans in the open with troops trained to fight in prepared positions.

Weygand succeeded in interviewing the King of the Belgians and Billotte but left without seeing Gort. He explained afterward that he was afraid that if he stayed, air attacks might prevent him from returning to Paris in time to attend a conference on the following day.[33] Billotte was mortally injured when his car crashed on the way back from his meeting with Weygand; his successor, General Blanchard, could give no orders to the Belgians or the British until he received formal notification of his appointment four days later. Meanwhile, Rundstedt's forces in the corridor were growing stronger, and Bock was threatening to drive a wedge between the Expeditionary Force and the Belgian Army. By the evening of May 23 the two divisions at Arras which Gort had earmarked for Weygand's offensive seemed so clearly threatened with encirclement that Gort decided to pull them back. Two days later the threat to his rear from Bock's advance posed so urgent a problem that he made the crucial decision to commit them to a defensive role.

On May 26 Weygand tacitly acknowledged that a counterstroke from the north was no longer possible by agreeing with Blanchard that the Belgian Army, the British Expeditionary Force, and the First Army should withdraw to a bridgehead covering Dunkirk.[34] Some forty-eight hours later the Belgians, unable to comply with this plan because pressure from Bock's forces was so strong, gave up the struggle and surrendered unconditionally.

The bridgehead to which the Expeditionary Force and the First Army were withdrawing was bounded on the west by a line of canals or canalized rivers running south and southeast from Gravelines to St.-Omer and beyond. Elements of Army Group A's armor approached the canal line on May 23, but Rundstedt ordered them on that day not to go beyond it.[35] On the following day Hitler endorsed Rundstedt's decision, adding that any further advance by the armored formations would restrict the Luftwaffe's field of action.[36] Later he authorized Rundstedt to resume his advance at his discretion, but Guderian, the commander of the 19th Panzer Corps, reported after visiting his forward units on May 28 that sending armored troops beyond the canal line would entail needless sacrifices. Although senior officers complained after the war that Hitler's order of May 24 prevented Army Group A from completing its task, there is little to show that they dissented at the time from the view that air attacks and pressure from Army Group B would do all that was necessary as long as Army Group A made sure that the Allies did not break out to the west.

Ironside believed until May 24 that Gort's best course would be to fight his way to Amiens, if the French could be persuaded to set him free by giving him an order to that effect.[37] Nevertheless, he proposed as early as May 17 that the Admiralty should collect and organize a fleet of small ships which could be used to embark as many troops as possible at Dunkirk, Calais, and Boulogne if the need arose.[38] Two days later Gort's Chief of Staff, Lieutenant General H. R. Pownall, warned the War Office by telephone that withdrawal by way of Dunkirk or its neighborhood might be the only course of action open to him.[39] Under the direction of the Flag Officer, Dover, Vice Admiral B. H. Ramsay, the Navy and the fraternity of seafaring men prepared themselves from that day for the task of saving as much as could be saved of Britain's only army. In the light of an impassioned plea from Air Chief Marshal Dowding, Churchill ruled on

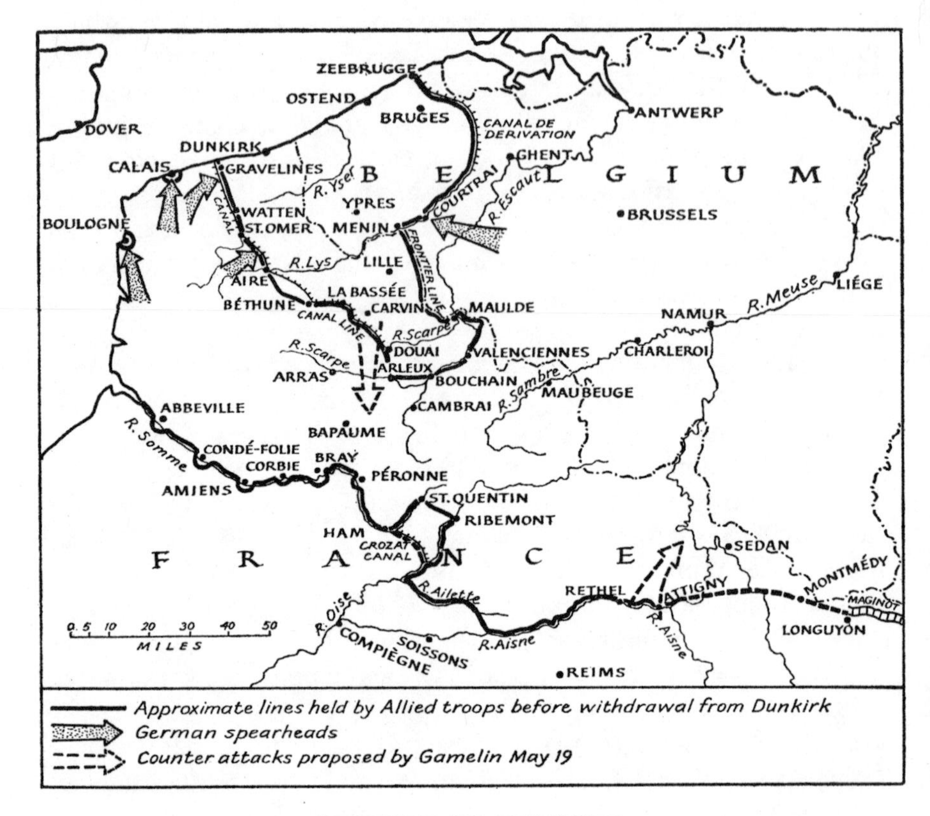

PRELUDE TO DUNKIRK

May 19, and the War Cabinet agreed on May 20, that no more fighter squadrons should be sent to France.[40] Most of the Air Component of the Expeditionary Force then returned to the United Kingdom but continued to cover as much of the battlefield as it could from bases in the south of England.

When embarkation of the main body of the Expeditionary Force at Dunkirk began on May 26, responsibility for providing fighter cover fell ultimately on Dowding, but immediately on his subordinate, Air Vice Marshal Keith Park, commanding No. 11 Group in the southeast. Park had at his disposal about 200 aircraft, or rather less than a third of the home-based fighter force. More could have been provided only at the cost of exposing vital areas in the north and Midlands to grave risks and—perhaps worse—of overcrowding

No. 11 Group's bases and saturating the system of control. By using forward airfields near the coast, Park was able to make about 300 sorties a day over the crucial area. This was not nearly enough to provide continuous cover at a useful strength throughout the long hours of daylight, and many units awaiting their turn for embarkation complained that Fighter Command's contribution was inadequate. But the results spoke for themselves. Helped by calm seas and by cloudy spells which hampered bombing, the British succeeded in bringing home between May 26 and June 4 not the mere 30,000 to 50,000 men of the Expeditionary Force whom they had hoped to save, but roughly 225,000, in addition to some 110,000 French troops and about 2,000 Belgians. A further 50,000 French troops made the crossing in French ships. The Luftwaffe's losses exceeded Park's, although not by so large a margin as was believed at the time.[41]

There remained south of the corridor well over 100,000 British troops employed on the lines of communication or at bases, in addition to the Advanced Air Striking Force, the newly arrived 1st Armored Division, and one infantry division. When France was on the verge of collapse, the government sent more troops in the hope of persuading the French to continue the struggle at all costs. The great majority of these men were successfully reembarked in the nick of time at Le Havre, Cherbourg, and ports farther west. Some 50,000 Allied troops who accompanied them brought the number of British and Allied fighting men carried from France to the United Kingdom in British ships in May and June to well over 500,000.[42]

This was an extraordinary feat, and it made a powerful impression on neutral opinion, not least in the United States. The loss of hundreds of tanks and thousands of guns and wheeled vehicles which had to be left behind or destroyed was nonetheless a serious matter for the British at a moment when France was about to drop out of the war and Italy to enter it. The return of the Expeditionary Force without its heavy equipment gave Britain a home defense army of some twenty-five to thirty divisions, with so few modern field guns, tanks, and antitank guns that it could not present a serious obstacle to a hostile armored force until it was reequipped. It was supplemented by a Home Guard of some 300,000 local defense volunteers, with little mobility and incompletely armed.

In any case, the fate of the Expeditionary Force was still in the balance when the government addressed itself, toward the end of

May, to the problem of survival in a single-handed war against the Axis Powers. Attempts to withdraw Gort's force and completion of the withdrawal from Norway were expected to result in heavy losses, not only of men, but also of warships and perhaps aircraft. The government's attitude to problems of home defense was influenced, too, by highly colored reports from the Low Countries and by the belief that treachery must have played some part in the swift collapse of the French forces on the Meuse. A consequent determination to foil paratroops and stamp out supposed fifth column activities in Britain led to some measures of dubious value. Signposts, milestones, and street signs were removed or defaced; retailers were compelled to part with stocks of maps and guidebooks; place-names were chiseled or painted out of war memorials and shopfronts. Large numbers of harmless aliens were interned; more than 1,000 British subjects suspected of a fondness for the Germans were detained without trial under emergency regulations which gave the government dictatorial powers.[43] The construction of defensive positions was felt to be so urgent a task that much of the work was entrusted to civilian contractors, some of whom built concrete pillboxes facing the wrong way or without means of entry for the troops who were supposed to man them.[44]

The Chiefs of Staff, reporting in the last week of May on the country's prospects of carrying on the war alone, assumed that Italy would join Germany as a belligerent, that the United States would give "full economic and financial support," and that Japan, if not actively hostile, would be unfriendly. They found it "impossible to say whether or not the United Kingdom could hold out in all circumstances" but came to the conclusion that the crux of the problem was the country's ability to withstand the air attacks which an enemy deficient in naval power must be expected to deliver before he tried to put his troops ashore.[45] Fighter Command had about 600 Hurricanes and Spitfires and roughly 100 other fighters in first-line squadrons throughout the country, but fighter losses in France and the Low Countries during the past three weeks had exceeded deliveries of new aircraft by at least a third.[46] Thus the strength of the fighter force seemed bound to fall in the course of the coming battle unless a substantial reserve could be built up without delay. The Chiefs of Staff proposed that the United States Army and Navy should be asked to comb their stocks for Fighter Command's benefit, but they did not explain how American aircraft were to be delivered and equipped to British standards or how British pilots and maintenance crews were to become familiar with them in time for a battle expected to begin at almost any moment.

Lord Beaverbrook, the newly appointed Minister of Aircraft Production, thought it more important to speed the arrival of British fighters, if necessary at the cost of retarding the growth of the bomber force. A willing response from the aircraft industry raised deliveries of fighter aircraft during the next four months from the 1,295 expected by the Chiefs of Staff when they drew up their report to 1,885.[47] * The result was that despite the loss of nearly 800 fighters in combat between the second week of July and the end of September, in no week during that period did the daily average of Hurricanes and Spitfires ready for immediate delivery from aircraft storage units fall below the number needed to meet at least three or four days' losses.[48] A varying number of aircraft which could be made ready for delivery within four days and small immediate reserves with squadrons provided further insurances against disaster.

The Chiefs of Staff, echoing a suggestion already made by Churchill, went on to propose that the Americans should also be asked to provide some destroyers and light naval craft.[49] This, too, was a proposal which smacked of desperation rather than calm reflection. Churchill and his advisers had in mind the difficulty of covering the long coastline of the United Kingdom with the number of patrol vessels they expected to have at their disposal when the campaigns in France and Norway were over and Italy had entered the war. As things turned out, the Germans emerged from the Norwegian campaign so painfully conscious of their naval inferiority that their planners could not contemplate landings outside the relatively short stretch of coast within reach of short-range dive bombers and single-seater fighters. Furthermore, the Admiralty, by requisitioning trawlers, drifters, and miscellaneous small craft, succeeded in mustering by the second week of July about 1,000 patrol vessels, of which some 200 to 300 were always at sea.[50] This did not save the Navy from being hampered in its task of protecting ocean trade by the diversion of cruisers and destroyers to counterinvasion duties, but whether

* Of the 1,885, 1,084 were Hurricanes and 582 were Spitfires. The rest were Defiants, Beaufighters, and Whirlwinds.

such diversion was necessary was another matter. According to the Admiralty's critics, the ships could safely have been left where they were until an invasion fleet was known to be assembling.[51]

President Roosevelt was reluctant to ask Congress to agree that American warships should be sold, lent, or given to a foreign power. He did not want the British to be defeated, but he wished to be sure that, if they were, their fleet would not be surrendered to the Germans but would be sent to Canada or the United States.[52] Churchill and his colleagues declined to give such an assurance. They pointed out that since they were determined not to abandon the struggle with Germany in any circumstances, the question of surrendering the fleet could not arise as long as they remained in office. Even so, they were not prepared to renounce the right to dispose of it as they pleased or to bind their successors not to use it as a bargaining counter if the need arose.[53] Churchill assumed that Roosevelt was Britain's "best friend" but reminded the British ambassador in Washington, Lord Lothian, that hitherto the United States had not given her any help worth mentioning. Whether such help was forthcoming in the future would depend, he thought, on her ability to show that she was capable of withstanding the onslaught to be expected within the next three months.[54]

Nevertheless, he continued to press for American destroyers. His pertinacity was such that Roosevelt and his advisers were moved to make a proposal so novel that probably few British statesmen would have been willing to consider it. This was that in return for a promise to deliver fifty overage destroyers of little commercial value, Britain should, in effect, renounce control of the western Atlantic and the Caribbean by ceding naval bases in that neighborhood to the United States. The British government jibbed at outright cession but suggested an "exchange of gifts" by which Britain would receive the destroyers and the United States the right to use the bases in question. Eventually it was agreed that the destroyers should be exchanged for ninety-nine-year leases of bases in the Bahamas, Jamaica, Antigua, St. Lucia, Trinidad, and British Guiana and that leases of bases in Bermuda and Newfoundland should be thrown in for good measure.[55] Despite a warning from the British that they could accept these terms only if they were assured that there would be no delay in concluding the deal,[56] none of the destroyers arrived in time to have taken part in repelling an attempted invasion in 1940, and only nine were delivered before the end of the year. Nevertheless the price did not seem to Churchill and his colleagues too much to pay for the economic and financial benefits they hoped to receive in the months to come.

The Americans had even better reason to be satisfied with their bargain. The Soviet Union, when she wished to improve her strategic position in the Gulf of Finland, incurred almost universal execration, spent 50,000 Russian lives, and killed or wounded perhaps 250,000 Finns before she gained the right to establish bases on Finnish as well as Estonian soil. The United States, when she wished to improve her strategic position in the Caribbean and the western Atlantic, gained the right to establish bases on British soil without odium or rancor and without firing a shot. Roosevelt described the destroyers-for-bases deal, not unfairly, as the most important contribution to national defense since the Louisiana Purchase.[57]

President Roosevelt's concern for the future of the British fleet was matched by a corresponding concern on the part of the British for the future of the French fleet.

The French promised, when Britain released France from her obligation not to make a separate peace with Germany, that they would not allow their warships to fall into German hands, but they would not undertake to put them out of harm's way by sending them to ports beyond Hitler's reach before opening negotiations for an armistice. When they laid down their arms, their ships were based in France, French North Africa, the British Isles, the eastern Mediterranean, the West Indies, and the Far East. A powerful squadron, consisting of the battleships *Bretagne* and *Provence*, the modern battle cruisers *Dunkerque* and *Strasbourg*, a seaplane carrier and six destroyers, was at Mers-el-Kebir, near Oran. The new battleships *Jean Bart* and *Richelieu*, almost complete but not yet in service, were at Casablanca and Dakar. Ships in the West Indies included the carrier *Béarn*, laden with aircraft bought in the United States on joint Anglo-French account.

The armistice terms provided that the French fleet should be "demobilized and disarmed" under German or Italian supervision. The British government feared that Hitler, either by putting his own interpretation on these terms or by issuing spurious orders in the name of the French Ministry of Marine, might gain possession of some of the most valuable ships and use them for his own purposes. If he did, the Axis Powers might be able to offer a serious challenge to the Royal Navy in the Mediterranean and elsewhere.

At the end of June the Admiralty assembled at Gibraltar a powerful detached squadron consisting of the battle cruiser *Hood*, the battleships *Valiant* and *Resolution* and the carrier *Ark Royal*, with one light cruiser and four destroyers. This force, commanded by Vice Admiral Sir James Somerville, was intended to replace the French fleet at the western end of the Mediterranean and cover convoy routes to Britain from Freetown and Gibraltar. Somerville, with his strength augmented by a second cruiser and seven additional destroyers, was also given the uncongenial task of proposing to Admiral Gensoul, the French commander at Mers-el-Kebir, that he should either join forces with the British, sail with reduced crews to the West Indies or to any British port, or scuttle his ships within six hours. Should Gensoul reject all these proposals but offer to "demilitarize" his ships under British supervision, Somerville was to satisfy himself, before accepting the offer, that the process could be completed within six hours and would put the ships out of commission for at least a year.[58] If all else failed, he was to engage Gensoul's squadron and destroy it.

Somerville was sure that no French officer would willingly allow his ship or his squadron to fall into German hands. He and his colleagues and subordinates viewed with "horror and incredulity" orders which might compel him to open fire on the French.[59] However, he duly took his force to Mers-el-Kebir on July 3, sending ahead in a destroyer an envoy, Captain C. S. Holland, who reached the harbor about 8 A.M.

The orders given to Somerville suggest that his superiors expected Gensoul either to accept one or other of the British proposals or to make counterproposals almost as soon as the matter was broached to him. As things turned out, more than the six hours specified by the Admiralty for completion of the whole business elapsed before Gensoul even consented to receive Captain Holland aboard his flagship. In the meantime, Holland had no choice but to give the proposals the disagreeable air of a threat by putting them in writing. Gensoul's written reply seemed to leave no loophole for negotiation, and he did not help matters by reporting to the Ministry of Marine that he had been asked to sink his ships within six hours, without adding that he had been given the choice of joining the British at sea or sailing with reduced crews to the West Indies or to any British port.[60] Since the French made no immediate attempt to leave harbor, Somerville nonetheless continued his efforts to reach a settlement long after the original time limit had expired. The most that could be extracted from Gensoul before Holland took leave of him at 5:25 P.M. was, however, a statement to the effect that his crews were being reduced and that "if threatened," he would make for the West Indies or the United States rather than allow his ships to fall into the wrong hands.[61]

Somerville, learning from the Admiralty of indications that Gensoul was about to be reinforced, warned him in the meantime that he would be obliged to open fire if no agreement were reached by 5:30 P.M. About that time Gensoul cleared his fleet for action. Somerville, although advised by the Admiralty to "settle matters quickly," held his hand until 5:54 P.M. Unhappily the brief exchange of shots which followed caused heavy loss of life among the French. The *Bretagne* blew up and the *Dunkerque*, the *Provence*, and a number of smaller ships were seriously damaged, but the *Strasbourg* escaped with five destroyers to Toulon.

Nine days later, after torpedo bombers from the *Hermes* had attacked and damaged the *Richelieu* at Dakar, the British government announced that no further action would be taken against French warships at ports outside France and not under German or Italian control. A British patrol off Martinique was then withdrawn, but steps were taken to withhold supplies of fuel oil from the *Béarn* and to impress upon the French, through the good offices of the United States government, the importance of keeping their warships in West Indian waters out of harm's way for the duration of the war.

Many British naval officers regarded the clash with Gensoul's squadron as the predictable consequence of an act of political unwisdom comparable with Lloyd George's attempt to force the pace at Chanak in 1922. Nevertheless, it did the British little or no harm in the eyes of neutrals. On the other hand, it ended such chances as they ever had of persuading any substantial part of the French Navy to join the Free French movement launched by the newly promoted General de Gaulle. It also contributed to the severance of diplomatic relations with the French government established by the veteran Marshal Pétain at Vichy, although British sponsorship of the Free

French movement would doubtless have made a rupture inevitable in any case. When British and Free French forces arrived off Dakar some ten weeks later in the hope of making a bloodless conquest of Senegal, the *Richelieu* contributed to the failure of the expedition by joining shore batteries in opening fire on them. General de Gaulle did, however, succeed by the end of the year in rallying the whole of French Equatorial Africa to his cause. This helped the British establish an air route from the Gold Coast port of Takoradi across the heart of Africa to Egypt and thus to build up their air forces in the Middle East at a time when nearly all shipborne reinforcements and supplies for the Army of the Nile had to be carried by the long route around the Cape. The case for withdrawing the Mediterranean Fleet from Alexandria to Gibraltar or Aden was discussed in London when Italy entered the war, but the conclusion reached was that any benefits derived from the freeing of the fleet for service in the Atlantic or the Indian Ocean would be more than offset by the sacrifice of Egypt and of Malta.[62] The fleet would stay, and Malta would be reinforced and supplied by fast convoys from Alexandria and Gibraltar. Not only Malta and Egypt but also Kenya, the Sudan, Iraq, Palestine, Aden, and the head of the Persian Gulf would be defended, and help would be given to Greece and Turkey should Germany attack them. These decisions were not affected by the refusal of the Turks, after the fall of France, to be bound by a promise to enter the war on the side of the Allies if Italy declared war on France and Britain.

In July and the early part of August, while plans for the invasion of Britain were still under discussion, the Germans delivered a series of air attacks on ports in the south of England and shipping in or about the Thames Estuary and the English Channel. These were intended to weaken Britain's air defenses in preparation for the main assault and to induce the British to thin out their light naval forces in the invasion area. The Admiralty responded to them by accelerating arrangements for the diversion of ocean traffic to west coast ports, changing the organization and timing of local convoys, and moving a destroyer flotilla from Dover to a less vulnerable station at Portsmouth. Between July 10 and August 12 the British lost 2 destroyers and some 30,000 tons of merchant shipping but destroyed 286 Ger-

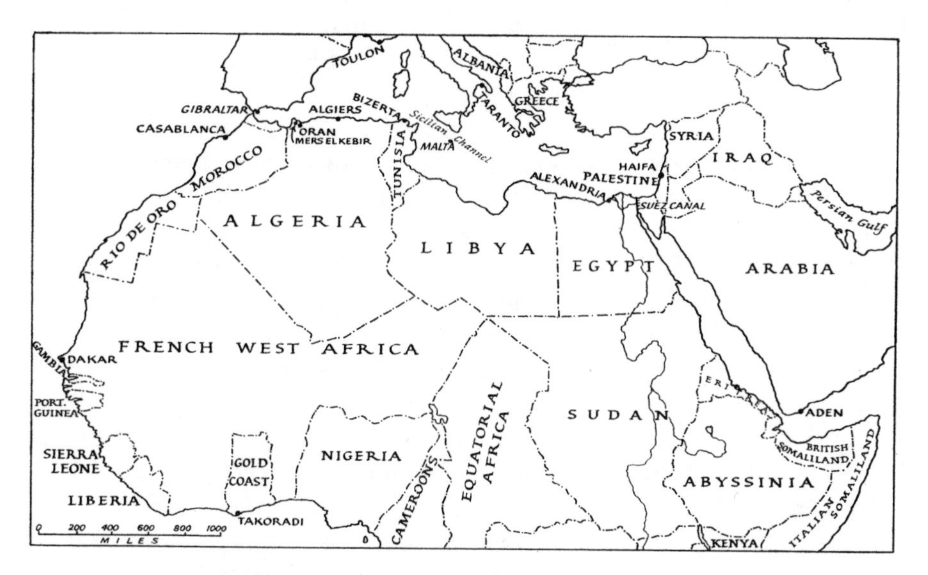

NORTHERN AFRICA AND THE MIDDLE EAST

man aircraft for the loss of 150 of their own fighters. The attacks did not weaken Britain's air defenses, which were stronger in numbers and experience at the end of the preliminary phase of the battle than at its beginning.

On the eve of the main assault, the British had some 750 first-line fighters fit for immediate use, some 350 undergoing routine maintenance or minor repairs in station or squadron workshops, and some 300 ready for immediate issue from stored reserves.[63] German aircraft stationed in France, Belgium, Holland, Denmark, or Norway and immediately available for operations against Britain included about 1,000 long-range bombers, some 300 dive bombers, about 700 single-seater fighters, and some 260 heavy fighters.[64]

The Germans hoped to begin their grand assault with massive attacks delivered in daylight on four successive days in the second week of August. In the outcome, uncertain weather led them to postpone the start from August 10 to August 13 and to forgo major attacks on August 14 and 17. On August 13, 15, 16, and 18 they flew about 6,000 sorties and lost 236 aircraft without making much impression on the British, who lost fewer than 100 fighters.[65] The heavy fighters on which the Germans had counted to give close escort to their bombers proved too few and too unhandy for the purpose, the dive bombers which had done so well in France too vulnerable to be used against well-defended targets.

Thereafter the Luftwaffe was obliged to confine its major attacks in daylight to targets within reach of its single-seater fighters. These aircraft were unsurpassed in speed and rate of climb by any contemporary fighter; but their radius of action was short, and they did not prove particularly effective in a close-escort role. During the second phase of the main assault, which lasted from August 24 to September 6, some damaging attacks were made on airfields in the south of England, but the loss of nearly 1,000 aircraft since early July made serious inroads on German striking power. On four of the first six days of September the British fighter force flew more sorties between dawn and dusk than the German bomber and fighter forces put together.[66]

Originally Hitler was to have decided on September 11 whether to give or withhold the preliminary order for landings in Britain.[67] If he gave an affirmative decision, the troops would land on September 21 unless an executive order to be issued a week after the preliminary order specified another date. Chiefly to give the Luftwaffe more time to gain the required air superiority, he afterward postponed the preliminary decision until September 17 and the provisional date for the landings until September 27.[68] Since disembarkation was feasible only in certain conditions of moon and tide, no further postponement would be possible if the landings were to be made before the second week of October, when high winds and rough seas might prevent the troops from going ashore even if air superiority were won. In effect, this meant that either Britain's air defenses had to be brought to the verge of defeat by the middle of September or the whole project might have to be put back until the spring of 1941. By that time the British would have had such ample opportunities of re-equipping their home defense divisions that success would be problematical even if the landings went without a hitch.

In the light of these considerations, the Germans decided to suspend their attacks on airfields at a moment when these were causing the British a good deal of anxiety. London would be the target for their bombers during a new phase of the battle, due to begin on September 7. This decision reflected a wish expressed by Hitler to retaliate for a recent attack on Berlin, but its strategic basis was the belief that attacks on London would induce the British to commit their entire fighter force to unprofitable encounters with the 600 German single-seater fighters massed between the Netherlands and Normandy.

That belief was founded on a misapprehension. The Germans, overestimating the losses suffered by the British since July and underestimating their output of new aircraft, assumed that they could not have more than a few hundred fighters left. In fact, their losses had been steadily replaced throughout the battle.[69] Air Chief Marshal Dowding, charged with the air defense of the whole of the United Kingdom, had many more squadrons under command than his bases in the south alone could handle. Consequently, he could not have committed his entire force to the defense of London even if he had wished to do so. Of the fifty-two squadrons of single-seater fighters at his disposal on September 7, twenty-one were stationed in the southeastern counties.[70] Air Vice Marshal Park of No. 11 Group would meet attacks on London with these twenty-one squadrons, supplemented by a maximum of nine squadrons from neighboring groups. Numerical strengths varied from squadron to squadron and from day to day, but in general each squadron had enough aircraft and pilots to take the air at its normal tactical strength of twelve aircraft, after all allowances were made for leave, casualties, and the grounding of aircraft for maintenance and minor repairs.

Thus Park would have, at most, about 360 single-seater fighters with which to defeat or circumvent the enemy's fighters and destroy or drive off his bombers. The German fighters would, however, be handicapped to some extent by the need to conform with the movements of relatively slow bomber forces and to conserve fuel for the return flight. Some 400 to 500 heavy antiaircraft guns, about 500 barrage balloons, and some hundreds of light antiaircraft weapons of various kinds deployed in the Greater London area and the southeastern counties would help Park by restricting the enemy's freedom of action, even if they did not directly destroy or damage any German aircraft.

About 300 bombers, escorted and supported by roughly twice as many fighters, delivered the first raid of the new series in the late afternoon and early evening of Saturday, September 7. Their arrival coincided with a meeting at which the Chiefs of Staff decided to call troops in the eastern and southern counties to instant readiness to meet invasion, but the decision was based on a report prepared earlier in the day and was not affected by the raid. All but two of twenty-three British fighter squadrons ordered into action engaged the enemy, but most of them arrived too late to interfere with the bombing. Even so, the destruction of 41 bombers and fighters was a serious setback for the Germans, who admitted after the raid that they had made "heavy sacrifices." [71] Another 28 aircraft were lost on September 9, when only about 90 bombers out of more than 200 sent to London reached the target area. Losses were, however, considerably lighter on September 11 and 14, when smaller bomber formations were used and the proportion of fighters to bombers was correspondingly increased.

The experience of these two days encouraged the Germans to hope that they might yet achieve a spectacular success before Hitler made his crucial decision on September 17. Accordingly Field Marshal Albert Kesselring, commanding Luftflotte 2 in the Low Countries and France east and north of the Seine, arranged to deliver on Sunday, September 15, two successive attacks by modest bomber forces escorted and supported by virtually every fighter he could muster. While the second attack was in progress Field Marshal Hugo Sperrle of Luftflotte 3, on Kesselring's left, would create a diversion by sending a small force to attack the naval dockyard at Portland. The day's events would also include an attack by bomb-carrying heavy fighters of Luftflotte 3 on an aircraft factory near Southampton.

A great weakness of this plan was that Kesselring, with his strength depleted by recent losses, could launch two major operations in one day only by calling on some of his units to make double sorties. An interval of about two hours had therefore to be allowed between his two attacks on London. The result was that Park, receiving ample warning of both attacks from the radar chain, was able to counter each of them with his whole force and thus on both occasions to meet Kesselring's fighters on terms of approximate numerical equality. The Luftwaffe, flying some 700 fighter sorties to cover the two attacks on London and the attack on Portland, lost not only sixty aircraft, but also its faith in official estimates of British strength. On September 17 Hitler postponed the invasion of Britain "until further notice." [72] Warned on the following day that a number of invasion craft had been sunk or damaged by bombing, he agreed that the assembly of shipping at the invasion ports should cease and that transports and warships should disperse to reduce the risk of further losses.[73]

The Germans continued until the winter to make occasional daylight raids on London, interspersed with fighter sweeps and attacks on shipping. But the bulk of their air effort during the next eight months went into night attacks on London, Liverpool, Birmingham, Glasgow, Plymouth, Bristol, Coventry, Portsmouth, Southampton, Hull, Manchester, Belfast, Sheffield, Newcastle, Nottingham, and Cardiff. These caused considerable inconvenience, distress, and loss of life, but they did not bring the Germans within sight of a decisive victory.

After winning the Battle of Britain, the British faced five major tasks. The first was to reconcile their overseas commitments with the need to retain in the United Kingdom forces strong enough to ensure that the invasion threat did not recur. The second was to keep their external communications open by preventing German and Italian submarines and aircraft from sinking their merchant shipping faster than lost ships could be replaced. The third was to reopen the Gibraltar-Suez route to regular convoys as soon as they were strong enough to do so and meanwhile to maintain their hold on the Suez Canal, the Red Sea, and the Persian Gulf. The fourth was to find, alone or in partnership with hypothetical allies, the means of compelling Hitler to surrender his ill-gotten gains. The fifth was to avoid or at least postpone a Far Eastern war for which they would be ill equipped as long as a substantial proportion of their naval strength was needed to dispute command of the Mediterranean with the Italians.

The third task was crucial, not only because existing commitments in the Mediterranean locked up warships needed elsewhere but also because the long haul around the Cape made extravagant demands on cargo ships and transports by adding some 10,000 miles to the effective distance between the United Kingdom and the Middle East. In the winter and spring of 1940–41 the British took the first step toward freeing the shores of the Mediterranean and the Red Sea of hostile forces by tackling the Italians on land and sea. On November 11 carrier-borne torpedo bombers of the Mediterranean Fleet, under Admiral Sir Andrew Cunningham, gave a new dimension to naval warfare by sinking three Italian capital ships in shallow water at Taranto. In the following month General Sir Archibald Wavell opened a series of offensives which drove the enemy from Cyrenaica, Eritrea, the Somalilands, and Abyssinia.[74] In Cyrenaica two of Wavell's divisions routed the Italian Tenth Army and took 130,000 prisoners at the cost of fewer than 2,000 British casualties.

In the light of the disaster to the Tenth Army and of Greek successes in Albania, Hitler came to the conclusion that he could not afford to see Italy knocked out of the war and must intervene in the Mediterranean theater not only by sending aircraft to Sicily and launching a lightning campaign in the Balkans, but also by sending troops to North Africa. Wavell had therefore to meet a counterattack in Cyrenaica by the redoubtable General Rommel at a time when orders from London compelled him to divert some 60,000 troops to Greece. By the end of April practically the whole of Cyrenaica except Tobruk was once more in Axis hands, and German forces advancing into Greece by way of Rumania, Bulgaria, and Yugoslavia had defeated the Greeks and pushed the British out. The Germans went on to capture Crete with airborne forces which narrowly escaped disaster.

In the summer of 1941 Rommel repelled a counteroffensive in the Egyptian frontier area, largely by making a skillful use of his artillery to pin down or destroy Wavell's tanks before committing the bulk of his own armor. Almost simultaneously Wavell reluctantly extended his northern flank by complying with orders to send British and Free French troops into Syria. Thus the first phase of the war ended with the Axis Powers in possession of Tripolitania and practically the whole of Cyrenaica, while the British, after suppressing a weakly supported pro-Axis rising in Iraq, held Malta, Tobruk, and the whole of the oddly named Middle East from the Western Desert of Egypt to Lebanon and Kurdistan. Naval and air control of the central Mediterranean was still in dispute, but access to air bases in Sicily, Crete, and Cyrenaica put the Axis Powers in a strong position.

Meanwhile, the British received from secret sources indications of a coming German attack on Russia. They passed the gist of their information to Stalin, who responded by publicly accusing the British government of trying to make mischief between him and Hitler.

13

The "Grand Alliance": I

AFTER signing the Anti-Comintern Pact in 1936, the Japanese made repeated attempts to replace it by an unequal partnership which would assure them of German and Italian support against Russia, without committing them to go to war with France and Britain should Hitler and Mussolini decide to do so. When these efforts failed, they turned to the United States. In the spring of 1939, after Ribbentrop had warned them that Germany might conclude a pact with the Soviet Union if Japan refused to cooperate with her on Hitler's terms, they proposed that the Americans should join them in trying to avert a European war by urging the British and the French to make concessions to the Axis Powers and Hitler and Mussolini to become less bellicose.[1]

Cordell Hull, the American Secretary of State, gave this proposal a cool reception. Believing that the professed desire of the Japanese to avert a conflict with the European democracies was insincere, he offered some adverse comments on Japan's foreign policy and in particular on her failure to come to terms with Chiang Kai-shek.[2] In July he went on to denounce, with effect from the following January, the treaty which had governed commercial relations between Japan and the United States since 1911.

Pro-Axis members of the Japanese government then urged the Prime Minister, Baron Kuchiro Hiranuma, to make fresh approaches to Germany and Italy. Hiranuma declined to do so but was soon swept from office by the backwash of dire events. On August 20 a clash with Russian troops in disputed territory on the borders of Outer Mongolia and Manchuria culminated in a humiliating defeat for the Kwantung Army. Only three days later, the Japanese government learned to its dismay that Germany had indeed concluded a pact with Russia.

In the light of these setbacks the Japanese renewed their overtures to the Americans. Again they were rebuffed. Those of their statesmen who still hoped to avoid a clash with France and Britain had thereafter to be increasingly on their guard against a political crisis which might open the door to a military dictatorship.

One point on which there was general agreement in Japan was that the long-standing dispute with Nationalist China must somehow be patched up on terms which did not sacrifice everything gained at Chiang's expense since 1937. Since the fall of Canton, Chiang had received supplies from Russia by an overland route through Russian Turkestan and Sinkiang. Nothing could be done to stop this traffic. On the other hand, British and French preoccupations in Europe held out the hope that the European democracies might be persuaded to starve Chiang of supplies from sources under their control. After the fall of France, the Japanese succeeded in forcing the French authorities in Indochina to close the port of Haiphong and its communications with Chungking to war matériel consigned to Chiang. At the same time, they moved troops to the neighborhood of Hong Kong and called upon the British to close the so-called Burma Road. This road, constructed by Chinese labor with British and American approval and support, was mostly in Chinese territory; but its terminus was in British-controlled Burma, and it linked Chungking with the Burmese transportation system and ultimately with Rangoon.

The British responded to the threat of an attack on Hong Kong by preparing their possessions there and on the mainland at Kowloon for a siege. But the defenses of Hong Kong were not designed to withstand a systematic assault, and in any case the British were not in a position to fight singlehanded against Japan, as well as Germany and Italy. At an interview with Cordell Hull on June 27 Lord Lothian proposed that the United States should help Britain to resist Japanese encroachments, either by sending warships to Singapore or by banning trade with Japan. If neither course was acceptable, then the Americans would, the British thought, be well advised to join in bringing about a settlement of the Sino-Japanese dispute on terms which would ensure the continued existence of an independent China, safeguard the interests of the treaty powers, and keep Japan out of the war in Europe.[3]

Hull did not take kindly to any of these proposals. The government had decided that the fleet should remain at Pearl Harbor on the conclusion of recent exercises in Hawaiian waters. The President and his advisers were not prepared either to move it back to the West Coast or to send part of it to Singapore. At the same time Roosevelt and Hull, although unwilling to negotiate a new commercial treaty with Japan or to take an active part in reconciling her with Nationalist China, did not feel that the time had come for an economic embargo. Hull undertook not to oppose attempts at mediation by the British and Australian governments but insisted that the mediators should not acknowledge the right of the Japanese to establish a New Order in East Asia or take it upon themselves to offer concessions at Chiang's expense.[4]

In July the Japanese press became so hostile to the Western powers that the British decided to close the Burma Road for three months during the rainy season, when little traffic would be able to pass along it in any case. By this means they hoped, without irreparably damaging Chiang's interests, to put moderate members of the Japanese government in a position to placate extremist colleagues by claiming a diplomatic success.

The Japanese went on to demand access for their armed forces to Indochina so that they could use the northern part of the country as a base for operations against Nationalist China. The British proposed that the Americans should join them in offering military aid to the French authorities on the spot as a means of helping them to resist such encroachments, but the United States government refused to hazard American neutrality by sanctioning so drastic a step. The French managed to spin out negotiations with the Japanese until September but were then obliged to sign an agreement which gave

Japan limited rights of access to the province of Tongking. Almost simultaneously, Japan concluded a Tripartite Pact with Germany and Italy.

During the second half of the year the United States government went some way toward the severance of economic ties with Japan by prohibiting the export of certain raw materials and manufactured goods except under license. High-grade aviation fuel and lubricants were included in the list. The Japanese took steps to meet the situation by increasing their capacity to treat low-grade fuels in their own refineries, but their stocks of oil began to fall off in 1940 after rising sharply between 1935 and 1939.[5]

Meanwhile, British success in the Battle of Britain convinced a growing number of Americans that their country's strategic frontiers lay on the far side of the Atlantic. By the third week of August it was clear that although the battle was not yet over, the British fighter force was punishing the Luftwaffe severely and was suffering far lighter losses than the Germans claimed to be inflicting on it. "Exploratory conversations" between British and American officers began in that month, although it was not until after the signing of the Tripartite Pact in September that authority was given for comprehensive staff talks which followed early in 1941.

In the same month Sir Henry Tizard, until recently scientific adviser to the Chief of the Air Staff, arrived in Washington as leader and precursor of a British technical and scientific mission which assembled in September. Dispatched at a moment when Britain's dollar resources were running low, Tizard had made it clear to his government that he would undertake the journey only on the understanding that his task was not to barter information for reciprocal benefits, but to tell the Americans what they needed to know in order to bring their armed forces to the highest level of technical efficiency.[6] Accordingly, he and his colleagues imparted to American service chiefs and scientists, without asking or expecting anything in return except such goodwill as might accrue, the secrets of radar, the cavity magnetron, the proximity fuze, and other British inventions and discoveries whose importance an American official historian summed up with the comment that the cavity magnetron was "the most valuable cargo ever brought to our shores."[7]

Soon after Tizard's arrival, President Roosevelt remarked to him that he was risking his political future by sponsoring a much-debated bill which broke new ground by introducing compulsory military service in time of peace.[8] Some two months later, after telling voters that "their boys were not going to be sent into any foreign wars," Roosevelt was reelected by a handsome majority.

The outcome of the Presidential election was widely regarded on both sides of the Atlantic as an endorsement of Roosevelt's policy of support for Britain.[9] A point which attracted less attention in England was that it also gave the President a mandate to build conscript armies whose needs might conflict with British demands for American supplies. Measures recommended by the American service chiefs during the last few months of 1940 not only went far beyond, but in some respects ran counter to, the policy of all-embracing material support for Britain which Churchill seemed to expect the Americans to adopt when he urged the United States to "give us the tools, and we will finish the job." Admiral Harold R. Stark, the American Chief of Naval Operations, and General George C. Marshall, Chief of Staff of the United States Army, were emphatically of the opinion that the national effort should be directed not toward a mere furnishing of supplies to the British, but toward "an eventual strong offensive in the Atlantic" in alliance with Britain.[10]

Stark and Marshall believed, too, that eventually both strong air forces and strong land forces would have to be sent from the United States to fight in Europe or Africa or in both theaters.[11] Since two years or more would certainly be needed to train and equip American armies suitable for the purpose, the presumption was that, so far as the Americans were concerned, no major attempt to defeat the Germans on land was to be expected before 1942 or 1943. The British hoped to weaken Germany in the meantime by a combination of blockade and bombing, but American strategists did not believe that such measures could be decisive.

The American service chiefs were also of the opinion in 1940, as in 1939, that, in the event of war with Japan, the United States—and by implication her prospective allies—should stand on the defensive in the Far East and the Pacific until the Germans were defeated. Discussions in which British, American, and Dutch officers with local knowledge took part failed, however, to produce a defensive plan which the authorities in Washington were willing to endorse. A glance at the map was enough to show that the Western powers could not hope to defend important sources of raw materials in Malaya and Indonesia or American interests at Manila without gaining command of the South China Sea or at least putting themselves in a position to dispute control of it with the Japanese. The only first-class naval base within striking distance of the South China Sea was Singapore, and the British did not expect to be able to send a balanced fleet to Singapore before the spring of 1942. The Americans clung to their decision not to send a squadron in the meantime, arguing that dispersal of the battle fleet concentrated at Pearl Harbor would be contrary to the accepted principles of naval strategy. British, American, and Dutch commanders on the spot had therefore to fall back on the hope that aircraft and light naval forces might prove an effective substitute for a balanced fleet or that, if all else failed, their land forces might be able to hold out until they were relieved.

In the meantime, a situation threatened to arise in which the British would be unable, for lack of dollars, to place further orders in the United States unless restrictions on credit were relaxed. More than 40 percent of all American exports since the autumn of 1939 had gone to the British Empire, and it seemed that only the granting of large loans or credits to Britain could avert a disastrous slump. Roosevelt was, however, very reluctant to propose such a step at the risk of creating tensions similar to those which had darkened the international scene immediately after the First World War. He wanted, he said, to "eliminate the dollar sign." [12] His search for a means of doing so led to the discovery that a statute of 1892 empowered the government to lease army property to people outside the public service at the discretion of the Secretary of War. On the strength of that precedent, Congress passed in March, 1941, an act which gave the President authority to arrange for the manufacture of war matériel for the government of any country whose defense he deemed a vital American interest and to lend or lease "any defense article" to such a government on terms to be decided at his discretion.

This measure, described by Churchill in oddly negative terms as "the most unsordid act in the history of any nation," averted an industrial crisis and relieved the British government of a great deal of anxiety. Because it did not apply to existing contracts, the British continued, however, to pay in gold or dollars for most goods supplied up to the time when the United States became an active belligerent. Moreover, American merchant ships could not yet be used to deliver cargoes to British ports, as they were still forbidden to enter "combat areas." A system of "neutrality patrols" introduced in 1939 was extended in the spring of 1941, but such patrols did not prevent German submarines from taking a heavy toll of British, Allied, and neutral shipping.

After the passing of the Lend-Lease bill, means were found of overcoming some of the restrictions which it failed to remove. At the end of March the United States government seized sixty-five Axis-controlled ships in American ports. On April 10, after Wavell's troops had entered Asmara and Massawa in Eritrea, the President declared the mouth of the Red Sea no longer a combat area, so that American ships were thereafter free to carry equipment and supplies to the British forces in the Middle East. Provisional plans for joint convoy in the Atlantic were concerted with the British, ten American Coast Guard cutters were transferred to the British flag, and American officers chose bases in Britain and Northern Ireland at which United States naval and air forces would be stationed in due course.[13] Finally, on May 27, the President proclaimed a state of "Unlimited National Emergency," announced that "strict naval and military necessity" required that all possible assistance should be given to the British, and promised that "all additional measures" needed to ensure the delivery of supplies to Britain would be taken.[14] Since the Americans were not yet prepared to sail their merchant ships to Britain in convoy, there was in fact very little in the way of additional measures that they could do.

In the late winter and spring of 1941 the volume of British, Allied, and neutral merchant shipping sunk by various means in all parts of the world rose from an average of less than 300,000 tons a month in the first sixteen months of war to 529,706 tons in March and 687,901 tons in April.[15] In March well over 500,000 tons of shipping were sunk in the North Atlantic and United Kingdom waters alone. The essence of the problem for the British was to extend the area in which protection could be given. Diplomatic pressure from London and Washington failed to persuade the government of Eire to allow the British to use bases in Ireland, but bases were developed in the Hebrides and in Iceland, occupied by British and Canadian forces in the previous year. The completion of escort vessels ordered early in the war, the growth of the Royal Canadian Navy, and improvements in the range and equipment of maritime cooperation aircraft helped the Admiralty keep the situation within bounds. By the last week of

May the Royal Navy and the Royal Canadian Navy were able to provide continuous escort across the whole width of the Atlantic. Losses were beginning to decline when the war entered a new phase in June; thereafter they fell off sharply.[16]

Meanwhile, the British Bomber Command continued the attempts at night precision bombing begun in the spring and early summer of 1940. Inaccurate reports from bomber crews and misleading accounts from informants abroad of the effects of bombing contributed to the belief that Germany's economy might be "disrupted" by night attacks on oil targets and communications.[17] Since the average number of aircraft available for strategic bombing was only about 200 in the early stages of the war and about 500 in the latter part of 1941,[18] this belief would have been on the hopeful side even if the precise location and accurate bombing of individual factories and installations, at night and in face of antiaircraft fire and searchlight dazzle, had not been a task beyond the skill of all but the best crews. By the early part of 1941 it was generally, though not universally, accepted in Britain that successful night precision bombing was not to be expected of Bomber Command with its existing equipment and standards of training.

German bomber crews, too, were ordered to bomb precise objectives during their night attacks in 1940 and 1941. Nevertheless, their performance fell so far short of the required standard that the impression received by the British was that their attacks were indiscriminate. On September 11, 1940, Air Marshal Sir Charles Portal—at that time Air Officer Commanding in Chief, Bomber Command, but soon to become Chief of the Air Staff—proposed in the light of a conversation with Churchill that indiscriminate attacks should, in certain circumstances, be made on German towns.[19] On September 21 the Air Staff instructed him that the disruption of Germany's economy by the bombing of oil targets and communications was still its primary aim but that attacks were to be made on Berlin for the purpose of causing "the greatest possible disturbance and dislocation both to the industrial activities and to the civil population generally in the area." [20]

Berlin had in fact been attacked on the night of August 25, but not with the intention of causing indiscriminate damage. The first raid delivered for the purpose of damaging a German town rather than individual factories or installations was made on the night of December 16, when Mannheim was the target and the center of the town the intended aiming point. One hundred and thirty-four aircraft were dispatched "in perfect moonlight conditions." One hundred and two crews claimed on their return that they had attacked Mannheim, and "all reports agreed in suggesting that the majority of the bombs had fallen in the target area." [21] Air photographs taken in daylight on December 21 showed, however, that the attack had been widely dispersed and had "failed in its primary object." [22]

The conclusion drawn from these and similar experiences was not that area bombing and attempts at night precision bombing were equally futile but that "the only target on which the night force could inflict effective damage was a whole German town." [23] During the greater part of the period from the spring of 1941 to the end of the war with Germany, Bomber Command's effort went mainly into area attacks at night.

Day bombing was felt by most British airmen to be impractical where bombers had to fly long distances over enemy-held territory to reach their objectives. On the other hand, it was still possible where they could be escorted by fighters to targets within easy reach. Early in 1941 medium bombers escorted and supported by single-seater fighters began a series of day attacks on objectives in northern France. These attacks were supplemented by fighter sweeps and "tip-and-run" attacks by fighter pilots, who relied on cloud cover and evasive action to enable them to escape interception. About 190 bomber and some 2,700 fighter sorties were made in the course of such operations between January 9 and June 13. The British hoped, as the Germans had done in the summer of 1940, to bring the enemy's fighters to battle and catch them at a disadvantage, but in fact their losses were heavier than the enemy's.[24]

By the middle of June, 1941, large numbers of German troops were massed along the Russian frontier from Petsamo to the Black Sea, and most of the German air units hitherto based in France and the Low Countries had moved or were moving to eastern Europe. The signs seemed to point so clearly to an imminent attack on the Soviet Union that the British made plans to step up their daylight air offensive over northern France, "particularly in the event of operations developing against Russia." [25] During the next five months their fighters, bombers, and fighter-bombers devoted many thousands of sorties to attempts to relieve pressure on the Russians by forcing the Germans to bring their fighters back. That object was not attained, and their attempt to "fight the Battle of Britain in reverse" cost the British heavy losses, especially among fighter pilots.[26]

On June 22 Hitler opened his attack on Russia by thrusting his center toward Moscow, his left toward Leningrad, and his right in the general direction of Kiev, Odessa, and Dnepropetrovsk. The Russians were caught with their troops widely dispersed and with relatively few modern tanks and aircraft.[27] They had received many warnings that a crisis was imminent but had clung until the last moment to a policy of appeasement, which they hoped would buy them time to complete their rearmament and redispose their forces.[28]

How long the Russians would hold out was hard to foresee. Sir Stafford Cripps, the British ambassador in Moscow, reported a week before the offensive began that the Red Army was not expected in diplomatic circles there to withstand a German attack for more than three or four weeks.[29] Experts in London and Washington believed that the campaign might last from one and a half to three months.[30] Stalin himself admitted in July that the situation was critical and that Russia would be crippled or defeated without help from the West.[31]

The British came to the conclusion that they must do everything they could to keep the Soviet armies in the field, not only by using their naval and air power to harass the Germans but also by sending weapons, equipment, and supplies to Russia, even at the cost of delaying the expansion of their own forces.[32] They followed up a formal promise to that effect by dispatching to Archangel a first consignment of ammunition and crated aircraft, accompanied by forty-eight uncrated Hurricanes which landed successfully at Murmansk from the carrier *Argus.* Thus encouraged, the Russians recovered from a bad start, overhauled their system of command, and put in hand elaborate measures for the removal of industrial plant and key workers to areas beyond Hitler's immediate reach. Much to the satisfaction of the British, who were rightly skeptical of claims that icebreakers could make Archangel usable in winter, they also assured themselves of an ice-free port of entry for goods shipped from the West by successfully defending Murmansk and its communications with the interior.

The German advance, the consequent loss of important centers of agricultural and industrial production, and the removal of factories to new quarters temporarily halved Russia's output, depleted her reserves, and left her with serious shortages of weapons, equipment, ammunition, consumer goods, foodstuffs, and raw materials.[33] Early in September Stalin estimated his immediate requirements at 30,000 tons of aluminum by the beginning of October and 400 aircraft and 500 medium and light tanks a month for an indefinite period. He also asked for a second front in France or the Balkans.[34]

The British were not in a position to satisfy all these demands. In effect, they were already holding down some thirty to forty German divisions in France by maintaining substantial forces in the United Kingdom, and they could not mount an offensive in the Balkans without first gaining control of the central Mediterranean by defeating the Axis forces in North Africa. They decided to send Stalin 5,000 tons of aluminum from Canada at the earliest possible moment and 2,000 tons a month thereafter and to find from their own resources half the tanks and aircraft he had asked for. The other half would, they hoped, be forthcoming from the United States.

The Americans agreed that "visible support" should be afforded to Russia. At the same time, they took a further step toward belligerency by agreeing that Iceland should become a staging post for supplies to Russia and an advanced station for American naval and air units. In August United States forces relieved the British garrison of Iceland, and American warships and air squadrons took up positions which would enable them to join the British in keeping watch on adjacent waters and to attack any German ship seen to enter the American defense zone. Authority was given for American warships to escort shipping of any nationality on passage between the United States and Iceland and, from September, to escort shipping of any nationality on passage between the United States or Canada and the United Kingdom. The first convoy bound for the United Kingdom with an American escort left Halifax on September 16. As a result of more active American participation in the Battle of the Atlantic, German preoccupations in the Baltic, and damage done to German warships at Brest by British bombers and torpedo bombers, the Admiralty was able to contemplate by August the dispatch of a powerful fleet to Singapore by the spring of 1942.[35]

The question of American supplies for Russia was more difficult. President Roosevelt wished to make the United States "the great arsenal of democracy," but was obliged to give priority to the American Army of 200 divisions at which he was aiming. The Americans had to warn the British in September not only that deliveries of lend-lease materials during the next nine months would fall short of expectations, but also that tanks and aircraft for the Russians would have to be found largely from allocations already promised to Britain.[36] Since their figures showed that even then the Russians would not receive their full quota, the British volunteered to make up the deficiency at the cost of still further reducing their own share.

Thus the British and the Americans were able to tell Stalin when they traveled to Moscow later in the month that all the tanks and aircraft he had asked for would be provided.[37] In addition, the British renewed their offer of 2,000 tons of aluminum a month and promised to meet the whole of Russia's demands for a wide range of other raw materials, including cobalt, copper, lead, tin, rubber, wool, and zinc. The Americans offered a variety of manufactured or partly manufactured products and promised to look into the possibility of finding the rest of the aluminum needed by the Russians. The Western powers did not undertake to deliver all or any of these goods at Russian ports, but in fact the British, with the active participation of the Americans, organized an elaborate system of convoys to Murmansk and Archangel. During the next three years the Russians received, according to their own published statements, 5,480 British and 3,734 American tanks, 5,800 British, and 6,430 American aircraft, many thousands of British and American motor vehicles, and large quantities of raw materials, ammunition, and miscellaneous supplies.[38] This investment by the Western powers yielded rich dividends in the shape of a series of staggering defeats inflicted by the Red Army on the Germans between 1942 and 1945.

In the spring of 1941 the Japanese Foreign Minister, Yosuke Matsuoka, traveled to Moscow and Berlin in the hope of transforming the Tripartite Pact into a quadruple alliance by bringing in the Russians. Ribbentrop, without actually saying that Germany was about to attack Russia, made it clear that such an attack was possible.[39] Nevertheless, Matsuoka persisted in his attempt to come to terms with Moscow. On the return journey he persuaded the Russians, with some difficulty, to conclude a five-year neutrality pact with Japan.

Despite Ribbentrop's hint and a warning from the Japanese ambassador in Berlin, Hitler's attack on the Soviet Union came as a great shock to the Japanese and led indirectly to Matsuoka's dismissal on July 16. In the meantime, he and his colleagues, alarmed by the failure of an attempt to ensure against the cutting off of American supplies by persuading the Dutch to grant them far-reaching economic concessions in Java and Sumatra, decided to occupy southern Indochina as a possible base for an invasion of Indonesia. At an imperial conference on July 2 it was agreed that this move should be made even at the risk of war with the British Empire and the United States.[40] Subsequent discussions, culminating in a reconstruction of the government and the appointment of a new foreign minister, led to the conclusion that further attempts should be made to reach agreement with the Western powers but that the nation must be prepared to fight if its existence were threatened by embargoes or encirclement.

The American authorities, having broken the Japanese diplomatic cipher, learned from intercepted signals of the decision reached in Tokyo on July 2. Later they deciphered orders to the Japanese forces in Indochina to occupy bases suitable for operations against the Netherlands East Indies and Singapore.[41] On the other hand, they did not know that the Japanese government had sanctioned active preparations for war with the Western powers or that a surprise attack on Pearl Harbor was being studied in Tokyo.

In the last week of July the British and United States governments decided in consultation, but on the initiative of the Americans, to freeze Japanese funds throughout the British Empire and the United States.[42] The Dutch, whose trade with Japan was based entirely on the dollar, reluctantly followed suit. Japan was thus deprived of three-quarters of her foreign trade and nearly nine-tenths of her supplies of oil. Rear Admiral Richmond K. Turner, of the War Plans Division of the United States Department of the Navy, objected to these measures on the ground that they threatened to embroil the country in a Far Eastern war at a time when the Navy had just accepted new commitments in the Atlantic.[43] However, he decided not to press his protest to the point of resignation when he learned that diplomatic representations had failed to persuade the Japanese to withdraw from southern Indochina.

The Japanese still did not abandon hope of a peaceful settlement. Prince Fumimaro Konoye, the leader of a government which included both moderates and extremists, persuaded his colleagues to agree that no decision for or against war should be made before the middle of October and that meanwhile he should do his best to come to terms with the Western powers. Later the deadline was put back until the last week in November. When the middle of October came, Konoye resigned in favor of General Hideki Tojo, the former Minister of War. He explained afterward that although the primary cause of his resignation was that he wanted the responsibility for subsequent developments to rest squarely on the Army, that was not his only motive. He was also influenced by the hope that the choice of a soldier as Prime Minister might convince the Western powers that the government had no intention of making promises which the armed forces might repudiate.

Thus the Western powers faced in the late summer and autumn of 1941 a situation in which the scales were delicately balanced between peace and war. On the one hand, there was obviously a risk that they might find themselves at war with Japan before the year was out. On the other, there were signs that the Japanese might be willing to abandon their designs on Indonesia and Malaya if the Americans agreed to lift their economic embargo and help them come to terms with Chiang Kai-shek. British, Dutch, and American possessions in the Far East and the western Pacific would be extremely vulnerable until the spring of 1942, when the British hoped to send a balanced fleet to Singapore and the Americans to establish in the Philippines a bomber force capable of presenting a serious threat to Japanese positions in Formosa. A great deal might turn, therefore, on the outcome of diplomatic exchanges initiated by Konoye and continued by his successor. In these a leading part was, with the assent of the British, to be played by the veteran Cordell Hull. Hull was a very experienced Secretary of State, but he was deeply suspicious of the Japanese and reluctant to concern himself with military matters.[44] Although he attended meetings between the President and heads of departments at which the Chiefs of Staff were present, it seems doubtful whether he understood how grave were the strategic disadvantages to which the Western powers would expose themselves if they went to war with Japan while their defensive preparations were still incomplete.

In the course of a visit to London in July the President's personal representative, Harry L. Hopkins, mentioned the difficulty some

Americans had in understanding why the British attached so much importance to the Middle East.[45] He added that the President would welcome a meeting with Churchill. The sequel was the Atlantic Conference, held at Placentia Bay in Newfoundland in August and attended not only by the President and the Prime Minister, but also by their naval and military advisers. The statesmen gave a good deal of their attention to a statement of war aims, drafted by Churchill on broad Wilsonian lines and eventually published, with substantial additions and amendments, as the Atlantic Charter. Strategic aims and plans were discussed at some length in the light of the staff talks held earlier in the year and of more recent developments. The British were preparing to deliver an offensive in the Middle East which they hoped would drive the Axis forces from North Africa and reopen the whole length of the Mediterranean to Allied shipping. At the same time, they recognized that they might have to defend the Suez Canal and the head of the Persian Gulf against an airborne expedition from the Balkans and the Aegean or, if Russia collapsed, against an advance through the Caucasus. Wavell's successor, General Sir Claude Auchinleck, had made it clear in July that he had no intention of taking the offensive in the Western Desert of Egypt until Syria was firmly in his hands and Cyprus secure against a seaborne or airborne assault.

As things turned out, the offensive launched under Auchinleck's direction in November was brilliantly successful but left the British with their communications so stretched that Rommel was able by a bold counterstroke to recapture most of the territory he had lost. Profiting by the tendency of Auchinleck's subordinate commanders to disperse their armor and by their lack of good antitank weapons and strong air support, he proceeded in the following summer to take Tobruk and compel the British to withdraw to a narrow front between El Alamein and the Qattara depression, less than 100 miles west of the Nile Delta. Thus it was not until the autumn of 1942, after two attempts by Axis forces to break through to Cairo and Alexandria had been vigorously repelled at the battles of First Alamein and Alam el Halfa, that the British were again in a position to take the offensive with a reasonable prospect of success.

The Far Eastern situation, too, was discussed at the Atlantic Conference. Churchill believed that Japan would "probably recoil before the ultimately overwhelming might of the United States."[46] He urged Roosevelt to make it clear to the Japanese that the United States would not stand aside if British or Dutch possessions in the Far East were attacked. The President, aware of the danger of forfeiting the support of Congress by appearing to exceed his constitutional powers, was reluctant to make such a declaration. Eventually he agreed that Britain, the Netherlands, and the United States should warn Japan that any further act of aggression on her part would force them to protect their interests even at the risk of war. A warning which avoided the word "war" was then drafted, but Hull insisted on toning it down when it was shown to him on August 15.[47] The note presented by the State Department to the Japanese ambassador two days later differed so much from the original that the British and the Dutch withheld their version rather than allow it to be known that the Americans were out of step with them.

Negotiations between Washington and Tokyo came to a head in November. On November 5 the Japanese agreed among themselves to make further attempts to come to terms with the Americans, to go to war with the British Empire and the United States only if no success were achieved by November 25, and in any case to make no attack on Russia.[48] Instructions to that effect were cabled to the Japanese ambassador in Washington and deciphered by the Americans. Thus Hull knew by the end of the first week in November that the ambassador had been warned of the importance of bringing the negotiations to a successful conclusion by November 25 and that in all probability the penalty of failure would be war.[49]

The ambassador, Admiral Kichisaburo Nomura, was not a professional diplomat, although he had some experience of diplomacy. He had been chosen because he was well liked in the United States. When he expressed doubts about the success of his mission, the Foreign Ministry sent a special envoy to join him in Washington. The choice fell on Saburo Kurusu, who had been Japanese ambassador in Berlin.

On November 7 Nomura submitted his government's proposals for a comprehensive settlement. Japan offered, in return for an undertaking from the Americans not to discriminate against Japanese trade in any part of the world, to concede the principle of the "open door" throughout the "Pacific region," including China. In addition, she would remove her troops from all parts of China, except the northern provinces, Inner Mongolia, and Hainan, within two years.

She would also promise informally to remove her troops from Indochina as soon as she made peace with Chiang Kai-shek and to do her best to prevent the war in Europe from spreading to the Far East.

Hull responded to these proposals by pointing out that the great obstacle to a comprehensive settlement was that Japan was Germany's ally. Kurusu tried to explain that his government, although not in a position to denounce the alliance with Germany, was willing to regard it as a nullity, but he failed to convince Hull of his sincerity. As ambassador in Berlin at the relevant time, Kurusu had signed the Tripartite Pact on Matsuoka's instructions and was therefore assumed by Hull to have approved of it.

On November 18 Hull finally rejected the proposals on the ground that public opinion in the United States would not tolerate a comprehensive settlement with Japan as long as her alliance with Germany remained in force.[50] The Japanese then fell back on proposals for an interim agreement. They proposed on November 20 that pending a final settlement, both they and the Americans should call a halt to military movements in the Far East and the western Pacific, and that the Americans should lift their embargo on trade with Japan, resume deliveries of oil, and help Japan obtain supplies from the Netherlands East Indies and come to terms with Chiang Kai-shek. As part of the bargain, Japan would withdraw her troops from southern Indochina and undertake to pull out of the rest of Indochina as soon as her differences with Chiang Kai-shek were settled.

A serious objection to this program was that the reference to Chiang Kai-shek was so framed as to make it clear that the Japanese expected the Americans to speed a settlement by withdrawing their support from Chiang. Hull afterward described the proposals as "quite unacceptable."[51] Nevertheless, he did not reject them out of hand. On November 22 he showed them to the British and Chinese ambassadors and the Australian and Dutch ministers in Washington. At the same time he produced the draft of a reply which did not commit the United States to do more about the Sino-Japanese dispute than provide facilities for a peace conference if asked to do so. He stipulated that a maximum of 25,000 Japanese troops should remain in Indochina after the signing of the proposed interim agreement and that Japan should purchase no more oil from the United States than she needed for civilian use.

Hull complained later that the Australians, the British, the Chinese, and the Dutch all were either actively hostile to his counterproposals or lukewarm about them. The record shows that in fact the only serious opposition came from the Chinese, who objected to any relaxation of the embargo on trade with Japan. The British, when they responded to invitations from Hull and Roosevelt to comment on the Japanese offer and the American counteroffer, questioned the wisdom of selling oil to Japan and stressed the importance of keeping faith with Chiang Kai-shek, but they added that a Far Eastern war was the last thing they wanted at the moment and that they would support any action the United States might see fit to take.[52] Nevertheless, the reception given to his draft seemed to Hull so disappointing that on November 26 he dropped all proposals for an interim agreement, his own included. He told the Japanese on that day that if they wanted a new commercial agreement, no embargo on trade, and American support in the international money market, they must withdraw their forces from the whole of China and Indochina, relinquish their extraterritorial rights, and recognize the sovereignty of the Nationalist government throughout China. As the result of an oversight, he omitted to add that these demands were not meant to apply to Manchuria.[53]

The President, convinced that it was essential to unite American opinion behind the government by avoiding any appearance of appeasing Japan at Chiang's expense, concurred in Hull's decision.[54] Neither he nor Hull expected the proposals made on November 26 to be accepted,[55] and in effect he staked his chances of postponing a conflict until the Western powers were ready on the hope that the Japanese would nonetheless be willing to continue the discussions rather than resort to war.

That hope was a slender one. As long ago as the beginning of July the Japanese service chiefs had insisted that if Japan went to war with the Western powers, she must do so not only before her strategic reserves became seriously depleted by the disruption of her foreign trade, but also before the northeast monsoon in the South China Sea and winter gales in the northern Pacific reached their full force.[56] The government had succeeded in convincing them that even so the decision for peace or war, originally to have been made in the middle of October, could be deferred until November 25. More recently Matsuoka's successor, Shigenori Togo, had persuaded General Tojo to agree that the date should be put back to November 29 so that Nomura and Kurusu should have time to negotiate an interim agreement. The news that Hull had refused even to discuss an interim agreement came as a great shock to the Japanese. Ministers and service chiefs agreed on November 27 that his offer of a comprehensive settlement on terms which amounted to an ultimatum could not be accepted.[57] At a meeting of former prime ministers, a veteran statesman summed up the outlook by saying that Japan would not be justified in fighting to realize Matsuoka's dreams of conquest but must do so if her national existence were at stake.[58] On December 1 the decision to go to war was formally ratified at a conference attended by the emperor.

Japan's aims were to gain possession of all-important sources of oil, rubber, tin, and bauxite in Malaya, Borneo, and the Netherlands East Indies; establish economic hegemony over "Greater East Asia"; and guard against a counteroffensive by seizing forward positions along a line running more or less southward from the foothills of the Himalayas to the Nicobar Islands, southeastward and eastward through the Indonesian and Bismarck archipelagoes to the Gilbert Islands, and northwestward by way of Midway Island to the Kurile Islands. Matsuoka had spoken of wresting India and Australia from the British Empire, but no such hope was reflected in the plan adopted in the second half of 1941.

The Japanese Army could spare only 11 of its 51 divisions and roughly 700 of its 1,500 first-line aircraft for offensive operations. The Navy's resources included 10 battleships, 6 large and 3 small aircraft carriers, 36 cruisers, more than 100 destroyers, about 60 submarines, and roughly 1,000 aircraft. Even though half the Navy's aircraft would be available to support operations on land, Japanese strategists agreed that they could not hope to reach and hold their objectives in the Netherlands East Indies without first defeating British and American forces in Malaya and the Philippines, eliminating the British outpost at Hong Kong, and seizing British Borneo. To reduce the risk of a naval counterstroke, the United States Pacific Fleet was to be crippled on the outbreak of war by a surprise attack on the lines of the British effort at Taranto. Only when the conquest of Malaya, northern Sumatra, British Borneo, and the Philippines was assured and after flanking positions in the Bismarck archipelago and southern Burma had been occupied would forces be released for the capture of Dutch Borneo, Celebes, Timor, Amboina, Java, southern Sumatra, and central and northern Burma.

The launching of the Japanese offensive on December 7 confronted the British and the Americans with just such a situation as they had agreed to meet by standing on the defensive against Japan until Germany was defeated. But the disposition of their forces was so unsatisfactory that a successful defense of their interests and possessions in the Far East and the western Pacific was not to be expected. From their bases in southern Indochina the Japanese could dominate the South China Sea. The United States Pacific Fleet, relegated to a base 5,000 miles from Manila, could have played no useful part in the defense of Malaya, Hong Kong, the Philippines, or Borneo, even if eight of its nine battleships had not been disabled at the outbreak of war by a carrier raid which caught the local authorities unprepared. At Singapore the British had only six destroyers, three light cruisers, two armed merchant cruisers, and two capital ships which the government had insisted on sending in the hope that they might exercise a deterrent effect on the potential enemy.[59]

With so weak and unbalanced a force at his disposal, the Commander in Chief of the British Eastern Fleet was powerless to prevent the Japanese from disembarking troops in Malaya and Siam. Indeed, he lost both his capital ships and his life in a vain attempt to do so. Hong Kong and British Borneo, defended by small garrisons without effective naval or air support, were virtually untenable. The Philippines were held by much larger forces under Lieutenant General Douglas MacArthur, but their defense became no more than a heroic delaying action when air attacks wrecked the navy yard at Cavite and destroyed more than half the bombers on which MacArthur was relying to make up for the lack of a strong fleet. The United States Asiatic Fleet, with only three cruisers, eleven serviceable destroyers, twenty-five serviceable submarines, and some thirty flying boats at Cavite and elsewhere, could do little to prevent the Japanese from disembarking troops in the Philippines and supplying them at will.

The British authorities in Malaya had foreseen before the outbreak of war that their naval and air forces might not be strong enough to prevent the enemy from coming ashore. They had therefore drawn up a plan to block the routes leading southward from the most probable landing places in southern Siam. The plan would be feasible only if troops could be sent into Siamese territory at least twenty-four hours before the enemy arrived. As things turned out the fear of political repercussions, especially in the United States, led the Commander in Chief of their land and air forces, who was not a soldier but an airman, to delay his decision so long that the plan could not be carried out. When at last he decided to abandon it, so much time had been lost that the success of the alternative plan which he then adopted was gravely prejudiced.[60] Under the alternative plan a force on the left was to occupy a partially prepared position at Jitra, in northwest Malaya, while a smaller force on the right protected its flank by advancing to a reconnoitered but unprepared position a short distance beyond the frontier. The force on the right, dispatched too late and delayed by an altercation with Siamese frontier guards, failed to reach the reconnoitered position and had to fight an encounter battle against Japanese infantry with light tanks. The force on the left received the order to go to Jitra after it had waited for forty-eight hours in pouring rain to move into Siam. Partially disorganized by the change of plan and weakened by preliminary skirmishes, it abandoned the Jitra position in face of probing attacks by the enemy's advanced guard. Its attempt to withdraw to a rear position under cover of darkness led to so much congestion on the only through route to the south that some units took to side roads or struck out across country, were forced to abandon bogged guns and vehicles, and in some cases became irretrievably separated from their parent formations. The British then faced the choice between reassembling their forces for a decisive battle in southern Malaya and fighting a series of delaying actions farther north in order to buy time for the arrival of reinforcements from the United Kingdom or elsewhere. A powerful argument against the first course was that it might enable the enemy to push his air forces close enough to Singapore to make the unloading of equipment and supplies extremely difficult.

It was therefore against a background of almost unrelieved disaster that Roosevelt and Churchill, with their service advisers, discussed the future at the Arcadia Conference in Washington toward the end of 1941 and early in 1942. They came to the conclusion that their policy must still be to defeat Germany before Japan and therefore to maintain in the Far East and the Pacific only such forces as would suffice to hold areas from which an eventual counteroffensive could be launched.[61] On the assumption that the Philippines could not be held indefinitely but that Singapore was still defensible, they decided to aim at holding a line from Malaya through southern Sumatra, Java, and the Indonesian archipelago to New Guinea in order to safeguard naval and air bases in that area and their communications with India, the Middle East, and the United Kingdom. At the same time Burma must, if possible, be held so that supplies could continue to reach Chiang Kai-shek by way of Rangoon and the Burma Road, Australia must be held as a base for the eventual recapture of the Philippines, and the Japanese must be prevented from severing communications between the United States and Australia, New Zealand, and the islands of the Antipodes. At the urgent request of the American General Marshall, the British General Wavell assumed responsibility for the defense of a vast area extending from Burma to the Philippines and as far south as the north coast of Australia. China, where American airmen had been serving for some time past in the guise of volunteers, was to form with Indochina and Siam a separate theater under the command of Chiang Kai-shek, with the American Lieutenant General Joseph W. Stilwell as Chief of Staff and military adviser. The British, still with many more troops in the field and a bigger output of war matériel than the Americans, successfully resisted American demands for direct control of the route from Rangoon to Chungking.

Wavell traveled at the end of the first week in January from India to his new headquarters in Java. Interrupting his journey to pay a brief visit to Malaya, he decreed that a crucial battle for Singapore should be fought on the mainland about a hundred miles northwest of the island. He also decreed that the leading part should be played by troops which had not taken part in the retreat. Lieutenant General A. E. Percival, commanding the land forces in Malaya, formed an *ad hoc* force of Indian and Australian brigades under the Australian Major General H. G. Bennett, placed it across the trunk road leading to Singapore, and withdrew the corps retreating from the north to a covering position about fifty miles to the rear.

Bennett was an energetic and resourceful commander who had served with distinction in the First World War. But he had no firsthand experience of Japanese methods and no corps staff. Nor had he had much opportunity of weighing the strength and weakness of most of the troops under his command. Putting his best troops in the immediate vicinity of the trunk road, he gave his least experienced brigade the task of holding a front of some twenty-four miles on both banks of a river to the left and rear of his main position. An immediate consequence of this move was that the Japanese, using their best troops against the weakest part of Bennett's line, broke through his left and threatened to reach the trunk road some miles in his rear. A further consequence was that Percival, at first reluctant to order a general retreat because the troops on the right were fighting well and afterward instructed by Wavell to "fight out the battle" while preparing in secret for a withdrawal to Singapore, felt obliged to shore up a crumbling front at the risk of increasing his losses when a general retreat became essential. The withdrawal was completed on January 31 at a heavy cost in men, guns, and vehicles.

Singapore, repeatedly described by Churchill as a "fortress," is in fact an island large enough to contain several townships. The town of that name, near the southern extremity of the island, was inhabited in 1942 by roughly 1,000,000 people, many of them refugees. Coast defense guns were sited to guard the naval base on the north coast against bombardment by warships, not to fire at troops crossing the narrow channel from the mainland in small boats. The British had provided fighters and antiaircraft guns to protect the town, the naval base, and other installations against air attacks; but three of the four airfields on the island could be brought under observed artillery fire from the mainland, and the early-warning system depended largely on posts captured by the Japanese during the first few days of February or earlier. The Japanese commander, Lieutenant General Tomoyuki Yamashita, had thirty-one infantry battalions to Percival's thirty-six regular, three volunteer, two Malay, and four airfield defense battalions, but most of Percival's battalions were either much under strength as a result of recent losses or had been brought up to strength from newly arrived drafts which included a high proportion of raw recruits.[62] Yamashita's troops were the pick of the Japanese Army, and he could count on receiving about ten times as much air support as his opponent.

Percival knew that he could not hope to defeat the Japanese by fighting a battle of maneuver after they had gained a foothold on the island and established themselves in strength. Even if his troops had been equipped for such a role, lack of room for tactical withdrawals and enveloping movements would have been against him. At the same time, mangrove swamps which fringed the shore in many places made observation of the surface of the water so difficult that he could scarcely expect to prevent Yamashita's troops from coming ashore. He came to the conclusion that he must rely on local counteroffensives to pin them to the coast. This meant that he had to disperse his forces widely and leave a great deal to the discretion of commanders on the spot.

The Japanese began to land late on February 8 in a sector held by the 22d Australian Brigade. The troops covering the beaches in that sector had been told not to use their searchlights unless they were expressly ordered to do so. They had also been told that if they were surrounded and could not rally at company headquarters, they were to fight their way to previously selected battalion perimeters. These instructions could not be amplified or revoked when the Japanese began to disembark under cover of darkness, since air and artillery bombardments had cut all telephone lines in the forward area. Some units, caught at a disadvantage and supposedly threatened with encirclement by invisible enemies, lost their way while trying to find the perimeters assigned to them. The result was that the prompt counterattack which was the essence of Percival's plan could not be delivered. In some places, therefore, the Japanese were able to push inland, although in others they made little progress. An attempt to confine them to the western part of the island failed when, early on February 10, a crucial position was abandoned in consequence of a misunderstanding. Wavell, paying a brief visit to the island, insisted that the lost position should be recaptured, but a counterattack in darkness by tired and scattered troops was unsuccessful.

Percival then fell back to a perimeter covering the town. Very nearly the whole of the built-up area thus became a legitimate target for Japanese aircraft and artillery. Bombing and shelling caused heavy civilian casualties, blocked streets with rubble, and fractured water mains at many points. By February 13 armed deserters, chiefly from administrative units or newly arrived drafts, were known to be lurking in the town and trying to force their way aboard ships bound for Sumatra and Java.

Two days later the municipal authorities reported that more than half the water from reservoirs outside the town was running to waste and that supplies were not expected to last more than another twenty-four hours. Civilians could still be fed, but rations for the troops were running short. Ammunition for field and antiaircraft guns and fuel for military vehicles were also scarce.

Percival came to the conclusion that he could restore the situation only by regaining control of the water supply and recapturing food and ammunition stored outside the built-up area. When his subordinate commanders reported that in their unanimous opinion, an offensive undertaken for that purpose could not succeed, surrender became his only course. Accordingly, his 80,000 combatant and noncombatant troops joined the 50,000 or so who had passed into captivity since December. Yamashita promised in return to protect the lives and persons of British civilians of all ages and both sexes who fell into his hands.

Without doubt the most serious setback ever suffered by British arms, this outcome greatly lowered Britain's standing in the Far East, and indeed throughout the world. If it occurred to the British to reflect that so appalling a disaster might have been averted had the Americans agreed to send a strong fleet to Singapore or if Hull had kept his head, they wisely refrained from saying so. The harm was done, and such reproaches could have served no useful purpose.

Nonetheless, the fall of Singapore was bound to affect both British and American views on the conduct of the war. Hitherto Wavell, although aware that the Japanese had begun their drive toward the Indonesian archipelago and that Borneo and Celebes could not be saved, had based his strategy on the hope of gaining time for the arrival of powerful air forces from the United States by holding a line from Malaya through Sumatra, Java, and Timor to Port Darwin in Australia. The loss of Malaya destroyed that hope. Less than a week after Percival's surrender the Anglo-American Combined Chiefs of Staff reminded Wavell that he would soon need to withdraw his headquarters from Java in order to escape capture. He pointed out in his reply that much of the territory he had been asked to defend was already past saving, that the Combined Chiefs had agreed that henceforth troops in Burma should be controlled from India, and that therefore his headquarters might be better disbanded than shifted to a new location. The British and the Americans could, he thought, do more for the defense of Java by putting their forces at the direct disposal of the Dutch than by maintaining the fiction that there was still an "American-British-Dutch Area" to be defended.

Accordingly, on February 25 Jonkheer Dr. Tjarda van Starkenborgh Stachouwer, governor-general of the Netherlands East Indies, assumed command of all surviving Allied forces in Indonesia. Stachouwer's chances of saving Java were, however, substantially reduced when, only two days later, his small fleet of British, Dutch, American, and Australian cruisers and destroyers was decisively defeated at the Battle of the Java Sea. In the second week of March he and the commander of his land forces decided to capitulate on terms which compelled all Allied units throughout the Netherlands East Indies to lay down their arms. The Japanese then completed their conquest of Indonesia by landing in northern Sumatra without opposition.

Meanwhile, troops of the Japanese Fifteenth Army had entered Burma from Siam. To gain time for the assembly of forces capable of defending Rangoon, the Irrawaddy Valley, and the Burma Road, the 17th Indian Division was ordered to make a fighting retreat through Lower Burma. The division had almost completed its task when it was overtaken by a series of disasters. On February 21, after it had broken contact with the enemy, its troops and vehicles were bombed and machine-gunned by Allied airmen who had been told to look for a nonexistent Japanese column on a road approximately at right angles to its line of retreat. On the following day, troops awaiting their turn to cross the Sittang River by a railway bridge wide enough for only a single line of vehicles were attacked from the flank and rear by Japanese who had made a forced march through the jungle. Finally, so alarming a situation seemed by the early hours of February 23 to have developed that the officer responsible for demolishing the bridge before the Japanese arrived in strength gave the order to blow the charges when only about a third of the division had crossed. Many of the troops left on the wrong side of the river eventually made their way to safety, but the division lost most of its transport and was deprived for the time being of more than half its infantry.[63]

Hitherto the British had hoped to stem the advance of the Japanese Fifteenth Army by disembarking at Rangoon an armored brigade and an Australian infantry division originally intended for service in the Middle East. The Australian government had agreed that the division in question should be diverted to the Far East, but on the day of the Sittang bridge disaster objected, in view of the fall of Singapore, to its going to Rangoon. This decision caused some dissatisfaction at the time, but was not unreasonable inasmuch as Lieutenant General T. J. Hutton, the commander of the land forces in Burma, himself doubted whether he would be able to maintain a force of the size proposed.

General the Honorable Sir Harold Alexander, who arrived early in March to succeed Hutton, believed when he first set foot in Burma that Rangoon could be successfully defended. Finding that more than half the native population had already fled and that he was likely to face awkward administrative problems if he tried to hold the city, he agreed after a day or two that he would be well advised to withdraw to the Irrawaddy Valley while his communications were still open and supplies accumulated by his predecessor in central Burma still intact. He completed his withdrawal on March 8, only a few hours before the enemy arrived.

After occupying Rangoon, the Japanese raised their strength in Burma to some four divisions. Alexander, pushed northward by numerically superior forces with strong air support, had soon to make up his mind whether to take his army by the Burma Road to China or attempt a difficult withdrawal along jungle tracks and waterways to India. Concluding after consultation with Chiang's principal liaison officer in Burma that he would have great difficulty in maintaining and reequipping his British, Indian, and Burmese troops if he went to China, he decided to make for India. Accompanied by many thousands of refugees whom he was determined not to abandon, he completed in May the longest retreat in British military history. Of three Chinese divisions which were unable to withdraw before the enemy cut the Burma Road, two made their way by independent routes to India and one reached China by marching across the foothills of the Himalayas from Fort Hertz, in the extreme north of Burma.

While the withdrawal from Rangoon was in progress, two Japanese naval forces made brief incursions into the Indian Ocean for the purpose of seeking out British warships and their bases and destroying merchant shipping. Admiral Sir James Somerville, the new commander of the British Eastern Fleet, withdrew his main base to Kilindini on the coast of Kenya but retained an advanced base for his faster ships at Addu Atoll in the Maldive Islands. The British did not try to stop the Japanese from seizing the Andaman and Nicobar

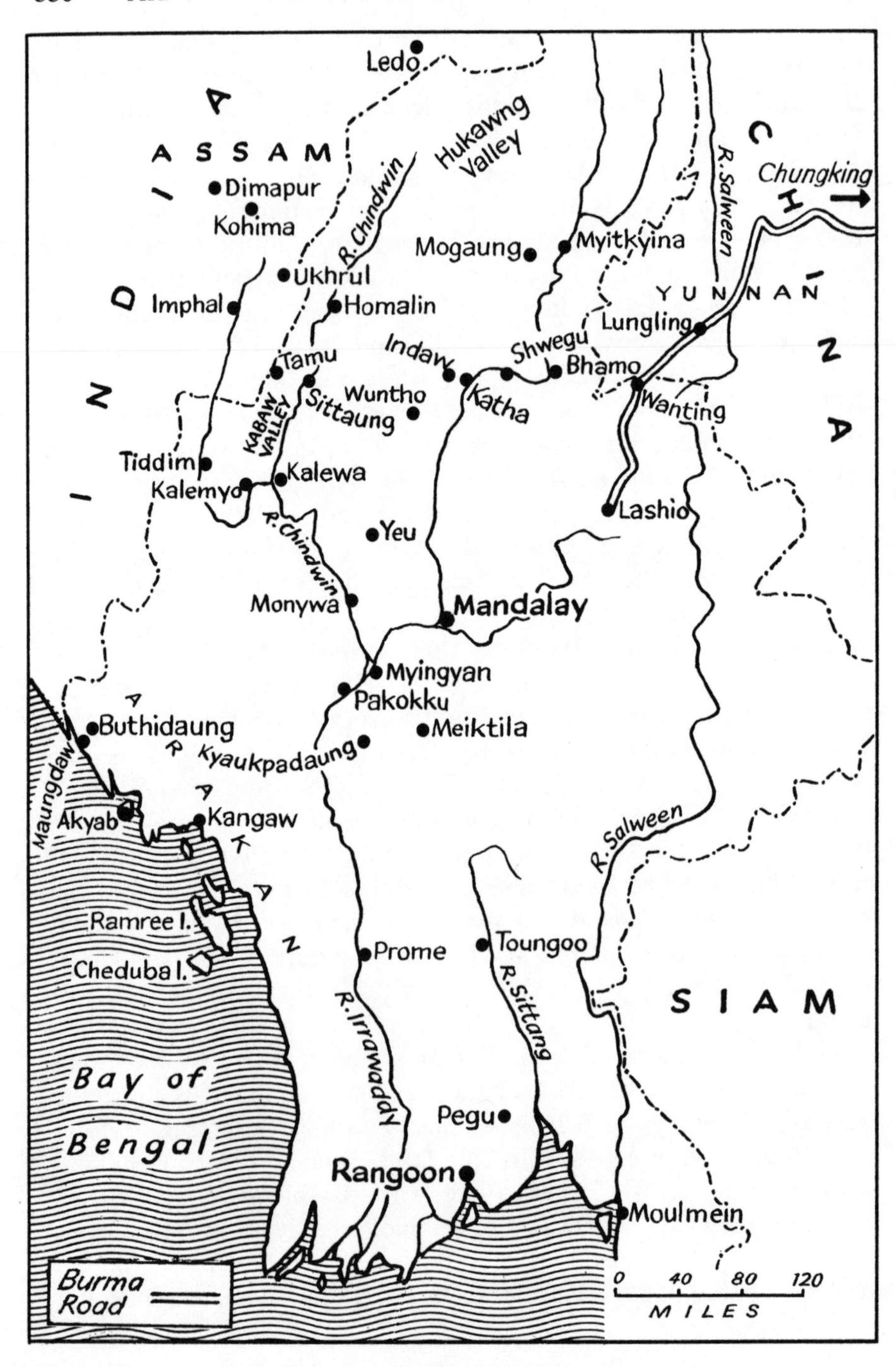
Ledo
ASSAM
INDIA
Dimapur
Kohima
R. Chindwin
Hukawng Valley
Mogaung
Myitkyina
R. Salween
CHINA
Chungking
Ukhrul
Imphal
Homalin
YUNNAN
Lungling
Tamu
Indaw
Shwegu
Bhamo
Wuntho
Sittaung
Katha
Wanting
KABAW VALLEY
Tiddim
Kalewa
Kalemyo
Lashio
R. Chindwin
Yeu
Monywa
Mandalay
Myingyan
Pakokku
Meiktila
Buthidaung
ARAKAN
Maungdaw
Kyaukpadaung
Akyab
Kangaw
R. Salween
Ramree I.
Cheduba I.
Prome
Toungoo
R. Sittang
SIAM
R. Irrawaddy
Bay of Bengal
Pegu
Rangoon
Moulmein
Burma Road
0 40 80 120
MILES

BURMA (1942)

Islands but occupied the French island of Madagascar in order to prevent them from using it as a submarine base and effecting a junction with their German and Italian allies.

With the capture of the Andaman and Nicobar Islands and the occupation in February and March of outposts in northern Papua, New Britain, and the most northerly of the Solomon Islands, the Japanese completed, for all practical purposes, the program of conquest and expansion on which they had embarked in the previous December. In the hope of still further strengthening their defensive perimeter and reducing the risk of a successful counteroffensive they decided, however, to establish a seaplane base at Tulagi in the central Solomons, attempt a landing at Port Moresby in southern Papua, and do their best to bring the remnant of the United States Pacific Fleet to action by sending an invasion force to Midway Island.

Admiral Chester W. Nimitz, the new Commander in Chief of the Pacific Fleet, received good warning of the Port Moresby venture. The outcome was the first considerable naval engagement in which all the damage suffered by both sides was inflicted by aircraft from ships which never saw each other. At the Battle of the Coral Sea on May 7 and 8 an American task force under Rear Admiral F. J. Fletcher lost the carrier *Lexington* but scored a strategic victory by sinking the Japanese light carrier *Shoho*, damaging the 26,000-ton carrier *Shokaku*, and forcing transports and warships bound for Port Moresby to turn away. The Japanese were not prevented from sending a small force to Tulagi, but projected attacks on Australian airfields had to be abandoned because the Japanese carriers failed to reach their launching area. In July a substantial force disembarked at Buna, on the far side of the Owen Stanley Mountains, with the intention of capturing Port Moresby by an overland advance, but Australian troops halted it some thirty miles from its destination and afterward drove it back to the shores of the Bismarck Sea.

The expedition to Midway Island was repulsed on June 4 with even more spectacular results. Admiral Nimitz, directing operations from his base at Pearl Harbor, more than 1,000 miles away, decided to use shore-based aircraft from the island to supplement the efforts of two task forces built around the carriers *Yorktown*, *Enterprise* and *Hornet*. The shore-based aircraft scored no hits on carriers or battleships, but their intervention at a time when Japanese carrier-borne aircraft had been sent to attack the island led the commander of the Japanese carrier force to direct that ninety-three bombers which he had been reserving for torpedo attacks on any American warships that might appear should be rearmed in preparation for further attacks on objectives ashore. Although the order was afterward revoked, the result was that the arrival of American carrier-borne aircraft to attack his carriers caught him with all his bombers refueling or rearming. Accurate dive-bombing by aircraft from the *Enterprise* and *Yorktown* destroyed all four of his carriers, ended the threat to Midway Island, and shifted the balance of naval power in favor of the Allies. In the course of a diversionary operation in the north the Japanese seized Attu and Kiska in the Aleutians, but these remote and almost barren islands proved of little value to them.

As the sequel to Wavell's relinquishment of his command in February, the British and United States governments agreed in March that henceforth operations in the area stretching westward from Malaya and Sumatra to the Mediterranean should be managed by the British, and operations in the Pacific by the Americans. Operations in the European theater and the Atlantic would be conducted by the British and the Americans in partnership, and China would be regarded as a separate theater. Commanders in all theaters would be expected to frame their plans in accordance with directives to be issued from time to time by the Anglo-American Combined Chiefs of Staff and approved by the British and United States governments. The Australians, the Chinese, the Dutch, and the New Zealanders would be entitled to present their views to advisory councils in London and Washington.

Outwardly the grand strategy laid down at the Arcadia Conference was not affected by these changes. The Combined Chiefs of Staff continued to stress the importance of defeating Germany before coming to grips with Japan. They still maintained that the Western Allies should aim at "drawing a ring round Germany" by reasserting control of the Atlantic, supporting Russia and Turkey, strengthening Britain's hold on the Middle East, and driving the Germans and the Italians from North Africa. At the same time, they conceded that the situation in the Pacific theater must be "stabilized" before a new front could be opened in Europe or Africa.[64] The American service chiefs had always held—and their British colleagues did not deny—that a defensive strategy need not preclude the establishment of bases from which offensive operations would eventually be launched. Not surprisingly, since for most Americans "the war" had already come to mean the war against Japan, the American Chiefs of Staff put a liberal gloss on that concession. In theory, priority was given to operations against Germany. In practice, the movement of large numbers of American troops and their equipment to the south and southwest Pacific in 1942 made such demands on the national resources and on Allied shipping as to rule out any major intervention by United States forces in Europe or Africa much before the end of the year.

How the "ring round Germany" should be tightened when the moment came to tighten it was not decided at the Arcadia Conference. Stalin had asked for a second front in France or the Balkans. Whether the Western Allies should open such a front by disembarking troops somewhere on the French coast or alternatively by sending a seaborne expedition from North Africa to Yugoslavia, Albania, or Greece or by invading the Balkans through Italy or Turkey was a question yet to be answered when the conference broke up.

However, in April General Marshall and Harry Hopkins traveled to London with proposals already sanctioned in principle by the President. The substance of these was that British and United States troops should disembark in the spring of 1943 on the French coast between Le Havre and Boulogne, occupy the line of the Oise, and advance toward Germany after establishing bases at Boulogne and Antwerp.[65] Some thirty American and eighteen British divisions, backed by nearly 6,000 first-line aircraft, were expected to be available for the purpose.

Of all the methods of giving effect to Stalin's wishes that might have been suggested, this was possibly the least attractive. The Germans had been firmly in possession of northern and western France and the Low Countries since the summer of 1940. Their reconnaissance aircraft visited the United Kingdom almost daily and sometimes twice a day. They were known to have established particularly strong defenses along the stretch of coast on which Marshall proposed that Allied troops should go ashore. These would doubtless be further strengthened, if only as a precaution against minor raids or diversionary landings, as soon as the Allies were seen to be building up forces and accumulating supplies in Britain. To oppose an Allied advance to the Oise and beyond, the Germans would be able to call not only on substantial numbers of troops already in France and Belgium, but also on reinforcements which could be moved to threatened areas with the help of an exceptionally well-developed system of roads and railways. Finally, the Allies would not be able to use Antwerp as a base and port of entry for troops, equipment, and supplies without capturing not merely Antwerp itself, but broad tracts of Belgian and Dutch territory which commanded the seaward approaches to the port.

Nor could disciples of Clausewitz argue that the operation proposed by Marshall would conform with a cherished principle of orthodox military doctrine by putting the Western Allies in a position to engage the main body of the enemy's armed forces. The main body of the German Army was likely to remain for a long time to come on the Eastern Front, 1,000 miles from Boulogne. From the standpoint of an academic strategist, a landing in Picardy would be just as much a diversion as a landing in Bosnia. Advantages which *could* be claimed for Marshall's plan were that the Allies would be able to use short-range land-based aircraft to cover the initial assault and that an advance from the Oise might put them in a position to threaten the Ruhr. To defend the Ruhr, the Germans might divert substantially larger forces from the Eastern Front than they would be willing to devote to the defense of their interests in Southern Europe, important though these were.

The British had few illusions about the difficulties which an assault on the strongest part of Hitler's "Fortress Europe" would entail. Moreover, they were not affected to the same extent as the Americans by an instinctive revulsion from Balkan entanglements. Their strategists had long recognized that an invasion of Southern Europe from North Africa might be profitable; Churchill himself had more than once expressed his interest in striking at "the soft under-belly of the Axis." Nevertheless, they were careful not to wound the susceptibilities of their allies by finding fault with Marshall's proposals. Recognizing that the Americans would have to find a high proportion of the troops needed for the liberation of Western Europe, they merely stipulated that no attempt should be made to give effect to the plan until the Western Allies were strong enough to carry it out without risking a series of humiliating setbacks. In the outcome this factor led to the postponement of the assault on Western Europe until the early summer of 1944, the substitution of landings in western Normandy for landings in eastern Normandy and Picardy, and the adoption of an elaborate deception plan which went a long way to ensure success.

During his visit to London in April Marshall also proposed that a small-scale landing in France, on lines already discussed, should be made in 1942 if the plight of the Russians became desperate or alternatively as a means of exploiting a German collapse. The British agreed that a favorable opportunity of putting troops ashore in 1942 ought not to be missed, but a detailed examination of the plan showed that it would be useless as a means of relieving pressure on the Russians since the Germans would be able to contain a force of the size proposed without moving any units from the Eastern Front. An experimental raid on Dieppe in August by some 6,000 Allied troops, of whom nearly 5,000 were Canadian and about 50 American, showed that a full-scale assault would pose formidable problems.

At a further high-level conference in June, Churchill sought to divert Roosevelt's attention from premature landings in France by reviving his interest in an expedition to northwest Africa. The President agreed that such an expedition might prove an acceptable substitute for the second front in Europe which he had incautiously allowed the Russians to expect in 1942. Marshall and his British counterpart, General Sir Alan Brooke, were at first far from ardent supporters of proposals which they feared might cut across their plans for 1943. After Rommel's offensive had been successfully halted at Alamein they agreed, however, that preparations to disembark British and American troops in French North Africa about the middle of October, 1942, should be pressed forward. Later the date was put back to November 8 in order to give the Americans more time to complete their preparations.

Since Roosevelt believed that, in view of past relations between Washington and Vichy, the French were less likely to fire on the American than on the British flag, he and Churchill agreed that the expedition should be represented as primarily an American venture and that the American General Dwight D. Eisenhower, formerly of the War Plans Division of the Department of the Army, should be Supreme Commander. Command of the land forces was to have gone to General Alexander or, failing him, to Lieutenant General B.

L. Montgomery. Ultimately another commander had to be selected, since Alexander was appointed to command the Middle East land forces when Churchill fell out with Auchinleck during a visit to Cairo in August, while Montgomery was appointed to command the Eighth Army in the Western Desert when an aircraft carrying its commander-designate to Cairo was forced down by the enemy.

The object of the expedition to French North Africa was to secure the whole of French Morocco, Algeria, and Tunisia, including the crucial port of Bizerte. Nevertheless, no initial landings farther east than Algiers, some 400 miles west of Bizerte, were included in the final plan. Partly because British as well as American planners attached some importance to the early capture of Casablanca as a port of entry for reinforcements and supplies, but also because landings outside the Strait of Gibraltar were considered less liable to interference from the enemy than landings in the Mediterranean, nearly 25,000 American troops carried straight from the United States were disembarked on beaches in western Morocco, 1,000 miles from Bizerte. Thus the Germans were able to rush troops and equipment from Sicily and Italy to Tunisia not only by air, but also by sea. The result was that although French Morocco and Algeria were occupied without great difficulty after little more than token resistance from the French, Tunisia did not fall to the Allies until the late spring of 1943.

About a fortnight before the landings in French North Africa, Montgomery took the offensive at Alamein with massive air support and a superiority of roughly two to one in men and tanks.[66] More fortunate than former commanders of the Eighth Army, he had nearly 1,000 field and medium guns and some 1,300 antitank guns on a front of forty miles. About 800 of his antitank guns were up-to-date 6-pounders with an excellent performance.

Montgomery's advantage in firepower was partly offset by topographical and tactical factors which restricted his main assault to a narrow sector between the coast and a ridge some fifteen miles to the south. At his first attempt, on the night of October 23, the engineer companies of his leading infantry formations were unable to complete the clearance of corridors through the enemy's minefields for an armored corps which was to have passed through a gap made by the infantry. Consequently the armored corps, coming under heavy fire from daybreak, made little progress and suffered fairly heavy losses. A second attempt on November 2 was more successful, but meanwhile, the armored corps had taken such a battering that the follow-up was very slow. Rommel, a sick man who had left the hospital to resume command of the Axis forces when his successor died of heart failure on the first day of the battle, succeeded in extricating about two-thirds of his troops but left some 30,000 prisoners and many damaged vehicles in British hands. Thus ended the battle popularly called the Battle of Alamein, but known to military historians as Second Alamein.

In the course of the next few months, Rommel completed a retreat of some 1,500 miles to Tunisia, making two long pauses on the way to rest and reorganize his troops. On March 6 he turned to attack the Eighth Army at Medenine but was repulsed with heavy losses. Resuming his interrupted spell of sick leave, he then relinquished command of his force to General Hans Jürgen von Arnim, commander of the Axis troops that had reached Tunisia since November by sea and air. On the Allied side, General Alexander assumed control, under Eisenhower's direction, of all land forces in Tunisia when the Eighth Army crossed the frontier in the middle of February.

In central Tunisia, an attempt by Axis forces to roll up the First Army's front from south to north was defeated by a narrow margin near the Kasserine Pass in the second half of February. In eastern Tunisia, the Eighth Army outflanked the powerful remnant of Rommel's force at Mareth in the last week of March and early in April tore a gap in the front near Gabès to which it had retreated. The whole of the Axis forces, about a quarter of a million strong, then withdrew under pressure to the neighborhood of Tunis and Bizerte. Meanwhile, the German bomber force, depleted by losses in Africa and Russia and an inadequate replacement program, had become too weak to prevent the British Mediterranean Fleet from asserting control of the Sicilian Channel. Thus Arnim's troops could no longer be reinforced, supplied, or withdrawn by sea. Since the loss of airfields needed to give fighter protection to his transport aircraft soon prevented him from receiving more than a trickle of supplies by air, he was left with no choice but to give up the struggle. By the middle of May the Western Allies were masters of the Mediterranean seaboard from Algeria to Lebanon.

The fall of Tunisia released nine American and thirty-one British, British-controlled, or French divisions for such tasks as might be allotted to them. Moreover, these divisions could be reinforced from Britain or the United States if the Combined Chiefs of Staff saw fit to release troops not yet committed to other theaters. Clearly a moment had come when the case for "striking at the soft under-belly of the Axis" deserved serious consideration. At the same time, the case for Operation Overlord, as the projected invasion of northern France was called, had become weaker than it appeared when the project was first mooted. Obviously, a second front in France or the Balkans was still desirable on political grounds, if only because the interests of the Western powers might suffer if Russia were left to defeat Germany single-handed and impose her own terms at the peace conference. But landings in France were no longer urgently needed to avert the collapse of an ally who had shown his staying power by encircling a quarter of a million Germans at Stalingrad, checking an invasion of the Caucasus, and resisting numerous assaults on Leningrad and Moscow.

Moreover, in the spring and summer of 1943 it was far from certain that Overlord was a practical operation of war. At the Casablanca Conference in January the Western Allies had decided that in order to make the assembly of their forces for such an operation possible, they must give priority to the defeat of German submarines.[67] They had also decided that British and United States air forces based in the United Kingdom must aim at "the progressive destruction and dislocation of the German military, industrial and economic system, and the undermining of the morale of the German people to a point where their capacity for armed resistance is fatally weakened." [68] The situation at the end of May was that the Royal Navy and the Royal Canadian Navy, by adopting aggressive tactics based on experience with Arctic convoys, had overcome the menace of the U-boat[69] but that Germany seemed in other respects as strong as ever. Much was expected of precise attacks on German factories by day bombers of the United States Eighth Air Force; but the resources of the Eighth Air Force were still fairly slender, its buildup was disappointing, and hitherto its efforts had done little to remove a well-founded suspicion that day bombers without long-range fighter escort would prove incapable of reaching objectives deep in the heart of Germany except at a prohibitive cost. While it was clear in the early summer of 1943 that no invasion of northern France would be possible for at least twelve months or so, it was far from certain that even at the end of that time Germany's capacity to fight would have been so much reduced as to make an assault on the strongest part of Hitler's "Fortress Europe" feasible. Furthermore, no argument adduced in favor of Overlord could alter the fact that troops disembarked at the head of the Adriatic would be much closer to Vienna than troops disembarked in Normandy would be to the Ruhr.

Opposition to any radical departure from the program sketched in 1942 was nonetheless extremely strong. Hitherto Britain and the British Commonwealth had provided the greater part of the forces deployed against the Axis Powers in the Mediterranean theater, in the Atlantic, and in European skies. Overlord was the operation on which the Americans based their hopes of playing a dominant role in the war with Germany. Unlike the Germans, who believed that control of the Balkans would be "decisive from the point of view of winning the war," [70] Roosevelt and his advisers regarded southeastern Europe as a blind alley. They feared that an attempt to seize the Balkans, even if successful—perhaps most of all if it were successful—might lead to the postponement or abandonment of Overlord. The British held other views but declined to press them to the point of open disagreement. When the veteran Smuts proposed that the Allies should shelve Overlord and concentrate for the time being on preparations for an advance through Yugoslavia to the Danube and the Sava, Churchill silenced him not by drawing attention to the administrative difficulties which an advance by that route might present, but by remarking that Overlord was "the keystone of the arch of Anglo-American co-operation." [71] Whether the experts who solved the problem of supplying troops disembarked on open beaches in Normandy in 1944 might equally well have solved the problem of supplying a force advancing from the head of the Adriatic to Vienna by way of the Ljubljana gap remains an unanswered question.

After debating the future of their forces in the Mediterranean at some length, the Allies agreed to move seven of Eisenhower's forty divisions to the United Kingdom as a contribution to preparations for Overlord. Sicily was to be invaded as soon as Eisenhower was ready, but no immediate preparations for landings on the Italian mainland or in Yugoslavia were sanctioned. The British pressed for an early invasion of Italy, increased support for subversive movements in the Balkans, and the seizure of islands in the eastern Mediterranean but were careful to add that they did not regard such operations as substitutes for Overlord.

The Allied invasion of Sicily on July 10 was instantly successful. It was followed within a fortnight by Mussolini's deposition and replacement by a successor who promptly entered into negotiations with the Allies. Nevertheless, it was not until September that Allied troops went ashore in the heel and toe of Italy and at Salerno, southeast of Naples. The delay gave the Germans time to strengthen their forces in Italy and prepare to disarm units of the Italian Army and the Regia Aeronautica which showed signs of going over to the enemy. Thus an agreement concluded between the Western powers and the Italian government on September 3 did not save the Allies from having to fight for possession of the country.

By the beginning of October the Allies held not only Naples, but also a group of airfields near Foggia from which their bombers could reach targets inaccessible from the United Kingdom or Africa. To the astonishment of the Germans,[72] they did not follow up their success by invading Yugoslavia but fought their way doggedly to Rome with forces weakened by preparations for Overlord. Since General Alexander would remain, until Overlord was launched, the only Allied land force commander in contact with German troops, he might have expected the highest priority to be given to his theater. In fact, he received only grudging support from the Combined Chiefs of Staff. When, early in 1944, he wished to disembark some 50,000 troops behind the German lines at Anzio, he had great difficulty in obtaining the necessary landing ships. Meanwhile, far-reaching offensive operations were in progress in the Pacific theater, although at each of four high-level conferences in 1943 Roosevelt and Churchill had declared that they still intended to defeat Germany before undertaking a major offensive against Japan.

Since British and American shipyards and boatyards produced about 18,500 assault vessels of all categories in 1943,[73] the inability of the Combined Chiefs of Staff to meet Alexander's needs except after prolonged haggling was remarkable. Still more remarkable was the inadequacy of the provision originally made for Overlord. The Overlord planners, when they framed proposals for what the Combined Chiefs called "a full-scale assault against Continental Europe," were given to understand that only about 3,300 assault vessels would be available.[74] On that basis, they proposed in the late summer of 1943 that three seaborne and two airborne divisions should land near Caen, in western Normandy. They pointed out, however, that an operation on so limited a scale was not likely to succeed unless the Germans had no more than twelve reserve divisions of good quality in France and the Low Countries on D day and that even then the chances of success would be no more than "reasonable."

At the Quadrant Conference at Quebec in August, the British and the Americans accepted this proposal, but with important reservations, tacit or explicit. Churchill spoke for others besides himself when he expressed the opinion that the scale of attack should be increased by at least a quarter and that landings should not be confined to the neighborhood of Caen but should be extended as far west as the east coast of the Cotentin Peninsula. General Eisenhower, who left the Mediterranean theater at the end of 1943 to become Supreme Commander for Overlord in default of General Marshall, who was needed in Washington, agreed that the scale of attack originally proposed was too light. So did Montgomery, who was to coordinate the operations of the British and American land forces during the assault phase.

The problem was to find the additional assault vessels needed to transport and disembark a larger force. In theory these vessels were allotted by the Combined Chiefs of Staff. In practice the American Chief of Naval Operations, Admiral Ernest J. King, was able to exercise more than his fair share of control over their allotment by reason of an Anglo-American agreement which provided that most of the larger vessels should be built in the United States. King believed that the interests of the Pacific theater should be paramount, suspected some of his colleagues of deferring too much to the British, and was always reluctant to see equipment which he could use in the Pacific theater diverted to other theaters. Although himself a member of the Combined Chiefs of Staff Committee, he went so far as to assert on one occasion that "what operations are or are not conducted in the Pacific is no affair of the Combined Chiefs of Staff since this theater is exclusively American." [75]

Eventually an answer was found as the result of a request from Stalin at the Teheran Conference in the early winter of 1943 that Overlord should be launched not later than the end of the following May.[76] The British and the Americans had expected him to insist that the operation should be launched not later than the beginning of May. They concluded that they would be justified in postponing D day until the first week of June. King then agreed that, by taking advantage of an additional month's production, he and his colleagues could safely increase the allotment of assault vessels for Overlord to 4,126. About three-quarters of these would be found from allocations made to the British. In response to an urgent request from Eisenhower, King afterward agreed to add about 200 American warships and light naval craft to the 1,000 or so contributed by the Royal Navy and the Royal Canadian Navy. Since the postponement also gave the Allies more transport, aircraft, and gliders to draw upon, they were able to raise the strength of the assault force to five seaborne and three airborne divisions. These were to be followed within the first five days by nine more seaborne divisions. About 5,000 medium bombers, fighters, and fighter-bombers would provide tactical support.

Acute controversy surrounded the contribution to be made by 3,000 to 4,000 British and American heavy bombers based in the United Kingdom and Italy. By the early part of 1944 it seemed clear that Germany's capacity for armed resistance was not likely to be seriously undermined by strategic bombing before D day. That her output of war matériel had increased markedly while attempts were being made to reduce it was not fully apparent, but losses inflicted on the Allied bomber forces by the German fighter force told their own tale. The adoption by the Americans of an excellent long-range escort fighter, the P-51B or Mustang, improved the outlook considerably, but no destruction of the German military, industrial, and economic system was yet in sight.*

However, if the Germans could not be seriously weakened before D day, they might still be prevented from applying their strength where it would do most harm. The Overlord planners proposed that the heavy bombers should be used for a limited period before D day

* The original version of the Mustang, known in the United States as the P-51, was built by an American manufacturer for the Royal Air Force. Its performance, except at low altitudes, was disappointing. On the initiative of the British, experiments were made with Mustangs powered by the Rolls-Royce Merlin 61 engine or alternatively by the Packard-Merlin engine, built under license in the United States. The Packard-Merlin version of the Mustang was the P-51B. Its performance was equal or superior to that of the best contemporary interceptor fighters; when fitted with large external drop-tanks, it could reach Berlin. As a long-range escort fighter it surpassed the P-38 (Lightning) and the P-47 (Thunderbolt), neither of which provided as good a combination of reliability, range, and all-round performance.

to attack the French, Belgian, and German rail systems, with the object of creating a situation which would prevent the swift repair of damage to be inflicted at a crucial stage by tactical bombers and fighter-bombers.

This plan was widely criticized on the ground that it was likely to cause heavy casualties to French and Belgian civilians and unlikely to yield quick results. Its advocates pointed out that it was not meant to yield quick results, but only to make quick results attainable by the tactical air forces.

Air Chief Marshal Sir Arthur Harris, of the British Bomber Command, objected to the plan on other grounds. He argued that "area" attacks on German towns were not merely the best but the only useful contribution he could make to the Allied offensive. Experimental attacks which he was ordered to deliver in March showed, however, that his force was capable of bombing rail targets with much greater accuracy than he had supposed.[77]

General Carl Spaatz, of the United States Strategic Air Forces in Europe, was also opposed to the plan. He believed that attacks on oil targets would do more harm to Germany's economy and give him better opportunities of wearing down the German fighter force. British experts, on the other hand, regarded attacks on oil targets as essentially a long-term measure, which could have no decisive effect until long after D day.[78]

In the light of these conflicting views, General Eisenhower decided to adopt the rail plan, on the understanding that its adoption would not prevent General Spaatz from aiming at the reduction of the German fighter force and that casualties to French and Belgian civilians would be carefully watched.[79] Attacks on oil targets were not mentioned in a rambling directive given to the commanders of the strategic bomber forces on April 17 by Eisenhower's deputy, Air Marshal Sir Arthur Tedder.[80] Such attacks were nonetheless delivered by the Americans from May, and by the British from June, with spectacular results. In the meantime, the British Bomber Command played the leading part in an offensive which went far to disrupt the French rail system by D day.[81]

Allied preparations for the invasion of Europe coincided with German preparations to bombard London and other targets with flying bombs and long-range rockets. Between August 17, 1943, and June 12, 1944, the Allies aimed nearly 36,000 tons of bombs at installations believed to have some connection with these weapons. Their attacks on flying-bomb launching sites in northern France caused the Germans to suspend work on the sites, except as a blind, and build modified sites which made poor targets for Allied bombers.

On June 6 about 83,000 British or Canadian and some 73,000 American troops landed in western Normandy, with the British on the left, near Caen, and the Americans on the right, near Carentan. Allied security and deception plans were so successful that the Germans did not know until the eleventh hour that an invasion fleet was at sea and continued long afterward to believe that the main thrust was coming farther east.

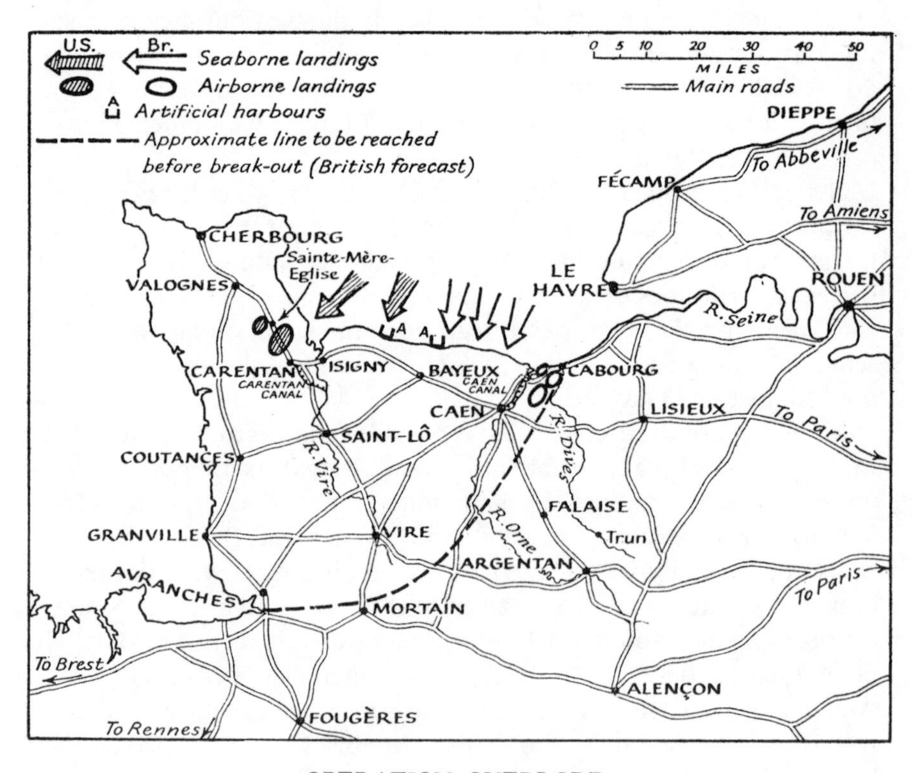

OPERATION OVERLORD

When the Allies went ashore in Normandy, many British and American sympathizers with the Russian cause expressed their satisfaction that the Western powers had at last opened their long-promised Second Front. The popular belief that hitherto the Russians had borne almost the entire burden of the war with Germany was, however, wide of the mark. Before D day the Western powers had not only shipped large quantities of war matériel to Russia but were holding in the western and Mediterranean theaters and the Atlantic about two-fifths of Germany's field army, at least two-thirds of her Air Force, and very nearly the whole of her effective naval strength.

The immediate aim of the Western Allies when they set foot in France was to occupy a large beachhead bounded by a line running eastward and northeastward from the base of the Cotentin Peninsula at Avranches to Cabourg, northeast of Caen.[82] Only when they were firmly established in that beachhead would their forces emerge from it to seize a broad tract of Brittany and Normandy as far south as the Loire and as far east as the Seine. Eisenhower hoped thereafter to meet and defeat the main body of the enemy's forces in the west, if he had not already done so, by making a major thrust to the Ruhr and beyond by way of Amiens and a subsidiary thrust in the general direction of the Rhineland by way of Metz. The three British members of his staff who drew up his "overall plan" did not recommend an advance by the more northerly route alone. They argued that it might put the Allies in collision with the enemy on a narrow front where they would have insufficient room for maneuver and no chance of concealing their intentions.[83]

Montgomery, as coordinator of the land forces, aimed during the assault phase and the buildup at drawing the better part of the enemy's forces to the British front so that the Americans should be free to seize Cherbourg and establish themselves securely in the Cotentin. In this he succeeded so well that Caen, which the British had hoped to take on the first day, did not fall until July 9. A few days later Rommel, whose command covered the whole of northern France and the Low Countries, reported to Hitler that in his opinion the end of an "unequal struggle" was approaching. Almost immediately afterward he was seriously injured in a road accident. Rundstedt, nominally supreme commander in the Western theater although in practice he had little authority over Rommel, had already been relieved of his post after asking permission to withdraw from Caen.

About a week after D day, the Germans opened a flying-bomb offensive against the United Kingdom from the modified launching sites built since December. London was the chief target, but a few missiles were dispatched to Portsmouth and Southampton. The launching of this offensive, which seemed likely to be followed by attacks with long-range rockets, caused so much anxiety in London that Eisenhower ruled on June 18 that countermeasures must take precedence over everything except the "urgent requirements" of the battle in France. During the next six weeks Allied bombers aimed about 74,000 tons of bombs at installations associated in intelligence reports with the flying bomb and about 8,000 tons at targets associated with the long-range rocket. Many bombs were wasted on unprofitable targets, but some useful attacks were made on depots where flying bombs were stored. Fighters succeeded from the outset in destroying many flying bombs before they reached the target area, but the performance of antiaircraft guns specially deployed for the purpose was disappointing until the commander of the air defenses, Air Marshal Sir Roderic Hill, took the bold step of moving all the guns to the coast. Outstanding contributions to the success of the guns thereafter were made by technical devices developed and manufactured in the United States. By the end of August the air defenses were destroying more than 80 percent of all flying bombs which did not fly hopelessly wide of the target or crash before coming within range.[84]

About the middle of July the situation in Normandy was that the Second Army, composed of British and Canadian divisions, had entered Caen but that the United States First Army on its right was making only slow progress toward the base of the Cotentin Peninsula. On July 18 the Second Army launched, on Montgomery's orders, an ambitious diversionary attack designed to pin the enemy to its front while the Americans came forward. A massive preliminary bombardment began with the plastering by heavy bombers of selected portions of the battlefield. This raised a cloud of smoke and dust which hampered subsequent attacks by medium bombers on precise objectives. The Second Army's armored spearheads made good progress at first but slowed down when they reached defended positions not effectively reduced by the preliminary bombardment. The result was that units waiting behind them to debouch from a bottleneck between the built-up area of Caen and wooded country to the east were unable to come forward. The Second Army failed to attain its tactical objectives on high ground south of Caen, although it did succeed in enlarging its bridgehead south and east of the Orne.

Nevertheless, the diversion served Montgomery's purpose. In the last week of July the Americans, aided by a further thrust by British and Canadian formations on their immediate left, advanced to the base of the Cotentin Peninsula on a narrow front which the Germans could have made almost impregnable had not much of their attention been devoted to the British sector.

On August 1 Eisenhower set up the Twelfth Army Group (General Omar H. Bradley) to control the United States First and Third armies on the right and the Twenty-first Army Group (Montgomery) to control the British Second Army and the Canadian First Army on the left. For the time being Montgomery was to coordinate the operations of the two army groups. This last arrangement was not much to the taste of Bradley or his army commanders.

Bradley intended to send the Third Army into Brittany and order the First Army to take up positions almost due south of the Cotentin. Montgomery, often accused by American critics of excessive caution, insisted on a more adventurous strategy. One corps of the Third Army turned westward to Rennes and Lorient. The rest of the Allied armies, with the exception of part of one American corps sent southward to the Loire, swung eastward, pivoting on Caen. About 30,000 German troops were trapped near Falaise, southeast of Caen, in the third week of August, but cloudy weather and a cumbrous maneuver which took two corps of the United States First Army across the British front allowed large numbers to reach the right bank of the Seine by ferrying themselves across the river.

Meanwhile, three American divisions, preceded by British and American airborne troops and followed by seven French divisions, had landed in the south of France between Cannes and Hyères. Such an operation had been projected earlier as a diversion for Overlord, but the British, predicting that it would weaken Alexander without helping Eisenhower, had persuaded the Americans to postpone it on the understanding that it was not to be permanently renounced. The Germans responded to the reduction of Alexander's strength in Italy by moving two divisions to the Western Front and almost immediately after the landings ordered practically the whole of their forces in the south of France to retreat northward and join Rommel's successor. The outcome was that thirteen divisions, some of them much under strength, were added to the forces opposing Eisenhower and that he received by a roundabout route ten American and French divisions which went to form a new Sixth Army Group on his extreme right.

During the second half of August Montgomery urged Eisenhower to strike a decisive blow at the Germans before they could recover. Arguing that limitations of supply made simultaneous advances along divergent lines impractical, he begged his chief not to split his forces when he reached the Seine, but to keep them together as "a solid mass of some forty divisions . . . so strong that it need fear nothing." With such a force at his disposal, Montgomery could advance confidently toward the Ruhr, directing his left on Antwerp and his right on Brussels, Aachen, and Cologne. Alternatively, the forty divisions could be put at Bradley's disposal for an advance to Frankfurt.

Eisenhower refused to be diverted by this argument from his "overall plan." At the same time, he could not deny the importance of Antwerp or that an advance on the Ruhr was more likely to lead to a decisive battle than an advance on Frankfurt. He ruled that the Twenty-first Army Group, supported for the time being by the United States First Army, should move north of the Ardennes; the United States Third Army was to move south of the Ardennes, by way of Metz. Priority would go, until further notice, to the northern group of armies. Montgomery was to coordinate the movements of the northern group, but after the end of August Eisenhower himself would coordinate the operations of the land forces as a whole.

This was not one of Eisenhower's happiest decisions. By allocating the United States First Army, but not the Third, to the northern group of armies, he split the American Twelfth Army Group without giving the northern group the strength which, according to Montgomery, it needed to secure Antwerp and reach the Ruhr. In other words, he disappointed Bradley without satisfying Montgomery. Similarly, by decreeing that the northern group should have priority and that Montgomery should coordinate its movements, he exacerbated American impatience of British control without in fact conferring on Montgomery the powers he needed to carry out his task. The only priority which could have been useful to the northern group of armies was priority for supplies. Supplies would, however, continue to be allocated to the American armies by the Twelfth Army Group. Thus it was not Montgomery but Bradley who would decide how much fuel and ammunition should go to the First Army to enable it to cooperate with the British and how much to the Third Army to enable it to take part in a purely American enterprise.

Finally, Eisenhower's assumption of direct responsibility for coordinating the operations of the land forces meant, in effect, that henceforth army group commanders would have to conduct their own operations in the light of such broad instructions as they might receive from time to time. Even if the Supreme Commander had been qualified by experience to direct the day-to-day operations of armies in the field, he could not have performed such a task from his headquarters far to the rear of the fighting front.

Montgomery, making the best of a bad job, crossed the Seine at the end of August and reached Antwerp in five days. Meanwhile, the United States Third Army (General George S. Patton, Jr.) advanced to the neighborhood of Verdun, meeting little opposition on the way. The Germans withdrew from their flying-bomb launching sites in northern France, made haste to bar Montgomery's route to the Ruhr, and reinstated Rundstedt in his old post. They still commanded the seaward approaches to Antwerp and held pockets of resistance at Brest and Lorient.

On September 4 Montgomery renewed his plea for a full-blooded thrust to the Ruhr and beyond. He believed that if the northern group of armies received an adequate share of the 7,000 tons of supplies a day which were going to the American armies, even twenty divisions would enable him to turn Germany's main defensive position in the west by cutting through the forces immediately in front of him while they were still assembling.

When this request was made, Eisenhower was immobilized at his headquarters 300 miles behind the lines by the aftereffects of a minor accident. His reply, much delayed in transmission, was to the effect that he would welcome a strong thrust by the northern group of armies but was not prepared to curtail the operations of the United States Third Army south of the Ardennes.

A few days later, on September 8, the Germans opened attacks on London with long-range rockets launched from The Hague, only sixty miles north of the Allied front near Antwerp. In the light of this new departure the Combined Chiefs of Staff, meeting at the Octagon Conference at Quebec on September 12, agreed to remind Eisenhower of the advantages of entering Germany by the northern route. On the same day Montgomery received Eisenhower's sanction for an attempt to force the crossings of the Maas, the Waal, and the lower Rhine between Eindhoven and Arnhem with his existing resources, supplemented by one British and two American airborne divisions and an additional 1,000 tons of supplies a day for a limited period.

A powerful argument in favor of this plan was that the airborne divisions were in reserve and that therefore Eisenhower could give them to Montgomery without taking any troops away from Bradley. As a substitute for the full-blooded eastward thrust which Montgomery had proposed earlier, however, the operation left a good deal to be desired. It involved moving the British 30th Corps along a single road to Eindhoven. The corps would then have to cross three broad rivers and five minor waterways by nine bridges, all of which were to be captured in advance by the airborne troops. When the corps reached the right bank of the Rhine at Arnhem, part of it was to wheel westward in order to cut off the rocket-launching units and other German troops in western Holland. Finally, the main body of the British Second Army was to follow the 30th Corps across the Rhine, establish itself north of Arnhem, and prepare to thrust eastward into Germany after throwing out a deep salient in eastern Holland. Clearly, a great deal would depend on the ability of the airborne troops to capture the bridges and hold them until the 30th Corps arrived.

The operation was launched on September 17. The two American airborne divisions captured seven of the eight bridges assigned to them, and the eighth was reached and crossed by leading troops of the 30th Corps on September 20 at a moment when the Americans were approaching its northern end. All the bridges, except the great steel bridge across the Rhine at Arnhem, were thus in Allied hands by the evening of the fourth day.

To capture the Arnhem bridge was the task of the British 1st Airborne Division. On expert advice, the division chose a landing area north of the river, about seven miles from the objective. Field Marshal Walther Model, the officer responsible to Rundstedt for the northern sector of the German front, happened to be present and saw the paratroops arrive. Some British units reached the bridge in time to seize its northern end; others were held off by a prompt counterstroke organized by Model. To make matters worse, a sudden change in the weather over British airfields delayed the arrival of part of the division. The result was that the Germans were able to put up a strong defense by calling on armored units which they had moved to the neighborhood sometime earlier without knowing that an airborne offensive was impending. The 30th Corps reached the south bank of the lower Rhine in time to rescue about 2,000 survivors of the First Airborne Division before daybreak on September 26 but could go no farther. The Germans, retaining their hold on the greater part of Holland, still commanded the seaward approaches to Antwerp and could still bombard London with long-range rockets launched from The Hague. Furthermore, until their aircraft were grounded in the spring for lack of fuel, they could still use airfields in northwest Germany as bases for bombers specially equipped to send flying bombs toward the United Kingdom. Antwerp became in September, and remained throughout the winter, a target for rockets and flying bombs dispatched from sites well behind the German lines.

For all practical purposes, the failure of the Arnhem operation ended Eisenhower's chances of defeating the enemy's forces in Western Europe before the spring of 1945. He claimed in his correspondence with the Combined Chiefs of Staff that his intention was still to envelop the Ruhr from the north but added that no deep drive into Germany would now be possible until Antwerp could be used as a port of supply. Nevertheless, he sanctioned in November an ambitious offensive whose avowed objects were not merely to defeat German forces west of the Rhine and establish bridgeheads on the right bank, but to capture the Ruhr and the Saar. When a German attack on the British front threatened to hold up the entire program, he allowed his armies in the American sector to go forward without waiting for the British. Thus in effect he substituted a frontal assault on the Siegfried Line for an attempt to outflank it. Except on the extreme right, where French and American troops of the Sixth Army Group reached the upper Rhine near Mulhouse and at Strasbourg but failed to take Colmar, the attacks were unsuccessful. Between Aachen and the Saar the Twelfth Army Group, hampered by atrocious weather, made little impression on prepared positions which the Germans had had ample time to improve since their withdrawal from the Seine.

At the end of 1944 nearly fifty-five percent of the employable population of the United Kingdom was either serving with the armed forces or directly engaged in war production. Both Germany and the

United States had larger armies than Britain's, but in neither country was so high a proportion of the national effort committed to the prosecution of the war.

The failure of the Western Allies to complete the destruction of Germany's armed forces in the West by the end of the year had, therefore, very serious consequences for the British. They had hoped, not unreasonably in the light of Allied progress in August, to be able to make their main effort in 1945 in the Pacific theater, where warships and aircraft would be at least as useful as large armies. Another spell of hard slogging in Europe would confront them with grave manpower problems and the prospect of lasting damage to their economy.

At the same time, the November offensive did not inspire confidence in Eisenhower's military leadership. The British admired and respected Eisenhower for his determination to take a broad view of his responsibilities but were not convinced that his attempts to hold the balance between the interests of British and American commanders in the field made for good strategy. It did not escape them that things seemed to have gone much better before than since he assumed direct responsibility for coordinating the movements of the land forces.

In the light of such reflections, the British Chiefs of Staff came to the conclusion that they must ask their American colleagues to join them in pressing for a statement of Eisenhower's intentions.[85] They had not yet done so when, on December 16, the Germans took the offensive in the Ardennes.

Hitler aimed at thrusting a powerful armored force across the Meuse near Liège and directing it on Antwerp for the twofold purpose of denying the port to the Allies and cutting off Eisenhower's forces in the north. A second armored force was to cross the river south of Namur and seize Brussels. Altogether twenty-eight divisions, of which seventeen were to take part in the armored thrusts, were assigned to the plan. Such air support as the weather allowed was to be provided by 300 to 400 bombers, supplemented by nearly 2,000 fighters drawn largely from the air defenses of the Reich.

The Allies received many indications that an offensive was impending, but these were not conclusive. The Germans were thought too weak, and Rundstedt too cautious, to act aggressively.

The brunt of the assault was borne by a single corps of the United

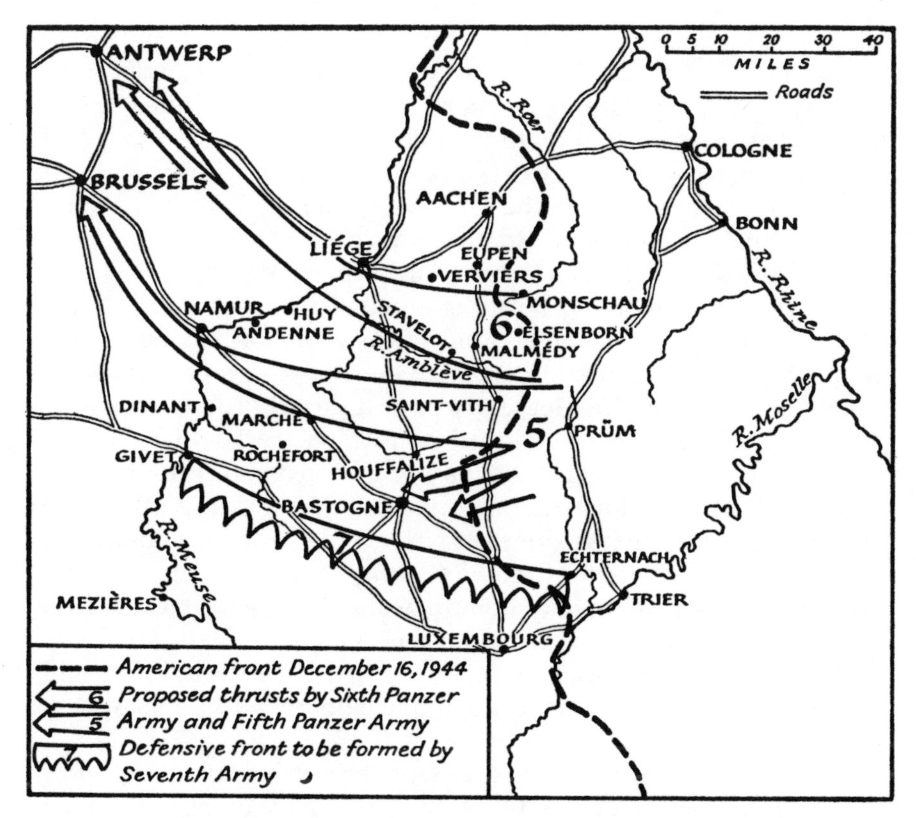

THE GERMAN OFFENSIVE IN THE ARDENNES,
(DECEMBER, 1944, TO JANUARY, 1945)

States First Army. With only four divisions on or immediately behind an eighty-mile front, the corps was too weak to prevent the Germans from punching two ragged holes in the Allied line.[86]

Bradley, having committed a great part of his forces to preparations for further offensives near Aachen and in the Saar, had practically nothing with which to fill the gap. For a time he and his subordinate commanders hoped that the enemy could be held by improvised measures and that counterattacks from north and south would then restore the situation.

After a few days it became apparent that Bradley was out of touch with events on the fighting front. He had not visited the First Army since the German offensive began, and his communications with its headquarters were precarious. On December 20 Eisenhower ruled that Montgomery should take charge of operations north of the German penetration and Bradley of operations south of it. In broad terms this meant that Montgomery, already in command of the Twenty-first Army Group, assumed control of the United States First Army, with such of its formations as were north of a specified line, and of the United States Ninth Army, which Eisenhower had placed in October between the First Army and the British. To compensate him for their loss, Bradley was given control of the Sixth Army Group's forces in addition to his own Third Army.

American troops were said to fight better offensively than defensively. Montgomery did not forbid offensive action by the United States First Army, but his immediate aim was to prevent the Germans from crossing the Meuse. By passing British troops across the Ninth Army's rear, he established himself on the left bank of the river between Namur and Givet, pushed armored patrols to the right bank, and set up a "long-stop" position south of Liège. At the same time he persuaded the Americans to make redispositions and tactical withdrawals which enabled the First Army to meet the enemy, with conspicuous success, more or less on the line on which Henry Wilson had hoped to halt the Germans in 1914. German spearheads came within fifteen to twenty miles of the Meuse between Liège and Namur and within four miles in the neighborhood of Dinant but could make no further progress.

Counterattacks then pushed the Germans slowly back. Deep snow handicapped both sides, but cloudy skies which hampered Allied bombers, fighters, and fighter-bombers helped the Germans extricate themselves from a bottleneck where disaster might have overtaken them in better weather. On January 16, exactly a month after the launching of the German offensive, Allied troops moving from north and south brought the campaign to a close by meeting at Houffalize. Since December 16 each side had lost about 80,000 of all ranks killed, wounded, or missing.[87] The Allies had lost more armored fighting vehicles than the Germans but could claim to have defeated what proved to be Hitler's last attempt to pass to the offensive in the West. Furthermore, they had attracted to their front the lion's share of the new or refurbished formations which Hitler had managed to scrape up since September. By the second week of January, when the Russians launched a vast offensive on a front extending from Lithuania to the Ukraine, the Western Allies were holding down almost as many divisions as there were on the Eastern Front from the Baltic to the Danube and beyond.[88]

14

The "Grand Alliance": II

WHEN the British agreed after the loss of Malaya and the Netherlands East Indies that the whole of the Pacific should be regarded as an American theater of war, they recognized that some such arrangement was inevitable if Allied resources were to be used to the best advantage in a global war. The employment of American forces to develop bases in islands of the South Seas where British or French influence had hitherto been paramount was nonetheless a striking commentary on the shifts of power which had come about in the past few years.

The appointment of the American General MacArthur to direct Allied operations in the southwest Pacific seemed at the time still more anomalous. With the exception of parts of New Guinea, Papua, and Borneo so inaccessible that scarcely any outsiders except a few explorers and missionaries had ever visited them, practically the whole of the territories assigned to MacArthur were either in Japanese hands or administered by British or Australian officials. Until reinforcements reached him from the United States, MacArthur depended largely on the Australians to provide him with an army.

The British accepted these arrangements in the belief that the overriding responsibility of the Combined Chiefs of Staff for all theaters of war would ensure that Allied resources were distributed in accordance with an agreed strategy and on the understanding that priority was to be given to the defeat of Germany. In practice, however, the Combined Chiefs of Staff had only a limited control over events in the Pacific theater. The distribution, not merely of American-built assault shipping but of shipping of all classes allocated to the armed forces of the United States, was largely in the hands of the American Admiral King. That the Pacific theater should have first claim on American resources and that American resources included almost everything made in an American factory or shipyard were to King self-evident propositions. Moreover, so reluctant was King to admit anyone outside his own service to his confidence that it was not until the autumn of 1942, when he wished to borrow a carrier from the British, that the naval authorities in London were able to obtain a detailed account of the disposition of the United States Pacific Fleet and the intentions of its commander.[1]

The decision to open a limited offensive in the Pacific early in 1942 was thus an American rather than an Allied decision, inasmuch as it was largely King's. This does not mean, however, that the British disapproved of it. They recognized, no less than the Americans, that the Allies would be in an intolerable position if their agreement to undertake no major offensive against Japan until Germany was defeated were understood to mean that in the meantime no attacks could be made on her outlying bases and possessions.

As it was, offensive operations began in February and March with the bombing and shelling of Japanese-held islands by carrier-borne aircraft and warships of the Pacific Fleet. In April sixteen Army bombers, stowed for the purpose aboard the new carrier *Hornet*, raided Tokyo and other objectives in Japan. The bombers were to have landed at Chuchow in Nationalist China, but a last-minute change of plan and the unreadiness of the Chinese prevented them from doing so.[2] All, except one which came down in Russian territory, either made crash landings or were abandoned by their crews in midair when their fuel ran short. Nevertheless, only eight of the eighty airmen who took part in the venture lost their lives. Most owed their survival to Chinese peasants who hid them from the Japanese.

The material results of the Tokyo raid were small, its moral effects substantial. The raid was one of the factors which led the Japanese to conclude that they would be unwise to extend their defensive perimeter to the South Seas by attempting the capture of Fiji and Samoa without first trying to bring the remnant of the United States Pacific Fleet to action.[3] Thus it helped the Americans establish themselves in the New Hebrides with little or no interference from the enemy and to score a decisive success at the Battle of Midway Island.

Early in July the American Joint Chiefs of Staff decided, on King's initiative, to open a series of offensives in British and Australian territory for the purpose of dislodging the Japanese from the Bismarck archipelago.[4] On the right, Vice Admiral Robert L. Ghormley, USN, to whom Nimitz had delegated responsibility for Allied operations in the South Pacific, was to begin by occupying the Santa Cruz Islands, driving the Japanese from their new seaplane base at Tulagi, and gaining a firm foothold there and in adjacent islands of the British Solomon Islands Protectorate. On the left, MacArthur was to expel the Japanese from eastern New Guinea and the northern part of the Solomon Islands before attempting the capture of New Britain and New Ireland.

Accordingly, the boundary between the Southwest Pacific Area and the South Pacific Sub-Area of the Pacific Ocean Area was redrawn so that the southern part of the Solomon Islands, formerly in MacArthur's area, fell within Ghormley's. MacArthur's resources did not include the transports, assault vessels, and aircraft carriers needed for expeditions to New Britain and New Ireland, but these were to be provided later.

MacArthur's offensive was delayed by the Japanese advance on Port Moresby in July and August. Consequently it was not until early in 1943 that his land forces, under the Australian General Sir Thomas Blamey, completed their occupation of the small part of eastern New Guinea which was their immediate objective. The campaign, conducted mostly in roadless country, provided a convincing demonstration of the importance of adapting methods of supply to circumstances. The Japanese were supposed to be adept at jungle warfare, but their communications broke down during their march to the south, and they suffered heavy wastage from malnutrition and tropical diseases. The Australians, when they counterattacked, were well served by Papuan porters who carried supplies along jungle trails. Later they and the Americans who joined them were supplied by aircraft which dropped rations and ammunition in well-marked clearings or delivered supplies and equipment, including artillery, to airstrips developed or constructed for the purpose.[5]

Only a few days after the Joint Chiefs of Staff had decided to send an expedition to the southern Solomons, they learned that the Japanese were building an airfield on the island of Guadalcanal, about twenty miles from Tulagi and separated from it by a sheltered roadstead in which a substantial fleet could lie at anchor. The capture of Tulagi and Guadalcanal then became the primary object of Ghormley's thrust. His forces visited the Santa Cruz Islands in due course but found them unsuitable for the development of naval and air bases.

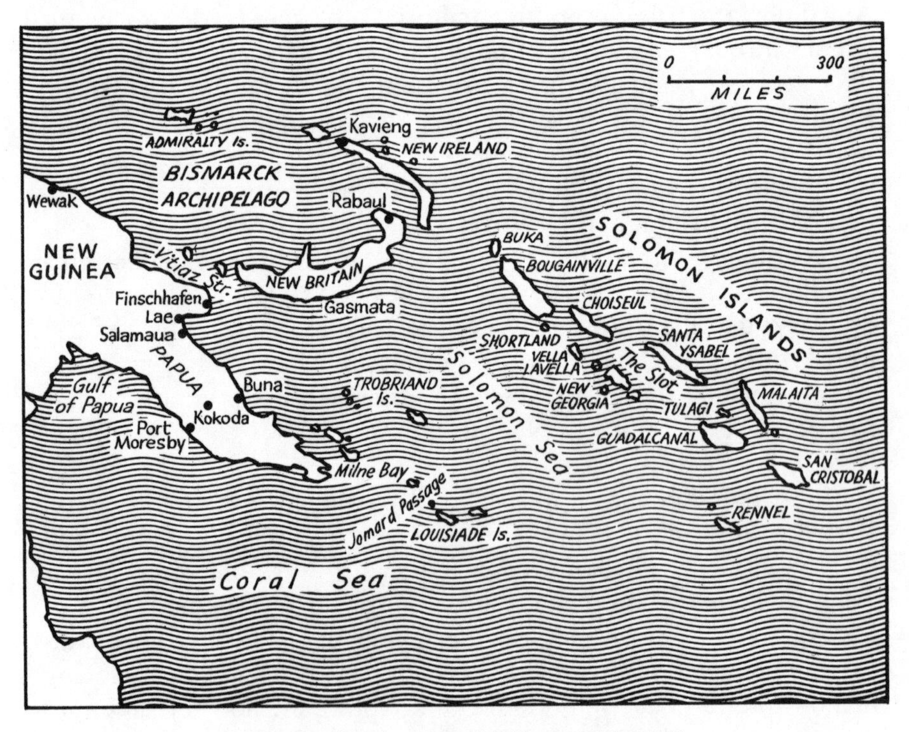

NEW GUINEA AND THE SOLOMONS

The Guadalcanal-Tulagi venture was the first expedition to enemy-held territory undertaken by United States forces since 1898.[6]

Since marines were to provide the landing force, most of the planning was done by naval officers. The planners seem to have assumed that success would be more or less assured if enough marines to outnumber the enemy by a comfortable margin could be safely disembarked. At the same time, they overestimated the strength of the enemy's land forces.* Thus the authorities were led not merely to budget on an unnecessarily lavish scale, but to disembark a larger force than they were capable of maintaining without straining their resources almost to the limit.

About 19,000 marines were assigned to the operation. Admiral Ghormley decided to carry all of them to Guadalcanal and Tulagi in one lift, leaving none in reserve to exploit a success or plug a gap. With their equipment and supplies, they would fill nineteen large and four smaller transports and supply ships. These were to be escorted by four cruisers and nine destroyers, supported by a further four cruisers and six destroyers organized in two fire-support groups, and accompanied by five minesweepers. Air support was to be provided by land-based aircraft from New Caledonia, the New Hebrides, Fiji, Samoa, and the Friendly Islands and by such aircraft from Australia and New Guinea as MacArthur could spare from his operations there. These would not include any short-range fighters, because the distances were too great. Additional air support, including fighter cover, would therefore be provided for a limited period by naval aircraft from three carriers, which in turn would be supported by a battleship, six cruisers, and sixteen destroyers. Ghormley was, however, so reluctant to risk these valuable ships for any length of time within reach of Japanese land-based aircraft that he ruled that the carrier force should withdraw after forty-eight hours. This ruling, although understandable, was highly illogical, since unloading was expected to take about four days and the transports and supply ships would need air cover just as much on the third and fourth days as on the first and second.

The arrival of the expeditionary force on August 7 took the garrisons of Guadalcanal and Tulagi by surprise, but they signaled a report to their parent formation at Rabaul in New Britain. Bombers from Rabaul attacked Allied transports and warships in the road-

* The planners estimated that there were 5,000 Japanese in Guadalcanal alone. In fact, there were about 2,500 there and some 1,500 at Tulagi, but only about 600 of those in Guadalcanal were combat troops.

stead on the first and second days but were beaten off by carrier-borne fighters after damaging two destroyers and one transport. On the second night a cruiser force, also from Rabaul, surprised and engaged warships patrolling the entrance to the roadstead, sank or disabled one Australian and three American cruisers, but withdrew without opening fire on the highly vulnerable transports and supply ships. In the meantime, the commander of the carrier force, alarmed by the loss of roughly a fifth of his fighters and fearing an attack by bombers and torpedo bombers, had asked permission to withdraw and had begun to do so without awaiting the favorable reply which reached him in the early hours of the morning. On the following day the transports and supply ships, accompanied by the surviving warships of the escort and fire-support groups, in turn withdrew, taking with them a great deal of equipment which they had not had time to unload.

Despite these setbacks, the marines made what seemed at the time a good beginning. Tulagi fell, after a stiff fight, on the second day. About 11,000 marines landed on the first day in Guadalcanal without opposition from the Japanese, who withdrew to another part of the island. They had then to deal with stores dumped more or less at random on the beach. On the second day they occupied the partially completed airfield but not the neighboring Mount Austen, a dominant feature which was to have been taken on the first day.

The departure of the transports and supply ships on the third day left the marines with rations for about a month, roughly half their initial allotment of ammunition, no radar or coast defense guns, and none of the equipment which was to have been used for the construction of permanent quarters. A first installment of nineteen fighters and twelve dive bombers arrived on August 20 in a converted merchant vessel, but it was not until a naval construction battalion reached the island at the beginning of September that the airfield could be made fit for use in all weathers. Thereafter the marines were able, as a rule, to dominate the roadstead and its immediate approaches during the daylight hours; but they were confined to a narrow beachhead, they were weakened by malaria and dysentery, and they could not prevent the Japanese from disembarking troops and supplies at night. To cover the passage of supplies and reinforcements, the American naval authorities had to make heavy demands on their aircraft carriers and their few surviving battleships.

The outcome was a long series of naval engagements which confronted the Americans with the danger of defeat by attrition. In the first six weeks, Japanese submarines sank the carrier *Wasp* and damaged the *Saratoga* so seriously that she had to be sent to Pearl Harbor for repairs. In the second week of October, Japanese aircraft and warships covering the arrival of reinforcements bombed and shelled the airfield so successfully that more than half the aircraft based there were knocked out, nearly all reserves of fuel were destroyed, and the surface became temporarily unusable by bomb-laden aircraft. The result was that on October 15 the Japanese were able to raise the strength of their land forces to some 20,000 men by disembarking between 3,000 and 4,000 men in daylight.

On the same day Admiral Nimitz observed that henceforth it would be possible to carry supplies to Guadalcanal only at great cost and that the situation was critical though not hopeless.[7] The Joint Chiefs of Staff came to the conclusion, and the President agreed, that withdrawal was out of the question and that a battleship, 6 cruisers, 24 submarines, and about 130 naval aircraft drawn from American resources should be added to the Allied forces in the South Pacific. At the same time Vice Admiral William F. Halsey, a distinguished task force commander, succeeded Ghormley as Supreme Commander, South Pacific Sub-Area, and Commander in Chief, South Pacific Force. The British contributed the carrier *Victorious* at the cost of leaving the Home Fleet without a single carrier, but she could not be adapted to carry American aircraft in time to take part in the struggle for Guadalcanal. On the eve of the Allied landings in French North Africa no additional troops could be found from theaters outside the Pacific, but arrangements were made to relieve tired by fresh marines, move some seventy-five aircraft of the United States Army Air Corps from the central Pacific to the South Seas, and reinforce Guadalcanal with infantry formations from New Caledonia and Hawaii.

Further naval battles, in which both sides suffered fairly heavy losses, led the Japanese to conclude about the middle of November that they could no longer afford to risk their heavy ships in the narrow waters leading to Guadalcanal while the Americans had a fleet in being. At the end of the following month they decided to reduce their naval commitment by withdrawing from Guadalcanal to New Georgia, some 200 miles closer to Rabaul.

On December 9 Major General (afterward Lieutenant General) Alexander M. Patch, of the United States Army, assumed command of the land forces in the American beachhead. Arrivals and departures during the next few weeks brought his strength to roughly 50,000 of all ranks. Aware that the Japanese were building an airfield in New Georgia but not that they intended to leave Guadalcanal, he began about the middle of December a series of thrusts designed to clear them from Mount Austen as the prelude to an attempt to round up their entire force. Strong rearguard actions, to which troops brought specially to the island for the purpose made important contributions, enabled them to embark nearly 12,000 survivors of their garrison without his knowledge. It was not until the afternoon of February 9, about thirty-six hours after the last of them had gone, that their departure became known to the Americans. Patch claimed that they had been "totally and completely defeated." That interpretation was not accepted by the Japanese authorities. According to them, their troops had accomplished their mission by pinning the Americans to a small part of the island for many months and had departed to fight elsewhere.

The British in India, like the Americans in the Pacific, were not content to maintain a purely defensive posture in 1942. Their problem was to frame an aggressive strategy compatible with means and circumstances. Mounting an offensive across the frontier between India and Burma would be extremely difficult, for there were no through roads in Bengal and no road or rail bridges across the broad, fast-flowing Brahmaputra. The authorities had drawn up plans in the early part of the year to overcome this handicap by accumulating stores and building airfields and strategic roads in the frontier area, but for some time after the fall of Burma most of the available labor force had to be used to build and stock camps for 400,000 refugees who entered the country just as the rainy season was beginning.[8] The difficulty of moving equipment and supplies across India was further increased by the diversion of ocean traffic from east to west coast ports to escape the attentions of the Japanese, since this put an added strain on the railways.

Work on a road which was to have linked India with China by way of Ledo in Assam and the Hukawng Valley and Myitkyina in Upper Burma had also to be suspended at the beginning of the rainy season because the 15,000 laborers assigned to the project were needed for more urgent tasks. In any case, Myitkyina soon fell to the Japanese and would have to be recaptured before the road could be completed. Meanwhile, war matériel could be sent to Nationalist China only by a hazardous air route across the foothills of the Himalayas. Whether priority should go to fuel and bombs for Major General Clare L. Chennault's American bombers in China or to equipment for new Chinese armies which the indomitable Stilwell was determined to create was a question of military policy which only the Combined Chiefs of Staff were qualified to answer.

Wavell, on resuming his post as Commander in Chief in India after his abortive attempt to coordinate the defense of Malaya with that of the Netherlands East Indies, came to the conclusion that until he had enough aircraft to ensure command of the air, he must be careful not to aim too high.[9] He proposed that during the dry weather between the early winter of 1942 and the late spring of 1943 he should advance to the line of the Chindwin between Kalewa and Homalin, in Upper Burma, and thence to Myitkyina. He would then be in a position to join hands with the Chinese for a subsequent advance to Rangoon by way of Mandalay and the Irrawaddy Valley.

Wavell had shown himself in the past a bold and successful planner of offensive operations. Nevertheless, his proposal to advance no farther in the near future than Myitkyina seemed to Churchill far too cautious. Churchill believed after the Battle of Midway Island that the Japanese were unlikely to offer any further challenge to British control of the Indian Ocean. Wavell ought, in his opinion, to aim at taking Rangoon and Moulmein by seaborne assault before the end of the 1942–43 dry season but should first seize Akyab Island, off the coast of Arakan, for use as an advanced base. He would need about 40,000 to 50,000 specially trained troops which could, according to Churchill, be provided if all went well in the Middle East and on the Russian front.

During the next few weeks Tobruk fell, the Eighth Army in the Western Desert retreated to the Alamein position, and the Russians suffered a series of setbacks in the Crimea and the Ukraine. The British Chiefs of Staff diverted substantial forces from India to the Middle East for fear of a German advance through the Caucasus but nonetheless expected Wavell to comply with Churchill's wishes by preparing for a thrust to Rangoon in the early part of 1943.[10] Civil disturbances in India, although soon suppressed, increased Wavell's difficulties by necessitating troop movements which threw an added burden on the railways. Furthermore, if Wavell mounted a seaborne expedition, he would have to compete for shipping and assault craft with the Pacific theater, the Anglo-American expedition to French North Africa, and the British expedition to Madagascar.

By the middle of August it was clear that the troops and equipment needed for seaborne assaults on Akyab and Rangoon could not be put at Wavell's disposal in the immediate future.[11] Believing that even so, they would reach him by the end of the rainy season, he decided in the following month to prepare for their arrival by driving the Japanese from a covering position between Maungdaw and Buthidaung, about fifty miles short of Akyab. To find a division for the purpose, he was compelled to reduce the scope of his proposed advance on the Chindwin front. Signs that the Japanese were very thin on the ground in the most northerly part of Burma suggested that nevertheless the recapture of Myitkyina might still be possible. The two Chinese divisions which had retreated to India after the fall of Rangoon were being trained under Stilwell's supervision for an offensive role. Wavell arranged that they should move on Myitkyina by way of Ledo and the Hukawng Valley when they were ready. He also arranged that work on the Ledo Road should be resumed under the direction of American engineers. The Chinese divisions would be supported by such troops as Wavell could still spare for the purpose. In addition, they would receive indirect support from the Chindits, a body of picked men who were being trained to maintain themselves for weeks at a time behind the enemy's lines and to disrupt his communications.

Moving across country or in river steamers, launches, and local craft, the troops assigned to the capture of the Maungdaw-Buthidaung position reached and occupied it about the middle of December. By that time Wavell was aware that there would be a further delay before everything he needed to mount a seaborne expedition reached him and that consequently he would not be able to use Akyab as a base for his assault on Rangoon unless he captured it with his existing resources in the meantime. He therefore ordered his troops to continue their advance in the hope that they would be able to storm the island by making the short crossing from the mainland in the small craft at their disposal. Their ability to do so was not put to the test, for they were unable to break through the Japanese defenses on the mainland.

Wavell also learned in December that the Americans would not be ready to start work on the Ledo Road much before the spring.[12] This meant that it would be almost impossible to supply Stilwell's Chinese divisions during the rainy season if they succeeded in establishing themselves in the Hukawng Valley. He concluded that their attempt to advance in that direction should be postponed and that the troops which were to have supported it should devote the rest of the dry weather to the improvement of communications on the Indian side of the frontier.[13]

Wavell recognized that this decision meant that the incursion into Japanese-held territory for which the Chindits were preparing could not be followed up and was therefore hard to justify on purely strategic grounds. After consulting their commanding officer, Brigadier Orde C. Wingate, he came to the conclusion that, even so, it would be wrong to deprive the Chindits of a chance of gaining valuable experience while their enthusiasm was at its height.[14] Accordingly, they crossed the Chindwin at two points about 40 miles apart in the middle of February and penetrated up to 150 miles or so behind the Japanese lines before receiving orders in the fourth week of March to return to base. About two-thirds of the men who had set out in February were back in India by the first week in June. Damage done to the railway linking Mandalay with Myitkyina was soon repaired, but the moral effects of the raid were considerable. The inference drawn from it by the Japanese was that their hold on Upper Burma was precarious and that they must either advance their defensive positions to the line of the Chindwin or, better still, seize the forward bases established by the British at Imphal and Kohima.[15] In the light of this verdict, it seems fair to conclude that Wavell might have scored a notable success on the Chindwin front during the 1942–43 dry season had he stuck to his original plan instead of allowing himself to be deflected from it by Churchill and the Chiefs of Staff.

The first attempt by the Combined Chiefs of Staff to frame a rational strategy for the Far Eastern and Pacific theaters in the light of developments since the spring of 1942 was made at the Casablanca Conference early in 1943. At that time the Western Allies had come to a standstill in Tunisia; they did not know when they would be able to land in northern France or whether such landings would be possible at all; the Americans, five months after their arrival in Guadalcanal, had yet to gain possession of an island on which the Japanese had never had a secure grip and whose inhabitants were loyal to the British. On the other hand, the Russians had won a crucial battle at Stalingrad and the British had held and counterattacked the Axis forces with considerable success at the Alamein position.

On balance, it seemed reasonable to assume that sooner or later the Western Allies would be able to defeat Germany in partnership with the Russians and that with or without Russian help, they would also succeed in defeating Japan. Japan's industrial capacity was much smaller than that of the British Empire or the United States. Her homeland was seriously deficient in raw materials; her Manchurian ventures and her undeclared war with Nationalist China had not yielded the benefits expected of them. Above all, her merchant fleet was barely sufficient for her peacetime needs. The territories she had captured from the British and the Dutch since the outbreak of war were rich in almost everything she lacked, but their acquisition would not save her from economic collapse if the Allies could prevent her from carrying their products home by sinking her shipping faster than she could replace her losses.

Even so, it was not to be expected that the Allies would be content to rely on air and submarine blockade as their sole means of putting pressure on Japan. Operations of quite a different character had already begun in Burma, New Guinea, and the Solomons; American naval strategists favored, in addition, a thrust from the central Pacific, with the Philippines, Formosa, or Japan as its ultimate objective. Other possible strategies included an advance from the Aleutians to the Japanese homeland by way of the Kurile Islands and an offensive through China. An advance by either of these routes would, however, pose formidable administrative problems.

A serious objection to a thrust from the central Pacific was that it threatened to make inordinate demands on the shipping and assault craft needed in all theaters. Moreover, by far the greater part of the Japanese Army was in China, Manchuria, Korea, Japan, and southeast Asia. An advance from island to island across half the breadth of the Pacific would not, therefore, enable the Allies to come to grips with any substantial part of the enemy's land forces until they reached some objective deemed by the Japanese so important that they were willing to reinforce its garrison on a massive scale. For these reasons, among others, the Combined Chiefs of Staff were not prepared, in the early part of 1943, to lay down a comprehensive strategy for the defeat of Japan. They recommended that MacArthur and Halsey should continue their operations in New Guinea and the Solomons on the lines proposed in the previous summer and that Nimitz in the central Pacific should aim at advancing when he was ready to a line from Truk in the Caroline Islands to Guam in the Marianas. In southeast Asia the British should, in due course, undertake a limited offensive on the Chindwin front, and additional transport aircraft should be sent to Assam for the twofold purpose of increasing the flow of supplies to the new Chinese armies and enabling Chennault to launch sustained attacks on Japanese shipping off the coasts of China and Siam. The British should also prepare for a major assault on Rangoon about the middle of November, but whether such an assault was feasible would have to be decided later in the year. Roosevelt and Churchill endorsed these proposals on the understanding that the Allies were still to aim at defeating Germany before undertaking a major offensive against Japan.[16]

As things turned out, lack of shipping prevented Wavell from receiving during the next few months anything like the quantity of supplies and equipment needed to mount a seaborne assault on Rangoon before the end of 1943.[17] He therefore decided to give priority over all other engineering projects in Assam to the building of enough airfields to raise the capacity of the airlift to China to the 10,000 tons a month demanded by Chiang Kai-shek as part of the price of his participation in an offensive in Burma. Auchinleck, who succeeded to the chief command in India when Churchill relegated Wavell to the post of Viceroy, bent his efforts in the same direction. At the Quadrant Conference at Quebec in August the British and United States governments agreed that Acting Vice Admiral Lord Louis Mountbatten (who held the substantive rank of Captain) should become Supreme Allied Commander in southeast Asia, with Stilwell as his deputy, but Mountbatten's appointment did not become effective until the middle of November.

MacArthur completed his capture of the north coast of Papua while the Casablanca Conference was in progress, but it was not until the end of June that he was ready to pass to the next stage of his offensive, which envisaged the capture of the part of New Guinea closest to New Britain. In the central Pacific, Nimitz needed even longer to assemble the massive fleet, large fleet train, and substantial body of troops required for a thrust to the Marshall Islands and beyond by way of the Gilbert Islands. Meanwhile, Halsey made only modest progress in the Solomons. Thus the strategic situation in the Far East and the Pacific had changed little since January when Roosevelt, Churchill, and the Combined Chiefs of Staff met in Washington for the Trident Conference in May.

In the meantime, Wavell had come to the conclusion that apart from the difficulty of amassing the equipment needed for a seaborne assault on Rangoon in competition with other commanders, the program sketched at Casablanca offered only the prospect of slow progress at a considerable cost.[18] During the voyage to the United States he proposed to Churchill that his forces and MacArthur's, instead of making separate attacks on the Japanese perimeter at points divided by a vast expanse of land and sea, should unite for a powerful assault on Sumatra.[19] Such an offensive could be mounted under the guise of continued preparations for the recapture of Burma and the Bismarck archipelago. If successful, it would drive a wedge into the Japanese positions in Malaya and the Netherlands East Indies by giving the Allies control of the channel between Sumatra and Java. Wavell added that the Americans and the Australians would, in his estimation, be far readier to cooperate in an assault delivered close to the boundary between the British and American theaters than to help him in Burma, either by sending troops or by releasing shipping and assault craft.

Churchill raised the question of an attack on Sumatra at the conference, but in terms which suggested that what he had in mind was a purely British attack on the northernmost part of the island rather than an Anglo-American attempt to blow a gaping hole in the Japanese perimeter. Nor did he press the matter when the Combined Chiefs of Staff asked that consideration of it should be deferred. When submitting their proposals at the close of the conference, the Combined Chiefs made no mention of an Anglo-American assault such as Wavell envisaged. They did, however, leave open the possibility of a purely British attack on Sumatra by indicating that the seaborne expedition which the British were expected to undertake need not necessarily take the form of an assault on Rangoon. Except that Wavell or his successor was now exhorted to make a "vigorous and aggressive" thrust from Assam in order to join hands with Chinese forces which would, it was hoped, move into Burma from Nationalist China, the program sketched in May was very much the same as that discussed in January.

At the Quadrant Conference three months later, Churchill renewed his plea for an attack on Sumatra, but again he spoke only of a British assault at one end of the island. The British Chiefs of Staff objected that the capture of northern Sumatra would give them no more than a base from which they might be able to bomb Singapore.[20] Roosevelt was even less enthusiastic. Likening the area held by the Japanese to a slice of pie with Tokyo as its apex and the Netherlands East Indies as its rim or crust, he described the attack proposed by Churchill as a mere attempt to nibble at the crust.[21] No such criticism could have been made of Wavell's project. He had not suggested in May that the British should nibble at the Japanese perimeter. His proposal was that they should unite with the Americans and the Australians to shatter it.

The true case for Wavell's project thus went by default. The Allies, seeing no acceptable alternative, agreed in August on measures which differed only in detail from those discussed in January and May. In the central Pacific, Nimitz was to aim at capturing the Gilbert Islands, the Marshall and Caroline Islands at least as far west as Truk, and the Marianas. In the southwest Pacific, MacArthur was to extend his hold on eastern New Guinea and gain a footing in the Bismarck archipelago but was no longer to take Rabaul, which his forces were to bypass. In southeast Asia, Mountbatten was to aim first at capturing northern Burma in order to reopen land communications with Nationalist China and make the airlift more secure. He was also to increase the capacity of the airlift by building more airfields. What else he should do, particularly in the way of a seaborne expedition, would have to be decided in the light of further study by the staffs concerned.

However, at the close of a conference of Foreign Ministers at Moscow in October, Stalin opened the eyes of the Allied statesmen to new possibilities by remarking "suddenly and in passing" to Cordell Hull that the Soviet Union would join Britain and the United States in defeating Japan when the war with Germany was over.[22] He expressed a similar intention at his meeting with Roosevelt and

Churchill toward the end of the year. The Western Allies, attracted by the prospect of using the Russian Maritime Provinces as a base for the bombing of Japan, persuaded him to agree on February 2, 1944, that large numbers of Allied bombers should be stationed in eastern Siberia once the Soviet Union had declared war on Japan.[23] Besides building six or seven new airfields near Vladivostok, the Russians afterward asked the Americans to send, in addition to their own bomber force, 540 heavy bombers to be manned by American-trained Russian crews.[24] Later the Russians made it clear that they no longer wished the Americans to take a hand in the training of their airmen, and at the Yalta Conference early in 1945 they withdrew their offer of bases near Vladivostok and offered bases about 500 miles farther north.[25]

During the months that followed the Quadrant Conference MacArthur made substantial progress in New Guinea, still using forces which were largely Australian. Meanwhile, Nimitz continued his preparations for an advance in the central Pacific. By November the forces at his disposal included six modern and seven older battleships, six large fleet carriers, five light carriers, eight small escort carriers, and more than 100,000 soldiers and marines. Opening his offensive in that month, he completed the capture of the Gilbert Islands in roughly a week at the cost of some 4,000 casualties. Since the islands were defended by fewer than 5,000 Japanese, his subsequent advance to the Marianas or beyond threatened to be so expensive a business that the interest taken by the Western Allies in the possibility of bombing Japan from Siberia or elsewhere was not surprising.

The assault on the Gilbert Islands had just begun when the Sextant Conference, attended not only by Roosevelt and Churchill and their service advisers, but also by a Chinese delegation led by Chiang Kai-shek, opened in Cairo on November 22. Meetings were held daily until November 26. The British and the Americans then left to meet the Russians at Teheran. The Sextant Conference was resumed on December 3 and broke up on December 7.

In the course of the discussions in Cairo, Chiang Kai-shek made it clear that he was not prepared to pass to the offensive unless the British undertook a major seaborne expedition in the Bay of Bengal. Roosevelt assured Chiang during the first round of talks that such an operation would be launched within the next few months[26] but was forced to retract when he found that neither his own advisers nor Churchill's could promise that the necessary resources would be forthcoming. The American Chiefs of Staff were not prepared to release assault shipping for an attack on Sumatra. Their British colleagues thought an expedition to the Andaman and Nicobar Islands the most promising course of action open to Mountbatten with his existing resources but were not satisfied that such an expedition would make the best use of equipment which might be usefully employed in the European theater.[27] The outcome was that the Combined Chiefs of Staff agreed that "major amphibious operations" in the Bay of Bengal should be postponed at least until the end of the next year's monsoon, that roughly half Mountbatten's landing craft should be sent to the Mediterranean, and that the main effort against the Japanese in 1944 should be made in the Pacific theater. They also proposed that warships of the British Eastern Fleet not needed in the Indian Ocean as a deterrent to the Japanese should move to the Pacific, insofar as they could be "supported and profitably employed" in an American theater.

The Combined Chiefs of Staff embodied these recommendations in a report submitted to the Allied plenipotentiaries at the last plenary session of the Sextant Conference on December 6. A significant feature of the report was the stress laid on measures calculated to bring Japan within reach of a new American long-range bomber, the B-29. The Combined Chiefs proposed that Nimitz and MacArthur should continue their operations in the central Pacific and New Guinea with a view to "a major assault in the Formosa-Luzon-China area" to be delivered in the spring of 1945, but they made it clear that they regarded the advance in the central Pacific not only in that light, but also as a step toward the bombing of Japan from bases in the Marianas. In southeast Asia, Mountbatten was to aim at capturing Upper Burma in the spring of 1944 but to give priority to the development of the airlift to Chungking and of bases near Calcutta for bombers capable of reaching Japan from forward airfields in China. Finally, Mountbatten's chances of launching a major offensive in the Bay of Bengal after the next monsoon were to be reviewed in the light of further discussions to which Chiang Kai-shek would be a party.

Both Roosevelt and Churchill initialed the report, but Churchill afterward denied that he had assented to a plan which relegated

Mountbatten's new Southeast Asia Command to a mere supporting role until the end of 1944.[28] He argued, not unreasonably, that his initials proved that he had seen the report, but not that he had accepted it in its entirety.

As things turned out, Mountbatten's forces had much more than a minor part to play in 1944. After the Chindit operation in 1943, Japanese officers in Burma succeeded in convincing their superiors that the Fifteenth Army, on the Chindwin front, ought to be reinforced and equipped for a tactically offensive but still strategically defensive role. Their plan was that, during the dry season between the autumn of 1943 and the spring of 1944, the Fifteenth Army (Lieutenant General R. Mutaguchi) should cross the Indian frontier and seize Imphal and Kohima under cover of a diversion in Arakan by the Twenty-eighth Army (Lieutenant General S. Sakurai) on Mutaguchi's left. In the extreme north, two divisions under the direct control of the Burma Army (Lieutenant General M. Kawabe) were to hold defensive positions in the Hukawng Valley and on the Salween front against the British to the west and the Chinese to the east. Since there were practically no roads in the neighborhood of the Chindwin front except those built recently by the British for their own purposes, Mutaguchi's approach march would have to be made largely along jungle tracks unsuitable for wheeled vehicles, even in dry weather. This meant that roughly half his troops would receive no supplies from the rear during the first three weeks of their advance.

In the hope of reinforcing the Fifteenth Army without exposing transports to air and submarine attacks in the Bay of Bengal, the Japanese made frenzied attempts in 1943 to complete during the rainy season a single-line railway linking the Siamese and Burmese rail systems. About 60,000 prisoners of war and large numbers of Burmese and Malayan conscripts were set to work on the project, but they suffered heavy wastage from starvation and disease and made slow progress. Troops dispatched from Siam to join Mutaguchi's army had to make long marches to reach his front. Consequently they arrived so late that he was unable to start his offensive until the diversion in Arakan was over, and even then he was short of men.

Mountbatten's land forces consisted mainly of British and Commonwealth troops. With the exception of troops in reserve, assigned to special formations or performing purely administrative duties, they belonged to the Fourteenth Army, commanded by the British Lieutenant General William Slim. In addition to a small army reserve and a small force in Ceylon, Slim had one corps of three divisions in Arakan, one corps of three divisions based on Imphal, and the equivalent of one corps of three American-trained Chinese divisions based on Ledo. The three Chinese divisions formed the Northern Combat Area Command under Stilwell, who was also Deputy Supreme Commander and Chief of Staff to Chiang Kai-shek. In addition, Stilwell was responsible, at least in theory, for the administration of all units of the United States Army and Army Air Corps in China, India, or Burma.

Slim had made a close study of Japanese methods. He had come to the conclusion that in jungle warfare, attacks could not be contained by the orthodox method of withdrawal to a continuous line of planned or improvised positions, since it was not possible to form in the jungle a line which could not be turned by infiltration. Instead of withdrawing, units outflanked by the enemy must stay where they were, and their parent formations or commands must be ready at all times to supply them by air. Even though completely surrounded, they would then form "an anvil against which reserves could destroy the enemy forces in their rear." [29]

Slim had no detailed knowledge of the Japanese plan but was aware by the early part of 1944 of indications that an offensive was impending and was likely to start in Arakan.[30] After discussing the situation with his immediate superior on February 2, he ordered his principal administrative officer to "start packing day and night" so that supplies would be ready for delivery by parachute to his troops on the Arakan front when they were needed.

Less than forty-eight hours later, General Sakurai began his diversionary attack in Arakan by dispatching about 5,000 infantry and engineers on a long march around the eastern flank of the 7th Indian Division near Buthidaung. Helped by early morning mists, his troops succeeded in passing across the rear of the 7th Indian Division and reaching the rear of the 5th Indian Division on its right. At the same time, Sakurai launched a frontal assault near the junction between the two divisions. By this means he was able, by the third or fourth day of the offensive, to cut the communications of the 7th Indian Division, invest its headquarters and administrative area, and threaten the communications of the 5th Indian Division.

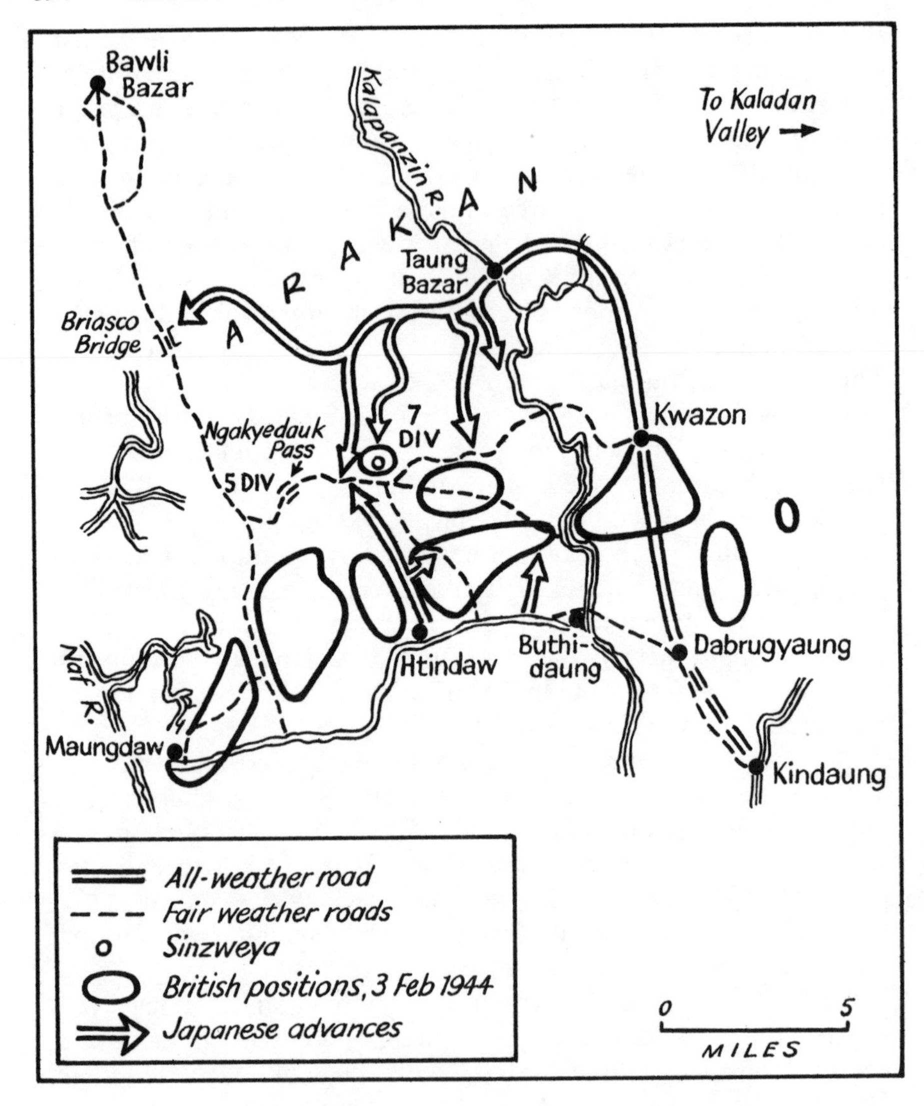

THE BATTLE OF THE NGAKEYEDAUK PASS

Slim's response was to order both divisions to stand fast and to promise reinforcements and supplies.[31] From the sixth day, troops surrounded and cut off by the enemy received daily airborne deliveries of food, ammunition, cigarettes, rum, mail, razor blades, and newspapers. The Japanese, on the other hand, had great difficulty in supplying their forward troops. On February 22 a counterattack drove them from the Ngakyedauk Pass, in the 5th Division's rear. On the following day they called off their offensive.

The Battle of the Ngakyedauk Pass marked a turning point in the war in the Far East. It also drew attention to a serious weakness in the structure of the Southeast Asia Command. The only air transport units at Mountbatten's disposal for the carrying of supplies to Slim's troops were the four British and two American squadrons of his Troop Transport Command. Since these became insufficient for his needs when a crisis arose in Arakan, he borrowed thirty to forty aircraft from the Air Transport Command of the Tenth United States Army Air Force. The primary task of this command was to carry supplies to China, and it was expressly excluded from the forces under Mountbatten's operational control. He had nonetheless been authorized, at a time when offensive operations in Upper Burma were in view, to make a limited use of its resources "in order to meet any unforeseen contingency arising in battle." The outcome of his conscientious attempts to discover whether this concession covered a defensive battle in Arakan was disappointing. Stilwell, having departed to take charge of his Chinese divisions in the north, could not be found when his advice was needed, and a telegram to the Combined Chiefs of Staff went unanswered until the crisis was over.[32]

In Upper Burma, Mutaguchi opened his offensive by sending about a third of his force across the Chindwin at Kalewa in the second week of March. Another two divisions crossed the river at points farther north about a fortnight later. At the end of the month and early in April, these two divisions gained control at several points of the road linking Imphal and Kohima with the British railhead at Dimapur.

The British, long expecting Mutaguchi's attack, had prepared for it by forming a defensive perimeter around Imphal and accumulating there enough supplies to maintain an army of 150,000 men for several weeks. When the offensive began, Slim further strengthened the perimeter by withdrawing troops from outpost positions and flying the whole of the 5th Indian Division from Arakan. All available transport aircraft, including some twenty to thirty borrowed from the Air Transport Command of the Tenth Air Force, were then used to supply the troops at Imphal and elsewhere and to carry noncombatants and wounded to the rear. This time Mountbatten took the precaution of making a direct appeal to the American Joint Chiefs of Staff. Their reply was to the effect that they agreed to the diversion of the aircraft he had borrowed but that in the future he must ask permission before acting. This was obviously unsatisfactory. If aircraft of the Air Transport Command were to be used in a tactical role at all, the decision to divert them to such a role at any particular time could be made only in the light of a tactical situation which could not be assessed from the standpoint of Washington.

By the middle of April Mutaguchi's two divisions in the north were already in poor shape. One had received no supplies since the start of the offensive, the other few. During the second half of the month both divisional commanders were forced to give up all thoughts of offensive action and devote themselves to attempts to escape defeat. Their opposite number in the south, although able to receive supplies from the rear, had proposed as early as the last week in March that the offensive should be abandoned.[33] On Mutaguchi's orders, he continued nonetheless to batter at Slim's defenses south of Imphal until, in June, even Mutaguchi was obliged to admit that only a general retreat could avert the loss of his entire force. By July there remained of Mutaguchi's army of 84,000 men only some 30,000 still fit to march.[34] Slim's battle casualties on the Chindwin front were roughly 16,000.

Meanwhile, Stilwell had begun his long-delayed advance toward the Hukawng Valley and Myitkyina. His three Chinese infantry divisions were supplemented for the purpose by a Chinese tank brigade and by Merrill's Marauders, a body of American troops organized on the lines of Wingate's Chindits. To cover Stilwell's left, a force of Burmese volunteers raised and organized by the British moved almost due south from Fort Hertz toward the Irrawaddy. On his right the Chindits, now with six brigades of which three were British, two Indian, and one West African, moved partly by air and partly by a long march through wild country to the neighborhood of Indaw, where they held up supplies intended for Japanese troops in the Hukawng Valley and contained a force equivalent to the infantry of one Japanese division. Wingate was killed in an air crash on March 24, and was succeeded by Brigadier (afterward Major General) W. D. A. Lentaigne.

In April Chiang Kai-shek, under the threat of an embargo on

American supplies, at last agreed to take the offensive against the Japanese 56th Division on the Salween front. Soon afterward his troops successfully resisted attacks which threatened airfields established by the Americans in China, but neither the Chinese divisions serving under Stilwell nor those which crossed the Salween in May proved of much value in an offensive role. The result was that on more than one occasion Stilwell was able to get forward only by entrusting to Merrill's Marauders, and later to brigades of the Chindits which were put at his disposal, tasks to which a less ruthless commander would not have committed lightly armed troops without artillery support. Even with this help, he made such slow progress that it was not until August 3 that Myitkyina was in his hands. His battle casualties during his advance from Ledo to Myitkyina were substantially greater than those suffered by Slim's forces during the whole of the fighting for Imphal and Kohima.

At the end of June Stilwell found fault with British arrangements for the relief of two brigades of the Chindits which had been in action or behind the enemy's lines for sixteen weeks without a break. He did not deny that tired troops must be relieved but thought that the withdrawal of entire brigades would mean that fit as well as unfit men were withdrawn and that this would be uneconomical even though the troops withdrawn were to be replaced by others. A medical investigation showed that in fact there were very few men still fit to fight in either of the brigades in question. The upshot was that both brigades, less one company, were withdrawn, and that Mountbatten warned Stilwell of the danger of keeping men in battle who could not defend themselves. Stilwell protested that he had never contemplated such a course.

Some weeks later Stilwell quarreled with Chiang Kai-shek and was recalled to the United States. The opportunity was taken to make changes which removed some of the anomalies arising from Stilwell's equivocal position, but which left Mountbatten still dependent on the Americans for two-fifths of his transport aircraft.

Slim, defying the convention which ordained that active operations should cease when the monsoon broke, continued his advance to the frontier and beyond during the first few months of the rainy season. By August his forces stood on a line from Maungdaw through Tamu in the frontier area to Myitkyina and the left bank of the Irrawaddy. Unless his forces were to be broken up for the benefit of other theaters, he could thus look forward to driving the enemy from the whole of Burma during the next dry season. By so doing, he would regain control of a country larger than France and Belgium put together, unhinge the whole of the Japanese positions in southeast Asia, and pave the way for the enemy's expulsion from Malaya, Sumatra, Siam, and Indochina.

The Japanese considered a voluntary withdrawal but came to the conclusion that although they need give only a low priority to attempts to prevent the Allies from reopening land communications with China, they could not afford to abandon the oil and rice of central and southern Burma without a struggle.[35] Accordingly their forces, some ten divisions strong, took up positions approximately on the line of the Irrawaddy from Rangoon and Akyab on the left to Bhamo on the right.

The British Chiefs of Staff, although still inclined to pin their hopes on a seaborne expedition to Rangoon rather than an overland advance, now recognized that the capture of Burma was the key to success in the Far East. The Americans, on the other hand, continued to regard a junction with Chiang Kai-shek's forces as the primary object of the campaign in southeast Asia. On September 16 the Combined Chiefs of Staff made a characteristic attempt to reconcile divergent views by directing Mountbatten to aim at seizing Rangoon by seaborne and airborne assault in the spring of 1945, but meanwhile to push forward on land with the object of improving the air route to Chungking and reopening land communications with China.

The Northern Combat Area Command, now with one Indian and two Chinese divisions, duly began about the middle of October a southward drive from Myitkyina, directing its right on Indaw and its left on Bhamo. Farther to the east a force controlled by Chiang Kai-shek, still moving in Chinese territory, made a leisurely advance along the axis of the Burma Road. On reaching the frontier at Wanting in the third week of January, the Chinese found that the Japanese 56th Division, warned of their approach and fearing envelopment by forward elements of Slim's forces, had withdrawn. The Burma Road was ceremonially reopened to Allied military traffic shortly afterward but proved of little strategic value. Chiang Kai-shek, still regarded in the United States as ruler of a great power and hence a valuable ally, had shrunk to the stature of a provincial warlord. Despite generous help from the Western Allies, he was powerless to expel the Japanese from China, and even in territories nominally under his control his authority was challenged by rivals who had taken a rich toll of supplies sent to him from Russia during the past few years. The whole of China, impoverished by war, corruption, maladministration, and natural disasters, was ripe for Communist penetration.

Until December, Slim intended to continue his advance in the general direction of Mandalay and destroy the reorganized Japanese Fifteenth Army between the Chindwin and the Irrawaddy. About the middle of that month he came to the conclusion that the Japanese would not stay to fight unless he found a means of compelling them to do so. The British Chiefs of Staff then proposed that Mountbatten should be given a new directive which would make the liberation of Burma his immediate aim and that of the whole of southeast Asia his ultimate objective.[36] Since the Americans, still intent on supporting Chiang Kai-shek, were reluctant to renounce their freedom to use their transport aircraft for purposes which might conflict with Slim's, the Combined Chiefs of Staff had some difficulty in arriving at a suitable formula. Furthermore, early in February Chiang asked that the three Chinese divisions still in Burma should be flown to China. Some anxious moments followed before all parties were persuaded to agree that Slim should have first call on the air transport squadrons until June 1.

Facing the need to complete his campaign before the means of victory were taken from him, Slim delivered what the commander of the Japanese forces in Burma afterward called his master stroke. Under cover of continued preparations for an assault on Mandalay, he sent an entire corps due south along the right bank of the Chindwin, passed it across the Irrawaddy at a point beyond the confluence of the two rivers, and in the first week of March cut the line of retreat of the whole of the Japanese forces north of that point by seizing vital road and rail junctions at Meiktila. After repelling a desperate attempt by the Japanese to regain possession of the town, he chased a beaten enemy down the valley of the Sittang toward Rangoon, twice overrunning the headquarters of the Japanese Thirty-third Army on the way.

At the end of April the 17th Indian Division reached Pegu, about thirty miles from the scene of the disaster which had overtaken it in 1942 and some forty from Rangoon. The Japanese were reported to be leaving Rangoon and to have turned their prisoners loose. Meanwhile, a seaborne expedition had, at Slim's request, been mounted as an insurance against failure to reach Rangoon by the overland route before the stipulated date. Two Indian infantry brigades, preceded by paratroops, landed unopposed at the mouth of the Irrawaddy on May 2. By the evening of the following day Rangoon was once more in British hands.

Inevitably the British were unable to exercise a comparable influence on Allied strategy in the European theater. Toward the close of the campaign in the Ardennes, the Combined Chiefs of Staff agreed that Eisenhower should be asked to state his intentions.[37] The substance of his reply was that he could not, for logistic reasons, concentrate his forces in the north to the extent favored by the British. Estimating that, even though supplies were now reaching him through Antwerp, not more than thirty-five of his seventy to eighty divisions could be maintained north of the Ardennes, he proposed to supplement his promised drive toward the Ruhr by thrusting as many divisions as he could spare across the middle Rhine toward Frankfurt and Kassel.[38]

Had Eisenhower said no more than this he would have had a strong case. His appeal to logistic necessity was, however, accompanied by a rather diffuse and long-winded attempt to defend his proposals on strategic grounds. This gave the impression that he was not convinced of the importance of striking hard at the Ruhr and was still inclined to subordinate strategic considerations to attempts to hold the balance between the interests and ambitions of British and American commanders.

However, toward the end of January the British and American Chiefs of Staff met in Malta before flying to the Crimea to confer with the Russians. In the course of long and frank discussions Eisenhower's Chief of Staff, the American Lieutenant General Walter Bedell Smith, succeeded in convincing the British that his chief had no ulterior motives and still intended to give priority to the northern group of armies.[39] Ultimately it was agreed that the British Second, the Canadian First, and the United States Ninth armies, all controlled by Montgomery, should begin the 1945 offensive by occupying the west bank of the Rhine from Emmerich on the left to Düsseldorf on the right. The United States First and Third armies, under Bradley, would then occupy the west bank from Düsseldorf to Coblenz. Finally, the Third and Seventh armies would clear the enemy from the Saar and the Palatinate while Montgomery crossed the Rhine at Wesel. The only serious disadvantages of this plan were that the crossing of the Rhine at Wesel threatened to be the most difficult operation undertaken by the Allies since they had landed in Normandy and that Bradley was not likely to be satisfied with a minor role.

Meanwhile, the Russians, with more than one and a half times as many divisions as Eisenhower, had begun a massive advance on a broad front from Königsberg to the Carpathians. Hitler had roughly the same number of divisions as the Russians on the Eastern Front but had weakened his center in order to maintain his grip on U-boat training areas in the Baltic and on sources of supply in Hungary. Moreover, in recent months he had starved his armies in the East of new equipment for the sake of the offensive in the Ardennes.[40] By the beginning of February the Soviet armies were on the Oder and their spearheads barely fifty miles from Berlin.

Thus the Russians had already overrun a great part of Poland by the time the British and the Americans left Malta for the Crimea. Since the Soviet authorities had refused to support a Polish uprising in Warsaw in the previous August and were backing a Communist-inspired Polish Committee of National Liberation which did not recognize the authority of the Polish government in London, their future relations with the Western Allies seemed likely to be difficult.

However, Roosevelt and Churchill had no intention of quarreling with Stalin. They relied on the Russians to play a big part in the defeat of Germany. They wished to reach agreement with the Soviet government about the postwar occupation of Germany on terms which would enable the Americans to remove their troops from Europe within two years. They also wished to ensure that the Russians joined, but did not dominate, an organization intended to supersede the League of Nations. Above all, they were eager to nail Stalin to his promise to declare war on Japan when Germany was defeated. To secure this benefit they were even willing—albeit with misgivings on Churchill's part—to concede terms tantamount to a complete restoration of the power and influence in the Far East which the Russians had lost in 1905.

Similarly, Stalin had nothing to gain by focusing attention on the gulf which divided him from Western statesmen. He counted on the

Western Allies to reduce the Japanese to a state which would give him an easy victory when he joined the war in the Far East. Furthermore, at a time when the Germans had yet to be driven from the whole of Hungary and the Soviet armies on the Oder were in danger of outrunning their supplies, clearly the armies of the West still had a useful part to play in defeating Germany. Thus the Russians had every incentive to purchase British and American goodwill at the cost of a few concessions. Besides undertaking to enter the war against Japan within two to three months of Germany's defeat, they accepted Anglo-American plans for the occupation of Germany and agreed to join the United Nations without insisting that each of the sixteen republics of the Soviet Union should have a vote. They were reticent about their long-term strategic plans and remained hostile to the Polish government but promised to broaden the basis of the Polish Committee of National Liberation, hold free elections in liberated countries, and respect the existing social order in Rumania.

Hopes inspired by these promises were soon shattered.[41] Within three weeks of Yalta the Soviet authorities forced the King of Rumania to dismiss the all-party government which he had set up with their approval and install a Communist government in its place. They did nothing to broaden the basis of the Polish Committee of National Liberation. They denied the Americans access to airfields near Budapest which were to have been used by Allied bombers. They excluded British and American officials from prisoner of war camps in Eastern Europe, although their own officials were allowed to visit camps in Western Europe. They announced that their Commissar for Foreign Affairs would not attend the inaugural meeting of the United Nations at San Francisco in April. Finally, they accused the Western powers of trying to make a separate peace with Germany, on the absurd ground that an invitation to the Soviet government to send an emissary to witness the surrender of the German forces in Italy had been issued after, not before, the credentials of the German officers who offered to surrender were verified.

These incidents did not lead the Western powers to conclude that the agreement they had made with the Soviet Union about the occupation of Germany would not be honored or that the Russians should be treated as enemies. They did, however, suggest very strongly that Eisenhower would be well advised to do everything he could to bring his campaign to a successful conclusion before large tracts of Western Europe were added to the territories in which the Russians were free to subject governors and governed to Communist indoctrination.

Eisenhower launched his offensive while the Yalta Conference was still in progress. On February 8 Montgomery began his advance in the northernmost sector through a narrow corridor between the Maas and a flooded area on the left bank of the Rhine. Hitler decreed that Rundstedt's forces on the left bank, instead of withdrawing across the river, should fight a desperate battle where they stood. In consequence Montgomery's initial advance was much harder, and his subsequent crossing at Wesel a good deal easier, than had been expected. The last survivors of the German armies on the left bank withdrew in the second week of March, and on March 23 the leading troops of two British and two American divisions crossed the broad expanse of the Rhine on either side of Wesel without great difficulty.

Farther south the leading formations of the United States First Army, meeting lighter opposition, reached the left bank at Cologne on March 5. Two days later one of its divisions captured an unblown railway bridge at Remagen, thirty miles upstream from Cologne. Eisenhower then gave Bradley authority to pass not more than five divisions to the right bank. Later he agreed that Bradley should move to the right bank as many divisions as he could support and that the United States Third Army, which had already reached Coblenz, should close up to the left bank as far south as Mannheim.

The broad effect of these decisions was that by the fourth week of March Montgomery held a bridgehead some twenty miles wide and nearly twice as deep on the right bank of the river north and south of Wesel, that the First Army was also across the Rhine at Remagen, and that the Third Army, too, had reached the right bank and had its leading troops at Darmstadt, less than twenty miles south of Frankfurt. About 290,000 Germans had surrendered since February 8, and another 325,000 were trapped in the Ruhr. Everything seemed ready, therefore, for Eisenhower to complete the capture of the Ruhr and continue his advance to Berlin while the Russians were still held up on the Oder. Politically and strategically there was everything to be said for such a move, and nothing in the Yalta agreements precluded the Western Allies from making it.

Eisenhower had complained in January that he found it difficult to plan current or future operations without knowing what the Russians were going to do.[42] At Yalta the British and the Americans had proposed an exchange of liaison officers, but the Russians had made it clear that such an arrangement would not suit them. Thus there was no obligation on any Allied commander to disclose his plans to the Soviet authorities unless his superiors ordered him to do so.

The Combined Chiefs of Staff were therefore astonished when, on March 28, they received "for information" a copy of a telegram in which Eisenhower asked the heads of the Allied Military Missions in Moscow to tell Stalin that he proposed to continue his advance not in the direction of Berlin but toward Leipzig and Dresden and to make a secondary thrust toward Regensburg and Linz.[43] Soon afterward the British learned, although not from the Supreme Commander or his British deputy, that Eisenhower intended to take the Ninth Army away from Montgomery and use it to support Bradley's advance on Dresden.[44]

The heads of the Allied Military Missions found Eisenhower's message so baffling that they asked for further information before complying with his request that they should deliver it as a "personal message" to Stalin. The British authorities in London, from Churchill down, found it worse than baffling. Convinced that no strategic advantages which Eisenhower might claim for an advance on Dresden could outweigh the political disadvantages of his not going to Berlin,[45] they asked that the Combined Chiefs of Staff should warn him of the danger to which he might expose the Western Allies by withholding his left.[46]

This request reached Washington at a moment when the United States had, in effect, no government. President Roosevelt died on April 12. Although the British did not know it at the time, for some weeks before his death he was too ill to do a full day's work. The question raised by the British was referred to General Marshall, who did not feel competent to decide an issue of high policy and was Eisenhower's immediate superior in the American military hierarchy. Although there was not much doubt that the Combined Chiefs of Staff ought to have been consulted before the fatal telegram was sent, loyalty to a subordinate impelled Marshall to defend Eisenhower on the ground of "operational necessity." Eisenhower himself, when taxed with a breach of his undertaking to give priority to the armies of the left, replied that he had never promised to go to Berlin and that an advance on Dresden was consistent with his "overall strategic plan." A point he seems to have overlooked was that the plan had in fact been drawn up on the assumption that Berlin was the objective.[47] He could not logically appeal to it as a justification of his strategy if he was not going to Berlin.

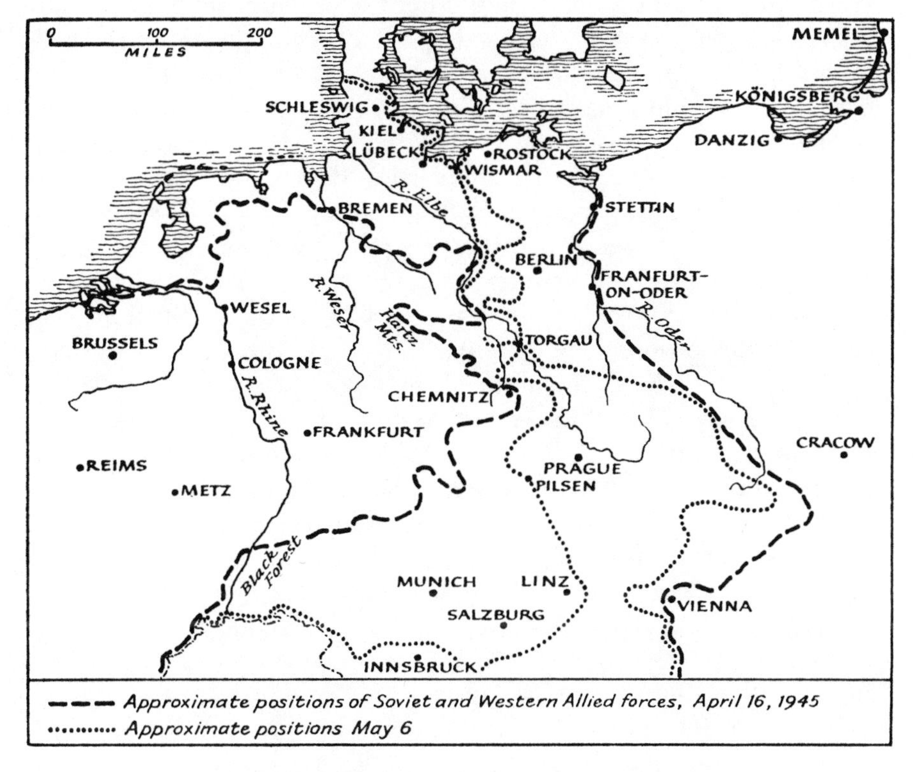

THE CONQUEST OF GERMANY (1944–1945)

In the light of Marshall's submissions, the Combined Chiefs of Staff decided to make no formal protest. Eisenhower did, however, respond to informal criticisms of his proposals by assuring the British, and afterward warning the Russians, that he still intended to push his left at least as far as Schleswig-Holstein. At the same time he refused to give up the plan announced in his telegram.[48] The result was that by the middle of April his forces were dispersed over an extremely wide front, with a ragged center and two long flanks stretching all the way from Chemnitz in Saxony to the Black Forest on his right and from the bend of the Elbe to Antwerp on his left.

The Russians, on the other hand, held a firm front with its right on the Baltic and its left on the Carpathians and were poised to thrust a broad, deep salient toward the heart of Germany.

On April 14 Eisenhower was obliged to confess to the Combined Chiefs of Staff that he could not, after all, sustain simultaneous advances in three directions and had to halt his center while he cleaned up his flanks.[49] On the following day the Russians, who had told him earlier in the month that they did not expect to pass to the next stage of their offensive before the second half of May, announced that they proposed to resume their advance in the central sector without delay.[50] Eisenhower sprang a further surprise in April by suggesting that on making contact with the Russians, his troops should withdraw to the zones they were to occupy after the defeat of Germany. On the initiative of the British, the Combined Chiefs of Staff scotched this proposal by directing him to dispose his forces in accordance with military requirements and without reference to the occupation zones. They did not forbid him to parley with the Russians but added that he must consult them before raising any important issue or making any major change of plan.[51] An existing instruction, which left him free to act as he thought fit in a case of urgent military necessity, was not rescinded.[52]

During the next few weeks Eisenhower took full advantage of these concessions. Doubtless considering that nothing was more important than to avoid any risk of a clash with the Red Army, he kept in close touch with the Soviet authorities, consulted them about his moves, and directed the Third Army, at their request, to advance only a short distance into Czechoslovakia. By April 25, when Russian and American forces met at Torgau on the Elbe, the Russians had Berlin at their mercy. Farther north the British crossed the Elbe on April 29, took Lübeck on May 2, and on the same day deprived the Russians of any pretext for an advance into Denmark by reaching the Baltic coast at Wismar a few hours ahead of them. On May 4, some seventy-two hours before the German Supreme Command tendered its formal submission at Rheims, Montgomery accepted at Lüneburg the surrender of the whole of the surviving German forces in Holland, Denmark, Schleswig-Holstein, northwest Germany, and the islands off Germany's North Sea coast.

In the Pacific theater, the Americans made much better progress in 1944 and 1945 than in 1942 or 1943. From the point of view of Allied strategy as a whole, a serious disadvantage of operations conducted on a vast scale in a remote theater was, however, that they made heavy demands on resources sometimes urgently needed in other theaters. By the summer of 1944 the United States Navy had at its disposal about eight times as many vessels of all classes as in 1942.[53] Since Britain, too, had a powerful navy, the Allies were not short of warships. On the other hand, they were sometimes hard put to find the assault craft needed to conduct simultaneous offensives in the Pacific, the Far East, the Mediterranean, and northwest Europe. They also faced the problem of finding the merchant shipping needed to supply their armies throughout the world without reducing the flow of food and raw materials to the United Kingdom below the danger level. On this problem was superimposed, as the war in Europe drew toward its close, that of feeding the inhabitants of liberated countries.

In the early part of 1944 Nimitz advanced with some 50,000 troops and a fleet of nearly 300 warships, transports, and auxiliaries to the Marshall Islands, which he captured by the end of February at a relatively low cost. In the course of naval and air operations conducted in support of the assault on the Marshall Islands 137,000 tons of Japanese merchant shipping were sunk and about 270 Japanese aircraft destroyed. Meanwhile, MacArthur, still using a high proportion of Australian troops, continued his operations in New Guinea and gained a firm foothold in the Bismarck archipelago. The ultimate effect of these and other operations in the southwest Pacific was that roughly 140,000 Japanese troops and disembarked seamen at Rabaul and elsewhere, including some 30,000 still in the northern Solomons, were cut off from the main body of Japan's armed forces.

On March 12 the American Chiefs of Staff, encouraged by reports that there were few Japanese in the western part of the Bismarck archipelago, agreed with MacArthur that he and Nimitz should be given new directives. MacArthur was to hasten the development of a strong naval base in the Admiralty Islands and to make a stage-by-stage advance along the north coast of Dutch New Guinea to the islands between New Guinea and Celebes, mainly for the purpose of establishing bases from which more valuable objectives could be reached.[54] Nimitz, besides giving MacArthur naval and air support, was to aim at capturing the southern islands of the Marianas about the middle of June and the Palau Islands about the middle of September. In November he was to seize Mindanao, in the Philippines, as the prelude to an expedition to Formosa in the early part of 1945. The advance to Formosa was to be made by forces under MacArthur, either directly from Mindanao or by way of Luzon.

The British objected that there was no place in this program for the strong fleet they expected to send to the Pacific within the next twelve months. The American service chiefs replied that Nimitz would not need the services of a strong British fleet before the second half of 1945. The British might, they suggested, use their warships to better purpose in their own Far Eastern theater.[55] The Americans soon made it clear, however, that they were not prepared to release the assault shipping needed for a seaborne expedition in the Bay of Bengal.

The British decided to propose that if their main fleet were not needed in the central Pacific, a Commonwealth fleet of ships drawn from the Royal Navy, the Royal Australian Navy, and the Royal New Zealand Navy should be assembled under a British commander and placed at the disposal of the Americans in MacArthur's area. On September 9 the American Chiefs of Staff accepted a proposal on these lines.[56] However, at the Octagon Conference at Quebec a few days later, Churchill renewed the offer of a British Pacific Fleet to serve under Nimitz. Roosevelt at once accepted it, overruling objections from the manifestly reluctant Admiral King.[57]

The British then pressed on with plans to send to the Pacific during the first half of 1945 a fleet expected to include six large and four smaller carriers and four battleships and to support it with a fleet train which would absorb more than 300,000 tons of shipping. Because the fleet train would enable the fleet to work from bases in Australia and the Admiralty Islands, the Australian government undertook to spend large sums on the development of Port Darwin as a first-class naval base and on the dredging of its seaward approaches.[58] In addition, the British proposed to move four divisions to Australia, and to station about a thousand bombers and long-range fighters in the Pacific theater as soon as the war with Germany was over.

As things turned out, Eisenhower's inability to bring his campaign in northwest Europe to a successful conclusion by the end of 1944 made serious inroads on these plans. The British heavy bomber force was still needed in the European theater in 1945. The British Pacific Fleet had to be reduced to a Carrier Task Force of four fleet carriers, two battleships, five cruisers, and some fourteen destroyers, and imports to the United Kingdom had to be cut to the bone so that the shipping needed to form a fleet train even on a reduced scale could be released. The British Carrier Task Force completed its assembly in Australian waters about the end of February. Less one carrier which remained temporarily at Sydney, it reported to Nimitz on March 15. Four days later it moved to Ulithi in the Caroline Islands.

In the meantime MacArthur challenged the decision of the American Chiefs of Staff to make Formosa the next major objective after Mindanao. He argued not only that the United States was under a moral obligation to liberate the whole of the Philippines as soon as possible, but also that Luzon was more valuable than Formosa as a base for future operations against Japan. Although Nimitz admitted later that MacArthur was right,[59] at the time he and King believed that Formosa should be captured with the least possible delay as a stepping-stone to the coast of China.

When President Roosevelt visited Hawaii in the summer of 1944 for a series of talks with senior officers, MacArthur succeeded in convincing him that attempts ought to be made to drive the Japanese from Leyte and Luzon at an early stage. Nimitz and MacArthur afterward agreed to propose not that Leyte should be captured after the fall of Mindanao, but that it should replace Mindanao as their first major objective after the completion of current operations brought their forces together on a line from the Palaus on the right to the islands between New Guinea and the Celebes on the left. Proposals in that sense were submitted to the Combined Chiefs of Staff at the Octagon Conference in the middle of September and were accepted with little more than an hour's delay.[60] This decision did not rule out a subsequent advance to Formosa and hence did not end the controversy. Early in October the American Chiefs of Staff agreed, however, that Luzon, not Formosa, should be the next step after Leyte. Thrusts toward Japan would then be made by way of Iwo Jima in the Volcano Islands on the right and the Ryukyu Islands on the left, but plans were still to be drawn up for a landing on the coast of China north of Formosa. An invasion of the Japanese homeland was expected to follow in the winter of 1945–46.

While these controversies were in progress, Nimitz assembled for the capture of the Marianas 14 battleships, 7 large and 8 smaller aircraft carriers, 10 escort carriers, 24 cruisers, about 140 destroyers and escort vessels, and more than 50 transports and supply ships carrying about 130,000 marines and soldiers and their equipment and supplies. As usual, Nimitz remained ashore at Pearl Harbor. Vice Admiral Raymond A. Spruance commanded the expedition while Admiral Halsey, who had reported to Pearl Harbor after completing his task in the South Pacific, prepared with a separate staff for the next stage of the offensive. The seven large and eight smaller carriers, with more than 900 aircraft, formed with other warships a Fast Carrier Force under Vice Admiral Marc A. Mitscher.

The Japanese had about 60,000 troops and disembarked seamen in the three largest islands of the Marianas but regarded the defense of the group as essentially a naval problem. They relied chiefly on land-based naval aircraft and on the prompt arrival of a powerful fleet from Tawitawi, between Borneo and the Philippines. Many of their land-based aircraft were, however, destroyed in preliminary attacks by Mitscher's carrier-borne bombers. Others were sent south about the beginning of June to take part in an attempt to halt MacArthur's progress toward the western extremity of New Guinea. They were recalled when the gravity of the threat to the Marianas became apparent, but few survived the return flight. Altogether, fewer than 100 land-based aircraft were available in the middle of June to supplement some 470 carrier-borne aircraft. Furthermore, the Japanese were outnumbered not only in carriers, but also in battleships, cruisers, and destroyers.

The Americans began to land in Saipan on June 15. On the following day Vice Admiral Jisaburo Ozawa, commanding the Japanese First Mobile Fleet from Tawitawi, made rendezvous east of the Philippines with a battleship squadron which had moved south earlier in the month. Admiral Spruance, warned that a Japanese fleet was approaching and that it included carriers, arranged to complete his landings in Saipan with the least possible delay, send his transports and supply ships out of harm's way as soon as essential equipment and supplies had been unloaded, and postpone landings elsewhere until the naval battle was over. His plan was that Mitscher should first knock out Ozawa's carriers and disable or delay his battleships and cruisers, which would then be finished off by a battle fleet to be formed from ships used at the beginning of the battle to cover Mitscher's carriers.

By the evening of June 18 Ozawa was less than 500 miles west of Guam. Spruance forbade Mitscher to close with him during the night at the cost of leaving the western approaches to Saipan uncovered. Mitscher was unable, therefore, to get within striking distance of Ozawa's carriers on the following day, but a good performance by his radar helped him punish the Japanese carrier-borne aircraft severely when they took advantage of their longer range to attack his own carriers, and he destroyed most of the remaining Japanese land-based aircraft by making further attacks on airfields. Two carriers were sunk by American submarines.

Ozawa, assuming that many of the aircraft which failed to return to his carriers had landed safely in Guam, was not aware of the full extent of his losses. He withdrew to the northwest, intending to make rendezvous with his tankers and renew the engagement when he had refueled. About 200 of Mitscher's aircraft came up with him just as the sun was touching the horizon on June 20. In twenty minutes they sank one of his carriers, damaged four, and put all but 35 of his surviving aircraft out of action.

Thus ended the two-day Battle of the Philippine Sea. Besides giving the Americans control of the approaches to the Marianas, it crippled the Japanese carrier fleet for the rest of the war. The aircraft lost could be replaced with little delay, but not their crews. Furthermore, by completing the capture of Saipan on July 9, the Americans gained a much more convenient base for the long-range bombing of Japan than the airfields near Calcutta and in China which they had begun to use in June.

Eight days after the fall of Saipan, Tojo and his colleagues were forced by pressure from a committee of elder statesmen to resign. Advocates of a negotiated peace urged a respected naval officer, Admiral Mitsumasa Yonai, to form a government, but he declined to do so. General Kuniaki Koiso, who spoke for the army, then became Prime Minister, but a place was found for Yonai, making him, in effect, Vice-Premier.

In September Nimitz and MacArthur duly assaulted the Palau Islands and the island of Morotai, northwest of New Guinea. Nimitz also seized Ulithi, in the western Carolines, as a forward base for his main fleet. On October 17 a large American expedition was seen to be approaching Leyte. Admiral Tejiro Toyoda, the Japanese Naval Commander in Chief, then put into effect a plan to lure the American carrier fleet to the north by sending his own weak and partially equipped carrier fleet in that direction and using his battle fleet to destroy the American invasion force. Admiral Halsey fell into the trap to the extent of leaving the San Bernardino Strait, between Luzon and Samar, unguarded at a crucial moment, but the Japanese failed to seize their opportunity of destroying his transports and suffered crippling losses in a series of naval battles known collectively as the Battle of Leyte Gulf. Losing three battleships, one large and three smaller carriers, ten cruisers, and seven destroyers, they were left with six battleships, but without a carrier force or a balanced fleet. In addition, two destroyers which did not accompany the fleet were sunk by air attacks. Halsey lost only one light fleet carrier, two escort carriers, three destroyers or destroyer escorts, one submarine, and one torpedo boat.

On land, a highly controversial decision to defend Leyte to the last ditch cost the Japanese their chances of making a prolonged stand elsewhere in the Philippines. After capturing the small island of Mindoro with ease in the middle of December, the Americans disembarked a powerful force in Luzon in the second week of 1945. MacArthur's troops entered Manila on February 4, just as the Yalta Conference was beginning.

Even so, the Western Allies were still far from satisfied that Japan would be defeated without a desperate struggle. The cost of capturing Saipan had been so high, the battle for Leyte so hard fought, that immense casualties would, it was thought, be incurred when the Japanese homeland was invaded. During the struggle for Leyte the Japanese had introduced a new and disturbing factor by launching so-called kamikaze attacks on warships by airmen willing to give their lives for a hit. At the same time, attempts by long-range bombers from southeast Asia and the Marianas to destroy industrial targets in Japan by delivering precise attacks in daylight had proved so unsuccessful that such attacks were about to be replaced by "area bombing" on the lines of the British air offensive against Germany. Of nine aircraft factories listed by the American Chiefs of Staff for destruction, only one had been severely damaged by the end of January.

The Western Allies were still anxious, therefore, to receive Russian help during the last stage of the war against Japan. The Soviet authorities had already announced, and they confirmed at Yalta, that the strategy they proposed to adopt if and when they entered the Far Eastern war was to assemble in the neighborhood of Lake Baikal about sixty divisions, backed by 1,000,000 tons of military stores which they expected the Western Allies to provide. Besides putting pressure on the Japanese along the northern and eastern frontiers of Manchuria, they would drive a wedge between the Japanese forces in Manchuria and China by sweeping with a highly mobile force from Lake Baikal through Outer and Inner Mongolia toward Peking and Tientsin.

The terms on which the Russians were prepared to carry out this plan were discussed on February 8 at a confidential meeting between Roosevelt and Stalin, in which the British took no part.[61] Three days later the British joined the Americans and the Russians in signing a formal agreement by which the Soviet Union undertook to enter the war against Japan "two or three months after Germany has surrendered and the war in Europe has terminated." In return the Soviet Union was to receive, without question, the Kurile Islands and the part of the Sakhalin Islands hitherto ruled by Japan, the use of Port Arthur as a naval base, recognition of her "pre-eminent interests" in Dairen, and joint control with China of the Chinese Eastern Railway and the South Manchurian Railway. Since the Russo-Japanese Neutrality Pact of 1941 would remain in force until 1946, secrecy was held to be imperative. Roosevelt undertook to obtain Chiang Kai-shek's concurrence,[62] but Chiang was not, in fact, informed until the following June of the terms of the agreement.

Thus the Western powers agreed, in effect, to restore to Russia the dominant naval position in Far Eastern waters of which Japan had deprived her forty years earlier. Churchill, recognizing that his colleagues would not concur without reluctance in so profound a readjustment of the balance of power, took the precaution of warning them before the terms were settled that the cost of Russian participation in the Far Eastern war would be very heavy but must be accepted.[63] Roosevelt, whose judgment may have been impaired by his impending illness, is said to have defended his part in the transaction on the ground that Stalin was "not an imperialist" and that the United States had more in common with Communist China than with colonialist Britain. No appeal to long-term British and American interest could, however, hide the discrepancy between the concessions made to Stalin and the assurance given to Chiang Kai-shek at the Cairo Conference in 1943 that the Western powers aimed at restoring Manchuria to China.

The Yalta Conference ended on February 11. On February 22 the Japanese ambassador in Moscow, Naotake Sato, asked the Soviet Commissar for Foreign Affairs whether Far Eastern questions had been touched upon at Yalta. Molotov replied that they had been "entirely excluded." [64] Six weeks later he warned Sato that the Soviet Union did not propose to renew the Neutrality Pact when it expired in 1946 but added that he would not forget in the meantime that it was still in force.[65]

On February 19 the leading elements of a three-division corps of the United States Marines assaulted Iwo Jima, a small island but important because its three airfields placed Japanese fighters on the direct route for American bombers flying from the Marianas to Tokyo. The island, defended by some 21,000 Japanese in prepared positions connected by tunnels, proved extremely hard to take. Resistance ceased on March 26, but American casualties, naval losses included, exceeded the entire strength of the Japanese garrison.[66]

The capture of Okinawa, in the Ryukyu Islands, proved an even more expensive business. The Americans, expecting heavy opposition from a garrison of unknown strength, assigned three divisions of marines and five of infantry to the task. The defenders, surviving a prolonged naval bombardment preceded by attacks on neighboring islands by British and American carrier-borne aircraft, allowed about 50,000 of the enemy to stream ashore without opposition on April 1 before counterattacking from prepared positions disposed in considerable depth. The battle for Okinawa continued until July and cost the Americans casualties equivalent to more than a quarter of the initial strength of their combatant troops.[67]

These experiences suggested that the capture of the Japanese homeland might cost the Western Allies as many as 1,000,000 casualties. Thus they had a strong incentive to end the war with Japan before November 1, when they were due to invade Kyushu, if they could do so on terms not flagrantly at odds with Roosevelt's boast at Casablanca that "unconditional surrender" would be demanded of their enemies. Since the behavior of the Russians in Rumania and Poland was far from reassuring, they also had an incentive to bring hostilities to a close before Stalin was ready to earn the large reward they had promised him if he went to war with Japan within three months of Germany's defeat. Furthermore, in the light of expert scrutiny of his proposals for an offensive from Lake Baikal, they were not satisfied that he really needed the supplies he had asked them to provide.[68] On the other hand, they did not wish to quarrel openly with the Soviet Union, for they still hoped that she would cooperate with them in the occupation of Germany and in making the United Nations an effective successor to the League of Nations.

Whether Russian participation in the war with Japan was still desirable from the strictly military point of view was a difficult question. Two points were, however, clear. The first was that American progress in the Pacific made it no longer essential that Allied bombers should be stationed in Siberia.[69] The second was that by the late summer the Western Allies might well be in a position to drop at least one atomic bomb on Japan if they wished to do so.[70]

For some years before and after the outbreak of the Second World War, a good deal of attention was paid in a number of countries to the strategic implications of nuclear energy. In Britain, the matter was discussed in governmental circles even before J. D. Cockcroft and E. T. S. Walton, two British disciples of the British-domiciled New Zealander Ernest Rutherford, first experimentally "split the atom" in 1932.[71] In Germany and among German and Austrian scientists who had gone into exile because they feared or disapproved of Hitler, the splitting of the nucleus of the uranium atom by Otto Hahn in 1938 stimulated interest in the possibility of initiating a chain reaction by which a useful amount of energy might be released. In France, the work of Frédéric Joliot-Curie and others focused attention on the possible application of nuclear energy to industrial uses. In the United States, where expatriate scientists such as the Italian Enrico Fermi and the Hungarian-born Leo Szilard made important contributions to the theory and practice of nuclear physics, a group of physicists and mathematicians sought to divert the government from an exclusive preoccupation with peaceful applications by persuading their veteran colleague Albert Einstein to warn the President in 1939 of the danger that Hitler might be first in the field with atomic weapons.

The problem of producing from uranium a nuclear weapon light and small enough to be carried in an aircraft and used as a bomb was, however, widely thought to be unsolvable until shortly after the outbreak of war, when Rudolf Peierls and Otto Frisch, two German-born scientists working for the British, suggested that it might be solved if useful quantities of the isotope uranium 235 could be extracted from commercial uranium, which consists essentially of uranium 234, uranium 235, and uranium 238, but contains only 1 part of uranium 235 to 140 parts of uranium 238. Early in 1940 Franz Simon, a German-born Jewish physicist who had settled in England in 1933, proposed a method by which this might be done. In the following year, after a committee of experts had reported that there was a reasonable chance that atomic bombs could be produced before the end of the war,[72] the British government set up a pilot plant for the production of nuclear explosives at Rhydymwyn in North Wales. This was intended as the precursor of a larger establishment to be set up in Canada, where commercial uranium was readily available.

As a result of Sir Henry Tizard's visit to the United States and reciprocal visits by American scientists to the United Kingdom, the Americans were informed in due course of the Peierls-Frisch calculations and the Simon process. American experts, impressed by the progress made in Britain at a time when the British could devote only a small proportion of their scientific manpower to nuclear projects, concluded that progress would be still more rapid if the venture were backed by the resources of the United States. In the summer of 1942 Roosevelt and Churchill agreed that the development of nuclear weapons should be continued as a joint Anglo-American enterprise, chiefly in the United States and Canada, on the understanding that neither Britain nor the United States should use such weapons against a third party except by mutual consent.[73]

During the Quadrant Conference at Quebec in August, 1943, Churchill complained to the President that apparently some of the American scientists and officials assigned to the project had not been told that it was a joint one and that they had withheld information from their British colleagues. The informal understanding of the previous summer was then replaced by a formal agreement between the British and United States governments.[74] Brigadier General Leslie R.

Groves, the officer charged by the American authorities with responsibility for all work done on the project in the United States, admitted after the war that nonetheless his policy at all times was to tell the British as little as he could.[75]

The Simon process relied on the filtering effect of a complex of sieves, or membranes. Groves had so little success with it that eventually he decided to try a method of thermal diffusion rejected as impractical by Frisch in 1939 but advocated by the distinguished American physicist Philip H. Abelson. This yielded only a slightly enriched form of uranium which needed further treatment before a satisfactory product was obtained. However, by a combination of methods his team of American, British, and refugee scientists and technologists succeeded in producing enough fissile material by the summer of 1945 to make three bombs. One contained uranium 235. The others contained plutonium, an artificial element obtained by a process developed with remarkable success in the United States. The experimental detonation of one of the plutonium bombs in New Mexico on July 16 left the Allies with one uranium bomb and one plutonium bomb to drop on Japan if they agreed to do so.

In the meantime, a swift end to the war had become for the Japanese an imperative need. By the beginning of 1945 the carrying capacity of their merchant fleet had declined by more than half since 1941.[76] Area attacks on their towns and cities in the late winter and early spring did immense damage. A growing shortage of aviation fuel threatened to make matters still worse by grounding their defensive fighters. For all practical purposes, the naval battles of the Philippine Sea and Leyte Gulf ended their hopes of turning the tables on their opponents by gaining a spectacular success at sea. Finally, the fall of Rangoon made it clear that their expulsion from the whole of southeast Asia could only be a matter of time.

On April 4 Koiso, discredited by the loss of Iwo Jima and repeated air attacks on the homeland, fell from office. He was succeeded by Admiral Baron K. Suzuki, president of the Privy Council. The seventy-nine-year-old Suzuki soon found that his mission was not to continue the war but to end it. A tentative request had already been made to the Swedish minister in Tokyo to act as mediator between Japan and the Allies.[77] Shigenori Togo, who returned to his old post at the Foreign Ministry when Suzuki came to power, had always advocated friendship with the Soviet Union and preferred to look to Moscow. On June 18 the Supreme War Council agreed that Japan should ask for peace on terms which allowed the emperor to keep his throne and that the Russians should be invited to act as mediators.[78] With the active concurrence of the emperor, Togo then made strenuous attempts to persuade the Soviet government to receive a special envoy from the imperial court. Sato reported on July 13 that he had been unable to arrange an interview with Molotov but had told the Deputy Commissar for Foreign Affairs that his government proposed to send Prince Konoye to Moscow and that Japan wished to make peace but not to surrender without conditions.[79]

Meanwhile, Field Marshal Sir Henry Maitland Wilson, head of the British Joint Staff Mission in Washington and a member of the Anglo-American Combined Policy Committee on Atomic Affairs, had advised the British government that the Americans proposed to drop an atomic bomb on Japan "some time in August." Apparently taking the government's assent for granted, he asked in the last week of April how he should convey it to the American authorities.[80] After a delay which seems to have been caused by preoccupations arising from the German collapse, he received a reply to the effect that the British government did not object in principle to the American proposal, but regarded the matter as one which Roosevelt's successor, President Harry S. Truman, might wish to discuss with Churchill at the Potsdam Conference in July.

Whether Japan should be subjected to nuclear bombing was thus regarded on both sides of the Atlantic as primarily a question for the Americans, even though they were not free to give an affirmative answer without British assent. Great weight attached, therefore, to a report submitted on June 1 by an all-American policy committee headed by Henry L. Stimson, the veteran Secretary of War. The report recommended that "the bomb" should be used against Japan as soon as possible and that it should be dropped, without prior warning of its nature, on a military objective surrounded by or adjacent to houses or other buildings.[81]

Probably in the light of an appeal circulated by a number of eminent scientists some time in June, Stimson added on July 2 that the Japanese ought, in his opinion, to be given a chance to surrender before extreme measures were taken against them. They should be told that "unconditional surrender" did not mean that they would be enslaved or deprived of the means of existence or that their country would be permanently occupied. They might also be told that they would be allowed to retain their existing form of government if they wished to do so. At the same time, they should be warned that refusal to surrender would entail "inevitable and complete destruction." [82]

During the Potsdam Conference Stalin told Truman and Churchill, at separate interviews, of the Japanese approach. He added that, the communication made by Sato contained no concrete proposals and that therefore the Soviet government had taken no action on it. Since the Americans had intercepted and deciphered Togo's instructions to Sato,[83] most of this was stale news. The most interesting feature of Stalin's disclosure was the light it threw on his own attitude to the prospect of an early peace. Churchill, feeling that the Western Allies ought not to brush aside an opportunity of coming to terms with Japan even though the Russians might wish them to do so, ventured to remind Truman that the cost of forcing unconditional surrender on the Japanese might be very heavy. He received the impression that the Americans would be willing to interpret Roosevelt's phrase in a liberal sense.[84]

Truman and Churchill also discussed the atomic bomb. On Churchill's advice, Truman told Stalin on July 24 that the Western Allies had a new weapon of extraordinary power but gave no details.[85] Stalin showed no more than a polite interest and "never asked a question," probably because he knew from his secret sources what was brewing. An American bomber unit specially trained for the nuclear bombing of Japan had arrived at Tinian in the Marianas, and final preparations for its first operational mission were sanctioned about the time when Truman made his disclosure to Stalin. The statesmen had, however, agreed some days earlier that no executive order for the dropping of the first bomb should be issued until the Japanese had been given a warning on the lines proposed by Stimson. Accordingly the Western Allies issued late on July 26 a declaration to the effect that they did not intend to enslave the Japanese, destroy their nationhood or permanently occupy their country, and that Japan would be allowed after the war access to raw materials and eventually to world markets.[86] On the other hand, refusal to surrender would bring retribution of a nature not precisely stated.

Unhappily the chances that the Potsdam Declaration would induce the Japanese to throw in their hand were greatly reduced by two omissions. In the first place, no reference was made in the declaration to the future status of the emperor, although the Allies were not unwilling that he should remain on his throne and were strongly advised by Stimson to make that clear.[87] Second, after going to all the trouble of drafting the declaration and submitting it to Chiang Kai-shek for his approval, they robbed it of much of its force by broadcasting it to the world, as if it were a mere propagandist statement of war aims, without first transmitting it to the Japanese government through a neutral intermediary whom they could trust. They did send a copy to Moscow, but the Soviet Union was not, as they well knew, genuinely neutral. The result was that the Japanese authorities, who did not share Truman's and Churchill's knowledge of Stalin's duplicity, learned of the declaration only from their monitoring service. Not unreasonably, they decided to do nothing about it until they received either a formal communication from its sponsors through diplomatic channels or an answer to their request to be allowed to send a special envoy to Moscow.

No word having come from Japan when the Potsdam Conference broke up on August 2, Truman authorized the use of nuclear bombs against Japan as soon as the weather was good enough for visual bombing. The Americans were aware that the production of radioactive dust by the explosion of a nuclear bomb might be held to contravene the spirit of a voluntary undertaking by the Western Allies not to resort to "chemical warfare" unless other nations did so. They arranged, therefore, that the uranium bomb released from 30,000 feet above Hiroshima on August 6 should be fused to explode some time before it reached the ground. They believed that this would not only ensure the maximum blast effect but would also reduce unwanted side effects to a minimum.[88]

As things turned out, rather fewer people were killed outright by the Hiroshima bomb than had died on a night in the previous March when Tokyo was attacked by a few hundred aircraft armed with high-explosive and incendiary bombs.[89] On the other hand, the precautions taken by the Americans did not prevent the Hiroshima bomb from condemning a number of survivors to a lingering death. Thus the Western Allies exposed themselves to a charge not only of ruthlessly slaughtering some tens of thousands of fellow creatures whose leaders were known to be anxious to make peace, but also of accomplishing nothing they could not have accomplished without recourse to nuclear weapons, except to add a new barbarism to the art of war and a new terror to existence.

On the day after the attack on Hiroshima, the emperor told Togo that he ought to make peace at once, without arguing about terms.[90] In Moscow, Sato had been eagerly awaiting Molotov's return from Potsdam but was unable to see him before the late afternoon of August 8. Molotov, doubtless reflecting that three months less one day had elapsed since the formal surrender of Germany, cut short his greetings by announcing that the Soviet Union would be at war with Japan with effect from the following morning.[91] Since it was already nearly midnight by Far Eastern time, only a few hours were left before Soviet troops poured into Manchuria and northern China. Almost simultaneously, a B-29 which had left Tinian during the night dropped the remaining plutonium bomb on Nagasaki after making three abortive runs over its primary target at Kojura.

The Japanese, recognizing at last that their faith in Russian goodwill had been misplaced, then addressed themselves to Washington through the Swiss government. On August 14, after some days of negotiation, punctuated by disagreements in high places and a short-lived uprising by a group of army officers, they agreed to lay down their arms. Their surrender, like that of the Germans, was described as unconditional, but some doubt attaches to the relevance of this term in the context of modern war. While in form the Japanese submitted themselves wholly to the will of the victors, in intention they doubtless relied on the Potsdam Declaration and on the knowledge that the British and the Americans, no matter what they might do or say at moments of stress, would never agree in cold blood that a whole nation should be punished for the sins of a few. Since the emperor was allowed to retain his throne, in practice the terms granted by the Allies were barely distinguishable from those on which Togo and probably most of his colleagues would have been glad to negotiate at almost any time since the middle of June.[92]

15

The "Special Relationship"

IN the spring and summer of 1945 the Western Allies celebrated their victories over Germany and Japan. When the celebrations were over, when the mists of illusion had rolled away, they looked upon a world divided and confused by conflicts of interest and sentiment for which it was hard to find a parallel in European history since the seventeenth century. Poland and the countries of the Danube basin had escaped the tyranny of Hitler only to fall beneath the sway of Russia. In the Far East, the economic and political bankruptcy of Nationalist China and the inability of the Western European powers to perform in recent years their cherished role as evangelists of material progress had created a fertile field for the dissemination of Communist doctrines, which in turn conflicted with nationalist aspirations stimulated by the failure of the Japanese to impose a new order on Greater East Asia. At the same time, the cost of maintaining and equipping fleets, armies, and air forces had increased so enormously since 1939 that only countries as rich in raw materials and manpower as the Soviet Union and the United States could henceforth be regarded as first-class powers. Few nations, it seemed in the early postwar years, could expect to preserve even the semblance of independence unless they either came to terms with one or other of those powers or somehow managed to come to terms with both.

In these circumstances the advent to power in Britain of Socialist statesmen traditionally suspicious of the American brand of capitalism did not prevent the British from drawing closer to the United States during the early postwar years by accepting a large American loan at a low rate of interest. Partly on grounds of financial and military expediency, partly in deference to political theories which reflected, to some extent, American distrust of paternal government, the British cut short their attempt to prepare the inhabitants of British India for responsible self-government by acquiescing in the creation of the separate, independent, and mutually antagonistic Hindu and Moslem states of India and Pakistan. Hailed by some Englishmen as a triumph for the principles of liberty and self-determination but regarded by others as a shameful abdication of responsibility, the lowering of the British flag and the withdrawal of British troops from the Indian subcontinent were followed, as indeed was expected, by riots and massacres on a vast scale. The effect, or at any rate the apparent effect, on India's economy, too, was far from reassuring. In 1938 the value of exports from British India had exceeded the value of imports by more than 100,000,000 rupees. In 1951 India and Pakistan had, between them, an adverse trade balance of nearly 2,000 million rupees.

The withdrawal from India resulted in some saving of troops, but this was more than offset by other needs. A substantial army of occupation had to be maintained in Germany; troops were needed to deal with uprisings, largely Communist-inspired, in Malaya and elsewhere. At a time when the British were striving to reduce their overseas commitments by promising early independence to colonies on which they had hitherto proposed to confer the privilege of self-government only after a long period of transition, they found themselves compelled not only to spend more on their armed forces than ever before in time of peace, but also to accept the disadvantages of compulsory military service.

In the United States the comfortable belief that the intransigence shown by the Russians during the last few months of the war was only the product of a passing mood was not abandoned without a struggle. George Kennan, the United States chargé d'affaires in Moscow, dealt a shrewd blow to such hopes when, early in 1946, he described the framers of Soviet policy, in a long cable to the State Department, as utterly convinced that there could be no lasting agreement between Russia and the United States and that the fabric of American capitalist society ought to be disrupted.[1] Churchill, visiting the United States no longer as Prime Minister but as leader of His Majesty's opposition, made a similar diagnosis when he remarked a few days later that an "iron curtain" had descended across Europe. Adding that the Soviet leaders did not, in his opinion, want war but that they did desire "the fruits of war and the indefinite expansion of their power and doctrines," he proposed a remedy in the shape of full military collaboration between Britain and the United States.

The sequel was the forging by President Truman and his successors of a network of alliances throughout the world. Largely on the initiative of General Marshall, who accepted the post of Secretary of State in 1947, the United States government offered massive aid to countries willing to stay outside the Russian orbit. Notwithstanding attempts by Truman's critics to represent this policy as the fruit of illicit passages between Wall Street and Downing Street, only four votes were cast in the Senate against a measure which authorized the government to associate itself with arrangements concerted between nations concerned to arrest the march of Communism.

It was therefore under the approving eye of the United States government that Britain, France, Belgium, Holland, and Luxembourg concluded in 1948 a defensive alliance clearly aimed at Russia. The Russians retaliated by cutting land communications between Berlin and the British, French, and American occupation zones in western Germany. Their offers of food and fuel failed, however, to persuade the inhabitants of West Berlin to accept incorporation in the Russian Zone, and they could not prevent the Western powers from supplying West Berlin by air or from proclaiming their solidarity by concluding at Washington the far-reaching pact of mutual assistance called the North Atlantic Treaty.

Thus the Russians lost, as they admitted, the first round of their cold war with the West. The Western powers celebrated their victory by welding their occupation zones into the West German Federal Republic.

Truman's repudiation of isolationism led to the recognition on both sides of the Atlantic that a "special relationship" existed between Britain and the United States. The term was appropriate for two reasons. In the first place, Britain was believed, when the North Atlantic Treaty was signed in the spring of 1949, to be the only power apart from the United States which possessed atomic bombs, Clement Attlee's Socialist government having decided soon after the war that Britain should manufacture nuclear weapons independently of the United States. Second, when the North Atlantic Treaty powers agreed in principle toward the end of 1950 that the West German Federal Republic should make a contribution to their land forces, great difficulty was experienced in reconciling the French to the practical details of the scheme until the British persuaded them to withdraw their objections by undertaking to maintain four divisions and a tactical air force in Continental Europe until the end of the twentieth century. The French thus received, after the lapse of more than a generation, the promise of lasting British support for which they had been angling since the end of the First World War.

How much the relatively small land and air forces maintained in Western Europe by the North Atlantic Treaty powers could do to stop the Russians from sweeping to the Channel coast if they had a mind to do so was a question often asked in the 1950's and later. Everyone who asked it knew, however, that the Western powers relied ultimately not on these forces but on the belief that the Russians would shrink from a course of action which might expose them to a counterattack with nuclear weapons.

How long the West could hope to retain a monopoly of such weapons was another question. It was answered in the autumn of 1949, when the American authorities announced that the Russians were known to have made and tested an atomic bomb. According to a well-informed source, the news came as a shock to many American scientists, who had assumed that "we had at least five more years of grace." [2] If that is so, the scientists concerned would seem to have been unduly complacent. The Russians, who numbered among their nuclear physicists such men as Pyotr Kapitza, considered by Rutherford his most brilliant pupil, were scarcely likely to be as much as nine years behind the West.

Meanwhile, a conflict had arisen in the United States between service chiefs who urged the government to sanction the development of a hydrogen bomb more powerful by far than any nuclear weapon yet produced and a body of civilian advisers who were unanimously of the opinion that the development and construction of such a weapon would be uneconomic and would damage the moral standing of the United States. Early in 1950 President Truman was informed that Klaus Fuchs, a German-born scientist working for the British, had imparted his very considerable knowledge of the project to the Russians. A few days later he gave orders that the hydrogen bomb should be developed and constructed as rapidly as possible. Later the British in turn decided to add the hydrogen bomb to their armory.

In the following summer the Communist rulers of North Korea invaded non-Communist South Korea with six divisions of the North Korean People's Army supported by Russian tanks and aircraft. The Americans, convinced that Communism ought to be fought wherever it became belligerent, persuaded the Security Council of the United Nations to agree, at a meeting not attended by any Russian delegate, that the North Koreans should be made to withdraw. General MacArthur, the American Commander in Chief in the Far East, had only a few lightly supported infantry companies within reach of the battlefield, but large reinforcements were sent from the United States. Other members of the United Nations were invited to make contributions, and some did so; but only the British sent much more than a token force. Even so, their contribution was very much smaller than that made by the Americans.

Later in the year Chinese Communist forces joined the North Koreans and inflicted a staggering tactical defeat on the United States Eighth Army. MacArthur asked permission to extend the war to China, and on November 30 President Truman was understood to imply at a press conference that the United States government might, in certain circumstances, authorize him to "use the atomic bomb at his own discretion." [3] The British, who were not in favor of any extension of the war and indeed believed that Communist China should be admitted to the United Nations, voiced strong objections. A long controversy culminated in open defiance by MacArthur of his government's policy. MacArthur was then relieved of his command. After further delay a cease-fire was negotiated, largely on the initiative of the Russians. By the time the Korean War ended in 1953 it had cost the United States more than 140,000 casualties and her allies about 17,000.[4] Besides lowering the standing of the United States in the eyes of nations not invincibly hostile to the Communist governments of Russia and China, the war exposed American service chiefs to the reproach that their preoccupation with nuclear weapons had deprived their country of the means of meeting its obligations to allies without subjecting the world to the threat of total war.

In the early winter of 1952 the Americans tested at Eniwetok, in the Marshall Islands, an experimental version of the hydrogen bomb, too large and too unwieldy to be carried in an aircraft. The Russians responded to the news that the test had been successful by claiming that they already had hydrogen bombs suitable for military use. The testing of a still more potent thermonuclear weapon in 1954 resulted in a heavy fall of radioactive dust and led to predictions that further tests in similar conditions would "poison life at the source for all mankind" within a quarter of a century. The sequel was an agreement between the powers possessing nuclear weapons that any further tests should be made below the surface of the earth. The development by the Western powers and the Russians of such immensely powerful and dangerous devices also led to the conclusion that both sides had provided themselves with weapons they would never dare use and that total war had therefore become improbable.

No agreement to abstain from the development and production of such weapons was, however, reached. On the contrary, much care was lavished, on both sides of the Iron Curtain, on the development of long-range ballistic missiles with nuclear warheads. The introduction of such missiles, and the consequent disappearance of the bomb-carrying aircraft, within ten years or so had been predicted in Britain at the end of the Second World War. Consideration had also been given at that time to the production of antimissile missiles capable of destroying long-range missiles before they reached their destinations. The vast cost and immense complexity of such projects made progress slow. Moreover, the intercontinental ballistic missile had yet to be perfected when the introduction of nuclear-powered submarines armed with medium-range rockets posed new problems.

The fact remained that no nuclear weapon had been used in war since 1945. The Americans, not only when they faced a setback in Korea but also in 1962 when the Russians threatened their security by proposing to establish missile bases in Cuba, were tempted almost to the verge of the abyss. On both occasions they stopped short of calamity, and on both occasions the British exerted their influence on the side of caution. The Cuban crisis was resolved precisely because neither the Americans nor the Russians were prepared, when they saw how much was at stake, to risk certain and perhaps intolerable losses for the sake of doubtful gains. The experience did not cause either side to relax its vigilance, but it did prompt the statesmen on both sides to ask themselves whether any circumstances could arise in which they would not think it better to negotiate than to fight.

For the British neither their own possession of atomic weapons nor the nuclear stalemate between the United States and the Soviet Union solved the problem of safeguarding the trade routes and sources of supply on which they still depended. On the contrary, the reluctance of the great powers to embark on total war made it all the easier for lesser nations to engage in limited wars or acts of lawlessness which threatened British interests. In 1951 a weak Persian government defied its contractual obligations by seizing the Anglo-Persian Oil Company's refinery at Abadan. The British government was, for all practical purposes, powerless to defend the company's interests by the threat of force, since it could not have done so without risking an international crisis whose effects might have been far worse than those resulting from a temporary stoppage of supplies. The outcome was that the company's assets were transferred to an international consortium in which American interests were prominent, that Persia's exports fell in 1951 to less than half the figure for 1950 and were halved again in 1952, and that the United States government was afterward compelled to pay large subsidies to Persia in order to keep her out of the hands of Russia.

Four years later a league of Arab states financed, with funds drawn largely from royalties paid in advance by American oil companies in Saudi Arabia, a revolt in Algeria, which had long been regarded not as a colony but as part of metropolitan France. Since the American authorities wished to retain the undisturbed use of bases in North Africa, the United States government was constrained to condone the revolt by advising the French to give way. That the French would probably have had to do so in any case did not make the action of the Americans less paradoxical.

Meanwhile, a complex situation had arisen in Egypt. At the beginning of the 1950's the British still had the right, conferred on them by the treaty they had made with the Egyptians in 1936, to maintain a force in the Suez Canal Zone and to strengthen it in case of need.

The Western powers, prompted by the United States government, contemplated replacing the British force by an international one, but their tentative advances were repulsed by the Egyptians. The Egyptians also rejected a proposal that they should themselves assume responsibility for the defense of the Canal Zone, using arms which the British offered to provide.

These negotiations coincided with a financial crisis and other troubles which culminated in the dismissal of King Farouk and his replacement, after a brief interregnum, by Gamal Abdel Nasser, a dictator who commanded wide popular support.

During the winter of 1951–52 the Egyptians obstructed the British troops in the Canal Zone by withholding their labor, refusing customs facilities, blowing up bridges, and attacking road convoys. The British raised the strength of their troops from 10,000 to 80,000 men and imported labor from Cyprus, Malta, and East Africa.

In consultation with the United States government and sometimes under strong pressure from it, the Conservative government which assumed power in Britain in 1951 made repeated attempts during the next few years to reach an understanding with the Egyptians. In 1954 they concluded with Nasser, largely on the initiative of the American Secretary of State John Foster Dulles, an agreement by which all British troops except a few technicians were to withdraw from the Canal Zone twenty months later. The military installations in the Canal Zone would then be maintained by civilian contractors responsible to the Egyptian government, and the British would return only in the event of an "armed attack" on Egypt, Turkey, or a member of the Arab League and if the Egyptians asked them to do so.

Dulles, in pursuance of his policy of forging defensive alliances against Russia, went on to persuade Britain, Iraq, Pakistan, Persia, and Turkey to conclude a treaty known as the Baghdad Pact. To the disappointment and indignation of the British, he announced only when negotiations had reached an advanced stage that the United States would not join the pact, as had hitherto been expected.[5] The pact caused intense alarm in Israel, where it was viewed as an incitement to Arab bellicosity. At the same time it was vigorously condemned by the Egyptians, and by Nasser in particular, as an imperialist maneuver and an affront to the Arab League.

Soon after the signing of Egypt's agreement with Britain, Nasser asked for American arms. On the instructions of the State Department, he was told that he could have them only if he paid for them in dollars and allowed the Americans to establish a military mission in Cairo for the purpose of satisfying themselves that he did not use them for purposes of aggression.[6] He then placed a large order for Russian arms on terms which imposed no restrictions on their use and allowed him to pay for them by exports of cotton.

Dulles described Nasser's arms deal with the Soviet Union as "the most serious development since Korea, if not since World War II." [7] He added that the Russians were, for the first time, making a determined effort to move into the Middle East, where two-thirds of the world's known oil reserves were located.[8] He refused arms to Israel on the ground that Americans would not consent to be parties to an arms race but agreed that the Israelis might be allowed to purchase French aircraft and British aircraft made in Canada.[9]

At the same time, Dulles sought to detach Nasser from the Russians by reviving, in consultation with the British, a long dormant project for the construction of a dam above the existing Nile dam at Aswan. The projected Aswan High Dam would, in the opinion of its sponsors, improve the lot of the Egyptians by increasing the area irrigated by the Nile. It might also help keep Nasser out of mischief. After protracted negotiations, Dulles announced on December 16, 1955, that Britain and the United States would help Egypt build the dam not only by arranging for her to receive a loan from the World Bank and themselves making loans, but also by giving her, as a free grant, the $70,000,000 needed to complete the first stage of the work.

The Russians, who had already tentatively offered to finance the project, then intimated that they would like to take a share if Russian participation were not ruled out by the terms of Egypt's agreement with the West. The State Department made it clear that this would not be allowed.[10]

Apart from discussing the matter with the director of the World Bank, Nasser made no attempt to close with the Anglo-American offer until the following July. He then sent his ambassador, who had been recalled to Cairo, back to Washington with instructions to clinch the deal. In the meantime, he angered Dulles by recognizing Communist China and by letting it be known that the Russians were willing to meet the whole cost of the dam. Dulles told a press conference on July 10 that it was improbable that his deal with Nasser would be completed, but later he made it clear to President Eisenhower and the British that the matter was still open to discussion.[11] The British agreed to leave the decision to him but begged him, if he did refuse the loan, not to do so in a manner which might lead to an explosion of anger on Nasser's part. They should, he suggested, "play it long." [12] The French ambassador in Washington, Maurice Couve de Murville, warned officials of the State Department that a blunt refusal might drive Nasser to seize the Suez Canal, but whether this warning was passed to Dulles is not clear.[13]

The Egyptian ambassador called by appointment on Dulles at the State Department on July 19. Dulles began by mentioning a number of objections to the scheme. The ambassador said that he hoped the offer made by the Americans and the British was not going to be withdrawn. He added, with extraordinary lack of tact, that he had a counteroffer from the Russians in his pocket. Dulles, remarking that in that case Egypt did not need British or American help, then abruptly withdrew the offer.[14] A week later Nasser, after making a violent speech in which he expressed the hope that the Americans would "choke to death on their fury," announced that he had seized the Suez Canal and proposed to use the assets of the Suez Canal Company to promote Egypt's glory.

Sir Anthony Eden, who had succeeded Churchill as Prime Minister on Churchill's retirement, soon made it clear that the British government regarded the seizure of the canal as illegal. Apart from any injury done to the shareholders of the Suez Canal Company, who might or might not receive the compensation promised by Nasser, it seemed to Eden intolerable that a waterway whose international character was established by treaty should pass into the hands of a single power. The nations of Western Europe received at least half their supplies of oil by way of Suez, and the security of the canal was vital to them since the giant oil tankers which afterward enabled them to use other routes without suffering any serious inconvenience did not yet exist.

Nasser's action was discussed in the House of Commons on July 27. Hugh Gaitskell, leader of the Socialist Opposition, described it as "high-handed and totally unjustifiable." [15] On the same day the Cabinet considered the matter in consultation with the Chiefs of Staff. After the meeting Eden sent President Eisenhower a telegram to the effect that he and his colleagues were "all agreed that we cannot allow Nasser to seize control of the canal in this way" and that he had instructed the Chiefs of Staff to prepare a "military plan" for use if force should be needed to "bring Nasser to his senses." [16]

Five days later Dulles arrived in London for discussions with the British and the French. He said that Nasser must be "made to disgorge what he is attempting to swallow." [17] He brought with him a letter from the President. The substance of Eisenhower's message was that while he did not rule out the *eventual* use of force against Nasser, he thought that every attempt ought first to be made to settle the dispute by negotiation. Above all, the powers opposed to Nasser must prove that any action they proposed to take was lawful.[18]

In the course of the discussions Dulles made it clear that he was not in favor of referring the dispute to the United Nations, at any rate until other methods had been tried, since not all member states could be relied upon to agree that pressure should be brought to bear on Nasser. His policy was first to ensure that any action taken against Nasser would be supported by all the powers whose interests were adversely affected by the seizure of the canal. He therefore proposed a conference of maritime nations. Proposals for the administration of the canal by an international board on which the Egyptians would be represented were then put to Nasser but rejected. Dulles next proposed that a further conference of interested powers should be held for the purpose of working out a scheme by which users of the canal would collect tolls and remit what they considered a fair proportion to the Egyptian government.

Meanwhile, the British called up about 20,000 reservists and moved troops, ships, and aircraft to the Mediterranean. The United States government raised no objection to these moves, of which it was informed in general terms. Early in September President Eisenhower warned the British that public opinion in the United States was opposed to the use of force against Nasser in any circumstances, but the British did not take this to mean that the attitude of the United States government had changed since August. In the absence of any precise restatement of American policy by the State Department, they assumed that the President and Dulles still believed that force might have to be used in the last resort.

On September 26 the dispute between Nasser and users of the canal was at last referred to the United Nations by the British and the French on the one hand and the Egyptians on the other. At a conference with British ministers in Paris on the same day, the French pressed for early action against Nasser.

At a further conference on October 16, the British and the French discussed not only their dispute with Nasser, but also what Eden afterward called "the growing menace of hostility by Egypt against Israel." [19] The British had feared that Israel was about to attack their ally Jordan with arms supplied largely by the French. They learned with relief that she was in fact preparing for war with Egypt. In the light of this disclosure they agreed with the French that hostilities between Egypt and Israel might provide an opportunity for British and French forces to prize the canal from Nasser.

War between Egypt and Israel duly began on October 29. On that day Israeli forces crossed the Egyptian frontier and pushed rapidly into the Sinai Peninsula and toward the canal. On the following day the British and French governments called on both belligerents to "stop all warlike action forthwith" and withdraw their forces to a distance of ten miles on either side of the canal. The Egyptians were asked, in addition, to accept a temporary occupation by Anglo-French forces of key positions at Port Said, Ismailia, and Suez. If satisfactory replies were not received within twelve hours, France and the United Kingdom would intervene in such strength as might be needed to secure compliance.[20]

The circumstances in which these demands were made were not propitious. Britain's gold reserves had been falling for some weeks as a result of heavy speculation against sterling. Public opinion, not only in the United States but in anti-imperialist circles in Britain and throughout the world, had moved sharply since July against the use of force to unseat Nasser. Above all, there was a serious lack of understanding between Washington and London. Dulles had spoken early in October of differences of outlook between Britain and the United States where "the so-called problem of colonialism" was concerned.[21] He had also disclaimed any intention of "shooting a way through the canal." These remarks were mysterious, as well as ominous, since no one had ever suggested shooting a way through the canal and Dulles had shown in the past that he was aware that the case against Nasser was founded not on any assertion of colonial claims but on international rights created by treaty. Nevertheless, the British believed that the understanding that force might have to be used in the last resort still held good. Conversely, Dulles and the

President were still confident—as the violence of their subsequent reaction showed—that the British and the French would make no major move without consulting them.

At a meeting of the Security Council of the United Nations on October 30, the Americans proposed a motion which, in effect, condemned the Israelis as aggressors for their part in the war with Egypt. This was vetoed by the British and the French. Later in the day the President and Dulles learned of the notes delivered to the Israelis and the Egyptians by the British and French governments. Both responded to the news with an intense anger which testified to their extreme astonishment. Dulles found it hard to believe that the British and the French had permitted themselves to act without consulting him.[22]

The Israelis accepted the ultimatum but resumed hostilities when they learned that the Egyptians had rejected it. Anglo-French intervention began on October 31 with attacks on airfields. These soon gave British and French aircraft complete mastery of the air. On November 5, three days after the Israelis had completed their occupation of the Sinai Peninsula, British and French troops disembarked near Port Said. Meanwhile, the General Assembly of the United Nations adopted, at an emergency session on November 1, a motion framed by Dulles which called on the British, the French, and the Israelis to cease fire. Against the background of threats by the Russians to use long-range rockets against the British and the French if they remained intransigent, the United Nations agreed on November 4 to send an international force to Egypt. At midnight on November 5 the Allied Force Commander received orders to cease fire on the ground that hostilities between the Egyptians and the Israelis were over.

Thus ended the ill-starred attempt of the British and the French to wage war without first making sure that they had, if not the approval, at least the tacit assent of the United States. Eden, shaken in health, soon laid down his office. It remained for his successors to patch up relations between the Lion and the Eagle and to resume, in cooperation with the Americans, the search for a means of peaceful coexistence with the Bear.

Appendix I

THE OIL OF THE MIDDLE EAST AS A FACTOR IN BRITISH MILITARY POLICY, 1914–1938

The Background

In the summer of 1917 and later, the Allied governments were accused by their critics at home and abroad of prolonging the war in the interests of British imperialism, and the British in particular of "fighting for the oil wells of Mesopotamia." At that time there were, in fact, no commercially productive oil wells in Mesopotamia or elsewhere in the Ottoman Empire, and no oil had yet been produced in commercial quantities in those territories. Until some years after the First World War the only commercially productive oil installations in what is now called the Middle East were those operated by the British-controlled Anglo-Persian Oil Company in western Persia.

To trace the antecedents of the Anglo-Persian Oil Company, it is necessary to go back to 1901, when the Shah of Persia granted a concession for sixty years to William Knox d'Arcy, a London solicitor who had made a fortune from Australian gold mines. It covered the whole of Persia except the northern provinces, where Russian influence was paramount.

Attempts by D'Arcy and his associates to exploit the concession involved heavy outlay and at first brought little or no return. At the end of about five years, when funds were getting low, help was obtained from the Burmah Oil Company, partly through the good offices of the Admiralty, which was interested in Persia as a possible source of fuel for its new oil-burning ships. The only other sources outside the New World were in Russia, Rumania, Burma, and the Far East.

In 1908, when drilling was about to stop because once again funds were approaching exhaustion, a fantastic strike was made at Masjid-i-Sulaiman, the site of an ancient fire temple in the midst of an otherwise unproductive waste. In the following year the Anglo-Persian Oil Company was formed with a capital of £2,000,000. Besides developing the wells at Masjid-i-Sulaiman and building an up-to-date refinery at Abadan, both on Persian soil, the company constructed a pipeline to the port of Basra, in Turkish territory. By 1914 production was of the order of a quarter of a million tons a year. It increased fourfold during the next four years.

On the eve of the war the British government acquired a 51 percent holding in the Anglo-Persian Oil Company in return for an investment which doubled the company's capital. The government appointed two directors with the power of veto, to be exercised only in matters of high policy. The largest shareholder apart from the government was the Burmah Oil Company.

On the shores of the Persian Gulf and the Arabian Sea outside Persia, the position on the outbreak of war was that the Sheik of Kuwait, the ruler of Bahrain, the sheiks of the Trucial Coast, and the Sultan of Oman all had undertaken to grant no oil concessions except to a British subject. The influential Ibn Saud, who claimed suzerainty over vast but sparsely inhabited territories in Arabia Deserta and was regarded by the British authorities in India as a more representative figure than Sherif Hussein of Mecca, was under no such obligation. However, the government of India did its best to secure his goodwill, and in 1915 he, too, signed a treaty with the British.

In parts of the Ottoman Empire still effectively under Turkish control, there had long been intense rivalry between British, German, and American interests. Many applications for concessions in these territories had been made to the Turkish government.

The history of these transactions goes back to 1888, when a railway concession was granted to the German-controlled Ottoman Railway Company of Anatolia. Thereupon the grand vizier promised the company or its associates priority with respect to all mineral rights, oil included. No definitive concession followed, but in 1904 the company obtained an option on oil rights for one year, with the prospect of a forty-year concession if oil were found while the option was still in force.

By 1911, at the latest, the Turkish authorities considered that any rights created by this arrangement had lapsed for want of performance. The Deutsche Bank, as successor to the railway company, maintained that £20,000 sterling had been spent on exploration and that it was entitled either to a concession or to compensation.

Rear Admiral Chester Colby, an American citizen representing the Ottoman-American Development Company and sponsored by the New York Chamber of Commerce, was no luckier. In 1909 he obtained a draft concession from the Turkish Ministry of Public Works. This concession seems never to have been ratified. Despite intervention on Colby's behalf by the United States Department of State, the Turkish authorities decided in 1911 that he had no valid claim.

In the same year African and Eastern Concessions Limited was formed with indirect backing from the British government for the purpose (among others) of developing the oil resources of the Ottoman Empire. To secure the cooperation of the Deutsche Bank, the company acquired the bank's worthless oil rights in return for a quarter of its issued capital of £80,000.

In 1912 the company was renamed the Turkish Petroleum Company. The companies or groups which held most of the shares undertook not to interest themselves in the production of oil in the Ottoman Empire except through the parent company.

At a meeting summoned by the British Foreign Office and held in March, 1914, all shareholders in the Turkish Petroleum Company, except one, agreed to a reorganization which involved the doubling of the company's capital and the following distribution of shares:

	£ sterling
Anglo-Persian Oil Company	80,000
Royal Dutch-Shell group	40,000
Deutsche Bank	40,000
	160,000

The dissentient was C. S. Gulbenkian, who had played an important part in the formation of the original company in 1911. He was associated with Royal Dutch-Shell but also held a block of shares in his own right. Since he naturally objected to being squeezed out, it was agreed that, in return for the surrender of his existing shares, he should be allotted a 5 percent holding in the reorganized company but that his 8,000 shares should carry no voting rights. To make this allotment possible, the holdings of the Anglo-Persian Oil Company and Royal Dutch-Shell were each reduced by 4,000 shares.

Having gained his point, Gulbenkian remained on excellent terms with his colleagues and with the British government. His expert knowledge, not only of the oil industry but also of the Ottoman Empire and the idiosyncrasies of its rulers, made him invaluable as a negotiator.

In the following summer, negotiations with the Turkish authorities at last came to a head. On June 28, 1914, the grand vizier agreed in a letter to the British and German ambassadors in Constantinople to lease to the Turkish Petroleum Company, on terms to be decided later, the oil deposits "discovered or to be discovered" in the vilayets of Baghdad and Mosul. These two districts had long been considered by experts among the most promising parts of the Ottoman Empire from an oil prospector's point of view.

On the outbreak of war with Turkey, the company's chances of enforcing the concession became doubtful. Irrespective of the outcome of the war, the validity of the lease was sure to be contested when hostilities were over. Even if the concession could then be revived or renegotiated, a long time seemed likely to elapse before the Turkish Petroleum Company saw any return. The Anglo-Persian Oil Company's installations in Persia, on the other hand, became in wartime an economic and strategic asset of great importance.

Under the Sykes-Picot Agreement between France and Britain, the vilayet of Mosul was included in that part of the future Arab state or group of states which the Allies proposed to treat as a French sphere of influence. The French ambassador in London promised that British oil rights would not be affected. So far as Mosul was concerned, this promise gave the Turkish Petroleum Company some hope of reaching agreement with a future Arab ruler who would, presumably, accept guidance from the French, but the terms on which a new concession might be granted remained uncertain.

Gulbenkian suggested that the problem might become simpler if the French interested themselves in the oil project by acquiring the Deutsche Bank's shares, which the British government had handed to the Custodian of Enemy Property. The outcome was a long correspondence between Walter Long, the British Colonial Secretary, and Henri Bérenger of the French Foreign Ministry. Eventually it was agreed that the Deutsche Bank's interest should be acquired by a French company in which the government held 35 percent of the shares and 40 percent of the voting rights. Mosul would not, however, fall within the French sphere of influence but would be allotted, with Baghdad, Basra, and the adjacent territories, to the area under British control or tutelage. The following distribution of shares in the Turkish Petroleum Company was accepted when the Allies and the Germans met at San Remo in 1920 to discuss the reparations problem:

	Percentage
Anglo-Persian Oil Company	47.5
French company	25
Royal Dutch-Shell	22.5
C. S. Gulbenkian	5
	100

In 1925, after a postponement owing to the Kemalist revolt in Anatolia and other disturbances which delayed the signing of an effective peace treaty with Turkey, the League of Nations confirmed the award of Mosul to the Arab state of Iraq. The government of Iraq then agreed to pay the Turkish government 10 percent of its revenue from oil for the next twenty-five years. Somewhat tardily, the Turkish Petroleum Company was renamed in 1929 the Iraq Petroleum Company.

Both before and after the San Remo Conference, the United States government pressed the British to open Mesopotamia to American oil interests. Lord Curzon, who had become Foreign Secretary in 1919, was not inclined to do so. He pointed out that the country was still in so unsettled a state that commercial exploitation of its resources would be difficult. He also argued that the Americans already had a disproportionately large share of the world's oil and were notoriously exclusive. They could not seriously fear competition from oil firms in the Middle East. These produced only about 1 percent of the world's output, had to pay Suez Canal dues, and were a long way from the best markets. Gulbenkian thought the best plan was to allow American oil companies to acquire an interest in the Turkish Petroleum Company, and eventually his solution was adopted.

The first commercial production in Iraq was in an area transferred from Persia to the Ottoman Empire shortly before the war. This area was covered by the Anglo-Persian Oil Company's concession.

In 1923 the Turkish Petroleum Company applied to the government of Iraq for a definitive concession. The company faced strong competition from rival interests but in 1925 was awarded a concession for seventy-five years. This covered the whole of Iraq except the former vilayet of Basra and the transferred territories. The company was, however, required to submit a number of plots to auction for the government's benefit. The Anglo-Persian Oil Company surrendered half its holding in favor of six American companies and was compensated by an overriding royalty on all oil produced by the parent company. With other adjustments, this arrangement gave by 1928 the following distribution of shares:

	Percentage
Anglo-Persian Oil Company	23.75
French company	23.75
American companies	23.75
Royal Dutch-Shell	23.75
C. S. Gulbenkian	5
	100

A further agreement provided that the company should make no profits, but should sell crude oil at cost to its shareholders. Since Gulbenkian was not in a position to derive any benefit from this arrangement, one of the constituent companies would buy his shares at a "just valuation."

In 1927 an immense strike was made at Kirkuk, about 150 miles north of Baghdad. The oil came out of the ground so fast that the company's engineers had great difficulty in bringing it under control.

The system of auctioning plots was disliked by the company, and objections were raised on the ground that it would encourage speculative bids. In 1931 the company negotiated a new agreement which gave it unrestricted rights in an area of 32,000 square miles east of the Tigris and left the government a free hand elsewhere. To save Suez Canal dues and provide employment, the company undertook to install pipelines connecting Kirkuk with Haifa in Palestine and Tripoli in Lebanon. The pipeline network was first used in 1934 and was formally opened early in 1935.

In accordance with the new agreement, the government granted a concession covering 46,000 square miles west of the Tigris to B.O.D. Limited, a British company originally controlled from London. The share capital was acquired toward the end of 1932 by Mosul Oilfields Limited, a holding company with British, Italian, German, Dutch, French-Swiss, and Iraqi shareholders. Control passed for a time to the Italians, but the wide distribution of shares enabled the Iraq Petroleum Company, by discreet purchases, to acquire a majority holding and eventually to absorb the operating company.

In the summer of 1938 the Iraq Petroleum Company was granted, for the benefit of a subsidiary company, a concession covering the former vilayet of Basra. The whole of the oil resources of the Tigris-Euphrates basin, apart from the transferred territories, thus passed, some twenty years after the conclusion of the Mesopotamian campaign, under the control of an international consortium which existed for the benefit of its American, British, British-Dutch, and French shareholding companies and of the Arab state of Iraq. Production was of the order of 4,000,000 tons a year, and oil royalties provided more than a quarter of the whole revenue of the state. Crude oil accounted for roughly two-thirds of the country's exports, and slightly more than 50 percent of all exports went to France.

In Persia output continued to increase after the First World War, but the country was vexed by internal conflicts. In 1932 the Persian government canceled the oil concession, and the British government appealed to the League of Nations. In the following year a new agreement was signed. This extended the Anglo-Persian Oil Company's concession until 1993 but limited it to a defined area in the southwest. An American company obtained a concession covering another part of the country but soon abandoned it. In the six years from 1933 to 1938 the Anglo-Persian Oil Company produced about 50,000,000 tons of crude oil and paid the government more than £17,000,000 in royalties. Crude oil and oil products accounted for nearly three-quarters of the country's export trade, and slightly more than a quarter of all exports went to the United Kingdom.

The main events during the period between the wars in the Arabian Peninsula and on its borders were as follows:

Kuwait. In 1934, after many years of rivalry, the Anglo-Persian Oil Company and an American company, the Gulf Oil Corporation, pooled their negotiating powers and obtained a joint concession for seventy-five years. A huge strike was made in 1938.

Bahrain. In 1927 the Gulf Oil Corporation bought an option from Frank Holmes, a New Zealander who had acquired rights in various parts of Arabia and had tried without success to dispose of them to British companies. Gulf was, however, debarred from retaining the option by the terms of an agreement governing relations between shareholders in the Turkish Petroleum Company. Furthermore, the ruler of Bahrain could grant a concession only to a British subject. Accordingly, a Canadian company was formed to take up the option, but control passed to the California-Texas Oil Company. Production of crude oil rose by 1937 to nearly 1,000,000 tons a year, and by that date a refinery afterward of great importance was also in operation.

Qatar. In 1935 the Anglo-Persian Oil Company obtained a concession for seventy-five years but assigned it to the Iraq Petroleum Company. The first strike was made in 1939.

Saudi Arabia. Ibn Saud granted a limited concession to Holmes in 1923, but it lapsed in 1927 after two renewals. In 1935 the Iraq Petroleum Company, offering payment in rupees, made a bid in competition with the Standard Oil Company of California, which offered gold. Standard obtained a sixty-year concession covering a large tract of eastern Saudi Arabia. This was developed jointly by two American companies. Oil was found in vast quantities, but commercial production did not get into its stride until shortly before the outbreak of the Second World War.

Altogether, the Middle East produced on the eve of the Second World War a little more than 6 percent of the world's output of crude oil. The United States produced about 60 percent, Russia and Venezuela each between 10 and 12 percent. Borneo and the Netherlands East Indies produced about 3 percent, Mexico some 2 percent. The vast resources of Kuwait and Saudi Arabia were, however, only just beginning to be tapped.

Policy and Strategy

In 1914 the British government at home wished to protect the Anglo-Persian Oil Company's interests in Persia and at Basra; the government of India and the India Office aimed at impressing Turks and Arabs. The difference was unimportant. A landing at the head of the Persian Gulf would, and did, serve both purposes. The oil installations were secured, and the Turks were driven from the port of Basra and its neighborhood.

The moral effects of the occupation of Basra were largely undone some twelve months later by the failure of the Allies to take Gallipoli. Meanwhile, the British and the French embarked on negotiations which led to the Sykes-Picot Agreement. When the negotiations began, they expected their attempt to capture the Dardanelles to be successful. In that case Russian troops would enter Constantinople, and Russia's position would be greatly strengthened by the reopening of her Black Sea ports to foreign trade.

The genesis of the Sykes-Picot Agreement was an invitation extended by the Russians to their allies in March, 1915. In effect, the British and the French were asked to say what their wishes in regard to the future of the Ottoman Empire would be if Russia succeeded at the peace conference in establishing her claim to Constantinople and the Straits. Discussion showed that the Russians also proposed to claim a tract of Asia Minor in the region of Erzerum, Trebizond, and northern Kurdistan.

Britain's chief preoccupation east of Suez was the defense of India. Russia was the only first-class power that could threaten India from the landward side. It followed that if the Ottoman Empire fell to pieces and Russia gained a foothold in Asia Minor, the British would have a powerful interest in preventing the sparsely populated territories between the western frontier of Persia and the Mediterranean from becoming a no-man's-land on which the Russians could encroach at will.

Britain's concern for the future of Mesopotamia, Transjordania, and Palestine, as expressed in the Sykes-Picot Agreement, must be seen in the light of this preoccupation, not merely of her rather tenuous interest in the oil deposits of Baghdad and Mosul. Grey and the permanent officials of the Foreign Office were, indeed, willing that France should claim Mosul as part of a French sphere of influence and offer no more in return than a vague promise to respect British interests.

The problem was further complicated by French claims to Syria and a large part of southern Anatolia and by British obligations toward Arab potentates. Consequently the Sykes-Picot Agreement envisaged a complex system of zones and spheres of influence, designed to give an acceptable balance of Arab, British, French, and Russian interests. Later an attempt was made in the Treaty of St. Jean-de-Maurienne to reconcile these interests with the promise, made to the Italians when they undertook to enter the war in 1915, of a "just share" of western Anatolia. But the Treaty of St. Jean-de-Maurienne, approved by the Western Allies in 1917, was never accepted by the Russians and became a nullity.

The Sykes-Picot Agreement was not a plan of campaign or a scheme of military conquest. It did not purport to do more than sketch the outlines of a settlement which the British and the French would be willlng to support at the peace conference in the circumstances postulated by the Russians. By January, 1918, and indeed a good deal earlier, it was clear that since the Russians had renounced their claim to Constantinople and the Straits, those circumstances would not arise. Consequently Lloyd George was not bound either by the Sykes-Picot Agreement or by the Treaty of St. Jean-de-Maurienne when he made his statement of war aims in that month. The promise made to the Italians in the Treaty of London, on the other hand, was still an obstacle which Lloyd George hoped to overcome by offering some suitable alternative.

The oil deposits of Baghdad and Mosul were not among the immediate objectives of the force which landed at the head of the Persian Gulf in 1914. At that time no advance beyond the confluence of the Tigris and the Euphrates was contemplated, and even the making of plans for a further advance was actively discouraged.

In the following spring the authorities in India raised the strength of the force to two divisions and appointed a commander in chief, General Sir John Nixon. They then told Nixon that he should make plans to occupy the whole of the vilayet of Basra and also for an eventual advance to Baghdad. The home government concurred in their refusal to make further additions to the force, counseled caution, and suggested that Nixon should concentrate for the time being on driving the remaining Turkish forces from the vicinity of the pipeline.

During the summer of 1915 a series of cautious advances took part of Nixon's force, under Major General Sir Charles Townshend, about 150 miles up the Tigris. On September 29 Townshend captured Kut-el-Amara, less than 100 miles from Baghdad. The home government concurred in these moves, but on October 6 the Secretary of State for India, Austen Chamberlain, refused to countenance an attack on Baghdad. Later in the month he agreed that it was reasonable to hope that Baghdad might be taken and held if two Indian divisions about to move from France to Egypt were diverted to Mesopotamia. Although no one could say when the divisions would arrive, the government of India was then told that Nixon might march on Baghdad.

Accordingly, Nixon gave Townshend permission to continue his advance. Townshend duly arrived in the last week of November within a few miles of Baghdad but was driven off by strong Turkish forces in entrenched positions. He retreated to Kut, where the Turks surrounded and besieged him. Nixon, with the two reinforcing divisions added to his strength, tried but failed to relieve him, and on April 29, 1916, he surrendered for lack of food.

In the light of these setbacks, the War Office relieved the military authorities in India of responsibility for the control and later for the administration of the Mesopotamia force. Lieutenant General Sir Frederick Stanley Maude succeeded Nixon, and General Sir Charles Monro became commander in chief, India. Criticism of the authorities in India by a parliamentary commission forced Austen Chamberlain to resign his post, although his responsibility for mistakes made thousands of miles from London was purely nominal.

After the fall of Kut the Mesopotamia force remained on the defensive until the Battle of the Somme was over. Sir William Robertson, the Chief of the Imperial General Staff, thought the troops should fall back some fifty miles. Asquith's War Committee, mindful of Moslem opinion and encouraged by the success of the Arab revolt on the shores of the Red Sea, refused to sanction a further retreat and insisted that the force should continue to improve its communications with a view to a possible advance on Baghdad at some future date. Accordingly, Robertson told Maude by cable at the end of September that his immediate task was to maintain his hold on the vilayet of Basra but that the government would like him to establish British influence in the vilayet of Baghdad if and when he found himself in a position to do so. For the present he could expect no reinforcements.

Both Maude and Monro felt that the situation called for something more in the meantime than a passive attitude toward the Turks. Largely on Monro's advice, Robertson gave Maude permission at the end of October to exert such pressure on the enemy as was possible with his existing resources. By such means Maude succeeded between December and February in taking about 4,500 prisoners, recapturing Kut, and driving the Turks in confusion to Baghdad. He then asked for fresh instructions.

Meanwhile, the Russian Army of the Caucasus, under the Grand Duke Nicholas, was engaging the Turks in Transcaucasia. Early in February the Grand Duke told the War Office that he proposed to send some of his troops through Persia and across the frontier to Mosul and Baghdad. Thereupon Robertson advised Maude to speed up his advance. Maude did so. After occupying Baghdad on March 11, his troops made contact with the Russians on April 2 at a village in the Persian frontier area, about 70 miles northeast of Baghdad and nearly 200 miles southeast of Mosul.

The British then offered to provision the Russian forces north of Baghdad if they would join Maude in pursuit of the Turks. The Grand Duke was unable to take advantage of the offer. Within a day or two of the capture of Baghdad, Russia was in the throes of a revolution and the Czar was off his throne. During the ensuing struggle for power, those aspirants to leadership who believed that the only hope for Russia lay in a negotiated peace with the Central Powers sought to recommend themselves and their policies to the war-weary masses by imputing discreditable motives to statesmen in all countries who were willing to carry on the fight. Wide currency was given to such innuendos outside Russia. In England, men opposed on humanitarian grounds to the continuance of the war or who wished for one reason or another to bring the government or the capitalist system into disrepute murmured that Lloyd George and his colleagues were really fighting not for the independence of Belgium, the sanctity of treaties, and the defeat of German militarism, but for the oil of Mesopotamia.

When these rumors began to circulate in the summer of 1917, the vilayet of Mosul was the only part of Mesopotamia not occupied by British troops. In view of its remoteness from Baghdad and the uncertain situation created by the defection of Russia, no serious attempt was made to bring it under Allied control until the war was almost over. In the meantime, the Mesopotamia force consolidated its hold on Basra and Baghdad while General Allenby drove the enemy before him in Palestine and Syria. On October 30, 1918, after suffering a calamitous defeat in northern Palestine and losing Damascus and Aleppo, the Turks gave up the struggle.

Arrangements had then to be made for the administration of vast tracts of the Ottoman Empire which the Turks had ceased to be able to govern and parts of which the Allies had undertaken not to return to Turkish rule. Attempts to hasten a settlement at a time when the statesmen of the Allied and Associated Powers were flushed with victory and beset by problems at home and abroad led to blunders which created a fresh set of problems, most of them not connected, or only remotely connected, with the oil question.

Ten days after the signing of the armistice agreement with Turkey, Britain and France undertook to encourage the formation in Mesopotamia and Syria of Arab states under rulers acceptable to the inhabitants.

The French set up such a state in the interior of Syria and agreed that the Emir Feisal, one of the sons of Sherif Hussein, should be its ruler. In the summer of 1920, after the League of Nations had awarded them the mandate for Syria, they abandoned the experiment, deposed Feisal, and bombarded his capital. Thereafter they ruled Syria as a French colony. An oil concession for seventy-five years was granted in 1938 to a subsidiary of the Iraq Petroleum Company, but no oil was found on a commercial scale.

The British, awarded the mandate for Mesopotamia, did almost the opposite. In 1921 they renounced their intention of governing the country as a British colony and set up the Arab kingdom of Iraq. They proposed the deposed Emir Feisal as a candidate for the throne, and in due course he was elected. The country's oil resources were developed by the Iraq Petroleum Company in the interests of British and foreign shareholding companies, but the task of helping Feisal to maintain order in territories inhabited largely by unruly tribesmen fell to the British.

In Transjordania the Arab kingdom of Trans-Jordan, ruled by Feisal's brother Abdullah, was established under British tutelage, and in Palestine the British tackled the daunting task of keeping the peace between Jews and Arabs. The oil pipeline from Iraq to Haifa passed through both countries.

In general, the collapse of the Ottoman Empire substantially increased Britain's commitment in the territories between the Caspian and the Red Sea without materially altering the nature of her strategic interest in those territories. Between the wars, as in 1914, her chief preoccupations in that area were the safeguarding of the landward approaches to India and the security of the Anglo-Persian Oil Company's installations at the head of the Persian Gulf.

Appendix II

THE BACKGROUND TO SUEZ

The Suez Canal in International Law

The status of the Suez Maritime Canal as an international waterway was established by a convention, or treaty, between Austro-Hungary, France, Germany, Great Britain, Italy, the Netherlands, Russia, and Turkey, signed at Constantinople on October 29, 1888.

The Constantinople Convention laid down the principle that the maritime canal should "always be free and open, in time of war as in time of peace, to every vessel of commerce or of war, without distinction of flag." The signatory powers undertook not to obstruct, by exercise of the right of blockade or otherwise, the passage of merchant vessels or warships of any nation, even in time of war and even though the Ottoman Empire (which included Egypt) should be among the belligerents.

The signatory powers also undertook not to commit any act of hostility in the canal, at its ports of access, or within a radius of three nautical miles of those ports. This undertaking was subject to the proviso that the Sultan of Turkey and the Khedive of Egypt should always be free to take such measures as might be necessary for the defense of Egyptian territory, the maintenance of public order, and (in the sultan's case) the defense of Turkish possessions on the east coast of the Red Sea. They were also free, and indeed might be called upon by the local agents of the signatory powers, to take such steps as might be needed to ensure the security of the canal and the execution of the treaty.

By an earlier convention, the right to operate the canal and to levy tolls had been conferred for a limited period on the Universal Suez Canal Company. Article 14 of the treaty of 1888 made it clear that the validity of the treaty was not limited by the duration of the concession. In other words, when the Suez Canal Company's rights expired in 1969, the maritime canal would still be an international waterway, and the signatory powers or their successors would still be bound by the obligations accepted on their behalf in 1888.

The Political and Strategic Background

In theory Egypt was ruled in 1888 by a khedive who owed allegiance to the Sultan of Turkey. In practice, the khedivial government had for some years been incapable of asserting its authority without a greater degree of moral and financial support than the sultan could provide.

In 1875 financial stringency compelled the Khedive Ismail to part with his foundation shares in the Suez Canal Company, and he found a buyer in the British government. Because he was still unable to pay his way, eventually the French, at Bismarck's prompting, joined the British in deposing him and establishing a system of government designed to safeguard the interests of Egypt's foreign creditors.

The voluntary withdrawal of the French from this arrangement in 1882 gave the British a free hand to regulate Egypt's external and internal policies, restore her commercial prosperity, and put her finances on a sound footing. The British claimed no colonial rights in Egypt, and they regarded themselves not as usurpers of the khedive's or the sultan's authority but as trustees and advisers. From 1888 to 1914 their representative in Cairo bore the modest title of Resident or Consul General. British officers and administrators who held key positions in the Army and the public services were, at any rate in theory, servants not of the British Crown but of the Egyptian government.

Throughout this period the avowed intention of the British was to relinquish their special position in Egypt as soon as an Egyptian government capable of ruling without their help could be installed in office. No such government had, however, been found when the outbreak of the First World War compelled Asquith's government to declare Egypt a British protectorate as the only means of ensuring that the country did not fall under the sway of the sultan's Central European allies.

After the war the Turks no longer claimed suzerainty over Egypt. Because the Egyptians were manifestly not strong enough to resist aggression with their own resources the British retained, when they recognized Egypt as a sovereign state in 1922, the self-imposed responsibility for the defense of Egyptian territory and the Suez Canal which they had assumed in 1914. Their insistence on stationing troops in Egypt made Anglo-Egyptian relations difficult until Mussolini's invasion of Abyssinia convinced the Egyptians of the danger of Italian encroachments across the Libyan frontier and by way of the Sudan. Egyptian statesmen of all parties then agreed, by appending their signatures to the Anglo-Egyptian Treaty of 1936, that the British should be allowed, in return for the withdrawal of their forces from Cairo and Alexandria, to station troops and air squadrons in the Canal Zone and to reinforce them without limit in an emergency.

The treaty of 1936 paved the way for a working agreement which survived the stresses of the Second World War. Before and immediately after the war British relations with the Arab world were, however, troubled by the inveterate hostility of the Arab inhabitants of Palestine to Jewish immigration. Britain was widely believed to have accepted the League of Nations mandate for Palestine in the belief that it would strengthen her military position in the Middle East. But this was not the motive which impelled her statesmen to agree in the first place that a national home for the Jewish people should be established in Palestine, and it would be difficult to prove that her strategic aims would not have been equally well served had Palestine become and remained a purely Arab state. As things were, clashes between Jews and Arabs became so frequent in the 1930's that an expert commission appointed by the British government reported that Jewish and Arab aspirations in Palestine were irreconcilable and recommended partition.

The outbreak of war in 1939 enabled the British to shelve the issue. After the war demands for the admission to Palestine of large numbers of Jewish refugees became so insistent and illegal immigration reached such vast proportions that it had to be faced. Clement Attlee's Socialist government relinquished the mandate for Palestine, and the state of Israel was carved out of Palestine under the aegis of the United Nations. The immediate outcome was an Israeli-Arab war which the powers had to stop by imposing an uneasy truce on the belligerents. Since hostilities between Israel and Egypt seemed likely to be resumed at any moment, the Americans, the British, and the French then agreed to sell arms to Israel, Egypt, Iraq, Jordan, Lebanon, Saudi Arabia, and Syria only for defensive purposes. On May 25, 1950, they announced their "unalterable opposition" to the use of force or the threat of force by Israel or any of the Arab states.

One consequence of the creation of the state of Israel and its recognition by the United States was that the Americans and the British came to be regarded throughout the Arab world as champions of Israel at a time when they wished to strengthen the ties with Arab states already established by the British. Two-thirds of the world's known oil reserves were in the Middle East, Western Europe drew at least half its supplies of oil from Middle Eastern countries by way of the Suez Canal, and one and a half thousand million dollars of American capital were invested in Middle Eastern oil wells and refineries. Moreover, the Americans wished to confront the Soviet Union with an eastern counterpart to their system of alliances in Western Europe. Comparatively inexperienced in Middle Eastern affairs, they relied largely on the British to win the Arabs to their side.

An upsurge of Arab nationalism stimulated by the conflict with Israel and sustained by a stream of propaganda from Cairo made this a difficult task. King Farouk's overthrow in 1952 at the hands of a military junta was preceded by a vigorous attempt on the part of his ministers to evade their obligations under the treaty of 1936 and to drive the British from the Canal Zone by fostering civil disobedience and encouraging acts of lawlessness and violence. Gamal Abdel Nasser, Farouk's supplanter at one remove, celebrated his accession to office by asking the Western powers for arms but waged a war of words against their alleged colonialism and imperialism. He also played a leading part in planning, organizing, and fostering Arab resistance to French rule in Algeria.

As Britain's Foreign Secretary from the end of 1935 to the early part of 1938, Anthony Eden had sponsored the Anglo-Egyptian Treaty of 1936. Holding the same post from 1951 to 1955, he negotiated in 1954 an agreement by which the British undertook to withdraw from the Canal Zone in 1956 on the understanding that they might be asked to return at any time within the next seven years in the event of an "armed attack" on Egypt, Turkey, or a country linked with Egypt by membership of the Arab League. The military installations they left behind them would be maintained by civilian contractors supervised by British technicians.

In the meantime, General Eisenhower had succeeded Harry S. Truman as President of the United States. Against Eden's advice, he chose as his Secretary of State John Foster Dulles, a distinguished lawyer with a considerable knowledge of international affairs, but, according to his American critics, too devious in thought and speech, too self-assertive, and too little endowed with the saving virtue of humility to make a success of so responsible a task.

Dulles and Eden agreed that the Western powers should do everything they could to strengthen their position throughout the world by coming to terms with suitable allies. It was therefore not solely at the prompting of the Americans but in the light of his own convictions that Eden negotiated the 1954 agreement with Egypt and concluded the complex of alliances between Britain, Iraq, Pakistan, Persia, and Turkey which became known as the Baghdad Pact. Eden believed, however, that the "collective security" at which he had always aimed would be attained only if the Western powers accompanied such moves by attempts to reassure the Russians and convince them that peaceful coexistence was possible. Dulles believed that the Western powers should aim at keeping the Russians guessing by subjecting them to a series of shocks.

In the outcome it was not the Russians but the British and the Americans who received a shock when they learned at the beginning of March, 1956, that King Hussein of Jordan had abruptly dismissed the British General Sir John Glubb, his family's trusted adviser for the past quarter of a century and Chief of Staff and Commander of Jordan's army, the Arab Legion. Afterward attributed to the youthful Hussein's jealousy of Glubb, this move was ascribed by many Western commentators at the time to the machinations of Nasser or the Russians or of both. Thereafter Dulles became increasingly doubtful of the wisdom of the offer to provide part of the cost of building the long-projected Aswan High Dam which he had made to Nasser on behalf of his own and the British government in the previous December.

In the meantime, Eden, deeply disturbed by the knowledge that Nasser had placed a large order for Russian arms, had proposed to Eisenhower and Dulles that Britain, France, and the United States, as signatories to the tripartite declaration of May, 1950, should take preliminary steps which would make it clear to all concerned that they would, if necessary, use force to prevent a clash between Israel and the Arab states. Eisenhower and Dulles had refused to cooperate in such a move.

During the next few months Nasser further angered Dulles by recognizing Communist China, arranging to barter Egyptian cotton for Chinese steel, and letting it be known that he had received an offer from the Soviet Union to finance the Aswan Dam project.

Nasser's envoy was to call at the State Department on July 19, 1956, to discuss, and supposedly to accept, the offer made in December. On the eve of his arrival the British strongly advised Dulles, if he came to the conclusion that the offer ought to be withdrawn, not to risk driving Nasser into the arms of the Russians by making an immediate announcement to that effect, but to spin out the negotiations so that the news could be broken to Nasser gently. As things turned out, the abrupt withdrawal by Dulles of the offer led Nasser to seize the Suez Canal and thus precipitate the Suez crisis.

Bibliography

ACHESON, DEAN, *Present at the Creation.* London, 1970.

ADAMS, MICHAEL, *Suez and After.* Boston, 1958.

ALLEN, H. C., *Great Britain and the United States: A History of Anglo-American Relations (1783–1952).* London, 1954.

AMRINE, MICHAEL, *The Great Decision.* London, 1960.

ANGELL, NORMAN, *The Great Illusion.* London, 1913.

ASPINALL-OGLANDER, CECIL, *History of the Great War: Military Operations, Gallipoli.* London, 1929–32. 2 vols. and 2 vols. of maps.

ASQUITH, THE EARL OF OXFORD AND, *Memories and Reflections.* London, 1928. 2 vols.

AVON, THE EARL OF, *Full Circle.* London, 1960.

———, *Facing the Dictators.* London, 1962.

BACON, ADMIRAL SIR REGINALD, *The Dover Patrol, 1915–1917.* London, no date.

———, *Life of Lord Fisher.* London, 1929.

BAILEY, T. A., *Woodrow Wilson and the Lost Peace.* New York, 1944.

BAKER, R. S., *Woodrow Wilson and World Settlement.* London, 1923. 3 vols.

BARNETT, CORRELLI, *The Desert Generals.* London, 1960.

———, *The Swordbearers.* London, 1963.

BEAL, JOHN R., *John Foster Dulles.* New York, 1957.

BEAUFRÉ, ANDRÉ *Strategy of Action.* London, 1967.

———, *The Suez Expedition, 1956.* London, 1969.

BEAVERBROOK, LORD, *Politicians and the War.* London, 1960.

———, *Men and Power, 1917–1918.* London, 1956.

Behrens, C. B. A., *Merchant Shipping and the Demands of War.* History of the Second World War, United Kingdom Civil Series. London, 1955.

Beloff, Max, *The Foreign Policy of Soviet Russia, 1929–1941.* London, 1947–49. 2 vols.

———, *Soviet Policy in the Far East, 1944–1951.* London, 1953.

Berle, Adolf, *The American Economic Republic.* London, 1963.

Blackett, P. M. S., *The Military and Political Consequences of Atomic Energy.* London, 1952.

Blake, Robert, *The Unknown Prime Minister: The Life and Times of Bonar Law, 1858–1923.* London, 1955.

———, ed., *The Private Papers of Douglas Haig, 1914–1919.* London, 1952.

Boyle, Andrew, *Trenchard: Man of Vision.* London, 1962.

Bradley, General Omar H., *A Soldier's Story.* London, 1951.

Bryant, Arthur, *The Turn of the Tide.* London, 1957.

———, *Triumph in the West.* London, 1959.

Bullitt, William C., *The Great Globe Itself.* New York, 1947.

Bullock, Alan, *Hitler: A Study in Tyranny.* London, 1952.

Bundy. *See* Stimson.

Butcher, Captain Harry C., *My Three Years with Eisenhower.* London, 1946.

Butler, J. R. M., *Grand Strategy Volume II. Grand Strategy Volume III, Part II.* History of the Second World War, United Kingdom Military Series. London, 1957 and 1964.

Byrnes, James F., *Speaking Frankly.* London, 1947.

Bywater, H. C., *Sea Power in the Pacific.* London, 1934.

Calder, Angus, *The People's War: Britain, 1939–45.* London, 1969.

Callwell, Major-General Sir Charles E., *Field-Marshal Sir Henry Wilson: His Life and Diaries.* London, 1927. 2 vols.

Carr, E. H., *The Bolshevist Revolution.* London, 1950–53. 3 vols.

Chatfield, Lord, *The Navy and Defence.* London, 1942.

———, *It Might Happen Again.* London, 1947.

Chennault, C. L., *The Way of a Fighter.* New York, 1949.

Churchill, Randolph S., *The Rise and Fall of Sir Anthony Eden.* London, 1959.

Churchill, Winston S., *The World Crisis.* London, 1928–29. 4 vols.

———, *The Second World War.* London, 1948–54. 6 vols.

Clark, Ronald W., *The Birth of the Bomb.* London, 1961.

———, *Tizard.* London, 1965.

Coakley. *See* Leighton.

Collier, Basil, *The Defence of the United Kingdom.* History of the Second World War, United Kingdom Military Series. London, 1957.

Colvin, Ian, *Chief of Intelligence.* London, 1951.

Connell, John, *The Most Important Country.* London, 1957.

———, *Auchinleck.* London, 1959.

Cooper, Duff, *Haig.* London, 1935–36. 2 vols.

Corbett, Sir Julian, *History of the Great War: Naval Operations,* Volumes 1–3. London, 1920–21.

Cruttwell, C. R. M. E., *A History of the Great War, 1914–1918.* Oxford, 1936.

———, *The Role of British Strategy in the Great War.* London, 1936.

DAVIES, J., *Mission to Moscow.* London, 1942.
DAVIS, GEORGE T., *A Navy Second to None.* New York, 1940.
DEANE, J. R., *The Strange Alliance.* New York, 1947.
DEMPSTER. *See* WOOD.
DERRY, T. K., *The Campaign in Norway.* History of the Second World War, United Kingdom Military Series. London, 1952.
DEXTER, DAVID, *The New Guinea Offensives.* Canberra, 1961.
DULLES, ALLEN W., *Germany's Underground.* New York, 1947.
DUROSELLE, J.-B., *From Wilson to Roosevelt.* London, 1964.
EDMONDS, BRIGADIER-GENERAL SIR JAMES E., *History of the Great War: Military Operations, France and Belgium.* London, 1922–48. 9 vols.
EHRMAN, JOHN, *Grand Strategy Volume V. Grand Strategy Volume VI.* History of the Second World War, United Kingdom Military Series. London, 1956.
EISENHOWER, GENERAL OF THE ARMY DWIGHT D., *Crusade in Europe.* London, 1958.
ELLIS, MAJOR L. F., *The War in France and Flanders, 1939–1940. Victory in the West,* Volume I. History of the Second World War, United Kingdom Military Series. London, 1954 and 1962.
EYCK, ERICH, *The Weimar Republic.* London, 1962.
FEILING, KEITH, *The Life of Neville Chamberlain.* London, 1947.
FEIS, H., *The Road to Pearl Harbor.* Princeton, 1950.
———, *The China Tangle.* Princeton, 1953.
———, *Churchill, Roosevelt, Stalin.* Princeton, 1957.
FINER, HERMAN, *Dulles over Suez.* London, 1964.
FISCHER, FRITZ, *Germany's Aims in the First World War.* London, 1967.
FLEMING, D. F., *The Cold War and Its Origins, 1917–1960.* Volume I. London, 1961.
FRANKLAND. *See* WEBSTER.
FULLER, GENERAL J. F. C., *The Second World War.* London, 1948.
GAFENCU, GRIGOIRE, *The Last Days of Europe.* London, 1947.
GARNETT, DAVID, ed., *The Letters of T. E. Lawrence.* London, 1938.
GAVIN, LIEUTENANT-GENERAL JAMES M., *War and Peace in the Space Age.* London, 1959.
GEORGE, DAVID LLOYD, *The Truth About Reparations and War Debts.* London, 1932.
———, *War Memoirs of David Lloyd George.* London, 1934.
———, *The Truth About the Peace Treaties.* London, 1938.
GERARD, JAMES W., *My Four Years in Germany.* New York, 1917.
GIBBS, N. H., *The Origin of Imperial Defence.* Oxford, 1955.
GLEASON. *See* LANGER.
GOOLD-ADAMS, RICHARD, *Time of Power: John Foster Dulles.* London, 1962.
GOUGH, HUBERT, *The Fifth Army.* London, 1931.
GOUTARD, COLONEL A., *The Battle of France.* London, 1958.
GOWING, MARGARET, *Britain and Atomic Energy, 1939–1945.* London, 1964.
GREENFIELD, KENT R., *American Strategy in World War II: A Reconsideration.* Baltimore, 1963.
———, ed., *Command Decisions.* New York, 1959.
GRENFELL, R., *Main Fleet to Singapore.* London, 1951.
GREW, J. C., *Ten Years in Japan.* New York, 1964.

Grey of Fallodon, Viscount, *Twenty-five Years.* London, 1925. 2 vols.
Grinnell-Milne, Duncan, *The Silent Victory.* London, 1958.
Groueff, Stephane, *Manhattan Project.* London, 1967.
Groves, Lieutenant-General Leslie R., *Now It Can Be Told.* New York, 1962.
Guinn, Paul, *British Strategy and Politics, 1914–1918.* Oxford, 1965.
Gwyer, J. M. A., *Grand Strategy Volume III, Part I.* History of the Second World War, United Kingdom Military Series. London, 1964.
Halifax, The Earl of, *Fulness of Days.* London, 1957.
Hall, H. Duncan, *North American Supply.* History of the Second World War, United Kingdom Civil Series. London, 1955.
Hamilton, General Sir Ian. *Gallipoli Diary.* London, 1920. 2 vols.
Hancock, W. K., and Gowing, M. M., *British War Economy.* History of the Second World War, United Kingdom Civil Series. London, 1949.
Hankey, Lord, *The Supreme Command, 1914–1918.* London, 1961. 2 vols.
Harris, Marshal of the R.A.F. Sir Arthur, *Bomber Offensive.* London, 1947.
Hart, Captain B. H. Liddell, *The Other Side of the Hill.* London, 1951.
Hassell, U. von, *The Von Hassell Diaries.* London, 1948.
Higham, R., *Armed Forces in Peacetime: Britain 1918–1940, a Case Study.* London, 1963.
Hoag, C. L., *Preface to Preparedness: The Washington Conference and Public Opinion.* Washington, 1941.
House, E. M., and Seymour, C., eds., *What Really Happened at Paris.* London, 1921.
Hull, Cordell, *The Memoirs of Cordell Hull.* London, 1948. 2 vols.
Ichihashi, Y., *The Washington Conference and After.* Stanford, 1928.
Imlah, Albert H., *Economic Elements in the Pax Britannica.* Cambridge, Mass., 1958.
Ismay, Lord, *The Memoirs of Lord Ismay.* London, 1960.
Jellicoe, Admiral of the Fleet Earl, *The Grand Fleet 1914–16.* London, 1919.
Joffre, J.-J.-C., *Mémoires, 1910–1917.* Paris, 1932.
Johnson, F. A., *Defence by Committee: The British Committee of Imperial Defence, 1880–1959.* Oxford, 1960.
Jones, F. C., *Shanghai and Tientsin.* London, 1940.
———, *Manchuria Since 1931.* London, 1949.
———, *Japan's New Order in East Asia.* London, 1954.
Jones, H. A., *The War in the Air,* Volumes 2–5 and 1 vol. of maps. London, 1928–35.
Kahn, Herman, *On Thermonuclear War.* Princeton, 1960.
———, *Thinking About the Unthinkable.* New York, 1962.
Kannengiesser, Hans, *The Campaign in Gallipoli.* London, 1928.
Kase, Toshikazu, *Eclipse of the Rising Sun.* London, 1951.
Kaufmann, William W., *Military Policy and National Security.* Princeton, 1956.
Kelly. *See* Macleod, Roderick.
Kennan, George F., *American Diplomacy, 1900–1950.* London, 1959.
King, E. J., and Whitehill, W. M., *Fleet Admiral King: A Naval Record.* New York, 1952.
Kirby, Major-General S. W., *The War Against Japan,* Volumes I to IV. History of

the Second World War, United Kingdom Military Series. London, 1957–65.
KISSINGER, HENRY A., *Nuclear Weapons and Foreign Policy.* New York, 1957.
———, *The Necessity for Choice.* New York, 1961.
KLUCK. COLONEL-GENERAL ALEXANDER VON, *The March on Paris.* London, 1920.
LANGER, W. L., *Our Vichy Gamble.* New York, 1947.
LANGER, W. L., AND GLEASON, S. E., *The Challenge to Isolation, 1937–1940.* New York, 1952.
———, *The Undeclared War, 1940–1941.* London, 1953.
LEAHY, FLEET ADMIRAL W. D., *I Was There.* New York, 1950.
LEIGHTON, R. M., AND COAKLEY, R. W., *Global Logistics and Strategy, 1940–1943.* Washington, 1955.
LOCKHART, R. H. BRUCE, *Memoirs of a British Agent.* London, 1932.
LODGE, H. C., *The Senate and the League of Nations.* New York, 1925.
LONG, GAVIN, *To Benghazi.* Canberra, 1952.
———, *Greece, Crete and Syria.* Canberra, 1953.
LONGRIGG, S., *Oil in the Middle East.* London, 1961.
LOWE, C. J., *The Reluctant Imperialists: British Foreign Policy, 1878–1902.* London, 1967. 2 vols.
LUDENDORFF, GENERAL ERICH, *My War Memoirs, 1914–18.* London, 1919.
LYTTELTON, OLIVER (VISCOUNT CHANDOS), *The Memoirs of Lord Chandos.* London, 1962.
MCCARTHY, D., *South-West Pacific Area, First Year.* Canberra, 1959.
MACLEOD, IAIN, *Neville Chamberlain.* London, 1961.
MACLEOD, RODERICK, AND KELLY, DENIS, eds., *The Ironside Diaries.* London, 1962.
MAGNUS, PHILIP, *Kitchener: Portrait of an Imperialist.* London, 1958.
MAISKY, I., *Who Helped Hitler?* London, 1964.
MATLOFF, MAURICE, AND SNELL, E. M., *Strategic Planning for Coalition Warfare, 1943–1944.* Washington, 1953.
MEDLICOTT, W. N., *British Foreign Policy Since Versailles.* London, 1940.
MERRIAM, ROBERT E., *The Battle of the Ardennes.* London, 1958.
MILLIS, WALTER, ed., *The Forrestal Diaries.* London, 1952.
MILNE, ADMIRAL SIR ARCHIBALD BERKELEY, *The Flight of the Goeben and the Breslau.* London, 1921.
MILNER, S., *Victory in Papua.* Washington, 1947.
MORISON, SAMUEL ELIOT, *American Contributions to the Strategy of World War II.* Oxford, 1958.
———, *The History of United States Naval Operations in World War II.* Boston, 1947–62. 15 vols.
———, *The Two-Ocean War.* Boston, 1963.
MORTON, LOUIS, *The Fall of the Philippines.* Washington, 1953.
MUGGERIDGE, MALCOLM (ed.), *Ciano's Diary.* London, 1947.
———, *Ciano's Diplomatic Papers.* London, 1948.
NAMIER, L. B., *Diplomatic Prelude, 1938–1939.* London, 1948.
———, *Europe in Decay.* London, 1950.
———, *In the Nazi Era.* London, 1952.

NEWBOLT, SIR HENRY, *History of the Great War: Naval Operations.* Vols. 4 and 5. London, 1928–31.
NICOLSON, HAROLD, *Peacemaking, 1919.* London, 1933.
———, *Curzon: The Last Phase.* London, 1934.
NISH, IAN H., *The Anglo-Japanese Alliance: The Diplomacy of Two Island Empires, 1894–1907.* London, 1966.
NORTH, JOHN, *Gallipoli: The Fading Vision.* London, 1936.
NORTHEDGE, F. S., *British Foreign Policy: The Process of Readjustment, 1945–1961.* London, 1962.
———, *The Troubled Giant: Britain Among the Great Powers, 1916–1939.* London, 1966.
NUTTING, ANTHONY, *No End of a Lesson.* London, 1967.
O'BRIEN, TERENCE H., *Civil Defence.* History of the Second World War, United Kingdom Civil Series. London, 1955.
OSGOOD, ROBERT E., *Limited War.* Chicago, 1957.
PLATT, D. C. M., *Finance, Trade and Politics in British Foreign Policy, 1815–1914.* Oxford, 1968.
PLAYFAIR, MAJOR-GENERAL I. S. O., *The Mediterranean and Middle East,* Volumes I to IV. History of the Second World War, United Kingdom Military Series. London, 1956–62.
POSTAN, M. M., *British War Production.* History of the Second World War, United Kingdom Civil Series. London, 1952.
POTTER, JOHN D., *Admiral of the Pacific: The Life of Yamamoto.* London, 1965.
PRITTIE, TERENCE, *Germans Against Hitler.* London, 1964.
RALEIGH, SIR WALTER, *The War in the Air,* Volume I. London, 1922.
RENTZ, JOHN R., *Bougainville and the Northern Solomons.* Washington, 1948.
———, *Marines in the Central Solomons.* Washington, 1952.
RITTER, GERHARD, *The Schlieffen Plan.* London, 1958.
———, *The German Resistance.* London, 1958.
ROBERTSON, FIELD-MARSHAL SIR WILLIAM, *Soldiers and Statesmen.* London, 1926. 2 vols.
ROOSEVELT, ELLIOTT, *As He Saw It.* New York, 1946.
ROSKILL, STEPHEN, *The War at Sea.* History of the Second World War, United Kingdom Military Series. London, 1956–61. 3 vols. in 4 parts.
———, *The Navy at War, 1939–1945.* London, 1960.
———, *Naval Policy Between the Wars.* Volume I. London, 1968.
ROTHFELS, HANS, *The German Opposition to Hitler: An Assessment.* London, 1961.
SAUNDBY, AIR MARSHAL SIR ROBERT, *Air Bombardment: The Story of Its Development.* London, 1961.
SCHLABRENDORFF, FABIAN VON, *The Secret War Against Hitler.* London, 1961.
SCHRAMM, WILHELM VON, *Conspiracy Among Generals.* London, 1957.
SCHRÖTER, HEINZ, *Stalingrad.* London, 1958.
SCHWARZ, URS, *American Strategy: A New Perspective.* London, 1967.
SEYMOUR, CHARLES, ed., *The Intimate Papers of Colonel House.* London, 1926–28. 4 vols.

SHERWOOD, ROBERT E., *The White House Papers of Harry L. Hopkins.* London, 1948. 2 vols.
SHIRER, W., *The Rise and Fall of the Third Reich.* London, 1960.
SIMONDS, FRANK H., *How Europe Made Peace Without America.* London, 1927.
SLIM, FIELD-MARSHAL LORD, *Defeat into Victory.* London, 1956.
SNELL. *See* MATLOFF.
SPEARS, MAJOR-GENERAL SIR EDWARD, *Liaison 1914.* London, 1931.
———, *Assignment to Catastrophe.* London, 1954. 2 vols.
STETTINIUS, EDWARD R., *Roosevelt and the Russians.* New York, 1950.
STIMSON, H. L., AND BUNDY, MCG., *On Active Service in Peace and War.* London, 1948.
TAYLOR, A. J. P., *The Struggle for Mastery in Europe.* Oxford, 1954.
———, *The Origins of the Second World War.* London, 1961.
TAYLOR, MAXWELL D., *The Uncertain Trumpet.* New York, 1959.
TAYLOR, TELFORD, *The Breaking Wave.* London, 1967.
TEMPERLEY, H. W. V., *A History of the Peace Conference of Paris.* London, 1920–24. 6 vols.
TEMPLEWOOD, VISCOUNT, *Ambassador on Special Mission.* London, 1946.
———, *Nine Troubled Years.* London, 1954.
TERRAINE, JOHN, *Douglas Haig: The Educated Soldier.* London, 1963.
———, *The Western Front, 1914–1918.* London, 1964.
THOMAS, HUGH, *The Spanish Civil War.* London, 1961.
TILLMAN, SETH P., *Anglo-American Relations at the Paris Peace Conference of 1919.* Princeton, 1961.
TIRPITZ, GRAND ADMIRAL VON, *My Memoirs.* London, 1919.
TREVOR-ROPER, H. R., *The Last Days of Hitler.* London, 1956.
TRUMAN, HARRY S., *Year of Decisions, 1945.* New York, 1955.
TUCHMAN, BARBARA W. *The Guns of August.* New York, 1962.
ULLMAN, R. H., *Intervention and the War.* Princeton, 1961.
WARLIMONT, WALTER, *Inside Hitler's Headquarters, 1939–1945.* London, 1964.
WATKINS, K. W., *Britain Divided: The Effect of the Spanish Civil War on British Political Opinion.* London, 1963.
WATSON, MARK S., *Prewar Plans and Preparations.* Washington, 1950.
WEBSTER, SIR CHARLES, *The Art and Practice of Diplomacy.* London, 1961.
WEBSTER, SIR CHARLES, AND FRANKLAND, NOBLE, *The Strategic Air Offensive Against Germany.* History of the Second World War, United Kingdom Military Series. London, 1961. 4 vols.
WELLES, SUMNER, *The Time for Decision.* London, 1944.
WERTH, ALEXANDER, *Russia at War, 1941–1945.* London, 1964.
WHEATLEY, RONALD, *Operation Sea Lion.* Oxford, 1958.
WHEELER-BENNETT, J. W., *The Nemesis of Power: The German Army in Politics, 1918–1945.* London, 1953.
WIGMORE, L., *The Japanese Thrust.* Canberra, 1957.
WILLIAMS, W. A., *The Tragedy of American Diplomacy.* New York, 1962.
WILMOT, CHESTER, *The Struggle for Europe.* London, 1952.
WOLFF, LEON, *In Flanders Fields.* London, 1959.
WOOD, DEREK, AND DEMPSTER, DEREK, *The Narrow Margin.* London, 1961.

WOODWARD, E. L., *British Foreign Policy During the Second World War.* London, 1962.
WRENCH, JOHN EVELYN, *Geoffrey Dawson and Our Times.* London, 1955.
WU, A. K., *China and the Soviet Union.* London, 1950.
YOUNG, DESMOND, *Rommel.* London, 1950.
YOUNG, G. M., *Stanley Baldwin.* London, 1952.

Source Notes

1. Before the Deluge

1. Lowe, *The Reluctant Imperialists*, 4.
2. *Ibid.*, 5.
3. Nish, *The Anglo-Japanese Alliance*, 248.
4. Guinn, *British Strategy and Politics, 1914–1918,* 13.
5. Statements in this chapter and in subsequent chapters about Henry Wilson's views and actions are based on his diaries, except where another authority is cited. For published extracts from the diaries see Callwell, *Field-Marshal Sir Henry Wilson: His Life and Diaries.*
6. Accounts of the origin and development of Plan XVII were given after the war by Joffre and others in evidence before a French parliamentary commission appointed to inquire into the loss of the Briey iron fields.
7. Churchill, *The World Crisis 1911–1914,* 516–18.
8. Grey, *Twenty-five Years*, I, 97–98.
9. Allen, *Great Britain and the United States*, 405–7.
10. This is the figure given by innumerable authorities (among them Lloyd George, who was Chancellor of the Exchequer at the time) and adopted by Imlah, *Economic Elements in the Pax Britannica*, 70–75. See also Platt, *Finance, Trade and Politics in British Foreign Policy.*
11. Allen, 64 and *passim.*
12. *Ibid.*, 550.
13. *Ibid.*, 551.

14. Seymour, *The Intimate Papers of Colonel House*, I, 157, 197, 247, 269–71, 325.
15. Allen, 608.
16. Seymour, I, 215.
17. Morison, *The Two-Ocean War*, 17.
18. Seymour, I, 199; Allen, 648.
19. Allen, 623.

2. *Disaster in Europe*

1. Ritter, *The Schlieffen Plan.*
2. *Ibid.*
3. These figures are based on the numbers of divisions actually used in August, 1914. Ritter describes the evolution and development of Schlieffen's and Moltke's plans.
4. Wilson's diary.
5. High-level documents apart, a fair indication of Germany's intentions was given by routine intelligence reports, visible preparations (*e.g.,* construction of barracks and rail sidings), and written and oral indiscretions by highly placed Germans. The Kaiser, notoriously outspoken, scarcely bothered to conceal his intention of marching his troops through Belgium in the event of war with France. He may, indeed, have hoped that threats uttered well in advance would help him overawe the Belgians when the time came to give them an ultimatum.
6. Quoted by Tuchman, *The Guns of August*, 83.
7. Pourtalès called on Sazonov in St. Petersburg at 7 P.M. by local time—*i.e.,* at 5 P.M. by Central European time. Thus the declaration of war and the issue of the mobilization order were almost simultaneous. The German military authorities had already taken preliminary steps under a "state of emergency" order issued on the previous day.
8. Quoted by Tuchman, 81–82.
9. Churchill, *The World Crisis 1911–1914*, 192–93; Lloyd George, *War Memoirs*, 33.
10. Lloyd George, 29; Guinn, *British Strategy and Politics 1914 to 1918*, 24; Hankey, *The Supreme Command*, 63.
11. Churchill, 220.
12. Wilson's diary.
13. Hankey, 169–70.
14. Churchill, 198.
15. *Ibid.*, 199.
16. Quoted by Churchill, 222–23.
17. Churchill, 255.
18. Kannengiesser, *The Campaign in Gallipoli*, 25–26.
19. Quoted by Tuchman, 153.

3. *Mons to Ypres*

1. Quoted by Tuchman, 128.
2. Tuchman, 173–74, 225–28, 313–22 (citing German, Belgian, and neutral sources).
3. Seymour, *The Intimate Papers of Colonel House*, I, 299.
4. Quoted by Tuchman, 338.
5. Tuchman, 337.
6. Seymour, I, 306.
7. *Ibid.*, I, 292.
8. *Ibid.*, I, 294–97.
9. Tuchman, 177.
10. Wilson's diary. Some accounts omit the reference to "aeroplanes."
11. The British, about 80,000 strong, suffered 1,600 casualties at Mons on August 23. The French, about 1,000,000 strong on all parts of their front, are believed to have suffered at least 140,000 casualties in the frontier battles between August 20 and 23.
12. Wilson's diary.
13. Tuchman, 408.
14. Or, according to another version, "which will go another step."
15. Quoted by Tuchman, 363.
16. Tuchman, 394, 406.
17. This was the official version. According to another account, French said: "Tell him we will do all we possibly can."
18. Churchill, 321.
19. *Ibid.*, 333–48; Guinn, *British Strategy and Politics 1914–1918*, 39–40.
20. Churchill, 359; Guinn, 40.
21. Hankey, 225, 260; Guinn, 59.
22. Hankey, 227–29, 246–47.
23. *Ibid.*, 252.
24. *Ibid.*, 244–50.
25. *Ibid.*, 252; Guinn, 48–49.
26. Asquith, *Memories and Reflections,* II, 63; Guinn, 48.
27. Guinn, 43.
28. Hankey, 176, 226.
29. *Ibid.*, 176–77, 222–25.
30. *Ibid.*, 237.
31. *Ibid.*, 238.

4. *The Way Round*

1. Hankey, 168, 249; Guinn, 40.
2. Hankey, 239.
3. *Ibid.*, 223.

4. Quoted by Guinn, 43.
5. Guinn, 44.
6. Hankey, 222.
7. *Ibid.*, 223.
8. *Ibid., loc. cit.*
9. *Ibid.*, 244–50.
10. *Ibid.*, 251.
11. Lloyd George, *War Memoirs*, 216–17, 222–23.
12. *Ibid.*, 224.
13. Hankey, 262.
14. *Ibid.*, 240–41; Guinn, 50–51.
15. Guinn, 51.
16. *Ibid., loc. cit.*
17. *Ibid., loc. cit.*
18. Hankey, 248–49, 253–54, 266, 271.
19. *Ibid.*, 263.
20. *Ibid.*, 263–65, 267.
21. *Ibid.*, 261, 262.
22. *Ibid.*, 265, 273, 274; Lloyd George, *War Memoirs*, 232, 239; Guinn, 54.
23. Hankey, 75, 280.
24. *Ibid.*, 279–80.
25. *Ibid.*, 223, 242.
26. *Ibid.*, 242.
27. *Ibid.*, 262.
28. *Ibid.*, 266.
29. Guinn, 56.
30. Hankey, 266, 271.
31. *Ibid.*, 271.
32. *Ibid.*, 267 n., 271.
33. *Ibid.*, 267.
34. *Ibid.*, 270; but see also 253–54.
35. *Ibid.*, 269.
36. *Ibid.*, 269–70.
37. *Ibid.*, 269.
38. *Ibid.*, 272.
39. *Ibid., loc. cit.*
40. *Ibid.*, 274.
41. *Ibid., loc. cit.*
42. *Ibid.*, 277–78.
43. *Ibid.*, 278–79.
44. *Ibid.*, 276, 279; Guinn, 58.
45. Hankey, 288; Lloyd George, *War Memoirs,* 255.
46. Hankey, 281.
47. *Ibid.*, 281–82.
48. *Ibid.*, 283–84; Lloyd George, *War Memoirs*, 247–48; Guinn, 62–64.
49. Hankey, 284.
50. *Ibid., loc. cit.*

51. *Ibid.*, 285.
52. *Ibid.*, *loc. cit.*
53. *Ibid.*, 286; Guinn, 66.
54. Hankey, 286.
55. *Ibid.*, 287.
56. *Ibid.*, 288.
57. *Ibid.*, 288–90.
58. *Ibid.*, 271.
59. *Ibid.*, 283.
60. *Ibid.*, *loc. cit.*
61. *Ibid.*, *loc. cit.*; Lloyd George, 248.
62. Hankey, 284.
63. Guinn, 67.
64. *Ibid.*, *loc. cit.*; Hankey, 291–95.
65. Guinn, *loc. cit.*
66. Hankey, 290.
67. *Ibid.*, 292.
68. *Ibid.*, 290–91; Guinn, 67–68.
69. Guinn, 68.
70. *Ibid.*, 69; Hankey, 292.
71. Guinn, 69–70.
72. Hamilton, *Gallipoli Diary,* I, 41–42.
73. Hankey, 294, 300; Guinn, 71.
74. Hankey, 293.
75. *Ibid.*, 304.
76. Guinn, 73; Hankey, 305.
77. Hankey, 308–10; Lloyd George, 75 ff.
78. Lloyd George, 84–87.
79. *Ibid.*, 87.
80. Hankey, 263.
81. *Ibid.*, 312.
82. *Ibid.*, 311–12.
83. *Ibid.*, 315.
84. *Ibid.*, *loc. cit.*; Lloyd George, 134–35; Blake, *The Unknown Prime Minister*, 244.
85. Hankey, 307, 335–36, 340–45.
86. *Ibid.*, 430, 456.
87. *Ibid.*, 457.
88. Guinn, 89; Hankey, 343.
89. Guinn, 90.
90. Guinn, 95–96; Hankey, 408.
91. Guinn, 115.
92. Hankey, 446, 481–82, 499, 502–3, 536, 607, 608, 637, 672, 676; Lloyd George, 467–69, 540, 573, 823, 859, 865–66, 1367, 1379, 1380, 1382–85, 1405, 1407–8, 1423–24, 1461–63. See also Robertson, *Soldiers and Statesmen, 1914–1918.*
93. Hankey, 467–69.
94. *Ibid.*, 471.

95. *Ibid.*, 476.
96. *Ibid.*, 477 n.

5. Blockade and Attrition

1. Hankey, 355.
2. *Ibid.*, 356.
3. Lloyd George, *War Memoirs*, 398.
4. Hankey, 375.
5. Grey, *Twenty-five Years*, II, 103.
6. Hankey, 369.
7. Seymour, *The Intimate Papers of Colonel House*, I, 447.
8. Hankey, 367–68.
9. Seymour, *op. cit.*, I, 324.
10. *Ibid.*, 375–76.
11. Hankey, 364.
12. Seymour, I, 414; see also 405.
13. *Ibid.*, *loc. cit.*
14. *Ibid.*, *loc. cit.*
15. *Ibid.*, 415.
16. *Ibid.*, 428–29.
17. *Ibid.*, II, 36.
18. *Ibid.*, I, 455.
19. *Ibid.*, I, 456; II, 16.
20. *Ibid.*, II, 81–101, 111, 117, 173–202.
21. *Ibid.*, II, 130, 135, and *passim.*
22. *Ibid.*, II, 200–2.
23. *Ibid.*, 165, 248 ff.
24. Allen, *Great Britain and the United States*, 681.
25. Fischer, *Germany's Aims in the First World War.*
26. Seymour, II, 179.
27. Hankey, 494–95.
28. Seymour, II, 318–19.
29. *Ibid.*, 215.
30. *Ibid.*, 219.
31. *Ibid.*, 227.
32. *Ibid.*, 241.
33. Hankey, 506.
34. Lloyd George, *War Memoirs,* 456–60; Beaverbrook, *Men and Power, 1917–1918,* 45–46.
35. Hankey, 514.
36. Quoted by Lloyd George, 507.
37. *Ibid.*, 509.
38. Hankey, 557.
39. *Ibid.*, 545.
40. *Ibid.*, 558.

41. Text in Lloyd George, 545–55.
42. Hankey, 557–61; Lloyd George, 555–56. Hankey (560) does not confirm Lloyd George's impression that Asquith knew in advance that the meeting at which he read the memorandum would be an informal one.
43. Lloyd George, 569, 572–74, 818.
44. *Ibid.*, 589–90; see also Beaverbrook, *Politicians and the War.*
45. Hankey, 567–68.
46. Letter reproduced in Lloyd George, 591–92.
47. The accounts of Bonar Law's dealings with Asquith in Beaverbrook, *Politicians and the War,* and Blake, *The Unknown Prime Minister*—the first by Law's friend and mentor, the second by his biographer—tell the story primarily from the standpoint of Bonar Law. Points which have continued to excite controversy are (a) how far Beaverbrook's (and Bonar Law's) impressions of Asquith's attitude to the war were correct or were colored by political or personal prejudice; (b) whether Asquith received from Bonar Law a fair impression of the attitude of the Unionist leaders other than Bonar Law himself.
48. Quoted in Lloyd George, *War Memoirs,* 596.
49. Quoted in Seymour, *Intimate Papers of Colonel House,* II, 317.
50. Seymour, II, 390–91, 414–15.
51. *Ibid.*, 390–91.
52. *Ibid.*, 389–95.
53. *Ibid.*, 393.
54. *Ibid.*, 394.
55. Text in Lloyd George, 653–54.
56. Lloyd George, 655–57; Hankey, 599–600.
57. Seymour, II, 403.
58. *Ibid.*, II, 404.
59. *Ibid.*, 395–96, 407.
60. Lloyd George, 661.
61. Hankey, 601.
62. Lloyd George, 660; Hankey, 602.
63. Seymour, II, 420.
64. *Ibid.*, *loc. cit.*
65. Letter reproduced in Seymour, II, 434–35.
66. Seymour, II, 442.
67. *Ibid.*, 445.
68. *Ibid.*, 467.

6. Soldiers and Statesmen: I

1. Letter reproduced in Beaverbrook, *Men and Power, 1917–1918,* 364–69.
2. Quoted by Beaverbrook, 151.
3. Hankey, 639, and *passim*; Lloyd George, *War Memoirs,* 670, 671.
4. Lloyd George, 690.
5. Hankey, 647–48.
6. *Ibid.*, *loc. cit.*; Lloyd George, 693, and *passim.*

7. Lloyd George, 682.
8. *Ibid.*, 683, 688.
9. *Ibid.*, 688.
10. *Ibid.*, 689.
11. Hankey, 643; Lloyd George, 690.
12. Lloyd George, 690–91.
13. *Ibid.*, 691.
14. Hankey, 650.
15. *Ibid.*, *loc. cit.*; Lloyd George, 693.
16. Hankey, *loc. cit.*
17. Lloyd George, 692.
18. Hankey, 653.
19. Lloyd George, 696–99.
20. Bacon, *The Dover Patrol, 1915–1917*, 343–44, and *passim.*
21. Lloyd George, 699.
22. *Ibid.*, 1442.
23. *Ibid.*, 633.
24. *Ibid.*, 1292, and *passim.*
25. Hankey, 531.
26. *Ibid.*, *loc. cit.*
27. Lloyd George, 1075, 1077; Hankey, 530–31, 532.
28. Lloyd George, 1083.
29. *Ibid.*, *loc. cit.*
30. *Ibid.*, 1086; Guinn, *British Strategy and Politics, 1914–1918,* 221.
31. Lloyd George, 1086 (quoting Murray's dispatch).
32. *Ibid.*, 1088 (quoting Smuts).
33. *Ibid.*, 1092; Beaverbrook, *Men and Power, 1917–1918,* 187, 367–68.
34. T. E. Lawrence did not, as is commonly supposed, complain when he championed the Arab cause in 1919 that either the Balfour Declaration or the Sykes-Picot Agreement was inconsistent with wartime promises made to Arab chieftains. On the contrary, he described the Sykes-Picot Agreement as, "in a sense," the charter of the Arabs. His objection to it was not that it was unfair to the Arabs, but that it was unworkable. The Arabs, he thought, would tolerate a Jewish national home under British supervision, but not one established under international auspices. His other criticisms related not to wartime agreements or declarations, but to steps taken or contemplated after the armistice. (Garnett, *The Letters of T. E. Lawrence*, 280–94, and *passim.*)
35. Lloyd George, 709, 710; Hankey, 650, and *passim.*
36. Hankey, 561.
37. *Ibid.*, 604; Lloyd George, 824.
38. Lloyd George, 824, 838; Hankey, 605.
39. Lloyd George, 841.
40. *Ibid.*, 843, 849–55.
41. Hankey, 608; Lloyd George, 853–55, 859.
42. Wilson's diary.
43. Lloyd George, 853, 854.
44. Hankey, 613 n.

45. Lloyd George, 887–88.
46. Hankey, 613; Lloyd George, 887.
47. Hankey, 614.
48. Nivelle's letter to Haig, Lloyd George, 881–83.
49. *Ibid., loc. cit.*
50. Lloyd George, 892.
51. Hankey, 615–16.
52. *Ibid.*, 616–17; text of memorandum in Lloyd George, 893–94.
53. Lloyd George, 898–99.
54. *Ibid.*, 890; but see Hankey, 621.
55. Hankey, 624.
56. Lloyd George, 899.
57. *Ibid.*, 901.
58. Wilson's diary. See also Hankey, 625.
59. Hankey, 678.
60. Lloyd George, 1251, 1252, 1292; Hankey, 679, 701.
61. Hankey, 680, 682.
62. *Ibid.*, 671; Wilson's diary.
63. Lloyd George, 1275, quotes Haig's instructions to his army commanders.
64. Lloyd George, 1296 (quoting Charteris).
65. *Ibid.,* 1268 (quoting Wilson's report to C.I.G.S., dated July 6, 1917); Wilson's diary.
66. Hankey, 684.
67. *Ibid.*, 683.
68. Quoted by Wolff, *In Flanders Fields*, 150.
69. Gough, *The Fifth Army*, 205.
70. Lloyd George, 1244.
71. *Ibid.*, 1230. See also Fischer, *Germany's Aims in the First World War.*
72. Lloyd George, 1316; Hankey, 699–700.
73. Wolff, 256 (quoting GHQ instructions).
74. *Statistics of the Military Effort of the British Empire during the Great War.*
75. See, *e.g.*, Edmonds, *Military Operations, France and Belgium, 1917*, II.
76. Wolff, 163, 166, 169, 201, 258, 259.

7. Soldiers and Statesmen: II

1. Wilson's diary.
2. Hankey, 703–7.
3. *Ibid.*, 713–14.
4. *Ibid.*, 715; Wilson's diary.
5. Lloyd George, 1390. Some sources give an even higher figure.
6. Hankey, 722–23.
7. *Ibid.*, 721–22.
8. Lloyd George, 1797.
9. *Ibid.*, 1797, 1799.
10. *Ibid.*, 1800.

11. *Ibid.*, 1797–1800, 1805.
12. *Ibid.*, 1797.
13. *Ibid.*, 1805, 1807.
14. Hankey, 745.
15. Lloyd George, 1803–9; Seymour, III, 311–12, 440–46; Hankey, 745, 764–65.
16. Lloyd George, 1809–10.
17. Hankey, 731.
18. *Ibid.*, 730.
19. Seymour, III, 325.
20. *Ibid.*, 302–23.
21. Text in Lloyd George, 1510–17.
22. Seymour, III, 347 and n., 350.
23. *Ibid.*, III, 328.
24. *Ibid.*, IV, 199–200.
25. *Ibid.*, *loc. cit.*
26. Quoted by Seymour, III, 354.
27. Text in Lloyd George, 1643–49.
28. Hankey, 769.
29. *Ibid.*, *loc. cit.*
30. *Ibid.*, 748–55, 770–73; Lloyd George, 1656, 1663.
31. Hankey, 772; Lloyd George, 1664.
32. Lloyd George, 1664.
33. Text in Lloyd George, 1670.
34. Lloyd George, 1676.
35. *Ibid.*, 1678.
36. *Ibid.*, 1671–72.
37. Hankey, 776.
38. Beaverbrook, *Men and Power, 1917–1918,* 198, 201–3.
39. Hankey, 776; Lloyd George, 1672–73.
40. Beaverbrook, 208–9, 412.
41. Lloyd George, 1697.
42. *Ibid.*, 1689.
43. *Ibid.*, 1715; Hankey, 782; Wilson's diary.
44. Hankey, 781–82.
45. Lloyd George, 1699.
46. *Ibid.*, 1704 (from Edmonds).
47. *Ibid.*, 1729–30.
48. Text of Haig's memorandum in Lloyd George, 1738–39.
49. Lloyd George, 1740.
50. Wilson's diary.
51. *Ibid.*
52. Lloyd George, 1740.
53. Quoted by Lloyd George, 1740.
54. Lloyd George, 1818; Seymour, III, 449–56.
55. Lloyd George, 1823.
56. *Ibid.*, 1825; Seymour, III, 458.
57. Lloyd George, 1743–49; Hankey, 791–92.

58. Hankey, 796–97.
59. Text in Lloyd George, 1784–86.
60. Beaverbrook, 261–63; unpublished material.
61. Hankey, 798–99.
62. *Ibid.*, 808, 813; Guinn, 308; Wilson's diary.
63. Hankey, 813.
64. *Ibid.*, 810.
65. *Ibid.*, 815.
66. Fleming, *The Cold War and Its Origins*, I, 18.
67. Text of order in Lloyd George, 1892–93.
68. Fleming, I, 19.
69. Milner as quoted by Guinn, 308.
70. Guinn, 309 n.
71. Quoted in Lloyd George, 1895–96.
72. Seymour, III, 399–427.
73. *Ibid.*, *loc. cit.*
74. Hankey, 825.
75. Fleming, I, 17.
76. Lloyd George, 1903.
77. Seymour, III, 420.
78. Quoted in Seymour, III, 428.
79. Seymour, III, 428 n.
80. *Ibid.*, *loc. cit.*; Lloyd George, 1908.
81. Estimates vary from 60,000 to 72,000.
82. Lloyd George, 1908.
83. *Ibid.*, 1860–62; Guinn, 314.
84. Guinn, 314, 315.
85. *Ibid.*, 315; Lloyd George, 1868–69.
86. Lloyd George, 1933. For a detailed account of events leading to the armistice between Germany and the Allied and Associated Powers see Temperley, *A History of the Peace Conference of Paris.*
87. Lloyd George, 1941–42.
88. *Ibid.*, 1917–19; Hankey, 836–37.
89. Lloyd George, 1950; Hankey, 840–41, 842; Guinn, 318.
90. Lloyd George, 1948.
91. The German communication was embodied in a misdated note transmitted to the President of the United States through the German Legation in Berne, the Swiss Federal Government, and the Swiss Legation in Washington. It had not yet reached the President when the Supreme War Council met at 5 P.M. on October 5.

8. War and Peace

1. Text in Temperley, *A History of the Peace Conference in Paris*; also in Lloyd George, 1953.
2. Seymour, *The Intimate Papers of Colonel House*, IV, 75.

3. Text in Temperley; also in Lloyd George, 1956–57.
4. Lloyd George, 1958; Seymour, IV, 167.
5. Lloyd George, 1958–59.
6. Seymour, IV, 84.
7. *Ibid.*, IV, 87–88.
8. Lloyd George, 1961–62.
9. *Ibid.*, 1960–61.
10. Seymour, III, 383.
11. Lloyd George, 1963.
12. *Ibid.*, 1977; text in Temperley.
13. Hankey, *The Supreme Command, 1914–1918*, 856.
14. *Ibid.*, *loc. cit.*; text in Temperley.
15. Wilson's diary.
16. Hankey, 857; text in Temperley.
17. Wilson's diary.
18. Lloyd George, 1967; see also Temperley.
19. Roskill, *Naval Policy Between the Wars*, I, 22–23.
20. Seymour, IV, 95–96.
21. Text of armistice terms in Lloyd George, 2044–53; also in Temperley.
22. Seymour, IV, 167.
23. *Ibid.*, 198–209.
24. *Ibid.*, 167–68. Temperley deals authoritatively with this point.
25. Seymour, IV, 68, 231.
26. *Ibid.*, 155–56.
27. *Ibid.*, 165, 169, 170, 173–74, 184; Roskill, I, 90.
28. Seymour, IV, 168–75, 184–93.
29. *Ibid.*, 169–70; Hankey, 859–63.
30. Seymour, IV, 171.
31. *Ibid.*, 184–90; Hankey, 862–63.
32. Seymour, IV, 175, 193; Temperley; Lloyd George, 1979.
33. Seymour, IV, 177–79.
34. *Ibid.*, 182–83.
35. Lloyd George, 1513, 1516; Seymour, IV, 127–29, 176, 182, 184.
36. Seymour, IV, 161, 204.
37. *Ibid.*, 176.
38. Text in Lloyd George, 2047.
39. Quoted from Lloyd George, 1981.

9. Versailles and After

1. Seymour, IV, 250; Henry Wilson's diary.
2. Seymour, IV, 226.
3. *Ibid.*, *loc. cit.*
4. *Ibid.*, 227.
5. *Ibid.*, 227–30.
6. *Ibid.*, 291; Allen, *Great Britain and the United States*, 706.

7. Seymour, IV, 142.
8. Seymour, III, 68–78.
9. Roskill, *Naval Policy Between the Wars*, I, 90.
10. *Ibid.*, I, 83.
11. Letter reproduced in Seymour, IV, 433–35.
12. Henry Wilson's diary.
13. Roskill, I, 79 n.
14. *Ibid.*, 79.
15. According to Henry Wilson, Foch expressed his conviction that such allegations were well founded and that furthermore the Americans were trading with Communist Russia.
16. Roskill, I, 78.
17. *Ibid.*, 95.
18. *Ibid.*, 94.
19. *Ibid.*, 92.
20. Henry Wilson's diary.
21. Seymour, IV, 396–97, 398, 413–18, 420.
22. *Ibid.*, 291.
23. *Ibid.*, 296.
24. *Ibid.*, 297.
25. Text of resolution in Seymour, IV, 302–3.
26. Seymour, IV, 303 n., 314–15.
27. Roskill, I, 88; Seymour, IV, 465–66.
28. Roskill, I, 85.
29. Seymour, IV, 320–21, 322, 323, 324, 325.
30. *Ibid.*, 366.
31. *Ibid.*, 401.
32. *Ibid.*, 400.
33. *Ibid.*, 400, 425–26, 439–43.
34. *Ibid.*, 432.
35. Roskill, I, 91; Henry Wilson's diary.
36. Seymour, IV, 411.
37. *Ibid.*, 416.
38. *Ibid.*, 417.
39. Text of cable in Seymour, IV, 418–19.
40. Seymour, IV, 419–25.
41. Roskill, I, 91; text of letters and memorandum in Seymour, IV, 433–39.
42. Seymour, IV, 438.
43. *Ibid.*, 444.
44. *Ibid.*, 465–69.
45. Roskill, I, 88.
46. Seymour, IV, 466.
47. *Ibid.*, *loc. cit.*
48. *Ibid.*, 467–71.
49. *Ibid.*, 449–50.
50. *Ibid.*, 450.
51. *Ibid.*, 460–61.

52. Roskill, I, 183–84.
53. Henry Wilson's diary.
54. *Ibid.*
55. Seymour, IV, 484.
56. Roskill, I, 183.
57. *Ibid., loc. cit.*
58. *Ibid.*, 184.
59. *Ibid.*, 185.
60. Seymour, IV, 502.
61. Memorandum of conversation between Colonel House and Lord Robert Cecil; text in Seymour, IV, 437–38. According to Seymour, the memorandum was drafted at President Wilson's request.
62. Seymour, IV, 510.
63. *Ibid.*, 517.
64. *Ibid.*, 512–13, 517–18.
65. *Ibid., loc. cit.*
66. Temperley.
67. Seymour, IV, 521–22.
68. *Ibid.*, 524–26.
69. Roskill, I, 215; Collier, *The Defence of the United Kingdom*, 6.
70. Roskill, *loc. cit.*
71. Roskill, I, 213.
72. *Ibid.*, 220–21.

10. Between the Wars: I

1. Collier, *The Defence of the United Kingdom,* 3; for capital ships, compare Roskill, *Naval Policy Between the Wars*, I, 71.
2. Collier, 21, 71.
3. Saundby, *Air Bombardment*, 41–45.
4. Collier, 11.
5. *Ibid., loc. cit.*
6. *Ibid.*, 12.
7. Roskill, I, 189–90.
8. *Ibid.*, 194,
9. *Ibid.*, 195.
10. *Ibid.*, 197.
11. *Ibid.*, 198.
12. *Ibid., loc. cit.*
13. *Ibid., loc. cit.*
14. Collier, 14.
15. *Ibid.*, 14–15.
16. *Ibid.*, 15.
17. *Ibid.*, 18.
18. *Ibid., loc. cit.*
19. O'Brien, *Civil Defence*, Chapter II.

20. *Ibid.*, 41.
21. Collier, 20.
22. Roskill, I, 216–17.
23. *Ibid.*, 216.
24. *Ibid.*, 219.
25. *Ibid.*, 221.
26. *Ibid.*, *loc. cit.*
27. Collier, 6.
28. Roskill, I, 293.
29. *Ibid.*, 225; Collier, 6–7.
30. Roskill, I, 226.
31. *Ibid.*, 292, 301.
32. *Ibid.*, 278.
33. *Ibid.*, 279.
34. *Ibid.*, 281–82.
35. *Ibid.*, 282.
36. *Ibid.*, 290.
37. *Ibid.*, *loc. cit.*
38. *Ibid.*, *loc. cit.*
39. *Ibid.*, 291.
40. *Ibid.*, 292–93.
41. *Ibid.*, 293.
42. *Ibid.*, 296.
43. *Ibid.*, 297.
44. *Ibid.*, 293, 297.
45. *Ibid.*, 274–75, 297–99.
46. *Ibid.*, 300–1.
47. *Ibid.*, 302.
48. *Ibid.*, 303.
49. *Ibid.*, 303–4.
50. *Ibid.*, 306.
51. *Ibid.*, 227.
52. *Ibid.*, 307.
53. *Ibid.*, 308.
54. *Ibid.*, 307.
55. *Ibid.*, 307–8.
56. *Ibid.*, 313, 314.
57. *Ibid.*, 314.
58. *Ibid.*, 315.
59. *Ibid.*, 319.
60. *Ibid.*, 316–17.
61. *Ibid.*, 325–26.
62. *Ibid.*, 353.
63. *Ibid.*, 326–27.
64. *Ibid.*, 328.
65. *Ibid.*, 333.
66. *Ibid.*, 352.

67. Schwarz, *American Strategy*, 20.
68. *Ibid.*, 19.
69. Collier, 23–24.
70. Roskill, I, 342.
71. *Ibid.*, 464.
72. *Ibid.*, 255, 256, 367–69, and *passim.*
73. *Ibid.*, 470–71, 491, 496–97, 525, 528–29.
74. Collier, 21.
75. Jones, *Japan's New Order in East Asia*, 10–11.

11. Between the Wars: II

1. Avon, *Facing the Dictators*, 523–24.
2. Jones, *Japan's New Order in East Asia*, 15.
3. *Ibid.*, 5, 15–16.
4. *Ibid.*, 4, 9, 26–27.
5. *Ibid.*, 23.
6. Collier, 24.
7. *Ibid.*, 25.
8. *Ibid.*, 26.
9. *Ibid.*, 27–28, 31.
10. *Ibid.*, 27.
11. Avon, *Facing the Dictators*, 141; Collier, *op. cit.*, 30.
12. Avon, 141.
13. Collier, 31–32.
14. *Ibid.*, 37.
15. *Ibid.*, 42.
16. Roskill, *Naval Policy Between the Wars*, I, 66–67.
17. Collier, 41; Avon, 249, 252, 253, 257, 264.
18. Avon, 123, 209, 224.
19. *Ibid.*, 230; Roskill, *The War at Sea*, I, 52.
20. Avon, 231.
21. *Ibid.*, 124, 230.
22. *Ibid.*, 320–21.
23. *Ibid.*, 324.
24. *Ibid.*, 323.
25. *Ibid.*, 332.
26. *Ibid.*, 332–33.
27. *Ibid.*, 332.
28. *Ibid.*, 347. See also Namier, *Europe in Decay*, 5–6, 11–25.
29. Avon, 337.
30. *Ibid.*, *loc. cit.*
31. *Ibid.*, 338.
32. *Ibid.*, 340.
33. *Ibid.*, 356.
34. *Ibid.*, 386.

35. *Ibid.*, 405.
36. See, for example, Fleming, *The Cold War*, I, 62.
37. Avon, 435.
38. Text in Avon, 431–32.
39. Avon, 432.
40. See, for example, Macleod and Kelly, *The Ironside Diaries*, 24–25, 35, 41, 45–46, 47, 52–53, 60, 64–70.
41. Avon, 445.
42. *Ibid.*, 460.
43. *Ibid.*, 485, 490.
44. Jones, *Japan's New Order in East Asia*, 31.
45. *Ibid.*, 33.
46. *Ibid.*, 30, 31, 33, 36.
47. *Ibid.*, 33.
48. *Ibid.*, 36.
49. *Ibid.*, 41; Chennault, *The Way of a Fighter*, 41–42.
50. Jones, 46.
51. *Ibid.*, *loc. cit.*
52. Testimony of Admiral Isamu Takeda (Jones, 47).
53. Jones, 49, 173, 174; Wu, *China and the Soviet Union*, 268, 269.
54. Jones, 74, 89.
55. Avon, *Facing the Dictators*, 540; Roskill, *The War at Sea*, I, 42, 553.
56. Avon, 534.
57. *Ibid.*, 536, 540.
58. *Ibid.*, 541–42, 544–45.
59. *Ibid.*, 545–46.
60. *Ibid.*, *loc. cit.*
61. *Ibid.*, 548–49. For a fuller account, see Welles, *The Time for Decision.*
62. Avon, 550.
63. *Ibid.*, 550–52.
64. *Ibid.*, 570–71.
65. *Ibid.*, 577–91.
66. *Ibid.*, 589.
67. Collier, *The Defence of the United Kingdom*, 48, 63.
68. Macleod and Kelly, *The Ironside Diaries*, 53–54.
69. Schwarz, *American Strategy*, 26.
70. Ritter, *The German Resistance*, 95; Rothfels, *The German Opposition to Hitler*, 59; Schlabrendorff, *The Secret War Against Hitler*, 91–92. For other aspects of German resistance to the National Socialist movement see books listed in bibliography under Colvin, Hassell, Prittie, Schramm, Wheeler-Bennett.
71. Schwarz, 27–28.
72. Avon, 520.
73. Warlimont, *Inside Hitler's Headquarters*, 20; Ritter, 131.
74. Gafencu, *The Last Days of Europe*, 145–46.

12. The Second World War: Phase One

1. Schwarz, *American Strategy*, 28.
2. Namier, *Diplomatic Prelude*, 350–52.
3. Butler, *Grand Strategy Volume II*, 58.
4. *Ibid.*, 178.
5. The account of the Scandinavian campaign in this chapter is based chiefly on Butler, *Grand Strategy Volume II*; Derry, *The Campaign in Norway*; Roskill, *The War at Sea*; Warlimont, *Inside Hitler's Headquarters.*
6. Roskill, *The War at Sea*, I, 158.
7. *Ibid.*, I, 159.
8. *Ibid.*, 160.
9. *Ibid.*, 161–62.
10. *Ibid.*, 159–60.
11. *Ibid.*, 161–62.
12. Macleod and Kelly, *The Ironside Diaries*, 253, 257–59; Roskill, *op. cit.*, I, 181–82. See also Derry, *The Campaign in Norway.*
13. Goutard, *The Battle of France*, 32.
14. *Ibid.*, 32–33, 35–36.
15. Collier, *The Defence of the United Kingdom*, 110.
16. Goutard, 112.
17. *Ibid.*, 111, 184.
18. *Ibid.*, 131.
19. *Ibid.*, 136–37.
20. Webster and Frankland, *The Strategic Air Offensive Against Germany*, I, 191–201.
21. *Ibid.*, 202.
22. Saundby, *Air Bombardment*, 98; Goutard, 138, 145.
23. Webster and Frankland, I, 144.
24. *Ibid.*, 145, 299–304.
25. Goutard, 200–5.
26. Macleod and Kelly, 311.
27. Goutard, 102, 208.
28. Macleod and Kelly, 320–21.
29. *Ibid.*, 321–22.
30. Goutard, 216.
31. Ellis, *The War in France and Flanders,* 1939–1940, 95; Goutard, 217.
32. Goutard, 218–19.
33. *Ibid.*, 210–11.
34. *Ibid.*, 222.
35. Ellis, 347–48.
36. *Ibid.*, 349–53; Goutard, 227–34.
37. Macleod and Kelly, 327, 330–32.
38. *Ibid.*, 314.
39. Ellis, 68–69; Collier, 111.

40. Collier, *loc. cit.*
41. *Ibid.*, 116.
42. Roskill, *The War at Sea*, I, 239.
43. Calder, *The People's War, 1939–1945*, 133.
44. Collier, 142.
45. *Ibid.*, 119.
46. *Ibid.*, 120–21.
47. *Ibid.*, 121; Wood and Dempster, *The Narrow Margin*, 462.
48. Wood and Dempster, 464.
49. Allen, *Great Britain and the United States*, 800; Macleod and Kelly, 309; Collier, 122.
50. Roskill, *The War at Sea*, I, 251.
51. *Ibid.*, 252–54, 257–58.
52. Allen, 800–5.
53. *Ibid.*, 801, 803, 804.
54. *Ibid.*, 803–4.
55. *Ibid.*, 806.
56. *Ibid.*, 805.
57. *Ibid.*, 806.
58. Roskill, *The War at Sea*, I, 243.
59. *Ibid.*, 244.
60. *Ibid.*, 243.
61. *Ibid.*, 244.
62. *Ibid.*, 296–97.
63. Wood and Dempster, *The Narrow Margin*, 463, 464.
64. Collier, 452.
65. *Ibid.*, 184–99, 456–57.
66. *Ibid.*, 459–60.
67. Wheatley, *Operation Sea Lion*, 72–73.
68. *Ibid.*, 80, 83–85.
69. Wood and Dempster, 463.
70. Collier, 472–74; Wood and Dempster, 326–27.
71. Quoted by Wood and Dempster, 338.
72. Wheatley, 88–89.
73. *Ibid.*, 89–90.
74. For detailed accounts of these campaigns see Playfair, *The Mediterranean and Middle East*, I.

13. The "Grand Alliance": I

1. Jones, *Japan's New Order in East Asia*, 122–23.
2. *Ibid.*, *loc. cit.*; Hull, *Memoirs*, I, 631.
3. Jones, 165–66.
4. *Ibid.*, 167.
5. *Ibid.*, 258; Kirby, *The War Against Japan*, I, 481.
6. Clark, *Tizard.*

7. *Ibid.*
8. *Ibid.*
9. Allen, *Great Britain and the United States*, 807.
10. Schwarz, *American Strategy*, 30–31.
11. *Ibid., loc. cit.*; Greenfield, *Command Decisions*, 14, and *passim.*
12. Allen, 810.
13. Roskill, *The War at Sea*, I, 454–55.
14. Allen, 816.
15. Roskill, Appendix R.
16. *Ibid., loc. cit.*
17. Webster and Frankland, *The Strategic Air Offensive Against Germany,* I, 146–47, 149, 153, 157–61, 163–64.
18. *Ibid.*, 129.
19. *Ibid.*, 153–54.
20. *Ibid.*, 153.
21. *Ibid.*, 226.
22. *Ibid., loc. cit.*
23. *Ibid.*, 233.
24. Collier, *The Defence of the United Kingdom*, 291.
25. *Ibid.*, 294.
26. *Ibid., loc. cit.*
27. Werth, *Russia at War, 1941–1945,* 137–41.
28. *Ibid., loc. cit.*
29. Gwyer, *Grand Strategy Volume III, Part I,* 90.
30. *Ibid., loc. cit.*; Sherwood, *The White House Papers of Harry L. Hopkins*, I, 303–4.
31. Gwyer, 96, 109; Sherwood, I, 332 ff.
32. Gwyer, 146–48.
33. Werth, 222.
34. Gwyer, 96, 109; Sherwood, I, 332 ff.
35. Roskill, I, 490–91, 555.
36. Gwyer, 151–55.
37. *Ibid.*, 155–61.
38. Werth, 625–26.
39. Jones, 211.
40. *Ibid.*, 260; Kirby, I, 66–67.
41. Jones, 211.
42. *Ibid.*, 264.
43. *Ibid., loc. cit.*
44. Schwarz, *American Strategy*, 32.
45. Allen, 819.
46. Churchill, *The Second World War*, II, 522.
47. Jones, 282, 283.
48. *Ibid.*, 297–98.
49. *Ibid.*, 300.
50. *Ibid.*, 304.
51. Hull, *Memoirs*, II, 1070.
52. Jones, 309–12.

53. *Ibid.*, 312.
54. *Ibid.*, 314.
55. *Ibid.*, *loc. cit.*
56. Kirby, I, 90.
57. *Ibid.*, I, 88; Jones, 317.
58. Jones, 318.
59. Roskill, *The War at Sea*, I, 554–59.
60. Kirby, I, 184 ff.
61. *Ibid.*, I, 263; Butler, *Grand Strategy Volume III, Part II,* 669–72.
62. Kirby, I, 210 ff.
63. *Ibid.*, I, 73, 445.
64. *Ibid.*, II, 223.
65. Butler, 572–81.
66. Playfair, *The Mediterranean and Middle East*, IV, 7–10, 30.
67. Roskill, II, 351.
68. Webster and Frankland, II, 12.
69. Roskill, II, 358–76.
70. Ehrman, *Grand Strategy Volume V*, 61.
71. *Ibid.*, 112–13.
72. *Ibid.*, 61–62, 68.
73. *Ibid.*, 37–38.
74. Ellis, *Victory in the West*, I, 10 ff.
75. Allen, 843.
76. Ehrman, 179, 180.
77. Webster and Frankland, III, 27–28.
78. *Ibid.*, 32.
79. *Ibid.*, 34, 35, 36.
80. *Ibid.*, 36–37.
81. *Ibid.*, 39–40, and *passim.*
82. Ellis, I, 357.
83. *Ibid.*, I, 82–83.
84. Collier, *The Defence of the United Kingdom*, 384, 523.
85. Ehrman, *Grand Strategy Volume VI*, 36–37.
86. Merriam, *The Battle of the Ardennes*, 73, 74, 99–105, 107, 128–29.
87. *Ibid.*, 199, 200.
88. Wilmot, *The Struggle for Europe*, 694.

14. The "Grand Alliance": II

1. Roskill, *The War at Sea*, II, 229–30.
2. Morison, *History of United States Naval Operations*, III, 393.
3. Kirby, *The War Against Japan*, II, 226.
4. Morison, *History of United States Naval Operations*, IV, 260.
5. Kirby, II, 286 ff.; see also Dexter, *The New Guinea Offensives.*
6. Morison, IV, 282.
7. Morison, V, 178.

8. Kirby, II, 53 ff.
9. *Ibid.*, 235.
10. *Ibid.*, 237.
11. *Ibid.*, 143.
12. *Ibid.*, 295.
13. *Ibid.*, 306.
14. *Ibid.*, 309–10.
15. *Ibid.*, 428–34.
16. *Ibid.*, 297.
17. *Ibid.*, 368 ff.
18. *Ibid.*, 363–64.
19. *Ibid.*, 363.
20. *Ibid.*, 420; Ehrman, *Grand Strategy Volume V*, 151–52.
21. Kirby, II 422.
22. Ehrman, 161.
23. *Ibid.*, 428–29, 430.
24. Ehrman, *Grand Strategy Volume VI*, 212.
25. *Ibid.*, 215–16.
26. Ehrman, V, 158 ff.
27. *Ibid.*, 153.
28. *Ibid.*, 427.
29. Kirby, III, 127.
30. *Ibid.*, *loc. cit.*
31. *Ibid.*, 140–41.
32. *Ibid.*, 145.
33. *Ibid.*, 240.
34. *Ibid.*, 372.
35. Kirby, IV, 58.
36. Roskill, III, Part II, 312.
37. Ehrman, VI, 72.
38. *Ibid.*, 72 ff.
39. *Ibid.*, 89.
40. Wilmot, *The Struggle for Europe*, 693.
41. Ehrman, VI, 137–38.
42. *Ibid.*, 80.
43. *Ibid.*, 132.
44. *Ibid.*, 133.
45. *Ibid.*, 137.
46. *Ibid.*, 144.
47. Ellis, *Victory in the West,* I, 82.
48. Ehrman, VI, 145.
49. *Ibid.*, 147–48.
50. *Ibid.*, 156.
51. *Ibid.*, 153.
52. *Ibid.*, 155–56.
53. Roskill, *The War at Sea*, III, Part II, 191 (Table 32).
54. Ehrman, V, 450–51.

55. *Ibid.*, 421 ff.
56. Roskill, III, Part II, 188.
57. *Ibid., loc. cit.*; Ehrman, V, 518.
58. Ehrman, VI, 221–22.
59. Roskill, III, Part II, 200.
60. Kirby, IV, 64.
61. Ehrman, VI, 218; Leahy, *I Was There*, 316–62.
62. Ehrman, VI, 219; Jones, *Japan's New Order in East Asia*, 478–79.
63. Ehrman, VI, 218.
64. Jones, 433.
65. *Ibid.*, 433–34.
66. Kirby, IV, 238; Morison, *The Two-Ocean War*, 524.
67. Morison, *The Two-Ocean War*, 556.
68. Ehrman, VI, 261.
69. *Ibid.*, 261.
70. *Ibid.*, 275.
71. Clark, *The Birth of the Bomb*, xiii.
72. *Ibid.*, 125–36.
73. Butler, *Grand Strategy Volume III, Part II,* 625; Ehrman, VI, 276.
74. Ehrman, *loc. cit.*
75. Groueff, *Manhattan Project*, 338.
76. Roskill, III, Part II, 367 (Table 40).
77. Jones, 429.
78. *Ibid.*, 436.
79. *Ibid.*, 437.
80. Ehrman, VI, 276, 296.
81. *Ibid.*, 277–78.
82. *Ibid.*, 285–88.
83. *Ibid.*, 304; Millis, *The Forrestal Diaries*, 86–88.
84. Ehrman, VI, 303.
85. Amrine, *The Great Decision*, 187.
86. Ehrman, VI, 305–6.
87. *Ibid.*, 288.
88. *Ibid.*, 296.
89. Saundby, *Air Bombardment*, 220, gives 70,000 as the figure for the Hiroshima bomb; about 80,000 to 85,000 were killed in the Tokyo raid.
90. Jones, 442.
91. *Ibid., loc. cit.*
92. *Ibid.*, 436.

15. The "Special Relationship"

1. Allen, *Great Britain and the United States*, 893–94.
2. Gavin, *War and Peace in the Space Age*, 116.
3. Allen, 971.
4. Gavin, 124.

5. Finer, *Dulles over Suez*, 18.
6. *Ibid.*, 26.
7. *Ibid.*, 28.
8. *Ibid.*, 33.
9. *Ibid.*, *loc. cit.*
10. *Ibid.*, 39.
11. *Ibid.*, 44–46.
12. *Ibid.*, 46.
13. *Ibid.*, 47.
14. *Ibid.*, 48.
15. Quoted by Finer, 63.
16. Eden, *Full Circle*, 470.
17. Finer, 97.
18. *Ibid.*, 90–91.
19. Quoted by Finer, 326.
20. Text of ultimatum to Egypt in Finer, 362–63; also in Nutting, *No End of a Lesson*, 193–94.
21. Finer, 288–90.
22. *Ibid.*, 370–71.

Index